DIRECTING THE
CHORAL MUSIC PROGRAM

KENNETH H. PHILLIPS
Gordon College
The University of Iowa

New York   Oxford
OXFORD UNIVERSITY PRESS
2004

Oxford University Press

Oxford   New York
Auckland   Bangkok   Buenos Aires   Cape Town   Chennai
Dar es Salaam   Delhi   Hong Kong   Istanbul   Karachi   Kolkata
Kuala Lumpur   Madrid   Melbourne   Mexico City   Mumbai
Nairobei   São Paulo   Shanghai   Taipei   Tokyo   Toronto

Published by Oxford University Press, Inc.
198 Madison Avenue, New York, New York, 10016
http://www.oup-usa.org

Oxford is a registered trademark of Oxford University Press

Library of Congress Cataloging-in-Publication Data

Phillips, Kenneth H. (Kenneth Harold)
    Directing the choral music program / Kenneth H. Phillips.
       p. cm.
    Includes bibliographical references (p.) and index.
    ISBN 0-19-513282-3
      1. Choral music—Instruction and study.   2. School music—Instruction and study.
    I. Title

MT935 .P529 2003
782.5'071—dc21   2002190848

Printing number: 19 18 17 16 15 14 13 12

Printed in the United States of America
on acid-free paper

Dedication

This text is dedicated to those people, mostly choir directors, who have made a significant impact upon my life, both musically and personally:

Kathryn Phillips, my mother, whose sweet voice was my first model of beautiful singing. Mom's renditions of "Jesus Wants Me for a Sunbeam," and "Climb, Climb up Sunshine Mountain" are among my earliest musical memories.

Celia Lattanzio, junior choir director, who nurtured my young singing voice and tolerated my antics in junior choir at Christ Lutheran Church (Beaver Falls, PA).

Philip Inman, choirmaster and organist (Christ Lutheran Church), who taught me the beauty of worship through choral music.

Robert Shoup, junior high choir director (Beaver Falls, PA), whose annual rendition of "Stouthearted Men" helped to keep many of us boys singing.

Bruce Keefer, senior high choir director, who gave me my first choral conducting experience at Beaver Falls Area High School (PA).

Clarence Martin, professor and choral director (Westminster College, PA), whose choice of inspiring choral literature instilled in me a love for quality choral music.

Ada Peabody, professor of music education (Westminster College), who instilled in me an admiration for Lowell Mason and his pioneering work in music education.

Joseph Golz, professor and choral director (West Virginia University), who taught me the value of conducting with clarity and efficiency.

Alfred Mann, professor and musicologist (Eastman School of Music), choral director (Bach Choir of Bethlehem), whose love for the music of J. S. Bach brought me new insight into the depths of Bach's genius.

Vance George, professor, choral director (Kent State University), and three-time Grammy Award winner (San Francisco Symphony Chorus), who introduced me to the highest standards of artistic achievement through the world of professional music making and the world's greatest choral literature.

All of these fine people, and more, have contributed to a life rich in choral music making. The value of music teachers can never be underestimated. Their lives reap a different kind of reward—one filled with great personal meaning and satisfaction. This world is a better place because they have made and continue to make a positive impact upon countless generations. Their song is never ending.

Contents

EPILOGUE   MOVING INTO THE WORKPLACE

Preface

Directing the Choral Music Program is a choral methods text intended primarily for undergraduate students preparing to become choral music teachers. It also will be of value to persons wanting to become church choir directors, children's choir directors, and directors of numerous other choral organizations. Although the text covers the basics of choral preparation, experienced conductors may find the content valuable in its presentation of established concepts from a new perspective. Others may find that the text helps to fill gaps in their own background. No text can claim to be completely comprehensive, however, and this text does not make that claim. Its purpose is to impart the knowledge necessary to lay a secure and proper foundation for the development of a choral music program.

This text does not cover the area of choral conducting. Most schools have separate courses for methods and conducting, and while both are interrelated, it is not necessary to have skill in conducting before studying the contents of this text. Some basic conducting knowledge is helpful if the instructor chooses to employ microteaching rehearsal strategies as part of Unit 3 ("Choral Techniques"). A basic conducting review can be accomplished using the author's text *Basic Techniques of Conducting* (Oxford University Press, 1997).

There are three units of study. Unit 1 relates the "nuts and bolts" of choral administration. Besides writing their own rationale for teaching choral music, students are to prepare promotional materials and learn how to audition singers. Unit 2 addresses the important area of "planning your work and working your plan." Developing a code of conduct, learning to choose quality choral literature, preparing the rehearsal schedule, and understanding basic show choir choreography are just a few of the many topics covered. Unit 3 reviews basic vocal skills development and energizing the warm-up. Sight-singing procedures are discussed as well as techniques for rehearsing the choir. After a look at the many other nonschool choral organizations available to direct, the text concludes with final words on preparing to enter the professional world of the choral music educator.

While a great amount of information is covered in this text, knowing about a topic and actually being able to demonstrate it are, as everyone knows, two different things. For this reason, it is important that the student be able to demonstrate the various skills, some of which are outlined at the end of each unit under "Optional Projects." These include public relations practices, auditioning singers, classifying voices, writing lesson plans, energizing the choral warm-up, teaching sight-singing, choosing music for a concert, working on choreography for a pop music group, rehearsing choirs, applying performance practices to music of various eras, job interviewing skills, and so forth. The more time spent in and out of class doing these various activities, the better. For example, students can learn to audition singers in class; it takes at least two times for most to become comfortable with the process. This activity is improved, however, when students are directed to find singers outside of class to audition. Also, as much as a third of class sessions may be devoted to Unit 3 and the learning of techniques for rehearsing choirs. Microteaching of five- to ten-minute lessons gives students the initial skills needed to communicate effectively in the rehearsal. If some type of real-world experience is possible outside the classroom, in addition to the microteaching, so much the better. This may not be possible, but at least students will have had some experience teaching choral music before a group of "real" people, and will learn what to say and how to say it.

The study and discussion questions at the end of each chapter are intended for directed reading purposes and may be required as homework. Using these questions as the basis for course content frees class time for the actual "doing" process. The questions can be used as the basis for class discussion, or they can be used solely as background to class activities. Students can be told to circle questions they do not understand, and time can be given when reviewing before an exam to address the circled questions. The study and discussion questions also can serve as the basic content for written exams. It is suggested that three written exams be given, one for each unit. Grades also may be given for written work and various demonstrations of skills.

Vocal students often have poor piano skills. The choral methods class is one more place where these skills can be improved. For example, when students audition others, they should be able to play scales and arpeggios up and down in all keys. When rehearsing choral music, students may take turns accompanying, or at least playing parts. Vocal students often do not understand how important it is to have piano skills until they are in their first teaching job.

Likewise, students who conduct need to use their singing voices confidently. They must be able to model and demonstrate what they want and how it should sound. Even voice students are found to be hesitant and nervous when providing vocal models. Nevertheless, this skill is extremely important and must be developed. Students need to understand that being a great singer is not a requirement for being a great choral conductor. Although a beautiful voice serves as a good model, a confident and leading voice is more important. On the other hand, students should be cautioned against singing with the choir, a practice that is all too common among choral directors. Conductors cannot accurately hear their choirs when they are singing with them.

The choral conducting profession has made great strides in recent years. Now there are choruses every bit as professional as orchestras, and choral singers who are well trained and growing as a profession. The amateur choral singer, however, continues to fill the ranks of choirs everywhere, and choral directors who know how to administrate, plan, rehearse, and conduct will always be needed. This book is for all those who aspire to having their own choirs and who will take their places among the ranks of music makers everywhere. The sound of voices united in song make for this to be a better world.

Music pitches are given throughout the text using the octave designations shown in Example P.1. The "great" octave uses capital letters, the "small" octave makes use of small letters, and the octaves above middle c are designated by the exponents 1, 2, and 3.

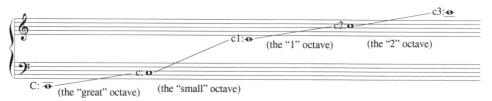

Example P.1. Octave designations.

ACKNOWLEDGMENTS

I have been a choral director for over thirty years, working with countless people, children and adults, who have enriched my life by their singing. To all of them I acknowledge my debt for their efforts in making this world a more beautiful place.

Numerous authors have been cited in this text for their insights, writings, and research. I am indebted to them for helping advance our knowledge of music making and learning. Special thanks goes to Dr. Alfred Mann for giving permission to reprint his program notes for Handel's *Messiah* in Chapter 19.

My appreciation is extended to a former doctoral student, Eugene F. Bechen, for his contribution of the final chapter, "Planning for Success." Gene's expertise in working with pre-service music educators is most evident in this writing.

I am also grateful to the Obermann Center for Advanced Studies at The University of Iowa, where I spent a semester's developmental leave working on this book. The "cookie breaks" were the best. Thanks, Lorna.

I am now professor emeritus at The University of Iowa. My time at Iowa was rewarding and challenging, and I am grateful to the colleagues there who supported my work. Now, as a faculty member of Gordon College (Wenham, Massachusetts), I am pleased to be among and working with their fine faculty and staff, most of all C. Thomas Brooks, Director of Choirs and Chair of the Department of Music. Tom's vision has given my life new meaning and direction.

Lastly, I am profoundly indebted to my wife, Donna, who has stood by me "in sickness and in health." King Solomon said it best, *He who finds a wife finds a good thing, and obtains favor from the Lord* (Proverbs 18:22).

CHORAL ADMINISTRATION

1 | Becoming a Choral Music Director

Welcome to the study of the choral music program. Most likely you have spent many hours singing in various choirs. Now you are embarking on preparation for a leadership role in choral music. Whether you become a public or private school music teacher, a church choir or community chorus director, or a college or university choral conductor, you are preparing for an exciting and challenging profession that many have found rewarding.

Every choral conductor automatically assumes the role of teacher. There is no escaping the responsibility of imparting knowledge in the choral art. The teaching profession is a noble calling, and those who are called to educate succeeding generations make a lasting, positive impact upon society. Think of the best teachers whom you have had and how they have contributed to your personal and professional goals. Perhaps you have had a choral director whose love of music so inspired you that you have chosen to follow in his or her footsteps. While the path to becoming a choral conductor is demanding, you may take pride in knowing that this profession enhances the human spirit and adds greatly to the quality of life.

A well-known newspaper columnist, Sydney Harris, once wrote a column titled "Teachers Live On." In it he discussed the obituary of a University of Chicago professor that ended with the statement, "He left no survivors." Harris related that a former student of the professor called to protest, noting that the professor had hundreds of survivors in his former students. A great teacher, stated Harris, even without writing a word is survived by generations, even centuries of people, whose lives become the ultimate reward. Not everything in life can be measured in dollars and cents—certainly not the most important things.

THE PROFESSIONAL CHORAL MUSIC EDUCATOR

What does it mean to be a member of a profession? The dictionary defines a profession as "a calling requiring specialized knowledge and often long and intensive academic preparation" (Merriam-Webster, 1985, p. 939). This definition certainly describes the requirements of a choral music educator. The general public, however, often lacks respect for education as a profession. Why is this?

To be treated as a profession, public perception must be that the members act like professionals. Teaching is often seen as a nine-month job with lifetime job security. While it is true that many teachers teach only for the regular academic year, and that teaching is a rather secure occupation, it is also true that many people never understand that teaching requires life-long learning. Good teachers are constantly upgrading their knowledge and skills and often spend summer breaks attending workshops or taking college or university courses. This is one of the characteristics that marks a professional—the willingness to spend the time and resources to remain up to date in his or her area.

One of the best ways an educator can stay on the cutting edge is to belong to professional organizations and to attend the meetings and conferences scheduled by those organizations. For the choral musician, belonging to the American Choral Directors Association (Lawton, Oklahoma) is an excellent way to stay current in the choral field. Founded in 1961, the ACDA has greatly improved the status of choral music in the United States; convention programs present the best in choral clinicians and choirs, and regular publications help to disseminate current information. Membership in ACDA helps strengthen the profession of choral music, and it helps members to grow as choral professionals. Many colleges and universities have ACDA chapters where students can begin their life-long membership in this inspiring profession.

The largest group of professional music educators in the United States is The National Association for Music Education (Reston, Virginia). Once known as the Music Educators National Conference (MENC), this organization of approximately sixty-five thousand members is the "umbrella" group for many other music teacher organizations. Begun in 1907 in Keokuk, Iowa, as the Music Supervisor's National Conference (Birge, 1939), MENC has firmly established the place of music in America's public and private schools. This organization was responsible for helping to establish national standards for music education (MENC, 1994) and has been active in promoting the benefits of a music education for all students. Most colleges and universities have student MENC chapters, where preservice students can learn the benefits of belonging to a professional music teacher organization.

QUALIFICATIONS FOR THE CHORAL CONDUCTOR

The definition of a profession implies specialized knowledge and intensive academic preparation; music students know how specialized the content base is in the music major. Knowledge of music, however, is only the beginning of a choral director's preparation. Vito Mason,

Figure 1.1. ACDA logo. (American Choral Directors Association. Used by permission.)

Figure 1.2. MENC logo. (The National Association for Music Education, formerly Music Educators National Conference. Used by permission.)

a former choral professor at the American University in Washington, D.C., gives the following ten qualifications in the article "On Being a Choral Conductor" (1985):

- Know the score thoroughly.
- Acquire the skill to speak precisely and inspirationally.
- Develop the ability to hear.
- Be a thoroughly trained musician.
- Acquire skill on an instrument.
- Develop a trained mind.
- Attain good physical coordination.
- Contain a musical imagination.
- Recognize the composer's rights.
- Be open minded to new ideas.

For the book *In Quest of Answers* (1991), Carole Glenn asked prominent American choral directors about the qualifications for being a conductor. Excerpts from some of the answers follow:

Eph Ehly: "Foremost, the conductor must be able to communicate and inspire."

Rodney Eichenberger: "The ideal conductor has a thorough understanding of musical style and a keen insight into interpersonal relationships."

Joseph Flummerfelt: "The conductor should have musicianship, intelligence, a passion to communicate . . . and an understanding of how people learn."

Margaret Hillis: "One must be able to analyze a score, to hear it, to know how the piece is put together."

Donald Neuen: "A conductor needs a vital personality. He or she also needs a zeal for hard work. A conductor must have a love of people and music, as well as an inner, honest sensitivity to all kinds of feelings."

Weston Noble: "I would deem it important that we . . . have a high feeling-function . . . accompanied by a strong intellectual background, and an awareness that the predominance of emotion can be negative as well as positive."

Robert Shaw: "Obviously, the most important musical qualifications are the ability and facility to study the score."

Dale Warland: "I think that one must be, first of all, as good a musician as is possible. That is primary."

All of the aforementioned qualifications develop over time, and the music major preparing to conduct should be well along in establishing a base of knowledge and skills. The challenge is to never stop growing and learning.

Great musical knowledge and conducting skill do little good unless choral directors develop the interpersonal skills that are needed to work with singers. More persons drop out of teaching because of interpersonal problems than for any other reason (Elrod, 1976). Teaching is a people-related process, and there is no way around the need for developing a personal means of communication that facilitates positive relationships.

Eph Ely states that foremost, the conductor must be an effective communicator. Good communication implies that the teacher/director has a businesslike attitude before a group. Louis Rossman (1989) states: "Be assertive, but not hostile" (p. 5); a conductor must have a take-charge attitude without being authoritarian or abusive. Most often this is reflected in effective use of the speaking voice. A beginning teacher may have trouble finding his or her "teaching voice" and speak too casually, using a conversational tone. Good teaching is similar to acting; a conductor must find and use an "acting voice" when in front of an ensemble. An effective speaker also stays away from such mannerisms as repeatedly saying "you know" and "OK." Conductors need to speak clearly, precisely, and loudly enough to be heard by all ensemble members.

The second characteristic Rossman gives for effective communication is good eye contact. "If a student is beginning to lose attention, make more eye contact to ensure intensity and maintain this contact a little longer than usual" (p. 5). Speaking over the heads of people or looking down at the floor are clear ways of communicating insecurity. Conductors must speak up and look up to communicate effectively.

Perhaps the greatest qualification needed to be a music teacher is a love of music. Persons who love music so much that they can't imagine doing anything else with their lives are headed in the right direction for a successful teaching career. Any others should perhaps rethink their future. Music teaching can be hard, exhausting work. There are days when the only thing that keeps a choral director going is his or her love of music. To those who have a passion for music, welcome to the world of choral leadership!

HISTORICAL PERSPECTIVES

Today's choral conductors have roots that extend far back in time. As beginning professionals, it is important to know something about these roots and the foundation of the choral art. Knowing the roots of a profession helps put the present and the future in perspective. It also develops a respect for how far choral directors have come in establishing choral music as a respected artistic endeavor.

Ancient Times

There is historical evidence that choral singing existed in many of the earliest civilizations. In ancient Greece music and gymnastics were considered to be the foundation of education. Plato and Aristotle valued the central place of music, noting its moralizing nature and effect on the senses. Because members of the general public were musically educated, they could participate in a wide-range of choral activities, including choruses that were integral to the performance of Greek drama. Music contests and festivals were prevalent, and concert societies and artists' unions were formed. By the end of the fourth century B.C.E., music education had reached the height of its influence, an importance that has yet to be found in modern civilization (Mark, 1982).

Music education in ancient Rome was valued as an intellectual discipline. The upper class included music in the basic education of youth along with arithmetic, geometry, and astronomy as part of what was known as the *quadrivium*. Roman citizens understood the benefits of a strong academic education in music but held musical performers to a lower status of servitude. Performance was relegated to slaves and foreigners and used mostly for celebrations and entertainment. This philosophy may be difficult to understand in contemporary society, where the general public shows little interest in the intellectual study of music, placing most of its value on music as entertainment.

Singing in biblical times is well documented in the Old Testament; the book of Psalms is known as the hymnbook of the Hebrews. Chief among composers was King David, who played the lyre and was himself a singer. While we do not know the music to which the Psalms were set, the texts of the Psalms represent some of the most sublime poetry ever written and remain a viable source of texts for composers of choral music.

The Levites are the first professional musicians named in the Bible—they were paid musicians. By the time King Solomon built the temple, there were as many as four thousand Levites involved in worship through singing and playing of instruments. Today, many choral musicians continue in this tradition by holding positions as choral directors in churches and synagogues.

The birth of Christianity led to new musical traditions in worship that were to climax centuries later in the form of the Roman Catholic mass. Early on, Christian chants were patterned after Jewish melodies, and psalm singing was retained as a major element of worship. After the Romans destroyed the Jewish temple in 70 C.E., instrumental music was banned from the synagogue as a gesture of mourning, and early Christians then carried over this ban to their services as well (Kegerreis, 1970, p. 319). The banning of instruments resulted in a style of unaccompanied singing that became embedded in the traditions of church music. The "a cappella choir movement" of twentieth-century America can trace its roots to this banning of instruments from Jewish and Christian worship.

In 313 C.E. the Roman Empire was Christianized under Constantine. Christianity spread quickly under Charlemagne, who not only conquered but established centers for learning throughout Europe. Christian chant began to conform and stabilize and singing schools, or *Schola Cantorum*, were established for the education of priests; these schools included instruction in music theory and singing. "The Schola is a very important entity to the choral musician because it represents the first official school for training vocal musicians in the medieval world" (Collins, 1993, p. 6).

The Medieval Era (c. 500 to 1450 C.E.)

By the end of the sixth century, Pope Gregory the Great had created the "Golden Age of Plainsong" (c. 500–1000 C.E.), which led to the codification of what is now called Gregorian Chant. The mass became standardized, and the need for singers and trained musicians was met through singing schools, monasteries, convents, and *orphanotrophium*; the latter were orphanages where boys were given singing instruction and a general education. By the eleventh and twelfth centuries, cathedral schools opened in urban settings for a rising civil servant class. These schools also provided a basic education and trained students in music for worship. Music education as public education had its roots in these cathedral schools.

The founding of universities further influenced the importance of music education. Major theorists such as Boethius of Ravenna (*De institutione musica*) and Guido D'Arezzo (*Micrologus*) produced writings and theories valued for their scientific and mathematical knowledge. Guido developed one of the earliest forms of music notation and introduced solmization syllables in relation to a person's hand to facilitate music reading (see Figure 1.3). The academic study of music (*musica speculativa*) was part of the seven liberal arts: the *trivium* (grammar, rhetoric, logic) and *quadrivium* (arithmetic, geometry, astronomy, music). Performance (*musica practica*) was studied outside of academia.

The study of music in an academic setting has never had such emphasis for all students as it had in the medieval university. Today's students who pursue a liberal arts degree rarely have any in-depth study of music. The general public does not understand the complex body of knowledge that music represents. Music educators need to inform people that music is an academic subject worthy of its place in the school curriculum.

Music performance was centered in the church during the Middle Ages, with the cathedral of Notre Dame in Paris becoming a leading center. In addition to the mass, the motet evolved as an important form of composition. Motets were generally short, polyphonic pieces based on sacred Latin texts and sung unaccompanied by a choir of four to six boys and ten to thirteen men. Organ, string, and wind instruments were gradually added, but protests against the use of instruments were common.

The medieval choir conductor typically was an adult member of the chorus. Early conducting used up-and-down motions of the hand to indicate the pulse; conductors also were known to have used a long wooden stick or roll of paper to keep the beat. As music became more polyphonic, a circular motion of the hand was used to indicate the flowing line; *arsis* (upward stress) and *thesis* (downward relaxation) motions reflected word accent rather than meter. This style of conducting, known as *chironomy*, remains appropriate for conducting the nonmetrical music of the Medieval and Renaissance eras.

The Renaissance (c. 1450 to 1600)

Music education in the Renaissance was either private instruction for children of the nobility or instruction for the talented poor at church schools. In England, guild schools were be-

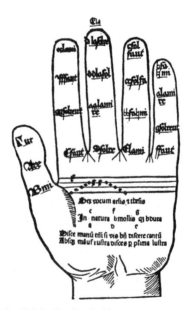

Figure 1.3. Guidonian hand. (Anonymous woodcut, 1488.)

gun for children of the merchant class. While these schools were taught by priests, the idea of public education began to blossom.

The Renaissance, known as "The Golden Age of Polyphony," produced the full flowering of choral singing in cathedrals and chapels of the nobility. The bass voice was added to the choral timbre, resulting in the four traditional voice parts (SATB). By 1625 the choir of the Sistine Chapel in Rome had grown to thirty-two singers, all of whom were boys or men. These well-educated musicians were products of the cathedral schools. In Venice, the great cathedral of St. Mark's with its five domes had up to five choirs, often singing or playing music of multiple voice parts.

The idea that Renaissance choral singing was always unaccompanied is somewhat mistaken. In the "da cappella" or chapel style of the Renaissance, instruments slowly became common in worship but most often doubled vocal lines; the pipe organ typically was used in this manner. Therefore, to speak of "a cappella" singing as always being unaccompanied vocal music is historically inaccurate. Kegerreis (1970) states, "It was during the eighteenth century that the term *a cappella* began to refer to unaccompanied choral performance " (p. 320). By the twentieth century, the term "a cappella" in America clearly meant unaccompanied singing.

Renaissance choral conductors had an important role in leading the various worship services of the Roman rite, both in cathedrals and chapels of nobility. Most had been trained in choir schools, and many chapel conductors became composers and organists of great wealth and fame. The choir often stood around a large, common choir book, where the conductor could easily communicate with the singers.

The Protestant Reformation added another dimension to choral music development: congregational singing. In the Roman Catholic tradition, singing was done mostly by the choir. Martin Luther, believing that worship should actively involve everyone, wrote many chorales (Lutheran hymns) for congregational singing. Lutheran choirs eventually were opened to women and members of the congregation. Luther believed in music literacy for the general populace and prescribed that music be taught in the church-sponsored schools. Music literacy became an educational objective for all children.

The great Anglican tradition of English choral singing was a continuation of the Roman Catholic model. Evidence from an early choir in Warwick (1415) documents that boys were allowed two pounds annually for food and clothing, were flogged when they disobeyed or were absent from rehearsal, and had their heads shaved each year at the beginning of Lent. King Henry VIII established and endowed numerous cathedral and collegiate choral foundations; cathedral choirs of twenty to thirty men and boys were thus secured as part of a national culture.

The Baroque Era (c. 1600 to 1750)

The centrality of choral music in the Renaissance gave way in the Baroque to an emphasis on solo singing and opera. In addition, instrumental music blossomed and became independent from vocal music. The "old" style of a cappella choral singing (*stile antico*) was gradually replaced with a new style (*stile moderno*) in which instrumental accompaniment no longer doubled voices but had a life of its own, providing a contrast (*stile concertato*) to the vocal parts.

Choral singing, though its dominance was being challenged, continued to be important. Multimovement forms such as the cantata and oratorio were composed in vast numbers and included solo sections alternating with choruses. The music was often of virtuosic quality and demanded excellent singing technique. In addition, the practice of in-residence choirs for churches and cathedrals continued. J. S. Bach not only was a choirmaster in Leipzig but also was responsible for the general education of the boy choristers under his direction. Such programs were costly, and the size of most choirs was rather small except when large numbers of singers were needed for special occasions.

Choirs during the Baroque era remained predominantly male groups, with boys singing treble parts. Whereas women were known to have participated in secular Renaissance court music, with the advent of opera roles for women, female participation in a wider range of music became more accepted, "and by the end of the Baroque many choirs in Europe, even church choirs were comprised of both women and men" (May, 1987, p. 121).

The choral conductor in the Baroque era often directed from the harpsichord or organ. Because Baroque music was metrically organized, beat patterns began to emerge that distinguished one beat from another in a repeated gesture. However, audible time beating (e.g., the tapping of a stick) was continued from the Renaissance practice when large or combined groups necessitated strong measures to produce order. Robinson and Winold (1976) comment: "It is very difficult for the twentieth-century conductor to conceive that performances in earlier times were probably given amid pounding, stamping, singing, and shouting on the part of the director. This practice, however, continued even into the nineteenth century in isolated places like the Paris Opera" (p. 38). Conductors of the Baroque era were mainly interested in holding secure the tempo and rhythm. No established system of conducting technique was taught or known at the time.

The emphasis on solo singing during the Baroque was of great importance to singing in general. Demanding vocal lines that employed improvisation, a wide range, and many embellishments elevated singing to a virtuosic art. Treatises on singing were written, and the necessity of singing instruction became apparent as the demands of vocal lines increased in solo and choral music. The art of singing was raised to a new level.

The Classical Era (c. 1750 to 1825)

The era of Haydn, Mozart, and Beethoven was a time in which instrumental music assumed a dominant role. The sonata-allegro and concerto forms became standardized, and improvements in instrument making made it possible to produce a fuller and richer orchestral sound.

Few new trends in choral composition were evident at this time. While the performance of choral music continued to flourish, it was by way of older forms established in previous generations. One new characteristic that evolved was the blending of sacred and secular styles of composition. Former compositional techniques were abandoned as choral compositions began to resemble composers' secular writing; choral part writing often paralleled instrumental writing, and vocal lines demanded greater vocal technique. Also, works like the Ninth Symphony of Beethoven, with its final choral movement, began to reflect the heightened level of drama and expressivity that was to follow in the nineteenth century.

During the Classical era the dominant place for music performance moved from church to concert hall and opera house. While Haydn and Mozart continued to depend upon the patronage of the courts and aristocratic society, composers such as Beethoven finally were freed to make a living in public venues. Beethoven was known to have conducted his own symphonic works in subscription concerts. The making of music more publicly accessible gave rise to singing societies that encouraged the participation of large numbers, including women. However, most music of this period was performed by relatively small ensembles. The typical orchestra contained no more than forty players, and choruses were of similar size.

One role of the conductor continued to be as a keyboardist, especially in churches where the organist assumed such a leadership role. When choral and orchestral forces were joined, dual positions often existed in which the choral director, seated at the keyboard, was assisted by the concertmaster. With the elimination of continuo parts from choral works by the late eighteenth century, however, the role of the concertmaster increased in importance. "[T]he violin-leader established a silent conducting style much like one would find today in European restaurants in which an orchestra plays for dining entertainment. It is thus not surprising that the early nineteenth-century conductors . . . were string players" (Robinson and Winold, 1976, pp. 42–43).

The style of continuous time beating with the hand became standardized in the eighteenth century. "By the end of the century the beat patterns in use today were well established among orchestral directors. Still lacking however were the attributes of the interpretive conductor. Conducting was still a metrical rather than an interpretive procedure" (Robinson and Winold, 1976, p. 40).

Beethoven, as a transitional composer, was noted to be quite expressive in his conducting, but in a rather unorthodox manner. In quoting Spohr, Stoessel (1920) writes:

> It was Beethoven's custom to insert all sorts of dynamic markings in the parts, and remind his players of the marks by resorting to the most curious bodily contortions. At every "sforzato" he would thrust his arms away from his breast where he held them crossed. When he desired a "piano" he would crouch lower and lower; when the music grew louder into "forte," he would literally leap into the air and at times grow so excited as to yell in the midst of a climax. (p. 3)

The Romantic Era (c. 1825 to 1900)

By the beginning of the nineteenth century, the time of the "stand-up" conductor had arrived; this necessitated the expansion of ensemble size and a compositional style that demanded more overt expressivity. The use of a conducting baton was introduced in Germany by Mosel in 1812, and its employment, while not universally appreciated, spread rapidly. "Spohr tells a most amusing anecdote of how the musicians of the London orchestra protested most vehemently when he first proposed to lead them with the magic little stick instead of playing the violin with them" (Stoessel, 1920, p. 3).

The technique of conducting also became a topic of debate, especially between the composers Mendelssohn and Wagner. Mendelssohn favored a more conservative style of classical conducting that adhered to the written page. Wagner, however, believed a conductor should make great use of tempo rubato, thus bringing his own ideas of interpretation to the score. Franz Liszt also preferred a freer style of conducting. "It was Liszt's desire to free the performance of orchestral and choral works from the limitations of bar-line rhythm and to effect this change his style of conducting became a sort of modern chironomy in which his gesture expressed his 'melos' and underlying spirit of the composition as well as fulfilling their mechanical function" (Stoessel, 1920, p. 5). The debate between adhering to the score and freedom from the score continued well into the twentieth century. "Since each view was carried too far, the end result was a controlled rubato that became a factor in the development of the virtuoso conductor of the twentieth century" (Robinson and Winold, 1976, p. 44).

Choral composition in the Romantic era was generally of three types: (1) part-songs or short choral pieces, (2) sacred music with liturgical texts, and (3) music on a grand scale for chorus and orchestra. These types of writing required choral organizations of vastly different proportions, from small, intimate groups to large symphonic choirs. The first category of composition was especially important for the growing number of amateur part-singing groups. Separate choirs for females and males existed, and singing societies and choral festivals flourished everywhere.

Singing technique began to reflect the demand for greater realism in opera. In Germany and Italy solo singing was cultivated, resulting in larger voices capable of being heard over an orchestra. This bravura style of singing was not appreciated in all circles of music making; a duality emerged between the lighter "classic" type of art song singing and the operatic, full-throated style. These two approaches also were heard in choral singing; the opera chorus demanded a more soloistic style, while the standard choral organization required a more "blended" approach.

The difference between these two schools of singing has presented problems for voice teachers and choral directors to this day. Should choral singers, in their attempt to blend, be required to pull back and not sing as trained soloists, or is the ideal choral blend advanced when all singers sing as soloists? This debate, begun in the nineteenth century, became further advanced with the a cappella choir movement in the twentieth century.

The American Scene (c. 1600 to 1900)

America's roots in choral singing are found in the various groups of Europeans who ventured to this new country. When the Franciscan friars settled in St. Augustine, Florida, in 1603, they brought with them the rich traditions of the Roman rite. The Puritans, reacting negatively to Roman practices, brought with them psalters, from which they sang only the texts of the Psalms in metrical form. A preacher or leader would "line out" a tune by singing a phrase at a time, and the congregation would imitate the line by rote. Little concern was given to music reading or singing instruction, and because there were no public schools, music education among these early settlers was, at best, informal.

When the country began to grow, professional music teachers arrived from Europe; a number of private academies and schools then offered a wide variety of music study. The Moravians who settled in Bethlehem, Pennsylvania, held music to be of great importance; all children were expected to sing and play an instrument. Records show that some of the earliest New World performances of symphonies by Haydn and Mozart occurred among the Moravians. Rich choral singing was fostered, and a number of Moravians wrote choral anthems. The Moravians were a musical oasis in cultivating musical taste.

For the most part, singing in churches was abysmal, so much so that in 1717 the Reverend Thomas Symmes preached a sermon in Boston on the need for reform in singing. This led to the establishment of "singing schools" and societies for the improvement of singing and music reading. Most schools were held at churches once or twice a week for six weeks, and were led by itinerant singing masters who traveled from town to town. While only psalters were used at first, eventually instruction books and songbooks were written by American authors and composers, among them the singing master William Billings (1746–1800). Singing schools became a major focus of social interaction.

The rural South also experienced the rise of singing schools, but their emphasis on "shape-note" singing was unique. The shape-note system employed different notehead symbols (e.g., diamond, square) as a memory aid for singing solfège syllables (see Figure 1.4). This system became so popular that shape-note conventions sprang up in which large groups of people would gather for a day-long singing fest of hymns, sung first by syllable, and then words. These singing conventions continue in the rural South.

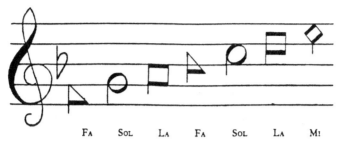

Figure 1.4. Shape notes. (Four-shape notation sequence used in the *Sacred Harp*.)

It would appear that singing and choral music were rather crude in early America. However, the desire to improve the quality of singing points to the importance that singing must have had for some early settlers. When the Massachusetts Bay Colony passed "The Old Deluder Satan Act" in 1647, public schools were mandated in towns of more than fifty households. But music in these schools was mainly recreational; serious music study was confined mostly to private and church schools.

The eighteenth and nineteenth centuries were witness to a growing support for public education in America, especially in the large industrial cities of the North. By 1750 the Latin grammar school curriculum was broadened to include teaching in English, and universal education was championed as the means to improve the lot of the poor. Music, however, continued to be viewed by the public as a recreational activity, and singing in these schools was not cultivated in any formal manner.

Lowell Mason (1792–1872), born in Medfield, Massachusetts, came from a family who valued music and who saw that Lowell had a rich education in singing and playing of instruments. After a brief move to Savannah, Georgia, where he worked in a bank and organized a church choir, Mason returned to Boston to become director of the Handel and Haydn Society, the oldest community chorus in America (1815). Lowell Mason became a prominent figure in the singing-school movement, and he and a friend opened a private music school: the Boston Academy of Music. It was Mason's belief that all people had a degree of musical talent, and that singing was a skill to be generally developed.

Basing his educational theories on those of the Swiss educator Johann Heinrich Pestalozzi, Mason produced his famous *Manual of the Boston Academy of Music for Instruction in the Elements of Vocal Music on the System of Pestalozzi* (1834), in which sight-singing and singing skills were developed in a sequential method. In 1837 Mason challenged the Boston school board to permit him to teach music, without pay, to the children in the Hawes elementary school. He wanted to show that he could teach all children to sing. The experiment was successfully demonstrated by a public concert of the children, and Mason was named the first public school music teacher in the city of Boston (1838). Music in the school curriculum then spread quickly to other cities, and Lowell Mason became known as "the father of music education." While it is true that there were music teachers in private schools before Mason, Lowell Mason is credited with being the first public school music teacher in the United States.

Choral singing flourished in nineteenth-century America, especially in Boston, where the Handel and Haydn Society dominated choral activity in America for one hundred years. In 1857 this group sponsored a choral festival for over six hundred singers, who presented Haydn's *Creation*, Mendelssohn's *Elijah*, and Handel's *Messiah*. Church choirs also flourished, many of them outside the main urban areas. In 1869 the Great National Peace Jubilee

Figure 1.5. Lowell Mason, 1792–1872. (Photo courtesy of MENC Historical Center, Special Collections in Performing Arts, Performing Arts Library, University of Maryland. Used by permission.)

was held in Boston; there were 110 participating choral societies and ten thousand singers. Included in the repertoire for the concert was the Anvil Chorus from *Il trovatore* by Verdi, accompanied by one hundred red-shirted members of the Boston Fire Department hammering on one hundred anvils. Although European repertoire was the mainstay of the concert, works of American composers were commissioned for later festivals and "represent an important step in the American composer achieving his 'Declaration of Independence'"(Colson, 1974, p. 21).

Another leading center of choral activity was New York City. There, in 1894, Frank Damrosch gave a concert with the Musical Arts Society devoted solely to the performance of great unaccompanied choral literature from Europe. The ensemble's style of unaccompanied singing was modeled after church choirs in Berlin (*Domchor*) and Leipzig (*Thomanerchor*), where a number of American choral conductors, including Lowell Mason, had traveled for study. "When they formed their choirs they copied repertoire, performance practices, mannerisms, and the basic sound of the two German choirs, which used boy sopranos and altos" (Kegerreis, 1970, p. 321). This a cappella choir sound was to have a tremendous influence on American choral singing in the first half of the twentieth century.

Twentieth-Century America (1900 to 2000)

Dean Peter Lutkin introduced the a cappella sound in 1906 at Northwestern University when preparing a lecture on music of the Renaissance. What began as an impromptu group for Lutkin's lecture became established as the Northwestern A Cappella Choir. The sound was then spread by the choir through important appearances at music teacher conferences.

The college choir that became most famous for a cappella singing was at St. Olaf College in Northfield, Minnesota. Under the direction of F. Melius Christiansen, the "St. Olaf sound" became the model for fine choral singing. The characteristics of the St. Olaf Choir included: (1) a spiritual emphasis found in church-related schools, (2) wearing of robes, (3) long, tedious try-out procedures, (4) flawless memorization of repertoire, (5) hidden starting pitch, (6) limited repertoire of about twenty selections, (7) repertoire taken generally from nineteenth-century German and Russian schools and Christiansen's own arrangements, and (8) cultivation of the "straight tone" (Kegerreis, 1970, pp. 322–23). This last characteristic, a tone without vibrato, caused much debate in the choral profession; many choral directors and voice teachers were critical of a sound that required students to suppress the natural vibrato of the voice. However, conductors currently associated with the Christiansen sound

Figure 1.6. F. Melius Christiansen, 1871–1955. (Photo courtesy of St. Olaf Archives. Used by permission.)

agree that "a free and natural vibrato reflects correct singing and is not necessarily detrimental to a balanced, homogeneous sound" (Aune, 1996, p. 16).

The a cappella choir movement spread quickly throughout the college ranks and also found great support in America's high schools, where it was responsible for bringing thousands of students into choral programs. In fact, the surge of choral singing in the schools elevated choirs to assume curricular status; no longer were choirs just glee clubs held before or after school. The movement brought a new prestige to the choral art and with it greater public support. On the negative side, however, the sole concentration on performance with little regard for comprehensive musicianship became so set a model that the academic side of music in many high school choirs was woefully neglected.

Another legendary figure in the development of choral singing in America was John Finley Williamson (1887–1964), the founder of the famous Westminster Choir College of Princeton, New Jersey. Williamson was a successful follower of the Christiansen model, and in 1926 he began a school in Dayton, Ohio, to train choral directors. "Williamson became convinced that competently trained directors could make tremendous strides in uplifting the quality and level of Protestant worship" (Van Camp, 1965, p. 236). Williamson moved the choir school from Dayton to Ithaca, New York, and finally settled it in Princeton, New Jersey, in 1932. His approach to choral sound changed when he found himself close to New York City and singers who were preparing for operatic careers. Instead of a "straight" tone that was easier to achieve with lighter, younger voices, Williamson shifted to a style that emphasized the solo quality of the mature voice. According to Williamson, the ideal choral sound was based on each voice singing as a soloist, with a rich and deep-throated tone. Williamson's approach had a great impact on choral directors. Most influenced were university choir directors who had graduate students with more mature singing voices. The "straight-tone" approach did not work as well with these singers. Today the sound of the Westminster Choir College choirs is one that continues to emulate the full-throated, soloistic, and highly energized sound identified with John Finley Williamson.

Howard Swan, in *Choral Conducting Symposium* (Decker and Herford, 1988), details six schools of choral singing that have influenced choral directors in twentieth-century America. Two of these have been discussed: St. Olaf and Westminster Choir. A third school was led by Father William J. Finn, author of *The Art of Choral Conducting* (1939). Father Finn's "sound" was based on the blending and classifying of voices as instrumental timbres (flutes, reeds, horns, strings). His ideal choral tone resembled a symphonic orchestra's varied distribution of tone colors.

Another school of choral tone is reflected in the work of the popular entertainer Fred Waring. Waring's "sung-speech" approach to vocal production, based on the belief that words should be sung as naturally as spoken speech, was put forth in the monograph *Tone Syllables*. The resulting "smooth" type of singing resembled that of popular artists of the day; it was particularly appropriate for very legato singing and ballads. The Fred Waring Pennsylvanians was one of the first professional choral ensembles to travel America and bring popular-style choral singing to the masses.

A fifth school of choral singing is represented by a much less known group of voice scientists: Douglas Stanley, John C. Wilcox, and Joseph J. Klein. These men, among the first to study singing from a scientific perspective, were responsible for creating a movement that stressed the development of the individual voice in the choral setting. From their work, choral directors were led to understand the importance of healthy singing and the need to teach voice in the choral rehearsal to choristers who would normally receive very little singing instruction.

Figure 1.7. John Finley Williamson, 1887–1964. (Photo courtesy of the Archives, Westminster Choir College of Rider University. Used by permission.)

Robert Shaw, often referred to as "the father of modern choral conductors," is at the center of the sixth school of choral tone development. Shaw began his career with Fred Waring but struck out on his own to New York City, where in 1948 he formed the Robert Shaw Chorale. Shaw toured the country with his chorus presenting masterworks, such as Bach's Mass in B Minor, in communities that had rarely heard such great music. Numerous tours to Europe under the aegis of the U.S. State Department further established Shaw's prominence, as did his work as associate conductor of the Cleveland Orchestra under George Szell, for whom he prepared the chorus. Shaw served as the music director and conductor of the Atlanta Symphony Orchestra and Chorus from 1967 to 1988, and upon his retirement was named music director emeritus and conductor laureate.

Robert Shaw received sixteen Grammy Awards, was the 1991 recipient of the Kennedy Center Honors, and in 1993 received the Conductors' Guild Theodore Thomas Award (Baxter, 1996, p. 9). Shaw, in his "retirement" years continued to direct choral groups and festivals throughout the world. He died in 1999, leaving the choral profession a great legacy.

Figure 1.8. Robert Shaw, 1916–1999. (Photo courtesy of Atlanta Symphony Orchestra. Used by permission.)

The choral tone associated with the choirs of Robert Shaw is a rich, mature one that comes from employment of only the best professionally trained singers. Like John Finley Williamson, Shaw worked mostly with adult singers whose depth of singing experience permitted a wider range of vocal colors than that of the a cappella school. Moreover, Shaw infused his choirs with a type of energy and rhythmic precision that created a vibrant sound, exciting and full of life. His attention to exacting intonation created a purity rarely found in adult singing groups.

> Shaw begins every rehearsal . . . the same way: octave unison on "nu" (noo) sung pianissimo . . . . More pitches are added and the dynamic range is expanded and contracted, but the groundwork is laid in the perfect-octave singing. The individual is directed to sing within the "sleeve" of sound being produced by the section, never allowing excessive vibrato to disturb the unison. (Jones, 1996, p. 20)

To this ideal of "pure" sound Shaw added a style of rhythmically oriented textual declamation that has become known as "rhythmic diction." This style of diction, unlike "sung-speech," requires that each syllable of each word maintain its individual rhythmic integrity. For music that is highly metric in its organizational structure (e.g., Baroque), this type of diction infuses a dancelike quality that is infectious and vibrant. Text is not permitted to "blur" the inherent rhythmic nature of the musical line.

Perhaps Shaw's greatest contribution to the contemporary art of choral music was his communication of stylistic authenticity in regard to the major historical periods of musical creativity. Shaw stated that his structural and analytical studies with the eminent musicologist Julius Herford "most profoundly affected my development" (Baxter, 1996, p. 11). With Herford, Shaw explored how the choral works of each style period should be performed so as to maintain their original character.

Shaw's concern with stylistic authenticity has had a tremendous impact upon the choral world; choral directors have become aware that no one "correct" sound will do for all choral music. A cultivation of varying color palettes is necessary if choirs in the twenty-first century are to sing music in a manner reflecting the way it was originally intended by the composer. The choral profession is deeply indebted to Robert Shaw for inspiring a higher level of music making.

FUTURE DIRECTIONS

The level of choral singing in America has risen throughout the twentieth century. There is now a global vision in choral music, and exposure to music and choirs of cultures from around the world has led to a new emphasis on multicultural music and higher singing standards in general.

Where will the choral music profession find its inspiration and direction in the twenty-first century? Perhaps in the younger generations of singers who are finding their voices in the ever expanding children's choir movement? Or maybe in professional groups such as the Dale Warland Singers, where members are actually paid to sing? Could it be in community and symphony chorus organizations who are committed to life-long music making? And what about school, college, and university choral groups, where the level of singing continues to rise? Will churches spend more money to attract really first-rate choral directors to build first-rate programs? Could an emphasis on diversity bring about a totally new choral repertoire? What does the future hold?

Whatever comes, it is bound to be an exciting continuation of growth and higher standards as the medium of recorded sound makes it possible for everyone to hear the best of choral singing. The First Art, a nationally syndicated radio broadcast by Chorus America (an organization of independent professional, semiprofessional, and volunteer choirs), is now making great choral programming available to millions of people each week. The Internet has made it possible for choral musicians to reach out around the world, sharing music and information that can help choral directors even in remote areas.

One thing is certain—the future will be filled with ever expanding technology, and choral musicians will be part of that world. Humanity, however, has a soul, and computers are not much good at caring for the spirit. Perhaps the challenge before the choral profession will be to cultivate a higher sense of public recognition of music as an activity that adds quality to life and makes living more than just existing—that makes life special.

It is a privilege to be part of a profession that since the dawn of time has recognized the arts and their benefits for humankind. Choral directors make a positive contribution to life and living, and all who practice this ancient art should think well of themselves and what they do. It is a profession worthy of its calling.

STUDY AND DISCUSSION QUESTIONS

1. Have you had a choral director who was a significant influence on your wanting to become a choral music educator? Describe the attributes of this person.

2. Why does the general public often perceive the field of education as not being a real profession? What can help to change this negative perception?

3. What do you think Vito Mason meant when he stated that a conductor "recognizes the composer's rights"?

4. What do you think Weston Noble meant when he stated that "the predominance of emotion can be negative as well as positive"?

5. What is one of the major reasons that people drop out of teaching, and why is this?

6. What are the characteristics of effective communication for teaching/conducting?

7. What may be the greatest qualification needed by someone who wants to become a music educator and conductor?

8. What was the role of music education in early Greek and Roman civilizations?

9. Where was music education centered during the Middle Ages, and for what purpose(s)?

10. Who were the medieval church choir members and conductors? Describe the style of conducting used.

11. How did the status of choral music in the Baroque change from that of the Renaissance, and what brought about this change?

12. What was the position of the choral conductor during the Baroque? Describe conducting style as it had evolved to this point in time.

13. What was the typical size of the Classical orchestra and chorus, and who conducted such ensembles?

14. What necessitated the expanded role of the conductor during the Romantic era, and what styles of conducting evolved during this time?

15. What was the general status of singing in early America, and what attempts were made to improve singing?

16. What was the status of choral music in late nineteenth-century America, and where was the greatest choral activity centered?

17. Who is called "the father of music education" and why?

18. What two major schools of choral singing evolved during the first half of the twentieth century, and who were the leaders of these schools?

19. Who is called "the father of modern choral conductors" and why?

20. What will be some major influences on choral music in the twentieth-first century, and how might the profession change in the future?

REFERENCES

Aune, G. J. (1996). The choral methodology and philosophy of F. Melius Christiansen: The tradition continues. *Choral Journal, 37*(4), 15–17.

Baxter, J. (1996). An interview with Robert Shaw: Reflections at eighty. *Choral Journal, 36*(9), 9–13.

Birge, E. B. (1939). *History of public school music in the United States.* Reston, VA: Music Educators National Conference.

Carlson, J. O. (1974). The performance of choral music in America from 1852 to 1872. *Choral Journal*, *14*(8), 20–21.

Collins, D. L. (1993). *Teaching choral music* (2d ed.). Upper Saddle River, NJ: Prentice Hall.

Elrod, W. (1976). Don't get tangled in discipline problems. *Music Educators Journal*, *63*(4), 47–50.

Finn, W. J. (1939/1960). *The art of choral conducting*. 2 vols. Evanston, IL: Summy-Birchard.

Glenn, C. (1991). *In quest of answers*. Chapel Hill, NC: Hinshaw Music.

Jones, A. H. (1996). Shaw: Simply and clearly the best. *Choral Journal*, *36*(9), 19–20.

Kegerreis, R. I. (1970). History of the high school a cappella choir. *Journal of Research in Music Education*, *28*(4), 319–29.

Mark, M. L. (1982). *Source readings in music education history*. New York: Schirmer Books.

Mason, V. E. (1985). On being a choral conductor. *Choral Journal*, *25*(6), 5–7.

May, W. V., Sr. (ed.) (1987). *Something new to sing about* (student text). New York: G. Schirmer, Glencoe.

Merriam-Webster's new collegiate dictionary (9th ed.). (1985). Springfield, MA: Merriam-Webster.

MENC (1994). *The school music program: A new vision*. Reston, VA: Music Educators National Conference.

Robinson, R., and A. Winold (1976). *The choral experience*. New York: Harper's College Press.

Rossman, L. R. (1989). *Tips: Discipline in the music classroom*. Reston, VA: Music Educators National Conference.

Stoessel, A. (1920). *The technic of conducting*. New York: Carl Fischer.

Swan, H. (1988). The development of a choral instrument. In H. A. Decker and J. Herford (eds.), *Choral conducting symposium* (2d ed.). Englewood Cliffs, NJ: Prentice-Hall.

Van Camp, L. (1965). The formation of a cappella choirs at Northwestern University, St. Olaf College, and Westminster Choir College. *Journal of Research in Music Education*, *13*(4), 227–38.

2 | Developing a Philosophy for the Music Program

What response would you give in a job interview to the question, "Why is music important in the school curriculum"? Have you formulated concrete ideas as to the value of a music education? Could you make a convincing argument, or would you resort to something like "music makes people feel good"? The fact is, principals and school boards are not much interested in spending money on a subject whose goal is to make people feel good. The general public wants "the basics," and unless a convincing case can be made for the place of music study in the school curriculum, the music program is among the first to be cut when budgetary restraints call for elimination of programs. Being able to defend music may be tantamount to being hired and retained in a school music position. If you do not have a viable rationale in mind, this chapter should help you to formulate one.

A critical reason for devising a strong rationale for music education is this: it will help you make decisions regarding the nature of the music program you plan and lead. For example, if you think the entertainment value of music is vitally important, then you will no doubt develop a curriculum with a strong show choir component. Likewise, if you believe that music is an academic subject with an in-depth body of knowledge, you will seek to educate your students about music, with various types of performing ensembles used as the learning vehicles. A strong rationale statement will give you focus and will keep you from becoming directionless or blown about by every new idea that comes along. Knowing *why* you do *what* you do will serve to direct *all* that you do.

THE NATIONAL STANDARDS

When the U.S. Congress passed the educational reform legislation of 1992 (Goals 2000: Educate America Act), it adopted a set of voluntary national standards for most areas of the school curriculum, including music. The nine music standards, developed by MENC with input from members nationwide, are published in the monograph *The School Music Program: A New Vision* (MENC, 1994). The following are the basic nine content areas:

- Singing, alone and with others, a varied repertoire of music
- Performing on instruments, alone and with others, a varied repertoire of music
- Improvising melodies, variations, and accompaniments
- Composing and arranging music within specified guidelines
- Reading and notating music
- Listening to, analyzing, and describing music
- Evaluating music and music performances

- Understanding relationships between music, the other arts, and disciplines outside the arts
- Understanding music in relation to history and culture

While these nine standards were adopted as voluntary, many states have now included them as part of their own state curriculum guides. The standards were written not as curriculum but rather as a guide to developing curriculum for all students in music.

The first standard states that all children will be able to sing, alone and with others, a varied repertoire of music. Singing has been the traditional core of the music curriculum from the days of Lowell Mason, and it continues to have much importance. But the success music educators have had in teaching *all* children to sing has not been great. The singing of the National Anthem at sports events is evidence that the general American public does not sing very well. Is this a reflection of poor teaching or an indifferent attitude among the public as to the value of singing? It is probably some of each. Vocal music teachers, in general, may need to learn better ways to teach singing, and to develop a clear rationale for why singing is such an important activity.

Choral directors cannot make the first standard their only objective if students are to receive a complete music education. The other eight standards can be woven throughout the choral curriculum so that students experience the playing of instruments, improvising, composing, music reading, listening, evaluating, interarts relations, and historical and cultural relations (see Chapter 4). Comprehensive musicianship requires a far greater vision for the choral program than typically encountered in the past.

Even with a strong music curriculum in place, a school music program may be in jeopardy when the public is unsympathetic to the program's goals or budgetary limits require program cuts. Unless music teachers can convince the public of music's importance, there will be little hope for the national standards' ever being met in America's schools. It comes down to this: people spend money on, and find time in their lives to do, the things they value. If people value something, they make time for it, even when their schedules are full. Therefore, it is the job of the choral music director to educate the public as to the value of music in people's lives. Value = time = money.

ADVOCACY FOR MUSIC IN THE SCHOOLS

The reasons for justifying music in the schools are many and varied. Music educators, when asked to name the benefits of a music education, often mention some of the following, which typically fall into three categories: personal, social, or educational.

- It increases appreciation for one's own culture.
- It promotes multicultural understanding.
- It creates self-discipline.
- It allows for self-expression.
- It fosters creativity.
- It uses "whole-brain" learning.
- It boosts self-confidence.
- It is a complex body of knowledge worth knowing.
- It encourages life-long learning.
- It integrates all areas of learning in the curriculum.

- It exalts the human spirit.
- It serves as a basic form of communication.
- It involves cooperative learning.
- It heightens school spirit.
- It raises community pride.
- It creates aesthetic sensitivity.
- It is cost effective for schools.
- It permits musical intelligence to be nurtured.
- It connects people to their traditions and heritage.
- It develops abstract thinking, problem solving, and higher-order thinking skills.
- It enhances the quality of life.
- It is conducive to better physical and mental health.
- It provides a means of employment.
- It allows for success in at least one area of study.

This list of twenty-four possible reasons, though not exhaustive, represents many positive outcomes, some of which are more generally recognized than others. All music educators should thoughtfully consider each of these statements (as well as others they might add) and decide for themselves which rationales they feel strongly about and which are most important to them. By committing a short list of five or six rationales to memory, they can, at a moment's notice, speak to parents, schools administrators, school boards, and students about the importance of a music education. Writing a brief paragraph about each rationale brings clarity and helps to commit pertinent information to memory. Teachers also need to be proactive by informing others without being asked.

The twenty-four rationales given here in support of music are among the most common, and others could be cited. Most of these rationale statements are easy to understand and need no further discussion. Several, however, may need further explanation and are discussed as follows.

Cost Effectiveness

The music advocate John Benham, in the video *School Music and "Reverse Economics"* (National Coalition for Music Education, 1991), makes a case for music programs' actually saving money for school districts. He notes that music classes, especially ensembles, often have two to three times the number of students found in regular classrooms. When ensembles are cut from the curriculum, the music students have to go somewhere. They typically go back to regular classrooms, where more teachers are needed to handle the influx of students. Evidence suggests that when elementary music programs are cut, in two to three years the high school ensemble program begins to suffer and shrink in size. As school boards understand that cutting music programs often means hiring additional teachers, they reconsider what seems to be an easy solution and find other ways to conserve costs.

Whole-Brain Learning

In the article "A Stronger Rationale for Music Education," the present author explains "whole-brain learning" as follows:

> *To study music is to study the learning process.* Music is an academic subject that involves learning in the major domains: cognitive (knowledge), psychomotor (skills), affective (attitudes and feelings), and kinesthetic (the senses). Music comprises its own complex body of knowledge, requires the development of motor coordination, shapes attitudes and feelings, and requires learning via the senses. Through music, people engage in the entire learning process and develop keener understandings and insights as to how knowledge, skills, attitudes, feelings, and the senses interrelate. (Phillips, 1993, p. 18)

Some schools teach foreign languages through music because such learning involves "whole-brain" activity. Children who study music actively engage the thinking process in its entirety.

Exalt the Human Spirit

The power of music to exalt the human spirit is sometimes difficult to explain. Carolynn A. Lindemann, a past president of MENC, describes it as follows:

> *Music study enables students to experience all that is human as it inspires them, turns on their senses and emotions, opens their minds, and reaches into their inner selves.* To be sensitive to the power and beauty of music, young people need to come face-to-face with a variety of musical experiences that will help them develop the musical understandings and knowledge necessary to extend the depth with which they think and feel. (Lindemann, 1998, p. 6)

The "power" that Lindemann mentions is something every musician has experienced, but it is difficult to put into words.

Thomas Moore, in *Care of the Soul* (1992), also comments on the power of the arts to help humanity, noting that "if we lack beauty in our lives, we will probably suffer familiar disturbances in the soul—depression, paranoia, meaninglessness, and addiction. The soul craves beauty" (p. 278). Moore also comments that technology's dominance of time and the belief that we can't live without technology creates psychological stress that often manifests as physical impairment. He calls upon art to bring about balance:

> Art, broadly speaking, is that which invites us into contemplation—a rare commodity in modern life. In that moment of contemplation, art intensifies the presence of the world. We see it more vividly and more deeply. The emptiness that many people complain dominates their lives comes in part from a failure to let the world in, to perceive it and engage it fully. . . . art *arrests* attention, an important service to the soul. Soul cannot thrive in a fast-paced life because being affected, taking things in and chewing on them, requires time. (p. 286)

Care of the soul releases the spirit to fly and find what it truly means to be human. What a wonderful experience can be found through the study of music, and how difficult it is to convince the public that money should be spent on such notions!

Transfer Learning

A reason that does not appear on the list of rationales is one that has caught the attention of the media—the effect that music has on learning other tasks or subjects, a phenomenon called "transfer learning." The "Mozart Effect" has received much attention following some research that indicates that college students who listen to Mozart's music before taking a test score higher than those who don't listen to such music. The lasting effects, however, have been found to be negligible. Similarly, the research done on music study and its relation to higher reading and math achievement (Hanshumaker, 1986) indicates a somewhat positive relationship, but hardly one that is conclusive. Music educators must take a "wait and see" attitude about the transferability of music study to achievement in other subject areas. If strong evidence surfaces, so much the better. But weak evidence is, in some respects, no evidence at all.

Of course it could be argued that there is little evidence to support any of the twenty-four reasons given for the importance of music study. Does strong research evidence show how music raises self-esteem among students? No. But music teachers have experienced this phenomenon so many times that collectively they know it to be true. Sometimes, common sense and wisdom through observation and experience must be relied upon when making claims for music's power to mold. But making out-on-the-limb claims such as "the boy who blows a horn will never blow a safe," that is, the study of music makes people better human beings, just can't stand the scrutiny of experience and observation. It is true that "good" people often choose to study music, and it is true that "bad" people also appreciate art. But there is no evidence of a cause-and-effect relationship. Music educators must be careful how far they go in making claims for music that cannot be validated either empirically or by common experience.

Music as a Vocation

Preparing students to enter the work force is central to the mission of secondary education. Hundreds of thousands of people make some type of musical activity their vocation, whether teaching, performing, selling, or promoting music. Do the schools, then, not have an obligation to expose students to the many and varied opportunities that music presents for meaningful employment? Yes, they do, but how often is this argument central to the cause of maintaining school programs? The music industry in all of its many facets generates billions of dollars in sales and salaries; students have the right to know how and where they might become part of this huge music network. And how will they know if they aren't involved in some type of musical activity? School music programs are vocational education, and the business side of music typically is staffed by people who have a background in music study and performance.

Cooperative Learning

One of the buzz words in education has become *cooperation*. People must learn to work together in the "real" world, and educators, in general, believe in fostering this skill and attitude from a young age. Therefore, schoolchildren commonly work in groups to solve problems.

Where else has cooperation been demonstrated better than in music classes, where students have always worked together for the good of the ensemble? Music educators have been leaders in stressing cooperative learning; large and small groups of students function as one with a singular purpose—communicating through music. General music class also becomes a place for group learning when students work together to produce a composition or put on a musical production. If cooperation is a desirable attribute for the adult business world, then students can learn it in music class.

Multicultural Sensitivity

Another leading theme in education today is that of multicultural sensitivity, which translates into learning respect and appreciation for the values and traditions of cultures other than one's own. Again, music educators have been leaders in exposing students to a wide variety of musical styles from around the world. Entire issues of the *Music Educators Journal* are dedicated to this objective, and MENC has been a leader in publishing multicultural resources for teachers. The culture of a people is tied directly to its arts, and through the arts students come to view what others value and how they live. Prejudice is often the result of narrow exposure to others outside of one's own culture; through music such barriers are removed as children come to understand that we are all God's children, valued because we exist on this planet together as part of the human race. While we may not look alike and differ in our beliefs and traditions, we all have the right to live and thrive as neighbors in a world community. We are like a tossed salad, each vegetable uniquely making a contribution to the whole. Through music we celebrate this diversity.

INTRINSIC VERSUS EXTRINSIC VALUES

The professional world of musicians is guided by one reason for music making: art for art's sake. The intrinsic value of music has little to do with the social and educational benefits mentioned earlier. Music is studied by professional artists because of its innate ability to capture the human element in a fixed form—the music composition. The sharing of great music becomes deeply personal; profound "feelingful responses" are valued as the outcome. The artist has little concern for any functional aspect of art other than its ability to create an aesthetic response from the listener or viewer. That, in itself, is sufficient reward for the artistic undertaking.

Music educators, by and large, are not professional musicians. While performance is often a part of what music teachers do, the outcomes of such experiences are focused as much on the process of learning as on the final product. A poorly sung concert may not be viewed as a failure if, in the process of learning the music, the students have gained insights and knowledge that they previously did not have. In other words, because a performance is a weak aesthetic experience does not mean that some personal, social, or educational objectives have not been met. Just because the baseball team had a losing season doesn't mean the players' time was wasted. No one plays a sport to lose, and no teacher prepares a concert to be weak or boring. But in education, the end product is not so much the focus as is the learning that has taken place along the way.

Every music teacher should strive to make each learning experience an aesthetic experience. This means planning for musical outcomes that are positive and meaningful. One way to ensure such an experience is to choose music that has artistic value beyond its sheer entertainment value. When music becomes "art" music it has a quality that sets it apart from the ordinary—musicians know it when they hear it. Students who do not respond positively to art music usually lack the guidance needed to understand what the music is trying to communicate—it may be like listening to a foreign language. It then becomes the teacher's job to lead the student into a knowledge of the composition so that a meaningful communication of thoughts and ideas takes place. All choral directors have had the experience of chorus members turning up their noses to a new work that is difficult, challenging, or in an unfamiliar style or language. Similarly, those same directors know that such compositions often become the choir's favorite pieces once mastered and understood. Unlocking the doors to a profound aesthetic experience takes time and patience, but it is the ultimate intrinsic goal of music teaching.

If the aesthetic experience is so important, why then do music educators continue to value the extrinsic outcomes of music study? It may be because the general public does not value nor understand the aesthetic principle in life (Phillips, 1983). Or it may be that music educators have come to recognize the aesthetic experience as only one of many diverse reasons for a music education. While it may be the most important reason, to deny the extrinsic values is to make a limited case for music's place in the school curriculum. Unlike the professional musician, the music educator has much broader objectives for teaching music that encompass the personal, social, and educational benefits previously discussed.

Utilitarian versus Aesthetic Approaches

Music education from the time of the Greeks and Romans was utilitarian; music was valued as a way of learning mathematics and science. In the medieval university music continued to be valued for its theoretical base; music performance was studied outside the academy. When Lowell Mason introduced music into the Boston public schools, the reasons given to justify its place were mainly utilitarian, and for a hundred years the utilitarian justification of music was unchallenged in America's public schools (Mark, 1982). With the advent of the child study movement in the early twentieth century, reformers such as John Dewey began to stress the need for school music classes that were focused less on drill and more on aesthetic pleasure. James Mursell (1934), a professor of music education at Columbia University, stressed human fulfillment through the aesthetic process as the top priority for music teaching. Professor Charles Leonard, a student of Mursell's and organizer of the graduate degree program in music education at the University at Illinois in Champaign-Urbana, based that university's program of teacher education on aesthetic education. In *Foundations and Principles of Music Education* (Leonard and House, 1959) he stated:

> After many years of justifying music education in the public schools on extramusical grounds and on extrinsic values, there has been a definite trend in recent years toward justifying the music program on the basis of the values of music itself. . . . many people became aware of the increasing alienation of music education in the public schools from music programs at the college level, which resulted in a growing dichotomy . . . between music education and professional music. (p. 113)

Moving from a utilitarian to an aesthetic justification tremendously influenced teacher education. Writers such as Abraham Schwardon (1967) and Bennett Reimer (1989) made convincing arguments that "art for art's sake" was the future of music education. Music educators enthusiastically embraced this new philosophy.

Why did music educators seek to base their rationale for music education solely on the aesthetic? Perhaps it was the 1957 launch of the Russian space satellite Sputnik that left Americans badly shaken and upset for not beating the Russians into space. Public leaders were calling for educational reforms, noting that American education had "gone soft." Music educators were looking for a raison d'être, some higher purpose for their place in the educational system. The time was ripe for change, and aesthetic education caught the attention of a profession badly in need of direction. The basic premise of aesthetic education was the uniqueness of music in the school curriculum. The arts were said to be the only place where students could develop aesthetic sensitivity (Riemer, 1989). While music educators never seemed to ask teachers of other subjects if this were true, "art for art's sake" became the banner under which music educators gathered for nearly two decades, from the mid-1960s through the mid-1980s.

After embracing aesthetic education for many years, though, music educators learned that aesthetic education as the sole justification of music in the schools did not work (Phillips, 1983). States Jorgensen (1994):

Justifying music in terms of its intrinsic as opposed to extrinsic worth might be appealing to musicians, but it posed difficulties for those charged with communicating these intrinsic values to educational policymakers. Seeing that the concept of aesthetic education remained fuzzy, many music educators were hard pressed to explain to skeptics what they meant by "aesthetic education." Moreover, many musicians had a sneaking suspicion that the notion of aesthetic education, often associated (at least in the philosophical literature) with the experience of listening to music, constituted too narrow a view. (p. 22)

Not only was the general public not interested in supporting aesthetic education, but music began to lose ground in the 1980s as tight economic conditions caused many school districts to cut music from the curriculum. In addition, educators realized that aesthetic sensitivity may be cultivated through many branches of study and is not unique to the arts. A finely crafted piece of furniture made in woodshop can be as aesthetically satisfying to one person as singing a Renaissance motet is to another. Educators learned that the arts do not have a monopoly on aesthetic education—all areas of study have some level of aesthetic quality.

The Praxialist Approach

The 1990s witnessed the beginning of a praxialist movement with writings by Francis Sparshott, Philip Alperson, and David Elliott. Alperson (1991) argued that a philosophy of music required one based in praxis, or musical experience through music making. It was David Elliott, however, in his book, *Music Matters: A New Philosophy of Music Education* (1995), who strongly challenged the philosophy of aesthetic education as the reason for justifying music's place in the curriculum. For Elliott, music exists to be practiced, and all musical learning and knowledge can flow from being involved in music as an active participant. Sitting on the sidelines as a music listener will not do; "musicing" (a term coined by Elliott in place of "music making") is the central focus of the musical/aesthetic experience.

A major problem with Elliott's praxialist philosophy is that it makes a case for process but fails to produce a defensible product. The process of music learning, he notes, should involve active participation of the "musicer" in aesthetic experiences. However, the product or outcomes of such an education are, according to Elliott: self-growth; self-knowledge; musical enjoyment (or "flow"); self-esteem; musical expressions of emotion; musical representations of people, places, and things; musical expressions of cultural-ideological meanings; building a sense of community; and multicultural sensitivity (p. 297). To these he adds happiness and the pursuit of life goals and values (p. 308). Missing here is any emphasis on aesthetic product or outcome. Is this a new philosophy of music education or just an old one revisited?

One of the fears that current music educators express concerning the praxialist philosophy is that it will set music education back half a century to the times when the focus of the general music curriculum was on performance, with little attention given to content. While this clearly is not David Elliott's intention, the making of every general music class into a chorus or instrumental ensemble is feared as a return to the old days when music was viewed more as a recreational activity. It is probably safe to say that this is not going to happen.

The praxialists state that historical and theoretical knowledge of music can be gained through performance and active listening. This is similar to the approach taken by those who foster comprehensive musicianship in ensembles. It is a worthy idea, but the time a conductor can give to developing a knowledge base in any rehearsal is limited. All historical and theoretical knowledge cannot be gained by active experience alone. Time for both music practice (*musica practica*) and music knowledge (*musica speculativa*) is needed if music is to be considered a viable part of the academic school curriculum.

A Balanced Approach

It is the aesthetic experience that draws most people, including music teachers, into the music profession. This experience is both process and product; a meaningful experience through performance or listening becomes a lasting impression that endures, often for a lifetime. It is a powerful intrinsic experience that is valued for itself alone.

Today music educators are realizing that there are both important intrinsic and extrinsic reasons for justifying the place of music in the schools. Bennett Reimer has stated: "Both are correct. These positions are not at all contradictory. The intrinsic versus extrinsic debate, I suggest, is fruitless" (1997, p. 9).

What is needed, however, is research into the many personal, social, and educational benefits, which involve the intrinsic and extrinsic values that are associated with music study and performance. Little is known about any of the twenty-four reasons listed in this chapter, except through general observation. Does the music program really increase community pride? Is music study beneficial to one's physical and mental health? Where is the evidence? Do students who study multicultural music develop greater sensitivity to and respect for other cultures? Does participation in music actually increase self-confidence? These and many other questions require answering if music education is to make a strong statement about the value of music in the school curriculum.

While little is known empirically about the value of music, it can be said that civilizations down through the centuries have valued music and its place in the lives of people. If it were not valued, it would long be gone. But music has yet to return to the central role it played in Greek civilization. Will it ever again? That depends upon future music educators who can clearly articulate a strong rationale for music education.

A RATIONALE FOR MUSIC EDUCATION

The following is a rationale that schools and music educators might adopt or use as a model for writing their own rationales for curricular guides, handbooks, and advocacy statements.

> A quality music education is a necessity for all students because of the many intrinsic and extrinsic values that the study of music has for all of humankind. Most important among these is music's potential for letting human beings share and communicate thoughts and feelings that transcend the written or spoken word—expressions of the spirit that make us uniquely human and bind us together as a people and a world of cultures. In addition, the study of music is beneficial for its many other outcomes, some of which include the development of social behaviors, such as cooperation and multicultural sensitivity; personal behaviors, such as self-discipline and self-esteem; and educational behaviors, such as integrated and "whole-brain" learning. While music has as its basis a complex body of knowledge, making it worthy to be called an academic subject, the study of music also enhances all areas of the school curriculum, making music central to the core of all education. Throughout history, advanced societies have included the study of music for their young people in order to prepare them for a life that is rich and varied. Music and a quality life are for everyone. (Phillips, 1998, p. 10)

STUDY AND DISCUSSION QUESTIONS

1. What are two reasons for having a strong rationale to defend the place of music in the school curriculum?

2. What are the nine national standards for music education, and what is the first of the standards?

3. What are other reasons besides the twenty-four listed in this chapter that you think are important justifications for music education?

4. How can the music program be cost effective for a school district?

5. What is the meaning of "whole-brain learning" in regard to music study?

6. How does music exalt the human spirit and care for the soul?

7. Can a case be made for transfer learning, that is, the effect of music study on other areas of learning?

8. Why is cooperative learning valued by society, and how does music teach such a desirable characteristic?

9. How does music foster appreciation for cultural awareness and diversity?

10. What are the three categories of benefits that encompass the twenty-four statements given as possible reasons for including music in the schools? Give examples of each.

11. What is meant by the intrinsic and extrinsic values of music study?

12. How does the job of the music educator differ from that of the professional musician?

13. Is the aesthetic experience part of the process or the product of the choral rehearsal? Explain your answer.

14. When and why did American music education move from a primarily utilitarian to a solely aesthetic rationale? What were the initial results?

15. What was the basic principle of aesthetic education in the school curriculum?

16. Why was aesthetic education as the sole rationale for music education not successful?

17. What is the praxialist philosophy of music education, and what are its strengths and weaknesses?

18. What does the author suggest is a more balanced approach to formulating a strong rationale for music education?

19. What is needed if strong intrinsic and extrinsic reasons are to be used to defend music's place in the curriculum?

20. What will help to determine the future of music education in the school curriculum?

REFERENCES

Alperson, P. (1991). What should one expect from a philosophy of music education? *Journal of Aesthetic Education*, *25*(3), 215–42.

Benham, J. (1991). *School music and "reverse economics."* Reston, VA: National Coalition for Music Education, video distributed by MENC.

Elliott, D. J. (1995). *Music matters: A new philosophy of music education.* New York: Oxford University Press.

Hanshumaker, J. (1986). The effects of music and other arts instruction on reading and math achievement and on general school performance. *Update: Applications of Research in Music Education*, *4*(2), 10–11,

Jorgensen, E. R. (1994). Justifying music instruction in American public schools: An Historical Perspective. *Bulletin of the Council for Research in Music Education*, *120*, 17–31.

Leonard, C., and R. House (1959). *Foundations and principles of music education.* New York: McGraw-Hill.

Lindemann, C. A. (1998). At the core. *Music Educators Journal, 84*(6), 6–7.

Mark, M. L. (1982). The evolution of music education philosophy from utilitarian to aesthetic. *Journal of Research in Music Education, 30*(1), 15–21.

MENC (1991). *Music makes the difference: Action kit for music education.* Reston, VA: MENC.

——— (1994). *The school music program: A new vision: The k-12 standards, prek standards, and what they mean to music educators.* Reston, VA: MENC.

Moore, Thomas (1992). *Care of the soul.* New York: Harper Collins.

Mursell, J. L. (1934). *Human values in music education.* New York: Silver Burdett.

Phillips, K. H. (1983). Utilitarian vs. aesthetic. *Music Educators Journal, 69*(7), 29–30.

——— (1993). A stronger rationale for music education. *Music Educators Journal, 80*(2), 17–19, 55.

——— (1998). A rationale for music education. *Music Educators Journal, 84*(5), 10.

Reimer, B. (1989). *A philosophy of music education* (2d ed.). Upper Saddle River, NJ: Prentice Hall.

——— (1997). Music's value. *Music Educators Journal, 84*(1), 9.

Schwardon, A. A. (1967). *Aesthetics: Dimensions for music education.* Washington, DC: Music Educators National Conference.

3 | Promoting and Recruiting for Choral Success

The place of music in the school curriculum is often uncertain. It is perceived by many as being a "frill" and not essential to a child's education. Therefore, music educators must actively promote the cause of music, always looking for ways to keep the music program and its benefits before the public. Chapter 2 was a guide to formulating a personal rationale for the benefits of music study; this chapter provides direction for promoting those benefits and for attracting students to the choral music program.

BUILDING A PUBLIC RELATIONS PROGRAM

The MENC publication *Promoting School Music: A Practical Guide* (1984) describes public relations as follows:

> Public relations involves conveying a message effectively through all available channels of communication to various segments of society. PR seeks to change the public's perception of a particular program, issue, or cause in a way favorable to the group sending the message and the purpose it represents. (p. 5)

Good public relations may not only change the public's perception about a program but also increase the value of programs that already have strong public support.

Tools for Promotion

MENC and ACDA have become especially effective in promoting music at the national, regional, and state levels, but it is up to every music educator to promote music in his or her own community. The necessary tools for such promotion include:

- A **self-study** to aid you in analyzing your situation and defining problem areas.
- A **fact sheet** or profile of your music program. It should capsulize the who, what, where, when, and why of the program—the facts you want your audience to know, including goals and objectives.
- **Media lists**, kept current, of all local media outlets. This includes radio, TV, newspapers, and magazines, with names of important contacts. Media lists are available from local utility companies, public relations and advertising firms, banks, and charitable organizations such as United Way.
- **Other lists**, such as PTA and board of education members, music supervisors, school newsletter editors, arts-related group leaders, music stores, and civic associations.
- **A planning calendar**, on which you can lay out your activities by the week or month.

31

This should provide a workable schedule for your PR program and offer an easy road map to follow. (MENC, 1984, pp. 8–9)

The National Coalition for Music Education, which includes The National Association for Music Educators (MENC), the National Academy of Recording Arts and Sciences, and the National Association of Music Merchants, has prepared another kind of tool for use by music educators, *Action Kit for Music Education* (1991). This advocacy kit contains two videos and a number of useful publications for helping music educators mount a successful advocacy program. Another publication, *Teacher's Guide for Advocacy* (MENC, 1992), is available to use with the *Action Kit* for building community support. The monograph *Tips: Public Relations* (Getto, 1988) is another MENC publication that contains numerous suggestions from experienced teachers on getting the word out.

Parents Groups

The first lesson that a music educator needs to learn about effective promotion is that you can't do it alone. A teacher's life cannot become consumed with ancillary activities when the main focus must be on teaching music. Involving parents in the promotion program can greatly facilitate the process, and in the end, the parents may know the community better than the teacher.

Some schools have established booster organizations, either separately for vocal and instrumental groups or combined as a music auxiliary. The parents who are involved are eager to be of service, and an ongoing program of music promotion is a good way to involve many people. One person needs to be in charge, and a PR committee is helpful, but promotion can involve everyone if all are aware of the need.

A promotion committee also may consist of a more informal group of parents who are called upon occasionally to speak out on the benefits of music study. In this case, no regular meetings are held, but a telephone "chain" list is kept for purposes of notifying parents when vocal support for the music program is needed. Rumors of an impending cut in music, to be discussed at the next school board meeting, should result in the "chain" being called and many parents attending the meeting. Rather than reacting to decisions already made, parents can be there ahead of a decision to speak out on the values of retaining the area in question. This type of organization may not be as effective as one working constantly on promotion activities, but on an emergency basis, it works well.

Print Media Relations

Most schools have media specialists whose job it is to send out news on current events to the news organizations. It is important to keep the media specialist informed of upcoming concerts, booster meetings, and so forth, with plenty of lead time. A minimum of two weeks often is required for information to find its way to the proper outlet.

When writing a news release, it is important to include such basic information as who, what, where, when, and if there is a cost involved. Also, it is good to be creative and to find a way to catch the listener's or reader's attention. The media like quotes and names of local people included. They also want statistics: how many students will be involved, the number of performances, and so forth. Long news releases will be cut; short and to the point is typically better (see example in Figure 3.1). It is important to include the name of a contact person and a telephone number where someone can be reached regarding the information in the news release.

DT: **April 10, 2003**
TO: **All News Organizations: For Immediate Release**
FR: **Music Department, West Sunbury High School**
RE: **Spring Choral Concert**
CONTACT PERSON: **Mr. John Wilkins (000) 444-4444**

"Everything's Coming Up Roses" is the theme for this year's spring choral concert at West Sunbury High School. The concert will be held on Friday evening, May 5, at 8:00 p.m., in the high school auditorium. John Wilkins, choral director, will conduct five choral ensembles encompassing over 150 students in selections ranging from madrigals to show tunes.

Tom Burke, senior and student music conductor, will lead the concert choir in their rendition of the spiritual "In Dat Great Gittin' up Mornin," with Greg Moses as tenor soloist. Junior Karen Williams will accompany all of the choirs, including the Junior Chorus, Show Choir, Choral Union, and Concert Choir.

Graduating seniors will be recognized and choir alumni will be asked to join in the final selection of the concert, "On Our Way Rejoicing." Regarding the program, high school principal Steven Gould states, "I always look forward to this annual event when the public and parents alike get to enjoy the sounds of much hard work on the part of our students."

Admission to the concert is $3 for adults, $2 for seniors, and $1 for students; tickets may be purchased from any choir member or at the door the evening of the performance. All proceeds will go to the choir activities fund.

Figure 3.1. Sample news release.

The inclusion of a photograph with the news release will make the information more interesting. Most newspapers prefer 5 × 7-inch glossy black-and-white photos, with borders. The pictures should be in sharp focus, and informal shots are usually better than posed ones. Also, newspapers like pictures where a few people can be seen accurately rather than pictures of entire choirs where people are hard to identify. All names should be correctly spelled and some background information provided—who is doing what and why. The back of the picture should not be written on because of possible damage to the photo. However, some type of identification taped on the back of each photograph is needed. When mailing photos, a piece of cardboard inserted inside the envelope provides protection. The envelope should be marked on the outside "PHOTOS ENCLOSED—DO NOT BEND."

Other outlets to consider when sending out news releases include chambers of commerce, civic clubs, churches, fraternal organizations, school newspapers, weekly papers, and suburban shopping supplements. The media specialist will have a listing of where news articles are regularly sent by the school. A school's activities calendar is also an important place to include upcoming events.

Radio and Television Broadcasts

The electronic media are a major source for most people's news; radio and TV are powerful means of disseminating information about school music programs. A personal contact is especially helpful when seeking to gain air time. A letter to the program director at the local

Figure 3.2. Publicity photo for kite-flying contest fundraiser.

and regional broadcast stations, followed by a personal visit, can be well worth the time and effort.

Radio and television stations provide a certain amount of free public service programming; they welcome newsworthy information in the form of public service announcements. The guidelines for preparing the news release are the same as for the print media. Broadcast time and space is very limited and announcements must be clear and to the point: who, what, where, when, and cost. Most public service "spots" are no longer than thirty seconds and are usually shorter.

Some stations will tape and rebroadcast concerts. This is a large undertaking for the choral director and the broadcaster; cooperation is of major importance among all personnel involved. Broadcast people have set ways of doing productions, and the choral director must work within their guidelines. Of major concern will be sound reproduction—microphones placed in the wrong positions will distort singing. The technician in this area needs to know of any special considerations. For example, should the piano have a microphone, and will one be needed for soloists? Do the microphones process sound evenly, or will individual voices stick out? Working closely with the sound technician is extremely important when the end result for a choral presentation should be more aural than visual. A nice picture will avail little if the sound is poor.

Local cable channels often provide good outlets to promote the school music program. Formats may include a panel discussion of music teachers, administrators, and parents on the value of music in schools; an interview with a music educator or student about the music program; a demonstration show where a typical rehearsal may be shown; and the one-person show where a music educator speaks about music in the schools.

Community Support

Most community members will be unaware of the school music program unless the program is taken to them. One successful way to do this is through performances at local service clubs and, where permitted, at local churches. While a student should never be required to sing as part of a worship service, evening and afternoon concerts in churches are widely accepted in most communities. The choral director needs to be aware of church policies regarding the music performed; some churches do not permit the use of secular music, even in concerts. It also must be clear that such presentations are concerts and not worship services. Churches often will permit a free-will offering for the guest choir.

One way to help community members understand the scope of the music program is to demonstrate a particular learning activity during a performance. This is especially helpful for groups such as the PTO, where the acquisition of skills and knowledge is uppermost in the minds of parents. If parents see and hear how music is learned, they will come to understand what a complex process it involves. An excellent type of demonstration is a voice-building sequence where different vocal exercises are practiced. Most people do not know that singing can be taught as a learned behavior. Similarly, a demonstration of a typical rehearsal sequence or classroom learning activity draws people into an understanding that singing is more than a recreational activity. When possible, some group singing should be included in a community presentation. Well-known songs or easy melodies, which can be taught quickly, make good choices. Group involvement is an excellent means of creating positive attitudes.

Many community businesses will permit announcements for school music events to be placed in windows and on bulletin boards. Some even permit groups to sing in lobbies and entrances. These same business often will sponsor advertisements in programs for concerts and musicals. It is a good idea to build bridges with the business community and to encourage parents to shop at places that support the music program.

Administrative Support

Communicating with the school administration is vastly important to a successful music program. A year-end report that flows from principal to superintendent to school board is a strong way in which to outline the achievements and goals of the music area. Citing facts and figures is always impressive, as the music teacher often sees many more students than the regular classroom teacher. Also, out-of-school hours that are spent in rehearsals, performances, and trips should be included. Administrators need to know what is happening, and the music faculty is the best source of this information.

Administrators and school board members should receive personal invitations to all school concerts. The inclusion of complimentary tickets, when appropriate, is important. School administrators may be asked on a rotating basis to make welcoming remarks at performances, and a public "thank you" from the director for administrative support goes a long way to building positive relations. The choral director should make it a point to meet school board members so they can recognize them in public and at concerts.

Learning to work with school counselors is of utmost importance for the music curriculum to thrive. If the school counselor does not view music as being important, it will become a low priority when counseling students on what courses to take. The MENC publication *Beyond the Classroom: Informing Others* (1987) suggests the following guidelines for working with school counselors:

- Read and respond to your professional correspondence promptly.
- Keep aware of proposed schedule changes.
- Try to anticipate problems.
- Try to understand the school counselor's position when problems arise.
- Work for the development and implementation of a policy that assures placement of students in music organizations and classes by the music teacher.
- Do not allow yourself to become involved in rivalries with other teachers.
- Work with counselors in helping students with appropriate career goals.
- Approach school counselors as professional colleagues.
- Talk with—not at—school counselors.
- Be considerate when asking for a meeting time.
- Make use of both verbal and a written summary after a meeting to restate the problem that has been solved.
- Work cooperatively to provide what's best for students. (MENC, 1987, p. 26)

Teacher Support

Establishing good working relations with other teachers also is of primary importance. Some teachers do not believe in the importance of music and would not mind if it were dropped from the curriculum. They become irritated when students are taken from class for trips or other events. The choral director must work to bridge this gap by establishing a good rapport with other teachers and by offering assistance for integrating music study into other subjects. Also, open and advanced communication is necessary to keep teachers informed of when students will be missing class. It does not make for good faculty relations when a teacher schedules a test and learns the day before that half the class will be missing to attend a choral festival.

Another way to bring teachers into an understanding of the music program is to involve them in it. Some schools have faculty choirs that perform in school assemblies, and teachers can be asked to serve as chaperones on trips. They also can be asked to oversee ushers, stage crew, and other duties. The all-school musical is a good opportunity to involve many faculty members in directing the staging, orchestra, costumes, makeup, programs, set construction and painting, props, tickets, dancing, and publicity. An after-musical party that includes these faculty assistants is a sure way to inspire cooperation and positive relations. Music teachers are just one part of the entire school process; respect for the other parts is vitally important to insure good faculty communications.

Arts Organizations

Local, state, regional, and national organizations are involved in arts advocacy throughout the United States. Music educators need to belong to these organizations and to support their efforts in bringing the arts to the public. Collaborative projects can include providing scholarships; arranging programs; providing artists-in-residency; placing announcements in newsletters, directories, and calendars to publicize arts events; and having representatives of arts organizations on school committees. In any collaborative venture, the official credit statement of the arts agency needs to be used and all funding sources recognized.

The Alliance for Arts Education is part of the educational division of the John F. Kennedy Center for the Performing Arts in Washington, DC. It has branches in every state that oversee the general status of the arts, working vigorously to support arts programs, including those in schools. They closely monitor legislative decisions at the state level and regularly lobby legislators for arts funding. These alliances are especially important to music educators when school music programs are threatened with cutbacks. They provide the moral support and documentation needed to help teachers make a good case for school music. If the location of a state division is unknown, the national office can be contacted for information by writing: Alliance for Arts Education, Education Department, JFK Center for Performing Arts, Washington, DC, 20566.

Other important organizations are the National Federation of Music Clubs, which sponsors a National Music Week, and the National Foundation for Advancement in the Arts, which awards monetary grants to high school seniors who are seventeen to eighteen years of age and who demonstrate excellence in dance, music, visual arts, theater, or writing. The National Federation may be contacted at 1336 North Delaware, Indianapolis, IN 45202, and the National Foundation at 100 N. Biscayne Blvd., Miami, FL 33132. These groups often have local or regional chapters that are important arts advocates.

Music in Our Schools Month

MENC began a program of school music national awareness in 1975. The program, Music in Our Schools Days, was expanded in 1977 to a week and now is a month-long celebration in March of each year. A Music in Our Schools Month (MIOSM) Teacher's Guide is available from MENC, as are a large number of awareness items such as T-shirts, ball caps, banners, pencils, notepads, and so forth. A MIOSM Starter Kit also is available.

Part of the MIOSM celebration is the World's Largest Concert (WLC), where thousands of children across America join together in a nationally televised singalong concert. Approximately five choral selections are chosen from the children's choir repertoire and serve as the basis of the WLC. The television program features an established children's choir accompanied by a student orchestra and is broadcast from nationally recognized venues such as Disney World's Epcot Center in Orlando, Florida. This is a terrific way to join students from around the country in unified support of music. Other activities that are appropriate for MIOSM include:

- Submitting MIOSM articles to state journals
- Supplying local newspapers with regular releases on all music activities
- Making initial contact with state officials for a governor's proclamation
- Contacting program chairpersons of civic organizations and suggesting a MIOSM program for their March meetings
- Setting up special programs with radio and television stations
- Contacting local chambers of commerce, telephone companies, banks—anyone who publishes a calendar of events—to ask that they include MIOSM dates (MENC, 1991)

MIOSM activities are important outlets for showing the local community that the arts are supported across the United States by millions of people.

THE CHOIR NEWSLETTER

Choir newsletters are becoming an increasingly effective means by which to promote the choral program and at the same time communicate important information about upcoming

February/March 2002
Choru♭Pondent: Lee Cline

Choru♭Pondence

Jefferson Choral Department
Director: **Michael Reese** [mreese@esc.cr.k12.ia.us]
Associate Director: **Andrew Eley** [aeley@esc.cr.k12.ia.us]

DUE TO A VOCAL MUSIC CONCERT ON THE NORMAL THIRD THURSDAY (2/21), THE NEXT CHORAL PARENTS MEETING WILL BE ON TUESDAY, FEBRUARY 19, 2002, AT 7:00 PM IN THE CHOIR ROOM. THIS IS THE LAST PARENTS MEETING BEFORE THE INVITATIONAL!!

HELP FEED THE CROWDS!!!

Each year at the Show Choir Invitational we sell food at three locations: auditorium, cafeteria, and new gym areas. We count on donations from the families of **ALL STUDENTS IN ALL OF OUR CHOIRS** to help feed the visitors at the Invitational.

Bring your items to the cafeteria. It is important that we have everything by 4:30 p.m. on Friday, March 8th. If there is no way you can have your items at school by 4:30, you can bring it before 9:00 a.m. on Saturday, March 9th. **PLEASE MAKE EVERY EFFORT TO HAVE THINGS AT SCHOOL BY FRIDAY AT 4:30 P.M.** There will a list of all choir members in the cafeteria. Be sure to check your name off the list and have your name on your item.

This year we are asking parents to contribute the following:

BOYS & GIRLS with the last names beginning with:

    A-BA – apples
    BE-H – seedless grapes (wash and remove stems from grapes)
    I-J – bananas
    K-L – seedless grapes (wash and remove stems from grapes)

GIRLS with last names **M-Z:** Bring one-gallon size plastic bag of **cleaned** vegetables. **Please include a combination of carrots, celery, cauliflower and broccoli.**

Figure 3.3. Choir newsletter. (Cedar Rapids Jefferson High School, Cedar Rapids, Iowa. Used by permission.)

events. The use of computers in the production of such vehicles has made the publication of a monthly newsletter a relatively easy task, although one that can be assigned to someone other than the choral director. Booster organizations have talented people who are computer literate and who make fine editors for such news publications.

A catchy title for the newsletter is appropriate. Something like "ChorusPondence" or "Valley Voices" lends quick identification to the choral program and brings about instant recognition of the publication (see Figure 3.3).

A newsletter can be as simple as several $8^1/2'' \times 11''$ pieces of paper stapled together. For a professional look, a folded magazine-type format is desirable. With a one-page insert the newsletter will be six pages; a folded and stapled insert permits eight pages but is more costly. Even a single sheet, front and back, is better than no newsletter.

Computer programs permit all types of interesting fonts and borders. A logo makes an attractive addition to the title area, and varying the size of type makes the format more eye-appealing. News items set in columns and boxes, rather than straight across a page, make for a more professional look.

Newsletter Contents

A number of ancillary items are standard from newsletter to newsletter. These include issue dates, names of the choral faculty, a listing of the choral auxiliary or booster officers, names of choir officers, names of the editor and publication staff, school and department telephone numbers, e-mail addresses, fax numbers, school address, and a half page for the recipient's address, school return address, and the nonprofit permit number (reduces postage). Newsletters are far more effective when mailed to parents. Sending them home with students does not guarantee delivery!

The purpose of the newsletter is twofold: to promote school choral music in general, and to promote current school choral events and performances. Items may include:

- Announcements of approaching choral concerts
- Announcements of auxiliary/booster meetings
- Choir expectations and requirements
- Announcements of fund-raising events
- Names of students who have made special honor choirs
- Sale of concert tapes
- Announcements of out-of-school rehearsals
- School eligibility rules for participation in music activities
- Descriptions of the various choirs in the choral program
- Information regarding choir apparel and T-shirt sales
- Choir fees and fund-raising expectations
- Solicitation of donations from patrons
- Remarks from the director(s)
- Choral Awards Night announcement
- Names of graduating seniors
- Special interest articles such as highlights of choir tour
- Requests for volunteer help

- Notes of appreciation
- Choral performances by other groups
- Rationale for music study
- Dates of standardized tests for college admissions

Fine Arts Calendar

One item that should be included in every newsletter is the monthly calendar. This can be typed in a straight list by date, or an actual calendar block can be used with events typed into each block (see Figure 3.4). It is helpful if this calendar is on a removable insert for easy posting in the home. A performing arts calendar, with all school fine arts events included, becomes a major source of communication between the choral director and the students and, equally important, between the choral director and the parents. Complaints of being uninformed become negated when a calendar is made available.

The Printed Product

The final product needs to be written in a simple, clear-cut manner with no grammatical or typographical errors and no misspelled words. Any written product that goes forth from a school should represent the school at its best. Just because the newsletter comes from the

March						
Sun	*Mon*	*Tue*	*Wed*	*Thu*	*Fri*	*Sat*
					1 WSD, Ovation, MST @ Pike H.S. Indianapolis, IN TBA	**2** WSD, Ovation, MST @ Pike H.S. Indianapolis, IN TBA
3 WSD, Ovation, MST @ Pike H.S. Indianapolis, IN TBA	**4** Musical Auditions TBA	**5** Musical Auditions TBA	**6**	**7**	**8** Jefferson Show Choir Invite	**9** Jefferson Show Choir Invite
10	**11**	**12**	**13** Meistersingers @ NCACDA Convention Des Moines, IA	**14** Meistersingers @ NCACDA Convention Des Moines, IA	**15**	**16**
17	**18**	**19** CC, MST, Middle Schools? Concert 7:00pm, Auditorium	**20**	**21**	**22**	**23**
24	**25**	**26**	**27**	**28**	**29**	**30**
31						**2002**

Figure 3.4. Fine arts calendar. (Cedar Rapids Jefferson High School, Cedar Rapids, Iowa. Used by permission.)

choral department does not excuse the printed product from being a good example of clear, errorless writing.

Every effort should be made to present the newsletter in as professional a format as possible. The sophistication of computer programs makes this an easy task. However, it is just as important that printing or duplication of the newsletter be clear, with sharp contrasts. The type should be large enough to be read easily, and the paper needs to be white or of a light color so print contrast is maximized.

Many schools have print shops where programs and announcements are generally produced for the entire school. This type of professional set-up helps in the production of a good product. It does no good to put time and effort into a newsletter if the final product is poorly printed. Going outside the school to a professional printing business will entail far more cost than an in-house publication.

Keeping a database for the names of recipients is relatively easy with a computer. The database should include the names of all parents and guardians who have students in choirs, and also all of those in administration, as well as regular patrons. It is a good idea to include on the mailing list local arts groups and nearby college and university music faculty. Visibility is a key factor in any successful music program, and the monthly or bimonthly newsletter is an excellent means by which to make the choral area visible in the community.

RECRUITING CHORISTERS

Choral directors always want to know how they can recruit more students. The best answer is that a quality program sells itself and attracts students to it. A quality program may take several years to build, however, and attracting students is often difficult given the negative attitude many students have to "school" music. Therefore, the following suggestions (Demorest, 2000; MENC, 1994; Phillips, 1986) are given for help in recruiting and building school choral programs.

Advertise the Choral Program

When it is time for students to join a chorus, advertise the choral program as being open to all students having a real desire to sing. Make a poster that can be duplicated on a copy machine. Keep the message simple; use a catchy slogan and bright colors. A student in choral methods designed the simple but effective poster shown in Figure 3.5. Place these posters in conspicuous places around the school. Also, use the school newspaper and public address system to advertise the program. Again, keep the message short and direct.

TONALLY AWESOME!

7th & 8th Grade Choir

See Ms. Marston in Room 121

Figure 3.5. Choir recruitment poster.

Talk with School Guidance Counselors about the Choral Program

Counselors may be unaware of the scope of the choral program and the requirements for the various choirs. Ask them to report new students who transfer to the school, especially those students who may have been in choir previously. Also, ask the counselors to provide a list of students who have excessive study halls. A hesitant singer may be waiting only for a personal contact.

Keep Schedule Conflicts to a Minimum

If concert choir is scheduled at the same time as honors English, conflicts are sure to arise, and students who are college bound will usually take the English course. Communicate to the school principal the necessity of scheduling choir for times other than when single-section courses are meeting.

Teach Singing in General Music Classes

Use the singing component of general music classes as a way to identify prospective choristers. Singing has been dropped from some general music curricula because of the negative attitude of students toward singing. This is a most unfortunate situation for the choral director and the students. Singing can be taught in the general music class if the teacher understands the voice and proper approaches to instruction. Students need not be intimidated by the singing of songs if a developmental sequence of voice skills is used in teaching kids to sing. The general music class is often the last time that many students ever take a music class, and it may be the last time when students can be encouraged to become singers. If students come to understand that singing is something that everyone can learn to do, they become more willing to participate.

Lay the Groundwork for Choir Recruiting in the Elementary Grades

Ask permission to take a small group of singers to different elementary schools for the purpose of presenting short, informal programs in individual classrooms. Have the singers circle the classroom to be closer to the listeners. Introduce the group to the children, explaining a little about a choir and the various parts that are sung. Have the different voice parts sing independently, and then together as a group. Then give the elementary students some "directed" listening by instructing them to listen for specific things in the music the group will sing. Following the presentation, solicit answers from the children as to what they heard. Keep the presentation short, and make it educational. Leave the students with the idea that all people can learn to sing, and that someday they, too, could be in such a choir. Elementary teachers appreciate this informative break from the regular routine, but clear this type of activity with the school principal.

Recruit Students from Study Halls

Seek permission from the study hall teacher to talk to all students as a group. Ask the students how many of them are bored each day in study hall, and how many would like to have an exciting experience (most hands will go up). Then explain that you are looking for students who would like to learn to sing, as singing is something that can be learned. Tell a little about the requirements, and stress that while being in a choir can be exciting and fun, it also is demanding and not for loafers! Learning to sing well demands physical coordination like that of an athlete, and the choral experience would help them to develop their bodies into great instruments. Then ask for volunteers and sign them up on the spot. Scheduling changes will be needed, but that is a minor irritation when compared to recruiting new choral singers.

Choose an All-School Musical with a Large Chorus

If the school presents Broadway musicals, the chorus for such a show is an excellent place to attract new singers to the choral program. Do not require that the show chorus be drawn only from those who participate in the school choral program. If it is truly an "all school" musical, then it should be open to all students. Singers can be drawn into the regular choral program once they experience the delight of singing in the chorus of a Broadway musical production.

Solicit Recommendations for Choir Membership from Students

Ask choir members to recommend friends who they feel might be interested in singing. Make personal contact with each of these students and explain the values of choir participation. Emphasize that singing is something one can learn to do and not some type of "gift" that only "gifted" people have. Find out who the leaders are in the school and contact them.

When accepting older students into choir, it is important not to intimidate them with a lengthy audition. However, some type of vocal evaluation is needed to determine part placement and choir assignment. Emphasize that an audition is not a graded evaluation, nor does it matter if the student sounds good by themselves because singing in a choir is a group experience. Always audition students individually, away from peers, and make the environment as nonthreating as possible by engaging the students in small talk before beginning. Also, interjecting a little humor helps to ease tensions.

Build Rapport with School Athletic Coaches

Attend school athletic events and make your presence known. Offer the choir for participation in pep rallies. Have the choir sing the National Anthem, school fight songs, or novelty presentations based on popular tunes. The author once heard of a football coach who directed all players to audition for the choir after he received a plea for help from the school choral director. Athletic coaches are powerful models, and music programs can be helped by sympathetic coaches. Music programs should not be in competition with athletic programs.

Maintain a Flexible Grading Policy

High school students with high academic standings have been known not to join choir in their junior or senior years for fear of lowering their grade point averages. While a B grade may be acceptable for most students, those with high averages do not want to take the chance of getting anything lower than an A. If a strict grading policy based on achievement is used in the choral program, it stands to reason that a student entering the program with little experience may not get an A. In this case, a pass/fail or audit system would be a good alternative to offer. Most students will want a regular grade in choir because of the high proportion of A or B grades usually earned. A few, however, may elect a grading system that will not interfere with their academic averages.

Work Closely with Band and Orchestra Directors

Some students may want to be in both choral and instrumental groups, which may cause scheduling problems. *Do not vie for students.* Working closely with instrumental teachers may result in creative ways that students can be in more than one group. A model for resolving scheduling conflicts can be found in an article by James E. Latten (1998) in the reference section of this chapter.

Encourage Male Singers

The problem of recruiting male singers to the choral program is a constantly challenging one for choral directors. Male singing has been on the decline in America since the 1930s (Gates, 1989), and the absence of males in most school choirs today is obvious. Concerning this problem Demorest (2000) states:

> Junior high is the time when many boys choose not to continue singing. It is the time when their voices are changing and don't sound particularly good. Singing involves taking a somewhat personal risk—not an easy thing for adolescents who already feel rather insecure. Peer pressure also intensifies around this time, and in the eyes of an adolescent boy, choir may not have the prestige of other activities. (p. 38)

One way to reduce the embarrassment boys feel while singing during the voice change years is to rehearse the boys as a group, separate from the girls, at least part of the time. This provides the opportunity to work on vocal technique peculiar to the voice change in a supportive environment. It also helps to create an esprit de corps that nurtures the fragile masculine ego. One study has shown that adolescent male participation in choir is highly related to male identity (Kennedy, 1999).

Steven Demorest (2000) details another approach to male recruitment in "a workshop for boy singers:"

> When the workshop was first offered in 1992, organizers at the University of Washington had no idea what the response would be. They were overwhelmed when more than 320 boys participated the first year. . . . Since that inaugural year, several changes in the preregistration process and a "no riding the elevator" rule have helped the workshop run more smoothly. (39)

Demorest notes that literature choice for the boys is critical; it must have masculine appeal and must "fit" vocally. Held on a Saturday, the day-long workshop concludes with a concert by the massed male choirs.

One of the interesting components of the workshop includes interaction of boys with college-age male singers. "Teachers consistently report that the concert by our guest group is the highlight of the day for the boys, their musical reward for a day of hard work and good singing" (p. 40).

Recruiting students can be a difficult and time-consuming task. However, choral directors are also music educators and as such have the responsibility of bringing the choral art to as many students as possible. It is well worth the effort when nonsingers find the joy of singing in a school choral program.

USING STANDARDIZED TESTS

Standardized tests of intelligence are commonly given in schools as indicators of student learning potential. Such tests also are available for determining music aptitude. As everyone has an intelligence quotient (IQ), so everyone has a music IQ, which can be measured and used for counseling students and parents about musical potential. Students with high musical aptitudes should be encouraged to consider music as a possible career.

Perhaps the strongest reason for choral directors to know students' musical aptitudes is to identify musically talented students who are not involved in the choral program. Students with high musical aptitudes who are not participating in music may never have received any encouragement to participate. Such students, when identified, are good recruit prospects. However, a low score on a music aptitude test should not be used as a reason to keep a student out of choir. Musical aptitude is only one component among a number of areas that contribute to success in music making.

Perhaps the best-known and most accepted tests of musical aptitude have been written by Edwin E. Gordon. Dr. Gordon has had a long and distinguished career in studying the psychology of music. Most important among his findings is that musical aptitude is developmental up to and around the age of nine, after which it becomes stabilized. Gordon believes that all people are born with a potential musical aptitude, which requires early development through a rich variety of musical experiences if potential is to be reached. Music educators and schools need to provide rich musical experiences for children from an early age if students are to reach their full musical growth. Gordon has shown that scores can increase on repeated tests of musical aptitude up to about the age of nine, but after that age, scores tend not to increase on repeated testings.

Gordon's theory of developmental and stabilized musical aptitude provides a strong reason to increase the contact time students have with music at an early age. Day care centers need to include a variety of informal music activities within an environment that encourages musical exploration. Similarly, students in the primary grades should have daily exposure to music from either a music specialist or the regular teacher.

Tests of musical aptitude by Edwin Gordon are available for use with students beginning as early as age three. Each test has a tonal and rhythm component that generates separate and composite scores. The test packages include a manual for test administration, scoring, and interpretation. Test administration requires a stereo cassette playback unit. Because the tests are standardized measurements, they are not available for purchase by individuals. Tests must be purchased by an institution, such as a school. The publisher of the following tests by Edwin Gordon is G. I. A. Publications, 7404 S. Wabash Avenue, Chicago, IL 60638. Each test comes in a box that includes the cassette tape(s), test manual, test forms, and scoring grids.

Audie

Audie is a test of developmental music aptitude for children three to four years old. It takes ten to twenty minutes to administer and is not to be given all at one time. Teachers or parents and guardians may give the test, which is in the form of a game. The adult listens to the cassette with the child and keeps track of the child's responses. The tonal and rhythm parts each take five to ten minutes to complete. Scoring information is provided. The test may be readministered periodically to check the developing aptitude of the child, and the test manual provides guidelines for making use of the test results, which may include providing greater opportunities for musical involvement by the child.

Primary Measures of Music Audiation (PMMA)

The PMMA is a test of developmental musical aptitude for use with children ages five to nine, or kindergarten through sixth grade. The test is given in a group setting; students do not need to know how to read or write, as the answer sheet uses pictures of smiling faces or frowning faces for identification of musical phrases that are "same" or "different." All that is required is for the child to draw circles around pairs of faces. The rhythm and tonal parts each take approximately twelve minutes to administer, and the entire test can be given at one time. The test is hand scorable, and national grade norms are presented in the test manual. As the test is rather easy, it is suggested that the next test level (IMMA) be used by fourth grade, especially when primary students are scoring high on the PMMA. This is an excellent test for determining the developing musical aptitude of students. It is short, easy to administer, and provides valuable insights into students' abilities and needs.

Intermediate Measures of Music Audiation (IMMA)

The IMMA is a more discriminating test than the PMMA. It is to be used with students in grades three through six who have had a fair amount of exposure to music, the majority of whom have scored above the eightieth percentile on the PMMA. A developmental musical aptitude test, it uses the same format and test-taking procedures as the PMMA, and it is as short and easy to administer as the other tests. Repeated administrations are appropriate as students progress through the grades. Grade level norms are presented in the test manual, and the tests are hand scoreable.

Advanced Measures of Music Audiation (AMMA)

The AMMA is a test of stabilized musical aptitude and may be used with students as early as grade five, although it is vastly more appropriate for secondary and college students. Like the other tests, the AMMA yields three scores—tonal, rhythm, and composite—and is recorded on cassette tape. It requires only fifteen minutes to take and may be given in group or individual settings. The test does not presume a knowledge of music. Respondents listen to paired musical phrases, choosing whether they sound the same or different because of a tonal or rhythm change.

Musical Aptitude Profile (MAP)

The MAP is the original test of stabilized musical aptitude developed by Edwin Gorden. It is for use with students from age nine through high school and differs from Gordon's later tests in that it includes a test of musical sensitivity. Unlike the other tests, the MAP is long; each of the three tests requires approximately forty minutes to administer. This is demanding for elementary students and is not meant to be given all at one time. For this reason the IMMA is preferable because of its short duration. Also, the IMMA is a developmental test of musical aptitude, which may be more appropriate when charting student growth. The short length of the AMMA also may make it more useful with high school students. The MAP is the first of Gordon's test of musical aptitude, and it remains a major achievement in the testing field.

The Iowa Tests of Music Literacy

Musical achievement differs from musical aptitude in that achievement is a measure of what a person knows as the result of instruction; aptitude is more a reflection of innate musical potential. Most achievement tests are teacher designed and vary according to what is being assessed. Edwin Gordon wrote the Iowa Tests of Music Literacy as a means of testing achievement in basic music functioning. There are three areas of concentration—listening, reading, and writing— each area containing two parts, rhythm and tonal. Each of the six tests takes approximately forty-five minutes to administer, and more advanced students can skip Level 1 for Level 2. The test kit contains enough materials to administer to fifty students, and additional answer sheets can be ordered separately (as is the case for all of Gordon's tests). Unlike the tests of musical aptitude, these achievement tests presume that students are experienced in music and read music to some degree. The benefits of using standardized achievement testing are to discover weaknesses in students' musical functioning that can be improved through instruction and curriculum enrichment, and to identify students with particular strengths.

Standardized tests of music are not commonly used among music educators. This may be due partly to lack of knowledge of such tests and the costs involved. However, the school guidance counselor should be able to include the costs in the school's testing budget. The use of such tests can yield valuable information in guidance and recruitment.

STUDY AND DISCUSSION QUESTIONS

1. Why is a proactive approach to public relations necessary for the music program?
2. Should the choral director be involved in public relations and to what degree?
3. What information is appropriate in a news release?
4. What technical aspect of a radio or TV broadcast should be of major concern to the choral director?
5. What types of radio and TV programs could involve promotion of the choral program?
6. In addition to the performance of choral music, what other activities might be included as part of a presentation to a civic group?
7. How can the choral director cultivate administrative support?
8. Of the guidelines given for working with school guidance counselors, which do you think is the most important and why?
9. How can the choral director cultivate support from other teachers?
10. What is the Alliance for Arts Education and what does it do?
11. What are some activities appropriate for Music in Our Schools Month at the high school and elementary levels?
12. Why is a choir newsletter important and to whom should it be sent?
13. What important element should be included in every newsletter?
14. What is the best means of recruiting students to the choral program?
15. Why is singing in the general music curriculum so important to the choral program?
16. Why is rapport with athletic coaches so important to the choral program?
17. Why should the choral director not vie for students with the instrumental director?
18. What is the difference between an aptitude test and an achievement test?
19. What benefits are there in giving standardized aptitude tests in music to all students?
20. What benefits are there in giving standardized achievement tests to music students?

REFERENCES

Demorest, S. M. (2000). Encouraging male participation in chorus. *Music Educators Journal, 86*(4), 38–41.

Gates, J. T. (1989). A historical comparison of public singing by American men and women. *Journal of Research in Music Education, 37*(1), 32–47.

Getto, E. O. (comp.) (1988). *Tips: Public relations.* Reston, VA: Music Educators National Conference.

Gordon, E. E. (1979). *Primary measures of music audiation.* Chicago: G.I.A.

———— (1982). *Intermediate measures of music audiation.* Chicago: G.I.A.

———— (1988). *Musical aptitude profile.* Chicago: G.I.A.

———— (1989). *Advanced measures of music audiation.* Chicago: G.I.A.

———— (1989). *Audie.* Chicago: G.I.A.

———— (1991). *The Iowa tests of music literacy.* Chicago: G.I.A.

Kennedy, M. (1999). It's cool because we like to sing: Junior high boys' experience of choral music. Paper presented at the Desert Skies Symposium on Research in Music Education, Tucson, AZ.

Latten, J. E. (1998). A scheduling-conflict resolution model. *Music Educators Journal, 84*(6), 22–25, 38.

MENC (1984). *Promoting school music: A practical guide.* Reston, VA: Music Educators National Conference.

———— (1987). *Beyond the classroom: Informing others.* Reston, VA: Music Educators National Conference.

———— (1991). *Action kit for music education.* Reston, VA: National Coalition for Music Education.

———— (1991). *Building support for school music: A practical guide.* Reston, VA: National Coalition for Music Education.

———— (1992). *Teacher's guide for advocacy.* Reston, VA: National Coalition for Music Education.

———— (1994). Recruiting singers for elementary chorus. *Teaching Music, 1*(6), 24–25.

Phillips, K. H. (1986). Recruiting high school choristers. *Choral Journal, 27*(5), 25–27.

4 | Planning and Building the Choral Program

It would be wonderful if all choral directors had to do was to rehearse music and conduct performances. Unfortunately, this is not the case. More time is spent doing paperwork than making music, and the paperwork cannot be ignored. Every successful choral music program is built on careful planning and management. While it may be possible to get by without strict attention to detail, doing so will show up eventually in a program that lacks focus and future. There is a saying that has great merit when it comes to administrative tasks: "Plan your work and work your plan."

School administrators are especially upset when teachers do not attend to the business of teaching. Lesson plans, reports, grades, budget requests—all need to be done in a timely fashion. The best program will not make up for an unauthorized bill that is submitted for payment by the choral director. Schools, in many ways, are businesses and run according to standard procedures and protocols. Learning to apply a school's guidelines for the many paperwork tasks that are involved in teaching is among the first duties of any new teacher. At first the requirements may seem overwhelming, but a general routine can be established quickly if the tasks are done daily and on a regular basis. A new teacher needs to read the school handbook thoroughly and should not be afraid to ask questions. There is much to be learned on a new job.

THE MASTER SCHEDULE

Before the choral director can design, redesign, and request a certain schedule for the choral curriculum, there must be a knowledge of the type of master schedule used in the school. Traditionally, high schools have days divided into six to eight periods of equal length, usually forty to fifty minutes. Courses are scheduled into these time slots, and the same classes meet in the same order on a daily and weekly basis. This type of schedule is simple and easy to understand; many school districts continue to use it (Walker, 1989). Its biggest problems are a lack of flexibility, short periods, and wasted contact time when students are changing classes.

The number of periods in the day is critical to the music education program. While the eight-period day has the least contact time per time slot, eight periods are the most beneficial when it comes to students taking music courses. Students in an eight-period schedule often can be in two ensembles and perhaps take an elective music appreciation or theory class. The six-period day is the worst, as college-bound students may not be able to schedule any music classes at all. While the seven-period day is better than six, eight periods provide maximum opportunity for a full music curriculum.

Some schools have eight rotating periods in the schedule across a seven-period day. This can be done by dropping a period each day (see Figure 4.1), or by rotating an eighth period

Time Slot	Day 1	Day 2	Day 3	Day 4	Day 5	Day 6	Day 7	Day 8
1	2	1	1	1	1	1	1	1
2	3	3	2	2	2	2	2	2
3	4	4	4	3	3	3	3	3
4	5	5	5	5	4	4	4	4
5	6	6	6	6	6	5	5	5
6	7	7	7	7	7	7	6	6
7	8	8	8	8	8	8	8	7

Figure 4.1. Schedule 1: Dropping a period each day.

across a seven-period day (see Figure 4.2). In both cases, an eighth period is added to the cycle of classes. "In the rotation approach, the length of the school day remains the same and every teacher prepares the same average number of classes each day, but students have the opportunity to elect a full program of eight classes" (Shuler, 1996, p. 24).

Block Scheduling

Much has been made in recent years of block scheduling, in which larger blocks of time, usually ninety minutes, are appropriated for each subject. Advocates of this concept point to the greater contact time for each course and note that students receive more in-class help from teachers because of the longer class period. Another benefit mentioned is that student pass time between classes is significantly decreased, as fewer course periods are scheduled each day. Also, there are no study halls (Kember, Wolfman, Mueller, George, 1995, pp. 35–36).

The straight block schedule has only four periods each day, and the same four courses are taken daily for ninety minutes each (see Figure 4.3). Teachers know that they cannot lecture or teach from a book for ninety minutes; student attention level requires alternative forms of teaching. There is much greater emphasis on small group projects, student demonstrations, field trips, library use, and so forth. An academic subject that typically requires one year to cover can be taught in one semester. "One clear advantage of the four-period day is that teach-

Time Slot	Day 1	Day 2	Day 3	Day 4	Day 5	Day 6	Day 7	Day 8
1	1	8	1	1	1	1	1	1
2	2	2	8	2	2	2	2	2
3	3	3	3	8	3	3	3	3
4	4	4	4	4	8	4	4	4
5	5	5	5	5	5	8	5	5
6	6	6	6	6	6	6	8	6
7	7	7	7	7	7	7	7	8

Figure 4.2. Schedule 2: Rotating the eighth period across a seven-period day.

Monday	Tuesday	Wednesday	Thursday	Friday
Subject 1 (90 minutes)	Subject 1	Subject 1	Subject 1	Subject 1
Subject 2 (90 minutes)	Subject 2	Subject 2	Subject 2	Subject 2
Subject 3 (90 minutes)	Subject 3	Subject 3	Subject 3	Subject 3
Subject 4 (90 minutes)	Subject 4	Subject 4	Subject 4	Subject 4

Figure 4.3. Straight block schedule.

ers are given one of the four periods for planning and evaluation, which is usually a big improvement over present practice" (Lehman, 1995, pp. 18–19).

The straight four-period block schedule may be a problem for high school music students wanting to take an ensemble. While it may be possible to elect chorus one semester, it may not be possible to do so for the entire year depending upon students' needs to take required college preparatory courses. A year on the straight block is like an eight-period schedule, but the eight courses occur four a semester. This can create a major conflict for music students.

The straight block also may be problematic in that rehearsals periods are ninety minutes long. Fatigue results in poor vocal technique, which results in poor vocal production. The longer period does permit greater concentration on music reading skills, however, and it permits time to teach the cultural and historical contexts of the music that are called for in the national standards. A survey of choral directors (Hook, 1995) whose traditional schedules changed to the block reports that 57.9 percent had taken advantage of the opportunity to present theory and history lessons, and "two-thirds of the respondents believed that the longer class period enhanced their students' preparation for music festivals" (p. 29).

The alternating block schedule has been found to be more useful for music educators (Hoffman, 1995). In this type of schedule, a four-period block "A" schedule is alternated daily with another four-period block "B" of different courses (see Figure 4.4). Each block remains ninety minutes, but now eight courses are taken each semester, permitting a choral ensemble to be scheduled for the entire year. The same problems still exist with the long period, but the possibility of a student's taking choir for both semesters make this alternate block more desirable for the music program.

Time Slot	Day A Subjects	Day B Subjects
1	1	5
2	2	6
3	3	7
4	4	8

Figure 4.4. Alternating block schedule.

Monday	Tuesday	Wednesday	Thursday	Friday
Subject 1 (45/45 minutes)	Subject 1 —	Subject 1 —	Subject 1 —	Subject 1 —
Subject 2	Subject 2	Subject 2	Subject 2	Subject 2
Subject 3 (90 minutes)	Subject 3	Subject 3	Subject 3	Subject 3
Subject 4 (90 minutes)	Subject 4	Subject 4	Subject 4	Subject 4
Subject 5 (90 minutes)	Subject 5	Subject 5	Subject 5	Subject 5

Figure 4.5. Split-block schedule.

A third type of block scheduling exists—the split block (see Figure 4.5). In this schedule the first block is split into two, forty-five minute blocks, and students may schedule two courses during this time. This schedule works well when both chorus and band are scheduled during the first block for forty-five minutes each; students who elect to be in both ensembles may then schedule each, back to back. Both the instrumental and choral directors can offer other forty-five minute courses for those students who do not elect both (e.g., theory, music appreciation, group lessons), or other courses may be taken (e.g., foreign language or physical education) that are offered for the shorter amount of time.

There are many variations in block scheduling. In one every-other-day model, two subjects alternate daily in block one. Some schools offer split blocks of more than forty-five minutes, and some split more than one block. Music teachers seem to favor either the alternating block or the split block.

The choral director should be actively involved in working with those who determine school scheduling. They can volunteer or ask to be appointed to a steering committee that may be considering a move to block scheduling.

> In pushing for split-blocks or alternating blocks rather than straight-block schedules, you should be able to find many allies among teacher colleagues. Alternating blocks tend to be supported by those teachers whose subjects are essentially elective, including teachers of the other arts and many teachers of the humanities. Split-blocks tend to be supported by these same teachers and also by those whose disciplines require regular practice to develop skills, such as foreign languages and physical education. (Lehman, 1995, pp. 20–21)

Whatever the form the schedule takes, music educators must guard against music ensembles' being pushed out of the school day to once again become "extracurricular." Music is an academic subject; it must maintain its place within the school curriculum with credit-generating courses. Without a flexible schedule, there will be little need to design an in-depth choral curriculum.

DESIGNING THE CHORAL CURRICULUM

What types of choirs are appropriate in the choral curriculum? There are a vast array of possibilities, most of which depend upon the master schedule and the amount of instructional time, the number of vocal music teachers, the size of the school population, and the willingness of the choral director to design and teach the program.

Senior High School Choral Curriculum

The high school (grades 9–12) choral curriculum can be broad and diverse and depends upon the number of faculty in choral music and the flexibility of the scheduling. Larger high schools often have two choral faculty members and professional accompanists. In most smaller schools there is likely to be one choral director who is responsible for the entire program. In this case, the choral curriculum may be less diverse depending upon the amount of time the choral director has in the day (especially before and after school) and is willing to commit to the program. The beginning choral director would do well to remember that having a life outside of the job is extremely important. Taking on too much responsibility can lead to quick burnout and health problems.

Most high schools have at least one or two choral ensembles. The "top" or best choir is typically an auditioned group comprising junior- and senior-level students. It is also a good idea to have a second choir that depends less upon audition for the less vocally developed.

> One important educational precept . . . is that every student, regardless of talent or age, should have the opportunity to participate in the choral music program. That philosophy takes into account the uncertain singer who has difficulty just matching pitches, the student who is out of the social mainstream . . . the student who may be mentally impaired but is being mainstreamed effectively in some areas, and the student who has a physical disability. (Michelson, 1994, p. 3)

Choral directors are educators and must remember that all students are entitled to a public education in America. Choral ensembles for only the best singers present an elitist image of the choral program.

Care must be taken that chorus not become a dumping ground for students who are lazy and not succeeding elsewhere in school. Such students may be disruptive and create frequent discipline problems. The choral director should have the final say as to who is accepted for choir.

It is good to have a feeder system in the lower grades in which students can gain experience and then naturally progress to the top choir. The choral director who has students from the seventh or eighth grades is at an advantage in being able to shape these students from an early age. These younger choirs are valuable assets to the entire choral program and should exist in the choral curriculum. Students who sing throughout the junior high/middle school years are more likely to continue their singing in senior high school.

Choirs that meet during the academic day should produce credit toward students' graduation requirements. There should be few exceptions, if any, to this policy. Choirs are academic and teach a subject matter that has a complex body of knowledge. Ensembles that meet before and after school are typically treated as other extracurricular activities and generate no academic credit.

There are numerous ways to organize high school choral ensembles. The following are some of the many possibilities.

Concert choir (known by many names). Membership in this choir is by audition and is reserved for male and female students of the highest musical and singing achievement. It may include only seniors, a combination of seniors and juniors, and even some talented sophomores. The number of students accepted into this group will depend upon choral balance and may be limited in number for purposes of traveling and touring. This is the top choral group in the high school and typically meets every day.

Chamber singers (or madrigal singers). This is a select group of the best singers, usually drawn from the concert choir. The size may vary from sixteen to twenty-four students. It is an optional ensemble in the choral program, but can be valuable for introducing members to a style of chamber and madrigal literature that is less effective with larger groups. Such choirs often meet before or after school and typically do not receive academic credit.

Mixed chorus (known by many names). This is the general high school chorus and should be open to all male and female students in grades ten to twelve regardless of audition outcome. When the school population is small, there may be fewer boys in this choir than girls, which may necessitate the use of three-part (SAB) music. This is a valuable feeder choir and typically meets three to five days a week.

Choral union. Some schools have such a small population that the mixed chorus is weak and not suitable for public performance. In this case, a "combined" choir including concert choir members and mixed chorus members is possible. The choral union is scheduled to have all singers meet together two or three days a week, while the concert choir members meet alone the other days at the same time. Combining these two choirs in a "union" permits the weaker students to experience the singing of music that they would not otherwise be able to do. However, the "mix" also limits the time that the concert choir meets by itself, which can be remedied with an additional after-school rehearsal time, if necessary.

Men's and women's choirs. There is a wealth of good literature for men and women separately, which can be experienced by separating genders for rehearsals of the concert choir or choral union. This can occur easily when two choral faculty work at the high school; asking for help from the instrumental directors is also a possibility. Because of limited student time, these choirs are not scheduled independently but rather as subgroups of another choir. The amount of repertoire will of necessity be small, but this type of singing experience is valuable for students.

Show choir (also swing and jazz choirs). This type of popular singing group has become a regular part of many choral programs. In most schools the group meets before or after school and receives no academic credit. Wise choral directors insist that students in this type of group also must belong to a choir in the regular academic curriculum. Sizes of such groups vary from relatively small (sixteen singers) to very large ensembles. Show choirs place much emphasis on choreography, while swing choirs may do some movement in standing formation. Jazz groups are usually small and include no choreography or planned movements.

Figure 4.6. Chamber singers ensemble. (Chamber Singers of Riverside High School, Ellwood City, Pa. Photo by Bud Dimeo, *Ellwood City Ledger*. Used by permission.)

Care must be taken that pop singing groups do not overwhelm the choral program and become its focus. While popular with students and audiences alike, the core of the choral curriculum must be choral music, not popular tunes arranged for group singing. Some choral directors are set against popular singing groups in the schools. David Itkin, in the article "Dissolving the Myths of the Show Choir" (1986), believes that reasons given for supporting such ensembles are just that—myths. In his concluding statement he says,

> Unquestionably, the influence of the popular arts cannot be ignored—so why should we strengthen it further? It is not our duty . . . to present a "rounded musical picture" when the influences on our students and community are already so far weighted toward the opposing side. (p. 41)

In rebuttal, both Gene Grier (1986) and Tim Sharar (1986) state there is room for all styles of music in the choral program, and that "beauty is in the eyes (and ears) of the beholder" (Sharar, 1986, p. 17). They note that any ensemble has the potential to become vocally abusive and that good singing is good singing.

Small groups (trios, quartets, octets). Building a choral ensemble around small groups of four to eight singers is an excellent way to encourage independence and to challenge singers to learn the music. Some choral directors regularly have students sing in front of the choir in quartets or octets, thus presenting an excellent vehicle for evaluating student progress and achievement. Students are more likely to study their music outside of class if they know they are going to sing in front of the group.

Other outlets for small groups are ensembles such as barbershop and beautyshop quartets, a women's trio, and so forth. Groups like these must be self-motivated and should be able to learn the music with minimal help from the choral director. Such groups are extracurricular and do not receive academic credit.

Treble choir. Sometimes the absence of boys in a choral program forces a choral director to create a separate choir for the many girls who, if included, would overbalance the boys in the mixed chorus or choral union. In large schools, this ensemble may be quite large, and some girls may prefer to be in a gender-specific choir. For legal purposes, however, the choir should not be called a "girls" chorus, as this makes gender the major criterion for choir membership, which is not legal (Merrill, 1976). Criteria for such a choir should include vocal ranges (treble) and quality. Care must be taken that girls or women in this chorus not be made to feel like second-class citizens. This ensemble should form a valuable part of the feeder program.

Ninth-grade mixed chorus (known by various names). Keeping ninth-grade students together in a mixed ensemble is especially appropriate, as true four-part music can now be sung. While schools may include some ninth graders among the older choir groups, a solid ninth-grade mixed choir is a tremendous part of the feeder program. These students feel more comfortable together, and their voices are not overshadowed by those of older students. This choir meets daily or sometimes three days a week.

Broadway musical chorus. The values of the all-school musical chorus were addressed earlier under recruitment (Chapter 3). Suffice it to say that such choruses usually rehearse after school and require much preparation time. Dancing is often required, and students should be auditioned with both singing and movement activities. However, great prowess in either area is not needed. It is surprising how much students can learn to sing and move with a little instruction and lots of encouragement.

Voice class. Instrumental directors have long had the benefits of giving group and individual lessons during the school day, so why should not the choral director? Voice classes

Figure 4.7. Broadway chorus from *South Pacific*. (City High School, Iowa City. Photo by Anne Craig. Used by permission.)

can be scheduled for one or two times a week, making small-group lessons a part of the academic curriculum. Such classes are not to be used for further teaching of choral music, but rather for the development of the singing voice and solo literature. A number of voice class books are available and can form the basis of the curriculum. One way to organize such classes is to introduce specific vocal exercises, vocalises, and song literature on one day, and then listen to students individually the second day. If not performing before the class, students may be given assignments from the class book while individuals are working with the teacher. A public recital for such students is an excellent outlet for those wishing to participate.

Individual lessons. Many choral directors give individual voice lessons to students when time permits during the school day. It is not legal to accept payment for such lessons. Some directors require that all students receive at least one or two lessons during the grading period. This is difficult to arrange, as students must attend either the lessons during a study hall or be taken out of class. However, the benefits of hearing every student individually are great.

Honors and festival choirs. Honors and festival choirs abound in most areas of the country, and many choral directors and students are actively involved in such activities. The responsibility of preparing the students usually falls to the choral director, who must find the extra time during the day or before and after school to teach the music. This can consume a large amount of time, and some directors make (or purchase) cassette tapes with students' vocal parts recorded. This saves much time and allows students to work more on their own.

Junior High/Middle School Choral Curriculum

The older junior high form of school organization (grades seven to eight or seven to nine) has mostly given way to the middle school concept, where upper elementary and lower high

Figure 4.8. Student in voice lesson. (Photo by Anne Craig. Used by permission.)

school grades are combined in one building. In such cases, the ninth-grade mixed chorus as a separate ensemble is still recommended. Also, because of the inherent problems of adolescence, it is best to keep the ensemble experience for students in grades seven and eight separate from that of the intermediate grades five and six when possible.

Seventh- and eighth-grade mixed chorus (known by various names, including junior choir and youth choir). Most seventh-grade boys still have unchanged, treble voices. The voice change usually occurs around the eighth grade, permitting boys to sing a lower range. If there are enough boys with changed voices, four-part music is possible, but traditionally three-part music is used: treble 1, treble 2, and changing.

This is a difficult time in the students' lives to be in a mixed ensemble. Boys become self-conscious of either sounding like girls or having their voices "crack." Girls also experience a type of voice change, which along with other physical changes can make them self-conscious around boys. For these reasons, a modified choir arrangement is recommended for students in seventh and eighth grades.

In a modified schedule, boys meet during the same time slot as girls, but on Tuesdays, Thursdays, and Fridays. Likewise, girls meet separately on Mondays and Wednesdays, but with the boys on Fridays. This arrangement permits the choral director to work with boys and girls separately and to attend to their individual needs during the maturation process. It also permits different music literature to be used with each group. However, a combined rehearsal on Fridays permits both groups to be brought together for a full musical effect on combined literature.

Some school principals believe that students are not to be separated by gender for any classes. This is not what the law stipulates (Merrill, 1976). Equal opportunity for choral participation must be available for both genders. Only one choir is on the schedule of courses, but it consists of two sections that meet separately and together. Care should be taken that sections not be called officially a "boys" chorus or "girls" chorus.

Where schools are large, it is possible to have separate choruses in seventh and eighth grades. The seventh-grade chorus will be of necessity a treble chorus, while the eighth-grade chorus will involve changing, and perhaps changed, voices. Whether these grades meet together or separately, it is important to keep adolescents singing during the voice change process. Many who drop out of choir at this age never return to singing.

Show choir. An increasing number of schools have show choirs for young adolescents. The wisdom of this move is yet to be determined. The question is often asked, "What will students have to look forward to if they begin singing in such groups at such an early age?" On the other hand, if the show choir helps to keep the students singing through this difficult time, why not include it, at least to a limited degree? Conventional wisdom is questioned, however, when such groups begin taking tours and presenting out-of-school performances like senior high school groups. The junior high or middle school choir director must resist the temptation to try and emulate their senior high school counterpart. Each age requires different handling, and the wise teacher knows this. Students are as likely to have burnout as are teachers; those who begin such activities early on may decide that it is just not worth the time when they become senior high students.

Musical chorus. Some middle school directors are now presenting musicals that are composed for young adolescents. Again, the temptation to emulate the senior high school program must be guarded. However, musicals that are performed as part of the choral program and that require little out-of-class rehearsal time can benefit students' interest in singing. Endurance is the key. Young adolescents should not be expected to sing for long periods of time, which may result in vocal fatigue.

Honors and festival choirs. More middle school and junior high choral directors are becoming involved in honors and festival choirs. Such events are excellent opportunities for students to hear other singing groups and for directors to share ideas. Out-of-school time is sometimes involved, but activities that are held during the school day are best for students at these ages.

Elementary School Choral Curriculum

The fastest growing movement in the choral area of late is that of children's choirs. Numerous groups independent of schools exist and often involve graded choir programs. Membership in these types of choirs is usually by audition, and those students who join are typically those who have developed an early love of singing.

The elementary school singing program has a long existence, but elementary music teachers have not regularly thought of themselves as choral directors. General music teachers foster singing in a group setting, but the song literature is rarely what could be called choral music. Elementary concerts usually feature whole classes singing songs, and this is good. What is most often lacking is the use of quality choral literature.

The children's choir movement has seen a rise in the number of elementary school choirs that meet separately from the regular music classes. A growing awareness of how to teach children to sing, exposure to good choral music for children, and the opportunity to hear excellent recorded examples of children's singing have all had a part in the expanding place of children's choirs in the elementary school music curriculum.

The question of selectivity arises with any discussion of elementary choirs. Should children be excluded from choir by audition, or should all children who want to sing be admitted? The answer is not an easy one. Certainly, every child should have the opportunity to sing in an ensemble, and this can be done through the regular general music program. But what about the students who show a real interest in singing and who demonstrate the ability to match pitch accurately with a suitable vocal range? Surely they will benefit from a separate choral experience. But what about the students who show a real interest in singing but do not match pitch accurately and have a limited vocal range? Will exclusion from chorus so keep them from thinking of themselves as singers that they will never audition again?

Perhaps the answer lies in a graded elementary choral program where willing students who are not singing accurately may receive extra help in a beginning group. This training choir then serves as a feeder choir for the more select group. If the select choir is limited to fifth and sixth graders, then the training choir could be the place where all younger students begin, thus eliminating the necessity of choosing among this age group. All students who want to join are accepted into the training choir. Students often know by the upper elementary grades if they want to sing or not, and hurting someone's feelings probably is more likely at an earlier age. Whatever is done, there always may be the chance of eliminating a singer who shows little potential.

Time to schedule elementary choirs also is a problem. Some schools have activity times where students may choose among a number of interests, choir being one of them. Other schools have general study times when students may be pulled from classes for choir. In some cases, choir is held before school.

It must be stressed again that a separate elementary choral program should not result in general music classes that do not include singing. The elementary years are the time to teach singing as a skill to all children. Choir can be a stimulating addition but should not supplant a music curriculum where singing is a focus. The first national standard for all children is "singing, alone and with others, a varied repertoire of music."

Children's choirs. Elementary choirs may be organized by individual grades, by two-level grouping (primary grades one to three; intermediate grades four to six), and by two-grade grouping (one and two; three and four; five and six). Choirs that encompass all grades are not easy to work with because of different skill levels and varying maturity of the children. Nevertheless, such groups can work if the repertoire is kept quite simple. Choirs for kindergartners are not encouraged, as such young children have very short attention spans.

Musical chorus. Many elementary choral music teachers direct annual musicals especially written for children. While the quality of the music is often questionable, when the production involves all the children of a certain grade as part of the general music class curriculum, then those students in the chorus can greatly benefit from this exposure to singing. In some schools children write their own musicals around a study theme chosen in cooperation with the regular classroom teacher. This makes for good staff relations and often involves many other teachers in the production of the musical.

Figure 4.9. Children's chorus. (Willowwind Children's Choir, Iowa City. Nancy MacFarlane, director. Used by permission.)

The number of possible choral organizations within a school curriculum from elementary through high school are numerous and varied. Choral directors should not include so many that they become married to their jobs. A life apart from music is important.

AUDITIONING THE SINGERS

Among a choral director's first musical jobs is auditioning singers and placing them in the various choral ensembles of the curriculum. The word *audition* or *tryout* often strikes terror in the hearts of students, and the choral director must be prepared for nervous students who feel insecure. Additionally it is important to complete the audition in as short a time as possible while still gathering all the pertinent information. The data collected are used to determine voice classification and choir placement. A smooth and businesslike process will greatly aid in calming students' fears and in creating an accurate voice-testing process.

The Audition Form

The audition form is typically in two parts: the top or front portion asks for basic identification information, and the bottom or back is for the director's use in recording audition data (see Figure 4.10). The basic ID section includes some or all of the following: student's name, address, telephone number, year in school, age, height, names of parents or guardians, and some indication of musical background. Other information could include voice lessons, instrument lessons, why the student wants to be in choir, part-time job and hours, interest in solo work, contests, all-state events, and something special about the student. The form should include as much information as the director finds useful.

VOCAL/CHORAL AUDITION FORM
MERCURY HIGH SCHOOL
Anywhere, USA

*Fill in **top** section of this form. Please print.*

Name _____ Telephone # _____

Address _____ E-Mail _____

_____ Zip _____

Names of Parents/Guardians _____

Part-time work _____ Hours _____

Voice Classification (if known): S1 S2 A1 A2 T1 T2 B1 B2 (circle one)

Year in School: 9 10 11 12 (circle one). Have you been in choir before? Yes No

Do you play an instrument? Yes No. If yes, what and how long? _____

Have you studied voice? Yes No. If yes, with whom and how long? _____

If you have other musical experiences (e.g., band) please list them on the back of this form.

Briefly state why you want to participate in the choral program _____

_____

_____

***Stop** here. Please present this form to the teacher upon entering the audition room. Thank you for your interest in the choral program of this school.*

(Key 1=very low, 5=very high)

1. Vocal Range: 1   2   3   4   5
2. Vocal Quality: 1   2   3   4   5
3. Sight-Singing: 1   2   3   4   5
4. Part Singing: 1   2   3   4   5
5. Singing Technique: 1   2   3   4   5
6. Confidence: 1   2   3   4   5
7. Over-all Rating: 1   2   3   4   5

Comments: _____   **Accept? Yes No**

_____

_____ Choir _____

_____ Voice Part _____

Figure 4.10. Vocal/choral audition form.

The data part of the form includes those skills that will be tested, some type of scoring indicators (e.g, 1–5) , and a key to interpret the indicators (e.g., 1 = low, 5 = high). The elements to be tested may include some or all of the following: voice quality, singing technique, range, tessitura, projection, tonal accuracy, rhythm accuracy, ability to carry a part, diction, vibrato, and sight-singing. A written staff is useful for indicating range and tessitura. Again, the form should have as much data collection as the director finds useful.

The audition form also needs to include whether or not the student is accepted, the voice part assigned, and choir assigned. It should be neat, legible, and easily reproduced. Any music or other materials that will be used in the audition process should be available in duplicate copies.

The Audition Process

It is better if the audition room is a private area where students will not feel so intimidated. Students should not be auditioned within hearing range of their peers. The audition process will be facilitated if the audition forms, with directives for filling out the ID portion, are available outside the audition room.

Upon entering the audition room, the director receives the audition form and engages the student in some light conversation to help quiet their nerves (Fenton, 1981). Typical ice breakers might include: "I like that sweater you're wearing," or "How was your summer"? If the student is unknown to the director the student may be asked about his or her singing background and other musical experience. It is also helpful for the director to say, "This audition involves no grade and all information is kept confidential—so relax."

The first singing element in the audition is a test of vocal range—the lower extent and then the upper. By using two standard vocalises (scale and arpeggio) the student is given a chance to warm up. This activity seems to be less intimidating than that of singing a song. The lower range is tested by singing a descending five-note scale (sol-fa-mi-re-do), on a neutral vowel (ah), beginning on g above (trebles) or below (changed male voices) middle c. The pattern is lowered by half steps until the singer reaches his or her lowest comfortable pitch. The upper range is tested by singing an ascending arpreggio to the octave (do-mi-sol-do), on a neutral vowel, beginning on or around middle c or an octave below for men. The pattern is raised by half steps until the singer reaches his or her highest comfortable pitch. The process may be repeated as necessary. The data for lowest and highest pitches are recorded on the audition form.

The range measure is followed by the singing of a simple, well-known melody, such as "My Country, 'Tis of Thee," in a comfortable key. This enables the assessment of a number of things, including voice quality and technique. Students can be asked to sing the first phrase from "My country" to "of thee I sing" on one breath as a measure of breath control. It is good to have a copy of the music and words available. When auditioning for an advanced choir, students may be asked to sing a prepared solo.

When checking for a student's ability to carry a part, a relatively unknown folksong or hymn can be used. The student watches the music as the parts are played together at the piano. Then the student sings his or her part while all parts are again played. If a student is unable to do this, the part should be played as he or she listens. Next, the student should sing the part while it is played. Finally, the student should attempt to sing the part with all parts being played. If he or she can carry the part after this instruction, the singer has sufficient ear and memory. The director then will assign the student to a choir based on the strength of the audition.

Sight-singing can be checked if students indicate they read music. A useful way to do this is to have five sight-reading examples available, each one progressively more difficult.

Beginning with number three, the difficulty level can be increased or decreased according to the student's performance. Students should be encouraged to use whatever system of sight-singing they know (e.g., syllables, numbers, neutral syllable, etc.).

Optional pitch memory and discrimination tests can be given. A disjunct melodic line is played, or primary triads in root and inverted positions, and the student asked to respond accordingly. Two melodic patterns are played in succession, the student indicating if the patterns are the same or different. Rhythm accuracy may be determined by asking students to clap rhythmic patterns of increasing difficulty, or by clapping back rhythm patterns they hear.

The audition concludes in one of two ways: (1) the director informs the student immediately of the outcome, or (2) the student is informed that a list will be posted by a certain date indicating choir assignment. The latter approach works well when the director must evaluate all of the auditionees in relation to each other before choosing the choir finalists. The student is thanked and dismissed, and the director then finalizes the data collection form. The entire audition should take approximately ten minutes. The following is a summary of the audition process:

- Student fills out identification data on audition form before entering audition room.
- Student is greeted by director and put at ease with "small talk."
- Vocal range test is administered, lower followed by upper limits.
- Simple song or solo is sung to determine quality, technique, etc.
- One vocal part of an unknown song is sung to determine ability to carry a part.
- Sight-singing is measured if student indicates some ability to read music.
- Optional tests of pitch memory and discrimination are given.
- Student is told the outcome of audition or when decision will be posted.
- Student is thanked for auditioning and dismissed.

GUIDELINES FOR VOICE CLASSIFICATION

As part of the audition, the director must assign the student to a voice part. Voices are classified by various means, and only experience will help the choral director make quick and accurate judgments. Common indicators of voice part include range, tessitura, vocal quality, voice lifts, and speaking pitch (Wolverton, 1993, pp. 31–32).

Vocal Range and Tessitura

Vocal ranges and tessituras are common indicators with which to begin and are presented for children (Figure 4.11), young adolescents (Figure 4.12), and older adolescents (Figure 4.13) (Phillips, 1992). Tessitura refers to the comfort zone for singing within the outer limits of the total range. Typically, it is found by singing a song such as "America" or another song with a fairly wide pitch range, first in one area of the voice and then another, making use of a variety of starting pitches.

Vocal Quality

Vocal quality is another important indicator of voice classification. Heavier, darker voices tend to be more bass, alto, and mezzo soprano. Lighter, brighter voices are likely to be baritone, tenor, and soprano. Sometimes a person knows that it feels more comfortable to sing a

	1st grade	2nd grade	3rd grade	4th grade	5th grade	6th grade
Range	c^1–c^2	b–d^2	$b^\flat$–$e^{\flat 2}$	a–e^2	$a^\flat$–f^2	g–g^2
Tessitura	d^1–a^1	d^1–b^1	d^1–c^2	d^1–d^2	d^1–d^2	d^1–d^2

Figure 4.11. Vocal ranges and tessituras for children.

	Treble 1 & 2 (unchanged)	Tenor (2) (changing voice)	Baritone (changing voice)	Bass-baritone (newly changed)
Range	$b^\flat$–f^2	g–c^2	c–e^1	G–c^1
Tessitura	d^1–d^2	a–a^1	d–d^1	A–a^1

Figure 4.12. Vocal ranges and tessituras for younger adolescents.

	Sop. 1	Sop. 2	Alto 1	Alto 2	Ten. 1	Ten. 2	Bass 1	Bass 2
Range	$e^{\flat 1}$–$b^{\flat 2}$	c^1–g^2	a–e^2	f#–$c\#^2$	d–a^1	$B^\flat$–f^1	G–d^1	E–b
Tessitura	$a^{\flat 1}$–$e^{\flat 2}$	f^1–c^2	d^1–a^1	b–$f\#^1$	g–d^1	$e^\flat$–b	c–g	A–e

Figure 4.13. Vocal ranges and tessituras for older adolescents.

certain voice part, and this information should be considered seriously when assigning a voice classification.

Young adolescent boys may try to sing with a lower range and darker quality in trying to imitate the voices of older males. These boys need to be encouraged to make use of the entire vocal range. They must understand that males with lower voices are not more or less masculine than males with upper voices. When all male voices are exercised into the male alto range (sometimes incorrectly called the falsetto), boys come to understand the upper voice as a natural extension of the lower.

Specific voice classification for young trebles is discouraged. The girl who becomes an alto in elementary or middle school because she can read music could have a wonderful soprano voice. It is recommended that young trebles be classified as I or II and parts alternated on different vocal selections between melody and harmony. In this way both the lower and upper voices are exercised and strengthened.

Voice Lifts

Some choral directors advocate listening for certain "lifts" in the vocal registers as a guide to determining voice classification. The chart in Figure 4.14 indicates the upper and lower lift points for each of the voice parts given. The lower lift point delineates that pitch in the voice where there is a clear downward shift to a fuller chest voice, or lower adjustment. The upper lift point delineates that pitch in the vocal range where there is a clear upward shift out

Lift	Sop. 1	Sop. 2	Alto 1	Alto 2	Ten. 1	Ten. 2	Bass 1	Bass 2
Upper	e^2–$f\#^2$	$d\#^2$–e^2	$c\#^2$–d^2	b^1–c^2	e^1–$f\#^1$	$d\#^1$–e^1	$c\#^1$–d^1	b–c^1
Lower	c^2–$c\#^2$	$a\#^1$–b^1	$g\#^1$–a^1	$f\#^1$–g^1	c^1–$c\#^1$	$a\#$–b	$g\#$–a	$f\#$–g

Figure 4.14. Voice-lift guide for singing.

	Sop. 1	Sop. 2	Alto 1	Alto 2	Ten. 1	Ten. 2	Bass 1	Bass 2
Speaking pitch	c^1–e^1	b–d^1	a–c^1	g–$b^\flat$	c–e	B–d	A–c	G–$B^\flat$

Figure 4.15. Speaking-pitch guide for singing. (from Wolverton, 1993).

of the middle voice into the lighter, upper voice. Untrained voices usually have noticeable "breaks" at these lift spots, but well-trained voices have smooth register shifts, making detection more difficult.

Central Speaking Pitch

Voice classification also may be aided by determining a student's central speaking pitch. Figure 4.15 shows a listing of central speaking pitches as matched to voice classifications. One way to assess speaking pitch is to have the student count backward from twenty, which provides the time necessary to match central speaking pitch to the keyboard (Wolverton, 1993, p. 32).

The vocal audition process can reveal a great deal of information about a voice in a short time. As choral directors become more experienced at auditioning, their skills improve, their ears begin to detect more vocal characteristics more quickly, and the process becomes efficient and easier. Only time and practice are needed.

STUDY AND DISCUSSION QUESTIONS

1. What is the meaning of the saying, "Plan your work and work your plan"?
2. In what two ways can an eight-period day be scheduled into seven time slots?
3. What are pros and cons of block scheduling for music educators?
4. What types of alternatives are there to the straight block schedule?
5. What are some general guidelines for designing the high school choral curriculum?
6. What types of choral ensembles are appropriate at the high school level?
7. What are some guidelines for using popular music ensembles in the choral program?
8. What guidelines should be followed when separating students by gender for choir?
9. What are some ways to organize a voice class in the choral curriculum?

10. Why is early adolescence a difficult time for students to be in a mixed ensemble, and how can this situation be avoided?

11. Why is it important to keep students singing throughout the early adolescent years?

12. What guidelines are helpful when planning for junior high/middle school events outside of the regular choral curriculum?

13. What is your opinion regarding select children's choirs at the elementary level?

14. What are some of the basic identification data included on the audition form?

15. What are some of the basic voice collection data included on the audition form?

16. What else besides the audition form is needed for the audition process?

17. What does the director do first as part of the audition process? Why?

18. How is the audition concluded, and how long should the audition last?

19. What criteria can be used to classify voices?

20. What two things are needed to become efficient at choral auditioning?

REFERENCES

Fenton, W. C. (1981). Choral auditions: Content and procedures. *Choral Journal, 21*(7), 33–36.

Grier, G. (1986). Room for all. *Music Educators Journal, 73*(1), 15–16.

Hoffman, E., comp. (1995). A closer look at block scheduling. *Teaching Music, 2*(5), 42–43.

Hook, M. (1995). Block scheduling and its effect on secondary-school music performance classes. *Choral Journal, 36*(4), 27–29.

Itkin, D. (1986). Dissolving the myths of the show choir. *Music Educators Journal, 72*(8), 39–41.

Kember, G., G. Wolfman, D. Mueller, and M. George (1995). The school music program and block scheduling. In *Scheduling time for music*, 35–40. Reston, VA: Music Educators National Conference.

Lehman, P. R. (1995). Do you have the time? In *Scheduling time for music*, 11–24. Reston, VA: Music Educators National Conference.

Merrill, M. L. (1976). Eliminating sex discrimination from school music programs. *Music Educators Journal, 62*(7), 75–77.

Michelson, S. K. (1994). *Getting started with high school choir*. Reston, VA: Music Educators National Conference.

Phillips, K. H. (1992). *Teaching kids to sing*. New York: Schirmer Books.

Sharar, T. J. (1986). Eyes of the beholder. *Music Educators Journal, 73*(1), 16–17.

Shuler, S. C. (1996). Why high school students should study the arts. *Music Educators Journal, 83*(1), 22–26.

Walker, D. E. (1989). *Teaching music*. New York: Schirmer Books.

Wolverton, V. D. (1993). Classifying voices for choral singing. *Choral Journal, 33*(9), 31–32.

5 | Processing the Flow of Information

Numerous informational tasks involve the choral director daily; many demand some form of written communication. While paperwork requires time that could be spent teaching, it must be done. The use of the computer for e-mail and word processing has made written correspondence easier and faster, but technology has not diminished the amount of written work in schools; it may have only increased it. There is no getting away from the fact that teaching involves keeping records, planning lessons, preparing tests, reporting grades, writing letters, and informing others. These tasks are all important parts of the choral director's job.

Some school districts hire a secretary for the music program. This is wonderful for freeing teachers to teach. When administrators understand the large amount of written work involved in music programs, they often are persuaded to provide at least a part-time secretary. If a secretary is not available, a volunteer from a booster group sometimes is helpful. Also, appropriate tasks may be delegated to students: typing, filing, repairing music, and so forth. The choral director cannot do it all and should not even try.

The choral director's office needs to be neat and organized. "An appearance of disorganization sends a message to students that you are not in control" (Althouse, 1986, p. 30). Details and sometimes major items tend to fall through the cracks when life is not orderly. Althouse (1986) recommends setting up a tickler file or "to do" list so that deadlines aren't missed. Prioritizing items on the basis of urgency also helps. Having a yearly and monthly master calendar prods the mind when memory fails.

WRITTEN COMMUNICATION

Every music office needs some type of computer hardware and software. If the school does not provide for such, a booster group can be asked to purchase the items. The efficiency that such technology brings to office work cannot be overestimated. It also adds a professional touch to documents that handwritten specimens do not.

Student Records

All schools are in the business of tracking students through a number of years of education; this requires accountability in the form of student records. Information about students is considered confidential unless permission is given by the student or parents and guardians to release a document. For this reason, students' records should be handled with care and safeguarded. Grade books must be private, and computer records should be accessed only by the proper authorities using the proper passwords.

Each school district has procedures for keeping school records, and beginning teachers need to learn them as soon as possible. A master file typically is kept in the main office for each student, and documents are maintained for future reference beyond graduation. The accuracy of these permanent records depends, for a large part, on the information provided by teachers. The accuracy of student records is extremely important—attendance, reports, and copies of letters to parents must be free of error and submitted clearly and legibly.

Every music director needs a complete list of students in the program with names of parents and guardians, addresses, and telephone numbers. This database will serve many purposes and should be updated regularly.

Letters to Parents and Guardians and to Students

Most choral directors would be wise to make use of more written communication to parents, guardians, and students. Whether writing to tell of a discipline problem, an award received, or an upcoming trip, formal letters command attention. Thank-you notes promote goodwill and keep open the lines of communication between school and home.

All formal and informal written communication should be free of spelling and grammatical errors. Letters coming from educational institutions reflect the choral director as an educated person who is interested in more than just music.

While "form" letters are sometimes appropriate (see Figure 5.1), people are more likely to pay attention to letters that are more personal in nature. Letters should be brief, when possible, and to the point; people tend to ignore long communications.

Everyone likes to receive mail, and students are no exception. One way to make students feel special is to send short notes thanking them for their extra efforts for the choral music program. Having a ready-made card or notepad aids the process and makes it easier to do. By setting a goal of two or three such communications per week, the discipline of this job becomes more automatic. Sometimes it takes a little looking for things about which to commend students, but the effort is worth it for the boost in students' self-esteem.

Writing to Administrators

Most choral directors would do well to communicate more in written form with school administrators. These people need to know what is happening in the program: students who have gained honors, summaries of trips, festivals, and contests. This information keeps the value of the program ever present before those who make important decisions regarding its success.

Communicating goals and aspirations for the choral program is another important reason to write occasionally to school administrators. A yearly evaluation of the strengths and weaknesses of the program helps to share the vision for future direction. These need not be long reports—short, one-page summaries are good. It takes work to keep the lines of communication open, but the benefits can be well worth the effort.

Goals and Objectives

Some form of written document ought to be available that outlines the goals and objectives of the choral program (see Figure 5.2). All students should have a copy in their music folders or choir handbook; it needs to be reviewed periodically as a means of evaluating the success of the curriculum.

RIVERSIDE HIGH SCHOOL
Choral Music Department
Anywhere, USA

May 10, 0000

Choir Parents/Guardians
Concert Choir
Riverside High School

Dear Choir Parents/Guardians:

This letter is to inform you of the Concert Choir tour to Florida, May 26–30, 0000. Please keep it for future reference.

Enclosed with this letter is an itinerary of where we will be and what we will be doing. Telephone numbers are given in case you would need to contact your student in an emergency. Also enclosed are forms for student Conduct and Dress Regulation, and Parental Permission. Sign the permission form and return it no later than May 22. **Observe that the medical portion of this form is to be notarized.** These forms must be taken on the trip.

Transportation to the airport is the responsibility of each student, and sharing of rides is recommended. Please note arrival and departure times as listed on the itinerary. Choir members must not be late!

Students will need to pay for their own breakfasts and lunches; dinner each evening is provided in the cost of the trip. Additional money for snacks and souvenirs will be needed. An emergency fund is provided in case any student would lose his or her money. Travelers checks are a good safety measure.

Please impress upon your student the importance of good discipline on this trip. Students are not permitted out of their rooms after curfew, nor are they permitted to drink alcoholic beverages at any time, no matter what they are permitted to do at home. The chaperones cannot be responsible for prowling or drinking students.

Thank you for helping provide this opportunity for your student. Love is demonstrated in many ways, and this must surely be one of them.

Sincerely,

Ken Phillips
Choral Director

Figure 5.1. Sample letter to parents.

GOALS AND OBJECTIVES OF
CHORAL PARTICIPATION

GOALS

1. Choral participation will enrich the quality of our lives and the lives of those for whom we sing with a deeper appreciation for the world's beauty.
2. Choral singing will lead us to make positive and meaningful contributions to our own lives and the lives of others.
3. Singing will help us to develop our voices in a healthy and confident manner.
4. A knowledge of music will help us to understand the historical and theoretical nature of music, both as an academic subject and in practical application.
5. Belonging to the choir will foster a cooperative learning environment and engender friendships based on shared musical experiences.
6. Singing great choral literature will lead us to understand that music is a powerful means of communication that often transcends the written word, exalting the spirit and celebrating the best of humankind.

OBJECTIVES
As a choir member, I pledge myself to the following objectives as part of my participation in this ensemble.

1. I will help to create a "safe environment" where each person is treated with respect and dignity, and each person's worth is valued and honored.
2. I will participate willingly and actively in the learning process, contributing my part to the success of the whole group.
3. I will remember to bring my music and a pencil to every rehearsal as well as an open and receptive mind.
4. I will not talk disruptively during rehearsals nor make inappropriate remarks at any time.
5. I will work to improve my knowledge of music and my skills of sight-singing and vocal production.
6. I will attend all rehearsals and performances (unless excused), and understand that a portion of my grade will be based on participation.

I have read the goals and objectives and agree, by my signature, to strive to fulfill these statements through self-discipline and a mature attitude.

_____

Signature   Date

Figure 5.2. Choir goals and objectives.

A teacher's set of goals also helps to focus the energies of the choral director on what he or she does and should be doing (Jorgensen and Pfeiler, 1995). When shared with parents, guardians, and administrators, a goal statement can provide clear evidence of the all-encompassing nature of the choral director's job (see Figure 5.3).

EVALUATING AND REPORTING ACHIEVEMENT

Grades in music ensembles do not always reflect achievement; this is not good if ensembles are to be considered part of the academic curriculum. However, the emphasis on comprehensive musicianship seems to be having an effect on how choral students are graded. Emphasis is placed more on actual achievement and less on the nonmusical aspects of choral performance, such as attendance.

CHORAL DIRECTOR'S GOALS

1. I will commit myself to bringing high-quality choral literature to all of my students.
2. I will implement a disciplined, professional approach to teaching on a daily basis, whether it be in rehearsal, performance, or listening.
3. I will employ a comprehensive approach in helping students to become fine singers and culturally literate citizens.
4. I will reinforce certain values, including manners, in my students. As they grow and mature, I will encourage personal responsibility, punctuality, and tolerance for others and others' ideas.
5. I will stress a drug-free lifestyle for all of my students, mentioning hazardous health decisions and stressing habits that will lead to a healthy productive, long life.
6. I will encourage students' strengths and talents, develop their leadership skills, and care about them as individuals, not just as singers.
7. I will provide students opportunities for personal growth outside the school setting, including career counseling, special auditions, and new musical venues and experiences.
8. I will continue to develop my knowledge of music and the many styles and cultures it contains. In addition, I will seek to improve my teaching and planning styles so as to be a more effective choral director.
9. I will belong to and attend the meetings of professional music organizations (MENC, ACDA, etc.) as a way of stimulating professional growth.
10. I will work with parents, administrators, and other colleagues to provide the best education possible for all students under my influence, and I will seek to make music a part of all students' lives.

Figure 5.3. Choral director's job description (adapted from Jorgensen and Pfeiler, 1995).

Grading Components

There are three appropriate areas for grading the choral student: (1) musical knowledge, (2) musical skills, and (3) nonmusical criteria. Achievement of knowledge is reflected in historical and theoretical information about composers, music, eras, and so forth. Achievement in skills is shown in how the singing voice is used. These two areas together can represent as much as 80 percent of a student's grade. The nonmusical area, which includes attitude, effort, and attendance, represents the other 20 percent.

A knowledge of music cannot be tested if knowledge is not imparted in the rehearsal. The common complaint that there is little enough time for rehearsing, let alone teaching about music, is unfounded. Research (Gleason, 1995) has shown that inclusion of some knowledge into the ensemble rehearsal does not weaken performance. Choral directors often are guilty of turning out singers who sing beautifully but know nothing about the music.

MENC has produced two guides (Small and Bowers, 1997; Swiggum, 1998) for implementing the national standards into elementary, middle-level, and high school chorus. Each guide presents strategies for including all nine standards in the choral rehearsal. Standard 9E (advanced) specifies,

> Understanding music in relation to history and culture: identify and describe music genres or styles that show the influence of two or more cultural traditions, identify the cultural source of each influence, and trace the historical conditions that produced the synthesis of influences. (MENC, 1994, p. 38)

Figure 5.4 is an example given at the advanced level for teaching and assessing this standard (Swiggum, 1998).

The evaluation of singing skill needs to be done at regular intervals and may be assessed individually or in quartets. The following areas typically are included: voice quality, singing technique, part independence, and sight-singing. Some form of objective measurement tool, as in Figure 5.5, is recommended. Of course, none of these four areas can be measured unless singing and sight-reading are taught in the rehearsal. Most choral directors do not have the luxury of having trained singers in their choirs.

The inclusion of the nonmusical criteria of attitude, effort, and attendance in a choral student's grade is a common practice. Some schools, however, do not permit the grade to reflect anything but academic achievement and provide a separate place on the report card for social indicators. There is some justification of nonmusical elements in an ensemble grade. Choir is a cooperative activity; the whole effort suffers if members do not attend rehearsals and concerts. Likewise, students who impede progress because of talking or not making a good effort should be held responsible for such behaviors. Grading only on nonmusical areas, however, is a poor practice.

Grading Systems

Peggy Dettwiler, in the article, "Grading the Choral Ensemble . . . No More Excuses!" (1995), relates a grading system where points are added for knowledge, skills, and attendance and deducted for absence, tardiness, and "negative contributions to the group" (see Figure 5.6). Such point systems are rather common in ensemble grading. However, some point systems become so labor intensive and require so much bookkeeping that they are rarely worth the effort. It helps to keep the grading system simple and objective.

John Metheny (1994) recommends a type of self-evaluation for junior high and high school performance groups (see Figure 5.7).

STANDARD 9E

<u>Advanced</u>: **Understanding music in relation to history and culture:** Students identify genres or styles that show the influence of two or more cultural traditions, identify the cultural source of each influence, and trace the historical conditions that produced the synthesis of influences.

Objective

Students will identify and contrast the influences of rural European American culture and African American spiritual.

Materials

"Amazing Grace," arr. John Newton and Edward Lojeski (Milwaukee: Hal Leonard Corp.), 8300531, SATB, Level 1

Video recording *Amazing Grace with Bill Moyers* (Princeton, N.J.: Films for the Humanities and Sciences, 1990)

Videocassette recorder

Video monitor

Chalkboard

Prior Knowledge and Experience

Students have been rehearsing "Amazing Grace"

Follow-up

Show students the entire video of *Amazing Grace with Bill Moyers.* Discuss with them the background of the song and help them to consider the influence of the lifestyles and socioeconomic conditions of these two cultures on their music-making traditions.

Procedures

1. Show students excerpts from the video *Amazing Grace with Bill Moyers* that feature the African American Wiregrass Singers and culture on performances of a the Sacred Harp Singers.

2. Discuss with students the differences they hear in the two groups' versions of "Amazing Grace." Have students discuss characteristics of the two different styles and contrast them as you list them on the chalkboard. If necessary, play the video excerpts more than once.

3. Point out to students the characteristics that are specific to the European America tradition.

4. Ask students to identify whether the style of the "Amazing Grace" arrangement they have been rehearsing is in the African American or European American tradition. Discuss the stylistic features they observed in the video that they can apply to their own music.

5. Have students sing through "Amazing Grace."

Indicators of Success

1. Students identify the characteristics of African American and European American performances of spirituals and describe the influence of the cultural traditions on each performance.

2. Students perform "Amazing Grace" in the proper style of the publication.

Figure 5.4. Implementing National Standard 9E (MENC, 1998).

VOICE ASSESSMENT

Name _____ Date _____

Voice Part _____ Choir _____

Quality of Voice (level of sound, projection, resonance, confidence)

1 - <u>Deficient</u>: very weak sound—no projection, lack of distinguishable quality, little or no confidence.

2 - <u>Below Average</u>: weak sound, no projection, some distinguishable quality, little or no confidence.

3 - <u>Average</u>: medium sound, some projection, individual quality apparent, may have typical problems such as breathiness, constricted sound, etc., little confidence.

4 - <u>Good</u>: strong sound, projects well, quality characterized by a fair amount of resonance, free tone, and few vocal problems, including breathiness. Sings with a good amount of confidence.

5 - <u>Excellent</u>: strong sound, strong projection, free tone with vibrato, good amount of resonance, no major vocal problems. Confident use of voice; solo quality.

Singing Technique (posture, breathing, vocal production, diction)

1 - <u>Deficient</u>: very poor posture, very shallow breathing, tight jaw/throat, very weak vowel and consonant production.

2 - <u>Below Average</u>: poor posture, shallow breathing, tight jaw/throat, weak vowel and consonant production.

3 - <u>Average</u>: singing posture evident, shows signs of diaphragmatic breathing, jaw and throat somewhat relaxed and open, vowels and consonants distinguishable.

4 - <u>Good</u>: beneficial singing posture, proper breath management, relaxed jaw and open throat, vowels and consonants properly formed.

5 - <u>Excellent</u>: superior posture, superior breath management, relaxed jaw and open throat, superior diction.

Part Singing (pitch, part, intonation, range)

1 - <u>Deficient</u>: no sense of pitch, cannot carry a part, very poor intonation, and range less than an octave.

2 - <u>Below Average</u>: some sense of pitch, trouble singing a part, poor intonation, and range of about an octave.

3 - <u>Average</u>: good sense of pitch, ability to sing part fairly accurately, sings mainly in tune, has a range of about an octave and a fifth.

4 - <u>Good</u>: accurate sense of pitch, sings part accurately, sings in tune, has a range of about two octaves.

5 - <u>Excellent</u>: superior sense of pitch, superior part singer, sings in tune, has a range of two to three octaves.

Sight-Singing (interpretation of written notation)

1 - <u>Deficient</u>: no ability to sight-sing.

2 - <u>Below Average</u>: shows some signs of interpreting notation, but very weak.

3 - <u>Average</u>: shows definite signs of using notation, but not highly accurate.

4 - <u>Good</u>: sight-sings accurately with few mistakes.

5 - <u>Excellent</u>: sight-sings with superior accuracy.

Figure 5.5. Voice assessment form.

POINT GRADING SYSTEM

91–100	A
81–90	B (All students begin with 81 points.)
71–80	C
61–70	D
00–60	F

Points are added for

Preconcert vocal evaluations ———————————————— **up to 5 points**
(*Choir will be tested in quartets or small ensembles.*)

Positive contributions to the group ———————————— **up to 10 points**
(*Individual shows energy and concentration in rehearsal, exhibits good posture, marks music with a pencil, and participates in class discussions or rehearsal evaluations. Consideration also given for perfect attendance.*)

Practice/listening sheets ———————————— **1 point for each 30 minutes**

Choral worksheets ———————————————————— **up to 3 points**

Attendance at other choral concerts ————————— **up to 3 points**

Points are subtracted for

Absence from regular rehearsal ——————————————— **−2 points**
(1 absence without deduction)

Tardy to regular rehearsal ————————————————— **−1/2 point**

Absence from dress rehearsal ————————————————— **−1/2 point**

Absence from concert ——————————————————— **−10 points**
(*Reasonable opportunities will be given to regain lost points in case of illness or family emergency.*)

Negative contribution to the group ———————————— **up to −10 points**
(*Music not prepared or memorized; individual talks in rehearsal, exhibits bad posture, forgets music, chews gum or candy, or does not mark music with a pencil.*)

Figure 5.6. Point grading system (Dettwiler, 1995).

Director Total _____   Student Total _____

Music Ensemble Self-Evaluation Form

Name _____ Class _____

Directions: *Answer each question by circling the appropriate number.*

1. Rate the regularity of your class attendance this _____ (year, semester or 9 weeks):

10 9 8 7 6 5 4 3 2 1

perfect   almost   quite a   excessive
       perfect few absences absences

2. Rate the regularity of your attendance at extra rehearsals and performances:

10 9 8 7 6 5 4 3 2 1

perfect   1   2 or 3   over 3   have attended
    absence absences absences   no extra
                       activities

3. Rate your contribution to the organization (10 = your participation is essential to the group's success; 1 = doesn't make a difference if you participate or not):

10 9 8 7 6 5 4 3 2 1

4. Rate your level of effort to make the choir outstanding (10 = effort 100%, always focused in class, never cause a class disruption or loss of rehearsal time; 1 = little effort; don't care if the choir is any good):

10 9 8 7 6 5 4 3 2 1

5. Rate your attitude toward the choir (10 = always positive; never speak, think, or act negatively toward the group or other members of the group; 1 = always negative; don't like anything the choir does, don't like most of the choir members, don't like the music the choir performs, don't believe that membership in the choir should demand anything you don't want to do):

10 9 8 7 6 5 4 3 2 1

6. Rate your willingness to make personal sacrifices for the group (10 = willing to arrange schedule to meet commitments of the group; 1 = group should not cause conflict in personal life or schedule):

10 9 8 7 6 5 4 3 2 1

7. Rate your musical skill (10 = very advanced, considerable experience, read music rather well; 1 = beginner, little prior experience, do not read music well):

10 9 8 7 6 5 4 3 2 1

8. Rate your technical skill (10 = considerable experience, good tone and singing technique, capable of solos; 1 = little experience tone rather weak, poor technique, limited range, not ready to perform solo):

10 9 8 7 6 5 4 3 2 1

9. Rate your performance skill (10 = considerable experience and confident, poised, can control nerves; 1 = little experience, very nervous on stage, don't like to appear in public in a group or as an individual):

10 9 8 7 6 5 4 3 2 1

10. Rate your desire to become an excellent musical performer (10 = willing to invest considerable time; 1 = have no real interest in becoming even a competent performer):

10 9 8 7 6 5 4 3 2 1

Figure 5.7. Student self-evaluation grading form (Metheny, 1994).

When students have completed their self-evaluation you go over their evaluations and compare them to your own to see where differences occur. You mark any differences in a colored pen. In most cases, differences of more than one or two points rarely occur.

The student's final grade is based on your rating; however, your grade will usually be quite close to the student's self evaluation. This closeness eliminates most of the "you gave me a low grade" complaints. (pp. 37, 39)

Kathleen Keenan-Takagi (2000) recommends "embedding" assessments in the regular activities of a choral ensemble. She uses a "What I Learned" activity for students and a "Concert Reflection" form to encourage higher-order thinking skills.

Louise Frakes (Draper, 1998) uses self-assessment a little differently from Metheny by having students evaluate their videotaped performances.

With their sheet music in front of them, they watch the tape and write detailed comments about each piece. They use measure numbers to pin down choral achievements. . . . They write comments such as, "At measure six, the bass entrance was exactly on time, with correct pitch and good tone quality," and they consider such questions as, "Did we actually achieve the key change on page three?" (pp. 35, 48)

Self-evaluation systems give students some "ownership" of their grade and involve them in the seventh national standard: evaluating music and music performances.

The use of percentages is a common practice in grading. A scale of 0–100 percent is distributed over categories (e.g., 92–100 percent = A), and letter grades assigned. If the three categories of knowledge, skills, and nonmusical criteria are used for collecting data, then each area is summarized by a percentage, which may be weighted for the final grade. For example, if a student receives 90 percent in both knowledge and skills, each of which represents 40 percent of the grade ($40 \times 90 = 36$ percent), the sum of both areas is 72 percent. If the percentage for nonmusical elements is 75 percent, and the weight is 20 percent, the percentage added to the total grade is 15 percent ($20 \times 75 = 15$ percent), which, when added to the total, makes a final grade of 87 percent, or a B.

Whatever system of grading is adopted, it is important that students know and understand how grades are determined. Written guidelines (see Figure 5.8) should be available and reviewed on the first day of class. The choir handbook is an excellent place for presenting grading procedures.

Written guidelines also may take the form of a rubric, or model describing behaviors and characteristics that students exhibit as they grow and progress through levels of proficiency. The rubric in Figure 5.9 by Rex Nelson (Anderson, 1995) is a good example of a model where Level 1 represents the desired behaviors and Level 3 the undesired behaviors:

The advantage of a rubric is that it is non-judgmental if used correctly. It is essentially positive because it is simply a description of where students are at a particular point in their development. "This is where you are now, and this is where you can go." Taken as intended, it is pure encouragement. (p. 42)

Choral directors should not assume that students know what is expected of them. Written guidelines or a rubric is essential for objectifying the assessment process. If choir is an academic subject in which students receive credit for graduation, then students should be graded as rigorously as they are in other parts of the curriculum. When students know the components of their grade, they are better able to focus their energies on meeting the objectives in each of the designated areas.

HIGH SCHOOL CHOIR
GRADING POLICY

Choir grades are based on objective assessment in three areas: knowledge, skills, and attitudes (including attendance). Each of these areas will be assessed during the grading period and averaged as shown below for the student's grade. Music is an academic subject and carries academic credit. All students are expected to study their music, practice, contribute positively to the group whole, and attend rehearsals and concerts. Missing a concert is the same as not showing for an athletic event–it is not excused without a written note from a parent or guardian. Choir is a team effort!

Grading Scale
A = 100–92
B = 91–83
C = 82–74
D = 73–65
F = 64–00

I. Knowledge (25%)

A. Quizzes or Tests (1–2 per grading period)
B. Worksheets (several per grading period)

II. Skills (50%)

A. Singing Evaluation (1 per grading period)
B. Sight-Singing Assessment (1 per grading period)

III. Attitudes (25%)

A. Cooperation and Interest (as reflected in daily participation)
B. Attendance (Attendance at all extra rehearsals and concerts is expected. Unexcused rehearsal and concert cuts result in deductions of 5 points and 10 points respectively.)

Figure 5.8. Choir grading policy.

Authentic Assessment

A number of states are now requiring that schools use authentic assessment in evaluating students, and music educators also are moving in this direction. The MENC monograph *Performance Standards for Music Grades Prek–12* (1996) states:

Authentic assessment means that assessment tasks reflect the essential nature of the skill or knowledge being assessed. The student should actually demonstrate a music behavior in an authentic or realistic situation rather than merely answer written questions about it.

Assessment does not need to be based on multiple-choice tests or even on paper-and-pencil tests, though those techniques have their uses. Portfolios, performance-based

Sample Rubric Statements for Choir

Level 1 (highest of 3 levels)

A. **Contributions** (to spirit, morale, effectiveness, etc.)
   - Brings a unique spirit and sense of humor to rehearsals.
   - Is aware of group spirit and so looks for ways to make choir a better and happier place.
   - Praises the contributions of others.
   - Loves to be in choir.

B. **Rehearsal Skills** (involvement, motivation, effort)
   - Does more than what is required. Challenges self to see how good he or she can become.
   - Follows/practices voice part when other parts are rehearsing.
   - Appreciates a group whose idea of fun is hard work.

C. **Group Skills** (working with others)
   - Is helpful toward others in a way that is not condescending.
   - Leads by example.
   - Works willingly with everyone, regardless of personal feelings.
   - Knows when to forgive; develops tolerance.
   - Asks how he or she can serve the group.

D. **Vocal Ability** (tone, range, color, etc.)
   - Sings beautifully in all but extreme ranges of the voice.
   - Changes style and volume as demanded by the musical style.

E. **Willingness to Try All Styles**
   - Enjoys the challenges of singing many styles of music.

F. **Music-Reading Skills**
   - Learns music independently with little help.
   - Corrects mistakes, works out problem spots immediately.
   - Understands most music notation and markings and uses them.

G. **Music-Marking Skills**
   - Always has a pencil in rehearsal.
   - Marks mistakes the first time through. Music is well marked.

H. **Auditioning Skills**
   - Gives best effort every time.
   - Tries out for every solo.
   - Never apologizes during an audition.

I. **Miscellaneous**
   - Discusses concert dates in advance with family.
   - Invites, friends, family, neighbors to concerts well in advance.
   - Promotes the school choir program.

Figure 5.9. Rubric for student grading.

assessment, and other techniques of authentic assessment have been successfully used by music educators for many years; however, these techniques cannot by themselves solve the assessment problem facing educators. A portfolio is simply a collection of samples of a student's work. . . . Those samples must still be assessed, and the assessment requires . . . great care in developing suitable assessment strategies and appropriate scoring procedures. (p. 8)

Choral directors who assess singing skills use authentic assessment by evaluating how students sing, which should reflect students' knowledge of singing. Using authentic assessment for evaluating knowledge of history and culture is more difficult. An example of the latter is given above in Figure 5.4 (Swiggum, 1998). The key to assessing knowledge is to have students apply or use the knowledge in some observable form. Nonmusical achievement is reflected in what students are doing in regard to attitude, effort, and attendance.

Grading for Elementary Choirs

There is a trend in elementary schools not to use traditional grading, opting for a narrative description of student progress. "With this focus on 'authentic assessment,' how will general music teachers and choral teachers manage at the elementary level and middle school levels? These teachers see as many as 700 students for as little as thirty minutes a week. How can they possibly perform standards-based assessment?" (Draper, 1998, p. 34).

Anita Draper presents a number of creative ideas for elementary and middle school music teachers. Addressing the failure of traditional paper-and-pencil tests, she urges teachers to include assessment on a daily basis in a continual, informal manner:

Thompson asks students to fill in assessment forms partially before coming to her in groups of five for singing assessment. "With their little forms in front of me, I can just jot things down or circle skills really fast and then move on," she says. MacLeod videotapes her students frequently, without "making a big deal about the videotape and then reviewing it myself later," to enter the information into checklists. (Draper, 1998, p. 35)

Draper recommends the use of rubrics and checklists for quick authentic assessment and gives a number of Internet websites where information can be found on assessment projects in music.

The MENC publication *Strategies for Teaching Elementary and Middle-Level Chorus* (Small and Bower, 1997), is an excellent source for finding examples of authentic assessment. Figure 5.10 illustrates a sample lesson for Standard 1A: "Singing, alone and with others, a varied repertoire of music: Students sing independently, on pitch and in rhythm, with appropriate timbre, diction, and posture, and maintain a steady tempo beat."

Grades may be given for participation in the elementary choir when the choir exists as a separate class. It is better not to use regular letter grades, as justifying a letter grade at this age is difficult to do and not necessary. The following indicators often are used:

O – outstanding (usually solo quality or a group leader)

S – satisfactory (majority of students will receive this grade)

U – unsatisfactory (usually not a musical judgment, but one of attitude or behavior)

Testing may be done informally in small or large groups. A good practice is to have the students sing a song individually, one phrase at a time. Each student sits down after singing his or her phrase; the flow of the song is not to be broken. This enables the director to hear individual voices without putting undue stress on the students. If children are called upon to sing this way on a regular basis, it will be perceived as a normal activity.

STANDARD 1A

Singing, alone and with others, a varied repertoire of music: Students sing independently on pitch and in rhythm, with appropriate timbre, diction, and posture, and maintain a steady tempo beat.

Objective

* Students will sing a call-and-response song independently and chorally with accurate pitches, clear diction, good tone quality, and appropriate dynamics and timbre while maintaining a steady tempo.

Materials

* "Oliver Cromwell," arr. Benjamin Britten (New York: Boosey & Hawkes), OCTB5893, unison, Level 1–also in *We Will Sing*, by D. Rao (New York: Boosey & Hawkes, 1993).

* Chalkboard, or chart, with notated rhythm and pitches (but not text) of the phrase "Hee, haw, buried and dead," from "Oliver Cromwell."

Prior Knowledge and Experiences

* Students can sing the basic solfège scale and use the Curwen hand signs for high *do, sol, fa, mi,* and low *do.*

Indicators of Success

* Students sing on pitch, with good posture, breath support, tone quality, and diction.

* Students use appropriate dynamics and timbre with various stanzas and keep a steady beat.

Follow-up

* During students' early choral experiences, introduce strophic art songs containing appropriate texts, pitch ranges, and tessituras for them.

Procedures

1. Using hand signs for the pitches high *do, sol, fa, mi,* and low *do,* improvise two-measure phrases in 6/8 meter and have students sing and sign them back to you. Present different rhythm patterns at slow to moderate tempos. Ask students to raise their hands when they sing the phrase notated on the chalkboard or chart. Gradually, work into the melodic and rhythmic pattern in the phrase "Hee, haw, buried and dead." Echo-sing that phrase. Ask students to echo the phrase several times using syllables and hand signs.

2. As students look at the score, ask, "On what words do you find the phrase we sang?" Sing the phrase again, using syllables to remind them.

3. After students discover that the phrase is "Hee, haw, buried and dead," sing it with text and, as the students echo, point to the notation. Challenge students to find the other places in the music that are like "Hee, haw, buried and dead." Have students echo-sing all these phrases using texts.

4. Now sing the calls and let students sing the responses using the texts. After the group sings the responses, call on volunteers to sing the responses individually. Give more than one chance if the pitches are not correct the first time.

5. Continue the call-response activity using correct dynamics and in styles appropriate to the texts throughout the song. Experiment with different vocal timbres as the text changes. Correct any incorrect pitches and insist on good breath support enhanced by correct posture. Be sure that students keep a steady beat throughout the piece.

6. For the last performance of the song, let students choose the best style or timbre to use for various portions of the text while not overdoing unusual tone qualities. After reminding students to use correct dynamics, good diction, and proper breath support, conduct a performance of the whole song, maintaining a steady beat.

Figure 5.10. Assessment of National Standard 1A (MENC, 1997).

LESSON PLANNING

Most schools require some type of formal lesson planning from all teachers. A commercial planning book often is provided, or teachers devise their own plans according to their own needs. A computer-generated form (see Figure 5.11) is an excellent way of standardizing lesson planning for including the teacher's name, period, type of class, objectives, structure, and so forth.

Student teachers and beginning teachers benefit from detailed lesson plans. Such plans specify the structure of the lesson or rehearsal, with the approximate number of minutes for each section or activity, and show how procedures reflect the stated objectives. While plans need to be detailed, they are only guides and may be modified as a class proceeds. As much as possible, lesson plans need to be memorized and used in teaching for quick reference only.

Introductory Activities

Two introductory activities are appropriate for the choral rehearsal plan: the warm-up, and sight reading. The warm-up is the time to teach vocal production. All of the following activities are appropriate: energize the body (posture and breathing exercises), energize the vocal registers (phonation exercises), energize the singing voice (vocalises for vocal accuracy, resonance, pure vowels), energize diction (articulation exercises), and energize expression (exercises and vocalises for tempo, dynamics, agility, phrasing, meaning, and mood). This topic is covered in greater depth in Chapters 13 and 14.

Although choral conductors often fall into the trap of teaching by rote because their students tend to have poor sight-reading skills, sight-singing should be taught as part of the choral curriculum. Students need to be given the opportunity of trying to read the whole piece before part work begins. They will never learn to read music if not given the opportunity. Part of the rehearsal plan should include sight-singing. This topic is covered in greater depth in Chapter 16.

Rehearsal Procedures

The main body of the choral lesson plan is the procedures section where the rehearsal of repertoire is outlined. The number of selections chosen for any rehearsal will be determined by the length of the rehearsal and the difficulty of the music. The master schedule for each concert's preparation (discussed in Chapter 9) will help determine which pieces need to be rehearsed and when.

A good rehearsal plan begins by reviewing a selection that the choir has worked on but that needs more work. It may not be necessary to sing the entire work, but something needs to be sung that is familiar and easily accomplished.

Following the review of familiar literature, rehearsal begins of a new work or continues on selections in progress. Care must be taken that the choir not become bogged down on any one piece for too long.

COMPREHENSIVE MUSICIANSHIP.   It is appropriate to introduce some historical, cultural, or theoretical knowledge when each selection of the repertoire is introduced. This should not be a long music history lesson, but rather, a short introduction that might include such items as composer, era, style, meaning of text, and so forth. When progressing to the next piece of music, the composer's name can be announced instead of the title. This sensitizes students to information that otherwise might not be communicated.

General Music Lesson Plan   Grade _____

                                              Lesson _____

Warm-ups

VOCAL HEALTH OBJECTIVES

RESPIRATION
_____Posture Development
_____Breathing Motion
_____Breath Management

Opening Activity

PHONATION
_____Lower Adjustment
_____Upper Adjustment
_____Adjustment Coordination

Music Skills

RESONANT TONE PRODUCTION
_____Vocal Resonance
_____Uniform Vowel Colors
_____Vocal Coordination

Lesson

DICTION
_____Vocal Tract Freedom
_____Word Pronunciation
_____Consonant Articulation

EXPRESSION
_____Phrasing
_____Dynamic/Tempo Variation
_____Agility and Range Extension

MUSICAL OBJECTIVES
_____Pitch   _____Texture
_____Duration   _____Form
_____Loudness   _____Style
_____Timbre

LEARNER OUTCOMES
_____Culturally Aware
_____Decision Maker
_____Knowledge Explorer
_____Lifelong Learner
_____Practitioner of Good Health

Ending Activity

_____Responsible Citizen
_____Autonomous Person
_____Wise Resource User
_____Effective Communicator
_____Positive Self-image

Materials

Figure 5.11. Lesson plan for elementary vocal music.

Comprehensive musicianship is accomplished through the performance of literature. Students learn about the music and acquire knowledge that may not be present in the music. The choral director identifies the knowledge to be taught and interjects it quickly into each rehearsal. Research has shown that time taken for comprehensive learning does not weaken choral performance.

WHOLE-PART-WHOLE. Beginning teachers often drill notes for long periods of instruction without periodically stopping to evaluate learning. This is problematic when one section of the choir is rehearsed while the others sit and wait. The remaining students can easily become bored and disruptive. All students need to be kept singing as much as possible. It is better to plan short segments of note drill, putting all parts together as quickly as possible.

In the *whole-part-whole* concept of teaching, all parts sing together a whole section, part work is done to correct problems, and the whole is put back together for evaluation. When the music is difficult, it is better to have several cycles of the whole-part-whole sequence when teaching a particular section. For example, the soprano and bass parts are taught and then put together, followed by the alto and tenor. Finally, all parts are combined. If a part breaks down, it can be reviewed and parts combined again.

Another name for whole-part-whole learning is *paragraph teaching*. Each section in the main body of the rehearsal plan is thought of as a complete paragraph, with a clear transition to the next. The topic sentence is the overview (whole). The paragraph then develops one idea (part), and the end of the paragraph summarizes what was learned (whole) before a new paragraph is begun. This type of "chunk" learning facilitates the learning process; people learn better when material is presented in small amounts over a period of time. It also fosters periodic assessment—each paragraph is evaluated before rehearsal of the next chunk begins.

CLOSURE. Every good rehearsal ends upbeat, with students feeling positive about the music. This does not happen by chance; it must be included as part of the rehearsal plan. There needs to be sufficient time at the end of the class to sing something that will be successful and uplifting. If too much has been planned, the rehearsal will not end as it should, with an aesthetic experience.

Evaluation

The choral conductor needs to spend time at the conclusion of each rehearsal in evaluating how it went and how it could have been improved. This may not be possible when another class follows the rehearsal. Tape recording is an excellent way to provide for assessment, especially when there is no time to do so following the rehearsal. Videotaping is another excellent option.

Good rehearsals demand careful planning, and choral conductors who regularly wing it rarely maximize the potential of their rehearsal time. While detailed plans may be less necessary for veteran conductors, some type of plan is essential if the rehearsal schedule for the next concert is to be maintained.

INFORMING OTHERS

It is a constant challenge to let students and parents know what the choral program stands for, what the expectations are, and how these objectives will be evaluated. The choir newsletter has been discussed in Chapter 3 as a way of promoting choral activities. In this section, the choir handbook and the music booster's association are discussed.

Choir Handbook

The choir handbook is an important tool for communicating inside the choral program. It serves as a reference place for numerous items of information that might otherwise become lost as separate entities. Computers and desktop publishing make handbooks easy to produce (see Figure 5.12); they are well worth the effort.

The content of the choir handbook may include but is not limited to the following:

- music department calendar
- philosophy/rationale for the music program
- performance requirements

Figure 5.12. Sample cover for choir handbook.

- concert attire
- basic class rules and concert behavior
- rehearsal and concert attendance policy
- grading procedures
- rehearsal procedures and requirements
- score marking techniques
- honors and festival choir opportunities
- solo and ensemble contests
- fund-raising activities and requirements
- choir officers and student director
- vocal music awards
- summer music activities
- music boosters association

Other information appropriate for the handbook includes units on voice production, music theory and literacy, and basic information regarding historical styles and cultures. The choir handbook is as small or large as the director wishes, and it can be added to and developed more each year. It should be placed in the hands of students at the first rehearsal and referred to often during the school year.

Music Booster Association

The help a music booster group gives to promoting the choral program is discussed in Chapter 3. This group also provides important internal support, relieving the choral director of much work with fund-raising, handbook production, uniform management, and so forth. MENC has produced an excellent guide in the *Music Booster Manual* (1989/1994), which provides a variety of information from "Starting a Booster Group" to a "Constitution and By-laws." In the Introduction (p. v) it presents the following directives to consider before starting a booster group:

- The booster program should always be thought of as an addition. The funds it raises are not a replacement for school funding to justified music programs. Rather, it provides means for students to have music experiences beyond what the school can supply.

- The goal of a booster program is to assist and support the music educator so that he or she can maintain a music program that will be educational, enjoyable, and rewarding. But its authority should never reach into the content and priorities of the music program.

- A booster group is a music education advocacy group. When possible, it should be involved in supporting the entire music program, not just chorus or marching band. After all, these are community members who have seen how important the arts are in children's education and in their school experiences.

- When you are very active in fundraising, you need to be more aware than ever of your relationship with the community. Fundraising can be viewed as a form of supplemental taxation.

The final sentence in the second statement above needs special attention. Some booster groups have been known to "run the music program," to its detriment. This can be avoided if the purposes of the group are clearly delineated in the constitution and effectively communicated to the members of the association.

Record keeping, grading, rehearsal planning, communicating information—all of these make demands on the choral director. Sometimes the paperwork seems endless, and much of it will need to be done at home after the school day. It goes with the territory of a successful program. Staying at it on a regular basis is the way to keep it from becoming overwhelming. Planning for work and working that plan is the way to succeed.

STUDY AND DISCUSSION QUESTIONS

1. What are the benefits of being an organized choral director?
2. What are some guidelines for handling student records?
3. What are some guidelines and benefits of written communications to parents and students?
4. What are the three basic components appropriate for student grading, and which one is sometimes problematic? Why?
5. Where can the choral director find help in implementing the national standards?
6. What areas are typically assessed in an evaluation of students' singing skills?
7. What are some grading systems options, and which do you prefer? Why?
8. How can self-evaluation be employed in choral grading assessment?
9. Why should students be informed of the goals and objectives of the choral program as well as procedures for grading?
10. What is meant by authentic assessment, and how can this process be used in evaluating knowledge, skills, and nonmusical criteria?
11. How is the grading practice changing in elementary schools?
12. What types of grades typically are given for elementary choristers? Why?
13. What are the main components of a choral rehearsal/lesson plan?
14. How should lesson plans be used in the rehearsal?
15. What two types of activities are appropriate for the beginning of a choral rehearsal?
16. What guidelines are presented for planning the procedures section of the rehearsal?
17. What is meant by "paragraph teaching," and how does this benefit planning?
18. How should the choral rehearsal end for the students and the choral conductor?
19. What categories of information are most appropriate for inclusion in a choir handbook?
20. What are the benefits of a music booster group?

REFERENCES

Althouse, J. (1986). *168 non-musical ways to improve your band or choral program.* Van Nuys, CA: Music in Motion, distributed by Alfred.

Anderson, K. (1995). Design a rubric for your choirs (by Rex Nelson). *Choral Journal, 36*(4), 42–43.

Dettwiler, P. D. (1995). Grading the choral ensemble . . . no more excuses! *Choral Journal, 35*(9), 43–45.

Draper, A. (1998). Making the grade: Authentic assessment in music, K–8. *Teaching Music, 6*(2), 34–35, 48.

Frakes, L. (1984). Differences in music achievement, academic achievement, and attitude among participants, dropouts, and nonparticipants in secondary school music (doctoral diss., The University of Iowa). *Dissertation Abstracts International, 46,* 370A.

Gleason, B. (1998). Effects of whole music instruction on knowledge, performance skills, attitudes, and retention of sixth-grade beginning band students. *Contributions to Music Education, 25*(2), 7–26.

Jorgensen, N. S., and C. Pfeiler (1995). *Things they never taught you in choral methods.* Milwaukee: Hal Leonard.

Keenan-Takagi, K. (2000). Embedding assessment in choral teaching. *Music Educators Journal, 86*(4), 42–46, 63.

MENC (1986/1994). *Music booster manual.* Reston, VA: Music Educators National Conference.

——— (1994). *The school music program: A new vision.* Reston, VA: Music Educators National Conference.

——— (1996). *Performance standards for music grades prek–12.* Reston, VA: Music Educators National Conference.

Metheny, J. (1994). A grading system for secondary music groups. *Music Educators Journal, 80*(4), 37–39.

Small, A. R., and J. K. Bowers (1997). *Strategies for teaching elementary and middle-level chorus.* Reston, VA: Music Educators National Conference.

Swiggum, R. (1998). *Strategies for teaching high school chorus.* Reston, VA: Music Educators National Conference.

6 | Managing the Choral Program

It takes a lot of money to run schools, and all parts of the curriculum are in competition for a piece of the pie. Choral music is expensive, as are choir folders, risers, and music stands. The choral director must know financially what it takes to run a successful program and be able to present requests in such a way as to receive approval.

BUDGETARY PROCEDURES

Among the first orders of business in a new position is to find out the established procedures for submitting budgets, requisitioning materials, and keeping records. More money is likely to flow to the choral program when administrators see the choral director paying careful attention to expenditures and maintaining care of those items already purchased.

Budget Requests

Robert Garretson (1998) recommends a three-step approach for projecting the choral program's needs in budget development. First, a list is made of essential items such as octavo music, music folders, music filing supplies, and so forth (see Figure 6.1). A reasonable estimate is expected for each budget line and a total for the area. Second, a list is made of highly desirable items such as new filing cabinets or additional classroom chairs. The third area contains a "wish list" of items that would greatly benefit the program such as a new piano or new risers. Reliable figures, obtained from current catalogs of music supplies and equipment have to be submitted for all items.

Most school administrators recognize the importance of budget essentials and grant those requests if funding is available. The cost of octavo music is the greatest expense in this category; it is good to provide a reminder on the budget of how many choirs and students will be serviced by this request. Schools cannot fund purchases for all new music for any choral program, and the choral library must be relied upon as a primary source of choral literature. Nevertheless, octavo music is essential for most choral ensembles, and the photocopying of music is illegal. A yearly increase of 5–10 percent in the octavo music request is not out of line; more funding should be sought if school spending in this area has been low.

Although not all items in the second and third parts of the budget are likely to be approved, one or two may be funded. If the list is submitted and updated yearly, there is the possibility of achieving more costly items over time. Patience and persistence are needed. Providing a written justification for large-ticket items based on educational benefits is good practice. Also, most school districts require that items in excess of a certain dollar amount be let for bid.

CHORAL MUSIC DEPARTMENT

Proposed Budget for the Academic Year _____ - _____

A. Essential and Necessary Items*   Amount

    1. Octavo Music (SATB, SSA, TTBB).. $_____
    2. Music Folders .... _____
    3. Music Storage Boxes... _____
    4. Choir-Robe Maintenance and Repairs .... _____
    5. Equipment Maintenance .... _____
    6. Choral Recordings and Recording Supplies......................... _____

                                                Total .... $_____

B. Highly Desirable Items†

    1. Additional Storage Cabinets.. _____
    2. Photographs (for publicity purposes).................................. _____
    3. Additional Rehearsal-Room Risers .... _____
    4. Additional Chairs... _____
    5. Additional Standing Risers .... _____
    6. New Bulletin Board.. _____

                                                Total .... $_____

C. Desirable and Helpful Items‡

    1. Audio-Visual Rentals.. _____
    2. CD Recording and Playback Equipment.............................. _____
    3. Computer Hardware and Software .... _____
    4. Transportation Expenses (Festivals and Contests) .... _____
    5. Additional Piano.. _____
    6. Fees for Visiting Clinicians and Conductors .... _____

                                                Total .... $_____

                                    Grand Total .... $_____

*Essential and necessary for operation of the department or activity during the ensuing school year.
†Highly desirable for the future growth of the program.
‡Desirable and helpful in terms of providing the best educational experiences for the students.

Figure 6.1. Three-part music budget (Garretson, 1998).

Another approach to setting up a budget requires only two categories: one for operating expenses and one for nonrecurring expenses (see Figure 6.2).

Under "Operating Expenses" list the items necessary for the efficient function of the department for the ensuing year. Under "Nonrecurring Expenses" . . . list the items that are important to the further development of the program. Since the funds for special purchases are not likely to be available in any one year for the acquisition of all special needs, the items in this category should be listed in the order of importance. This will be of considerable assistance to the administrator in making the final budget allotments. Any items that the school is unable to acquire in a particular year may be included on the following year's budget request and perhaps ranked higher in the order of importance. (Garretson, 1998, pp. 303–4)

CHORAL MUSIC DEPARTMENT

Proposed Budget for the Academic Year _____ - _____

A. Operating Expenses   Amount

    1. Octavo Music (SATB, SSA, TTBB).. $_____
    2. Music Folders .... _____
    3. Music Storage Boxes... _____
    4. Choir-Robe Maintenance and Repairs .... _____
    5. Equipment Maintenance .... _____
    6. Choral Recordings and Recording Supplies.......................... _____
    7. Photography (publicity)... _____
    8. Audio-Visual Rentals... _____
    9. Transportation Expenses.. _____

                                           Total .... $_____

B. Nonrecurring Expenses

    1. Additional Storage Cabinets.. _____
    2. Additional Risers.. _____
    3. Additional Chairs... _____
    4. Additional Piano.. _____
    6. Choir Robe Replacement... _____
    7. CD Equipment... _____
    8. Computer Hardware and Software .... _____

                                           Total .... $_____

                            Grand Total .... $_____

Figure 6.2. Two-part music budget (Garretson, 1998).

Requisitioning Materials

Once budgetary figures are approved, the proper protocol must be followed for the requisitioning of materials and equipment. Schools most often operate on an academic rather than calendar year for financial expenditures. If the fiscal year runs from July 1 to June 30, nothing can be paid for the coming school year until after July 1; schools discourage requisitions against the new budget much before July 1.

Schools use requisition forms that are to be completed (usually in triplicate) and sent to the proper offices for approval, processing, and ordering. The school is under no obligation to pay any bill for any item ordered by a teacher without proper approval. Schools may permit teachers to place emergency orders by telephone using a requisition number; most companies require an order number when taking an order by telephone.

When ordering anything, accurate catalog item numbers are important. For ordering octavo music, all of the following should be included in the request: title, composer or arranger, publisher, octavo number, voicing (SATB, SSA, etc.), the number of copies needed, and the method of shipment. Without the octavo or edition number another arrangement may be sent by the same title.

After items have been received and checked by the choral director for accuracy and damage, a copy of the shipment order and requisition needs to be signed and returned to the proper school office for approval and payment. Teachers should be timely in returning this paperwork, as companies often apply penalties when bills are not paid on time.

Many schools have an activity fund where income is placed from fund-raising. Use of this money for the choral program (e.g., paying for a tour bus) is often at the discretion of the choral director and requires no formal request procedure. Payment, however, is processed through some type of voucher system where the bill is attached and presented for payment. School policy for the use of these funds must be strictly followed.

The handling of public expenditures is serious business, and teachers need to be careful how they appropriate and regulate money. Teachers have been dismissed from jobs for creating large debts that were not approved by the administration.

Keeping Records

The choral director should keep records of all expenditures approved during the school year. This is easy to do with a computer. A ledger or spreadsheet may be set up in accordance with the sections and items of the budget, and approved budgetary amounts entered for each line item. When an expenditure is made, the cost should be deducted from the balance once the bill has been approved. Shipping and handling charges are unknowns until a shipment has been received, and these costs are part of the total bill. By keeping a running balance for each line of the budget the teacher will know how much remains to be spent.

Teachers should work at spending the budget amounts approved. When balances remain at the end of the fiscal year, requests for increases are harder to justify. There is rarely enough funding provided for any choral program. Therefore, it is good policy to spend what has been allotted even if it won't be used until the coming year.

Choral directors often keep records of money raised by student fund-raising activities. Again, the ledger or computer spreadsheet is used to provide a page to enter each student's efforts. Accurate records must be kept and current balances available so students will know how much they have raised toward their individual goals.

A third use of the ledger or computer program is to keep a record of the activity fund, both for income and expenditures. This information should be available to administrators at their request and must be clear and accurate.

It is good if the choral director does not have to handle any money from fund-raising or concert ticket sales. Some schools have a person who handles all income from such activities. When choral directors must handle money, they should be very careful to document everything that comes in and goes out. The public demands that all funds used in schools be accounted for and used with discretion.

MUSIC SUPPLIES, EQUIPMENT, AND CONCERT ATTIRE

When purchasing music supplies and equipment, it is better if the purchases can be made through a local music business. Most communities have music stores whose taxes support the school system. It is common courtesy to support these businesses when possible. These types of stores rarely carry large stocks of choral music, but they will order anything requested.

Music Supplies

Large metropolitan areas often have outlets that publish their own line of choral music and also carry music of many other publishers. They typically have a large stock of choral music readily available. These businesses may have their own catalogs in which they advertise their wares and often provide approval services where music can be ordered to peruse and return if unwanted. Accompanying cassette tapes or compact discs frequently are available.

National music dealers are large-scale operations with outlets in a number of areas of the country. They carry a large stock of choral music of all publishers and produce a catalog of music often by season, voicing, and difficulty. Music packets are available on approval, as are cassette tapes and compact discs. These companies also may carry other music supplies and equipment, such as music stands.

Choral music may be ordered directly from a specific publisher (see names and addresses in Appendix A). Rental music most often must be secured through the specific publisher. Many music companies have been bought out by other publishers, and it is difficult to keep an up-to-date listing of names and addresses. Choral directors most often choose to order through a local, regional, or national music operation where all of their music can be ordered at one time.

Music publishers will send catalogs of publications upon request. However, most publishers now have websites, and catalog information is directly accessed through the Internet. The Music Publishers Association, at ⟨http://www.mpa.org/publist.html⟩, provides names, addresses, telephone numbers, and websites for all those publishing companies who belong to the association. Similarly, Indiana University has a worldwide music resource list through which all types of music information can be accessed, including publishers, at ⟨http://www.music.indiana.edu/music_resources/⟩. Information specific to choral resources may be found at ⟨http://www.choralnet.org/⟩. MENC has a chorus network accessed through ⟨http://www.menc.org⟩, where members may contribute ideas and recommend repertoire. Choral music in the public domain is at ⟨http://www.cpdl.org⟩.

Music Equipment

Some companies do not carry choral music but supply music equipment, instruments, filing supplies, and so forth. Catalogs are available upon request, and websites provide direct access to this information (see Appendix B).

MENC has produced guidelines for music equipment for music rooms at all levels in the document *Opportunity to Learn: Standards for Music Instruction* (1994). Included in the recommendations are the following for choral ensemble rooms:

- High-quality sound reproduction system
- CD-ROM-compatible computers and MIDI equipment
- Music library file cabinets or shelving
- High-quality acoustic piano tuned at least three times a year
- Set of portable choral risers
- Chairs designed for best choral posture
- Conductor's stand, podium, and optional music stands for students

One other piece of equipment that may be needed in a choral program is an acoustical shell. A shell is used to help project the sound of the chorus in the performance area. Shells are especially important on stages where the ceiling of the stage includes a "fly gallery" for storing stage scenery. Such areas trap the sound, causing projection to be weak, and students are unable to hear one another. Acoustical shells are expensive but last a long time if properly treated.

Chairs for choral rooms should be of the type that foster good singing posture. The Wenger Corporation makes one of the finest chairs for this purpose, and it comes in a variety of styles and costs (see Figure 6.3). If the choral room doubles as a regular classroom, posture-enhancing chairs are available with folding tablet arms. While such chairs are more expensive than chairs used in regular classrooms, they are well worth the cost when students' singing posture is enabled.

Special consideration should be given to having a good piano in the choral room. This instrument receives a lot of use, and a poor instrument will go out of tune quickly. Unfortunately, the school bidding process often results in the purchase of the cheapest instrument. If

Figure 6.3. Wenger posture chair. (Photo courtesy of the Wenger Corporation. Used by permission.)

the specifications are set high enough before the bid goes out to retailers, however, then bids must reflect these higher standards. A local piano tuner can provide the needed specifications. Also, the piano should be moved as little as possible to preserve the tuning. Additionally, it is good to have a performance piano that is stored under lock and key, and a portable electronic piano is useful for rehearsals outside the choir room. Students must not be permitted to bang on pianos. Pianos are costly instruments, and schools do not replace them quickly.

The vast majority of college graduates today are proficient in computers and know the tremendous benefits of technology. Computer work stations are common in all schools, and most teachers have them in their rooms for managerial uses and instructional purposes. MENC and ACDA publications have kept a steady flow of information on technology available (Kassner, 1998; McAdams and Nelson, 1995; Mueth, 1993: Oglesby, 1997; Sebald, 1997), and publications like these are invaluable for keeping up to date in this quickly changing area.

The Music Industry Conference, a nonprofit organization of publishers and manufactures that supply music-related products, publishes a guide that offers suggestions for choosing, purchasing, and maintaining music supplies and equipment. The guide also contains the names and addresses of members who sell concert attire, music room equipment, classroom instruments, and tour organizations. This helpful guide is published every other year in the January issue of the *Music Educators Journal*.

Concert Attire

Choral groups traditionally have worn some type of concert attire. This helps to present a uniform, pleasant appearance and keeps the focus of attention on the singing and not on what people are wearing. Robes became popular during the a cappella choir years, and many schools continue to use choir robes. Some high school choirs have changed to wearing gowns for women and tuxedos for men.

When finances are a concern, students may wear concert attire from clothing in their own wardrobes. White shirts or blouses and dark pants or skirts are a common form of attire, sometimes dressed up with a scarf or sash. Some children's choirs provide a common-color T-shirt and permit students to wear jeans and sneakers. High school boys in sweaters or sports coats and ties, with girls in white blouses and dark skirts, also make for a nice appearance. A uniform look does not need to cost a lot, and unless the school is providing the attire, cost will be a factor for some students.

CHOIR ROBES.   Schools usually provide choir robes at the secondary level, and this traditional look is a good one. A number of choir robe companies provide a variety of styles, colors, and fabrics; their names and addresses may be found in Appendix B. The choral director should send for catalogs and review prices and styles with a committee of students. Company representatives are available for on-site visits and presentations. When several styles and colors are decided upon, these can be modeled for the choir and input sought as to choices. In the end, the choral director makes the final decision, but a democratic process provides valuable information.

Who pays for choir robes? In many schools robes are purchased through the revenues of student fund-raising. This is not a good tradition to establish. Football players do not purchase their own uniforms. Funding for choir robes should come directly through the school music budget. Additional funding is needed each year to replace worn robes or supply robes for students for whom there are no correct sizes, and to supply garment bags, which help protect robes when traveling.

Something that students can be required to pay for is the dry cleaning of robes. This is a large expenditure when robes have been soiled because of student use. Schools may require that students pay a rental fee for robe use and repair, part of which is refunded when the robe is returned in good, clean condition. An end-of-year cleaning is important to maintain the look and freshness of robes.

FORMAL ATTIRE.   When considering more formal attire (see Figure 6.4), cost is an important factor. Local clothing stores often are willing to rent tuxedos at a reduced rate to choir members, and a number of wholesalers (see Appendix B) sell or rent tuxedos at low prices. In some cases, schools purchase used tuxedos from companies who are selling them off at reduced cost. If students are responsible for their own formal attire, some type of arrangement needs to be made for those students who are financially unable to meet this obligation.

Formal attire companies also make dresses for women. The designs can leave something to be desired, and it is hard to find one style that looks good on all shapes and sizes. A cheaper alternative is to choose a pattern and material, and each young woman either makes her own or has someone make her dress. Bright-colored dresses are less desirable than muted colors; the focus should be on the music and not on the dress. Also, dresses should be conservative in style; low-cut dresses are inappropriate. Again, there should be some way to help females who cannot pay for a special concert dress.

Dress shoes are sometimes a problem for students. Some schools choose styles of dress shoes for men and women and require that such shoes be worn with robes and formal attire. Local shoe stores will often maintain an inventory of these shoes at a lower-than-normal cost, and students are expected to purchase their own footwear, which they sometimes sell to younger students at the end of the year. Sneakers are not appropriate dress with either formal wear or robes!

Figure 6.4. Singers in formal attire. (Gordon College Choir, Wenham, Mass., C. Thomas Brooks, conductor. Used by permission.)

The maintenance of all concert attire is important. Strict checkout procedures should be in place so students may be identified and contacted when attire is not returned. It must be communicated before any attire leaves the school that students are responsible for the cost of replacing lost or damaged school property. A robe or dress committee is helpful for the processing of garments in and out of storage.

THE CHORAL MUSIC LIBRARY

The storage and processing of choral music is an important area of choral management. Music is expensive, and fortunate is the choral director who has a large choral library. Every effort should be made to maintain the choral library in an orderly and organized manner so that music can be found, retrieved, and stored efficiently. Appointing a student librarian will aid greatly in this process, and computer database programs have made the cataloging of music easier and more efficient.

Music Storage

Octavo music should be stored in either special music boxes or envelopes that can be closed (see Figure 6.5). Less expensive file folders can be used, but such folders are not closable, and music falls out easily. Each box or envelope should be labeled with the file number, title and composer of the composition, and voicing (SATB, SSA, etc.). Some directors like to write on the container the date of when the piece was last used as a quick reminder when perusing the choral files.

Filing boxes are best stored on shelving units where the maximum number of shelves are spaced per unit. This type of arrangement requires much room. Filing envelopes are cheaper but not as sturdy and are best stored in filing cabinets. Boxes often waste space when not filled to capacity, while envelopes can be compacted in a filing drawer rather easily. Boxes should have lids to prevent dust from accumulating on the music.

How the boxes or envelopes are arranged for storage is critical to how easily the choral library is managed. It is not recommended that music be stored in alphabetical order by title. Such an arrangement requires whole shelves or drawers of music to be moved periodically when there is insufficient space to insert a new composition. The easiest way to store

Figure 6.5. Music filing boxes. (Photo courtesy of Valiant Music Supply. Used by permission.)

music is to assign it the next number in the order of its purchase and to place it in the drawer or on the shelf in numerical order. This prevents periodic moving of files because new music is always placed at the end of the numbered sequence and not inserted between existing numbers. A separate storage room for the choral library is best.

Music Identification

All new music should be stamped with two identifying codes: the school property stamp and the file identification number. The music belongs to the school and should be identified as such in case it is lost outside the school. The filing number on each piece of music will speed the filing process when individual pieces of music are returned late to the choral library. New music should then be numbered by hand in ink from "1" to the number of copies purchased. This is extremely important, as this number is the way music loaned to students is identified when it is lost or not returned. Every student receives a numbered music folder registered in his or her name. All music that goes into that folder has the same number written on it.

When music is not returned to the choral library, the person responsible for the loss can be identified and charged with the cost of music replacement. Students need to know from the first day of choir that the music in their folders is on loan, and a fee in the amount of its value will be assessed for unreturned or damaged music. Many students will hold on to their music, if only for sentimental reasons, if there is not a strict enforcement of this rule. This is the only way the choral director can insure that the library will continue to have multiple copies for use in future years. When music is not returned, the fee paid should be used to repurchase the music immediately. If the computer database records that fifty copies of a selection were purchased, fifty copies need to be in the file. It is discouraging to retrieve music from the files and find fewer copies than listed.

The student music librarian repairs any damage done to the music before the music is filed away. Glossy cellophane tape is not good for this purpose; transparent varieties are readily available that hardly show once the music is repaired. Music that is greatly soiled may be either generally restored with a soft gum eraser or replaced.

Master Files

It is most helpful if one piece of music from every cataloged selection is located in the music office as a conductor's file. The file may be arranged by sections according to voicing (SATB, SSA, etc.) or by use (general sacred, general secular, etc.). This will aid the choral director when perusing the contents of the choral library for future programming. It negates having to pull boxes off shelves and envelopes out of drawers on a music hunt.

Schools in the past maintained card files to locate music in the choral library. Computer databases now make this an obsolete practice. One complete record of each selection is easily entered, including number of copies purchased, date of purchase, and dates of use. Lists may then be generated by titles (in alphabetical order), composers (see Figure 6.6), voicings, occasions, sacred, secular, and special accompaniments (Smith, 1979). Most important is the identification number to locate the music in the choral library. If a choral library is not databased, this makes an excellent project for the music librarian.

Music Folders

There are a number of ways to distribute music to students. Passing music in and out each time is necessary when music may be needed in different sections of the same group.

Choral Library
Index by Composer

Composer	Title	Language	Voicing	Accompaniment	Type	Publisher	Copies	Code
Britten, Benjamin	Song of the Fishermen	english	SATB	piano	opera chorus	Boosey & Hawkes	144	H 5
	Succession of the Four Sweet Months,	english	SATB	a cappella	song	Breitkopf & Härtel	61	529
	Te Deum in C	english	SATB/S or T	organ		Oxford Univ. Press	4	1149
	There is no Rose	english	SATB	harp or piano	fr A Ceremony of	Boosey & Hawkes	15	M 235
	This Little Babe	english	SATB	harp or piano	fr A Ceremony of	Boosey & Hawkes	11	M 236
	To Daffodils	english	SATB	a cappella	part song	Boosey & Hawkes	27	1207
	War Requiem	english	Boys Choir	voice part	mass	Boosey & Hawkes	30	D 5
	War Requiem	english	SATB	chorus score	mass	Boosey & Hawkes	155	D 5
	War Requiem	english	SATB	piano reduction	mass	Boosey & Hawkes	4	0
	Wolcum Yole	english	SATB	harp or piano	fr A Ceremony of	Boosey & Hawkes	4	M 237
Brockway, Howard	Hey Nonino	english	SSAATTBB	a cappella	madrigal	Schirmer	57	317
Brooks, Barrington	Betelehemu	nigerian	SATB	percussion	carol	Lawson-Gould	51	1293
Bruch, Max	Gruss an die heilige Nacht, op.62	ger/eng	SATB/S	piano reduction	Christmas-Hymn	N. Sinirock (xerox)	56	J 3
	Schön Ellen	ger/eng	SATB/B	piano reduction	cantata	Schirmer	75	F 5
Bruckner, Anton	Ave Maria	latin	SAATTBB	a cappella	motet	Marks Music	106	572
	Ave Maria/Tota pulchra es Maria	latin	SATB	a cap/organ	2 Marian	Peters	8	1130
	Christus factus est	latin	SATB	a cappella	gradual motet	Peters Edition	7	825
	Ecce sacerdos magnus	lat/eng	SATB	organ, brass	motet	Augsburg	17	904
	Libera me, Domine	lat/eng	SSATB	chorus score		Carus-Verlag	53	K 6
	Locus iste a Deo factus est	latin	SATB	a cappella	motet	Peters Edition	38	662
	Messe in E moll	latin	SSAATTBB	piano reduction	mass	Peters Edition	79	C 6
	Missa Solemnis	latin	SATB	piano reduction	mass	fr. the collected work	41	J 1
	Os Justi	latin	SSAATTBB	a cappella	motet	Schirmer	34	734
	Te Deum	latin	SATB	piano reduction	cantata	Arista	183	I 7
	Te Deum Laudamus	latin	SATB/SATB	brass	cantata	Schirmer	2	M 337
	Two Motets: Offertorium, Ecce Sacerdos	latin	SATB	piano reduction		Peters Edition	107	E 4
	Virga Jesse floruit	latin	SATB	a cappella	motet	Peters Edition	19	409
	Virga Jesse floruit	latin	SATB	a cappella	motet	Schirmer	50	409
Bruhns, Nicolaus	Zeit meiness Abschieds, Die	german	SATB	parts		Henry Litolff	UP	877
Brumel, Antoine	Mater patris et filia	latin	TBB	a cappella	motet	Schirmer	1	M 366

Figure 6.6. Sample computer printout of choral music repertiore.

Otherwise, it is inefficient and time consuming. Students do not receive the same piece of music each time, and any markings are not their own and become irrelevant or misinterpreted.

Most choral directors use some type of music folder in which music is placed for each student. When there is insufficient funding for each student in the group to have his or her own music, students may need to share music folders. This is not the best practice, but it can work. Extra folders of music are needed for the partners of those who are absent from rehearsal and have the folder.

Students carry their music folders home in some programs, and in others the folders are returned to a filing cabinet at the end of each rehearsal. Keeping the folders in the choir room cancels the problem of missing folders when students are absent or forget their music. However, permitting students to carry music home implies a responsibility for studying the music outside of class. It also places ultimate responsibility for loss of music on the students, who cannot claim that someone else took their folder when it turns up missing from a file cabinet in the choral room.

Sturdy choir folders are needed to protect music. Manila filing envelopes are a poor substitute, as they quickly become worn and damaged. A number of companies (see Appendix B) make folders especially designed for use by choir members, and such folders come in various styles and prices. A heavy and well-constructed folder costs more initially but will last much longer than a cheaper variety. All folders need expandable pockets on the insides to hold quantities of music, especially when larger works such as cantatas are included. Folders with pockets that do not expand are best avoided. It is further recommended that choir folders have some type of reinforced binding at the edges and the center seam. A strong binding will extend the life of the folder.

A suitable and less expensive alternative to a ready-made choir folder is the three-ring notebook with inside pockets. Such notebooks are inexpensive and easily purchased through any office supply outlet. All music placed in the notebooks must be punched using a three-hole punch; although this requires additional process time, the music is securely "locked in." Larger works such as oratorios are usually so thick that they cannot be punched; notebooks are not good for carrying this type of music, as the inside pockets are not expandable.

One type of folder on the commercial market has a handle strap attached for ease of holding (see Figure 6.7). This carrier is held in one hand and frees the other to turn pages and move music as needed. Choirs that regularly use printed music in performance find this folder convenient.

No matter what type of music folder is used, every folder should be identified with the person's name to whom it is assigned; additional identification such as school name or choir also is helpful. As mentioned previously, each folder needs an identification number that matches the number on all the music placed in it. When single selections turn up missing or are found apart from the folder, they can be traced to the rightful person. Keeping track of music is a major responsibility of the choral director, who must diligently protect the public's investment in music resources.

Copyright Law

It is against federal law (the copyright act of 1976, which became law in 1978) to photocopy music for performance purposes. Unfortunately, the practice goes on all the time where insufficient funding is provided for the purchase of music. Nevertheless, it is against the law, and fines of at least $250 per copy are payable by the person who does the copying, not the school district or choral organization. The law does provide for *fair use* by educators, which

Figure 6.7. The Black Folder. (www. musicfolder.com. Photos courtesy of Small World, Ian C. H. Bullen. Used by permission.)

means that portions (no more than 10 percent) of a work may be copied for use in a classroom setting. For example, it is permissible to copy a chorus from Handel's *Messiah* for study in a music appreciation class. But multiple copying of choral octavos for public performance is strictly forbidden. Choral directors may photocopy in an emergency to replace purchased copies "not available for an imminent performance, provided purchased replacement copies shall be substituted in due course" (Althouse, 1997, p. 45).

Works copyrighted before January 1, 1978, are protected for a maximum term of seventy-five years. This means that copyright has expired for publications with a copyright date of 1907 or earlier. These works are now in *public domain* and may be used at will, unless the copyright has been renewed by the publisher. Sometimes music has gone out of print and can no longer be purchased. In this case, the publisher must be contacted for permission to photocopy the music. Publishers often grant this permission for a nominal per-copy charge. Copyright for works registered on or after January 1, 1978, continues until fifty years after the death of the author or composer, or seventy-five years for anonymous works.

If there is photocopied music in the choral library, it should be destroyed. ACDA has taken a strong stance against the use of illegally photocopied music and will not permit its use at organization-sponsored events. Every choral director needs to serve as a model for students by not proliferating the unlawful use of copied music. A detailed account of copyright provisions can be found in the handy guide *Copyright: The Complete Guide for Music Educators* (2d ed., 1997) by Jay Althouse.

REWARDS TO STIMULATE PRIDE AND MOTIVATION

A choral group that is motivated and high spirited is an exciting organization and attracts new students to it. A lively esprit de corps comes first from a good program in which students take pride. Other, more tangible ways may also stimulate student interest and, while secondary, can be used successfully for motivating students.

Choral Recordings

Many school choirs now make CD or cassette recordings and use them as a source of fundraising. A recording may feature just one choir or selections from all choirs in the program.

Figure 6.8. CD jacket. (Cedar Heights Singers, Cedar Falls, Iowa, Joyce Spande, director. Cover art by Nancy Barsic. Used by permission.)

The more choirs involved, the greater potential for sales. Pride in a choral organization is greatly enhanced when there is a CD or cassette representing the group.

Most schools do not have the types of sophisticated recording equipment required for producing good recordings. Sound technician specialists will record with their own equipment in the school auditorium or other venue, and recording studios are available in some larger communities. When the master tape is made, a manufacturer is necessary for mass duplication. Names of businesses that provide this service are available in such publications as the *Choral Journal*. Recording and duplication costs can be quite high but are added into the final cost of each CD or cassette.

There is another cost involved in the mass production of a recording—the royalty fee. A royalty must be paid to the publisher for each work recorded.

Under the terms of the Compulsory Mechanical License, a copyright owner . . . cannot, after the first recording of a musical work, prohibit any subsequent recordings. So you don't have to worry about getting permission to record—assuming the work has been previously recorded and you're prepared to pay a royalty. Nevertheless, your first step should be a letter to the copyright owner before you record and request a license to record the work. In the event the work has never been recorded the copyright owner does have the option of denying your request but chances are he would grant you a license anyway.

The copyright owner will then issue you a license to record the work and you may proceed with the recording. Actually, if you're prepared to pay the required royalty there is no need to wait until you receive the license before making the recording. Some publishers use the services of . . . an agent for small recordings made by schools and churches. Others issue their licenses directly. The most widely used agent is The Harry Fox Agency, Inc., in New York City. If you're planning a recording project with several songs, one letter or phone call to the Fox Agency may save a lot of time. (Althouse, 1997, pp. 66–67)

Some copyright owners will waive the royalty fee when the recording is made for a "worthy cause." Nevertheless, royalties must be researched by schools and permission sought before sales of recordings are legally possible. It is up to the director to make a good case for "worthy cause" exemption. Again, fair use makes it possible for one recording of a concert to be made for study, but not duplication.

Group Photographs

An annual choir picture hung in the "choir gallery" is a positive way to increase pride in the choral program. Students are pleased to see their picture added to the others that have come before and feel a special part of the total organization. School photographers often are available for this project.

Some choral directors collect individual pictures from graduating seniors and make a collage or large picture out of the group. Placed conspicuously in the choral room, this also establishes a sense of tradition and pride in the choral program.

Figure 6.9. Choir in robes. (Riverside High School Concert Choir, Ellwood City, Pa., Kenneth Phillips, conductor. Photo by Joseph Yost. Used by permission.)

The Rehearsal Room Bulletin Board

The bulletin board in the choir room makes an excellent place for displaying newspaper articles about the choir and its members. Articles and photographs of choristers involved in the arts, sports, and other parts of the curriculum show that the director is interested in the students and their total educational program.

Thank-you notes and letters to the choir also can be displayed on the bulletin board. Students benefit from having access to such written communication, which every group receives on occasion. A positive note from the school principal, parent, or member of the community makes students feel that their hard work is appreciated.

Student Awards

The awarding of pins, keys, or letters to deserving students has a long tradition in choral programs. Some type of point system is usually established, and students earn points for participation in various groups, concert attendance, special rehearsals, singing a solo, serving as group leaders, officers, and so forth. The music booster group is a good source of funding for such an award program. Award plaques often are seen in music rooms and contain the names of outstanding choral students from successive years.

Many schools have end-of-the-year awards ceremonies for graduating seniors. The top male and female vocalists often are acknowledged with some type of gift or plaque. Again, a point system is needed to make the outcomes perfectly objective. It can create hurt feelings among students if the choral director just picks someone for the award. There needs to be established criteria for the choices, which can be defended if questioned.

Figure 6.10. Students wearing choir t-shirts. (1998 Texas Choral Directors Association Children's Chorus, Kenneth Phillips, guest conductor. Photo courtesy of Omni-Video, a division of Next Saturday Productions, San Antonio, Tex. Used by permission.)

T-Shirts

Choir T-shirts, using a choir logo or some musical expression, have become a popular and rather inexpensive way to build group spirit and pride. Vendors are available in most communities who produce unique creations for choir identity. T-shirts can be worn when presenting informal programs, for various fund-raising events, and when the group is traveling (see Figure 6.10).

Social Events

Many high school choral programs include various social events for students as a type of reward for their active participation. End-of-the-year awards banquets, after-musical parties, bowling and skating parties, and other mixers are ways in which students can socialize and feel good about being part of a successful choral organization. Again, the music boosters group can aid in the planning and directing of such fun activities.

Providing students with rewards is highly motivating and says thanks for working so hard to make choral music great in our school. It takes time to develop and manage such incentives, but it is all part of being a grateful choral director.

STUDY AND DISCUSSION QUESTIONS

1. What are some general guidelines for developing a music budget?
2. What clerical items must be included when ordering choral music for purchase?
3. What are some general guidelines for the handling of students' activity money?
4. What value does the Internet have for choral directors, and what websites are available?
5. What are some basic equipment needs for the choral room?
6. How can computers be used in the choral program?
7. What are some general guidelines for choosing concert attire?
8. What are some guidelines for maintaining the choral library?
9. What types of master files are recommended for the music library?
10. What guidelines are recommended for distributing music to students?
11. What guidelines are given for choosing choral folders?
12. What does the Copyright Act of 1976 stipulate for choral directors?
13. What costs are typically associated with the production of a choral recording?
14. What are the copyright requirements for choral recordings made for sale, and how can such obligations be more easily transacted?
15. What types of photographs are possible to stimulate group pride and tradition?
16. How can the rehearsal room bulletin board be used effectively?
17. What types of student awards are appropriate in the choral program?
18. What precaution is necessary when deciding vocalist-of-the-year awards?
19. What benefits are there for having choir T-shirts?
20. Why are social events and others types of rewards so important to the choral program?

REFERENCES

Althouse, J. (1997). *Copyright: The complete guide for music educators* (2d ed.). Van Nuys, CA., Music in Action.

Garretson, R. L. (1998). *Conducting choral music* (8th ed.). Upper Saddle River, NJ: Prentice Hall.

Kassner, K. (1998). Funding music technology. *Music Educators Journal, 84*(6), 30-35.

McAdams, C. A. and M. A. Nelson (1995). A beginner's guide to the Internet. *Music Educators Journal, 82*(1), 17–24.

MENC (1994). *Opportunity to learn: Standards for music instruction.* Reston, VA: Music Educators National Conference.

Mueth, L. (1993). MIDI technology for the scared to death. *Music Educators Journal, 79*(8), 49–53.

Oglesby, D. (1997). Technology for the choral director: A new *Choral Journal* column. *Choral Journal, 38*(5), 27.

Sebald, D. (1997). Web your program: an Internet primer for choral musicians. *Choral Journal, 37*(9), 9–13.

Smith, J. A. (1979). Be wise—computerize. *Choral Journal, 20*(3), 23.

Walker, D. E. (1989). *Teaching music.* New York: Schirmer Books

Unit 1

Optional Projects

1. A Rationale for Teaching Music

  a. Consider the many reasons for justifying music and choose five that are most important to you and for which you can build a strong advocacy statement. Write a two-page, double-spaced paper detailing your five reasons. Each reason should be no more than one paragraph in length. You may include introductory and closing statements if you do not exceed the two-page limit. Be careful about making "out-on-the-limb" statements, which cannot be supported reasonably.

  b. Present your "Rationale for Teaching Music" paper orally in class.

2. Preparing Promotion Materials

  a. Prepare a choir recruitment poster for any desired grade level. Follow the guidelines in Chapter 3 for content and style.

  b. Prepare a written newspaper release announcing a choral concert. Follow the guidelines in Chapter 3 for content and style.

3. Choral Auditioning

  a. Prepare a high school choral audition form according to guidelines in Chapter 4. Collect or write the necessary materials that students will need (sight-singing exercises, music to sing, etc.), and include them with the audition form.

  b. Audition a class member in class using the audition form and ancillary materials.

  c. Audition a number of high school students outside of class to gain experience in the audition process.

4. Lesson Planning

  a. Write a choral rehearsal lesson plan (any age level) for a forty-five minute period with four choral selections (your choice) to be rehearsed. Include time for warm ups and sight-singing, and follow the outline in Chapter 5. What you list to do at this point is not as important as the structure you use, but forty-five minutes is not a long time.

  b. Revise your plan, if needed, when returned by your instructor.

UNIT 2

REHEARSAL AND
PERFORMANCE PLANNING

7 | Working with
    Adolescent Singers

The adolescent years encompass approximately grades six through twelve. Students in these grades are going through difficult stages as they mature to adulthood. Physical and psychological changes make it hard to predict what students will do from one day to the next, and much patience and understanding is needed if educators are to succeed in helping students along this mercurial passageway.

Adolescents present even greater challenges for the vocal music educator. The inevitable voice change for both genders requires special considerations when choosing music, classifying and assigning voice parts, rehearsing groups, and establishing confidence. These dimensions change as students mature, and the choral director must be knowledgeable of the process if success with adolescent singers is to be attained.

Teachers at the junior high or middle school levels are sometimes referred to as a "special breed" of educators. It takes special skills to work with younger adolescents, as noted in the following anecdote:

> When I recently questioned my seventh-grade mixed choir as to the number of phrases in the first verse of "It's time to fly away" and received the responses, "When is this period over?" and "I really like your shoes," I was, indeed, teaching junior-high students. Some days the answers just don't fit the questions! (Jackson and Booher, 1985, p. 27)

Teachers of adolescents must be flexible and quick thinking and combine the interpersonal skills of a counselor with the loving concern of a parent. Most of all, they really have to love kids.

Not all choral directors have the temperament necessary to work with younger adolescents and prefer to work at the senior high level. It is good if they know this about themselves. However, some directors desire senior high positions because of the status. Junior high and middle school directors are not inferior to senior high directors. They really are a special breed, who demand the respect of the profession for their diligent and successful work in keeping students singing through these often traumatic years.

THE NATURE OF ADOLESCENTS

The physiological changes that accompany puberty are well known and documented. Boys are typically less mature than girls, and it is common to see girls towering over boys who have yet to experience a growth spurt. Physiological changes are accompanied by or even may cause psychological changes. It is the psychological parameter that concerns all teachers, for psychological problems can manifest as behaviors acted out in the classroom. Understanding the mind of the adolescent is a prerequisite for successful teaching at the middle and high school levels.

Self-esteem

Puberty can be terribly devastating to a student's self-esteem. Bright, outgoing elementary children sometimes become withdrawn and brooding as self-doubt and insecurity emerge in the teenage years. Many of these kids have no idea what is happening to them and feel lost in a new world of feelings and emotions. For an alarmingly high number of them, these years can be so traumatic that suicide becomes the only way out.

Numerous studies have shown that girls are less likely than boys to have a healthy self-esteem (AAUW, 1992). The American Association of University Women conducted a survey of three thousand students between the ages of nine and fifteen (AAUW, 1991). When asked to respond to the statement "I'm happy the way I am," 67 percent of boys and 60 percent of girls at the elementary level answered "always true." However, the percentages declined to 56 percent for boys and 37 percent for girls in the middle school years, and to 46 percent for boys and 29 percent for girls of senior high school age. This radical drop in the middle school years, especially for girls, is troubling. Comments Patricia O'Toole (1998):

> Whether girls believe they are good at a lot of things does not seem to matter. It is more important that girls do not acknowledge their abilities, so they are perceived as feminine by the boys (and teachers to some extent) and, therefore, will have a better chance at succeeding at what counts most in middle and high school—social acceptance. (p. 12)

Gender expectations are strongly rooted in family and social life, and teachers reinforce these models. "By early adolescence boys and girls choose to adhere more strictly to gender roles, as girls are less likely to consider themselves similar to boys, and boys rarely consider themselves to be like girls, having learned the emasculating consequences of doing so" (pp. 12–13).

Gender expectations are part of traditional choral practices and policies. Women's choirs generally are viewed as being at the low end of the choral hierarchy, and the majority of choral music is written from a male perspective. Boys are expected to cause the most behavioral problems in choirs, while girls are expected to sit passively while the director's attention is on the boys. Because girls so outnumber boys in most choral programs, boys are made to feel special if they sing. For girls it is a normal expectation. O'Toole relates, "There is no time, space, or concern for what might irritate, annoy or disturb a female singer in choir" (p. 26).

Gender-specific groupings were recommended in Chapter 4 as a way to rehearse boys and girls in the early junior high and middle school years. Patricia O'Toole agrees:

> The best solution suggested by method textbooks is rehearsing junior high boys and girls separately, during which time they can learn both common and individual repertoire. This scenario allows boys the privacy to work out their vocal (and emotional) difficulties, while the girls develop at their own pace, unhindered by disparity in abilities. When these stu-

dents move on to the integrated high school chorus, they are more confident in their vocal abilities, thus reducing undesirable tensions and behaviors in rehearsals. (p. 22)

Peer Approval

Adolescence is the time when peer approval is so important that students will do harmful or foolish things in a group that normally they would not do alone. Roe (1983) states that young men have a stronger need in this area than young women, and that need may be responsible for the "gang" mentality that is prevalent among adolescent males. "He is not usually willing to be different. The teacher must attempt to convince *all* the young men in order to influence their behavior" (p. 161). For young women, the need to conform also is strong. However, girls tend to be more individualistic if convinced of the merit or value of an action.

One problem peculiar to adolescent males is the identification of singing in general American culture as a feminine activity. Stereotypical models disputing manliness create conflicts that can result in hostile and aggressive behaviors. Patricia O'Toole relates the following story about directing a junior high summer honor choir:

> I asked the students about the benefits of singing at camp versus singing in their school music programs. Without hesitation, the young men blurted out, "support and acceptance from other guys for wanting to sing." To my horror, they told of being punched in the hallways and called fags, just because they sang in choir. If this physical violence is a common experience among young male singers (and not an urban myth), it is not surprising that they feel the need to be assertive, domineering, and aggressively heterosexual in choral rehearsals. (1998, p. 22)

O'Toole recommends that teachers help "struggling young men find an alternative choral singer identity—one that separates singing and sexuality and includes a critique of male privilege in the choral program" (p. 22). Young men need to experience male singing groups such as the King's Singers, and they need to realize that in many cultures (e.g., the Welsh) male singing ensembles are prominent and valued by the general populace.

Choral directors should make a conscious effort at building a mutually supportive group environment. They must ban verbal put-downs in rehearsals and encourage a genuine appreciation for the efforts of others. Students will participate more actively when they feel safe in the classroom. Likewise, the director needs to be free with verbal support. Adolescents want to know how they are doing and require much positive reinforcement. Having the school principal visit after a performance to give positive comments and constructive criticism boosts the importance of choir and helps students to feel respected.

Stanley A. Carlson (1993) relates how he creates a spirit of friendly competition in middle school choirs (separated by gender) through a challenge system. The challenge involves students' successfully clapping rhythms or sight-singing vocal exercises that appear each day on the board. While the students are having fun challenging each other, they are bettering their sight-reading skills. The entire choir sings each exercise following several challenges.

Emotional Natures

Adolescents tend to have extreme mood swings. Girls will let their emotions show more readily than boys, and tears are commonplace. Boys are no less affected, but they tend to act "cool" as a defense mechanism. Likewise, girls will do anything asked of them for a teacher they like, while boys often hold back and participate with less enthusiasm. Child psychologists Dan Kindlon and Michael Thompson (1999) comment:

One of the most common complaints heard about boys is that they are aggressive and "seem not to care." We have heard the same complaint from veteran teachers who are stunned by the power of boy anger and disruption in their classes. Too often, adults excuse this behavior as harmless "immaturity," as if maturity will arrive someday—like puberty—to transform a boy's emotional life. But we do boys no favor by ignoring the underlying absence of awareness. Boys' emotional ignorance clearly imposes on others, but it costs them dearly, too. Lacking an emotional education, a boy meets the pressures of adolescence and that singularly cruel peer culture with the only responses he has learned and practiced—and that he knows are socially acceptable—the typically "manly" responses of anger, aggression, and emotional withdrawl. (p. 5)

Boy-girl relationships also begin to blossom, and mating rituals are played out everywhere. Boys vie for attention by acting silly, and girls act coy. Personal hygiene is important, as students constantly comb their hair and look in mirrors for the latest blemish. The dress uniform of blue jeans and T-shirts shows the need to be part of the crowd.

Many students feel terribly alone, and choral participation is a wonderful antidote. An esprit de corps occurs with everyone working toward a common goal. The school music program makes a positive contribution to students' emotional health.

It is easy for students to become lost in the crowd. Teachers are busy with teaching and sometimes miss the telltale signs of a student who is in depression. Adolescents need to know that choral directors care about them as individuals and not just as choristers. A kind word, a simple thank you, a knowing smile—easy ways to tell students they are appreciated. Sometimes one-on-one counseling is required. The reward for teachers is group affection and respect. Adolescents can be intensely loyal to teachers who create a positive and accepting classroom environment.

THE FEMALE VOICE CHANGE

Males and females experience a voice change as part of puberty. Much more is written about the male, and the choral profession has rather neglected the special needs of females during adolescence (O'Toole, 1998). While the female voice change may be less noticeable, it is real and requires attention. A small but growing amount of research concerns the adolescent female voice, and this is encouraging for the profession (Bottoms, 1995; Fett, 1994; Gackle, 1987; Maddox, 1986; May and Williams, 1989; Phillips and Fett, 1992; Sipley, 1994; Williams, 1990).

Physiological Changes

The pubertal voice change for girls begins as early as ten or eleven years old and can require up to four years to complete the transition. During this time hormonal development increases the girl's estrogen level. Near the midpoint of puberty (between 12.5 and 14.5 years) menarche begins, as well as the growth of the larynx and vocal folds.

The larynx of the female does not undergo as radical a change as that of the male (Kahane, 1978). The girl's larynx thickens and grows more in height and laterally (side to side). Her vocal folds average a three- to four-millimeter increase, accompanied by a slight lowering of the speaking voice and singing range.

Stages of Voice Change

The female voice goes through a transition, according to Lynn Gackle (1991, pp. 22–23), in somewhat definable stages:

Stage 1. Prepubertal

Age:	8–10 (11–13) years
Vocal quality:	light, "flutelike," singing between upper and lower ranges is achieved with ease
Range:	b♭ to f² (octave and a fifth)

Stage 2A. Pubescent/premenarcheal

Age:	11–12 (13) years
Vocal quality:	breathiness; trouble singing in lower register; volume in middle and upper ranges is difficult to achieve; voice "cracks" are common
Range:	a to g² (octave and a seventh)

Stage 2B. Puberty/postmenarcheal

Age:	13–14 (15) years
Vocal quality:	huskiness or heaviness in the vocal timbre; a five- or six-note range is most comfortable to sing; lower tones of the vocal range are easiest to produce
Range:	a to f² (octave and a sixth)

Stage 3. Young adult female/postmenarcheal

Age:	14–15 (16) years
Vocal quality:	inconsistent sound; voice "cracking" common; breathiness decreases; greater consistency between registers; richer tone; gradual appearance of vibrato; overall increases in volume, resonance, and agility.
Range:	a to a² (two octaves)

Female pubertal stages begin earlier than male's, and the female voice settles more quickly into an adult model.

Vocal Quality

The beginning of female voice change often is signaled by huskiness or unsteadiness of the speaking voice. This is caused by thickening of the vocal folds and congestion within the muscles of the larynx; it results in the well-known characteristic of the adolescent girl's voice—breathiness. William Vennard (1967) describes a "mutational chink" forming in the female voice when the vocal folds are unable to close sufficiently to keep air from escaping during phonation. This results in a singing tone that is weak in upper partials and generally light and airy. Teachers long have accepted the adolescent girl's breathy voice as a fact of life—something girls will outgrow as they mature.

Recent investigations (Bottoms, 1995; Fett, 1994; Phillips and Fett, 1992) have sought to determine if breathiness is present in all pubertal girls' voices, and if help in the form of phonatory exercises can reduce the amount of breathy quality. In one study (Bottoms, 1995), one hundred girls were studied for incomplete glottal closure and absence of upper partials in the singing tone. Results showed the majority of girls to have the presence of these two characteristics, while 14 percent did not. Another study (Phillips and Fett, 1992), reported that 75 percent of fifteen-year-old females still "evidenced a fair amount of breathiness in the voice, and 28% of those exhibited considerable breathiness of the voice" (p. 9). However, 25 percent were judged to have good to excellent tone quality. These studies seem to indicate that while breathiness is present for most adolescent girls, it is not present for all of them.

An experimental investigation by Darlene Fett (1994) of the effects of vocal instruction on the singing performance of ninth-grade girls used exercises from the vocal method *Teaching Kids to Sing* (Phillips, 1992) with the treatment group. The control group performed vocalises, with no specific vocal instruction given. The treatment exercises included the areas of posture and breathing development, phonatory control, and resonant tone production, which were distributed over twenty-two weeks of rehearsals. Fett found that "the treatment group experienced less breath in the tone over time, while the control group's breathiness increased slightly" (p. 75). Results of this study seem to indicate that breathiness in the adolescent female voice may be helped with instruction that increases phonatory efficiency.

Vocal Instruction

The vocal method of Phillips (1992) works to increase energized breath management and provides phonatory exercises for strengthening the glottal closure muscles. One such exercise is the "sustained bleat."

> Direct students to imitate the sound a bleating sheep with *ba-a-a-a*, using a firm contraction of the abdominal musculature while emitting short, light grips of the vocal folds. Do not prolong group practice, but listen for individual performance. Students who cannot execute this exercise (i.e., make one long breathy sound instead of a string of little bleats) should be encouraged through proper vocal modeling by other students or the instructor. They need to learn to firm the vocal folds with breath energy, and often this will happen through repeated modeling and practice. (Phillips, 1992, p. 249)

Phonatory exercises that focus on clear glottal closure can, over a period of time, reduce breathiness in the adolescent female voice.

DeYoung (1985) relates that choral directors can abuse girls' voices by: (1) demanding loud singing for extended periods of time, (2) requiring that pitches be sustained for too long a duration, (3) seeking too wide a mouth opening, resulting in a stiff jaw, and (4) encouraging very soft singing, resulting in a weak, lifeless, out-of-tune sound (p. 104). Vocal instructors must be careful to protect singers' voices, especially those of the young.

Richard Alderson's *Complete Handbook of Voice Training* (1979) is one of the few voice books to comment on the young female singer. Alderson makes the following four recommendations for instructing girls through the voice change:

1. *Breathing exercises.* The girl's enlarged vocal bands will require more breath support than before, so she should continue to develop her breathing muscles. Also, as her breasts enlarge she will have to remind herself to stand up straight with her shoulders back. Her skeletal muscles will become stronger, and good posture will become easier after awhile.

2. *Humming, ringing quality.* The concept of a humming, ringing sound is important during this period, because of the tendency in most girls toward breathiness. Descending scales and arpeggios which mix head voice with the middle and low registers are vital to good vocal technique during mutation.

3. *Light approach.* The girl's voice which is supported well with a humming, ringing quality should be light. This does not mean weak or child-like, but implies a high, forward placement which is focused above the hard palate. The voice should "spin" and be flexible. There should be no feeling that the voice is caught in the throat or is "sitting on the vocal bands." Alternate bright and dark vowels may be incorporated into vocalizes to blend the brilliance and depth of the voice.

4. *Practice the upper range.* Young women should sing in all parts of their ranges to maintain the entire voice. Too many girls are allowed to sing exclusively in the lower two-thirds of their voices during vocal mutation, creating great difficulties in their late

teens with their high registers. Vocalizes such as the fire siren and songs which require a few excursions into the high range are highly recommended. (Alderson, 1979, pp. 239–40)

Alderson also recommends: (1) choose songs to explore the various registers, (2) have girls sing neither too high nor too low for very long, (3) avoid vocalizing on closed vowels such as "oo," and (4) vary the dynamics. "Frequent auditions also help the choral director place each girl in the proper choral section, thus satisfying the need for good choral balance and blend and the obligation to treat each singer as an individual" (p. 240).

Voice Classification

Voice classification for pubertal girls is problematic, as the voice is yet unsettled. It is recommended that vocal exercises in upper and lower registers be practiced, and that girls not be labeled as altos or even mezzo-sopranos until the ninth grade. Girls can be assigned equally to one of two groups, with frequent alternation of girls on the soprano and alto parts. All girls should be vocalised from $b^\flat$ to f^2, with a song tessitura of d^1 to d^2.

Teaching the Whole Person

As noted earlier, the adolescent female not only is experiencing physiological changes but is dealing with major psychological changes as well. Returning to the important article by Patricia O'Toole in the December 1998 issue of the *Choral Journal:*

> Parents, religious leaders, and teachers work to instill in teenagers a strong sense of self-worth, with the hope they will make the right choices when confronted with drug use, driving while intoxicated, and unprotected sex. Unfortunately, research indicates that girls are not weathering the pressures well, which is not surprising given the messages of self-worth received in school. Compounding the pressures are harmful messages from television, movies, magazines, and billboards. The media set a standard for attractive women at waif-thin or highly "buff" and promote an obsession with dieting. While boys and girls consume these beauty ideals, girls are more discontent with their body image than boys and are literally killing themselves (bulimia, anorexia) to achieve this ideal. (p. 30)

O'Toole notes that low self-confidence and negative body image often cause depression, something girls seem to suffer from twice as much as boys. What is frightening is that adolescent girls "are four to five times more likely than boys to attempt suicide; however, more boys succeed because they choose more lethal weapons" (O'Toole, 1998, p. 30).

Clearly, choral directors must be as concerned with the psychological as they are the physiological changes that occur in the lives of all adolescents. Failure to do so may result in students who become lost in the process, drop out of music, and miss the opportunity music can provide for a life-enriching experience.

THE MALE VOICE CHANGE

Much has been written about the adolescent male voice change, but the topic remains an enigma for many teachers. The various stages of transition and how best to handle this voice are problematic. No attempt is made here to address in any depth the various factions of this debate, as this has been done elsewhere (Emge, 1997; Phillips, 1992). Rather, recommendations are given to help choral directors devise their own plans for helping boys to sing in the early adolescent years. Experience is the best teacher.

Physiological Changes

During puberty the male hormone testosterone is produced by the testes, causing a growth spurt and other noticeable physical changes such as growth of facial hair, development of acne, physical awkwardness, and voice "cracking." The larynx of the pubertal boy grows dramatically in the anterio-posterior (front to back) direction, causing a protrusion of the *pomum Adami*, or "Adam's apple." The vocal folds lengthen considerably (to approximately ten millimeters), with a drop in pitch of about an octave.

The physical changes experienced by the adolescent male can take place quite suddenly and in a relatively short period of time, or they can progress slowly and almost imperceptibly, depending upon the boy's own body clock. Great variation of size and shape are seen, and it is not uncommon to have "late bloomers" looking like elementary children and "early bloomers" appearing as senior high guys.

Stages of Voice Change

Voice maturation begins typically between the ages of twelve and fifteen, and seems to peak in the eighth grade for most boys. Some voices are known to begin to change as early as the intermediate grades (four to six), and a few change as late as ninth or tenth grade. The boy who is about to enter puberty often displays a brilliance and power in both speaking and singing voices. Boys in early pubescence can be mistaken for females when speaking on the telephone, much to their consternation!

There are two schools of thought regarding the stages of voice change for males (Emge, 1997). The first, or "limited range," school believes that boys' voices change rather predictably, lowering gradually until the soprano range of c^2 and above is replaced with a full octave and more below middle c^1. This school is represented by Ayres and Roduner (1942), Barresi (1984), Coffman (1987), Collins (1993), Cooksey (1992), Cooper (1953), Groom (1979), McKenzie (1956), Rutkowski (1984), and Yarrington (1990). The second, or "extended range," school believes that boys' voices may change slowly or quickly and may not be limited to a midvoice comfort range of an octave or less during puberty. Authors in this school include Emge (1997), Herman (1988), Joseph (1959), Mayer and Sacher (1964), Phillips (1992), and Swanson (1959; 1977a).

One factor often overlooked in discussing the stages of adolescent male voice change is the area of vocal registration. Most prepubertal boys sing in a mixed register between middle c and an octave above. As their voices begin to lower, they carry their "boys" voice below middle c in a continued mixed registration; that is, they do not sing in a full chest register. Singing below middle c without the shift to a full chest tone results in a weaker sound the lower one sings. For boys whose voices are changing slowly, the absence of a real chest sound may be indicative of a poorly developed thyroarytenoid muscle within the vocal folds (the muscle that governs lower pitch production), or it may be a lack of exposure to the chest voice mechanism.

Similarly, pubertal boys can continue to sing in the octave c^1 to c^2 if they employ the cricothyroid muscle and produce an upper-register sound like the one used by sopranos for pitches c^2 and above. However, if this register is not exercised during puberty—and many boys resist singing "like a girl"—the upper range of the adolescent male will be limited. Thus, if boys sing neither in a full chest registration below c^1 nor in a predominately upper registration from about e^1 and up, they will be limited to a midvoice registration in which they can sing neither very high nor very low. This has been shown in the work of Mayer and Sacher (1964), Phillips and Emge (1994), and Swanson (1959).

Boys whose voices change quickly seem to have such a quick growth spurt that the thyroarytenoid muscles within the vocal cords gain dominance of vocal production. This results in a full chest register production that is sometimes limited to pitches around an octave below c^1. These boys seem to lose use of the cricrothyroid muscles, which cause pitch to rise, and results in an extremely limited range of approximately a fifth around $B^\flat$ to f. They may, however, have use of the cricothyroid muscle for pitches in the upper register, approximately a^1 to c^2, with no pitches in between. Both Herman (1988) and Swanson (1959; 1977a) attest to this phenomenon.

Boys whose voices change slowly either have a much slower growth of the thyroarytenoid muscle or are not experiencing kinesthetically what it is to sing with a chest voice mechanism. It does seem that boys whose voices change more slowly become tenors, while boys whose voices change more quickly become baritones and basses. In either case, chest voice registration, which is produced by the thyroarytenoid muscle, must be in use for the voice to produce pitches to the lowest extent possible. Swanson (1977b) has argued that low basses are vanishing from the choral scene because boys are not taught to use the lower register in high school.

It seems reasonable to suggest that pubertal boys' voices may change slowly or quickly, predictably or unpredictably. It also may be that pubertal voices have more range capabilities than evidenced for lack of proper use of vocal registers. One thing is certain: in a typical middle school group, there will be boys with unchanged, changing, and newly changed voices; they should not all be singing the same voice part.

Vocal Quality

All types of vocal qualities are heard from adolescent choirs—from strident and loud to whisperish and weak. While adolescent singers are incapable of a mature sound, they are capable of greater richness and depth than is commonly heard. They need to learn breath support, to produce a tone that is energized, and to sing with an open throat.

Students can experiment with changing vocal color by altering the size and shape of the vocal tract. Vocal imitation of an opera singer produces a large and pharyngeal sound, while imitation of a country singer may produce a thin and nasal sound. Experiencing how a yawn or a smiling position affects tone demonstrates the great range of timbres of which the voice is capable. Choral directors should encourage students to sing through the feeling of a "sigh," to keep the larynx relaxed, and to maintain depth of jaw position (not necessarily a more open mouth) for all vowels. The resulting sound, when supported with energy, will be warm, full, and resonant.

Loud singing should be avoided in the formative years. A dynamic level of *mezzo piano* to *mezzo forte* still is warranted. Soft singing requires greater breath management, if done correctly, and very soft dynamic levels are to be avoided. Occasional levels of *forte* are suggested as students progress in their vocal technique. Senior high school students should be able to sing at more extended levels of dynamic variation if technique is good.

The appearance of a vocal vibrato is common to the experience of a well-produced voice. The vibrato will appear naturally when the throat and larynx are relaxed and breath support is energized. Students of all ages should be encouraged to "let the vibrato happen" when it appears on its own. A "manufactured" vibrato using some type of vocal exerise is to be avoided. When the laryngeal muscles are relaxed, the vocal folds will be able to respond to the intermitent nerve energy of the body.

Vocal Instruction

The same types of instruction recommended previously for girls also is appropriate for boys. Exercises in posture development, breath management, resonant tone production, diction, and expression all are warranted. Every choral rehearsal should begin with a singing lesson that builds instruction in a sequential manner.

Boys need to explore and experience the full chest voice sound in phonatory exercises and vocalises (refer to Chapter 14). This is the voice they predominantly will sing in as adults, and the sooner it is explored the quicker the lower voice will extend and resonate. Likewise, boys need to actively exercise the upper voice so as to strengthen it for a full vocal compass. Alderson (1979) states:

> While the boy's voice is changing he should rely on head voice techniques for his highest notes. . . . The young man should probably not try to sing above the second lift in chest voice, even with modified vowels, as the extralaryngeal muscles are not strong enough in the mid-teens. As the young man matures, he will be able to reinforce his upper notes by blending chest voice with the head voice he has already learned, thus achieving a good upper register in chest voice. (p. 234)

For boys who have difficulty singing above d^1 it is highly recommended that they use only two registers: lower and upper. As they approach the upper voice, they should be taught to switch to pure upper production at around pitch e^1, thus making a slight break between registers. Medical authorities Sataloff and Spiegel (1991) concur, suggesting that boys in early adolescence sing with an audible shift from one register to another, without a blending in the middle: "This produces a tolerable choral sound, and they can continue singing safely in whichever mode is most relaxed for any given note" (p. 60). As Alderson relates, the strengthening of the upper notes will come in time. For young men, it is easier to ignore the middle register until technique is sufficient to produce a *passaggio* that is different from the prebupertal boy's "mixed" voice. A male alto sound that is cultivated from e^1 and up is an easy sound to float without vocal strain.

Strengthening the upper voice is the way to develop future high school tenors. It also is the way to fill in the middle of the voice for the boy whose voice has changed quickly. "Bring the top down" through descending scales to restore the full vocal range for boys who have experienced a loss of middle notes. It does not work to vocalize up from the bottom when trying to connect the two vocal registers.

Voice Classification

Vocal ranges and tessituras are given for all voices in Chapter 4 and are further discussed in the latter part of this chapter in relation to appropriate voicings. Suffice it to reiterate that continual monitoring of the vocal compass is needed throughout the adolescent experience, and that labeling voices too early in students' singing experience may result in voices that are limited in range and confidence.

The following technique for classifying young male adolescent voices is based on that of Sally Herman (1988, pp. 87–88). The process assumes there will be as many as four voice types, which will be labeled first tenor, second tenor, baritone, and bass (not to be confused with their senior high school counterparts).

- Each boy states his name and the school he was in last year. Director assigns a "1" to unchanged voices and a "2" to changed voices.
- Arrange students on the risers by group, 2s on the left, 1s on the right.
- Group sings "My Country, 'Tis of Thee" (G major) several times, and students are encouraged to sing with a more mature sound.
- Director listens to group 1 as all sing. Boys that sing first half of song at pitch written are labeled first tenors, with approximate range of $b^\flat$ to a^1. Boys that sing about a fourth below become second tenors, with approximate range of $a^\flat$ to d^1.
- Director listens to group 2 as all sing. Boys that sing on pitch one octave below the treble part are labeled baritones, with approximate range of f to c^1. Boys that sing about an octave and a fourth lower are declared basses, with approximate range of G to c.

Teaching the Whole Person

Patricia O'Toole (1998) has noted that boys are privileged characters in most choral programs because there are fewer of them and they know it. Therefore, the contributions that boys make should be openly recognized and appreciation expressed often for their willingness to participate in the arts. Boys need to know that manhood is based on maturity and strength of character, and that men have been liberated from the old stereotypes.

Boys are typically the troublemakers in choir; they act out because of insecurity and emotional mood swings. They do need a lot of attention and positive reinforcement, but not to the exclusion of girls. Choral directors must strive to maintain gender balance when it comes to making everyone feel appreciated.

As noted earlier about girls, some boys become so self-absorbed during adolescence that they withdraw and become easily depressed. Boys need to know that what they are experiencing is common for the human race, and that "this too shall pass." They should be informed in the elementary grades about what is ahead for them in adolescence, especially regarding the voice change. It is important for boys to know that there are adults who care about them and what they are experiencing.

APPROPRIATE PART VOICINGS

By the time students reach the ninth grade, the traditional voice parts of soprano, alto, tenor, and bass are commonly assigned. Students in the middle school grades (six through eight) or early adolescent years require some special handling, however, when it comes to appropriate voicings and choral balance.

Unison Singing

Most vocal authorities agree that unison singing is not recommended for middle school students, as it is almost impossible to find music that fits the limited range of b to g^1 (doubled at the octave for baritones). Even canons often incorporate more than an octave and quickly are out of range for many boys. Some canons that have voice parts starting on the tonic and dominant, e.g., *Non nobis, Domine* by William Byrd (see Example 7.1), are the exception.

Two- and Three-Part Treble (SA, SSA)

Two-part treble music is commonly used with choirs in the sixth and seventh grades. Boys as well as girls can sing both parts, although boys may resist singing the higher (soprano) part if their upper voices have not been exercised through the elementary grades. In this case,

Non nobis, Domine

William Byrd (1543–1623)

Example 7.1. *Non nobis, Domine* by Wm. Byrd. (Public domain.)

all boys will be assigned treble 2. It is recommended that parts be called treble 1 and treble 2, and not soprano and alto. Also, voice parts should be alternated between groups so that both groups learn to sing melody and harmony.

When there are a few changing or changed male voices in these grades, some directors place these boys in an eighth-grade chorus. The changing voice is not a problem when the seventh and eighth grades are combined in one choir. Sally Herman (1988) recommends that first tenors (unchanged male sopranos) sing the alto part at the pitch written in two-part music, and that changed basses sing the alto part down one octave. Second tenors (unchanged male altos) and baritones (changing male voices) are placed close to the sopranos and sing the soprano part down one octave in most two-part music.

Three-part treble music also can be used effectively in middle school choirs. When boys are included, or for all-male groups, the parts must be low enough for the boys to sing the pitches as written, for the alto part transposed down an octave will be too low. In the SSA arrangement of *Song for the Mira* by MacGillivray (see Example 7.2), the three treble parts can be sung by tenor 1 (unchanged males), tenor 2 (unchanged male altos) and baritones (changing voices). It is unfortunate that most three-part music is labeled SSA, as adolescent boys do not want to be considered or called sopranos or altos. A recent move for publishers has been to label three-part music for younger voices as parts 1, 2, and 3.

SAB and Three-Part Mixed

SAB voicing is typically not the same as three-part mixed voicing designed for choirs with few or inexperienced male singers. In traditional SAB writing the "B" range is typically too

Example 7.2. *Song for the Mira* (excerpt) by A. MacGillivray/S. Calvert. (Copyright © by CABOT TRAIL MUSIC. Gordon V. Thompson Music/Warner Chappell, VG-326. Reprinted by permission.)

low for young males. However, a high baritone part may easily fit the range of changing voices when there are no basses in the group (see Example 7.3). SAB selections with this type of high baritone range are hard to find.

The newer three-part mixed writing (see Example 7.4) has the following distinctions: a part 3 for males with a compromise range of f to d^1, a limited soprano range that keeps the three parts closer together, and an alto part that may be sung by females and males. This style of voicing has become popular among middle school directors, as the third part seems "to meet the adolescent male's social need to sit with other males and to sing the same part" (Beery, 1996, p. 17).

The problem with this type of voicing is that many choral directors put all the boys on part 3, even in seventh grade, whether their voices are changing or not. The results can be unpleasant—a droning where many boys are trying to sing the part but only approximate it. This is not the fault of the music. "Perhaps it is because the profession has become fixated on the term 'cambiata' (changing) to the exclusion of other vocal-part possibilities for young adolescent males. It also may be due to a lack of knowledge about how to instruct boys in the use of upper and lower vocal registers" (Phillips, 1995, p. 26).

A three-part mixed voicing with optional baritone part (see Example 7.5) is gaining greater popularity. Beery (1996) suggests a range of B$^\flat$ to b for the optional baritone part. He gives the following advantages of this voicing:

1. *Flexibility.* The director may use these pieces with various ensembles depending on the number and ranges of male singers.

2. *Development.* Because they can be performed with either three or four parts, these are ideal pieces for moving students from unison and two-part singing on to three-part music and toward the standard four-part literature.

3. *Recruitment.* Such pieces allow choral directors to combine the middle and high school (or adult) choirs together for festivals or recruitment purposes. (p. 18)

Beery presents a list of three-part mixed music with an optional baritone part that is worth exploring. Music of this voicing is not readily available.

Two- and Three-Part Male

For an all male group, some two-part TB music is appropriate for seventh- and eighth-grade boys when the parts are relatively high (tenor 1 and baritone). The first and second tenors sing the tenor part down an octave, and the baritones (changing voices) and basses (if any) sing the baritone part as written. Some higher TB music fits this voicing rather well, as in the duet by J. S. Bach from Cantata 196 (Example 7.6).

Frederick Swanson worked for years as a junior high music teacher in Moline, Illinois, and was famous for his public school boy choirs. He believed that boys and girls should be separated for music by the eighth grade and recommended a "bass-clef chorus" for boys with changing voices. He also believed that boys whose voices had not begun to change by eighth grade should be included in the all-male group, as these boys feel out of place in a younger, all-treble chorus.

Traditional TTB music does not work for this all-male choir, and directors must do a lot of their own music arranging. To begin, Swanson has the baritones (really tenor range) singing in traditional root positions of I, IV, and V chords (see Example 7.7). The tenor part (changing voices) harmonizes above, and the unchanged voices (altos) sing an easy descant part. As

Example 7.3. *The Wassail Song* (excerpt) arr. R. Forester. (Copyright © by Schmitt, Hall & McCreary/Warner Bros. Co., 5538. Reprinted by permission.)

Example 7.4. *Let Me Ride* (excerpt), traditional spiritual arr. R. Emerson. (Copyright © 1988 EMERSONGS, Jenson Publications, Inc./Hal Leonard, 403-12080. International Copyright Secured. All Rights Reserved.)

Brighten My Soul With Sunshine

For Three-Part choir,* accompanied

Joyce Elaine Eilers
A.S.C.A.P.

*While intended for SAB (high baritone), part three could be sung or reinforced by low altos, making the piece very useful to Training Choirs.

Example 7.5. *Brighten My Soul with Sunshine* (excerpt) by J. Eilers. (Copyright ©1975 by HAL LEONARD CORPORATION, 08541000. International Copyright Secured. All Rights Reserved. Reprinted by Permission.)

The Lord Bless You
(Cantata 196)

J. S. Bach

Example 7.6. *The Lord Bless You* (excerpt) by J. S. Bach. (Music in public domain. English translation by Z. Philip Ambrose. Reprinted by permission.)

On the Trail

F. Swanson

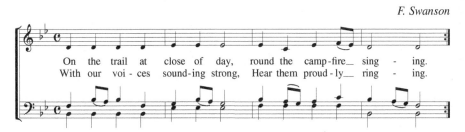

Example 7.7. *On the Trail* by F. Swanson. (second verse by K. Phillips.)

the boys become more comfortable at singing parts, they are moved to more traditional music with the melody in the top part.

Three-part selections especially written for young male adolescents are commercially available (see Example 7.8). Tessituras for this music typically need to be as follows: tenor 1 (treble unchanged): d^1–d^2; tenor 2 (treble unchanged or just beginning to change): a–a^1, and

This Old Hammer

Three-Part Chorus of Young Voices
with Piano Accompaniment

American Folk Poem   *Michael A. Gray*

Example 7.8. *This Old Hammer* (excerpt) arr. M. Gray. (Copyright © 1983 by G. Schirmer, Inc., Hal Leonard S-003-12473-00. International Copyright Secured. All Rights Reserved. Reprinted by permission.)

Lebenslust
(Joy of Living)

for Mixed Voices, S. A. T. B., with Piano

Text: Anonymous
English Text by Ray Robinson

Franz Schubert (1797–1828)
Edited by Ray Robinson

Example 7.9. *Lebenslust* (excerpt) by F. Schubert. (Copyright © 1980 by Hinshaw Music, Inc., HMC-425. Reprinted by permission.)

Wenn ich ein Vöglein wär
(Were I a Little Bird)
for S. A. T. B. and Piano

Robert Schumann
Op. 43, No. 1

Translation: Robert Carl

Edited and Arranged by William Hall

Example 7.10. *Wenn ich ein Vöglein wär* (excerpt) by R. Schumann. (Copyright © 1978 by National Music Publishers, WHC-97. Reprinted by permission.)

baritone (changing and newly changed): d–d^1. Some young baritones will be able to sing lower than d, but with little volume. In any case, c should be the lowest occasional note in the baritone part for eighth grade.

Four-Part Voicings

It is difficult to find four-part SATB music that works well at the middle school level. It is not impossible (see Example 7.9); it is just hard to locate music where the tenor and bass parts are within the ranges and tessituras of young male voices. However, some directors do use four-part music as early as the eighth grade. These directors cultivate the chest voice of boys earlier than most and keep the upper or male voice active also. Subscribers to the tenets of the "extended range" school believe in the presence of the adolescent bass voice and cultivate it according to the principles espoused by Herman (1988) and Swanson (1973, 1977).

Sally Herman recommends the use of four-part music in seventh and eighth grades. The music she lists is of the highest quality (see Example 7.10); she does not permit the vocal ranges of parts to deter her when it is possible to make adjustments. Herman advocates a voice-pivoting approach in which males sing a combination of voice parts as dictated by their present ranges. A second tenor may shift to first tenor or baritone parts for a few notes or even measures, and the first tenor may need to sing the alto part for a measure or two. This requires frequent vocal testing in order to know how to pivot voices.

Learning to place students by appropriate voicings takes much experience and a real knowledge of student voice ranges. There are a number of possible solutions at the middle school level, and much of the voicing will depend upon the available students and their vocal stages. What works one year may not work the next. The key is to be flexible, and when nothing fits, to arrange music that does!

STUDY AND DISCUSSION QUESTIONS

1. What are the personal characteristics needed to be a choral director for adolescents?
2. What can happen to students' self-esteem during adolescence, and for which gender does it appear to be a greater problem? Why?
3. How do choral programs traditionally shortchange girls? Why does this happen?
4. Why is peer approval so important to most adolescents?
5. What is the emotional nature of most teenagers, and how can they be helped?
6. What are the physical characteristics of the female voice change?
7. What is the dominant characteristic of adolescent female voice quality, and how can this quality be improved?
8. How should younger female adolescents be classified for singing parts?
9. What are the physical characteristics of the male voice change?
10. What are the two schools of thought regarding the stages of male vocal maturation?
11. What does vocal registration have to do with the male voice change?
12. What can be done to improve the voice quality of adolescents in general?
13. How can boys be taught to sing with ease above pitch e^1?
14. How many male voice parts are possible in an eighth-grade chorus, and what are the approximate ranges according to Sally Herman?
15. What is meant by the phrase "this too shall pass," and why do teenagers need to be reminded of this often?

16. When might canons be appropriate song material for middle school choirs?

17. How can boys be assigned to sing two-part treble music and two-part male music?

18. How does traditional SAB music differ from three-part mixed music and from three-part mixed with optional baritone?

19. What voicings are appropriate for an all-male chorus in the middle school?

20. What practice makes it possible to use some easier four-part (SATB) music in the middle school chorus? Describe this process.

REFERENCES

AAUW (1991). *Shortchanging girls, shortchanging America*. New York: American Association of University Women.

———— (1992). *The AAUW report: How schools shortchange girls*. New York: Marlowe.

Alderson, R. (1979). *Complete handbook of voice training*. West Nyack, NY: Parker.

Ayres, L. Y., and K. Roduner (1942). *Adolescent voice ranges and materials published for adolescent voices*. Eugene: University of Oregon Monographs.

Barresi, A. L. (1984). From uncertainty to understanding: A new approach to instruction about the changing voice. In M. Runfola and L. Bash (eds.), *Proceedings: Research Symposium on the Male Adolescent Voice*, 155–65. Buffalo: State University of New York.

Beery, L. (1996). Appropriate voicings for middle school chorus. *Choral Journal, 36*(8), 15–20.

Bottoms, J. F. (1995). Investigation of William Vennard's light mechanism principle in the adolescent female voice (doctoral diss., University of Colorado at Boulder). *Dissertation Abstracts International, 56*(09), 3493.

Carlson, S. A. (1993). Want the boys in your middle-school choir? Use a competitive challenge system to motivate and teach. *Choral Journal, 33*(9), 27–29.

Coffman, W. (1987). The changing voice: The elementary challenge. *Choral Journal, 28*(3), 5–7.

Collins, D. L. (1993). *Teaching choral music*. Englewood Cliffs, NJ: Prentice Hall.

Cooksey, J. M. (1992). *Working with the adolescent male voice*. St. Louis, MO: Concordia.

Cooper, I. (1953). *Changing voices in junior high: Letters to Pat*. New York: Carl Fischer.

DeYoung, R. (1958). *The singer's art: An analysis of voice principles*. Chicago: DePaul University Press.

Emge, S. W. (1997). The adolescent male: Vocal registers as affecting vocal range, register competence and comfort in singing (doctoral diss., The University of Iowa). *Dissertation Abstracts International,* 57(05), 1987A.

Fett, D. L. (1994). The adolescent female voice: The effect of vocal skills instruction on measures of singing performance and breath management (doctoral diss., The University of Iowa). *Dissertation Abstracts International, 54*(07), 2501A.

Gackle, M. L. (1987). The effect of selected vocal techniques for breath management, resonation, and vowel unification on tone production in the junior high school female voice (doctoral diss., University of Miami). *Dissertation Abstracts International, 48*(04), 862A.

———— (1991). The adolescent female voice: Characteristics of change and stages of development. *Choral Journal, 31*(8), 17–25.

Groom, M. D. (1979). A descriptive analysis of development in adolescent male voices during the summer time period (doctoral diss., Florida State University). *Dissertation Abstracts International, 40*(09), 4945A.

Herman, S. (1988). *Building a pyramid of musicianship*. San Diego, CA: Curtis Music Press, Neil A. Kjos Music, distributor.

Jackson, R. Q., and L. D. Booher (1985). Junior-high choral directors: a special breed. *Choral Journal, 25*(7), 27–28.

Joseph, W. A. (1959). The relationship between vocal growth in the human adolescent, and the total growth process (doctoral diss., Boston University). *Dissertation Abstracts, 20*, 1388.

Kahane, J. C. (1978). A morphological study of the human prepubertal and pubertal larynx. *American Journal of Anatomy, 151*, 11–19.

Kindlon, D., and M. Thompson (1999). *Raising Cain: Protecting the emotional life of boys*. New York: Ballantine Books.

McKenzie, D. (1956). *Training the boy's voice*. New Brunswick, NJ: Rutgers University Press.

Maddox, D. (1986). A study for developing the head voice to improve pitch singing accuracy of adolescent girls classified as non-singers (masters thesis, University of Missouri, Kansas City).

May, J. A., and B. B. Williams (1989). The girl's changing voice. *Update: Applications of Research in Music Education, 8*(1), 20–23.

Mayer, F. D., and J. Sacher (1964). The changing voice. *American Choral Review, 6*(2), 8, 10–12.

O'Toole, P. (1998). A missing chapter from choral methods books: How choirs neglect girls. *Choral Journal, 39*(5), 9–32.

Phillips, K. H. (1992). *Teaching kids to sing*. New York: Schirmer Books.

——— (1995). The changing voice: An albatross? *Choral Journal, 35*(10), 25–27.

Phillips, K. H., and D. L. Fett (1992). Breathing and its relationship to vocal quality among adolescent female singers. *Journal of Research in Singing and Applied Vocal Pedagogy, 15*(2), 1–12.

Roe, P. F. (1983). *Choral music education* (2d ed.). Prospect Heights, IL: Waveland Press.

Rutkowski, J. (1984). Two year results of a longitudinal study investigating the validity of Cooksey's theory for training the adolescent male. In M. Runfola and L. Bash (eds.), *Proceedings: Research Symposium on the Male Adolescent Voice*, 86–96. Buffalo: State University of New York at Buffalo.

Sataloff, R. T., and J. Spiegel (1991). The young voice. In R. T. Sataloff and I. R. Titze (eds.), *Vocal Health and Science: A Compilation of Articles from the NATS Bulletin and the NATS Journal*. Jacksonville, FL: National Association of Teachers of Singing.

Sipley, K. (1994). The effects of vocal exercises and information about the voice on the tone quality and self-image of adolescent female singers (doctoral diss., Texas Tech University). *Dissertation Abstracts International, 54*(08), 2940A.

Swanson, F. J. (1959). Voice mutation in the adolescent male: An experiment in guiding the voice development of adolescent boys in general music classes (doctoral diss., University of Wisconsin). *Dissertation Abstracts, 20*, 2718.

——— (1973). *Music teaching in the junior high and middle school*. Englewood Cliffs, NJ: Prentice Hall.

——— (1977a). *The male singing voice ages eight to eighteen*. Cedar Rapids, IA: Ingram.

——— (1977b). The vanishing basso profundo and fry tones. *Choral Journal, 17*(5), 5–6.

Vennard, W. (1967). *Singing: The mechanism and the technique*. New York: Carl Fischer.

Williams, B. (1990). An investigation of selected female singing- and speaking-voice characteristics through a comparison of a group of pre-menarcheal girls to a group of post-menarcheal girls (doctoral diss., University of North Texas). *Dissertation Abstracts International*, 51(11), 1544A.

Yarrington, J. (1990). *Building the youth choir: Training and motivating teenage singers*. Minneapolis: Augsburg Fortress Press.

8 | Planning for Discipline and Choir Conduct

Discipline—just the thought of this word makes even veteran teachers uncomfortable. "Student teachers and beginning teachers usually cite either discipline problems or the possibility of losing class control as their number one concern as they approach teaching assignments" (Elrod, 1976, p. 47).

It is not uncommon for students to display a lack of control and poor manners in school. Much of this stems from poor discipline habits in the home and society in general. "A cursory glance at the state of modern education shows that teachers are asked to assume more and more of the responsibilities that used to be the teaching province of the family" (Jorgensen and Pfeiler, 1995, p. 7). Teachers must be prepared to deal with disruptions in the learning environment if learning is to take place. An orderly classroom, free from distractions, is a primary requirement for educational progress.

Good discipline does not just happen. It requires forethought and planning on the part of the choral director. The teacher who walks into the classroom unprepared for behavior problems is asking for trouble. Students are going to misbehave, and it is the purpose of this chapter to recommend ways in which choral directors can anticipate the inevitable, have a plan of action, enforce the plan, and move on without disrupting the entire educational process. This plan of action involves knowing and employing the characteristics of good teaching, understanding the basic modes of discipline, establishing basic rules and consequences, enlisting help, and managing the classroom setting.

ATTRIBUTES OF GOOD TEACHING

Everyone has had good teachers and poor teachers, and it isn't difficult to tell the difference when sitting in a classroom. It is sometimes more difficult to be objective about good teaching when trying to describe it in words. The following characteristics often are mentioned (Acheson and Gall, 1997, p. 24):

Characteristics of a Good Teacher

- Has positive relationships with students
- Deals with students' emotions
- Maintains discipline and control
- Creates a favorable environment for learning
- Recognizes and provides for individual differences
- Enjoys working with students

- Obtains students' involvement in learning
- Is creative and innovative
- Emphasizes teaching of reading skills
- Gives students a good self-image
- Engages in professional growth activities
- Knows subject matter in depth
- Is flexible
- Is consistent
- Displays fairness

The above list of effective teaching characteristics has been summarized by Acheson and Gall (1997) as follows:

> The tasks of teaching include: (1) providing instruction in academic knowledge and skills; (2) providing an instructional climate that helps students develop positive attitudes toward school and self; (3) adjusting instruction in response to students' ability, ethnic identification, home background, and gender; (4) managing the classroom context so that students are engaged in learning; (5) making sound decisions and plans; and (6) implementing curriculum change. (p. 44)

These six tasks must be done well if the choral director is going to be effective, especially the fourth, "managing the classroom," which is a challenge when ensembles are large.

Effective Discipline

Carolyn Evertson (1987) has summarized several practices that effective classroom managers use:

> (1) careful analysis of the rules and procedures that need to be in place so that students can learn effectively in the classroom; (2) a statement of the rules and procedures in simple, clear language so that students can understand them easily; (3) systematic teaching of the rules and procedures at the start of the school year; and (4) constant monitoring and careful record keeping of students' academic work and behavior. (pp. 52–53)

These practices were observed by researchers in elementary and junior high classes but are equally applicable to senior high classrooms.

In characterizing good music teachers, Frederick Swanson (1973) gives the following five qualities:

> (1) The students have to feel that the teacher is on their side, that he/she wants them to succeed; (2) These good teachers are very explicit in what they expect; (3) There is an established routine; (4) These good disciplinarians are fair and consistent, and (5) Around each of these good disciplinarians is an aura of dignity, of being a person of special worth and authority, a person definitely in charge and quite capable of being in charge. (pp. 268–69)

This last characteristic—an aura of dignity—is perhaps the most difficult for new teachers to cultivate. In some cases, the beginning teacher will not be much older than the students. The best recommendation is that new teachers need to be businesslike and go about their duties with a sense of confidence, even when confidence is lacking. The old adage "don't smile until Christmas" has significance. It doesn't mean that teachers cannot be pleasant, but it does imply not acting like friends with students. To do so undermines the very teacher-student relationship that is necessary for classroom order. Once that line is crossed, it is most difficult to regain the necessary respect for being the one who is running the class or conducting the rehearsal. Telling jokes in class may work for veteran teachers, but it should be avoided by beginning teachers.

Appropriate Attire

Another way to establish an "aura of dignity" is to dress appropriately as a professional. Teacher dress codes have relaxed in the last several decades, and this may work against young teachers who look similar to older students. A male teacher need not wear a coat and tie, nor a female teacher a dress, to look professional. However, the more teachers look like students in their attire the greater chance the "aura" will be missing. Dress typically reflects the occasion, and when people are dressed up they tend to act with more dignity, which in turn engenders greater respect from those being addressed.

Teachers should avoid wearing trendy clothing reflective of styles that are "in" or "cool" among students. Such clothing is often a fad worn to establish identity. Many students have a strong need not to dress like adults. They are striving for independence, and attire is one way they make such a statement. When teachers dress like students or in fashions that are unusual for the average teacher, they are placing themselves in positions to be ridiculed or talked about behind their backs.

Commanding Voice

The level or command of voice with which a teacher speaks is extremely important in running an orderly rehearsal. New teachers frequently make the mistake of speaking in a conversational tone that is easily tuned out. A voice that is well modulated, easily understood, and loud enough to be heard in all parts of the room is necessary for the effective teacher.

Students who study basic acting learn to project the voice without straining the vocal mechanism. This ability to project should come naturally to singers, but students often do not realize the necessity of using the same breath support for public speaking as is used for singing.

It may help students who have trouble with voice projection to think of teaching as a form of acting. Actors cultivate many voice types to accommodate the various roles they play, and so, too, teachers need to cultivate voices that are different for the roles they occupy. "Group leader" is one voice that needs to be in every teacher's repertoire.

Teachers use their voices constantly and need to safeguard the vocal mechanism. Choral directors who shout instructions over the choir's talking and singing, or who sing along with the choir, are candidates for vocal fatigue. It is highly recommended that all teachers speak somewhat higher when teaching than for normal conversation. Speaking in a slightly elevated manner thins the vocal cords and causes them to make less contact. This results in vocal folds that do not swell with repeated use. The less contact the vocal folds make, the healthier the voice.

Some teachers develop vocal nodules from speaking too low and too loudly on a consistent basis. Voice rest is mandated for this disorder, and speech therapy may be needed to correct faulty speech habits. The speaking voice for a teacher is the major vehicle of communication; it should be protected by using good speech habits. Dr. Morton Cooper has written a helpful book, *Change Your Voice, Change Your Life* (1984), for those experiencing vocal problems.

Enthusiasm

No one wants to sit and listen to a boring teacher, especially adolescents whose attention spans are notoriously short. Effective teachers are stimulating; their enthusiasm for what they teach is infectious and easily caught by their students. Likewise, choral directors who love the music they are teaching need to show it in the manner they rehearse and conduct.

There are "Type A" and "Type B" personalities. The Type A can have a natural advantage in teaching—they are typically more outgoing people. When Type A directors are in front of a choir they easily command attention; the rehearsal room is electrified by their enthusiasm and high-paced teaching. They are fun to work for, and students become charged.

One danger of Type A leadership is the director who ends up working harder than the students. In fact, these directors may feel as if they are constantly "whipping" the choir into shape. Such a style becomes exhausting for the director and choristers alike. While enthusiasm is desirable, it should not result in pushing the rehearsal pace so fast that exhaustion is inevitable. Hard work—yes. Exhaustion—no.

Type B personalities can be very effective choral directors if they learn to move beyond their own reserved manner to one that is outward and demonstrative. While this requires some acting ability, it greatly stimulates a choir when the leader is excited about what he or she is teaching. The Type B needs to cultivate a higher level of communication if students are to be excited about singing. One way to do this is to use the voice effectively in a well-modulated, projected manner. Another is to learn the art of exaggerated conducting. Type B tends to underconduct, while Type A often overconducts. Good balance is needed to inspire singers and, at the same time, stay out of the way of the music.

Whatever personality type the choral director displays, a positive attitude and high expectations are paramount for success. Even when feeling ill or psychologically "down," the choral director must be "up" and positive when approaching the choir. Students will mirror the conductor's attitude, good or bad. A choral conductor who goes into rehearsal with a negative attitude often reflects a negativity that is picked up by the students; the results are typically less than satisfying. Sometimes it takes a conscious effort on the part of the choral conductor to "psyche" themselves up for yet another rehearsal. This is not acting phony—it is just acting the part.

FOUR MODES OF DISCIPLINE

Four basic modes of discipline are observed in the teaching profession: (1) authoritarian, (2) neglectful, (3) permissive, and (4) authoritative. Each of these modes or styles of classroom management has two main characteristics: (1) high or low control and (2) orientation toward either the teacher or the student (see Figure 8.1).

Authoritarian

The authoritarian style is indicative of teachers who have a high level of control in the classroom but whose motivation for teaching stems from meeting their own needs first. This is the type of teacher who, in demanding quiet, may use insults, put-downs, or abusive language. They appear to have little regard for students' feelings and generally do not care what students feel or think. The rule is to be obeyed, and there are few exceptions. If a student does poorly on a test because of illness or other extenuating circumstances, there is no latitude in permitting extra work or a test retake. Such teachers often are feared by students, who typically do not feel free to communicate on a more personal level with authoritarian types.

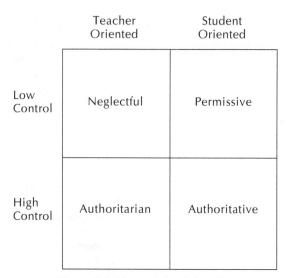

Figure 8.1. Four modes of discipline.

The authoritarian style of discipline does have one advantage—a high level of classroom order. By ruling with an iron fist, teachers who use this mode of management have little trouble with classroom disruptions. Solutions are simple—students are assigned detention or sent to the office. Little effort is made to get to the heart of the problem. Students are expected to behave, and if they don't they are punished.

Regarding the authoritarian discipline style, R. Louis Rossman states in the MENC publication *TIPS: Discipline in the Music Classroom* (1989):

> Remember that students are valuable individuals with a right to self-respect, pride, and dignity. They deserve to be treated with respect and politeness, and their personal integrity should not be questioned or attacked. Sarcasm and causing embarrassment are not appropriate and are often interpreted as ridicule by sensitive adolescents. (p. 4)

Rossman also reports that depersonalization "is the most frequent cause of disruptive behavior in schools" (p. 3). Teachers who are not motivated first by students' concerns are likely to depersonalize the educational process.

The authoritarian mode of discipline is faulty and should be avoided. While it may result in good control, it does so at the expense of students and a healthy and stimulating classroom environment.

Neglectful

The neglectful mode of discipline is, again, teacher oriented. However, teachers adopting this style show little control in the classroom. They have a typical "don't care" attitude and expect little from students as long as students expect little from them. These teachers may be burned out or are so lazy and unmotivated that little is accomplished in their classrooms. They use the same old lesson plans, allow students a great deal of freedom in disrupting class, are easily taken off the subject, and are more eager for the class to end than the students.

Neglectful teachers give the teaching profession a bad reputation. While every profession has its misfits, neglectful teachers stand out; adolescents are very critical when it comes to voicing opinions regarding such people.

A neglectful teaching style can be a hazard to students' well-being, both physically and mentally. Students in such environments often fool around in class, with the possibility arising of someone's becoming physically injured. The greater injury, however, is when students are poorly motivated and lose interest in the subject matter. Neglectful teachers should be identified by school administrators and given help or counseled out of the profession. They either entered the profession for the wrong reasons or were mistaken in their choice of a vocation.

Permissive

Permissive teachers love kids—they just don't know how to make students behave. Somewhere in their teacher preparation background, or in the models they have witnessed, these teachers have failed to understand the necessity for law and order. Their classrooms are legendary for breeding chaos, and anarchy seems to rule. They may be very much loved by their students, as these teachers are rarely demanding or abusive, and yet little is accomplished. The teaching environment is so noisy and disruptive as to make educational progress all but impossible.

In their love for students, permissive teachers let students have their own way. These teachers are regularly inconsistent in what they demand and in how they enforce the rules. They will make threat after threat but rarely follow through on any demand. When they do enforce a rule, it may be so unexpected that students become openly hostile and turn against them.

Beginning teachers are likely to adopt the permissive mode when they try to get students to like them. By becoming "friends" they hope to win students over, thus making the classroom environment positive and friendly. The opposite happens—students have so much freedom that they become noisy, often abusive, and generally out of control. Such teachers want to do the right thing; they just do not seem to know how. They also may be mismatched to the age level they are teaching or to their chosen vocation. In any case, they need help, and school administrators should work with them to get things under control, or they should be dismissed. Learning cannot progress well in such an environment.

Authoritative

The fourth mode of discipline, authoritative, is characterized by a high student orientation and a high level of order in the classroom. A teacher using this style of management is said to be assertive but not domineering. "The most successful teacher . . . is one who is patient, conscientious, and honest and who teaches with authority and kindness" (Rossman, 1987, p. 4).

Authoritative teachers choose teaching as a profession because they like to work with people, especially young people, and are dedicated to making life better through the process of education. They understand that a high level of order and control are necessary if education is to take place, and they plan accordingly. The assertive teacher does not wait for discipline problems to happen but anticipates disruptions and appropriate actions as needed. As much as possible, they do not permit behavioral problems to interrupt the flow of learning in the classroom.

The following twelve guidelines are given as areas of human relations that authoritative teachers maximize (Elrod, 1976, pp. 48–50):

1. Attempt to be firm and fair in your treatment of students.
2. Be consistent in your behavior in the classroom.
3. Attempt to be thoroughly planned and well organized each day that you teach.
4. Make few rules in the beginning.
5. Try to maintain a sense of humor.
6. Make your class interesting.
7. Provide your students with feedback about their work and attempt to make it quick and positive.
8. Know your students.
9. Be yourself. Know yourself.
10. Be flexible.
11. Know your subject.
12. Practice what you preach.

Elrod states, "Research indicates that more teachers fail because of inability to cope with personal relationships with people than fail due to a lack of subject matter knowledge" (p. 50). Teaching is a people-oriented field. Assertive teachers like people and work to maximize relationships with students while maintaining that "aura of dignity."

Rossman (1989) provides the checklist in Figure 8.2 as a self-check for the authoritative teaching style. Teachers occasionally should check themselves against these characteristics to see how well they are doing at being effective teachers.

Checklist for Teacher Self-Assessment

_____ Organized		_____ Has effective lessons
_____ Establishes rules		_____ Has sense of humor
_____ Knows the students		_____ Praises
_____ Consistent		_____ Predictable
_____ Self-aware		_____ Self-controlled
_____ Self-assured		_____ Knowledgeable
_____ Sensitive		_____ Sensible
_____ Enthusiastic		_____ Energetic
_____ Sincere		_____ Fair
_____ Flexible		_____ Friendly
_____ Observant		_____ Specific
_____ Respects		_____ Prevents

Figure 8.2. Teacher self-assessment, from *TIPS: Discipline in the Music Classroom*, comp. R. Louis Rossman (MENC, 1989).

BASIC RULES, CONSEQUENCES, AND ENLISTING HELP

Carefully formulated rules and procedures are at the center of good classroom management. Such rules and procedures should be decided upon before classes begin and are best when brief and phrased in a positive manner. Regulations should be posted in the classroom, included in the choir handbook, and reviewed regularly, especially when new classes begin. Rules need to be as few in number as possible, explicit, realistic, enforceable, and consistent with school regulations.

Code of Conduct

The choral director establishes a set of rules that govern rehearsal conduct before the students ever enter the classroom. The following is a list of twenty-one possible regulations that are commonly used by choral directors in building a code of conduct:

- Be on time.
- Demonstrate a positive attitude.
- Show respect for others and their property.
- Always bring a pencil (not a pen) to mark music.
- Respect the opinion and discretion of the director.
- Study your part while others are rehearsing.
- Leave all food (including gum) and drink outside the rehearsal room.
- No disruptive talking.
- Accept criticism positively.
- Leave the room only when dismissed by the director.
- Speak properly without the use of profanity.
- Follow instructions.
- Demonstrate a desire to learn and a willingness to succeed.
- Maintain your grades for eligibility.
- Place your music folder in the proper location in the folder cabinet.
- Be physically and mentally prepared for rehearsal.
- Be courteous to all.
- Be responsible for music that is assigned to you.
- Maintain orderliness and patience.
- Keep criticisms to yourself.
- Permit the director to direct.

While all of these rules may be important to a well-disciplined rehearsal, there are too many for a basic list of regulations. Choral directors need to review these examples and others and make a short list (no more than six is recommended) that they feel are most important to an efficient rehearsal process.

One way to shorten the list of rules would be to have input from student leaders. When students have some ownership of the rules, and this knowledge is shared with the choir, a sense of fairness is established. The rules, then, are not dictated but rather agreed upon by the director and the student leadership council.

Sometimes directors have another set of regulations for concert behavior. Rules might include the maintenance of good stage presence, wearing the appropriate attire, exhibiting good audience skills when not performing, remaining on task, and so forth.

Rules and regulations must be enforced without favoritism if they are to be respected by students. If it becomes clear that some students are treated more harshly than others, or if some students get away with breaches of conduct, the code of conduct will soon become meaningless.

With younger groups especially, it is a good practice to place the code of conduct at the front of the room in large letters and in a conspicuous place (e.g., above the chalkboard). In this way the rules are always before the students, and the code can be referred to easily when offenders must be cautioned—for example, "Kyle, that was a violation of rule number two," and the student has his or her first warning.

Consequences

The consequences for violating the choir's code of conduct also must be explicitly written, available in published form, and reviewed with students before a problem occurs. Ignorance of the law is not justifiable when students and parents have been advised of the rules and consequences at the beginning of a school year.

The following process is recommended when establishing a plan for attending to discipline problems:

- *Leave things alone*. Brief and minor disturbances may not be worth the interruption of classroom learning. Sometimes, just a look at the offender(s) with nothing said will stop the violation.

- *End the offense indirectly*. If learning is being disrupted, give a simple warning to the offender(s). Cite the rule being violated. With younger students a "time out" area in the room may be used to isolate the problem.

- *End the offense with a penalty*. A verbal warning may be accompanied with a demerit or "strike." Some directors use a baseball system: three strikes and you're out, which means an hour of detention. Avoid giving schoolwork as punishment, as something that should be a positive will take on a negative connotation.

- *Attend more fully*. When serious disruptions occur, send a student to the office for help, if warranted. This may stop the offense immediately. Address the offenders in a firm voice and separate them from their regular seats, but do not place them in the hall. (Teachers are responsible for all students assigned to them at any given time, and it is not possible to tell what students may do in the hallway.) Following the rehearsal, speak to the students individually. Indicate a dislike for the behavior and not the person. Detention or in-school suspension may be assigned, or more serious consequences considered. Calls the parents *before* the student goes home. A written warning is appropriate.

- *Remove the offender*. Students who constantly violate the code of conduct should have their membership terminated in the ensemble. Choir is a group activity requiring cooperation from all its members. A person who constantly impedes the flow of learning should be removed, even if he or she is one of the best singers. There can be no special privileges for repeat offenders. Removal should be preceded by active communication with the student's parents or guardians, and permission to terminate the student should be received from the proper administrator.

All infractions of the rules should be documented with the date for each student offense. This needs to occur immediately following rehearsals, or it may be done with a check-list system that the director has available during the rehearsal. If a recurrent problem becomes serious enough that detention is assigned, a student's grade is affected, or a student is removed from choir, the documentation will be there to back the decision in case the teacher's decision is challenged.

Enlisting Help

The choral director can receive help with discipline in a number of ways and from a variety of sources that include parents, colleagues, administrators, and student leaders. "Going it alone" is not necessary when it comes to classroom management.

HELP FROM PARENTS. A telephone call to parents is one of the most useful discipline tools that a teacher can employ. One phone call is all it usually takes to stop an offender from repeated disruptions. When calling parents or guardians, it is important to be professional and factual. Emphasis must be on how the learning environment is being disrupted and not on the director's emotional well-being. Some people are very defensive of their children; arguments are to be avoided at all costs.

When cooperation is not forthcoming, the choral director should suggest a personal conference with the offender and parents. If this fails to materialize or resolve the problem, the director requests a conference with the appropriate administrators, parents or guardians, and student. Proper documentation will be extremely important at this level, especially if removal of the student from choir is being recommended.

The following guidelines are for use in meetings with parents and guardians (Woolfolk, 1993, p. 417):

- Begin with a positive comment.
- Be able to give specific examples of misbehavior.
- Avoid characterizing the student, e.g., "Kim is lazy."
- Listen actively. Parents will usually respond.
- Establish a partnership by offering specific ways in which the student can be helped.
- Plan follow-up contacts.
- End with a positive statement.

HELP FROM COLLEAGUES. New teachers should turn to veteran colleagues for help when discipline becomes challenging. Some beginning teachers are afraid to do this; they do not want to appear weak or unsuited for the job. This is not a good reason to resist asking for advice. There are programs where new teachers are mentored by veteran teachers in other school districts. This relieves the worry of someone in the same school district knowing too much about a colleague, and it provides a great link to a music teacher in another district.

HELP FROM ADMINISTRATORS. Beginning teachers should not hesitate to seek help from the appropriate administrators when discipline problems are becoming a major distraction. Help should be available through mentoring, workshops, and videotaping of lessons. However, teachers need to be careful about "dumping" their discipline problems on the main office. Administrators want to know that teachers are in control of their classrooms and want to see evidence of actions' being taken before they are called to evaluate a given situation. Part of a teacher's responsibilities includes the handling of discipline problems.

HELP FROM STUDENT LEADERS.   Student leaders may be called upon to provide some indirect help in curtailing behavior problems. When a section leader is asked to help with unrest in a section, a subtle type of peer influence can do wonders for focus and discipline. Rossman (1989) states: "Give leadership responsibility to as many students as practical. When individuals assume responsibility for some portion of the organization, they invest something of themselves in the outcome of that endeavor" (p. 13). Some potential leadership roles include student director, accompanist, section leaders, librarians, and wardrobe managers.

GUIDELINES FOR CLASSROOM MANAGEMENT

Once the rules and consequences have been established and communicated to students and parents, consideration must be given to managing the choral rehearsal in an orderly and efficient manner. A good lesson/rehearsal plan is the first step in providing for a well-managed rehearsal. Objectives, content, procedures, flow—all are important elements to be considered before the rehearsal begins.

An Exemplary Music Educator

What is it that outstanding music educators do in their teaching that can serve as a model for all music teachers? This was the research question asked by Gerald King in "a 10-month naturalistic study of a teacher who has gained an international reputation as an exemplary educator in a single setting for more than 25 years" (1998, p. 57). The subject of the investigation was David I. Dunnet, a distinguished and honored Canadian music teacher. In observing and recording Dunnet's teaching style, King identified four major themes as being significant in helping to understand the characteristics of the exemplary music educator. The following are excerpts from the article (pp. 62–68):

- **Theme 1: High level verbal and non-verbal language is essential to become an exemplary teacher.** . . . excellent communication skills are crucial to quality teaching and . . . the ability to express oneself is an asset.

- **Theme 2: Routines and organization provide the framework for artistry in teaching**. Other researchers also have found that routine and organization are characteristics of expert teachers (Brand, 1990; Lautzenheiser, 1990; Merrion, 1990).

- **Theme 3: Humor is essential for exemplary teaching**. Many future educators reading the literature may interpret a sense of humor to mean the ability to tell jokes. It is my experience with undergraduate education students that many believe that if they can tell a few jokes they will have greater success in the classroom. Dave's humor is not haphazard; it is based on thought. Dave's humor is subtle, natural, and intellectual. It requires students to listen carefully and make meaning of the humor. Dave uses humor to keep students on task, to explain and reinforce concepts, and to nurture relationships.

- **Theme 4: A quality environment is conducive to quality teaching and learning.** Purkey and Novak (1984) state that the environment greatly affects student self-concept. They also state that a quality school environment is similar to a quality family environment; that is, an environment whereby individual respect, cooperative spirit, sense of belonging, pleasing habitat, and positive expectations are fundamental qualities.

The Classroom Environment

It may come as a surprise that one of King's four themes for exemplary teaching is a quality environment. This includes not only a social environment that is conducive to learning but the physical environment as well.

REHEARSAL ROOM.   The classroom setting should be prepared before students enter. The neatness and orderliness of the room sets the stage for an orderly rehearsal. "Both you and the students will respond to a productive environment in which the needs and functions of the class have been considered and in which an aura of purpose and order is apparent" (Rossman, 1989, p. 10).

NAMES OF STUDENTS.   Students are real people and expect to be called by their correct names. Teachers need to learn students' names as quickly as possible. Instead of calling the roll and stumbling over pronunciations, Sally Herman (1988) suggests that students be requested to pronounce their own names. This gives the teacher the opportunity to listen to the correct pronunciation and to find the name on the record sheet.

ORDER OF REHEARSAL.   Writing the order of music on the chalkboard gives students an overview of what is to be accomplished. It also helps them to put their music in the correct order, saving precious rehearsal time. Some directors even go so far as to indicate the approximate time at which each selection will be started. This practice makes for fine-tuned organization and helps the director to move ahead when the rehearsal may be bogging down on one choral selection.

OPENING ACTIVITIES.   The choral director who meets students at the door upon entry to the classroom discourages prerehearsal disruption and horseplay. This takes some discipline on the part of the director, but it is a technique worth cultivating. It also presents a time for the director to interact individually with students.

Upon entering the room, older students can begin the warm-up process on their own with a series of physical stretching exercises. This procedure puts this part of the warm-up out of the way before the late bell rings and saves rehearsal time. It also discourages prerehearsal disruption and general fooling around.

The rehearsal needs to begin on time; students entering late should not be permitted to disrupt the flow of the warm-up. Some system of accounting for tardiness and absence must be in place. It should require little time and effort from the director. A student secretary can be used to take attendance.

ANNOUNCEMENTS.   It is better if the rehearsal does not begin with announcements. If necessary, announcements may follow the introductory activities, or be planned for the middle or end of the rehearsal. Placing announcements on the chalkboard saves rehearsal time. A choir newsletter also saves time. When presenting announcements verbally, the director should not talk over the students' talking. If the announcements are important enough to take rehearsal time, they are important for all students to hear.

ATTENTION SIGNAL.   An opening routine of warm-up and sight-reading activities brings focus to the beginning of the rehearsal. Some type of attention-getting signal is appropriate, and the choral director must avoid yelling over students' talking to get them quiet. If students are stretching before the class begins, focus already will have been established. The conductor stepping onto the podium may be a signal, or the clapping of a rhythm pattern that is echoed. A simple posture gesture to indicate standing is another signal that the rehearsal is beginning.

REHEARSAL PACING.   The pace of the rehearsal should be as fast as possible without being rushed. The rehearsal plan provides a guide to pacing but may be modified as needed. Transitions between selections for some directors is a "down time" when quiet talking is permitted. This is a matter of personal choice, but a uniform policy needs to be established and communicated to the students. Again, some signal that the rehearsal is about to resume is needed if a brief period of talking is permitted between selections.

DISRUPTIVE TALKING.   Talking seems to be a big aggravation in some choral rehearsals. Students become bored when sitting and listening to other parts rehearse. A firm rule in the code of conduct should discourage this practice, but students may talk if they have nothing to do. Therefore, choral directors should resist having nonrehearsing students sit for longer than a couple of minutes without an activity being assigned. Such activities can include studying the text, writing in phonetic symbols above the text, working on a comprehensive musicianship worksheet that pertains to the pieces being studied, working on music theory worksheets, following one's own part while another part is sung against it, and so forth.

Sally Herman (1988) recommends rehearsal time be saved and talking minimized by having each section of the choir rehearse in a different corner of the room. A cassette tape and battery-powered playback equipment is necessary for each group. The director must make as many tapes as there are voice parts. Section leaders then lead the groups using the tapes as the director moves from group to group as needed. "The singers learn to focus in on their part and develop the skill of being able to execute that part with many other sound distractions" (p. 93). Herman does not recommend that every choral selection be learned this way but recommends it for more challenging literature. Tapes are especially helpful when learning a foreign text and when a substitute teacher is present.

POSITIVE NATURE.   The choral director needs to be positive and allow for times of humor. As noted previously, humor does not mean telling jokes, which typically leads to class disruption. Negativity and harsh comments breed an unsettling and unproductive environment. Even when under stress, the conductor must maintain a quiet disposition:

> When you are tempted to completely "blow your top," count to ten, and try to act as unemotionally and objectively as possible. Teachers must never lose their tempers. They may sometimes seem to become angry, but they must *never* actually lose control of their emotions. (Rossman, 1989, p. 18)

The maintenance of a positive demeanor also keeps teachers from overreacting to disruptions. When nothing else works, the rehearsal should be stopped until the disruptive behavior ceases, even if that means the termination of the rehearsal for the day. Working in chaos is to be avoided at all costs.

CONFRONTATIONS.   Teachers must avoid confrontations with students. It is counterproductive to argue, and students should never be threatened. In cases of violence or destructive behavior, directors must send someone for help. If a fight occurs between students, the director should not break it up alone—they are likely to be caught in the middle and used as a punching bag. Names of participants and witnesses must be written down and school authorities notified. Any audience that may have collected should be dispersed and school policy followed.

ANTICIPATE ACTIONS.   Becoming a good disciplinarian takes time, and new teachers will make many mistakes if they have not planned and anticipated their handling of discipline. It is recommended that beginning teachers run through "worst case" scenarios in their minds and practice deciding on courses of action. For example, what should teachers do if they pick the wrong suspect in a class disruption? Should they try to cover it up, or blame both people? Perhaps they should admit that they are human and make mistakes. By anticipating problems and consequent actions, a game plan will have been established as a guide for the real thing.

A Responsibility to Teach Discipline

Choral directors have many responsibilities, and one of them is to teach students how to act in a musical setting. Rossman (1989) states:

> Teach them how musicians treat one another personally, approach one another's music, rehearse, and behave at concerts. Music teachers share with other faculty members and parents the responsibility to teach general social behaviors to their students, who are citizens of the school, the community, and the world. (p. 23)

Teaching discipline is a big job, but it can be learned. Successful choral directors do it every day. They are successful because they have a philosophy of discipline and have thought through their expectations and plan of action before entering the first rehearsal.

STUDY AND DISCUSSION QUESTIONS

1. What element of teaching do student teachers and new teachers usually cite as their number one concern? Why?

2. Which two of the "characteristics of good teaching" do you think are most important, and why?

3. Why is an "aura of dignity" often difficult for new teachers to cultivate, and how can this be done by them?

4. Should teachers attempt to befriend students? Why or why not?

5. What are some guidelines for appropriate use of the voice by teachers?

6. What are some problems that Type A and Type B personalities may experience as choral conductors?

7. What are the two basic characteristics of each of the four modes of discipline, and which is the best model for teachers to emulate?

8. What does research indicate that more teachers fail at than anything else? Why is this?

9. What are some general guidelines for formulating rules and procedures for classroom discipline?

10. Which of the twenty-one rules for choir conduct do you think are most important? Are there rules that you would include that are not on this list? If yes, what are they?

11. What practice must be avoided by the director so as not to undermine the code of conduct?

12. Why should students not be placed in the hall for discipline purposes? Where could they be placed if removal from the class is necessary?

13. Why is documentation of student infractions of the discipline code necessary?

14. Who are some people to enlist help from in discipline matters?

15. When are phone calls to parents and guardians justified, and when should a parental conference be initiated by the choral director?

16. What are the four major characteristics of classroom management evidenced by an exemplary music educator? Is joke telling generally appropriate?

17. What elements of the classroom environment must the choral director attend to when preparing for and conducting a rehearsal?

18. What are some appropriate activities for the beginning of the rehearsal that will bring focus and a smooth beginning?

19. What are some suggestions for the elimination of talking during rehearsals?

20. Why is anticipating discipline action and planning rules and consequences so important to effective classroom management?

REFERENCES

Acheson, K. A., and M. D. Gall (1997). *Techniques in the clinical supervision of teachers*. New York: Longman.

Brand, M. (1990). Master music teachers: What makes them great? *Music Educators Journal, 77*(2), 22–25.

Cooper, M. C. (1984). *Change your voice, change your life*. New York: Macmillan. (paperback reprint, Scranton, PA, Harper Collins, 1985).

Elrod, W. (1976). Don't get tangled in discipline problems. *Music Educators Journal, 63*(4), 47–50.

Evertson, C. M. (1987). Managing classrooms: A framework for teachers. In D. C. Berliner and B. V. Rosenshine (eds.), *Talks to teachers*, 52–74. New York: Random House.

Herman, S. (1988). *Building a pyramid of musicianship*. San Diego, CA: Curtis Music Press, Neil A. Kjos Music, distributor.

Jorgensen, N. S., and C. Pfeiler (1995). *Things they never taught you in choral methods*. Milwaukee, WI: Hal Leonard.

King, G. (1998). Exemplary music educator: A case study. *Bulletin of the Council for Research in Music Education, 137*, 57–71.

Lautzenheiser, T. (1990). Motivation and the master music teacher. *Music Educators Journal, 77*(2), 34–36.

Merrion, M. (1990). How master teachers handle discipline. *Music Educators Journal, 77*(2), 26–29.

Purkey, W., and J. Novak (1984). *Inviting school success: A self-concept approach to teaching and learning*. Belmont, CA: Wadsworth.

Rossman, R. L. (1989). *TIPS: Discipline in the music classroom*. Reston, VA: Music Educators National Conference.

Swanson, F. J. (1973). *Music teaching in the junior high and middle school*. Englewood Cliffs, NJ: Prentice Hall.

Woolfolk, A. E. (1993). *Educational psychology*. Boston: Allyn and Bacon.

9 | Choosing the Music

Choosing music for teaching and performance is one of the most difficult jobs for the choral conductor. What may work with one group may not work with other groups; it remains a constant challenge to find the right music for the right set of circumstances. Music is expensive, and little money can be wasted on music that turns out to be a mistake. The objective is to build a library of quality choral music that can be used repeatedly.

Most vocal music majors have experienced a considerable amount of choral music by the time they graduate from college. This can be a help or a hindrance. Beginning choral conductors sometimes choose music for their own school choirs that they have sung in college. This music usually proves to be too difficult, and the novice can become discouraged by choosing music that is beyond the achievement level of his or her own choir. It is safe to say that a new choral director should err on the side of choosing music that is easy, rather than difficult. Finding something that singers can learn quickly and perform successfully provides a tremendous energy boost for a group and a conductor who are just getting used to one another. Difficulty level always can be increased once the strengths and weaknesses of a group are known.

GUIDELINES FOR CHOOSING QUALITY CHORAL LITERATURE

Quality choral literature is available today from numerous publishers (see Appendix A for a list of choral music publishers and websites). There is also much inferior literature, and the choral director must learn to tell the difference. In general, the music of well-known and respected composers will be better literature. Walter Ehret, in *The Choral Conductor's Handbook* (1959), provides the following checklist of general guidelines for the selection of good choral music:

Text

- Does it have literary value?
- Are the words easy to sing?
- Is the translation a good one?

Music

- Is it original in concept?
- Is it melodically, harmonically, and rhythmically interesting?
- Is its appeal lasting or only ephemeral?
- Is the musical setting in keeping with the style and mood of the text?

- Do the basic ideas grow as a whole?
- Is the part writing vocal rather than instrumental?
- Is it a good arrangement or overarranged?
- Are the ranges and tessituras suitable?
- Are the vocal lines interesting?
- Will it appeal to both performers and audience?
- Is it worth the effort to prepare for performance?
- Does the work fit into a balanced repertoire?
- Is it within the ability of the group to learn?
- Can its meaning be understood by the group so that a mature, emotional performance can result?
- Does the accompaniment enhance rather than detract?

Importance of the Text

Choosing music with a good text is important to the success of any choral composition. Is the text of literary value, are the words easy to sing, and if using a translation of a foreign text, is it a good translation? There is nothing wrong with using a good translation, but use of original languages is especially appropriate in a school setting where foreign languages are part of the curriculum. The choral conductor can emphasize the importance of foreign-language instruction by singing in foreign languages. This is a good way to build a working relationship between the choral area and the foreign-language department. Also, by retaining the original language, the beauty of the original setting is maintained—word syllables more closely match the notes. While an audience may not understand a foreign text, this can be overcome by providing a good translation.

Textual consideration is extremely important when choosing music for young teenagers. Adolescents will object to singing music they view to be textually immature or sentimental. Also, gender biases creep in as directors tend to look for music that is male oriented, feeling that girls will go along with the repertoire if the boys are happy. "This Old Hammer" will be a winner for most boys, who usually respond to more earthy texts, but girls may find it unappealing. Patricia O'Toole (1998) reflects this point of view when she writes:

> The majority of choral repertoire is about male experiences and written from the male perspective—even women's choirs' repertoire. Furthermore, it is expected that girls will comply with any repertoire choice. . . . One has to wonder how long boys would tolerate singing songs primarily about girls and songs written from the female perspective. Just as textbook companies have rethought the presentation (or lack thereof) of women in history, literature, social studies, and science, choral directors and music publishers need to respond to the same problems with choral music. As choral directors, we need to search for better texts for women to sing, even in the mixed-voice choir. (p. 20)

It takes great wisdom to choose choral music at all levels, and gender bias is an issue that has come of age. O'Toole's article provides some excellent resources and websites for locating choral materials and literature for women.

Importance of the Music

The second major element to consider when choosing literature is the quality of the music itself. The question must be asked, is the music worth the effort to prepare? It is not uncommon to work on a difficult piece, only to have the performance produce a weak aesthetic impression. Sometimes such an outcome cannot be predicted until the music has been sufficiently experienced. Selections that sound good at the piano may not sound nearly so good when sung by voices. Trying to avoid such an outcome is one of the demands placed on the choral director in choosing the music to learn and perform.

A good recording of a selection is an excellent way to gain the whole picture of a piece before selecting it for study. What is not apparent initially often becomes visible once the piece is experienced aurally. Much choral music is available today on cassette tape and CD, and many publishers now make available sample recordings of new releases. The *Choral Journal* contains a regular column titled "Compact Disc Reviews."

Considerations of range and tessitura are important when choosing music. Directors must know the "comfort zone" (tessitura) for the age level with which they are working and depart from it only when the music is not too demanding or taxing on the voice. Young tenors cannot abide a tessitura that "hangs high," and young altos should not be kept singing so low that they develop a break between their lower and upper vocal registers. Appropriate vocal ranges and tessituras are discussed in Chapter 4.

Choral Arrangements and Editions

There is a lot of choral literature to perform, and choral directors today can avoid choosing music of master composers that is arranged by someone else for other voicings. An SSA arrangement of Handel's "Hallelujah Chorus" is not a good idea—why tamper with genius? With sufficient SSA music available, choosing an arrangement that misrepresents an SATB masterwork is not necessary. Some arrangements merely simplify a work for use at a less demanding level. Again, the choral director needs to be suspicious of arrangements of masterworks unless it is known that the original ideas of the composer have not been violated.

Choral directors also should avoid choosing arrangements of instrumental works to which words have been added. This was a common practice in the days when good choral music was not so readily available. The second movement of Dvořák's *New World* Symphony does not need words (e.g., "Going Home"). The music of Dvořák stands on its own merit without any tampering. The choral art has a tremendous heritage of music from many centuries, and there is no need to resort to instrumental music with added words.

Walter Collins (1988) addresses the need for identifying and using excellent choral editions in "The Choral Conductor and the Musicologist." While this article may be more interesting to the college or university conductor, Collins's explanations of what to look for in good musical arrangements, transcriptions, and critical editions makes for valuable reading. Many works formerly available only in highly edited versions are now available in "cleaner" editions in which editorial markings have been removed.

Music of Lasting Value

One of the most important issues that choral directors must address when choosing choral music is its lasting appeal. Sally Herman states (1988):

> There seems to have been a push, in the junior high particularly, to look for "quick fixes" in terms of literature. There are *no quick fixes* in anything! The trend toward literature that the students can learn quickly and "like" has greatly disillusioned many teachers. The students may like a piece of music that they learned rapidly for the moment, but the long lasting effects are superficial. They will never "hold on" to the memories of that piece as they will one that they had to work feverishly on before they could even pretend to "know" it. (p. 90)

Herman further states that directors should choose a variety of music representing a range of styles and cultures. Jorgensen and Pfeiler (1995) agree: "Even when the literature is challenging, a diet of any one style is boring. A sound educational program demands a widely varied repertoire" (p. 15).

Is the programming of pop music a sell-out to audience tastes and popular culture? Some choral directors think so, but many believe that a certain amount of popular music in the choral curriculum is acceptable, as long as the arrangements are done well. The Tanglewood Symposium held in 1967 (sponsored by MENC, the Berkshire Music Center, Theodore Presser Foundation, and Boston University) issued a declaration of goals for guiding the future of music education in the United States. Goal number two states:

> Music of all periods, styles, forms, and cultures belongs in the curriculum. The musical repertory should be expanded to involve music of our time in its rich variety, including popular teenage music and avant-garde music, American folk music, and the music of other cultures. (Choate, 1968, p. 139)

This Tanglewood declaration opened the way for popular music to become an acceptable part of the school music curriculum. Because of it, music educators no longer label popular music as being inferior or poor, but rather recognize that all genres of music, including classical, have musical compositions that are superior and inferior.

The problem with any movement is those people who jump on the band wagon and take things to extremes. Some choral directors, in their attempt to include popular music in the curriculum, so embrace this genre that their choral programs become little more than venues for entertainment. Choral directors are not professional entertainers—they are music educators. If popular music is included in the choral program, it should be chosen because it has something to teach students.

The Tanglewood declaration also stimulated a multicultural movement within the choral curriculum. While music of great Western composers remains the core of the traditional choral program, a greater diversity is now possible because music of non-Western composers is becoming readily available. The study of choral music is an important way in which appreciation for cultural diversity is taught.

LOCATING QUALITY CHORAL LITERATURE

Where does the choral director find good choral literature? It is difficult to sort through the tons of literature produced by music publishers. To help, many publishers offer reading sessions for new choral works and make recordings and preview copies available.

Recommended Lists

An excellent source for finding choral music is to peruse recommended lists published in various periodicals or other sources. A recommended music list for junior high choirs by Sandra Chapman appears in the February 1991 issue of the *Choral Journal,* and Guy Webb's compilation of ACDA Honor/Festival Choir music used at national and division conventions appears in the September 1994 issue of the *Choral Journal.* A listing of high-quality but easy choral works for the developing high school choir is presented by Larry Torkelson in *Melisma,* a publication of the North Central ACDA. These three lists of recommended literature appear in Appendix C. In addition, yearly lists of music performed at all-state choral festivals now appear in the *Choral Journal.*

Multicultural music is becoming easier to locate, and recommended lists are being published. A "Selected List of Published Multi-Cultural Ethnically Inspired Choral Music" by Lawrence Kaptein (*Melisma*, winter 1995), is representative of the wide variety of world music now available to the choral profession. This list also appears in Appendix C. Choral conductors are becoming more aware of the need to avoid editions of multicultural music that are overly arranged and inauthentic.

For advanced senior high school literature, ACDA offers *An Annotated Inventory of Distinctive Choral Literature* (Hawkins, 1976) as the second in a series of monographs on choral topics. MENC publishes *Choral Music for Children* (1990), an annotated listing of over two hundred choral selections for children's choirs. Both of these lists include music of the highest quality.

A number of state choral directors' associations have provided tremendous service by making available lists of music recommended by many of its established members. Repertoire lists often are based on a certain categorization of music (e.g., music for chamber choir, SSA, boys' chorus, SATB secular, SATB sacred, and so forth). A check with state-level ACDA organizations will determine if such lists are available.

Library Resources

Music publishers often permit music to go out of print because costs of maintaining high inventories are prohibitive. The *Choral Music in Print* series (Daugherty, 1996), available in most college and university libraries, is an excellent source for determining if a choral selection is in print, who the publisher is, and in what voicings it exists. Updated supplements have been forthcoming since the original series began in 1974.

Reviews and Reading Sessions

Reviews of more recently published choral works regularly appear in the *Choral Journal*. These reviews are helpful in learning about appropriate age and difficulty levels. *The American Choral Review* is a monograph that contains scholarly discourses on choral music, including reviews of newly composed literature. Once published separately, it is now published as a quarterly supplement to Chorus America's *The Voice*.

Reading sessions at organizational conferences and conventions are another place to find new literature. Such sessions often include recommendations of "old chestnuts" by the clinicians and recommendations of newer works that have been used and found worthy for performance.

Personal Contacts and Concert Attendance

Perhaps the best idea for finding literature that works is to ask other directors what they have found to be successful. Word-of-mouth recommendations still seem to be the best way of finding out about unknown gems. Exploring another director's choral library is an excellent way to learn about choral literature.

Attending choral concerts to learn what other directors are performing is another good way to learn of literature. Outstanding choral groups appear at ACDA and MENC conventions, and the convention programs regularly contain the necessary publication information needed to order the music programmed by these choirs.

Music Clearinghouses

A number of music publishing houses sell music from many other firms. These are clearinghouses for all types of music. Most of these publishers will send out music on review for thirty days; it can be reviewed and retained or returned. Often they make available recommended lists of their best-sellers. While this music is not always the best, it may give an idea of what might work in a given situation.

The hunt for quality music is never-ending for the choral conductor. New directors should not feel overwhelmed by the task, but do need to find help when looking for high-quality literature. Knowing where to begin the search is the first step.

PROGRAMMING OBJECTIVES

There needs to be balance in the choral literature chosen for any choir. Programming nothing but "heavy" works can tax the students beyond their endurance and may leave the audience bewildered. Likewise, a program of all lighter works will have little educational benefit. Balanced programming objectives include: (1) teaching comprehensively, (2) performing a variety of styles, (3) developing the singing voice, and (4) entertaining the audience.

Programming to Teach Comprehensively

When choosing music as an educator, choral directors are responsible for more than choosing music that is aesthetically satisfying—they are responsible for choosing music that also educates students about music. It is not good music education when a choral music educator turns out students who sing beautifully but know nothing about the music they are singing. Thinking and learning about music in the contemporary choral classroom is known as comprehensive musicianship.

John Hylton (1995) describes comprehensive musicianship for the choral musician as follows:

> Comprehensive choral music education is inclusive, in depth, and *educates* the participant through experiences in choral music. This education is not limited to the learning of pitches and rhythms, but occurs through the provision of aesthetic experiences, the refinement of critical thinking skills, and the development of a fuller understanding of self. Comprehensive choral music education is not limited to the teaching of three pieces for competition or twelve selections for the spring concert, but rather seeks to facilitate student development in the areas of music reading, languages, and the historical and stylistic context of music. (pp. 2–3)

The additional responsibilities of comprehensive musicianship for today's choral teachers certainly would seem to increase the work load. It was easier when choral directors concerned themselves only with excellent performances outside the classroom. Today's educators must be as concerned with what is happening in the classroom as with performances outside. Why is this?

Today, more than ever, the place of music in the school curriculum is being challenged. More emphasis is placed on "basics," and the general public does not view music as a basic. What the general public does not understand is that music's core body of complex knowledge is basically academic. School administrators are demanding that each school subject worthy to be counted for academic credit must produce academic achievement. Simply grading students on attendance or attitude will no longer suffice. Grades in choirs must represent solid academic achievement that can be tested.

How does a choral teacher test students for academic achievement if nothing academic is being taught? Choral directors are so busy preparing students for concerts, contests, and festivals that little time seems to remain for teaching anything about music. Teachers complain that taking rehearsal time for teaching music history and theory weakens the performance program. However, research (Gleason, 1996) shows that performance is not weakened when teachers take time to emphasize knowledge about the music being studied. Knowing that J. S. Bach was a great composer of the Baroque period, the dates of the Baroque era, and what it represented musically, would seem to be minimal knowledge for students when singing anything by the great master. Also, knowing what key the music is in and what the musical terminology means (e.g., dynamics and tempo) is minimal theoretical knowledge. Teaching to include this information has not been common practice, and only a change in the attitude of choral directors to include a knowledge base in the choral curriculum will change future practice.

Why should a choral director choose music to perform that also has a solid base of knowledge? It may be the best way to guarantee music's place in the curriculum. When a choral teacher can say that grades in choir represent academic achievement, it places music on par with other academic subjects. Performance should remain the major objective of choral classes—students join choir to sing. However, a complex body of knowledge should be imparted along with performance so as to insure a balanced approach to music learning. Choral directors must be responsible for turning out singers who sing well and know something about what they are singing. That is the challenge—to be a musician and an educator.

Programming to Perform a Variety of Styles

Choral singing is almost as old as humankind, and history has produced a great heritage of choral music for the choral conductor to sample. Students, however, will initially dismiss musical styles with which they are unfamiliar, and choral teachers sometimes succumb to picking music only of the contemporary era to please students. Choral directors must remember—they are not hired by schools to act like professional entertainers, they are hired to be educators. Giving in to students' demands for a diet exclusive of anything but pop music is like going to a smorgasbord and choosing only desserts. Students need to be taught about the tremendous variety of musical styles that exist from all eras; they need to learn about music that is not so readily available to them through MTV and other popular media sources. The job of the music educator is to program a variety of choral music styles so that students will learn about this variety and come to understand and appreciate it.

Programming to include a variety of styles also means including music of non-Western composers. The use of multicultural music in choral programs is increasing, and choral conductors need to know where to find suitable literature. The *Choral Journal* is most helpful to this end. An article by Ronald M. Kean (1996) provides a listing of multicultural music according to the cycle of life (e.g., birth, childhood, work). The *Music Educators Journal* also has devoted numerous articles to multicultural music; one such article by Patricia Shehan Campbell (1995) focuses on the gospel music of African Americans.

Programming to Develop the Singing Voice

A third objective for programming music is to help students develop vocally. The choral director, most likely, will be the only voice teacher students ever have for vocal instruction. While a great deal can be accomplished in private lessons (if students have lessons), the regular teaching of voice in the rehearsal assures that all students are reached.

The music chosen for students must be matched to their singing skill. Programming music that is beyond their technique will lead to damaged voices and frustration. However, the music needs to present some technical challenge for vocal growth. Choosing music with extended musical phrases can be an excellent means of teaching good breath control. If the phrase lengths are too demanding, no vocal development will take place. Music with a wide range can aid in developing an expanded singing range if the notes are not so high or low that students must strain to sing them. When judging the technical difficulty of a choral piece, the director must ask if the degree of difficulty matches the technique of the students, and if the music provides opportunities for singing technique to grow. Music chosen to begin the year will of necessity be less vocally challenging than music programmed as the year progresses.

Programming to Entertain the Audience

The audience cannot be ignored when programming a school concert. Some choral conductors do not believe the audience should be considered when choosing music. Such an attitude may result in a sparse audience when most of the music programmed is beyond the comprehension of those in attendance. Music educators have an obligation to educate audiences, and such a task is best done slowly. This does not mean the choral director should assume the role of entertainer. It does require directors to choose a balance of music and styles, some of which will be more accessible.

There is nothing wrong with a spring pops concert that features popular music, if during the remainder of the year the choirs have worked on a balance of musical styles from the major historical eras. Choruses from America's musical theater are appropriate, as are popular ballads and folk music. But trying to make a fifty-voice choir sound like the latest six-member rock group just does not work. A choir is a choir, and most popular rock arrangements do not fit the choral idiom. When singing this music, students often complain that it does not sound like the recording. Of course not—it can't. This is a choir singing, not a rock group.

It is important for the audience to understand the choral director's job as educator and not entertainer. Each concert is really a "recital" or presentation of what has been learned in class. Sadly, many school choral concerts show little evidence of anything worthwhile having been learned. When parents and students understand a concert as a recitation and not a show, educational objectives are served.

The back of a concert program is a good place to explain the educational objectives of the concert. Learning to sing in a foreign language could be one goal, or having students experience a variety of musical styles could be another. Part of the job of a music educator is to educate the audience, informing them about music education and helping them to find meaning in the music. There is nothing wrong in programming an old patriotic war horse such as "The Battle Hymn of the Republic." But the audience should be challenged with something that will stretch them a little; the program should demonstrate that students are maturing in musical understanding. Parents respond positively when they learn about educational objectives for the choral program—objectives that include musical growth and knowledge.

PROGRAMMING SACRED MUSIC IN THE SCHOOLS

Much of the music in the choral heritage is set to sacred texts, and in an era of separation of church and state, this can present a problem for the choral conductor. *Religious Music in the Schools* (1987) states:

It is the position of Music Educators National Conference that the study of religious music is a vital and appropriate part of the total music experience in both performance and listening. To omit sacred music from the repertoire or study of music would present an incorrect and incomplete concept of the comprehensive nature of the art. (p. 1)

Sacred music does have a place in the public school setting. How that place is to be determined has been set forth in varying guidelines based on Supreme Court decisions and on constitutional and ethical considerations (Reynolds, 1984).

Supreme Court Decisions

A number of Supreme Court decisions have been made regarding the teaching of religion in the public schools. Generally, these decisions state that schools may teach about all religions but may not sponsor the practice of any religion. Therefore, the school's approach to religion must be academic and not devotional. A public school choral teacher cannot use choral music in a way that would lead anyone to believe that some type of religious rite was being practiced or advocated.

At the center of the constitutional consideration is the question. Does the activity have a secular purpose? In other words, is sacred music being used because it represents a genre that is historically significant? If so, it is allowed. If, however, the use of a piece of music may be construed to be the practice of religion, it is not allowed. The government has gone to great ends to discourage the excessive entanglement of public schools and religion. Sacred music is not considered an entanglement so long as there is no perceived entanglement by the public.

Guidelines for Using Sacred Music

Ethically, a choral director must work not to offend anyone of any faith when programming sacred music. Contemporary Christian gospel music usually has a very personal message and, as such, may offend non-Christians in the choir. Such music is best avoided in a public school setting. The question should be asked, "Has this music been chosen because of its educational value or because of some other reason that may be construed to be religious?" There should always be educational objectives for all programmed music.

The following guidelines are given to help choral directors who choose to program sacred music in the public schools:

- Sacred music should be selected on the basis of its musical and educational value rather than its religious context.
- Traditions of different people should be shared and respected.
- The excessive use of sacred music, religious symbols or scenery, and performance in devotional settings is to be avoided.
- The role of sacred music should be a neutral one, neither promoting nor inhibiting religious views.
- School policies regarding religious holidays are to be observed.
- Students who object to the singing of sacred music because of a conflict with their own religious beliefs should not be penalized.

Christmas and Holiday Concerts

Is it wrong to have a Christmas concert in the public schools? That depends on the policies of the school district and the common disposition of the people within the school district.

Some schools in the "Bible Belt" still have Christmas concerts with apparently no objections from the general public. Many schools have gone to "holiday" concerts in which music selections of various faiths and secular music are included. Some choral directors avoid the problem by having a "midwinter" concert in January or February, instead of the traditional December concert. This relieves some of the pressure people feel during the holidays, and it makes a fall concert an alternative.

Program to Educate

Whatever is done as a public school choral music educator, it must be done to educate, not proselytize. Wise judgment is needed, but there should be no trouble defending sacred music for school performance. Of course, if it is a parochial or private school, all of this discussion is moot. Choral directors in such schools are free to follow whatever religious practices are honored and choose music accordingly. Even here, however, all music chosen for study should have educational benefit, increasing knowledge, skills, or both. In addition, the music should be of lasting value—of excellent quality no matter what genre or style.

STUDY AND DISCUSSION QUESTIONS

1. When choosing music for the first time for a choir, should the director choose music that is generally easier or generally more of a challenge for the singers? Explain your answer.
2. Ehret asks if the text of a choral composition has literary value. How do you determine literary value?
3. What advantages are there for singing in the original language of a composition? What can be the disadvantages if the language is foreign to the singers and audience?
4. What does Ehret mean when he asks, "Is the part writing vocal rather than instrumental"? Do you know of a master composer whose vocal lines often tend to be like instrumental parts?
5. How could an accompaniment detract from a musical composition?
6. Do you believe there is a gender bias in choral music?
7. How can gender bias affect the choosing of choral music?
8. What can choral directors do to avoid gender bias?
9. What is the difference between vocal range and tessitura?
10. Why are arrangements or highly edited versions of masterworks usually to be avoided?
11. Where can you go to find lists of recommended choral music?
12. What does comprehensive musicianship involve for the choral class, and why is this important to the choral curriculum?
13. What does research say about the inclusion of comprehensive musicianship in music rehearsals?
14. What is the overall objective for "programming to perform a variety of musical styles"?
15. What are the general guidelines for "programming to develop singers vocally"?
16. Why is "programming to entertain" one legitimate objective of the choral program?
17. What happens when "programming to entertain" becomes the sole objective?

18. What is the position of each of the following regarding sacred music performance in the public schools: MENC, Supreme Court, U.S. Constitution, ethics?

19. What are some options to programming the traditional December Christmas concert?

20. What should be the overall guideline when choosing all choral music for programming?

REFERENCES

Chapman, S. (1991). Selected choral literature for junior high choirs. *Choral Journal, 31*(7), 23–29.

Choate, R. (ed.) (1968). *Documentary report of the Tanglewood Symposium.* Reston, VA: Music Educators National Conference.

Collins, W. S. (1988). The choral conductor and the musicologist. In H. A. Decker and J. Herford (eds.), *Choral Conducting Symposium* (2d ed.). Englewood Cliffs, NJ: Prentice Hall.

Daugherty, F. M. (1996a). *Sacred choral music in print: Master index, 1996.* Philadelphia: Musicdata.

———— (1996b). *Secular choral music in print: Master index, 1996.* Philadelphia: Musicdata.

Ehret, W. (1959). *The choral conductor's handbook.* New York: Edward B. Marks.

Gleason, B. P. (1996). The effects of beginning band instruction using a comprehensive, multicultural, interdisciplinary method on the knowledge, skills, attitudes, and retention of sixth-grade students (doctoral diss., The University of Iowa). *Dissertation Abstracts International, A 57*(01), 145.

Hawkins, M. B. (1976). *An annotated inventory of distinctive choral literature for performance at the high school level.* Lawton, OK: American Choral Directors Association (Monograph no. 2).

Herman, S. (1988). *Building a pyramid of musicianship.* San Diego, CA: Curtis Music Press, Neil A. Kjos Music, distributor.

Hylton, J. B. (1995). *Comprehensive choral music education.* Englewood Cliffs, NJ: Prentice Hall.

Jorgensen, N. S., and C. Pfeiler (1995). *Things they never taught you in choral methods.* Milwaukee, WI: Hal Leonard.

Kaptein, L. (1995). Selected list of published multi-cultural ethnically inspired choral music. *Melisma, 13*(2), 14–15.

Kean, R. A. (1996). A global celebration of life: Programming multicultural and ethnically inspired choral music according to the cycle of life. *Choral Journal, 36*(9), 45–48.

MENC (1987). *Religious music in the schools.* Reston, VA: Music Educators National Conference.

———— (1990). *Choral music for children: An annotated list.* Reston, VA: Music Educators National Conference.

O'Toole, P. (1998). A missing chapter from choral methods books: How choirs neglect girls. *Choral Journal, 39*(5), 9–32.

Reynolds, C. (1984). Sacred music: How to avoid cooking your holiday goose. *Music Educators Journal, 71*(3), 31–33.

Shehan Campbell, P. (1995). Mellonee Burnim on African American music. *Music Educators Journal, 82*(1), 41–48.

Torkelson, L. (1994). Accessible choral works for the developing high school choir. *Melisma, 13*(1), 12–13.

Webb, G. B. (1994). Repertoire performed by ACDA honor/festival choirs, 1983–1994. *Choral Journal, 35*(2), 25–40.

10 | Preparing the Choral Rehearsal and Music

Long-range planning of the rehearsal schedule is required for a successful choral program. The choral conductor also must consider a rehearsal format, prepare and mark the music, and decide how to place the singers in an effective seating plan. All of this requires extensive preparation and a large time commitment. The degree of success in any choral program is determined by how seriously the choral conductor plans everything.

THE REHEARSAL SCHEDULE

Before any rehearsal scheduling can take place, the concert dates for the year need to be determined. Typically, senior high choirs will present three to four programs annually, sometimes in combination with instrumental groups. Junior high, middle school, and elementary groups most often present two concerts a year, and some elementary schools present only one program in the spring.

Concert dates need to be set well in advance, preferably in the spring before the following academic year. Consulting the all-school calendar, as well as any community calendar, helps to minimize schedule conflicts. This is true especially at the high school level, where sporting events and standardized test days are projected several years in advance. Once the concerts dates are set, long-range planning can begin.

Choral Repertoire

If possible, music for the entire academic year should be chosen over the summer months. While changes and substitutions can be made during the rehearsal process, the sooner the big picture is in place, the better. The selection of music a year at a time permits the choral director to make decisions about programming for a wide variety of styles, difficulty levels, languages, and educational benefits. The music, when ordered at one time, saves clerical work and permits substitutions if certain selections are no longer available. Purchasing early in the school year also means a greater chance of having requests approved, rather than later in the year when school funds become depleted.

Jorgensen and Pfeiler (1995) recommend for the director to chronicle literature by keeping a chart for each ensemble, including the following for each selection:

- Title and composer
- Sacred or secular
- Language
- Accompanied or unaccompanied

- Historical era and style (motet, folksong, spiritual, etc.)
- Meter and tempo
- Key and tonality
- Texture: monophonic, homophonic, polyphonic
- Basic dynamic level(s)
- Educational benefits
- Level of difficulty

"Using the chart prevents the possibility of singing too many songs from one period; it forces the director to look for the Romantic piece that is sometimes ignored or the vocal jazz chart that is intimidating because it requires extra research or risk" (p. 16). Whether or not a formal chart is used, conscious consideration should be given to all of the above descriptors when planning music for the year.

Another factor to be considered when choosing music is the possibility of a unifying theme. "A Sampler of Folk Songs and Spirituals" would require the choice of various multicultural and American folk song literature, as well as spirituals. Themes make for good publicity interest and lend a sense of unity to any program. Using the generic "Spring Concert" also works as a type of theme.

Long-Range Schedule

Each performance is preceded by a number of weeks or months of rehearsal preparation. Whether the choir meets once a week or five times a week, the total number of rehearsals before the concert must be known for a logical long-range plan to be made. Without a long-range plan, it is difficult to decide just how much music can be accomplished in any given time period.

The prominent university choral conductor Donald Neuen presents the following formula for determining the amount of time needed when planning rehearsals:

> Although the allotted rehearsal time is 50 minutes per day, we must subtract an average of 12 minutes for daily warm-ups, vocalizing, other technical study, and business details. This leaves 38 minutes for the rehearsal of songs. Thus, the total rehearsal time for the Christmas concert is actually:
>
> 6 weeks × 5 days per week × 38 minutes per day = 1140 minutes.
>
> We must now subtract 38 minutes each for three days, during this rehearsal segment, on which there is no school. The new total: 1026 minutes.
>
> 6 songs divided into 1026 minutes = 171 minutes per song.
>
> Since we have 2 difficult, 2 medium, and 2 easy songs in this group of 6, we can begin by cutting the 171 figure by a third, for the easy songs, and adding that third to the difficult ones. We now have:
>
> 2 difficult songs @ 228 minutes,
>
> 2 medium songs @ 171 minutes,
>
> 2 easy songs @ 114 minutes.
>
> We must remember that this figure represents the total number of minutes we can spend on each song. *This cannot be exceeded!* If we have spent our allotted 114 minutes on an

easy song, and it is not completely learned, our only options are to take additional minutes from another song that might be progressing ahead of schedule, shorten the program,
or add extra (or sectional) rehearsals. This system of rehearsing confirms, on a daily basis, whether or not we are on our charted course toward a successfully prepared performance. (Neuen, n.d., p. 86)

Such careful planning also makes it clear how little rehearsal time there is for any given
concert.

Once the number of selections has been chosen according to the amount of time available, it is necessary to make a long-range schedule. This schedule reflects the number of rehearsals or weeks of preparation prior to the concert. Such a schedule (see Figure 10.1) is an
overview of what is planned day to day and week to week. Excessive departures from the
schedule mean that careful planning has not preceded its execution, or extenuating circumstances (e.g., illness, school closings) have forced a reconsideration of time allotments. It is
not unusual in these cases for music to be dropped from the schedule; this is most unfortunate when rehearsal time has been expended on music that is eliminated.

A long-range rehearsal plan keeps the choral director focused and accountable. Veteran
choral conductors have a sixth sense about how much music can be accomplished in any one
time period. They know the capabilities of their groups, and recognize how long it takes for
singers to learn the average musical score.

Choristers who sight-read are going to require less time on any given piece than those
who must be spoon fed every note. If sight-singing skills are being taught, the benefit of
accomplishing more in less time is evident as students become more proficient at reading
music.

It takes new conductors some time to develop the intuition needed to balance all of the
factors that influence long-range rehearsal planning. Objective planning is, therefore, the key
to success. Following the plan is also important.

THE REHEARSAL FORMAT

The ability to structure each rehearsal to meet the desired objectives is an art in itself. Careful planning is required, and a knowledge of rehearsal format is essential. The outline for the
rehearsal lesson plan is presented in Chapter 5. Deciding the content and order for that plan
is an activity required before each rehearsal. Choral directors who choose to wing it without
thoughtful planning often waste time.

Rehearsal Objectives

Every rehearsal plan begins with identifying the objectives to be accomplished. Typically, vocal warm-ups and sight-reading exercises are used as beginning activities. Written objectives
for each need not be specific, that is, an objective is not necessary for every exercise used. It
is enough to state the first objectives as "improve vocal skills through warm-up exercises"
and "improve sight-reading skills through sight-singing activities." However, it is important
for the director to know the objective of each exercise and to relate the objective informally
to students. All exercises and vocalises, as well as any written material used, should be listed
under the "procedures" section of the rehearsal plan.

The choral selections to be rehearsed are dictated by the long-range rehearsal schedule.
Objectives for learning these pieces will cover most of the rehearsal time and must be specific. It is not enough to state, "Rehearse *In Stiller Nacht*." Rather, the objective should be

Chamber Singers of Iowa City
Kenneth Phillips, conductor
Rehearsal Schedule: March 9–May 16
7:15–9:30 P.M. Monday (unless noted otherwise)

AN AMERICAN PORTRAIT: Music of 20th Century American Composers

3/09	Music Distribution New: Circus Band New: Willow Tree New: Chichester 1	5/04	**Board Meeting: 6:15 P.M.** Rev: Alice—3 choruses Rev: Alleluia Rev: The Pasture (men) Rev: God's Bottles (women) Rev: Beginning
3/16	Rev: Circus Band Rev: Willow Tree New: 3 Madrigall Rev: Chichester 1 New: Chichester 2	5/11	**Ext. Reh., 7:15–10:00 P.M.** 7:15 P.M.—1st half of concert 8:15 P.M.—Chichester Psalms 9:15 P.M.—In the Beginning
3/23	Rev: Circus Band Rev: Willow Tree Rev: 3 Madrigals Rev: Chichester 2 New: Chichester 3	5/15	**Dress Rehearsal, 7:15–10:00 P.M.** 7:15 P.M.—1st half of concert 8:15 P.M.—Chichester Psalms 9:15 P.M.—In the Beginning
3/30	Rev: 3 Madrigals New: Alleluia Rev: Chichester 3 New: Beginning	5/16	**Concert—8:00 P.M., Clapp RH** 7:00 P.M.—report 1077 8:00 P.M.—Concert Ives—Circus Band Barber—Under the Willow Tree
4/06	**Board Meeting: 6:15 P.M.** Rev: Alleluia New: Lobster Q. New: Beginning		Diemer—Three Madrigals Thompson—God's Bottles Thompson—The Pasture Thompson—Alleluia Fine—Choruses from "Alice" Intermission
4/13	Rev: Alleluia Rev: Lobster Q. New: Lullaby Rev: Chichester 1–2 New: Beginning		Berstein—Chichester Psalms Copland—In the Beginning 9:45 P.M.—Turn in music Break stage
4/20	Rev: 3 Madrigals Rev: Lullaby New: Father William Rev: Chichester 3 New: Beginning		10:00 P.M.—Party! Have a great summer! Look for a letter in July announcing au- ditions for fall.
4/27	**Solo Tryouts—6:45 P.M.** Rev: Father William Rev: Beginning New: The Pasture (men) New: God's Bottles (women)		

Figure 10.1. Sample of long-range rehearsal schedule.

161

specific: "Rehearse *In Stiller Nacht*, mm. 1–8, for correct < > and soft dynamic level." This type of planning requires knowing what the director wants from the singers before the music is rehearsed. Interpreting the music as one goes along is not acceptable, but at-the-moment inspiration is certainly permissible.

As pieces are learned, objectives may become more general, or holistic, for example, "Sing through *In Stiller Nacht* for expressivity and phrasing." Every repetition of a choral selection should be motivated by some objective that is communicated to the students, for instance, "Repeat *In Stiller Nacht*, and this time maintain the soft dynamic level, but don't back off your breath support—project the sound."

Objectives also need to include the bits of knowledge that are to be taught during rehearsal, for example, "Review the composer of *In Stiller Nacht*, the era in which Brahms lived, and the mood of the folk song." Added to these knowledge-based objectives might be the form of the song or another music theory element such as key or tonality. Long discourses on music history and theory are not necessary to impart important bits of information.

Every rehearsal should reflect three major goals: (1) knowledge gained, (2) skills improved, and (3) a meaningful, musical experience. Knowledge of the music means more than learning the notes. Improving skills means more than singing the notes. A meaningful, musical experience means more than getting through all the notes without breaking down. Knowledge of the music includes information about the music, skill improvement leads to improved singing, and a meaningful experience involves aesthetic satisfaction. All three have to be consciously planned for if these major goals are to be accomplished in every rehearsal.

Rehearsal Structures

Research on effective choral rehearsal structures (Cox, 1989) has identified three basic organizational strategies used by choral conductors. Rehearsal style A is presented in Figure 10.2. Fast-paced activities exist at the beginning and end of the rehearsal, but the middle of the rehearsal is marked by a rather long period of slow-paced activities. This rehearsal style is prob-

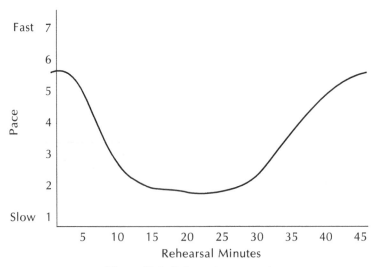

Figure 10.2. Rehearsal structure A.

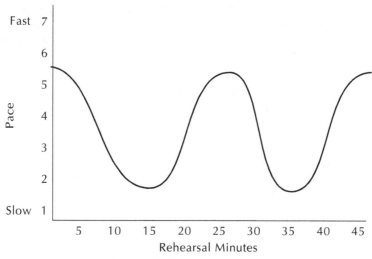

Figure 10.3. Rehearsal structure B.

ably the least effective for maintaining high interest among students. It is apt to result in behavior problems when singers are bored and sections of the choir become restless when not
singing for some time.

Rehearsal structure B (see Figure 10.3) represents fast-paced rehearsing at the beginning,
middle, and end of the rehearsal. In this case, all students are occupied with singing during
the middle by performing together a piece in progress, or by attending to voice-building or
sight-singing exercises. Because the middle of the rehearsal is typically the time when rehearsing becomes bogged down, the director using this format recognizes the need to increase
the pace of the rehearsal to keep things moving.

The third rehearsal structure, type C (see Figure 10.4), again has fast-paced activities at
the beginning and end of the rehearsal. However, the middle section consists of a rapid al-

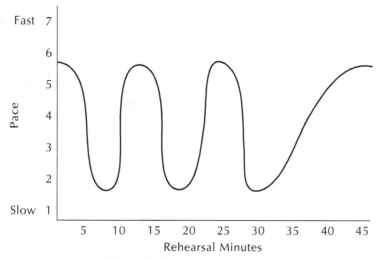

Figure 10.4. Rehearsal structure C.

ternation of fast-paced and slow-paced activities. Limited time is spent on each activity, and frequent changes of pace occur within the rehearsal structure. Rehearsal planning of this type appears to be most conducive to maintaining the interest of the singers and accomplishing rehearsal objectives (Cox, 1989).

Time Allocation

Translating rehearsal structure C into blocks of time might result in the following distribution for a fifty-minute rehearsal:

Activity	% of Time	Minutes
Warm-up/voice instruction	10%	5
Sight-singing instruction	10%	5
Sing a familiar piece (polish)	10%	5
Introduce a new work or one in progress	20%	10
Rehearse a work in progress	20%	10
Rehearse a work in progress	20%	10
Sing a familiar piece (polish)	10%	5

The middle section of the above rehearsal structure accounts for 60 percent of the time allotted. It may be that only two selections are rehearsed during this time, in which case each selection could be rehearsed for fifteen minutes. There can be more time in the middle section if the two familiar pieces require less time. Nevertheless, it is important to plan for an aesthetic experience near the beginning and end of every rehearsal. A sense of accomplishment is thereby gained, and choristers have a sense of the progress being made.

More time will be given to polishing music the closer rehearsals are to the concert; sight-singing and knowledge-based activities may be suspended in the last few rehearsals. No specific time in the above allocation is stipulated for the teaching of historical or theoretical knowledge. Such instruction is considered part of those segments of the rehearsal as identified in the objectives. However, this is not to say that some portion of a rehearsal could not be used for more detailed instruction of voice development or historical and theoretical knowledge. Time for such teaching is at the discretion of the choral director and is guided by the progress made in maintaining the rehearsal schedule.

Regarding the allocation of time in planning the choral rehearsal, Deral Johnson (1997) states:

> An efficient conductor, no matter how experienced, will go into rehearsal with specific time allotments for each composition to be rehearsed. Flexibility in realizing the set plan of action is the name of the game, however, for one composition could require less rehearsal time than originally planned, and another composition may not rehearse comfortably during that particular rehearsal. A change of time scheduling must be instantly implemented to accommodate these altered requirements. No apologies are needed for a change of scheduling or for misreading the time it will take an ensemble to work out a composition. (p. 37)

Johnson further recommends that when possible the choir should begin and end the rehearsal singing as a unit, and that beginning repertoire be easy on the voice. Also, placing the order of music on a chalkboard reveals good planning.

PREPARING THE MUSIC

A thorough understanding of the music to be rehearsed is required before the choral conductor enters the rehearsal. Learning the music along with the singers is not acceptable. Studying the score is time consuming but necessary if rehearsal time is to be used efficiently. Knowing the work in detail provides insights to guide the teaching of each selection in progress.

Marking the Score

Some type of system for marking the score is necessary to guide the eye in score interpretation. The late Margaret Hillis, the well-known director of the Chicago Symphony Chorus, prepared the guidelines in Figure 10.5 for her choristers for use in score marking. These are commonly used signals that every conductor and singer should know and employ.

The marking of music should be a regular activity to which choristers are accustomed. For this reason, each singer needs a pencil at every rehearsal; markings must never be made

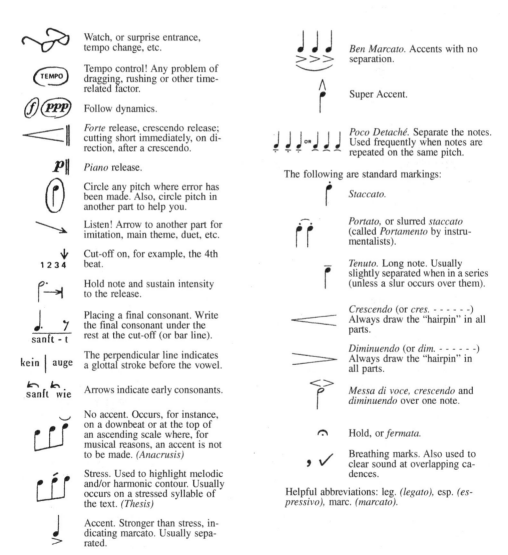

Figure 10.5. Score markings from *At Rehearsals* by Margaret Hillis (American Choral Foundation, 1969).

in ink. Choristers should be directed to mark the music lightly and to erase all markings before the music is returned to the music library.

Score Analysis

Before a choral conductor begins to analyze the score in detail, the whole picture is to be understood. It is helpful if a recording is available. If not, the selection can be played through at the piano and melodic sections identified and sung to gain understanding of the overall shape of the piece.

In the MENC monograph *Teaching Choral Music: A Course of Study* (1991, p. 4), sixteen elements are identified for score analysis:

- Tempos and tempo markings
- Meter and meter changes
- Notation and musical signs and symbols
- Key and key changes
- Voice ranges
- Entrances, cutoffs
- Movement of inner voices
- Dynamic levels and changes
- Beginning pitches of parts (initial pitches, as well as those after interludes or long rests)
- Length of introduction
- Length of interludes
- Phrase and harmonic analysis
- Implied mood
- Understanding of text (translation, if necessary)
- Language: diction, enunciation, pronunciation
- Style (period, background information on and intent of the composer)

The above elements are not in any implied order, but some order is necessary if the approach to score analysis is to be logical.

TEXT.   Perhaps the first element to be analyzed is the text. Points to consider include the source, the mood, language problems, diction problems, accuracy of the translation (if appropriate), textual repetition, and so forth. What style of diction will be appropriate, sung-speech or rhythmic? Is the meaning of the text obvious or will it require some explaining to the choir?

FORM.   The structure of the piece should be the next consideration. The late distinguished German choral conductor Wilhelm Ehmann (1968) states the importance of understanding the form of a composition when it comes to teaching it:

> The approach of allowing the essential style and character of the musical work to determine the method of practicing the parts in the order in which they probably were composed, of taking note of the musical structure . . . turns the whole learning process into a musical experience. (p. 201)

Steven Demorest (1996) concurs: "Approaching a piece structurally offers numerous opportunities for guided listening, analytical thinking, and conceptual understanding that go beyond the literature under study" (p. 25).

Julius Herford was one of the greatest choral musicologists of the twentieth century. His work with Robert Shaw is well known, and Shaw's reputation for meticulous score study and preparation is directly related to the influence of Herford. The "analytical graph" was employed by Herford as a tool for score analysis. While a detailed description of this technique is not possible here, choral directors should be aware of this approach to detailed score analysis as presented in "The Choral Conductor's Preparation of the Musical Score" by Julius Herford (1988).

The analytical graph presents the structural features of a work in a form that is easily visible and comprehensible, helping the choral conductor to understand the overall form, various sections, and elements such as dynamics, tempos, and textures. It also aids memorization.

A list of symbols and interpretations for use in graphing choral compositions is presented in Figure 10.6. Symbols and abbreviations are used for clarity.

The graphs indicate formal design by bar groupings, with the largest groupings at the top and subdivisions in successive lower levels (see Figure 10.7). Beneath the bar groupings are shown the metric, tempo, dynamic, motivic, textual, textural, and harmonic elements that contribute further to the structure of the piece.

Creating an analytical graph leads to an in-depth understanding of a choral work; it also requires much time. While such a process may not be practical for every small work, the need to at least identify all of the components represented in the graph is necessary if the choral conductor is to make sense of each piece. This knowledge also helps to define ways to teach toward a successful performance.

When analyzing the form of a composition, it is necessary to discover if the piece has repeated units as found in strophic, ABA, rondo, and other designs, or if it is through-composed, with no repeated sections. The texture helps in making this decision; for exam-

Symbol	Interpretation
1——4 4	Bar grouping spans mm. 1–4 and is four measures in length
1^2	Second beat of m.1
1^{2+}	Subdivision of the second beat of m.1
$5,6^1$	The melodic materials of m.5 ends with the downbeat of m.6
$5,6^1$	The melodic material of m.6 begins with the upbeat from m.5
$5,6$	A structural "pivot bar;" material simultaneously ends with the downbeat of m.6 and begins with the upbeat from m.5
1——4 2 + 2	Bar grouping spans mm. 1–4 and is internally subdivided into two plus two measures
1——6 3 × 2	Bar grouping spans mm. 1–6 and is internally subdivided into three two-measure units
5——8 = 1——4	Mm. 5–8 are structurally indentical to mm. 1–4
2 + 2	The second unit of two measures is a descending sequence

Figure 10.6. Symbols used in an analytical graph.

Analytical Graph: *O Süsser Mai*—Johannes Brahms

Form:	(A)	11 mm.	(B)	10 mm.	(A)	17 mm.
						coda

Measures: 1 -------------- 11, 12 ---------------------- 21, 22 --------------------------- 38

Phrasing: 1–2 3–4 5–6 7–11, 12–13 14–15 16–18 19–21, 22–23 24–25 26–27 28----38
 2 2 2 5 2 2 3 3 2 2 2 11

Melodic a a a a ext. b b b b a a a a ext.----
Motives:

Meter: 3 --
 4

Tempo: Flowing ($\quarternote$ = 84) espr. -- rit. ----

Dynamics: f $\rangle$ p $\langle\rangle$ mf $\langle\rangle\langle\rangle$ p $\rangle$ f $\rangle$ $\rangle$ p   pp dim.

Text: O süsser mai---   ich-----   O süsser-- wie den----------

Voices: SATB --

Accomp.: Unaccompanied --

Texture: Homophonic --

Harmonic
Structure: C   vii/V   4-3 sus. C   V/II chrom. 4-3 sus. C   vii/V   chrom.   C
 V   B sus.   V

Figure 10.7. Analytical graph for *O Süsser Mai* by J. Brahms.

ple, homophonic folksongs are typically strophic. Also, the presence of a unifying element, such as a rhythmic or melodic motive, text structure, or a single melodic idea will help to determine the formal design. College music majors typically have coursework in form and analysis; its practical application becomes apparent when preparing music to teach.

Finding the natural breaks in a composition helps the director organize the rehearsal into blocks of music that can be learned by the singers in each rehearsal segment. Some blocks will be more difficult than others, and it is a good idea to begin with an easier block that will be learned quickly. It is not necessary to rehearse the blocks in sequential order. However, when rehearsing pieces in smaller blocks, the conductor must work out the transitions between sections so the choir can sing easily from one to the next.

Major structural divisions should be shown in the score and the overall form indicated at the beginning of the composition (see Figure 10.8). Such breaks are divided with hash marks and labeled as to their structure, e.g., "B" section.

KEY, TONALITY, METER, AND TEMPO. The key and tonality of the music is marked at the beginning of each piece (see Figure 10.8). Capital letters indicate major, and lowercase letters indicate minor. Any changes in key or tonality are marked clearly in the music. The meter should be marked as to the number of beats that will be conducted per measure. Meter, as it is conducted, is sometimes different from the meter signature; for example, a piece in four may be more comfortably conducted in two. Changes in meter and beat note also are circled in the score.

Gloria in excelsis Deo

Figure 10.8. Choral score marked for rehearsal: "Gloria in excelsis Deo," from *Heiligmesse* by F. J. Haydn. (Earthsongs publication. Used by permission.)

Figure 10.8. (*continued*)

Figure 10.8. (*continued*)

171

Figure 10.8. (*continued*)

Figure 10.8. (*continued*)

All tempo indications and changes are highlighted; using a colored marking pen is help-ful to this end. The metronome marking needs to be checked with a metronome to determine if the tempo indicated requires modification for the ability of the group or the acoustics of the hall. Metronome markings are to be followed as closely as possible, but conductors fre-quently alter tempos for many reasons, including interpretation. If a metronome marking is not indicated, one should be chosen and marked in the score.

MELODY, RHYTHM, AND HARMONY.   The melodic, rhythmic, and harmonic content that fill in the formal structure of a composition are what students have to learn first—the notes. If the melody appears in different voice parts at different times, this needs to be noted so that all parts can learn the melody together. Sometimes entire melodic, rhythmic, and har-monic sections are repeated, perhaps with different words. Again, rehearsing these segments in succession helps to reinforce the learning process. If the melody has disjunct leaps or for-eign notes, these need to be circled in the score and isolated in rehearsal. All cues and cut-offs are marked indicating phrase length.

Important entrances, such as, the subject of a fugue, should be marked in the music. All such melodic entrances need special attention and typically are marked as cues in the choral score (see Figure 10.8). Awkward intervals and unusual or chromatically altered pitches are circled and isolated.

Rhythm problems are to be highlighted; the director must determine some system to re-hearse such spots (e.g., counting aloud, tapping the rhythm, speaking the rhythm with text). Any recurring rhythmic motives require identification, as the isolation and repetition of such passages can facilitate the learning process.

Difficulty of the harmonic language of any given selection needs to match each group's achievement level. Typically, twentieth-century art music makes more demands for singing nontonal music. Mildly dissonant music is easily sung when the dissonances are identified and isolated and the singers are instructed to hear the tension as something desirable. While writing in a complete harmonic analysis of every chord may not be practical for every se-lection, the choral conductor does need to know the harmonic language, including changes in tonality, altered chords, and modulations. These should be clearly marked and special at-tention given to them in rehearsal. The harmonic rhythm also is an important element, but consideration of this should be part of the process when choosing music to be performed. Music with a fast-changing harmonic rhythm (e.g., the music of J. S. Bach) may be too de-manding for some choirs to perform.

TEXTURE.   Choral compositions often contain more than one type of texture, and changes in texture should be noted in the score to facilitate rehearsing. For example, a unison passage where everyone has the melody is often a good place to begin the rehearsing of a new piece. However, a good unison can be the hardest to achieve, as voices must tune to each other to blend. Homophonic sections are typically easier to teach than polyphonic sections, unless the polyphony is a round or canon.

The type of texture also will dictate the balance of parts. In homophony, voice parts singing the harmony support the melody, and the melody must be distinguishable. In polyphony, the subject or melodic motive should stand out in each part when it is present. Analyzing for texture is extremely important to developing choral balance.

EXPRESSIVE INDICATIONS.   The varying of dynamics is essential to expressive singing. All dynamic symbols are marked in the score and highlighted. One way to do this is to use a red marking pencil for loud dynamics and a blue marking pencil for soft ones. *Crescendo* and *decrescendo* terms and abbreviations (e.g, *cresc.*) may be expanded on the music with the appropriate hairpin symbols (⟨ ⟩) to increase clarity.

Articulation indicators (*legato, staccato, marcato, tenuto*) ought to be highlighted for attention, and articulation symbols (phrase marks, dots, short lines, etc.), given special consideration (see Figure 10.8). As phrase length affects musical expression, all phrase lengths are determined by the conductor and proper breathing places marked with large commas or slashes.

Character terms, such as *leggiero, dolce,* and *pesante*, need to be highlighted in the score and changes noted. The interpretation of such terms is paramount to a performance that is musical. Rehearsing with such indications highlighted provides guidance and builds in the correct feeling for each piece from the beginning. To ignore character indicators until close to a performance almost guarantees failure. Choristers, especially young ones, tend to interpret a selection in performance the way it was sung in the first rehearsal.

Score Analysis Applied

Score analysis and accompanying markings are parts of rehearsal planning that yield excellent results when applied in the choral rehearsal. All types of problems in the music can be anticipated, saving time in the process of teaching; problems that might become ignored in the rehearsal are identified beforehand for concentrated work. Detailed knowledge of a choral score helps determine the flow of the teaching plan, and disruptions are minimized when the class moves quickly and smoothly.

Markings placed in a score will be of tremendous help to the choral director when conducting the performance. The eyes scan each page and pick up the symbols that are transformed into the conducting gesture: cues, cutoffs, dynamic indications, tempo changes, articulation styles, and much more. Without a well-marked score, the conductor easily may miss many of the musical aspects that bring music to life. Score analysis and marking are essential to guiding singers through the rehearsal process and in making the final performance a satisfying experience.

PLACEMENT OF SINGERS

The placement of singers in rehearsal and concert formation is part of the choral director's planning. Good blend, accurate intonation, and the overall quality of the ensemble will be influenced by choir seating and standing arrangements. To permit choristers to sit or stand anywhere within a section is to show little understanding for how a beautiful choral tone is developed. The choral director needs to know the vocal quality of each singer and the overall characteristic of each choral part if choral tone is to be improved.

Individual Voice Placement

There are as many vocal qualities in the average choir as there are singers. Some voices project and others do not. Some voices have much vibrato and others have little. Some voices are full and resonant, while others are thin and whispery. The choral director's job is to blend these various qualities into a uniform sound.

The first step in developing a choral seating plan is to make singers aware of the need for balancing voices within a choral section. A simple explanation of the objectives (blend, intonation, timbre) should suffice.

The second step is to experiment with voice placement within a section. The objective is to closely match voices that work together. Singers with voices of similar quality, when placed side by side, take greater pleasure from singing in an ensemble. This is known as acoustic voice matching (Ekholm, 2000).

Some voice qualities tend to be rather harsh and stick out. The excessive vibrato is a problem often found in an older group of singers. When persons with these types of voices are seated next to voices of a more blending quality, the rough edges of the choral sound can be lessened.

Most volunteer and school choirs have people with strong, average, and weak voices. These three vocal qualities should be mixed within each section, but care should be taken that strong and weak singers are not isolated. Dearl Johnson (1997) states,

> Usually, better results can be achieved if singers are placed in "circles" or "zones" of influence within the ensemble, the number of circles depending on the size of the choir and the range of talent among choir members.
>
> Within each circle the stronger singers are surrounded by more average singers, who in turn are placed next to the weaker members of the group. . . . This arrangement provides a solid core of singing, and at the same time permits some growth on the part of the most talented members of the choir. (p. 23)

Some singers feel lost within a section when they cannot hear themselves sing. Johnson recommends that each singer be given enough physical space to retain vocal identity.

The sound of a choral ensemble often is determined by the front row of singers. Voices to the rear tend to be "soaked up." Therefore, persons with vocal problems should not be in the front row, as there are no buffers for their vocal quality. Singers whose voices closely match and who have good voice quality are the best candidates for the front row of the choir.

Acoustic voice matching takes considerable time during initial rehearsals. Each section is worked with individually, and when possible, members can be asked to come early to rehearsal. A short vocalise or a phrase from a song is used for the matching process. An excellent singer is chosen to begin, and others are requested to sing individually until a close match is found—one that is similar in timbre, projection, and vibrato. Another match is chosen to sit on the other side of the original singer. Then, matches are found for these outer voices, and so forth. It is interesting to hear how some voices naturally fit better with others.

Another procedure for building the desired choral sound is to teach good voice production as part of the choral warm-up. Many choristers have no formal voice instruction in their backgrounds; they are in choir because they enjoy singing. When singers are taught to energize the voice and sing with a relaxed throat, choral tone is immediately improved.

Sectional Characteristics

The soprano and tenor sections are heard more easily than the alto and bass because higher frequencies are easier to detect and sound clearer. Therefore, choral balance will be affected by the number of singers in each section. Generally, for school choirs there should be more altos and basses because these parts tend to be overbalanced by the higher voice parts. However, when mature singers are involved, strong voices in the alto and bass sections will balance the sopranos and tenors with an equal number of singers. The choral director must know the vocal strengths of the choristers to determine the correct balance as far as numbers of persons on a part.

SOPRANO.   A good soprano sound is youthful, clear, and lyric, devoid of heavy vibrato, but not necessarily straight. The desired vocal timbre is typically bright and full but not edgy.

Sopranos typically have trouble vocalizing in the area above f^2 because they attempt to carry the weight of the voice too high. They need to sing lighter in this area and learn to shift into pure upper-voice production. Sopranos should sing one dynamic level less than marked in loud passages, and only *mp* to *mf* above the treble staff. They also need to modify closed vowels toward "ah" on pitches above the staff.

ALTO.   The alto voice is warm and less bright than the soprano. It should be full, well rounded, and able to project. A certain dark quality is desirable.

Most altos in choirs are really mezzo-sopranos. These women should be encouraged to drop their jaws more, increasing the depth of vocal quality. An overly dark alto sound may be the result of a depressed larynx and a small mouth opening. The younger alto typically has a voice break around the pitches a^1 to c^2. She needs to be vocalized from the top down, so the upper voice merges and blends with the chest register. Altos never consistently sing the tenor part.

TENOR.   The typical tenor sound is characterized by lightness and vitality. It also has a certain ring that makes it easily heard. While the quality is full, it is not as warm a sound as the baritone.

Amateur tenors tend to push the chest voice too high, with the designation "necktie tenor" being quite justified. Tenors need to sing lighter above e^1, with a pure upper-voice production. This sound blends beautifully and works well in lighter-voice singing such as that required for Renaissance music. When a fuller sound is desired, tenors must enter the upper register through the lighter, upper voice, and immediately support the sound for a greater fullness. Pushing the weight of the lower voice upward does not work. A sense of projection in the mask is important to cultivate an upper-voice ring.

BASS.   The bass voice is the fullest in the choir and has a robust quality. A certain warmth and darkness is desirable, without the sound's being hooty or overly dark. The baritone voice is lighter in quality, while the true bass has a richness that is easy to distinguish.

The bass section tends to sing flat more than any other section of the choir. This is because bass voice production is often overly dark or muffled. Basses need to sing with a forward focus and brighter vowel colors, especially for darker vowel sounds on pitches in the lower register of the voice. A lighter and softer vocal quality in the upper voice above middle c also is recommended. To develop pitches below the bass clef, basses are vocalized in the pure chest register below c. Many would-be basses never learn to sing very low because they fail to shift out of the mixed registration they use for pitch production in the middle voice. The pure chest register has to be cultivated for the development of the low bass voice (Swanson, 1977).

Seating Arrangements

The director decides the choral seating plan before the first rehearsal. Even if specific seat assignments are not yet made, the initial seating plan reflects the organization of the rehearsal room into rows, aisles, and number of seats per section.

Figure 10.9. Two-part chorus formation 1.

Figure 10.10. Two-part chorus formation 2.

A variety of choir formations are possible. When considering the placement of sections, the director needs to consider such things as the strengths of the various voice parts, repertoire, acoustics of the room, room design, eventual performance venue, and the conductor's personal preference for choral timbre. Wilhelm Ehmann (1968) indicates his priority when he states:

> The formation of the choir should . . . be determined by the structure of the music that is to be sung. Arranging the singers in such a way, they represent the structure of the music in a visible, physical manner—they stand "right in the structure of the piece" as it were. All relationships to the music and the unleashing of musical energies are represented in a visual and demonstrable form. Singing and listening are greatly facilitated by such formations. (pp. 8–9)

Ehmann further recommends that "the same singers should always stand next to each other" (p. 14). Thus it is important that the choir not rehearse in one formation and stand in another for the performance. Placing singers by height for a concert, when they do not sit that way for rehearsal, can disturb the singers' security and typically affects the performance in a negative manner.

When possible, the overall choir formation should be in the form of a semicircle, rather than a straight line. This formation improves the ability of singers to hear and see one another. It also permits those on the fringes of the group to feel more connected to the entire choir. Most choral risers of the standing type are made to form a semicircle when joined together.

Two-Part Formations

Many children's choirs stand in two-part formations. Two arrangements are possible. In Figure 10.9, the first part is placed in front of the second part when the "*first voice has the unrestricted lead* while the second voice moves along in a *faux bourdon* manner" (Lehmann, 1986, p. 9). This position also works well when the first part has a cantus firmus and the second part has a free, contrapuntal part against it.

The second possibility for a two-part formation, where the two parts are equal, is that shown in Figure 10.10. This is a common arrangement when part 1 sings the melody and part 2 the harmony. (Note: choir formations for young adolescents are discussed in Chapter 7.)

Three-Part Formations

Two formations work well for three-part choirs. The first (see Figure 10.11) places the three parts in sections from left to right, where the melody is predominantly in part 1, and parts 2

Figure 10.11. Three-part chorus formation 1.

Figure 10.12. Three-part chorus formation 2.

and 3 sing harmony. This implies an almost equal importance of the three parts. It also provides for flexibility when two-part music is sung. The middle voice part is split so that half sings with part 1 and half with part 2.

It is sometimes advantageous to divide the two harmony parts by placing the melodic part in between them (see Figure 10.12), especially when the voice parts are of the same gender (e.g., SSA) or quality (e.g., all treble). In this way, singers of the two harmony parts are less likely to confuse one another; that is, each harmony group stands next to the melody and not the other harmony part.

Four-Part Formations

The traditional four-part formation for an SATB choir is shown in Figure 10.13. This assumes voice parts of approximately equal strength; if the voice parts are divided, the second part is placed behind the first. Having the soprano and bass sections in close proximity helps to anchor intonation while alto and tenor parts relate in filling out the inner voices.

The men's sections of a mixed choir often are weaker in numbers and sound than the women's sections. When this is the case, the men can be placed in the center of the choir, with the tenors on the right and the basses on the left (see Figure 10.14). When there are more women than men, the women's sections extend to behind the men's sections as shown in Figure 10.15.

When the tenor section is relatively weak in relation to the other parts, the formation in Figure 10.16 is helpful in projecting the tenor sound. This plan shows the tenors in the center front, with basses behind them. Care must be taken, however, that tenors in the front row have a vocal quality that matches other singers in the front row. A big voice will tend to stick out, something to be avoided in all front-row placements.

In recent years choral directors at the college and university levels have placed singers in quartets (SATB) or in fully scrambled arrangements (SBATSBATSBAT). These types of formations are more appropriate for homophonic music and are excellent for developing the independence of singers and for improving intonation. These formations do not work well with inexperienced or average singers.

A modified scramble is possible in which sopranos and basses alternate in rows, front to back, on the left, and tenors and altos do likewise on the right (see Figure 10.17). This provides the singers with an opportunity to grow in independence while keeping the sections more together. Mixed formations do not work well with polyphonic music, where individual voice parts are of equal importance and need to be heard and seen as units within the contrapuntal texture. A sectional seating or standing arrangement is preferable for this type of texture.

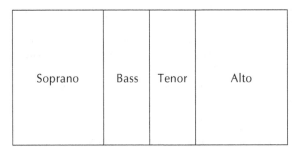

Figure 10.13. Four-part chorus formation 1: Traditional.

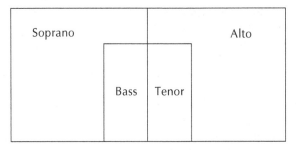

Figure 10.14. Four-part chorus formation 2: Men in center.

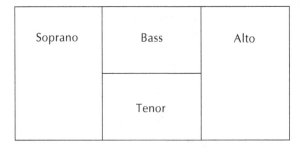

Figure 10.15. Four-part chorus formation 3: Men in center.

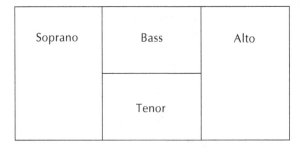

Figure 10.16. Four-part chorus formation 4: Tenor section front and center.

Figure 10.17. Four-part chorus formation 5: Modified staggered order.

The Seating Chart

It is helpful if the choral conductor has a seating chart prepared before the first rehearsal. It is even better if singers know where they are to sit as they enter the rehearsal room. This can be done through a prerehearsal letter, or a large chart can be posted outside the rehearsal room with the designated seating. If each singer has an assigned folder number, the use of that number on the seating chart helps to facilitate communication of choir placement. Singers have but to find their numbers in order to know where they will sit.

Preparing for the choral rehearsal is a big task. Planning can take as much or more time than the rehearsal itself. Without a plan, the rehearsal is likely to be directionless and inefficient. The greater the preparation, the more likely that rehearsal objectives will be met and satisfaction derived by everyone. A well-organized choral director who implements a well-thought-out plan has charted a path to success.

STUDY AND DISCUSSION QUESTIONS

1. What are some general guidelines for scheduling concert dates?
2. What are some general guidelines for choosing the choral repertoire for the year?
3. Why is having a long-range rehearsal schedule important?
4. How should rehearsal objectives be stated?
5. What are the three main types of rehearsal formats, and which one appears to work best? Why?
6. Approximately how much time should be spent on warm-ups and sight-singing activities in the fifty-minute choral rehearsal?
7. When is it appropriate to suspend sight-singing and historical knowledge instruction in the choral rehearsal plan?
8. With what type of choral music activity should the rehearsal begin and end? Why?
9. Why should singers be instructed to mark their scores, and how should this be done?
10. With what element of a choral composition does the choral director begin score analysis?
11. Why is it so important to know the formal structure of a choral selection?
12. What are the main reasons for using an analytical graph?
13. Why is the harmonic rhythm an important consideration when studying a choral composition?
14. What are the expressive elements that should be highlighted in a conductor's score?
15. When should possible problems in the music be discovered? Why?

16. What aspects of the choral sound are affected by the placement of singers?

17. What is the process of acoustic voice matching, and why is it important for arranging the singers?

18. What major vocal problems does each voice part of an SATB ensemble often exhibit, and how should each of these problems be corrected?

19. What type of choir formation can be used with a choir in which the men's sections are weaker than the women's sections?

20. When should a seating chart be devised, and why is such a chart important?

REFERENCES

Cox, J. (1989). Rehearsal organizational structures used by successful Ohio high school choral directors. *Journal of Research in Music Education, 37*(3), 201–18.

Demorest, S. M. (1996). Structuring a musical choral rehearsal. *Music Educators Journal, 82*(4), 25–30.

Ekholm, E. (2000). The effect of singing mode and seating arrangement on choral blend and overall singing sound. *Journal of Research in Music Education, 48*(2), 123–35.

Ehmann, W. (1968). *Choral directing*. Minneapolis: Augsburg.

Herford, J. (1988). The choral conductor's preparation of the musical score. In H. A. Decker and J. Herford (eds.), *Choral conducting symposium* (2d ed.), 199–265. Englewood Cliffs, NJ: Prentice Hall.

Hillis, M. (n.d.). *At rehearsals*. Chicago: Chicago Symphony Chorus.

Jorgensen, N. S., and C. Pfeiler (1995). *Things they never taught you in choral methods*. Milwaukee: Hal Leonard.

Johnson, D. J. (1997). *Choral techniques: Beyond the basics*. San Diego, CA: Neil A. Kjos Music.

MENC (1991). *Teaching choral music: A course of study* (1991). Reston, VA: Music Educators National Conference.

Neuen, D. (n.d.). Choral techniques. Unpublished handout document for workshop presentation at The University of Iowa.

Swanson, F. J. (1977). The vanishing basso profundo and fry tones. *Choral Journal 17*(5), 5–6.

11 | Organizing Performances

The major goal of any choral program is the performance. Weeks, months, and even years of preparation can precede any given musical event. While the process of music learning is important to music educators, a choral program that does not result in a product is lacking the very element that drives the program forward—the satisfaction derived from singing music in a polished performance for an appreciative audience.

The success of the choral curriculum does not depend upon achieving a wonderful concert. Cognitive objectives (i.e., knowledge gained) and psychomotor learning (i.e., improved skills) are important aspects of choral music education. However, if rehearsal preparation does not end in a sense of satisfaction for the singers, then the objective of planning for an aesthetic musical experience has not been achieved; it is this need that draws most people to choral singing in the first place.

Organizing for performances is part of the tremendous preparation effort required of choral directors. The goal of this chapter is to draw attention to the many details that need consideration when planning for effective concert presentations, choir tours, festivals, and competitions.

CONCERT PREPARATION

The first requirement of successful concert preparation is to choose the literature for the program. (The challenges of this process have been addressed in earlier chapters.) As stated previously, of paramount importance is that music choice be governed by educational objectives. However, a concert need not be stiff and formal to be educational. Audiences are accepting of programs that demonstrate student learning when the programming is done in such a way as to make the experience interesting and appealing. A balance of musical styles helps achieve an appealing performance package.

Programming

Once the literature has been chosen, it must be programmed into a sequence that is interesting, diverse, flowing, and without glaring clashes. Deral Johnson (1997, p. 40) presents the following guidelines:

1. Work for proper key alignments throughout the program. (Compositions which clash in key structure should not be used next to each other.)

2. Begin and end the performance with big, loud, and fast-tempo considerations.

3. Do not program many slow-moving compositions in sequence.

4. Strive for visual appeal as well as aural interest.

183

5. Try to create a fast pace when programming in order to maintain audience interest.

6. Consider using a central theme as one interesting way of organizing a program.

All of the above recommendations are worth considering. Ending a concert "big, loud, and fast" may seem a little like playing to the audience, but this is a common and successful practice in choral programming. Beginning a program with soft and reflective Renaissance music may work for sophisticated audiences, but a rousing opener is more apt to stimulate interest among the general public.

Slower, more intense, and difficult music needs to come near the beginning of the concert when the audience is fresh and attentive. The transition from such music must be carefully planned. For example, programming *The Circus Band* by Charles Ives after *Ave verum corpus* of W. A. Mozart would be quite a stylistic shock.

The problem of programming sacred and secular music in juxtaposition is to be considered carefully, as some styles work together and others do not. One piece of serious sacred music will not fit in a grouping of upbeat, secular works. Similarly, a light and bubbly madrigal in the midst of a sacred set is not good programming. Grouping pieces by similar styles is desirable.

The flow of a program can be thought of as similar to a drama. The characters are introduced, a variety of emotions are developed as the action proceeds, and a peak experience brings the drama to a close. Therefore, the director chooses a good opener, provides for a variety of styles, tempos, keys, and moods as the concert progresses, and ends it all with a memorable closing selection. Handel's *Messiah* is an excellent example of one musical work that reflects this outline of development. The challenge for the choral director is to program concerts that contain such unity and variety.

The use of a theme to unify a program is quite common, such as, "Echoes from a Cathedral," or "Melodies of Broadway." Themes can reflect certain musical eras (e.g., "The Glorious Baroque") or the music of one composer (e.g., "Schubertiade"). Programming according to the progression of historical eras also can be unifying if selections are arranged with dramatic intent.

> The tonal transparency of the Renaissance period moves smoothly into the changing tone color of the Baroque era, which proceeds beautifully into the searching for tonal richness and shading possibilities of the Romantic period. All of the above lead quite logically to experimentation with varieties of tonal concepts to satisfy the contemporary appetite. (Johnson, 1997, pp. 40–41)

Johnson also notes that chronological programming can be less satisfying when various styles require a variety of standing formations or when a number of choirs are involved.

Not all music that is rehearsed must be scheduled for performance, especially if it is not going well. It can be quite demoralizing for a choir to perform poorly, and the choral conductor should not hesitate to cut music from the concert, even if it appears on the concert program. A simple announcement to the audience that a selection is being deleted will suffice. Sometimes, directors will choose a difficult piece by which to challenge a choir, with no intentions of programming it. This can work when there is enough other music to perform.

When there are a number of choirs on a program, the younger groups should appear somewhere near the beginning or middle of the concert. The opening and closing positions must be strong, and more mature choirs should be scheduled for these places. The first group the audience hears sets the expectation for the remainder of the concert. Likewise, the audience should leave having just experienced the best possible singing. A combined choral presentation sometimes is programmed for the final selection.

The programming of concert music is an art. Without careful planning the presentation will likely be haphazard and without unity. The programming goal should be a concert that is a satisfying whole.

Length of Program

When programming for a general audience, it is better to have too short a program than one overly long. "Keep concerts short and sweet. Patrons will leave wanting more and return eagerly for the next performance" (Jorgensen and Pfeiler, 1995, p. 64).

A school concert that is longer than an hour and a half is self-defeating, no matter how good the quality of the singing. Parents and the general populace are used to watching television, where ten-minute segments are the norm. Many people become restless and uninterested when a traditional choral concert exceeds an hour. The programming of an intermission is necessary for longer concerts, where a natural break is warranted. However, audience members are typically lost during intermissions when students from choirs that already have performed are free to leave. By keeping the total concert between an hour and an hour and a half, an intermission is not needed.

A timing sheet should be prepared for each concert. Not only the times of each selection are to be listed but also time for applause, time for entering and exiting the performance area, and time for any greeting or announcements.

The Printed Program

A printed program is an asset to any performance. It presents a visual picture of the presentation and helps the audience follow the order of the concert. An attractive cover should include the name of the school, the theme (if appropriate), and the date, time, and place of the event. It also should include the choral conductor's name. Titles such as "Mrs.," "Mr.," "Dr.," and so forth are not used.

The program must be neat and the print easy to read, with good contrast on the page. Spacing is important, and divisions of the program should be discernible. All titles and names need to be checked for proper spelling. The use of a computer to assist in program layout is a tremendous asset.

Students' names should be included in the program when possible. The printed program serves as a historical document and records student participation in choir; students enjoy seeing their names in print. All names need to be double checked for spelling accuracy. Also, the names of soloists, accompanists, small ensemble members, choir officers, ushers, stage crew, school administrators, and anyone else who helped with the concert should be included.

The back of the program cover is a good place for comments from the director. This space can be used for providing program notes and items of special interest (e.g., a testimony to graduating seniors), and it is an excellent place for arts advocacy statements. Also, objectives of the choral music curriculum can be highlighted.

Audience etiquette leaves something to be desired during many school performances. A simple printed statement (e.g., "The audience is asked to neither leave nor enter the auditorium while groups are performing," or "Please refrain from the taking of flash pictures while the choirs are singing.") can do much to educate the audience.

> If audience deportment is a problem, use program notes to thank the audience for not walking in and out during performances, for leaving crying babies at home and for their

energetic and kind applause. The soft sell can work small miracles. If you are still not satisfied with audience behavior, do something about it. Teach each choir member about correct and acceptable behavior at concerts, hoping the message will reach the audience indirectly. (Jorgensen and Pfeiler, 1995, p. 64)

Audiences should never be lectured about their deportment, but students must be given direct instruction about being a good audience member.

A listing in the program of forthcoming school arts events makes for good advanced publicity. The inclusion of all events (instrumental concerts, dramas, art exhibits, etc.) helps to provide a sense of cooperation and goodwill among all arts faculty. Including events from other schools (elementary, middle school, high school) is helpful, as parents often have students at different grade levels.

Concerts provide excellent venues for honoring parents and administrators for their continued support. School administrators may be asked to provide a brief welcome to the audience; this ensures their attendance and gives them some much-needed recognition. Parents may be thanked in the program ("Our thanks to all those attending today's concert for supporting the choral students at Piedmont High.") or thanked publicly for backing the music program. Choral directors should never miss an opportunity to express gratitude to those people who make their jobs possible.

Technical Concerns

A number of technical matters must concern the choral director before the date of the concert. Among these are:

- Ushers
- Tickets
- Piano tuning
- Student attire
- Sound system
- Stage crew and equipment

USHERS.   Some high schools have an ushers club that regularly provides ushers for school events. The faculty sponsor works from the school calendar, but a personal contact is advisable prior to the event in case the concert has been overlooked. If ushers are not available through such a source, some other arrangement is required, such as asking students from the Student Council or other club organizations. Proper recognition of the ushers is needed in the concert program.

One purpose of the ushers is to hand out programs. Someone from the ushering group should be told where the programs will be located before the concert. Ushers also need to know that any remaining programs are to be returned to the choral room for students who desire another copy, perhaps to send to a relative.

A time for the concert venue doors to open is typically set at forty-five minutes to an hour before the concert is to start. If there is an admission charge and tickets sold, the ushers collect tickets and hand out programs as persons enter. Upon a given signal (e.g., lowering of lights), ushers ask those arriving to take their seats quickly, close the doors, and remain posted inside the doors. When latecomers arrive (as they always do), they may be requested to remain standing at the back until there is a planned break in the program, or they can be seated in available places at the rear of the seating area. Late arrivers should not be permitted to walk in and interrupt singing; a notice to this effect in the program will help educate the audience to the proper procedures for late arrival.

Student ushers are often timid about insisting that people not interrupt the program once the concert begins. Therefore, a meeting of the ushers and choral director before the day of the concert can provide the directives and encouragement they need to enforce the rules. Much time, planning, and effort go into a concert, which all can be ruined by people who are insensitive to audience performance behavior. The ushers are responsible, to some degree, for audience control. They also need to know the locations of public restrooms, telephones, and any room available for someone wanting to lie down because of sudden illness.

TICKETS.   If reserved seating is used, as for musical productions, the ushers have the additional duty of guiding people to their seats. Ushers must know the master outline of the seating plan and the proper procedures for ushering. The use of a small pen flashlight is recommended for the reading of seat assignments.

Whether or not to charge admission to regular school concerts is something decided upon by the choral director and the school principal. Some schools charge for most events, and others do not. A ticket purchased, no matter how small the charge, is a commitment to attend the concert. It is one of the best forms of advertising, and it provides a source of income for the choral activity fund. Typically, each student in a choir is given a number of tickets to sell and is accountable for the money or returned tickets. A student's sales can be applied to his or her individual credit when a quota is being raised for choir tour. Tickets for regular choral concerts are usually of the general admission type.

PIANO TUNING.   If a piano is being used for a concert, it needs to be tuned before the dress rehearsal. When the climate from where the piano is moved is different from the performance venue, it should be moved twenty-four hours before the tuning to permit time for adjustment to the new environment. Once the piano is in place and tuned, it is not good to move it before the concert; some pianos go out of tune quickly when moved. The piano must be placed so the pianist has easy sight of the conductor and the choristers can hear it.

Most school districts have a regular contract for the services of a piano tuner, but contact is made by the choral director. It is helpful to have a yearly schedule of piano tunings set before the academic year begins. Piano tuners require a quiet environment in which to work, and every effort must be made to guarantee a time free from distractions.

STUDENT ATTIRE.   The attire for a concert should be decided upon well in advance of the concert date, as well as any needs for special garments. If robes, tuxes, vests, or other attire are stored at the school, time needs to be set aside for the orderly distribution and collection of these things. Student aids can be helpful in this area. If garments are to be taken home before a program, some decision is necessary as to how the attire will be transported without being soiled.

SOUND SYSTEM.   Nothing can ruin a concert more quickly than a high-pitched squeal from a sound system. If sound amplification is needed for the performance, every effort must be made to have the system operated by a person who knows what he or she is doing. It is helpful if that person can do basic repairs or replace equipment that fails to operate properly.

Many performance venues have sound systems designed only for speaking purposes. Such modes of amplification distort music, especially at higher frequencies. When such a system is the only one available, it is best not to use it. It is possible to rent good-quality sound equipment, and this needs to be done when needed.

Choral directors often have their concerts audio or video recorded. Again, good-quality equipment is needed to produce an accurate recording. When possible, the recording should be done by someone with expertise in this area. It is not enjoyable to listen to a tape that has been under- or overrecorded, or where the piano is louder than the choir. Likewise, most video cameras have poor sound capabilities. A high-quality system and an excellent technician are required for maximizing all uses of amplified and recorded sound.

STAGE CREW AND EQUIPMENT. Choral risers and a conductor's podium with music stand are the two basic equipment needs for most choral concerts. These and any additional properties should be assigned for handling to some group of people, typically the stage crew. Some schools have stage crew clubs that take care of all staged performances. When not available, another group of students can be used. However, students in stage crews need to understand the seriousness of their jobs. Curtains that don't open at the correct time, lights that go out, leaving people moving in the dark, crashes of chairs from backstage—all are signs of an amateurish production.

The stage crew is invaluable for taking care of many of the technical concerns before, during, and following the concert. Their names are placed in the program for proper recognition, and they are thanked individually by the choral director for their help.

Dress Rehearsal

Public performance can be traumatic for students who are inexperienced in standing before people. Therefore, the dress rehearsal must be as much like the concert as possible. Jay Light (1995) states:

> The overriding rule about practicing performing is to simulate "battle conditions" as much as possible. What you want to do is to get as close to matching what the performance is really going to feel like when you're practicing, so that at the performance nothing that happens is a surprise. (p. 10)

Even when something happens that is a surprise, the dress rehearsal can help choristers learn to handle it.

One directive that all students need to hear before performing is "Don't advertise your mistakes." Problems occur in many concerts that are unanticipated—someone fails to cut off at the right time, the soloist falters, the pianist turns too many pages at once, someone becomes ill. Many of these incidents will go unnoticed by the audience if choir members do not give them away by looking at the mistake maker, laughing, or rolling their eyes. Students should be admonished to act professionally—"the show must go on." Choristers who advertise mistakes are often immature; they need to understand performance etiquette. The choral director must take the time to address concert behavior before the day of the performance.

The dress rehearsal should proceed as much as possible without stopping. The time for correcting note problems is over—all focus needs to be on a polished performance and smooth transitions. The practice of entering and leaving the stage area is as important at the dress rehearsal as singing the music. A good musical performance can be ruined by students who appear undisciplined and lacking in direction.

Similarly, if the stage crew has jobs to do during the concert, the dress rehearsal is the time to practice those specific tasks and to make adjustments. The dress rehearsal is as much about technical concerns as it is about music. If students are blinded by stage lights, then adjustments in lighting are needed immediately.

Planning for a concert must be as organized and focused as preparing for the rehearsals leading up to it. It takes experience to learn the process completely, but giving advanced thought to the many areas indicated previously will help in preventing important details from falling through the cracks. Jay Light (1995) relates this anecdote:

> Lee Trevino, the famous golfer, once won a sudden-death playoff match by sinking a seemingly impossible putt from a great distance. He was asked by a commentator afterwards "Surely, Lee, you must agree that was a really lucky shot you made?" Trevino replied without hesitation, "Sure, it was a lucky shot, but you know, I've found that the more I practice, the luckier I get." (p. 11)

So it is with concert planning and successful program presentations. The more the choral director performs and learns from each experience, the easier it becomes.

CHOIR TOURS

Out-of-school concert events can be both motivating and rewarding for students who are the best singers in the choral program. While activities such as choir tours, contests, and choral festivals are exciting and bring special recognition, they also involve much preparation that typically goes beyond the school day for both choral director and students. Choral music educators who include these types of experiences in the choral program are wise to think about the time commitment before becoming involved in too many out-of-school events. They also need to be dedicated to making all such activities educational and not just fun-driven.

The annual choir tour has become quite common for senior high school choral programs, and even some children's choirs take annual tours. This event can be the highlight of the year, or it can result in a negative experience if not properly planned. There are numerous pitfalls, and the inexperienced director may succumb to many of them without the proper guidance. The following tips are expanded and freely adapted from an article by the author (Phillips, 1996) and are presented for consideration by the choral director who is organizing and planning successful tours.

Educational Objectives

A choir tour must be an extension of the curriculum and the educational objectives of the choral program. To take a trip for the sake of taking a trip is not justifiable. School choral conductors are music educators and as such are employed to teach music—they are not professional entertainers.

Examples of justifiable objectives include: (1) understanding the life of professional musicians who spend much time on the road, giving numerous concerts in a short time span, (2) having a highly intense performance schedule that results in a higher level of musical achievement, (3) experiencing a diverse audience and wider appreciation for the arts, (4) learning to live and cooperate with others in a restricted environment, (5) gaining knowledge of the world outside students' immediate surroundings, and (6) becoming self-sufficient in meeting time demands, schedules, packing and unpacking, use of money, and so forth. Whatever objectives the choral director identifies should be communicated in writing to students, parents, and the school community at large.

Extent of Tour

Choir tours include everything from short, overnight exchange concerts to extended European tours. When they have no previous tour experience, a one- or two-day tour can be just as exciting for students as a one- to two-week tour. However, once students take big tours, or the place of longer tours becomes common in the program, it is difficult to turn back to smaller ventures. The beginning choral director is wise to keep initial tours short and may be wiser to keep all tours short.

The extent of any tour comes down to how much time and effort the choir director is willing to expend. Tours are costly, and the longer the tour the greater the cost. Since fund-raising is typically involved, the longer the tour, the more fund-raising is necessary. Extended tours require much work, and most of this will be during out-of-school hours. However, a tour to Europe can be a "dream trip" for those involved and may be well worth the hours of planning and preparation.

Professional Help

Professional booking agencies will arrange a tour for a price; these agencies regularly advertise in music publications such as the *Choral Journal* and *Music Educators Journal*. Some of the activities they offer include competitions and performances at famous venues such as Carnegie Hall in New York City and Epcot Center in Orlando, Florida. Using a tour agency saves a tremendous amount of work for the choral director, but it substantially increases the overall cost. When choosing a professional agency, background and reliability should be checked to insure good service. The choral director can ask for names of other groups who have booked tours to obtain references. If the company will not supply this information, it is best to stay away.

Tour Dates

Choosing the time for a choir tour is extremely important; the dates should not conflict with other school activities in which students may be participating. Neither must the tour come at a time when students will be taking semester exams, or are involved in standardized tests such as the SAT. Also, the choir should be at its peak performance time. Some choirs tour at the end of the school year, when classes are ended. Whatever dates are chosen, they should be decided upon and placed on the school calendar at least by the spring preceding the new academic year.

Financing the Tour

Most school boards will not finance tours for choirs, and the required funds are raised by the choral area. A budget is established as one of the first organizational procedures, and the total cost of the trip is projected. The budget includes such items as transportation, housing, food, performance hall fees (some venues will charge a fee for stage hands and security personnel), and admissions to attractions planned for the group. The total cost is then divided by the number of students going on the tour (not all may elect to go), and this figure becomes the prorated cost per student for the trip. (This figure typically includes the additional cost of chaperones and director). If using a professional agency, they will figure this cost for the group. A date of six to eight weeks before the event is set for students to have their quotas paid.

It is not wise to raise money for the tour on a "one for all—all for one" basis. This often results in 10 percent of the students (and parents) doing all of the work. Rather, students are required to raise individual quotas through various activities planned for the choir. Even the sale of concert tickets can be applied to students' quotas. It needs to be understood from the beginning that if a student's quota is not raised by the stipulated date, then the balance will be paid out of pocket. Some students may elect not to participate in fund-raising activities and instead write a check for their amount.

No student should be denied tour participation because of financial hardship. However, a good effort in fund-raising activities must be demonstrated by any student needing financial help. Community groups and even the school board may be contacted to help with a scholarship fund.

Numerous professional fund-raising organizations help school groups raise money. Most provide good service, but references should be checked before employing any agency. Some schools limit fund-raising, and school policies must be followed. However, booster groups often carry out their own activities outside of school governance. Choir tours require large sums of money, and the choral director must be cautious that all funds are handled appropriately.

Housing

Students can be housed in the homes of other students at school-sponsored festivals and for exchange concerts. This requires no cost and is easily administered. Sometimes students are placed in housing that is very different from that of their home environment and need to be warned against reacting negatively in such circumstances. Most places can be endured for a night. However, it should be normal practice that all host families are routinely screened, especially when unknown by anyone connected with the choir. Booster groups are good for providing this service.

When students are housed in hotels or motels, close supervision is required by chaperones. Most school-aged students are minors, and the choral director may be held responsible for their negative actions. Strict rules need to be written about behavior in the hotel, a curfew established, and regular room checks conducted. Long-distance services should be disconnected by the hotel and personal calls made only at pay phones.

Daily Schedule

The daily routine should reflect a balance of performance, sight-seeing, and recreational activity. Students are not to be given free time away from the group and must not fraternize with strangers. All recreational activity should be planned for group participation. If students do not elect to swim at the hotel pool, they can lounge in the area. Their presence needs to be accounted for at all times. The schedule should not be packed with so much activity that students become exhausted and present a poor performance. Neither can the schedule be so light that students have time to get into trouble. Above all, a preplanned schedule of events and times is necessary for students to observe.

Chaperones

A choir tour cannot be managed by the choral director alone. Help from chaperones is needed, and enough chaperones should be included to easily manage the group. A meeting for chaperones before the trip is a good way to help introduce the tour and make assignments. Chaperones need to understand their role. The tour is not for their fun and enjoyment, even though it is hoped they do enjoy the trip. Rather, they are present to help insure the success of the tour by enforcing rules and helping with equipment, attire, and so forth. Typically, the younger the group the more chaperones needed. Parents, other teachers, and administrators often serve in this capacity.

Rules of Conduct

Guidelines for behavior need to be set and communicated before the choir leaves on tour. Students must understand their role as ambassadors of the school and while on the trip are under the school's authority. Consequences for breaking rules must be clearly stated, and students who misbehave should be disciplined according to school policy. Students need to be told how to act on the bus or plane, how to conduct themselves in the hotel, and what is and is not appropriate boy-girl activity. As some students may be dating in the group, public displays of affection are to be discouraged.

Students get on each other's nerves quite easily. Personality types emerge, and students start complaining. Everyone needs to know from the beginning that a tour places people in close confines that are atypical; they have to learn to get along. Learning tolerance of others may indeed be one of the objectives of any choir tour.

Guidelines for managing money also are helpful. Some students will want to buy every souvenir they see and won't apportion their funds for the entire trip. If they are required to provide for any of their own food, they may go hungry near the end of the tour. The choral director should plan to have extra money along in case a student runs out, loses, or has money stolen.

Rules about student attire definitely are needed. Students need to look good when performing, and when not, their attire should reflect well upon the group. Choir robes are not appropriate in environments such as Disney World, and choir robes are difficult to pack and transport. Some type of performance apparel that is neutral is recommended for all performance venues.

Parental Consent

It is extremely important that parents and guardians sign a parental permission form, and this form be notarized by a notary public. Hospitals may refuse treatment to a minor when a permission form is lacking the official notary stamp. A medical consent statement is to be included granting any hospital or medical staff the permission to administer medication, medical treatment, allergy shot, immunization or emergency surgical care. Hospital staff will want to telephone parents or guardians regardless of the notarized form.

Even though a parent or guardian signs a consent form, persons cannot sign away their rights. The choir director may be found negligible in a court of law when he or she has acted (or not acted) in such a way as to place a student in harm's way. For example, a music teacher was sued by the parents of a student who was badly injured on a tour while crossing the street in the middle of a city block. Before dismissing the students from the bus, the director had told the students to walk to the corner, wait for the light, and cross only at the crosswalk. One student disobeyed and ran across the street from between parked cars, was struck by a truck, and lay bleeding in the street. Fortunately, the student did not die. Because there was evidence that the students had been told the correct place to cross the street just moments before exiting the bus, the charges against the music director were dismissed. No parental consent form would have saved a director who had not acted in such a way as to protect the students before dismissing them.

A letter should be sent to parents and guardians informing them of the trip. Included must be the consent form and a schedule that includes dates, locations, and telephone numbers for emergency contacts. When possible, the entire tour handbook, if used, should be sent to parents as well as given to students (see below regarding the handbook).

Musical Preparation

No choir tour is worth the effort if students perform poorly. Choirs that perform abroad are ambassadors of their country and should present the best they have to offer. While the planning for a choir tour is momentous, even more important is the musical preparation. If rehearsal time is spent on choir tour concerns, the results will show in performance. Rehearsals should be for rehearsing the music. Written communication is best for detailing choir tour procedures. Rehearsal time also can be placed in the tour schedule as part of the daily routine. Students need to be reminded that the focus of the tour is singing, not having fun. Anyway, it is more fun when the choir sings well.

Tour Handbook

A tour handbook can be a valuable asset for any choir tour. Such a booklet is easy to produce with the use of a computer. Contents may include some or all of the following:

- Luggage guidelines
- Safety guidelines
- Packing checklist
- Conduct on the bus, hotel, trip
- First aid and medications
- Performance venues
- Sight-seeing attractions
- Chaperones and duties
- Hotel housing list
- Daily schedule (with telephone numbers for emergency contact)

Choir Tour Success

Choir tours can create wonderful and lasting memories, or tours can turn into big headaches. Careful planning is necessary for each step from beginning to end if a successful trip is to be realized. Hundreds of choirs tour every year. It is a huge responsibility for the choir director but a great educational opportunity for students and everyone involved.

CHORAL FESTIVALS

The noncompetitive choral festival is a standard part of today's extended school choral program. It exists in two typical formats: (1) entire choirs from a few schools come together at one site to perform individually and as a combined group, and (2) a smaller number of students from many schools join to form a massed choir that presents the entire program. Examples of the latter include college- and university-sponsored honor choirs; ACDA or MENC sponsored all-state, regional, and district choirs; and festivals sponsored by individual schools. The event may be one day in duration or encompass two to three days, with a concert on the final afternoon or evening. A guest conductor most often is employed to conduct the massed choir and, in clinic-type festivals, works with individual choirs for a limited amount of time. Some festivals involve individual choirs performing for a panel of choral experts, who provide written comments about their performance. This is not a competition, and no rankings are given.

Benefits of Festival Participation

Choral festivals are often "mountaintop" experiences for students who have a deep love for singing. To gather with other students who are serious about music making is a unique opportunity, and it can motivate students to choose choral music as a career. An inspiring guest conductor combined with outstanding choral literature results in a performance that demonstrates to students just how fulfilling the arts are to humanity.

Students participating in choral festivals develop new friendships and achieve a camaraderie that is spontaneous and infectious. Instead of competing against one another, they learn to work cooperatively toward a common goal.

The benefits from this experience carry over to the home choral program, as students are more aware of what can be accomplished with concentrated work and discipline. Their level of expectation is increased, as well as their ability to discriminate and make value judgments about choirs and choral singing. An outstanding festival can help the school choral program achieve growth and prominence in the curriculum.

Student Preparation

Once a choral director commits his or her choir or students to a choral festival, the director must take responsibility for preparing the students musically. Most high school choral members are unable to learn new music by themselves adequately and must have help. When only a few members of a choir are involved, some directors make practice tapes or purchase commercially made rehearsal tapes. Most directors will schedule after- or before-school rehearsals.

It is unfair to students and guest conductors alike for the choral director to take students to choral festivals when not prepared. Dennis Cox (1985) states, "Students often say that they received the music immediately prior to the festival. Others report that while they received the music earlier, they received no individual instruction from the teachers prior to the event" (p. 23). This is a sad but not infrequently encountered experience.

Festival participation requires extra work from students and directors. Some schools will go together to hold pre-festival rehearsals in which different directors will conduct sectionals. Such dedication to making the festival a success is admirable and results in a positive experience for everyone, as related in this vignette from a festival guest conductor:

> Last March I conducted a choral festival which consisted of three high-school choirs. Each choir performed individually under its own director, and then three combined for a performance of the Rutter *Gloria*. The teachers in the district had hired a fine brass ensemble for the combined choral finale. The students forming the combined choir were not selectively taken from the individual choirs; all were involved. The choir consisted of 240 members. The students were superbly prepared, and perhaps half of the group did not use scores. The performance was what a festival should be. The students, teachers, audience, and I returned home feeling that we had all contributed to an effort that was more than a large festive occasion. We had been a part of something aesthetic. (Cox, 1985, p. 23)

Festival Organization

Planning and organizing a choral festival is a huge task requiring an excellent leader and many helpers. State music organizations often are responsible for such events, but individual schools also host festivals. The following guidelines, expanded and freely adapted from an article by Dennis Cox (1985), are presented for consideration by those serving as festival organizers, hosts, and participating directors. It is not meant to be exhaustive, but it is an exhausting list!

- Form a committee to help with the many details of festival preparation.
- Consult or write a festival handbook detailing the committee's responsibilities.
- Establish the date and location of the festival one year in advance. Choose a festival venue that has good acoustics for singing.
- Formulate a festival budget to include guest conductor's fee and expenses, music, mailings and postage, meals, ticket and program printing, guest musicians, student awards, and recording costs.
- Secure a guest conductor as soon as festival date and location are established.
- Supply the guest conductor with programs from the past three festivals, the age and musical level of students participating, and expectations of the festival chairperson.
- Choose music at least six months before the festival date; check on its availability.
- Order music and distribute to participating schools, or make a music list available for schools to order. Order music for each student; do not have students share music.
- Determine a rehearsal schedule for learning the music before the festival. Expect students to memorize the music unless the guest conductor decides that this is unnecessary.
- Arrange student housing venues or assignments as needed.
- Arrange for meal preparation as needed.
- Arrange for guest musicians as needed.
- Hire a recording technician and make provisions for the sale of recordings, if applicable.
- Prepare a festival schedule that includes sufficient rehearsal time but does not result in vocal fatigue for the singers.
- Prepare mailings and announcements for participating schools.
- Prepare the program and publicity materials.
- Appoint some directors to be present at all rehearsals to help with sectionals, equipment, student illness, and other unexpected problems.
- Immediately following the festival, convene the committee to discuss strengths and weaknesses of the event and ways to improve for the coming year. Establish a new organizing committee to begin work on the next festival.
- Prepare and file a festival financial report.

While all of the above items cannot possibly be done by the host or chair of the choral festival, the person in charge must be sure that all of these things are being accomplished by someone. A booster group is a good source of help for implementing festival plans, but the success of any festival rests upon the organizational skills of the host. It is a daunting task, but well worth the educational benefits.

COMPETITIONS

Whether music competitions are worth the educational benefits has been debated for years among music educators. Some say that competition is a fact of life; students need to learn to compete in the big marketplace. Others believe that "many of today's music educators are immersed in the race to be number one, and at times it is difficult to tell where the athletic field ends and the music classroom begins" (Austin, 1990, p. 22). Jorgensen and Pfeiler (1995) relate the following anecdote:

> Our choir had a reputation for seeking out and enjoying competition. When the phone call came from California that our choir had been chosen to represent Wisconsin in a national competition, everyone was ecstatic. The next eight months were devoted to doing everything possible to win this national competition. In Wisconsin, where devotion to the winning ethic of Vince Lombardi dominates all competitive ventures, few argued with the established goal. The choir rehearsed an inordinate amount of time, practicing over both Holiday and Spring break, and in the face of such a vigorous schedule, two students dropped the competitive venture at semester. Every learning opportunity focused on a strategy that would win in Los Angeles. When the dust settled in May and we were forced to buy an extra airline seat to accommodate the nine trophies for the trip home, many felt an admirable goal had been attained. First runner-up in a national competition by anyone's standards is grand. The goal was achieved; however, the wrong goal had been established. In retrospect the pride in winning remains, but it is regrettable that so much time was invested into an eight minute performance. The students were pushed too long and hard for the wrong reasons. This emphasis on winning at all costs was a huge mistake. (pp. 60–61)

The authors further relate their belief in competition, but competition that results in learning. "Those who compete for the sake of learning will not fret over a disappointing score. Veteran competitors relate many wonderful experiences that happened at events where the group didn't win" (p. 62).

James Austin (1990), in discussing the benefits of competition, disputes three prevalent myths: (1) competition is inevitable, (2) competition motivates, and (3) competition builds character and self-confidence. Austin argues that competition is not innate but a learned behavior. He further argues that competition may actually impede motivation, especially when higher-order thinking skills are involved. Finally, Austin states that competition can undermine confidence and character when the "win at all costs" mentality is prevalent, even among teachers. "Unfortunately, research indicates that competition may corrupt teachers to a greater degree than their students" (1990, p. 24).

One of the great educational benefits of any type of competition or festival is the opportunity to hear other groups perform. Sometimes, a tight time schedule does not permit this activity. When this is the case, it is difficult to justify the cost and time involved in participation. Students benefit most when they can compare their own efforts to that of others, and this activity alone can justify participation in a contest or festival.

Students also benefit when they hear the comments of judges and clinicians. A contest that does not provide for such feedback is not an educational experience. Some events have the adjudicator making remarks into a cassette tape recorder as the choir sings. This type of feedback is then directly related to the music, and students can effectively relate the comments to the music as it is heard.

Does competition provide for student motivation? Yes, it can, if handled properly. If the motivation is to do the best job possible without "killing the opposition," students will thrive and be challenged by the opportunity to demonstrate what they can do. If the motivation is one of being the best, whatever the cost, some students may actually develop a fear of failing. The difference is in how the choral director sets the goals and challenges students' efforts.

Guidelines for Competitions

If a choral director is going to participate in choir competition, Jorgensen and Pfeiler (1995) offer eight practical suggestions:

1. Avoid making a single competition, no matter how prestigious, an entire year's focus.
2. Emphasize that the trophies and travel surrounding a competitive venture are secondary to everything learned along the way.
3. Keep a realistic perspective. Think of it as another chance to learn, rather than report card day.
4. Avoid placing too much stock in one person's opinion. Clinicians and judges are only human.
5. Insist on good deportment and impeccable sportsmanship at competitive events.
6. Spend time after the competitive event discussing everything learned, everything that improved along the way, and everything for which you feel pride.
7. Because students take their cue from the director, it is important to be honorable and admirable in accepting criticism.
8. Be a class act. Wherever you go, wherever you place in the competition, make a good impression. (1995, pp. 61–62)

Preparation for Contest

When preparing for a competition, Morgan and Burrows (1981) relate the most common artistic criteria to be judged as: (1) intonation, (2) precision of ensemble, (3) diction, (4) tone and blend, (5) interpretation, (6) suitability of music to group, (7) vocal technique, and (8) stage presence and appearance. All of these elements must be thought out and built into each practice. "The last day of rehearsal, and especially the warm-up before the performance, is not the time for the director to badger the chorus about minor music flaws that should have been corrected much earlier" (p. 47).

Choral directors must seriously consider the amount of time it takes to prepare music for contest. When an inordinate amount of rehearsal time is focused on contest literature to the exclusion of learning a more varied repertoire, educational goals suffer. The emphasis of the choral curriculum must be on music education; anything less relegates music to the position of an activity and not an academic subject.

A Word to the Wise

Preparation for concerts, tours, festivals, and competitions requires a large time commitment, both in and out of school, for the choral director and students. Are such events worth the effort? Yes—if they result in a stronger educational program. No—if they detract from the regular choral music curriculum. The key is balance—something not easy for the beginning choral music educator to learn. Burnout will quickly follow those who take on too much too soon.

All goals of the choral program are to be advanced through the regular curriculum; outside events can be great fun and highly stimulating, but in the end they are all extracurricular. Music is a curricular subject; music educators must protect its rightful place in the education of all students.

STUDY AND DISCUSSION QUESTIONS

1. Why are concert performances so important to the overall choral program?
2. What are some general guidelines for programming choral literature?
3. Where should the more intense or difficult music be programmed in a concert? Why?
4. When and for what reasons would a choral director not program or cut from the concert music that has been rehearsed?
5. When multiple choirs are included in a concert, when should the younger or less experienced ensembles be programmed? Why?
6. What are some general guidelines for determining the length of the average school concert?
7. What are some general guidelines for preparing the printed concert program?
8. How can the concert program be used to educate and thank the audience?
9. What technical concerns must be attended to by the choral director before the concert?
10. Why are ushers important to a successful concert, and what general procedures should ushers follow?
11. What are some general guidelines for piano tuning before a performance?
12. Why is it important that the dress rehearsal be as much like the concert as possible, and what does this involve?
13. What three educational objectives of the six given in the text do you consider most appropriate for defending the place of a choir tour in the choral program? Are there other objectives you would include that are not given?
14. What are some general guidelines for the financing of choir tours, and how should fundraising be handled?
15. Why must a parental consent form be notarized, and what must the consent form stipulate?
16. What is the most important part of choir tour preparation, and how can choir tour concerns be communicated to students without the excessive use of rehearsal time?
17. What are some benefits of choral festival participation?
18. Why is student preparation of the music so important prior to the festival, and who is ultimately responsible for students' knowing their music?
19. What are some pros and cons of students participating in choral competitions?
20. How can the "winner takes all" philosophy be avoided in choral competitions?

REFERENCES

Austin, J. R. (1990). Competition: Is music education the loser? *Music Educators Journal, 76*(6), 21–25.

Cox, D. K. (1985). The choral music festival: Some thoughts on how better to achieve high-level educational and musical goals through a well-planned festival. *Choral Journal, 26*(2), 23–25.

Johnson, D. J. (1997). *Choral techniques: Beyond the basics.* San Diego, CA: Neil A. Kjos Music.

Jorgensen, N. S., and C. Pfeiler (1995). *Things they never taught you in choral methods.* Milwaukee: Hal Leonard.

Light, J. S. (1995). Practicing performing. *Melisma, 13*(2), 10–11.

Morgan, J., and B. Burrows (1981). Sharpen your edge on choral competition. *Music Educators Journal, 67*(8), 44–47.

Phillips, K. H. (1996). Tips for choir tours. *Teaching Music, 4*(3), 30–32.

12 | Popular Music Presentations

The job does not stop at the end of the school day for the choral director. Most opportunities for presenting concerts are outside of school time; often these include presentations other than standard choral concerts, such as Broadway musicals and pop entertainment shows. Directing beyond the classroom is a fact of life for choral music educators.

BROADWAY MUSICAL PRODUCTIONS

The Broadway musical has become a staple in most high school choral programs. Even some junior high/middle and elementary schools present yearly productions specifically written for these age groups (Packer, 1986). For some choral directors, the place of the musical remains questionable; they cite possible vocal abuse as an outcome (White, 1978). The practice of presenting musicals in the schools is so widespread and commonplace, however, that prospective choral directors need to have some basic knowledge in this area before embarking on their first production.

Benefits from Musicals

A number of authors (Jorgensen and Pfeiler, 1995; Mitchell, 2000; Packer, 1986; White, 1978) believe that students benefit greatly from participation in musical productions. Among the benefits cited are the following:

- Musicals are a truly American art form and provide students with specialized knowledge and instruction.
- Musicals can integrate many areas of the school (vocal, instrumental, art, drama, industrial arts, home economics, business, physical education) and create a bond among faculty and students that encompasses the entire school.
- Musicals instill self-discipline, self-confidence, responsibility, sacrifice, and appreciation for hard work.
- Musicals are one of the best ways to show off the choral program to students and the community.
- Musicals provide an opportunity for the development of self-expression and creativity.
- Musicals can create a sense of magic; participation is often one of the biggest highlights in the life of students.
- Musicals create a school tradition that results in a sense of loyalty among students and community.

Choosing a Musical

Selecting a musical is a difficult task. Typically, the show is chosen by a committee consisting of the vocal music director, the instrumental director, and the drama director. The committee members may or may not have a lot of experience with musical productions. When possible, they should try to see a presentation of any show that is under consideration. Many musicals are available for rent or purchase in video format. Almost all musicals are available in sound recordings, and students will learn their parts more quickly when a professional recording is available.

Directors often choose a musical with a large cast and big chorus; this provides the opportunity for many students to participate. However, the choice of a musical must reflect the type and quantity of students available. Even when musicals are "all-school" (students do not have to be in chorus to participate), the likelihood of attracting numerous students outside of the choral program is not great. An evaluation of the students who sing in the choral program is the best way to determine numbers and talent available.

When evaluating personnel needs, some musical roles require stronger acting than singing, some place more emphasis on singing, and some require strength in both. For example, the female lead in Rodgers and Hammerstein's *South Pacific* requires a strong actress for the part of Nellie Forbush, but a beautiful voice is not necessary. However, the male lead (Emile de Becque) requires a very good bass. This type of knowledge is paramount when evaluating a show. While the faculty committee does not want to be accused of casting the show before auditions, it would be foolish to choose *South Pacific* for a school that did not have at least one outstanding bass singer who could perform the male lead.

Besides personnel considerations, numerous other criteria must be considered when choosing a musical. One is audience appeal; lesser-known musicals (e.g., *The Boy Friend* by Sandy Wilson) are not likely to attract as large an audience as the big-name musicals. However, if a school develops an outstanding reputation, "the theater will be filled to capacity because of the tradition of excellence cultivated through repeated successes" (Jergensen and Pfeiler, 1995, p. 34).

Another criterion is the cost of producing a show. If elaborate stage sets, properties, and costumes are needed, the budget will be high. Some schools have to pay string players for the orchestra, which entails additional expense. Then there is the royalty payment (based on seating capacity, number of performances, and ticket price), which must be paid to the owners of the copyright. School boards typically expect musicals to break even, and provide little or no budget for a musical production. Schools that have excellent reputations for their presentations can be more extravagant with expenditures (e.g., purchase or rent background drops), while programs that attract smaller audiences must be more cautious when projecting expenses.

Included among the many other criteria to be considered when choosing a musical are the following:

- Difficulty of the choreography (if any)
- Age and maturity of the singers needed and involved (e.g., are children needed)
- Difficulty of the accompaniment
- Limitations and availability of the performance area
- Experience of the directing staff (the more experience, the easier the job)
- Time of year for the musical in relation to maturity of students, school conflicts, and adequate preparation time

- Number of set changes
- Elaborateness of costuming
- Special effects such as trap doors or apparatus for "flying" characters
- Sound system for amplifying voices

One other concern regarding the choice of a musical is the subject matter. Not all musicals work well with high school students, and some musicals, such as *Evita*, are best performed by adult groups. Also, if the text contains profanity, as many do, members of the community at large may take offense. Students sometimes object to the omission or changing of swearing, as they think it "cool" and adultlike to swear. The school, however, must present to the public an image that is wholesome and respectful. Students need to understand that a public performance authorized by the school must maintain higher moral standards than that often portrayed in the professional theater; people who attend professional events are typically more accepting of society's conventions. The school should not be in the position of offending the public, whose support it needs, especially in the arts. Likewise, some students will find it offensive to use profanity and should be spared any embarrassment from having to use such language. If a musical depends upon profanity and lewd characterizations, it would be wise to omit its consideration for presentation by secondary students. There are plenty of wholesome scripts available that are classics in the repertoire.

Rental Agencies

Musicals are owned by various agencies; music rental, royalty costs, and perusal copies are available upon inquiry. The following are the names, addresses, telephone numbers, and in some cases, websites, for the major suppliers of Broadway musicals:

Music Theatre International
421 West 54th Street
New York, NY 10019
(212) 541-4684; www.mtishows.com

The Rodgers and Hammerstein Theatre Library
229 West 28th Street
New York, NY 10001
(212) 541-6600 or (800) 400-8160; www.rnh.com

Samuel French, Inc.
45 West 25th Street
New York, NY 10010
(212) 206-8990

Tams-Witmark Music Library, Inc.
560 Lexington Ave.
New York, NY 10022
(212) 688-2525 or (800) 221-7196

All rental agencies will send perusal copies for two weeks, which can be studied in the process of choosing the musical. Once a contract is signed, chorus and vocal parts typically are shipped for use two to three months before the production (vocal scores with piano reduction often are available for purchase). Scripts are for sale and nonreturnable. Orchestral parts and score are for rent, usually for a shorter duration (one month). Some shows have a

Figure 12.1. Leads in high school musical production of *South Pacific*. (City High School, Iowa City. Photo by Anne Craig. Used by permission.)

stage manager's guide, choreography, costume specifications, and set designs, for which a rental charge is applicable. At the conclusion of the rental period, all materials must be erased and returned immediately to the rental agency. Failure to do so results in late fees and charges for erasure of scores.

The royalty fee for permission to produce a musical is not the same as the rental cost of the music. The royalty is determined by the number of seats in the auditorium, the number of performances scheduled, and the cost of tickets. All rental costs and fees are payable before any agency will send out music. Additionally, most contracts require a notation in the program indicating that permission has been given to produce the musical, for example, *This musical has been produced by permission of Tams Witmark Music Library, Inc.*

Tryouts

Announcements regarding tryouts appear several weeks in advance of the actual audition dates, and students sign up at the designated location. If the musical is an all-school event, audition times are scheduled after school. Auditions can be held during chorus if the musical is open only to chorus students. However, it is better if the regular choral rehearsal is not used for the musical. A number of choral students may elect not to participate in the musical for various reasons, one of which is the large amount of out-of-school time involved.

A two-week time period is typical for auditioning. Early in the tryout process a time is set for all students to learn and practice one or two selections from the musical. This gives students an equal chance at learning the audition selections. The beginning of tryouts is set aside for an introduction of the show, the characters, the rehearsal and performance dates, and the overall demands for being in the musical. Students need to understand the large time commitment and the importance of maintaining academic work during the rehearsal period. The remainder of the audition schedule is then announced, and students can sign up for principal roles or chorus.

Tryouts for singing and speaking usually are done on different days. Some students elect only to audition for the chorus, and others indicate their interest in different roles that involve speaking and singing. Auditions occur before the entire group; if students are unable to audition before peers, they most likely will be too insecure to sing before an audience. The reading of various short scenes or segments of the script representative of the various speaking parts is done on one day, with call-backs scheduled as needed. Each reader should have at least two opportunities to read.

Tryouts for singing follow speaking auditions; this gives students time to prepare musically. Solos from the musical are used for the leads, while those auditioning for the chorus sing the selections previously rehearsed. Call-backs often are necessary before the final cast is announced. In addition to choosing the lead parts and chorus, understudies should be selected for each of the major roles.

It is important that all members of the audition committee be present for all auditions, and that the cast be chosen by committee consensus. Hard feelings result when a student is thought to have been chosen for a lead role because of favoritism, real or imagined. The use of an objective evaluation form is encouraged to help in the selection process (see Figure 12.2). When disagreement occurs among the committee for the casting of a role, "final authority should rest with the choral director or voice teacher, who can best assess the vocal requirements of the part and the corresponding ability of the student" (White, 1978, p. 30). If the role has more dramatic emphasis than musical, however, the drama teacher (who is often the general director) may make the final decision.

When a show requires extensive choreography, some type of dance audition is warranted. The person in charge of choreography (often the physical education instructor) teaches a brief routine to all those students for whom dancing is required; this evaluation is included in the final choice of cast and chorus.

Most students are nervous during tryouts, and this condition must be recognized when auditioning. Some good talent may be obscured by initial jitters. Therefore, the audition committee always should appear friendly and encouraging of students' efforts. It is good for the committee to evaluate student potential when auditioning, as many students bloom during rehearsals.

Production Staff

There are numerous important roles to be played by many people in the successful presentation of a musical. While many of these positions are best filled by adults (teachers and par-

---

MUSICAL AUDITION FORM
MERCURY HIGH SCHOOL

Name _____ Telephone _____

Address _____ Grade: 9   10   11   12

_____ Zip _____

Are you free to rehearse evenings and weekends the length of the production? Yes No

If no, explain possible conflicts _____

Voice part you sing (if known): S1 S2 A1 A2 T1 T2 B1 B2 ? (unsure)

For what type of part are you auditioning?

_____ female leading role   _____ male leading role

_____ female supporting role   _____ male supporting role

_____ chorus   _____ dancer

Please list any previous acting or singing experience _____

_____

_____

Stop. *Do not go beyond this point. Please present this form at the audition.*

Key: 1=very low,   Comments
      5=very high
Singing Voice Quality: 1   2   3   4   5
Singing Voice Projection: 1   2   3   4   5
Speaking Voice Quality: 1   2   3   4   5
Speaking Voice Projection: 1   2   3   4   5
Appearance for Part: 1   2   3   4   5
Interpretation of Lines: 1   2   3   4   5
Movement and/or Dance: 1   2   3   4   5
            ACCEPT: YES   NO   ?   PART _____

Figure 12.2. Broadway musical audition form.

ents), student committees can do a lot of work when properly supervised. A brief summary of staffing needs is as follows:

- **General director:** oversees the entire production; selects other staff members
- **Stage director:** blocks and rehearses the drama; often the same person as the general director
- **Assistant director:** assists the director; often filled by a responsible student

- **Costumer:** arranges for all costumes, rentals, upkeep, etc.; oversees committee
- **Makeup designer:** oversees makeup committee and makeup supplies
- **Properties manager:** secures props and organizes committee
- **Musical director:** rehearses vocal and instrumental personnel
- **Choreographer:** designs and teaches dancing
- **Technical director:** responsible for scenery, lighting, and stage crew; often serves as stage manager
- **Stage manager:** oversees all backstage business; sometimes filled by assistant director
- **Prompter:** follows script in stage wings for missed cues and lines
- **Business manager:** oversees budget, ticket sales, publicity, program, and payment of bills; oversees committees for publicity and program
- **Box office manager:** manages ticket sales; oversees committee
- **House manager:** supervises ushers and provides cues for beginning the show, intermissions, and general house protocol

Planning Rehearsals

Once the cast is announced, a rehearsal schedule is given to all of those involved (see Figure 12.3). Most rehearsal times are after school or in the evening. By carefully organizing the time slots and requiring to be present only those students who are needed, students' time can be carefully managed and not wasted. Early in the production the musical portions, or at least the chorus portions, are rehearsed in the choir room by the vocal director while the drama is blocked onstage. Then the chorus can be called to the staging area when needed. Choreography rehearsals also appear on the master schedule, but a separate rehearsal schedule for orchestra players is provided by the orchestra director.

A real problem can occur during rehearsals when students not onstage are permitted to roam school hallways, go outside, and generally fool around. Rules of conduct need to include where students are to go and what they are to do when not actively involved in the production. Homework must not suffer during a musical, and students should be encouraged to bring such work to rehearsals.

The length of time for the entire production may vary (depending upon the number of rehearsals each week), but six to eight weeks is typical.

> To produce a show within such a time frame, acts and scenes must be broken down into workable rehearsal units that fit into the time limitation, and every rehearsal should be preceded by enough advanced work by the director so that the objective . . . is clearly understood. For example, blocking and movement should be worked out . . . so that the rehearsal is simply a matter of telling people where to go and what to do. Cuts in the score, da capos, transpositions, and potential trouble spots must be anticipated before the rehearsal begins. Of course, allowances will be made for creativity and spontaneity. (White, 1978, p. 30)

There often are dead times in musical production when something planned just doesn't work. At such times the director must stop and determine what to do. With careful planning, such times are limited.

The rehearsal schedule in Figure 12.3 has notations of "NO BOOKS" at specific times. Students need to learn their lines as soon as possible; this frees the action onstage. Also, there

SOUTH PACIFIC REHEARSAL SCHEDULE

March 20—7:30 Block Act I, scs. 1–2, pgs. 4–13 (boys chorus reh. in choir room)
     8:15 Block Act I, scs. 3–4, pgs. 14–29 (girls chorus reh. in choir room)
March 21—7:00 Line Rehearsal Act I, scs. 1–4 (boys chorus reh. in choir room)
March 22—7:00 <u>NO BOOKS</u> Act I, scs. 1–4 (boys chorus reh. in choir room)
March 23—3:00 Character Reh. Act I, scs. 1–4 with solos and boys chorus

March 27—7:30 Block Act I, scs. 5–6, pgs. 30–35 (girls chorus reh. in choir room)
     8:00 Block Act I, scs. 7–10, pgs. 36–49 (girls chorus reh, in choir room)
March 28—7:00 Line Rehearsal Act I, scs. 5–10 (girls chorus reh. in choir room)
March 29—7:00 <u>NO BOOKS</u> Act I, scs. 5–10 (girls chorus optional rehearsal)
March 30—7:00 Character Rehearsal Act I, scs. 5–10 with solos and girls chorus

April 03—7:30 Block Act I, scs, 11–13, pgs. 50–61, with chorus on stage
April 04—7:00 Line Rehearsal Act I, scs 11–13, with girls chorus only
April 05—7:00 <u>NO BOOKS</u> Act I, scs, 11–13 (girls chorus optional)
April 06—7:00 Act, scs, 1–13 with solos and chorus - run the complete act

April 10—7:30 Block Act II, scs 1–3, pgs 62–74 (chorus rehearses in choir room)
     8:30 Block Act II, sc. 4, pgs. 74–79
April 11—7:00 Line Rehearsal Act II, scs. 1–4 with boys chorus
April 12—7:00 <u>NO BOOKS</u> Act II, scs. 1–4 with boys chorus
April 13—7:00 Character Rehearsal Act II, scs. 1–4 with all solos and full chorus

April 17—7:30 Block Act II, scs. 5–9, pgs. 80–89 (full chorus reh. in choir room)
     8:30 Block Act II, scs. 10–12, pgs. 90–97
April 18—7:00 Line Rehearsal Act II, scs. 5–12 (no chorus rehearsal)
April 19—7:00 <u>NO BOOKS</u> Act II, scs. 5–12 with chorus
April 20—7:00 Character Rehearsal Act II, scs. 5–12 with chorus
April 21—7:00 Act II complete, scs. 1–12 with solos and full chorus

April 24—7:30 Acts I & II complete with music. Orch. and Crews all week
April 25—7:00 Acts I & II complete with music
April 26—7:00 Acts I & II complete with music
April 27—7:00 Acts I & II complete with music

May 01—6:30 Complete Production: all crews for dress rehearsal (no make-up)
May 02—6:00 Dress Rehearsal: make-up crew report
May 03—6:30 Final Dress Rehearsal (no make-up)
May 04—06 **THREE PERFORMANCES OF SOUTH PACIFIC**
     6:00 Cast reports for make-up and dress
     6:30 Crews report (orchestra reports at 7:30)
     8:00 Curtain!

NOTE: Highlight all dates requiring your attendance. Bring homework to do while not involved in rehearsal. Do not wander to any other part of the school other than the music/auditorium wing. You must contact either the drama director or the vocal music director if you are sick and cannot attend a rehearsal. The cast and crew party will follow the final performance. As many of the costumes are rented, please be certain that you take care of them and return them to the wardrobe members.

Figure 12.3. Rehearsal schedule for *South Pacific.*

are times designated for line rehearsal, when only the text is practiced. This encourages the memorization process; a prompter can help cue students if they forget cues or lines. The director must be firm about the memorization schedule, as students cannot develop their characters with scripts in hand.

Staging or Blocking the Musical

When the choral director is involved in staging the musical, some terminology for basic blocking (the process of staging the actors' positions and movements) is needed. "Upstage" refers to the rear of the stage or away from the audience. "Downstage" is the opposite—the front of the stage toward the audience. "Stage right" refers to the actor's right onstage, and "stage left" is the actor's left while facing the audience. Combined with "center stage," there are fifteen approximate areas onstage where the action is blocked (see Figure 12.4). The abbreviations include the following letters: U = up; D = down; C = center; R = right; L = left. Therefore, an indication of "DRC" represents a position of "down-right-center" onstage. When a person walks "in" onstage, they walk toward the center of the stage; "out" is away from the center. A "cross" is moving from one area to another and is typically marked in the script with "X."

Inexperienced students often look awkward when introduced to blocking arrangements. They will turn their backs on the audience while delivering lines, use ineffective gestures that appear artificial, and move at inappropriate times. Much patience is required of these amateurs as they learn to be comfortable onstage. Most of them quickly adapt to the requirements of the blocking when they receive clear and consistent directives.

The blocking of dialogue is better done separately from the musical scenes. This saves time and possible vocal fatigue, as all students are not required to attend every rehearsal. When blocking the music, care must be taken not to place students in physical or stage positions that may cause vocal strain.

> In one instance I restaged a scene that was originally for one singer to sit while another stood alongside for a rather extended duet. The seated singer simply could not master the technique of looking up while singing with the head at a normal or slightly downward cast. Consequently, she allowed her uptilted chin to pull up on the strap muscles below the jaw and as the tessitura of the song rose her larynx rose with it, creating vocal strain. Changing the staging to have both singers seated may have proved less effective visually, but it

UR	URC	UC	ULC	UL
R	RC	C	LC	L
DR	DRC	DC	DLC	DL

AUDIENCE

Figure 12.4. Diagram of stage areas for blocking purposes.

did prevent vocal strain and was compensated by the aural beauty this produced. (White, 1978, p. 32)

While professional singers have developed a singing technique that permits them to sing in sometimes unadvantageous singing positions, students will sing better when good singing posture is maximized. Also, as much as possible the blocking needs to be as far forward onstage as possible. Students' voices will be heard better, even when amplified, if they are nearer the audience. Forward staging also brings a greater sense of immediacy to the action.

Amplification

It is standard practice to amplify musical productions electronically. Using microphones is important for adolescents whose voices cannot carry over an orchestra without producing vocal strain. The typical high school auditorium's sound system is rarely installed with the objective of amplifying singing and often distorts musical sound. It is better to rent or borrow a good system. The use of cordless microphones for the principals is highly recommended, and multidirectional microphones make for optimum sound projection of the ensemble. These microphones usually are hung above the stage area, though some models are placed directly on the floor. Visible microphone stands placed in front of the cast should be avoided; this looks amateurish, and microphones on stands may pick up sound off the stage floor. Placement of the sound panel at the rear of the auditorium provides for adjustment of sound levels and good control of the all-important sound element.

The orchestra is not amplified, and specific electronic instruments such as guitar, piano, or bass, should be kept to minimum volume level. High school instrumentalists have little experience with accompanying singers and must be reminded to play softer when accompanying voices. If there is no orchestra pit and players sit at floor level, a railing built around the orchestra and draped with a heavy material will help absorb sound. No matter how good the production, the final results will be poor if the singers are drowned out by the players. In some cases it may be desirable to reduce the instrumentation when the accompanying forces are so large as to make vocal-instrumental balance impossible.

Final Rehearsals and Performance

The final rehearsals are extremely important in bringing focus to the performance; this is not the time to be making major changes in blocking, music, and so forth. A technical rehearsal is needed to make sure the stage crew members know their jobs, the sound system works, properties are in place, and all the myriad details come together. This is followed by two dress rehearsals in which costuming and makeup are checked for correctness. (When funds are limited, makeup can be limited to one rehearsal.)

Every attempt must be made to allow the dress rehearsals to flow without interruption. Although it is tempting to stop and correct problems as they occur, it is better for the staff of directors to make notes as the show progresses, meeting with the cast following the rehearsal for notes. If the final dress rehearsal is continually interrupted, the cast will have no sense of the whole production. Nor will they be challenged to work forward even when problems occur. At this point, the directors have to place the responsibility for the entire production on the students involved, and students typically rise to the occasion.

Performances of musicals most often are scheduled for at least two presentations. These shows take much work to produce, and repeated performances give students a chance to develop their dramatic and musical achievements further. The cast party following the final performance is a traditional time for celebrating this exciting event.

As mentioned earlier, the musical can be the highlight of students' high school careers. A great excitement and even tears will follow the close of a successful production. Learning the joy of music making in a cooperative learning environment fulfills one of the most important objectives of the music program: valuing a variety of musical styles. The Broadway musical may be one of the greatest instructional tools that music educators have for teaching the value of American music.

Maintaining a Balance

Sometimes high school choral directors become so caught up in producing a Broadway musical that the educational focus central to the choral program suffers. Some directors go so far as to produce two musicals an academic year. While the musical has a rightful place in the choral curriculum, to allow it to dominate students' education is to deny one of the overall goals of the choral program: the development of a broad appreciation for choral music as a legitimate art form. When the musical dominates the choral program, the curriculum becomes unbalanced.

Most choral directors do not let Broadway musicals detract from regular educational programming. However, the requirements for producing a musical are demanding; the work involved may exact a price in time lost with family, health problems, and burnout. Because of this, some schools elect to produce a musical on alternate years. This permits the focus to remain on the traditional choral curriculum. The choral director needs to consider and weigh the consequences of becoming involved in out-of-school performances to the exclusion of having any other life. Music educators are not professional entertainers, even though much of the public may think of them that way. In the profession of choral music education, the correct focus is on education. Therefore, even the Broadway musical becomes a vehicle for imparting knowledge, improving skills, and developing a love for music. Maintaining the proper balance is the key to many things in life.

Resources

Numerous books and resources are available to help the choral director in producing a Broadway musical. Among the best is *A Practical Handbook for Musical Theatre* (4th ed., 2000) by Larry Mitchell. This excellent guide contains information for (1) show selection, including the analysis of numerous musicals suitable for secondary school production, the cast and chorus requirements, best-known songs, extent of choreography, technical demands, and possible problems; (2) duties of the various production committees; (3) selected references for each subject where additional information might be found; and (4) directing techniques that can be used in preparing the show for the stage. Larry Mitchell is an experienced high school teacher who has produced and directed musicals for over thirty years; this guide represents all those years of practical experience.

A selected list of sources is presented at the end of this chapter. No book, however, can give all the information needed; only experience will develop the knowledge and skills necessary for the successful directing of a musical.

SWING CHOIRS

Groups singing popular music are a standard part of contemporary American choral programming. Swing, show, and jazz vocal ensembles are vehicles by which students learn to communicate in a mass-media idiom that is overwhelmingly prevalent in today's society. To ignore this music is to ignore a large part of youth culture. Ignoring popular music also forces the issue of "our" music (students') versus "their" music (adults'). Most high school choral directors now openly program popular music but work to maintain a balance among the various styles of choral literature available from all centuries.

When pop ensembles are present in the choral program, they should be an integral part of the curriculum and share equal importance with all other groups. "In such a program, there is no choir that dominates the choral program. This choir [pop group] should have the same standing as the other choirs" (Robinson, 1994, p. 1). Also, it is important to remember that music is music; whatever is sung should be sung well.

Educational Objectives

The inclusion of popular music groups in the curriculum must be based on strong educational objectives. Some benefits worth considering for both students and program are as follows:

- A knowledge of contemporary culture and its music
- Further development of singing skills and choral techniques
- Enthusiasm and motivation that carries over into the entire choral program
- Nurturing of students' self-esteem and self-confidence
- Positive public relations for the music area
- Focus for students' abundant energies
- Recruitment enhanced for the regular choral program

The last benefit in this list requires greater attention: Students who belong to pop ensembles must be enrolled in the regular choral curriculum. This is vital when working to provide a balance of musical styles in students' education. Some students are drawn to choral music because of interest in the show aspect of the pop group. If the only way they can become members of such an ensemble is to be part of a regular choir, however, they often will choose to do so, even when their intent is to make the pop ensemble. Once they become a member of a choir that sings art music, they often grow to value this type of musical experience.

Popular Music in the Schools

The swing choir was among the first pop music ensembles to become part of the choral music curriculum. Beginning in the 1940s, some school choral directors began to form small groups of twelve to sixteen singers for the singing of popular music. The early swing choir repertoire consisted of mostly Broadway tunes and original arrangements. A presentation consisted of singers standing in a semicircle, accompanied by piano, with maybe bass and drums. It was a very static look until the advent of television, which required greater action. Movement now was included in such shows as the *Hit Parade* and *Sing Along with Mitch* (Anderson, 1978, p. 7). Using these shows as models, choral directors arranged singers on stools, boxes, and layered platforms and risers, and limited body movements and gestures were employed. By the 1960s choreography was introduced by such groups as Fred Waring and the Pennsylvanians and the Johnny Mann Singers.

The 1970s witnessed the spread of the swing choir movement throughout the schools of America. Publishing companies were making popular music arrangements available at an unprecedented rate, and the Tanglewood Symposium (1976), a national meeting of music educators, endorsed the concept of including all types of music in the school curriculum, including jazz. Many music educators were appalled that schools would teach anything but the best music (meaning the classics). Others believed: "There are no good or bad styles of music. Rather, good and bad music exists within every style, and all genres are worthy of study." The adoption of this philosophy coincided with the flood of popular music being heard via the media. It was, perhaps, indicative of the feeling, "if you can't beat 'em, join 'em." By the 1970s popular music dominated the attention of America's students and could not be ignored by music educators.

Contemporary Swing Choirs

Today's swing choirs contain sixteen to thirty-two singers, with an equal number of boys and girls to facilitate forming partners for choreography. Groups typically are accompanied by a small band (piano, bass, guitar, drums, and perhaps, some winds), and the staging area is a combination of open space in front of risers, boxes, or platforms. The traditional swing choir places less emphasis on movement and choreography, and much of the repertoire is sung in grouped formations on risers. This style may appeal to a director who wishes not to spend hours on elaborate dance rehearsals but who does wish to include a variety of music in his or her program. The repertoire for the contemporary swing choir includes anything from swing arrangements, Broadway show tunes, country-western ballads, popular music from different eras (e.g., the 1950s and 1960s), gospel, and patriotic to funk and hip-hop.

Because the swing choir places less emphasis on movement, it is possible to include this type of experience for an entire choir when a separate ensemble is not possible or desirable. Junior high and middle school directors can use a swing choir approach for programming popular music. All students can be involved in some relatively simple gestures and movements that require little space. While not a true swing choir, the experience enables all students to have some contact with a medium that calls for more overt physical action than the straight choral concert.

SHOW CHOIRS

The transition from swing choir to show choir occurred in the 1970s and is seen today in the elaborate staging and choreography effects that have become the hallmark of school show choirs. Such groups often are large (forty to fifty members) and are accompanied by full back-up instrumental groups. With synthesizer and computer technologies available, complete accompaniments or individual instrumental sounds can be made electronically.

Unlike the swing choir, where individual music selections may not be linked or represent any type of flow, the show choir gives a show. The entire effect is of a seamless presentation and includes colorful lighting, bright and coordinated costuming, props (hats, canes, etc.), backdrops, and tremendous energy. Numbers follow with smooth transitions, and a variety of musical styles alternate. The pacing and unifying of the show are important, as most show choir selections are only three to four minutes in length. A typical show begins with a fast, upbeat, eye- and ear-catching tune with choreography. This is followed by a selection that is upbeat but not as "hot" as the opener. A slow ballad pulls the audience in; ballads usually do not involve choreography. The remainder of the show alternates between these styles and solos by the students. A novelty number like "The Telephone Hour" from *Bye, Bye, Birdie* (Adams and Strouse) provides contrast and humor. The closing selection is energetic and done well; the audience leaves the show enthused and with good vibes.

Costumes

Costuming for the show choir is important. Some groups make their own costumes, and a number of professional companies provide apparel for such groups (see Appendix B). It is important to remember that high school students should look like high school students and not Las Vegas dancers. Low-cut, revealing dresses for young women may appear sexy, but such costuming will not flatter all of the girls, nor will it be appropriate stage attire for them. Among other considerations are the following:

- Durability: Will the costume last for repeated performances?
- Versatility: Can the costume be worn for a number of musical styles and performance venues? Will a simple change of some item like a scarf or vest give added versatility?
- Movability: Can students move with ease during dance routines?
- Accountability: If students are accountable for the cost of costumes, are the costs prohibitive for some?
- Presentability: Do the costumes and colors make a good appearance under lights and onstage?

Who selects the costumes? It is often a committee matter, but adult supervision is required. Having members model a variety of costumes (especially for the women) is helpful when making a final decision. John Jacobson (in Robinson, 1994) states:

> It is almost always a bad idea to have a few of the cast members get together, go to a mall, and decide on the costume. You are the producer. Their input may be helpful, but spare yourself and them the embarrassment of choosing an inappropriate costume that looks good on a mannequin or magazine cover but flatters nobody in your cast. (p. 40)

In the end, the choral director has the final word regarding the choice of costumes.

Another and often costly part of costuming the show choir involves the need for dance shoes. High school boys may not have black dress shoes, which are a requirement for a uniform look. A special, thin-soled lace-up style called a jazz shoe is particularly good for dancing. Likewise, girls will need some type of black shoe with a moderate heel in which it will be comfortable to dance. Local shoe stores often will make special orders available to students at a discount, and students can sell their shoes to new members upon graduation. The costs of costuming a show choir can be quite high.

Good Singing Is Good Singing

The strength of the show choir is in its high-energy performance. Unfortunately, some directors put so much emphasis on staging that singing becomes secondary. However, singing should be the top priority for any choral conductor. "Therefore, one of the challenges facing the show choir director is to be sure that the musical aspect of the show is of equal impact with the visual aspect" (Anderson, 1978, p. 9).

A common criticism of pop singing is that it leads to vocal abuse. This is a valid criticism, as many popular singers end up with vocal nodules. The choral director constantly must monitor for strained vocal production in all rehearsals, choral or otherwise. Three areas are of particular concern: (1) excessive amplitude or belting, (2) lack of proper breath management, and (3) physical exhaustion.

When students have to project over a loud instrumental background they are apt to sing with excessive loudness. This results in a "pressed voice" condition, in which the vo-

Figure 12.5. Typical costuming for show choir. (City High School, Iowa City. Photo by Anne Craig. Used by permission.)

cal folds are making maximum contact, which leads to swelling of the vocal folds, hoarseness, and eventual loss of voice and vocal damage. Directors should never ask students to sing louder than the level at which they are comfortable. The use of amplification is highly recommended if not a necessity for pop groups. When possible, singers should have their own microphones. Wireless mikes make it possible to dance without the interference of wires or mike stands.

One other problem leads to vocal strain—physical exhaustion. When students are not well rested and healthy, their approach to singing will be hampered. Many students do not recognize their own physical limitations and continue to work and rehearse when they should be home resting. The choral director must not permit students to abuse themselves for the sake of the show. It is impossible to breathe correctly when physically exhausted, and when breath support is lacking, vocal abuse is inevitable.

Good singing is good singing, no matter what the style of music. The well-known jazz/show choir arranger Kirby Shaw (in Robinson, 1994) states:

> It cannot be too strongly emphasized that the jazz/show choir bases its standards of tone production, blend, and balance upon the same Western-European–derived choral practices found in the vast majority of American public school choral organizations. From this base of sound music making, all styles of American popular music are possible. The foundation stays the same; the styles are different. (p. 10)

Stylistic Accuracy

Just as there are many different eras and styles within the domain of art music, so are there numerous popular music styles. Students often are more knowledgeable of current sounds than the choral director, and their knowledge can be helpful when determining styles and repertoire. The director must become aware of stylistic differences if more than the notes of popular arrangements are to be communicated. Kirby Shaw (in Robinson, 1994) comments:

> Don't plan on doing any Broadway pieces unless you've heard Liza Minelli (rent the video "Cabaret"); any black gospel music until you know Arethra Franklin's renditions; any jazz without admiring Carmen McRae and Sarah Vaughan; any scat singing without listening to Jon Hendricks and Ella Fitzgerald; or any blues without hearing B. B. King. A lot of music educators will tell you to listen, listen, listen. Take it one step further and don't stop until you can reasonably approximate a whole host of sounds that the great artists make on a regular basis. The better you can imitate, the better your teaching abilities will be. (pp. 15–16)

While the task of learning the many popular music styles in the repertoire may seem overwhelming, students know the difference when a director does not know the difference.

When choosing any vocal arrangement of a popular song, the choral director and students need to remember that an arrangement for choir, no matter how stylistically accurate, is not going to sound as authentic as the original group's performance. Some songs just do not fit into a choral idiom, and some choral arrangers are better than others. The choral director needs to become familiar with the names of successful arrangers. Among the better known in the profession are Dick Averre, Phil Azelton, Don Besig, Alan Billingsley, Mark Brymer, Teena Chinn, Roger Emerson, Anita Kerr, Jack Kunz, Ed Lojeski, Phil Mattson, Jerry Nowak, Gene Puerling, Kirby Shaw, and Carl Strommen.

Some choral directors have the skills necessary to arrange tunes for their choirs. Since most popular music is not in public domain, arranging without permission from the copyright owner is illegal. In some cases, a payment will be required if permission is given to arrange a copyrighted tune. All arrangements of copyrighted material must include the statement "arranged by permission." A standard form for "request for permission to arrange" is available from most music copyright holders. These publishers will grant permission more readily to arrange older tunes, rather than current hits that are being played on the radio and MTV.

Choreography

A show choir is not a show choir without choreography, and while it is not necessary to choreograph every selection (e.g., a ballad), the dance routines typically make the show (see Figure 12.6). However, some directors overplan; it is not necessary that every line of music be choreographed. If the movement is too busy or active, it can become distracting and interfere with good vocal production. Sometimes, a nice tableaux or standing arrangement will suffice.

Figure 12.6. Typical show choir choreography. (City High School, Iowa City. Photo by Anne Craig. Used by permission.)

When the show choir is large, not all singers must be involved in all choreography. For special routines, certain couples can be featured downstage while the remainder of the group sings from upstage on risers or platforms. The upstage group may even use hand gestures, turns, and so forth, without being overly active. In a sense, this becomes a picture within a picture.

Some choral directors have little or no experience when it comes to choreography. They often will turn to professionals in the community for such help, or may have talented students in the group assist. Others may elect to take workshops and build a repertoire of movements they can teach. Two popular clinicians in this field are Sally Albrecht and John Jacobson. Both have made materials available to the profession for helping choral directors learn the basics of choreography (Albrecht, 1984, 1990; Jacobson, 1986). Beginning directors are encouraged to avail themselves of such materials when seeking help with choreography. John Jacobson (in Robinson, 1994) states:

Watch MTV. Go to festivals and concerts where the choirs use choreography and borrow ideas. Go to a dance hall, line-dance party, a dance class, a Broadway-style show, or a video store to pique your creativity. Don't be intimidated. You can do this. (p. 27)

It is true—most choral directors are creative enough to learn the basics of choreography. Many of them even become quite proficient at it.

Sally Albrecht (in Robinson, 1994, pp. 21–22) presents the following checklist for making choreographic decisions:

- Theme: come up with a theme or main concept for each number.
- Key lyrics: pick out favorite movement-oriented words that suggest activity.
- Rhythms and rests: accent interesting rhythms and rests in the music with movement.
- Position of singers: change standing arrangements for each number.
- Simplicity and variety: keep movements simple and clean.
- Facial work: maintain eye contact with the audience and speak with the face.
- Style: know the moves that work well in any given style of music.
- Vocal considerations: don't choreograph movements that will hurt the vocal sound.
- Upper torso versus footwork: use fancy footwork during nonvocal times, such as, interludes.
- Props/costume additions: try something new like puppets, flashlights, aprons, and so on.

Scheduling

Most show choirs are scheduled before or after school and are not offered for academic credit. In some schools, however, these choirs are included in the regular school day. The latter situation helps to relieve the pressure that choral directors often have with extended school hours. In most cases, the show choir involves much out-of-school time for rehearsals and performances.

As for all other out-of-school activities and concerts, the choral director must judge wisely as to the amount of time that can be invested in pop music groups. While such ventures can be exciting for students and director alike, there is a limit to which directors can give of themselves without feeling the adverse effects. Remember, the major objective of the choral director is to educate, not entertain.

VOCAL JAZZ ENSEMBLES

The vocal jazz ensemble is not found as frequently as the show choir in the contemporary secondary choral program. Most choral directors lack training in the special jazz idiom (Robinson, 1994, p. 2), even though college and university courses and workshops are becoming more available in vocal jazz. Also, while the jazz ensemble is sometimes thought of as appropriate for large choirs, Carl Strommen (1980) states:

Although larger choirs are certainly capable of performing music scored for the smaller jazz unit, the sheer weightiness of the concert choir can present some problems in intonation, particularly within the rich and sonorous harmonic structures typical of jazz arrangements. Also, the larger group will not have the "snap" and feel of a smaller group, especially when dealing with highly syncopated rhythmic figures that are so prevalent within the idiom. (p. 1)

The vocal jazz ensemble typically has a size limitation of between sixteen and thirty members, with twenty to twenty-four singers in the average-size group.

Vocal jazz finds its roots in the musical heritages of various cultural and ethnic groups in the United States. It draws much of its style from the instrumental jazz band, and the musical arrangements typically are more complex and challenging than those of the show choir. Jazz groups do not use choreography, although free but limited movement on the part of the singers is encouraged in response to the music.

Improvisation is one of the main characteristics of any jazz ensemble. For singers, a type of scat singing is required in which certain syllables, or nonsense words, are used as the vehicle for improvised solos. Regarding the ability to sing in this style, a teacher of improvisational scat singing states:

> It may seem to some teachers that scat singing is so individualized or requires so much creativity that it is out of reach for most performing groups. Moreover, teachers may not know how to improvise themselves and may have limited training in vocal jazz. The art of improvising, however, is a skill that teachers can learn, as well as encourage and develop in their students. (Madura, 1997, p. 26)

Madura relates some simple steps to encourage exploration of the jazz vocal style and gives this basic requirement: "extensive listening experiences with jazz recordings and live concerts" (p. 28).

Like show choirs, jazz ensembles are almost always amplified. They make use of a smaller instrumental accompaniment of piano, bass, and drums, which is augmented when needed. Some vocal jazz groups wear coordinated outfits, while others use a color theme with a variety of patterns and styles. Singers typically stand on choral risers in a more stationary style, and various grouping arrangements are reflective of the music.

Vocal jazz requires a special sound; the tone is very forward, "right at the teeth, with *no vibrato*" (Anderson, 1978, p. 53). The vocal technique needed to produce this sound would seem contrary to what is taught for healthy choral singing. The fundamental support system is the same, but how the singer controls the sound at the laryngeal level is very different. Adolescents can learn to sing stylistically with different vocal productions when they are taught the correct ways to go about each process. However, this requires much instructional sophistication on the part of the director, who is responsible for building the sound and at the same time protecting the voice.

The National Association of Jazz Educators (NAJE) was founded in 1968 and is the major agency of support for jazz in schools today. Its membership is committed to making jazz groups more prominent and visible among young people. While jazz bands abound in schools, vocal jazz ensembles are not as prevalent, but interest is increasing. Jazz is a distinctive American art form; inclusion of jazz study in the choral curriculum provides students with the opportunity to experience a highly creative and personal form of musical expression. A vocal jazz ensemble represents one more opportunity for music educators to diversify the music curriculum in today's schools.

STUDY AND DISCUSSION QUESTIONS

1. Which two of the seven benefits listed for students' participation in a Broadway musical production do you think are most important? Why?

2. How should a musical for school presentation be chosen?

3. When there is profanity in the script of a musical, how should this be handled?

4. How does the royalty fee differ from the rental cost of a musical, and how is the royalty fee determined?

5. What are some important parts of the process that need to be considered during tryouts and casting of the musical?

6. In what types of committees may students be involved for the Broadway show, and who should be in charge of such committees?

7. How much time should be scheduled for the production of a school musical?

8. When students are attending rehearsals but not directly involved for a period of time, what types of directives should be provided for this down time?

9. Why must musical decisions take precedence over blocking decisions when staging a musical?

10. What are some general guidelines for sound amplification of the show?

11. Why should the dress rehearsals for the musical continue without interruption from any of the directors involved?

12. How can the production of a musical show keep from dominating and overshadowing the regular school choral curriculum?

13. What philosophy for the inclusion of popular music in the music education curriculum was outlined in the Tanglewood Symposium?

14. Why must student members of school pop groups be required to enroll in the regular choral program?

15. What are the major differences that characterize the swing choir, show choir, and vocal jazz ensemble?

16. How and by whom should costumes be selected for the members of pop music groups in schools?

17. What three conditions often lead to vocal abuse among students in pop music groups?

18. How can a school choral director become current with the many popular music styles if lacking sufficient knowledge in this area?

19. What can beginning directors of show choirs do when they have little experience and can't provide instruction in choreography?

20. What group of professionals is organized to provide support and information for jazz educators in the schools?

REFERENCES

Albrecht, S. K. (1984). *Choral music in motion*. Vol. 1. *Adding movement to your choral program*. Van Nuys, CA: Alfred.

———— (1990). *Choral music in motion*. Vol. 2. *Movement for larger groups*. Van Nuys, CA: Alfred.

Anderson, D. (1978). *Jazz and show choir handbook*. Chapel Hill, NC: Hinshaw Music.

Jacobson, J. (1986). *Gotta sing . . . gotta dance! A glossary of movement for the new singer-dancer* (a set of four videos, each available separately). Milwaukee, WI: Hal Leonard.

Jorgensen, N. S., and C. Pfeiler (1995). *Things they never taught you in choral methods*. Milwaukee, WI: Hal Leonard.

Madura, P. D. (1997). Jazz improvisation for the vocal student. *Teaching Music, 4*(6), 26–28.

Mitchell, L. (2000). *A practical handbook for musical theatre: A guide for selecting, producing and directing the Broadway musical* (4th ed.). Fort Dodge, Iowa: Comedia Publishing (P.O. Box 1739, Fort Dodge, IA 50501).

Packer, G. (1986). Putting on the musical—junior high style. *Choral Journal, 27*(5), 21–23.

Robinson, R. L. (1994). *Getting started with jazz/show choir.* Reston, VA: Music Educators National Conference.

Strommen, C. (1980). *The contemporary chorus: A director's guide for the jazz-rock choir.* Van Nuys, CA: Alfred.

White, R. C. (1978). High school musicals: Accentuate the musical and eliminate the voice abuse. *Music Educators Journal, 64*(9), 27–33.

SELECTED BIBLIOGRAPHY FOR BROADWAY MUSICAL PRODUCTION

Allensworth, C. (1983). *The complete play production handbook.* New York: Harper and Row.

Boardman G. M. (1978). *American musical theatre.* New York: Oxford University Press.

Corson, R. (1986). *Stage makeup* (7th ed.). Englewood Cliffs, NJ: Prentice Hall.

Engle, L. (1983). *Getting the show on: The complete guidebook for producing a musical in your theater.* New York: Macmillan.

Franklin, M. A., and J. O. Dixon III (1983). *Rehearsal: The principles and practice of acting for the stage* (6th ed.). Englewood Cliffs, NJ: Prentice Hall.

Green, S. (1976). *Encyclopedia of the musical theatre.* New York: Da Capo Press.

Mitchell, L. (1992). *A practical handbook for producing and directing the Broadway musical* (3d ed.). Fort Dodge, IA: Comedia Publishing (P.O. Box 1739, Fort Dodge, IA 50501).

Parker, W. O., and H. K. Smith (1979). *Scene design and stage lighting* (4th ed.). New York: Holt, Rinehart and Winston.

Sellman, H. D., and M. Lessley (1982). *Essentials of stage lighting* (2d ed.). Englewood Cliffs, NJ: Prentice Hall.

Sievers, W. D., H. E. Stiver Jr., and S. Kahan (1976). *Directing for the theatre.* Dubuque, IA: Wm. C. Brown.

Terry, T. (1985). *Create your own stage sets.* Englewood Cliffs, NJ: Prentice Hall.

Tumbusch, T. (1969). *Theatre student: Complete production guide to modern musical theatre.* New York: Richard Rosens Press.

Welker, D. (1971). *Theatrical direction: The basic techniques.* Boston: Allyn and Bacon.

———— (1977). *Stagecraft: A handbook for organization, construction, and management.* Boston: Allyn and Bacon.

Wilfred, T. (1965). *Projected scenery: A technical manual.* New York: Drama Book Specialists.

Unit 2

OPTIONAL PROJECTS

1. Code of Conduct

a. Prepare a list of rules to govern conduct in the choral classroom at the secondary level. Frame the statements positively rather than negatively, and keep the number of rules as few as possible. In addition, include disciplinary measures for infractions of the code of conduct.

b. Share the code of conduct and disciplinary measures with the class and compare statements. Are statements clear, reasonable, and enforceable?

2. Show Choir Choreography

a. As a group, learn the choreography for part of a show choir selection provided by the instructor. A class member who has had experience with choreography can design and lead the instruction, or someone from outside the class may be chosen. Students may use three class sessions for learning this show choir project.

b. Execute the show choir choreography as a group for the instructor. The objective is not a flawless performance but evidence that everyone has participated in the choreography experience. When possible, the use of a prerecorded audio example can be used to facilitate this project.

3. Choral Rehearsal Observation

a. Observe representative examples of elementary, junior high/middle school, and senior high school choral rehearsals. As a courtesy, obtain permission from the directors before actually going to rehearsals. Also, a telephone call before the rehearsal may result in knowledge of any change in the rehearsal schedule.

b. Prepare a choral rehearsal observation summary for each observed rehearsal. Divide the summary into the following areas: (1) rehearsal facilities, (2) director's rehearsal procedures, (3) response of singers, and (4) overall evaluation of rehearsal. Include the name and grade level of each choir observed, and have the director sign the notes at the end of each observation report.

UNIT 3

CHORAL TECHNIQUES

13 | Vocal Development, Part 1

Singing is a learned behavior. Most people are not natural singers, and most choral students are going to require vocal instruction to reach their singing potential. The general public continues to believe that singing is some type of gift, which some people have and others do not. This is an unfortunate attitude, as public support for school music is based on the premise that all persons have musical ability. If this were not true, public tax dollars could not be used for school music. While some people have more artistic aptitude than others, music educators need to convince the public that a common denominator for musicianship exists among all people; it is the vocal music teacher's responsibility to help all students experience success in singing.

Choral directors must have a thorough understanding of the voice as an instrument. It helps if they are able to sing well, but it is not an absolute requirement. Many fine-sounding choruses have been produced by directors for whom voice was not the major instrument. However, producing a fine choral sound requires the director to have an ear for excellent vocal quality and a knowledge of how to produce that sound.

Aspiring choral conductors should avail themselves of vocal instruction. Like any other instrument, singing cannot be learned from a book or video. One has to experience personally the process of tone production to understand what the process involves and what it feels like to be singing well. Because the vocal instrument is part of the human body, correct kinesthetic feeling for tone production has much to do with successful singing. All choral directors need private voice study as part of their preparation.

Outside of the college or university setting there is often little opportunity for people to locate private voice teachers. Even when teachers are available, most choral singers do not avail themselves of the opportunity to study privately. Therefore, choral conductors find themselves in the role of voice teacher. Depending upon the age level of the group, choral directors may have to teach the choral literature and develop the vocal instrument simultaneously. Teaching only the notes without attention to vocal production often results in singers not reaching their vocal potential and may produce vocal strain.

Voice teachers are sometimes critical of the demands placed upon young singers by choral singing, and this concern is legitimate. Children tire easily, and their voices become strained when required to sing beyond their technique. Choral directors must monitor for vocal fatigue and recognize the limits of vocal endurance. The voice cannot be used for long periods of time without having a period of rest. In the block scheduling that is becoming prevalent in many high schools, it could be problematic to have students sing for an entire ninety-minute block. Likewise, festival and all-state choirs that rehearse all day become real opportunities for vocal abuse. Good choral music educators recognize the voice as an instrument that is easily damaged and take the proper precautions to keep vocal abuse from happening when conducting a choir.

There are five basic areas for which voice instruction generally is prescribed: respiration, phonation, resonant tone production, diction, and expression. A thorough education in all five areas is necessary to become a successful voice builder. It is beyond the scope of this book to present an exhaustive discussion of each area. A number of texts are available on the topic of vocal teaching, and several are recommended here for further investigation (see the list of references at end of chapter): Alderson, 1979; Haasemann and Jordan, 1991; Henderson, 1979; Miller, 1986; Nesheim and Noble, 1995; Phillips, 1992. Vocal students should explore numerous sources as they seek to improve their knowledge about the voice and techniques for vocal instruction.

Research has provided much detailed knowledge on how the voices works (Titze, 1994), but much remains to be learned. As research advances, choral directors need to remain current in their knowledge and techniques of vocal pedagogy, not only by reading but also by attending sessions on vocal instruction at music conferences. The voice is a wondrous instrument, and choral music educators have an obligation to study singing in-depth in order to excel as vocal music teachers.

POSTURE DEVELOPMENT

The singing voice is a wind instrument; it depends upon a breath source for the production of sound. Many singers, however, understand neither the importance of the breath nor the ensuing problems that result when the breath is not managed correctly. Proper breath management is the foundation of good singing technique, and the beginning of proper breath usage is correct posture development.

When singers do not stand or sit properly they are unable to breathe sufficiently to support the voice. For singers the body is the instrument, and the physical body must be carried in such a way as to maximize the potential for positive voice production.

The seven characteristics of good singing posture for standing are as follows:

1. Feet on the floor, comfortably apart, one foot slightly ahead of the other, weight distributed toward the ball of each foot
2. Knees relaxed slightly, with hips tucked under
3. Vertically stretched spinal column
4. Shoulders back and down
5. Elevated sternum
6. Head held high and level
7. Hands and arms down at sides and slightly back

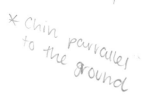

It helps to remind students: "ears over shoulders, shoulders over hips, and hips over knees." This will encourage the proper alignment of the body (see Figure 13.1).

The characteristics of posture for sitting are similar to those for standing, except the singer sits forward in the chair with hands in the lap, as shown in Figure 13.2. While students may at first object to sitting forward in their chairs, they soon will find this to be the position most conducive to good singing.

Figure 13.1. Standing posture for singing.

Figure 13.2. Sitting posture for singing.

A deterrent to good singing posture is the holding of music, which tends to pull the singing stance inward; the rounding of shoulders with lowered sternum and head is seen often. By insisting that singers hold their music up (see Figure 13.3), choral directors will help students maximize the singing posture. Music should be held high enough that singers can see just over the top to the conductor, looking down at the music only with the eyes. If the head is moving up and down from conductor to music, the music is being held too low.

Figure 13.3. Music placement for singing.

Good singing posture demands a state of alertness and readiness. The physical body should be neither tense nor totally relaxed, but held in dynamic balance between an ease and state of preparedness that is similar to what a gymnast uses before executing an exercise. Singers need to stay loose while remaining physically alert.

It does little good to remind students constantly about good posture or the lack thereof. Choristers often stand or sit tall for a minute or so but quickly revert to a slumped position unless proper singing posture becomes a habit. Habitual singing posture is encouraged by having students practice regularly the elements of good posture during the warm-up period. Spending a little time at the beginning of each rehearsal on postural exercises, especially in the early stages of students' choral experience, will produce benefits that last a lifetime. The following exercises are models for the development and practice of proper singing posture. A number of these exercises have been adapted from the author's methodology in *Teaching Kids to Sing* (Schirmer Books, 1992).

Posture Development Exercises

Stretching exercises, or muscle movers, are a good way to prepare the body for singing. Physicians recommend that people stretch each day; stretching is known to produce positive health benefits. Older students and adults should be instructed to stretch before the actual warm-up begins; each person does the stretches he or she finds most comfortable and beneficial. With elementary children, it is more helpful to have a stretching routine or set that everybody does together. Such sets should include no more than four exercises that focus on stretching the spinal column, loosening the lower limbs and arms, relaxing the shoulders, and elevating the head. Stretching needs to be executed slowly so as not to tear a muscle.

Stretches are not meant to induce great physical activity; rather, they are to open the body to a position conducive for good singing. Such activity should take no longer than a minute in most rehearsals, and will take no time from the warm-up period if begun by singers before the actual rehearsal starts.

The following stretches, all done in a standing position, are grouped by category. One exercise from each category forms a set of muscle movers.

BACK CONDITIONING

• SPINAL STRETCH. Feet comfortably apart, extend arms and interlock fingers with palms inward. Turn hands to palms outward, bend at waist and stretch forward with arms parallel to the floor; hold a few seconds. Move arms to over the head and stretch upward; hold a few seconds. Bend over and stretch the arms and hands down to the floor; hold a few seconds.

• SIDE STRETCH. Feet comfortably apart, hands on hips, stretch to one side (left) by raising the opposite (right) arm over the head in the direction of the side stretch; hold a few seconds. Reverse by stretching to the opposite side with the opposite arm stretching over the head in that direction; hold a few seconds.

• ROPE CLIMBING. Smoothly alternate (left-right) arm stretches above the head, reaching to the ceiling as if climbing a rope. Sides and shoulders alternately elevate on each stretch, and each hand should open and close while reaching upward.

SHOULDER CONDITIONING

• SHOULDER ROLL. With elbows extended to sides, gently roll shoulders in large circular motions; roll slowly back three times and forward three times.

• SHRUG. Elevate shoulders, hold briefly, let drop. Raise one shoulder, hold, and drop; alternate shoulders. Do the "wave" by raising and dropping alternate shoulders in succession.

• SHOULDER FLEX. Clasp hands in front of body and move shoulders alternately forward and backward; flex slowly.

HEAD CONDITIONING

• HEAD ROLL. Roll head gently forward and to one side and hold; repeat the roll forward to the other side and hold. Do not roll the head backward in a complete circular motion, as it is possible to pinch a cervical nerve.

• YES AND NO. Alternate nodding the head up and down with alternately turning the head from left to right, and vice versa. Move slowly and do not move the head back too far when nodding.

• THE TURTLE. Elevate shoulders while pulling the head down into its "shell." Drop the shoulders quickly as the head pops up; hold the head high and turn slowly from side to side.

LOWER LIMBS AND ARMS CONDITIONING

✓ • **HEEL MARCH**. With hands on hips, march slowly by alternately lifting one heel then the other, with a corresponding flexing of the opposite knee; do not lift the entire foot from the floor.

✓ • **SHAKE IT OUT.** Vigorously shake the arms and legs alternately to stimulate blood flow and flexibility.

✓ • **THE LUNGE**. One step forward, bend at the knee while keeping the rear leg straight. Alternate leg stretches.

POSTURE CUES.   The following visual cues help to activate good singing posture.

• SITTING FORWARD. Extend both hands forward, palms up, as if asking for something. Students respond by sliding forward and sitting tall.

• SITTING BACK. Extend both hands forward, palms outward, as if saying "stop." Students respond by sliding back and relaxing in chairs.

• SITTING TO STANDING. Hands forward and palms upward, make a circular motion beginning upward with both hands (right hand moves clockwise, left hand moves counterclockwise), hands pause briefly at bottom of circle, separate slightly and lift. Students stand on lifting motion.

• STANDING TO SITTING. Hands forward with palms downward, make a circular motion beginning downward with both hands (right hand moves counterclockwise, left hand moves clockwise), hands pause briefly at top of circle, lift slightly, and push down together. Students sit on pushing-down motion.

• REMINDER TO STAND TALL. Make "thumbs-up" motion with one hand in front of body.

POSTURE PRACTICE.   The following exercises are for the development of the seven basic characteristics of proper singing posture. All are executed while standing.

• **FOOT SLIDE**. Feet comfortably apart on the floor, move one foot slightly forward, with weight distributed to the ball of each foot. Move foot back and repeat exercise.

• **KNEE FLEX**. Lock the knees by stiffening; follow by a slight relaxation and repeat several times. Students must be warned against locking the knees while singing; it hampers flow of blood and creates tension in the whole body.

• **HIP ROLL**. With hands on hips (thumbs forward), rotate hips under as if beginning to sit down. Hip rotation places the abdominal muscles in a better position for breath support (inward), and helps relieve spinal curvature.

• STERNUM STRETCH. Palms of hands together in "praying" position, move hands back and to the sides until no further movement is possible; note elevation of the sternum in this stretch. Lower arms to sides without lowering the sternum. Repeat exercise with inhalation of air upon stretch to sides.

- SHOULDER ROTATION. Roll shoulders up, back, and down, as if falling into a groove. Let shoulders fall forward and repeat with less observable rolling motion.

- HEAD ELEVATOR. Elevate the head with an imaginary motion of lifting the head by a strand of hair. Drop head down into shoulders, and repeat lift without the imaginary lift of hair.

- HAND PLACEMENT. Hands down at sides, find seam lines of pants and hold on to clothing while singing, becoming accustomed to a position that is farther back than usual for the hands. Elevation of sternum and back/down position of shoulders will aid this side/back hand position.

FACIAL POSTURE.   The following exercises are to help students develop more expressive facial posture.

- EYEBROW SIT-UPS. Raise and lower the eyebrows, noting the role that eyebrows play in facial expression. Sing something "up" that will be aided with elevated eyebrows. The director points to the eyebrows as a reminder to elevate them for singing.

- BIG FACE, LITTLE FACE. Make the biggest face possible (drop jaw, open eyes, lift eyebrows), and follow by a very little face (reverse actions). Note all muscles of the face that are available for use when modifying facial expressions.

- MIME. Make facial expressions reflective of various emotions: happy, sad, melancholy, anger, surprise, and so forth. Relate the importance of facial expression to effective communication in singing.

ACTIVE AND MENTAL POSTURING.   The following exercises help develop good posture as a habitual way of life.

- LIGHT WALK. Walk in a circle in a normal fashion with no emphasis on proper posture. Switch to a walk that is more upright, springing, with a bounce to the step. Return to normal position and note the heavier, more lethargic feeling. Cultivate a lighter, upward posture for walking.

- FORWARD MOTION. Standing tall, lean slightly forward on the peak of a musical phrase; press into the musical line. Note the added strength this forward motion adds to the support of the musical line.

- FREE FLIGHT. While seated, close eyes and drop arms to sides. Consciously relax the major muscle groups of the body by focusing mentally on each area as it is commanded to let go. Imagine muscular tension flowing out of the upper body through the arms and fingertips to the floor. Repeat the same process as tension in the lower limbs drains through the feet. Drop head to chest and imagine mental tension draining out the top of the head. Cultivate a sense of peace and relaxation as a warm feeling of freedom fills the body. Breathe deeply. Stand and assume correct singing posture with a renewed sense of well-being.

BREATH MANAGEMENT: BREATHING MOTION

Breath management involves three areas of psychomotor development: breathing motion, breath control, and breath support. In breathing motion, students simply learn to breathe in and out correctly using the proper muscular action. For breath control, students learn to control the slow emission of the air column. Breath support involves energizing the air column with the correct breath pressure. Taken together, these three areas of breath management build on an expansive and upright singing posture.

Many people do not know that correct breathing for singing also is conducive to better health. Learning to breathe with the correct motion is, then, an objective of vocal instruction that has benefits beyond the music classroom. Deep breathing is known to aid digestion, cleanse the body of toxins, and massage the heart muscle. When someone sighs deeply, the expelled breath can relieve stress.

Vocal authorities generally agree on the following muscular action for a deep breathing motion:

• INHALATION. The diaphragm descends (contracts) and the lower ribs expand outward, with a corresponding enlargement of the body around the waistline.

• EXHALATION. The diaphragm ascends (relaxes) and the lower ribs contract inward, with a corresponding contraction of the body around the waistline.

Note that the diaphragm *contracts* upon inhalation and *relaxes* upon exhalation. It is a mistaken idea that the diaphragm also contracts upon exhalation; this is an impossible action. Physiologically, the diaphragm must relax for exhalation in order that air be expelled. This principle will be returned to when addressing the topic of breath control.

Children often practice a "chest heaving" breath when asked to take a big breath. This type of clavicular breathing (raising and lowering of the clavicle bones) becomes so habitual at an early age that often it is difficult to teach students later on to breathe correctly. However, research in this area (Brody, 1948; Cox, 1992; Fett, 1994; Gackle, 1987; Henry, 1995; Phillips, 1983; Phillips and Aitchison, 1997; Phillips and Vispoel, 1990) has shown repeatedly that students of all ages can learn to change their mode of breathing from high and shallow to low and deep with the proper instruction.

The physiology of the breathing motion is really quite simple. The diaphragm has a double-dome shape and is positioned within the rib cage under the lungs. When the diaphragm receives a signal from the brain to contract, it moves downward upon the abdominal cavity, causing the contents of that cavity (stomach, liver, intestines, and so forth) to compact and move outward. The drop of air pressure within the thoracic cavity brought upon by the lowering of the diaphragm causes air to rush into the lungs. Upon relaxation, the diaphragm returns upward to its normal dome-shaped position, pressing against the lower lungs and causing expiration of air. For this motion to occur smoothly and without interference, the abdominal muscles must be relaxed during the inhalation phase. If the abdominal muscles are held tight or contracted during inhalation (as some figure-conscious students, athletes, and ballet dancers are known to do), the abdominal contents will not be able to shift down and move out slightly as the diaphragm contracts downward. Students need to be reminded to relax the abdominal region when practicing the correct breathing motion.

Breathing Motion Exercises

Caution: students sometimes become light-headed from deep breathing exercises. Before beginning breathing study, singers need to be warned that if this happens, they need only stop doing the exercise momentarily; the light-headedness will clear quickly.

The following natural breathing exercises are given to help students discover and practice the deep breathing motion needed for good breath control and support. All breathing exercises begin with the *exhalation* phase of the breathing motion.

- SLOW SIP. Standing with feet comfortably apart, bend at the waist, placing palms of hands over kneecaps. Blow air out slowly, then inhale slowly through pursed lips as if breathing in through a straw; note movements of the abdominal area: inward for exhalation and outward for inhalation. Repeat several times. (The beginning position helps to keep the upper chest anchored so it will not rise during inhalation).

Exhale, then straighten up without inhaling; place two fingers of each hand into the abdominal area slightly above the navel. Inhale (sip) and consciously move the fingers outward with the incoming breath. Exhale and move the fingers inward with the out-going breath. Repeat several times. Using the fingers to monitor the movement of the abdominal area helps the students to feel and observe the desired motion.

The slow sip exercise also may be done in a sitting position. While seated, cross the arms over the thighs in the lap; bend at the waist so the abdominal area pushes into the arms. Exhale and feel the arms move inward upon the abdomen; inhale through the slow sip and feel the body lift from the arms. Repeat the cycle while sitting up, again placing the first two fingers of each hand into the abdominal area and moving the fingers accordingly in and out upon exhalation and inhalation.

- EAGLE SPREAD. Standing with hands clasped behind the head, bend at the waist and exhale; stand and inhale. Repeat several times. On the final exhalation, stand without inhaling, wait to deprive the body of oxygen, and then gasp. A deep, fully induced breath will occur as the body seeks to replenish the oxygen quickly.

- SILENT ROWING. The following is a more aggressive breathing motion exercise to help induce a flow or rhythm to the breathing cycle. While seated, extend elbows to the sides with hands clenched as if grasping oars for rowing a crew boat (long, narrow racing boat). Lean back, as if pulling on oars with a corresponding exhalation. Lean forward lifting the oars up and inhale through slightly pursed lips. Repeat several times. The leaning forward action upon inhalation helps keep the chest from rising.

- PANTING. With two fingers of each hand resting gently on the abdomen, exhale and inhale through the mouth with a slow but continuous cycle of breaths; monitor for the correct movement of the abdomen. Increase the pace of panting until a fast, reflexive action is possible. If students are introduced to this fast panting too soon, they may revert to clavicular breathing. In a group, pant slowly, gradually increasing the pace.

BREATH MANAGEMENT: CONTROL

Breath control may be defined as the slow emission of air while singing. Excellent breath control is necessary to sing long musical phrases. Once students have developed the habit of correct breathing motion, they are ready to learn to control the exhalation phase of the breath cycle.

A more vigorous breathing approach is needed for singing than for normal life functions. The thoracic cavity contains the lungs, ribs, and heart and must be expanded *before* inhalation begins; this permits a greater volume of air to be inhaled. This expansion is aided by an elevated sternum, which is a practice of good posture. It also is helped by the contraction of the *external intercostal muscles*, which lie between the ribs. The contraction of these intercostal muscles before the act of inhalation enlarges the rib cage and actually causes some air to enter the lungs because of the greater area made available. Once the external intercostals are activated, the diaphragm may contract to pull in a deep breath.

Breath control for the singer begins when the diaphragm starts to relax slowly upward. Because the diaphragm's movement is difficult to feel, it is best not to control the diaphragm directly. Rather, the pace of relaxation can be controlled by the lower rib line, to which the diaphragm is attached at its perimeter. Thus the singer must strive to keep the rib cage open and expansive while singing, resisting the countering effects of the *internal intercostal muscles* to pull the ribs down during exhalation. If the lower ribs are permitted to move in slowly, the diaphragm will not be able to rise quickly and the slow ascent of the diaphragm can be accomplished. This action has been demonstrated successfully in research by Miller and Bianco (1985). Therefore the singer must strive to maintain a feeling of inhalation while exhaling; not permitting the chest or rib cage to collapse while singing will greatly aid the slow emission of the breath. The external intercostals continue to contract, keeping the ribs expanded, and relax only as the internal intercostals contract ever so slowly, pulling the ribs down and inward. The breath may thus be controlled more directly by monitoring the action of the rib cage than by the direct action of the diaphragm.

A word of caution is necessary: *The rib cage cannot be held out continuously without any movement.* It must eventually lower, especially for long musical phrases. But singers can counter the practice of immediately collapsing the rib cage upon exhalation by learning to maintain an expansiveness of the rib line while slowly and gently permitting it to contract. Only then will they know how to control the breath effectively.

Breath Control Exercises

The following exercises aid in developing the slow emission of air while maintaining a full and expansive thoracic cavity.

• SLOW LEAK. Standing tall with elevated sternum and expanded rib cage, place hands on the lower rib line (not waistline), exhale, inhale with a slow sip, and exhale on a soft *ss* sound for varying counts of ten to thirty seconds. Monitor for a rib cage that moves in slowly. Students may sit as they run out of air to determine who can sustain the longest. (*ss, sh*)

• STOPPED LEAK. Follow the plan for the "slow leak" above; this time stop the leak every five seconds followed by five seconds of the *ss* sound. The director may say "stop—start," or touch the first finger to the thumb to indicate the stopped leak, opening the finger and thumb for the leak to continue.

• CONTROLLED COUNTING. With hands on the lower rib line, exhale, inhale, and begin counting at a tempo of one count per second. Determine how long students can count on one breath, sitting down as they run out of breath.

• BREATH SUSPENSION. The following exercise is intended to help students learn to suspend or hold the breath between inhalation and exhalation with the contracted diaphragm rather than the closed throat. Yawn deeply, pause while keeping the throat open; exhale with no glottal click. This is the feeling of an open glottis (space between the vocal folds) that should be maintained prior to vocal onset (when vocal folds close). Repeat but close the vocal folds momentarily before exhaling; a glottal click will be heard upon exhalation. Do not suspend the breath by closing the vocal folds before onset. If glottal clicks persist, inhale briefly before exhaling to find the feeling for exhaling without glottal noise.

BREATH MANAGEMENT: SUPPORT

Breath support can be described as the "energized breath column" for singing. The physiological source of this energy comes from the abdominal muscles, which, when contracted upward and inward against the diaphragm, create a state of balanced resistance resulting in firm breath pressure. Women often have greater difficulty in developing breath support, as they are, as a whole, longer-waisted than men, and must more actively lift the abdominal muscles in the support process.

There are four sets of abdominal muscles in the abdominal cavity. The outermost muscle is the *rectus abdominis*, which extends from the end of the sternum area to the pubic region. This muscle is a flexor, and when contracted hardens outward to protect the abdomen from a blow to the region. Pushing outward with this muscle for singing results in throat constriction; the function of the *rectus abdominis* is postural rather than for support. Some singers confuse pushing outward with the diaphragm with flexing the *rectus abdominis* muscle. The diaphragm cannot be pushed outward during singing; it must relax upward upon exhalation, and it cannot be controlled directly.

The *transverse abdominis muscle*, the innermost layer of the abdominal set, makes direct contact with the diaphragm. When it contracts, it lifts the abdominal area upward and inward; it is an important muscle in the support process. Its action can be consciously felt by contracting or flattening the abdominal area.

The two *oblique* muscles, *external oblique* and *internal oblique*, are positioned on either side of and under the *rectus abdominis* muscle. When these muscles contract, they lift the outer areas of the abdominal region, aiding the *transverse abdominis* in applying an even pressure to the diaphragm.

While a student cannot control the breath directly, it is possible to apply the pressure of the abdominal muscles directly to the support process. It is necessary to learn to contract the abdominal set (*transverse abdominis* and *oblique*) ever so evenly against the diaphragm, which, if relaxing slowly, will resist the pressure of the abdominal muscles with just the correct amount of suspended action, creating a balance between the two sets of muscles (those of control and those of support). This technique, labeled by the Italianate school of singing as *appoggio* (Miller, 1986), is the support system used by many fine contemporary singers, as noted by the Metropolitan opera star Jerome Hines in *Great Singers on Great Singing* (1982).

The outward hold of the rib cage for breath control should not be confused in the *appoggio* technique with a pushing out of the abdominal region for breath support. The uplifted rib cage and elevated sternum maintain an expansiveness while the abdominal muscles gently contract inward. Sometimes the pressure needed for a musical phrase is so slight that little contraction of the abdominal area is readily observable. At other times, a more conscious contraction is needed for greater breath energy. At no time, however, should a singer push the abdominal area outward for singing; the result will be unwanted throat constriction. Singers must stand tall, maintain an expansive posture, breathe deeply, and begin to sing with a gentle "lifting-up" thought from the center of the body. This will engender a feeling for breath support and energized singing.

Breath Support Exercises

The following exercises are intended to help students activate the abdominal muscles used in the breath support process and to help them feel the internal pressure known as breath support.

• FORCED EXHALATION. Exhale, inhale, and attempt to blow out the air forcefully through tightly closed lips. Repeat and permit some air to escape through the pursed lips; note the feeling of internal pressure created by this exercise. The abdominal muscles are trying to rid the lungs of air while the diaphragm cannot relax because the air is being held back at the lips. A similar but more gentle feeling occurs when there is a balance of slowly relaxing the diaphragm and gently contracting the abdominal muscles. Repeat the procedure for the forced exhalation exercise with a more gentle exhalation through pursed lips; note the feeling of fullness in the abdominal area. This exercise also may be done on an individual basis by blowing out through a straw.

• BREATH PULSING. This exercise will help students to activate the contractions of the abdominal muscles for breath support. Exhale, inhale, and lightly pulse the breath four times on a slight *ss* sound. Gradually increase the power of the crunches every four counts until a very firm level of abdominal contraction has been reached.

• POWER BREATH. Exhale, inhale, and forcefully expel the air on one long *ss* sound; do not bend over while exhaling. Monitor for strong contraction of the abdominal muscles. This exercise may be used to conclude the above breath-pulsing exercise.

• BREATH ARTICULATION. Exhale, inhale, and exhale the air with five quick soundless "bumps" on *huh-huh-huh-huh-huh*. Put up five fingers on one hand and blow them down one at a time (as if blowing out candles) with five continuous puffs of air.

• COSTAL CONTROL. This is a more advanced breath control exercise and should not be used until basic breath control action has been accomplished. It is used to teach the outward hold of the ribs, which cannot be used indiscriminately but must match the level of pitch being sustained. With hands on the lower rib line, exhale, inhale, and sing a sustained *ah* on middle c or an octave lower for changed male voices. Maintain the outward expansiveness of the lower ribs for as long as possible. Singing in the lower voice requires less breath pressure than singing in the upper voice, making sustained breath control easier in the lower voice.

Place first fingers and thumbs at midrib position with remaining fingers resting on lower ribs. Sing a sustained *ah* on the pitch g^1 (g an octave below for changed male voices) for as long as possible without contracting the middle rib line. Note that more breath energy is needed for a higher pitch, and the lower ribs begin to contract more quickly than for singing lower in the scale. With thumbs under armpits and fingers stretched across the upper chest, sustain an *ah* on c² (c¹ for changed voices) while keeping the upper chest expanded. Do not attempt to keep the lower or middle ribs out; higher pitches require greater breath energy, and the lower ribs will coordinate automatically if the upper rib cage is kept elevated.

Vary the upper-rib hold by sustaining an *ah* on the upper c² pitch while holding out the lower rib cage. Note how this lower hold counters successful support of the pitch in the upper voice by an almost choking action of the throat. For the upper voice, the lower rib line acts more like a bellows, generating more breath pressure from the lower rib line as it contracts more aggressively.

All of the breathing exercises presented in this chapter establish only a foundation for adding the breath to the voice. The exercises should be used extensively at first and then may be combined with phonation and tone production exercises. Unless students have a good understanding of the breathing process and are able to demonstrate correctly the breathing motion, breath control, and breath support exercises, it is unlikely they will correctly apply the breath to the voice for optimum vocal results. Even when students know how to breathe correctly, bad habits develop from laziness or fatigue. The choral director must monitor students constantly for correct use of the breathing process.

STUDY AND DISCUSSION QUESTIONS

1. What is meant by the statement "Singing is a learned behavior"?
2. Why must choral directors also think of themselves as voice teachers?
3. What has engendered the dispute between choral directors and voice teachers? What is one probable solution to the problem?
4. What are the five basic areas of vocal instruction in which the choral music educator must be a competent instructor?
5. What are the seven characteristics of good singing posture?
6. What is a deterrent to good singing posture, and what can be done to correct the problem?
7. What is the purpose of muscle movers, and what are the four categories of these exercises?
8. What is the main objective of facial posture exercises?
9. What are the three components of successful breath management, and why is each important?
10. What is the action of the diaphragm for a proper breathing motion?
11. What is the definition of the term *breath control*?
12. What muscles are involved in the breath control process, and how does each function?
13. How should students be taught to suspend the breath correctly, and why is this an important technique?
14. What is meant by *breath support*, and what muscles are the major source of breath energy?
15. What part does the *rectus abdominis* muscle have in the breath support process?
16. How should the diaphragm be controlled during singing?
17. What is meant by *clavicular breathing*, and why is this a poor technique for singing?
18. What condition results when the abdominal muscles are pushed out for breath support?

19. Why is it impossible to keep the rib cage fixed in an expanded mode when singing in the upper part of the voice?

20. Why is it important to monitor the breathing process frequently and practice breathing exercises apart from vocalization?

REFERENCES

Alderson, R. (1979). *Complete handbook of voice training*. West Nyack, NY: Parker.

Brody, V. (1948). An experimental study of the emergence of the process involved in the production of song (doctoral diss., The University of Michigan). *Doctoral Dissertations, 15*, 90.

Cox, M. J. (1992). An investigation of how vocal exercises affect the range, respiration, and pitch accuracy of junior high students (masters thesis, University of Nebraska, Omaha).

Fett, D. L. (1994). The adolescent female voice: The effect of vocal skills instruction on measures of singing performance and breath management (doctoral diss., The University of Iowa). *Dissertation Abstracts International, A54-7*, 2501.

Gackle, M. L. (1987). The effect of selected vocal techniques for breath management, resonation, and vowel unification on tone production in the junior high female voice (doctoral diss., University of Miami). *Dissertation Abstracts International, 48*(4A), 862.

Haasemann, F., and J. M. Jordan (1991). *Group vocal technique*. Chapel Hill, NC: Hinshaw Music.

Henderson, L. B. (1979). *How to train singers*. West Nyack, NY: Parker.

Henry, J. E. (1995). The effectiveness of Kenneth Phillips' strategies on the singing development of students in grade five (masters thesis, Pennsylvania State University).

Hines, J. (1982). *Great singers on great singing*. Garden City, NY: Doubleday.

Miller, R. (1986). *The structure of singing*. New York: Schirmer Books.

Miller, R., and E. Bianco (1985). Diaphragmatic action in three approaches to breath management in singing. In V. Lawrence (ed.), *Transcripts of the fourteenth symposium: Care of the professional voice*, vol. 2, *Pedagogy*, (357–60). New York: The Voice Foundation.

Nesheim, P., and W. Noble (1995). *Building beautiful voices*. Dayton, OH: Roger Dean.

Phillips, K. H. (1983). The effects of group breath control training on selected vocal measures related to the singing ability of elementary students in grades two, three, and four (doctoral diss., Kent State University). *Dissertation Abstracts International, 44A*, 1017.

——— (1992). *Teaching kids to sing*. New York: Schirmer Books.

Phillips, K. H., and R. E. Aitchison (1997). Effects of psychomotor instruction on elementary general music students' singing performance. *Journal of Research in Music Education, 45*(2), 185–97.

Phillips, K. H., and W. P. Vispoel (1990). The effects of class voice and breath management instruction on vocal knowledge, attitudes, and vocal performance among elementary education majors. *Quarterly Journal of Music Teaching and Learning, 1*(1&2), 96–105.

Titze, I. (1994). *Principles of voice production*, Upper Saddle River, NJ: Prentice Hall.

14 | Vocal Development, Part 2

Research has shown a strong, positive relationship between the speaking and singing voices. "Poor speech habits often result in poor singing habits, and medical authorities are reporting numerous cases of vocal nodules in children as a result of improper use of the speaking voice" (Phillips, 1992, p. 221).

The physiology for speaking and singing are very similar. Energized breath is directed through the vocal folds, which vibrate at various rates, producing pitch. These sound vibrations (or waves) are shaped within the vocal tract into distinct vowel colors. The vocal tract also adds resonance frequencies to each vowel, and the resulting sound is the unique vocal quality of each individual.

How a person coordinates the vocal process determines the overall beauty of the voice. If breath support is lacking, both speaking and singing will be devitalized. Lack of good breath energy typically results in one of two states: (1) a whispery sound or (2) a harsh, driven sound. Lack of proper breath support also may result in poor pitch control. Vowels that are poorly shaped often distort intonation and intelligibility. When the vocal tract is tense and not relaxed, the quality and resonance of the voice suffers. Good vocal production requires an understanding of how the voice works and many hours of guided practice.

VOCAL REGISTERS

It is possible to phonate in at least three vocal registers. (A vocal register is a series of pitches produced by the same adjustment of the vocal mechanism.) These registers typically correspond to the upper, middle, and lower singing ranges. Most people speak in or near their lower vocal register; this is an enculturation process. Singing, however, requires an individual to experience all of the vocal registers if the vocal range is to expand. While adult males generally sing in their lower and middle voices, the use of the upper register assists the proper production of the upper male singing range.

*low: chest/full voice/heavy mech.   * high: M falsetto/ W whistle
*upper: head/light mech.

The Vocal Folds

The larynx contains two vocal folds (or cords) that vibrate when air is passed between them; this produces vocal sound. The pitch of the voice is varied by the changing shape of the vocal folds. Pitch in the lower register is produced when the vocal folds are shorter and thicker. This action is caused by the contraction of the thyroarytenoid muscles within the vocal cords. Pitch in the upper register is produced when the vocal folds are longer and thinner. This action is caused by the contraction of the cricothyroid muscles, which are located at the base of the larynx. Pitch in the middle register is produced by the cooperative use of both the thyroarytenoid and cricothyroid muscles. Changes in pitch from upper to lower and vice versa are produced when more or less of each muscle is used to balance the contraction of the other muscle.

A singer must have a kinesthetic knowledge of what it feels like to sing in each of the three vocal registers. Once this feeling becomes innate, the process of pitch matching at all three levels becomes automatic. It takes time and practice, however, before a person is able to sing with a wide vocal range. The vocal muscles are like all other muscles of the body—they take time to develop for maximum efficiency.

Vocal Register Exercises

It is helpful if singers practice phonating in the three registers of the voice as a warm-up to singing. This opens the voice, helping the singers to experience the highs and lows of vocal production. The application of firm breath support is necessary if phonation is to be clear and unconstricted in the vocal tract.

- ACCENTED PULSE. Begin by pulsing the rhythm pattern in Example 14.1 in the lower or chest voice (speaking pitch) on the vowel *ah* at a moderate tempo. The abdominal musculature is consciously contracted on each pulse. Care must be taken that the jaw be dropped sufficiently from the posterior of the jaw so as to free the vocal tract of tension. Repeat the pulsing pattern in the middle voice, and then the upper voice. Boys with changed voices need to develop the use of the male alto register in the upper voice. This is not hard to do and is an excellent means by which to develop the upper male vocal range.

- WHEELIES. The lower wheelie, upper wheelie, and spiral wheelie help to develop the flexible application of breath support to the three registers of the voice. The lower and upper wheelies each constitute five vigorous breath and corresponding voice pulsations. For the lower voice use a rolling pulse on *yo-o-o-o-o*. The sound produced should be similar to that of a car's low, cranking battery turning over. The upper voice uses *yoo-oo-oo-oo-oo*. The spiral wheelie spirals downward from the upper to lower voice without a register break. Using the rolling pulse, begin with *yoo* in the upper voice, change to *youh* (as in *book* or *your*) in the middle voice, and *yoh* in the lower register. The abdominal support contractions should be firm and vigorous, resulting in strong vocal pulses.

- SIGH. This exercise imitates a descending vocal glissando. A deep breath is a requisite for a well-supported glide from top to bottom. Begin high in the upper voice on *ah* and glide smoothly down from the upper to the middle to the lower voice. Repeat twice and begin the glide higher and higher. Care must be taken to keep the sound light and unforced. The glissando should be one continuous sound with no audible voice break between the upper and lower vocal registers.

- DOWN FIVE. This exercise develops the lower extension of the vocal range and follows the vocal pattern 5–4–3–2–1; each repetition descends by half steps (see

(pulse *ah* on each note)   (gliss.)

Example 14.1. Vocalise: Accented pulse.

Yah - yah - yah - yah - yah

Example 14.2. Vocalise: Down five ("How Low Can You Go?").

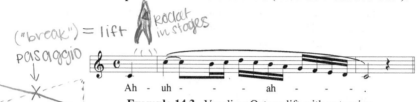

Ah - uh - - - ah - - - .

Example 14.3. Vocalise: Octave lift with extension.

☒ = head voice
☐ = middle voice

Example 14.2). It is necessary to shift into exclusive use of the lower register if the lower voice is to find its true extension. Care must be taken that the voice not be pushed on the lower pitches; however, students enjoy playing "how low can you go." Exercise in this part of the voice is to strengthen the thyroarytenoid muscle, which governs the production of the lower voice.

• OCTAVE LIFT WITH EXTENSION. The vocalise shown in Example 14.3 is excellent for developing extended upper range. Beginning in the lower voice, the registers must shift quickly to the upper voice by maintaining a light vocal quality. Men will sing the exercise an octave lower than shown, and will need to cultivate an upper male alto quality as the exercise is repeated higher each time by half steps.

• OCTAVE LIFT. "I know, I know, I know" is an octave lift exercise for developing the upper vocal range (see Example 14.4). The octave lift must be initiated with firm breath support, but the upper voice needs to be light on top. The *n* sound in "know" helps to produce a forward placement of the voice. Modulate the exercise upward by half steps.

RESONANT TONE PRODUCTION

A beautiful voice is one rich in resonance; it is characterized by uniformity of vowel color, depth and fullness of tone, and projection or "ring." These terms are highly subjective but are recognized by vocal authorities (Alderson, 1979; Appelman, 1967; Klein and Schjeide, 1972; Miller, 1986; Phillips; 1992, Vennard, 1967) as being characteristic of the resonant voice.

Resonance is produced above the level of the larynx in the vocal tract, which comprises the pharynx and oral cavity. Phillips (1992) states:

> Resonance may be defined as "constructive interference" of sound waves within the vocal tract. As energy is generated from the vocal folds, a complex sound wave is produced. This wave travels through the pharynx (throat) and out of the oral cavity (mouth), resulting in a loss of energy. A portion of the wave, however, is according to the shape of the vocal tract for the sound (vowel) being phonated. It is this interference of waves within the vocal tract that transforms a rather indistinguishable sound at the laryngeal level into a resonant tone. Thus, the vocal tract has acoustic properties apart from the pitch and harmonics produced by the vocal folds. Without this property of resonance, all voices would tend to sound alike and variation of vowel color would be impossible. (p. 253)

I   know, I know, I know, I   know.   I   *(etc.)*

Example 14.4. Vocalise: Octave lift ("I Know").

Formants and Vowel Production

The fundamental frequency (f) of the voice is the pitch one hears. Above this frequency are harmonic frequencies known as formants (F). While formants are similar to overtones, they are not "fixed" frequencies, i.e., at the octave, 5th, 4th, and so forth. Formants are better understood as frequency regions or bands of frequencies. Therefore, each pitch produced by the voice is a combination of fundamental and formant frequencies.

The formant frequencies of the voice raise or lower according to the shape of the vocal tract. By modifying the position of the articulators (tongue, jaw, lips, etc.), it is possible to change both the identity of a vowel (e.g., *ah* or *ee*) and increase or decrease its resonant quality. Because the vocal tract is capable of numerous changes resulting in numerous formant possibilities, the human voice is able to produce language.

The first two formant regions above the fundamental pitch provide most of the identity for the vowel (Titze, 1994). When choral directors strive to have singers produce uniform vowels, they are trying to have the singers shape the vocal articulators in such a way as to produce a match of similar vowel sounds among the various voices. This may mean dropping the jaw more, protruding the lips slightly, raising the tongue, and so forth. Singers need to be aware that vowels can and should be shaped across the choir in order to achieve similar colors for each of the vowels sung. Choirs that sound flat often do so not because of poor pitch but because vowel frequencies are not matched and therefore "beat" against each other, producing problematic intonation.

The third and fourth formant regions above the fundamental pitch are the main determinants of tone quality (as are the higher formants), enabling the listener to distinguish one voice from another. These quality formants can be shaped by the choral director to produce various tone colors that beautifully match the style of the music being sung. Most choirs tend to sing with a monochromatic timbre, that is, one sound that rarely varies. Choral directors should at least experiment with developing light and dark contrasts of tonal color, and may explore all of the variations between these two. Adjusting the vocal tract to produce varying choral sounds is much like the actions of a ventriloquist, who shapes the vocal cavity to sound like someone else. Singers also can do this shaping as they seek to find vocal tract formations that work well for certain resonant qualities. It takes time and practice, but it is worth the effort when a more beautiful voice is the result.

Teaching singers to sing with an open throat is conducive to producing a greater resonance in the voice. The relaxed and open pharynx is essential to this process. The pharynx comprises three parts: the *laryngopharynx*, the area below the level of the tongue; the *oropharynx*, the area behind the oral cavity and tongue; and the *nasopharynx*, the area above the soft palate behind the nasal cavity. Powerful constrictor muscles in the walls of the pharynx help to move things along in the swallowing process. When these swallowing muscles are contracted for singing, the tone becomes pinched and constricted. Similarly, when the tongue is tensed and drawn backward in the throat, the tone again becomes constricted. A gentle lift or arch in the soft palate helps to open the throat for greater resonance. Also, the jaw must be relaxed to produce a free tone. Tension in any of the vocal articulators will result in a less resonant voice.

Singers who tense the swallowing muscles in the process of singing often are not aware they do so. The use of these muscles can be a compensatory technique developed from not using the proper breath support. When breath management is wrong, the singer will compensate by using more tension in the vocal tract. Primary in this action are the muscles of the tongue (glossus). The tip of the tongue should be kept forward, resting on the fleshy ridge at the base of the lower front teeth. The back is kept forward and high enough to keep it out of the throat. It is common to see a singer whose tongue is drawn back with tip up, as in the position of the American *r* sound.

> The tongue must remain relaxed for singing. Any rigidity will cause a constriction of the vocal tract and reduce vocal resonance. A rigid or trembling tongue signals that the swallowing muscles are being used to compensate for poor breath support and control. (Phillips, 1992, p. 259)

Positioning of the larynx also can change the color of the voice. When a person swallows, the larynx rises; a yawn will result in its lowering. As the larynx is lowered for singing a darker sound is produced. A larynx that is too low or depressed results in a sound that is hooty. When the larynx is raised for singing it makes the formants higher, thus producing a brighter sound. Popular singers often have bright or twangy voices from using a high laryngeal position.

> A relaxed larynx that remains in its normal, at-rest position throughout the singing range is to be cultivated. It allows for maximum pharyngeal resonance and maximum development of resonant vocal tone. Singing with the larynx elevated activates the swallowing process, which in turn causes throat constriction. For an open throat, the larynx must remain relaxed in its normal position. This condition is greatly aided by proper support of the breath and consistent breath pressure. (Phillips, 1992, p. 260)

The position of the lips also is important for shaping vowel color and resonance. Drawing back the lips as for the *ee* sound shortens the vocal tract and raises the vowel formants; this produces a bright sound. Lips that are slightly flared forward, as for the *oo* vowel, lower vowel formants and produce a warmer sound. Lips that are extended too far forward muffle the sound. Singers need to find a uniform position of the lips (e.g., an oval position) to enhance uniform vowel quality.

Telling students to open their mouths often leads to overt tension in the jaw. What really helps vocal resonance is a jaw that is lowered from the back. When the hinge of the jaw is free, and the jaw can move without restriction, tone quality improves. If the jaw is tight it limits the "shower room" effect of the voice; the space within the vocal tract is constricted and so is the tone.

Singing with an open throat means singing with relaxed jaw and lips, forward and relaxed tongue, a larynx that stays at rest, a soft palate that is arched, and pharyngeal muscles that are relaxed. The human voice becomes an incredibly beautiful instrument when it flows through an open and free resonator.

Vocal-Tract Freedom Exercises

The following exercises are helpful in teaching students to sing with an open and relaxed throat.

• JAW DROP. This exercise teaches singers to drop the jaw from the back/hinge. Place the tips of the index fingers in front of the ears at the pinna (small cartilage outside the ear canal). Put the thumbs at the base/rear of the jaw. Drop the jaw from the synovial hinge and feel the indentations that occur at the synovial joint. Move the jaw up and down several times to effect a free jaw movement. Direct students to maintain a light pressure on the indentations while vocalizing on vowel sounds.

• NO-AH NO. The vocalise in Example 14.5 is helpful in establishing jaw fexibility. The jaw closes slightly for each "No" and springs open for each "ah." Concentration should be placed on the springing action at the hinge or rear of the jaw. Modulate upward by half steps.

• LARYNGEAL ELEVATOR. This exercise helps students learn to relax the larynx for singing. Pull the lips back (smiling) and speak a high laryngeal *uh* in the speaking voice. Notice the elevation of the larynx. Through a deep yawn speak a low laryngeal *ah* in the lower voice. Notice the dark and hooty quality and the depressed position of the larynx. Now speak as for sighing a medial to upper pitch using *ah*. Let the pitch naturally descend on a sigh; note the relaxation of the larynx (at rest) and the open-throat feeling. Preface the singing of vocalises with this exercise until students become used to the feeling of an enlarged pharyngeal area as for the sigh.

• INNER SMILE. This exercise helps to lift and arch the soft palate. With the lips lightly together and teeth parted, smile on the inside at the back of mouth. Nostrils will flare slightly. This inner smile creates a larger oropharngeal area. Preface the sigh exercise with this inner smile, and then employ both exercises before the singing of vocalises.

• TONGUE TIP. This exercise teaches students to keep the tip of the tongue forward and down when singing. Rest the tip of the tongue at the base of the lower front teeth. Speak the vowels *oo-oh-ah-eh-ee* without moving the tip of the tongue. All five vowels should be made by moving the sides and back of the tongue. Direct students to sing the vowel sequence *oo-oh-ah-eh-ee* on a sustained pitch, keeping the tongue forward in its resting position.

• MUSCLE MASSAGE. The muscles under the chin (geniohyoid and mylohyoid) aid the swallowing action and should not be used for singing. Tension in these muscles can be detected by resting the first finger on the chin with the thumb pressing lightly underneath. These muscles of the chin and neck should remain relaxed for singing. If tension (stiffness) is detected while sustaining pitches, the tension can be massaged away by gently rotating the thumb throughout the under-chin area. Both thumbs can be used simultaneously if the tension is excessive. Tension of the geniohyoid and mylohyoid muscles for singing indicates an elevated larynx.

• TONGUE FLEX. The tongue can be the arch enemy of the singer. It often has some degree of tension, causing it to be drawn back into the pharyngeal area. This reduces the size of the vocal tract and decreases vocal resonance. To check for tension in the tongue muscle, flex the tongue forward and back, slowly at first, while keeping the tip of the tongue anchored at the base of the lower front teeth. The jaw must not

No - ah,   no - ah,   no - ah,   no - ah,   no - ah,   no - ah,   no.

Example 14.5. Vocalise: No-ah no.

move while the tongue is flexing. Failure to move the tongue independently from the jaw is a sign of muscle tension. Once the tongue flex can be done easily and quickly, use it while singing simple vocalises such as the "Down five." Again, care must be taken that the jaw be down and relaxed, not moving while the tongue is moving. The goal is to relax the swallowing muscles and avoid their use in the singing process.

DICTION

Most singing involves the communication of language. The blending of music and words can produce incredibly beautiful results. If the listener cannot understand the text, however, then the singer has failed to give enough attention to the declamation of the words, and the performance suffers. Why sing at all if the text cannot be understood?

The pronounciation of a language in general is called the study of diction. Vocal music students often are required to take courses in the diction of English, Italian, French, and German. In these courses students are taught how to pronounce the sounds peculiar to these languages. They learn how to enunciate the vowels and articulate the consonants. The International Phonetic Alphabet (IPA) symbols are frequently used as a foundation for interpreting the sounds that are common to many languages of the world. The IPA designates one symbol for each vocal sound, regardless of the spelling. Many resources contain the IPA symbols (e.g., Phillips, 1992), and sources abound for the study of foreign-language diction (e.g., Cox, 1970; Hall, 1971; Marshall, 1953; May and Tolin, 1987; Moriarity, 1975; Uris, 1971).

Style of diction is dependent upon the choral literature being sung. Sung-speech diction is more suitable for popular music and ballads, where the rhythmic integrity of the music is not as important as is the stylized continuity of the music's flow. In sung-speech, word blends into word as final consonants are connected to initial consonants of following words. Double consonants become single consonants as every attempt is made to maintain a beautiful legato. Sung-speech diction was first popularized by Fred Warning (1951) and the Pennsylvanians, one of the early popular choral groups in America.

A second style, *rhythmic diction* (Fisher, 1986) is used to maintain the rhythmic integrity of the music and is particularly useful when performing music of the Baroque and Classical eras. In this style, even the syllables of individual words are spaced individually so as to emphasize the rhythm of each individual note. Care is taken not to smear syllables, especially across slurs. Sixteenth-note melismatic passages bring out the recurring pulse of the vowel on each note; words are not connected and double consonants are articulated separately. The music dances to a clarity enhanced by diction that does not blur the rhythm but rather enhances it.

Much of the choral art repertoire exists in foreign languages. When possible, choral directors are encouraged to use the original foreign texts with singers. The accent of the music more readily matches the textual accent when original languages are used. Also, the syllables of translated words often do not match the syllables of the original words, necessitating a change in note values. Students are encouraged to study foreign languages in school; the choral director can affirm this part of the curricula by using foreign texts. An accurate translation is a necessity, and choral students should know the meaning of the words. When an English translation is required, it should be a good one, accurate and faithful to the original text.

Uniform Vowel Enunciation

The beauty of the vocal tone is in the vowel. Therefore, every choral director must have a basic understanding of how vowels are best produced and must work with choral members to enunciate vowels correctly. Five basic guidelines are as follows: (1) Vowels are uniform in shape (oval with slightly flared lips), producing a uniform choral tone. (2) Vowels are deep-set (pharyngeal), producing a rich, resonant choral tone. (3) Vowels are focused forward (in the "mask"), producing an energized choral tone. (4) Vowels are modified when necessary to maintain vowel integrity. (5) Diphthongs are executed with correct balance, producing greater uniformity of vowel production. 2 vowels on 1 syllable   *timbre:* quality of sound

VOWEL UNIFORMITY.   Most people do not give much attention to how they speak in daily conversation. Final consonants are dropped, words are "chewed," and little effort is given to projecting the voice. When these lazy speech habits are brought into the choral rehearsal, the results are typically a choir that has a less than beautiful timbre. Unless the choral director knows how to go about changing this tone color, the choir members will be doomed to sing as they speak. This cannot be if a beautiful choral tone is the objective. People cannot sing as they speak. They have to understand the need to modify vowel production in what is called "singers diction." If the choir does not understand the difference between conversational speaking and singers diction, beauty of tone will never be achieved. The more inexperienced the choir, the more time the director must spend on developing uniform vowel production.

Vowels are produced by different shapes of the vocal tract. The jaw, lips, and tongue are mainly responsible for the changes that result in a variety of vowel colors. The difference between *ah* and *ee* is caused by changes in the vocal articulators that affect the formant frequencies in the vocal tract. The tongue is low in the mouth and the jaw is open for the *ah* sound. For the *ee* vowel, the tongue is higher on the sides and the jaw less open. Changes of the vocal articulators make changes in the formant frequencies, resulting in a change of vowel sound.

Because vowel formants exist as regions rather than fixed frequencies, choristers of different sizes can adjust their vocal articulators to match the sound of any vowel being produced by the group. Once an aural model is established by the director, the singers can adjust their own vocal tracts to reflect the model sound. Sections of the choir need to listen to other sections in order to develop good aural discrimination as to vowel uniformity.

DEEP-SET VOWELS.   The pharynx (throat) is the major resonator of the voice. Singing with an open throat means the muscles of the pharynx are open and relaxed. Singers often unconsciously tense these throat muscles when they overcompensate for lack of breath support. The result is a sound lacking in warmth and richness. The activation of the swallowing muscles for singing is to be avoided.

Deep-set vowels are rich sounding. Achieving richness is helped through the following techniques: (1) Maintain an "at rest" laryngeal position. If the larynx rises for singing, the sound becomes brighter because the vocal tract is shortened. Depressing the larynx will overly darken the sound, resulting in a "hooty" quality. (2) Maintain an arch in the soft palate. A feeling of surprise or the beginning of a sigh or yawn helps to keep the soft palate up or arched. (3) Maintain a forward tongue position. When the tongue is stiff and pulled back, it stifles pharyngeal resonance. (4) Maintain a jaw position that is lowered from the back or hinge of the jaw. Lowering the jaw from the rear opens the pharyngeal area. (5) Maintain a slightly flared lip position for all vowels as for the *oo* sound. A slight lip flare lengthens the vocal tract, lowers all formants, and makes the sound richer.

FORWARD PLACEMENT OF VOWELS.   It is common to speak of singing "in the mask" as opposed to singing in the throat. While the pharynx can provide a rich resonance to tone, the sound must be projected forward to the mask if the tone is to have energy and life. This is as much an imagery process as it is a physical one, but there is no doubt that mentally thinking the sound out in the mask helps to draw the sound forward in the vocal tract. This placement can be felt by sustaining an *n* while phonating. The tongue presses against the hard palate, and the concentration of vibration is felt forward, as if a person had on a surgical mask and it was being filled with sound. Singing through the mask gives the voice great carrying power.

VOWEL MODIFICATION.   When the frequency of the fundamental pitch being sung is higher than the first formant frequency of any vowel, it is difficult for a singer to maintain purity of vowel. This occurs especially in the upper ranges of sopranos and tenors, where greater depth of jaw opening is needed for pure vowel production. As pitches ascend above the treble staff, it becomes difficult to sing the closed vowels *ee* and *eh* without modifying them to either an *uh* or *ah.* Alderson (1979) notes that singers must continue to think the pure vowel sound so that understanding may not be lost. "There seems to be only a small fraction of the pure vowel necessary in the modified sound to be correctly identified" (p. 145).

DIPHTHONG EXECUTION.   There are six diphthongs in the English language, and many times these vowel combinations are problematic for singers. For example, the word "bright" uses a combination of *ah* and *ee* sounds for the one single vowel *i.* However, most people will substitute an *uh* sound for the *ah* when speaking and singing. The *uh* is a more shallow sound, and the word loses resonance when this substitution is made. The six diphthongs and the correct vowels for each are as follows:

i	= *ah* + *ee*, as *white*
ay	= *ēh* + *ee*, as in *gray*
o	= *oh* + *oo*, as in *rose*
ow/ou	= *ah* + *oo*, as in *brown*
oy/oi	= *aw* + *ee*, as in *turquoise*
ew/u	= *ee* + *oo*, as in *fuchsia*

For the first five diphthongs, the initial vowel is sustained as long as possible, with the vanishing or second vowel added very quickly at the end of the syllable. Singers often "chew" these two vowels, sustaining the second vowel much too long. This is especially true in popular music. The sixth diphthong is rarely a problem for singers; the *ee* sound is passed through quickly, with the *oo* being sustained. This combination is the exception to the rule. Choirs need to be vocalized on diphthongs to form the habit of correct production. Choral conductors typically use the "pure" or long vowel sounds for warm-ups, when short vowels and diphthongs also need practicing.

Resonant Tone Production Vocalises

Choral directors often use the *ah* sound to begin vocalization. It is, however, a difficult vowel with which to achieve uniformity. The variation of this sound, from bright *uh* to dark *aw*, is problematic. The *oo* sound is recommended as the first vowel for uniform vowel production. The lips form a natural oval and the back of the throat is naturally open. The larynx also is relaxed, which helps to make the sound warm and rich. If singers fail to extend the lips for the *oo* sound, placing the lips around the little finger can produce the correct model. Blowing out through pursed lips also will activate the correct lip formation.

oo____ oh____ ah____ eh____ ee__*etc.*
[u] - [o] - [a] - [e] - [i]

Example 14.6. Vocalise: Unison movement on long vowels.

[U]   [I]   [ɛ]   [æ]   [ʌ]

Example 14.7. Vocalise: Unison movement on short vowels.

• VOWEL UNIFORMITY. Direct students to speak the vowel sequence: *oo-oh-ēh-ay-ee*. Maintain the slight lip flare of the *oo* throughout the vowel sequence. Notice that the jaw drops from *oo* to *oh* to *ah*, and then begins to close on *ēh* and *ee*. Try to maintain a more vertical position for all vowels, especially the *ēh* and *ee*.

• UNISON MOVEMENT: LONG VOWELS. Sing in unison the vocalise in Example 14.6. Work to maintain the slight flare of lips and the oval or vertical positioning of all five vowels. Repeat this vocalise with the tuned consonant *n* at the beginning of each vowel. This helps to bring focus to the sound. Monitor for a larynx at rest.

• UNISON MOVEMENT: SHORT VOWELS. The short vowels in English are all shallow sounds and do little to enhance the choral tone. All short vowels must be sung with greater vertical positioning, that is, more drop of the jaw. A slight flare of the lips also will help to warm and make these vowels richer. The sequence in Example 14.7 begins with the *oo* sound (as in *soot*), which has a natural flare of the lips in its formations. The jaw drops more in the sequence for each successive short vowel in the vocalise.

• FOUR-PART MOVEMENT. The vocalise in Example 14.8 is easy to teach and produces quick results in vowel uniformity. It also can be sung using the short vowels as noted in Example 14.7. Varying the dynamics and tempo adds variety and keeps the vocalise fresh.

• OO-OH-AH. Speak the vowel sequence *oo-oh-ah*, noting the vertical positioning of the vowels and the greater drop of the jaw for each successive vowel. Sing the vocalise in Example 14.9 maintaining lip flare and vertical positioning. Be careful to sing a true *ah* (as in *father*) and not the darker *aw* (as in *ball*).

• OO-ĒH-EE. Speak the vowel sequence *oo-ēh-ee*, noting the vertical positioning of the vowels. Maintaining the lip flare of the *oo* for the *ēh* and *ee*, as well as keeping the jaw lowered, adds warmth to these bright vowels. Remember that the *ēh* vowel is not the diphthong *ay* in these vocalises. It is sung pure without the vanishing *ee* sound. The vocalise in Example 14.10 can be alternated with that in Example 14.9.

• SINGING DIPHTHONGS. The vocalise in Example 14.11 aids the correct singing of diphthongs. Sustain the initial vowel (except for number 6), adding the vanishing vowel quickly before moving to the next word. The initial vowel for each word in numbers 1, 4, and 5 is an *ah* sound, not an *uh*.

• VOWEL FOCUS. The vocalise in Example 14.12 develops a forward, "in the mask" placement. Direct students to produce a strong *vvv* with upper teeth against

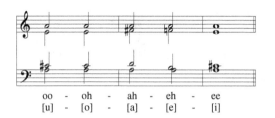

oo – oh – ah – eh – ee
[u] – [o] – [a] – [e] – [i]

Example 14.8. Vocalise: Four-part movement.

oo - o - ah   oo - o - ah   oo - o - ah   oo - o - ah   oo - o - ah
[u] - [o] - [a]

Example 14.9. Vocalise: Oo-oh-ah.

oo - eh - ee   oo - eh - ee   oo - eh - ee   oo - eh - ee   oo - eh - ee
[u] - [e] - [i]

Example 14.10. Vocalise: Oo-ēh-ee.

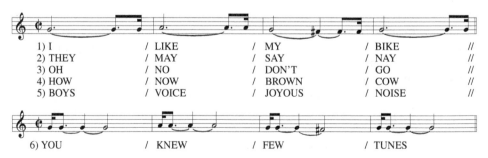

1) I   / LIKE   / MY   / BIKE   //
2) THEY   / MAY   / SAY   / NAY   //
3) OH   / NO   / DON'T   / GO   //
4) HOW   / NOW   / BROWN / COW   //
5) BOYS   / VOICE   / JOYOUS / NOISE   //

6) YOU   / KNEW   / FEW   / TUNES

Example 14.11. Vocalise: Diphthong production.

Vvvvvvvvvvvvvvvvvvoo - - - -

Example 14.12. Vocalise: Vowel focus.

lower lip. Sing down the first measure on the *vvv*, opening to the *oo* in the second measure, rising to a long or short vowel in measure 3. Sing the final vowel with much energy, lip flare, and vertical positioning.

Intelligible Consonant Articulation

If vowels make the beauty of the tone, then consonants make the sense of the word. Without well-articulated consonants, intelligibility of language is compromised. Regular attention to consonant production helps a choir to use good articulation habitually.

There are six classifications of consonants for singing in English. These classifications aid the rehearsal of consonants by group, and are a good memory tool.

Voiceless plosives:	*p, t, k, ch*
Voiced plosives:	*b, d, g, j* ← *sub-glottal*
Voiceless sibilants:	*f, s, th, sh*
Tuned continuants:	*m* and *n* (sustained), *l* and *r* (not sustained)
Voiced continuants:	*v, z, th, zh*
Aspirates:	*h, wh* (voiced) ★ *used for phrases starting with a vowel, or repeated vowels (malismas)*

consonants with pitch should be used as islands your group holds on to

Rules That Govern Articulation

Four basic rules govern good articulation: (1) Consonants are to be exaggerated (with some exceptions). (2) Consonants are to be executed quickly (with exceptions). (3) Consonants that are voiced or tuned are to be sung on pitch. (4) Consonants that begin words occur slightly ahead of the beat.

EXAGGERATE CONSONANTS.   Most consonants (except for *s* and *sh*) need to be exaggerated when sung. These sounds get lost in the tonal envelope, which tends to be more powerful than the consonant "interruptions." Singers bring lazy speech habits to choral singing; plosives (bursts of air) are imploded, voiced consonants are sung under pitch, and a lack of energy prevails. Choristers should not sing the language the way they speak it. Unless they learn to exaggerate consonants in general, they will not communicate the text. The choral director has to judge how much exaggeration or energy is needed. This depends upon the size of the ensemble, the acoustics of the performance hall, and the style of diction (sung-speech or rhythmic). Rehearsing singers in proper articulation is a constant challenge for the choral director. The payoff, however, is a choir that not only sounds good but also is intelligible.

ARTICULATE QUICKLY.   The majority of consonants should be produced quickly (the exceptions being two of the tuned continuants: *m* and *n*). Speed of production moves the consonant quickly out of the way of the vowel. This is especially necessary for the consonants *l* and *r*, which typically are sustained too long and under pitch; "scooping" is the product. To produce quickness of articulation, the articulators themselves must be relaxed and flexible. The use of exercises such as tongue twisters to aid in this process is recommended. Quick articulation requires the articulators to be facile.

★ *Consonants - short & quick*
★ *Vowels - long & pure*

SING ON PITCH.   Voiced and tuned consonants are to be sung on the pitch that follows. When singers do not "think" these consonants on pitch they tend to sing under the pitch; the result is scooping or flatting. Vocalises that include the singing of voiced plosives, tuned continuants, voiced continuants, and the aspirate *wh*, can help singers learn to sing these consonants in tune. Great care must be taken that the consonants *l* and *r* be sung on pitch. Because they can be sustained, under-pitch singing of these two consonants often results in flatting of the choir.

BEGIN AHEAD OF THE BEAT.   Some directors adopt a technique in which the consonant actually sounds ahead of the beat. Taken to extremes, this technique becomes distracting when a new vowel becomes inserted, e.g., *G(uh)-od*. It is important that vowel sound occur on the beat, however, especially when singing with instrumentalists. Teaching singers to use a quick and facile response to initial consonants maximizes length of vowel and beauty of tone. Most consonants are just noise.

★ Vowel on the beat, consonant right before the beat.

Articulation Exercises

The following exercises will help singers to develop greater exaggeration, speed, facility, and tuning of articulation. Remember: Consonants make the sense.

• ECHO CONSONANT DRILL: The choral director improvises a four-beat rhythm pattern using the consonants in each class, which the choir then echoes. Writing the consonants on the chalkboard helps to focus this rhythm drill. Repeat a number of times by varying the rhythm pattern. Students also may lead these consonant drills.

Voiceless plosives: p, t, k, ch. There should be no voiced sound in these consonants, only strong puffs of air.

Voiced plosives: b, d, g, j. All consonants have a subglottal buzz. Vary this consonant drill by singing the consonants on pitch.

Voiceless sibilants: f, s, th, sh. Alternate heavy and light stresses, heavy on *f* and *th*, and light on *s* and *sh*.

Tuned continuants: m, n, l, r. This class of consonants is better sung on a sustained pitch. To work on sustaining the *m* and *n* sounds, sing the word "amen" and "squeeze" the *m* and *n* by slightly extending these sounds. The *l* and *r* are not sustained. To practice a quick *l*, sing up and down a quick scale (1–5) passage on *la*. The same can be repeated for the *r* on *run*.

Voiced continuants: v, z, th, zh. All consonants have a subglottal buzz. Vary this consonant drill by singing the consonants on pitch.

Aspirates: voiceless h, voiced wh. The *h* is a true aspirate—air only. For the *wh* sound, the aspirate precedes the *w* (i.e., *hw*), and the *w* is really a vowel (*uh*).

• TONGUE TWISTERS.   Articulator flexibility can be advanced through the use of the following tongue twisters:

Momma made me mash my M&Ms. (Sing on sustained pitches).

Aluminum, linoleum, aluminum, tin.

Tip of the tongue, the teeth, the lips.

• KARATE CHOP. Practice exaggerating final consonants by speaking words with final sounds that need emphasis: *Lord, think, church, sob, hid, dog, judge.* Sustain each word for three counts and place the final consonant on beat four. All students may practice the feel of these final consonants by striking one hand against the other as in a karate chop gesture.

• HISSING SIBILANTS: S, SH, AND C. The troublesome elongation of these consonants can be helped by deemphasizing the sound and by parting the teeth immediately upon execution. When the teeth are parted it is impossible to make these sounds. Rehearse students in singing words with these hissing sibilants by parting the teeth immediately after the sound is initiated: *this, fish, peace, loves, sanctus.* As a visual cue, the director can touch the thumb to the first finger to indicate the beginning of the sound, springing the finger and thumb apart to stop the sound.

• THE THREE RS. The consonant *r* is pronounced three ways: in the American form with tongue pulled back (e.g., *run*), as a "soft" *r* with tongue forward (e.g., *father*), and as a "flipped" *r* between vowels (e.g., *spirit*). Typically, students sing all words with the American *r* sound, which tends to be hard and burred. The American *r* is sung when preceded by a consonant or when it begins a word, but it is never sung when it appears before a consonant. It is a tuned continuant and should be sung as quickly as possible. Sing words like *try* and *run* using the American *r*.

The *r* should be softened when followed by a consonant, pause, or rest. This is done by keeping the tip of the tongue forward. Sustain a hard (American) *r*, then gradually move the tongue forward until the *r* is softened. Sing the words *arm, father, Lord,* and *for,* keeping the *r* softened by keeping the tongue forward.

Madeline Marshall (1953) recommends that the *r* before a consonant be dropped, and also the *r* in final syllables, e.g., *winter.* This is a plausible alternative to using a soft *r* sound. However, when a word ending in *r* is followed by a word beginning with *r*, the first *r* is dropped.

The "flipped" *r* is sung when it appears between two vowels within a word, or between a word ending in an *r* and a word beginning with a vowel. Only one flip of the tongue is required; this should not be confused with the double *r* in Italian, which is rolled. Sing the words *spirit, very,* and *redeemer of* on sustained pitches, flipping the tongue once for the *r* between vowels. Students who cannot flip the tongue may substitute a *d* for the *r*, e.g., *veddy* for *very.*

EXPRESSION

All the good technique in the world cannot produce a great performance when expression is lacking. Outstanding performers are characterized by their ability to communicate effectively with an audience. This matter of musical interpretation is at the heart of the aesthetic experience. Music plumbs the depths of human feeling, connecting with the world of the spirit. To experience great music performed well is to experience the fuller reality of being human; it defines and connects people to one another.

Interpretive Preparation

Choral directors typically assume the role of music interpreter; they convey to choristers the meaning and mood of the selections being sung. All too often, however, choral performances are heard that have all the right notes but are boring for lack of expression. If the choral conductor does not give some forethought to what the composer is attempting to express, the whole purpose of the performance is undermined. An expressive performance is always the ultimate goal of choral singing.

Effective musical expression takes much preparation on the part of the conductor. Items to be considered before rehearsal are: (Be able to name at least 5)

- Origin of the text: poem, prose, scripture, mass, motet, madrigal, etc. What might the origin of the text indicate about the style of the period and the setting?
- Meaning of the text: What do the words convey, if anything?
- Mood of the text: Is there a basic sentiment or feeling from the words?
- Word accent: What is the natural stress of syllables?
- Word importance: Which words are important and need to be emphasized?
- Word painting: Are certain words characterized musically by special settings?
- Match of music and text: Has the composer done a good job at using music that works with the text? What is the overall mood being conveyed?
- Diction style: Will sung-speech or rhythmic diction be used?
- Pronunciation: What vowels will be modified and which consonants given special emphasis?
- Foreign language: Is a suitable translation available? Can the director provide a suitable phonetic model of the language?
- Style of music: What style and era of musical composition is represented, and how should this knowledge affect the musical performance?
- Musical phrase: How are the phrases delineated and where is the "peak" of each phrase?
- Breathing points: Where do the breaths occur for each part?
- Articulation: Is the music legato, staccato, marcato, or a combination of these?
- Texture: Is the music monophonic, homophonic, or polyphonic, and how will these textures affect the choral balance?
- Dynamic indicators: Where are the loud and soft passages, crescendo, decrescendo, and sudden changes in dynamics? How will these be indicated in the conducting gesture?
- Tempo indicators: Are metronome indications given? How will the tempo indicators be translated in the conducting gesture?
- Effective communication: How will expressive interpretation be communicated to the choir using effective body language (posture, facial expression, conducting gesture)?

Planning for all of the above takes much time and preparation. Conducting is a big job. Not spending time to find the heart of the music results in a final product that is uninspired. Why put all the time and energy in rehearsing music when the payoff is not meaningful? Begin planning with the end in mind.

Expression Exercises

Meaningful interpretation is the goal of both the conductor and the choral singer. However, students often are lacking in their knowledge of how to sing expressively. Like most other things, expression can be taught. It just takes time to develop a technique for expressive choral performance. The following exercises help to develop an awareness of expressive performance among choral singers.

• MEANING AND MOOD. The choral director leads a discussion of the text's meaning and mood. The text should be read aloud by one individual, or as a group. How does the author use the words to express the various sentiments in the writing? Are there phrases that are obscure or vague in meaning? Is there historical or social background material that will aid the understanding of the text? How can the words best be reflected in facial posture? Where does the peak of the song occur? How do the singers want the audience to respond? What will it take from the ensemble to achieve an expressive performance? How do the pieces in the current repertoire differ according to mood and what might be a good concert order for these selections?

• FACIAL POSTURE. Students need to practice varying their facial posture to match the sentiment of what they are singing. The eyebrows are an expressive element of the face; have students raise and lower the eyebrows—up for bright and happy, lower for pensive or sad. Students can be asked to reflect other moods in their facial expression: anger, joy, desperation, hurt, pride, and so forth. The conductor needs to remind students periodically about looking the part.

• BODY POSTURE. How students stand in chorus is reflective of whether or not they are connecting to the music. Body posture can be exercised by directing singers to perform a series of mirror-imaging postures where students reproduce the stance and look of the director. Again, such sentiments as surprise, elation, sorrow, melancholy, and so forth should be used to reflect how the physical body responds naturally to such emotions. A choir that looks expressive will sing expressively.

• SPIN THE PHRASE. A sense of "spinning" the phrase is necessary for the flow of musical expression. A phrase should always be thought of as traveling or going somewhere. As students are singing, they can be directed to conduct what they are singing by using a simple, continuous rolling motion of one hand, one roll per beat in tempo. This gesture may stop and lift at the breath. The rolling or rotating of the hand conveys visually and mentally that the musical phrase is continuous. It connects the choir to the music using an easy physical gesture.

• DYNAMIC VARIATIONS. Singing everything at one dynamic level is boring. Direct students to sing a tonic chord with moderate loudness. The director should adjust the level as needed. Then proceed to sing loudly, softly, very softly, gradually louder, and so forth. Students should not be permitted to force, or oversing. Very soft singing is most difficult because the breath support must remain firm.

Students should learn to interpret the Italian dynamic terms and symbols. Some basic drill may be needed to master these terms and symbols. Circling loud dynamic indicators in red pencil, and soft with blue is good for both conductor and students.

• TEMPO MARKINGS. Students need to learn to interpret the basic Italian tempo terms. This process can be aided by asking the students to count *1 an' 2 an' 3 an' 4 an'* as the director conducts a four-pattern at various tempos. This exercise easily becomes troublesome because students want to rush ahead of the tempo. The director makes a smaller pattern for faster tempos, and a larger pattern for slower tempos. Drawing circles around tempo terms in the music helps students to highlight the importance of following the given tempo. This also can be done with a marker or highlighter. The

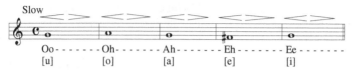

Example 14.13. Vocalise: Messa di voce.

Example 14.14. Vocalise: Portamento.

choral conductor is well served in deciding the exact pace of a tempo by using a metronome and marking the speed in the music. This is especially true when a metronome marking is not given. Even if a metronome marking is given, it may be too fast or slow for the ensemble in question. Decide upon the tempo before the first rehearsal.

• MESSA DI VOCE. Long notes require life—that is, a slight give and take of dynamic level—if the musical line is to be energized and interesting. The *messa di voce* (swell, ⟨ ⟩) requires much breath support technique, and singers should practice the vocalise in Example 14.13 in order to understand how to give inner life to long tones. Notes that only sit there do little for musical expression. HPBG

• PORTAMENTO. The smooth, almost inaudible connection of notes is known as *portamento*. The classic vocalise by Seiber in Example 14.14 is excellent for developing this glide between pitches. The second note of each group of two is softer on the ascent and descent. Work to make a beautifully connected line.

STUDY AND DISCUSSION QUESTIONS

1. How does the speaking voice influence the singing voice?

2. What is a vocal register, and what are the basic registers in the human voice?

3. How do the vocal folds work, and what muscles produce pitch in the singing voice?

4. What are the characteristics of the resonant voice?

5. How does "constructive interference" create formant frequencies, and what do the first four formants produce in the voice?

6. How can the quality of the voice be made lighter or darker?

7. How does a person sing with an "open throat"?

8. What happens to tone quality when the larynx is raised or lowered too much?

9. What lip position extends the vocal tract, helping to warm the vocal tone?

10. How should the jaw be lowered for singing?

11. How do the following terms differ: diction, pronunciation, enunciation, articulation?

12. What is the difference between "sung-speech" and "rhythmic diction"? Where is each style more appropriate?

13. What are the five basic guidelines for vowel enunciation?

14. How are deep-set vowels and vocal resonance achieved?

15. What is "singing in the mask"?

16. What is vowel modification and when is it necessary to use it for singing?

17. What are diphthongs and how are they generally executed for singing?

18. What are some guidelines that govern articulation?

19. Why must the choral conductor pay much attention to the expressive elements in the choral score?

20. How can expressive interpretation become part of a choir's basic performance technique?

REFERENCES

Alderson, R. (1979). *Complete handbook of singing.* West Nyack, NY: Parker.

Appelman, R. D. (1967). *The science of vocal pedagogy: Theory and application.* Bloomington: Indiana University Press.

Cox, R. G. (1970). *The singer's manual of German and French diction.* New York: G. Schirmer.

Fisher, R. E. (1986). Choral diction with a phonological foundation. *Choral Journal, 27*(5), 13–18.

Hall, W. D. (ed.) (1971). *Latin pronunciation according to Roman usage.* Anaheim, CA: National Music Publishers.

Klein, J. J., and O. A. Schjeide (1973). *Singing technique: How to avoid vocal trouble.* Anaheim, CA: National Music Publishers.

Marshall, M. (1953). *The singer's manual of English diction.* New York: Schirmer Books.

May, W. V., and C. Tolin (1987). *Pronunciation guide for choral literature (French, German, Hebrew, Italian, Latin, Spanish).* Reston, VA: Music Educators National Conference.

Miller, R. (1986). *The structure of singing: System and art in vocal technique.* New York: Schirmer Books.

Moriarity, J. (1975). *Diction: Italian, Latin, French, German: The sounds and eighty-one exercises for singing them.* Boston: E. C. Schirmer.

Phillips, K. H. (1992). *Teaching kids to sing.* New York: Schirmer Books.

Titze, I. (1994). *Principles of voice production,* Upper Saddle River, NJ: Prentice Hall.

Uris, D. (1971). *To sing in English: A guide to improved diction.* New York: Boosey and Hawkes.

Waring, F. (1951). *Tone syllables.* Delaware Water Gap, PA: Shawnee Press.

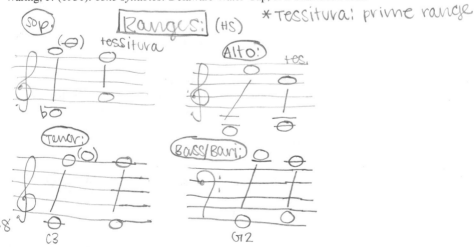

15 | Energizing the Choral Warm-Up

The choral rehearsal typically begins with some type of choral warm-up. The term "warm-up" is traditional and covers numerous activities. If the beginning of a rehearsal is just a warm-up, it may consist of little more than light vocalizing to prepare the voice for more rigorous singing. This is especially appropriate just before performances. However, the typical warm-up permits little time for actual voice development. Vocal and aural skills and sight-reading may be developed through an organized series of exercises and vocalises that progresses through the logical development of singing technique. While a warm-up may get the juices flowing, a vocal skills protocol teaches singing.

A variety of exercises and vocalises should be used for developing vocal skills. Not every exercise will work for every student, and a variety of approaches permits greater success. Singing the same vocalise over and over, day after day, is boring and does little to help students sing better. The choral director needs to be armed with a variety of exercises and vocalises that will develop posture and breathing, phonation, resonant tone production, range, agility, diction, expression, aural acuity, and sight-reading skills. This chapter presents only sample exercises and vocalises, mostly drawn from *Teaching Kids to Sing* (Phillips, 1992); numerous others are among the references listed at the end of this chapter (see especially Ehmann and Haasemann, 1981; Haasemann and Jordan, 1991; Nesheim and Noble, 1995; Robinson and Althouse, 1995). By trying out a variety of exercises and vocalises, choral directors can find out what works well for their students and can shape a plan of action that builds voices.

In most cases, the choral director must teach voice in the choral rehearsal; a clear and objective rationale helps to guide this process. The philosophy espoused in this chapter is that warm-ups should begin with energizing the body, energizing the breath, energizing the ear, and only then energizing the voice.

ENERGIZE THE BODY

The sound of a great chorus is of one that is energized (Neuen, 1988). This energy begins with a physical foundation of body and breath. Too often the warm-up begins with vocalises that are not built on a prepared, physical foundation. The result is often flat and lifeless singing. An energized voice is one that is buoyed by physical energy from the instrument itself.

Physical Conditioning

Singers often bring into the choral rehearsal a lot of physical stress from daily activities. This stress usually manifests as muscle tension, which is a hindrance to the vocal process. Therefore, it is recommended that every rehearsal begin with some type of overt physical activity that helps to relieve muscular tension. The following exercises are suggestions for this type of activity.

- MUSCLE MOVERS OR STRETCHES. All stretching exercises should be done slowly with emphasis on relaxing the lower limbs, torso, shoulders, neck, and head. Only gentle exercises should be chosen that do not require much movement (see Chapter 13). Students may choose their own stretches according to what works best for them. Only a little time need be given to this important beginning of the rehearsal (usually less than a minute), but it is invigorating for tense and tired choristers.

- MASSAGE AND KARATE CHOP. Older students and adults enjoy a shoulder massage and light "chops" up and down the back. Singers face one direction and massage the shoulders of the person in front of them, and then reverse direction and repeat. Care must be taken that the karate chops not become too vigorous; keeping the fingers spread helps for a lighter touch.

- BODY SHAKE. Direct students to give the body a thorough shaking; begin with the hands, then the arms, shoulders, torso, and legs. Finish by bending over at the waist like a rag doll. Stand slowly into an upright posture.

- FREE FLIGHT. This exercise encourages release of physical tension (see Chapter 13).

- THE SQUEEZE. Direct students to tighten/tense the body in the following order: feet (curl toes), legs (lock knees), buttocks (squeeze), hands (make fists), arms (pull to sides), shoulders and head (pull down), pursed lips, squeezed eyes, and frown. Hold the position for a short duration and release, feeling the rush of blood and relaxation that follows. Finish this exercise with a body shake (see above).

Posture Development

The seven characteristics of good posture are presented in Chapter 13. Taken together, they produce an alert and flexible position for singing. It does little good to constantly nag students to stand or sit tall. Good posture is a habit that results from much practice. The following exercises are suggested for developing proper singing posture.

- THUMBS UP, THUMBS DOWN. The director gives a "thumbs up" cue, and students respond by standing or sitting tall. "Thumbs down" is given and students slump. Periodic "thumbs up" cues from the director should engender an upright singing posture.

- POSTURE PRACTICE. Each of the seven postural elements can be practiced separately as individual exercises (see Chapter 13): feet, knees, hips, sternum, shoulders, head, and hands.

- FACE LIFT. This exercise practices various facial postures and expressions (Chapter 13).

- ACTIVE POSTURING. This exercise encourages students to make their posture a physically active part of their singing (see Chapter 13).

ENERGIZE THE BREATH

Energizing the breath is an important part of the warm-up routine. Breath management consists of three basic parts: breathing motion (deep breathing), breath control (slow emission of the breath), and breath support (energized exhalation). Students who do not know how to manage the breath will never learn to sing with vocal efficiency or freedom. Choral directors must take the time to teach breathing and to activate the breathing process at the beginning of rehearsals. When people are tired. the breathing muscles become sluggish and do not actively engage for singing. Therefore, regular attention to breathing action helps the singer to consciously recognize the importance of using the proper breath management techniques. The following exercises are suggested for engaging the breathing process during the warm-up routine. Typically, only one or two exercises can be used in any one vocal skills lesson plan.

Breathing Motion

The "deep" or diaphragmatic mode of breathing is described in Chapter 13. It has been called the "natural" breath and is necessary for the singer to use habitually. While some extensive time is necessary for students to discover this breath initially, the following breathing motion exercises may be used to help focus students' attention on the deep-breathing process. Note: breathing exercises typically begin with the exhalation first.

- HORIZONTAL BREATHING. Direct students to bend at the waist, placing the palms of the hands on the knees. (This position anchors the chest and keeps it from moving up and down during the breathing cycle.) Exhale first, noting the upward lift of the abdominal area. Inhale, permitting the abdominal area to fall toward the floor. Repeat this cycle. Following the third exhalation, stand without inhaling. Release the abdominal muscles and note the inhalation of air. Follow with several cycles of exhalation and inhalation.

- SLOW SIP. This exercise encourages a gentle, deep-breathing action (see Chapter 13).

- TWO-FINGER BREATHING. Standing, direct students to place two fingers of each hand on the abdominal area just above the navel. Exhale and move the fingers inward, even if they don't move naturally inward. Sip the air in through pursed lips and move the fingers outward with the expanding abdominal area. Repeat this cycle.

- EAGLE SPREAD. This exercise discovers the low breath through a gasp (Chapter 13).

- SURPRISE! Direct students to inhale quickly on *ah*, as though surprised. Note the expansion of the abdominal area. Exhale easily and repeat.

- SILENT ROWING. This exercise imitates rowing a boat as the breath moves in and out (see Chapter 13).

- SNIFFS. Direct students to do a short series of five sniffs through the nose on one inhalation. The diaphragm responds with a series of short contractions as it draws the air into the lungs. Exhale gently and repeat.

- PANTING. Reflexive panting encourages deep breathing motion (see Chapter 13).

Breathing motion exercises bring the students back to the fundamental breathing cycle for practice and conscious invigoration of the breath. When students can pant reflexively in automatic mode, their breathing mode becomes habitual; that is, they use the diaphragmatic breath without thinking about it.

Breath Control

Singers must learn to control the emission of the air column upon exhalation. This process is described in Chapter 13. The following exercises will help students to develop the technique of a slowly relaxing diaphragm, resulting in the slow emission of the breath.

- SLOW LEAK. This exercise emits the air in a controlled manner (Chapter 13).

- STOPPED LEAK. Greater control can be gained in this variation of the slow leak (see Chapter 13).

- BREATH STREAM. Exhale, inhale, and blow the air out through pursed lips for as long as possible. Place one finger approximately six inches in front to the lips and feel the breath stream as it centers on that point. As with all breathing motion exercises, maintain an expansive posture to keep the diaphragm from relaxing too quickly.

- CONTROLLED COUNTING. Counting as long as possible on one breath builds breath control. (Chapter 13).

- LIP TRILL. Exhale, inhale, and blow the air out through vibrating lips. This exercise requires relaxed lips and steady breath control. For those students who cannot vibrate the lips, direct them to make short bursts of the lips as if imitating a motorcycle. This helps to relax the lips for more sustained vibrating.

- COSTAL CONTROL. Place the hands over the ribs at about the midrib line (fingers forward and thumbs to the back). Exhale, inhale, then exhale slowly by keeping the ribs slightly outward against the hands. The exhalation should come from the relaxing diaphragm. When the ribs begin to lower, inhale and begin the process again. This helps the students to learn a full-bodied posture for the control process.

Breath Support

Exhalation on an energized air column is the ultimate goal of breath support. The interaction of contracting abdominal muscles with the slowly relaxing diaphragm (*appoggio*) creates this energy. The singer must never push out in the abdominal region; this is a flexing action of the *rectus abdominus* and only causes the swallowing muscles to engage (see Chapter 13). The abdominal area contracts gently and lifts easily upward for supported singing. The following exercises aid in developing the abdominal support action.

- FORCED EXHALATION. In this exercise the student feels the *appoggio* technique as the powerful contraction of the abdominal muscles is met by the slowly relaxing diaphragm (Chapter 13).

- BREATH PULSING. This exercise aims to build strength in the abdominal musculature used in the support process (Chapter 13).

- POWER BREATH. Strong contraction of the abdominal support system is the objective of this exercise (Chapter 13).

• BREATH ARTICULATION. This exercise helps to refine the support process (Chapter 13).

• MAGIC CANDLES. Spread the fingers and thumb of one hand in front of the mouth. Exhale, inhale, and blow out each "candle" with five puffs of air flowing from one breath. As the "candles" go out each finger contracts into a fist, at which point they all flare up on the in breath, and the puffs begin again. Vary this routine by blowing out all of the "candles" on one breath (swift contraction of the abdominals). Again, the candles relight (pop up) on the quick inhalation.

• ABDOMINAL PULSING. Plant a fist into the abdominal area slightly above the navel. Cover the fist with the other hand and gently pulse the abdominal region. A rigid muscle wall is a sign that the flexor muscle (*rectus abdominis*) is being engaged. Pulse the abdominal area until it is relaxed and gives easily. Next, sustain an *ah* sound in the voice and pulse the abdominals. The voice should shake or pulse with the compressions of the support musculature.

Learning to support the voice "on the breath" is one of the most important things a singer can learn to do. Without the correct breath pressure the voice never realizes its optimum beauty or strength. The choral director should make breath management exercises part of the voice-building skills section of each rehearsal.

Breath-to-Voice Activation

Exercises to hook up the breath to the voice engage the support process in active phonation. They wake up the vocal registers and free the vocal sound in an overt manner.

• WOOFERS. Students bark like big dogs (*woof-woof*), medium-size dogs (*roof-roof*), and little dogs (*yip-yip*). The size of dog corresponds with the lower voice, middle voice, and upper voice. Keep the barking light and under control! Each imitation requires a swift contraction of the abdominal support muscles.

• WHEELIES. These exercises apply a rolling support to the upper, middle, and lower voices (see Chapter 14).

• SIGH. Begin a sigh in the upper voice and glissando through the vocal registers from top to bottom (see Chapter 14). Feel the expansion of the pharyngeal area.

• ACCENTED PULSE. Apply firm contractions of the support muscles in everincreasing dynamic levels on *ah*. Maintain a relaxed jaw (see Chapter 14).

• MAMA MIA! Speak this phrase with an elevated and projected voice. Listen for the clear ring of the voice.

• SONG TEXTS. Speak the texts of choral literature as interpretive readings. Use an "acting" voice that is supported, modulated, and projected. Students should not be permitted to drone.

The speaking voice is a natural link to the singing voice. Application of breath to voice helps to coordinate the process of active phonation. The voice must ride on the breath column. All too often the voice is pressed from lack of proper support. The laryngeal muscles overwork for lack of adequate breath pressure. The breath-voice coordination technique must be actively pursued by the choral director.

ENERGIZE THE EAR

Singing is an aural skill that involves the mental processing of pitch. The music psychologist Edwin Gordon (1999) has demonstrated in his research the importance of audiation for the development of music aptitude and musical skills:

> Audiation takes place when we hear and understand in our minds music that we have just heard performed or have heard performed sometime in the past. When we merely recognize or imitate what we have heard, or memorize what we intend to perform, we live in the past. In audiation, the past lives in us. (p. 42)

Gordon makes an important distinction between music memory and audiation; if someone audiates they remember *and understand* what they hear.

Aural skills exercises in the vocal warm-up aid in-tune singing because students become aware of pitch and pitch relationships. Aural acuity also lays the foundation for sight-reading skills. Gordon's learning sequence hearkens back to that of Lowell Mason—it develops the ear before the eye. Unfortunately, many students have no aural conception of pitch relationships when they are introduced to written notation. Most singers are thus poor sight-readers. Many states do not include sight-reading at festivals because students do so poorly. Choral singers benefit from a program of aural skills development that provides a foundation for reading notation. As Gordon relates, children develop listening and speaking vocabularies before developing a reading vocabulary: "Without your first two vocabularies (developed by age three) serving as a basis, your ability to learn to read would have been severely jeopardized" (1999, p. 42).

Inner Hearing

The mental process of singing requires pitch perception (the ability to hear pitch), pitch memory (the ability to retain pitch), and pitch discrimination (the ability to detect differences and similarities among pitches). By the high school years, most students in choir hear pitch with no difficulty. Pitch memory also has developed, sometimes to such a high degree that many students learn their vocal parts by rote. What often is lacking in the mental imaging process is a high level of pitch discrimination. For example, students may be unaware of singing out of tune, which is a common problem among school choirs. Exercises that focus on the mental imaging process of pitch teach students "singing on the inside" before "singing on the outside."

The following exercises develop students' inner hearing. They are especially important for less mature singers for whom the mind-body connection is still developing. All choristers, however, will benefit from time spent on these mental imaging exercises.

- TUNING PITCH. Orchestras tune to A (440), and bands to B flat. To what do choirs tune? Choose a tuning pitch, perhaps the first note of a familiar song, and ask students periodically to sing the pitch on the "inside" and then on *loo* on the "outside." Compare to a well-tuned piano or tuning fork. It is surprising how adept students become at finding the correct pitch. Work for a very secure unison.

- SINGING ON THE INSIDE. At some point in their singing of a song, direct students to switch to "singing on the inside" (director points to ears). Switch back to "singing on the outside" (director points to lips). This exercise helps students learn the value of thinking pitch at a conscious level.

• SAME OR DIFFERENT? The director plays at the keyboard or sings two patterns that are either the same or different. Students signal with one finger against the chest for "same" or two fingers for "different." The better the students become at this exercise, the more difficult the exercises used.

• CHORDAL DEGREES. Play triads at the keyboard and direct students to sing 1, 3, or 5 on a neutral syllable. Do not tell the choir what chord degree they are to sing before sounding the triad. Give them "listening time" before asking for a response.

• SINGING SCALES INSIDE. Direct students to sing in their minds (from a given pitch) an ascending or descending scale, stopping on one scale degree as directed, e.g., stopping on scale degree 6 (or *la*). The director must cue the moving from one scale degree to the next. On another signal from the director, students sing "outside" the given scale degree upon its arrival, and adjust as necessary. This exercise can be varied by the director's playing up or down a scale and omitting a scale degree. Students may signal (showing the number of fingers against the chest) indicating the missed pitch.

Intonation

Getting a choir to sing in tune can be a real challenge. Even choirs with considerable technique fall into the trap of poor intonation. The most common intonation problem in choral singing is flatting. Barbara Doscher, in the article "Exploring the Whys of Intonation Problems" (*Choral Journal*, November 1991), gives some "easy-to-fix" causes. For example, flatting may occur if the room is too hot. Bending the neck to look down at music held too low may interfere with functioning of the larynx. Singing for too long a time may cause fatigue. Being insecure of the notes can produce hesitancy and tire the voice. Doscher's other directives include: Have patience with voices that are adjusting to pubertal change. Choose music in which the tessitura is comfortable and not too high. Work on breath management and guard against excessive pressure on the larynx. Maintain an open throat and a relaxed jaw. All of these directives are addressed in Chapters 13 and 14.

Rhythmic accuracy and vitality were the foundation of the choral technique used by the late Robert Shaw, who believed that "almost 50 percent of poor intonation is due to poor rhythm" (Decker and Herford, 1988, p. 42). Shaw worked incessantly with his singers to maintain the integrity of each note; his choirs sang impeccably in tune. He also worked to develop a fine sense of pitch memory. The following exercises are given as aids for in-tune singing. They combine the process of mental imaging with vocal production. Singing is a psychomotor skill.

• SIXTEEN PULSES. Shaw frequently used a very challenging intonation exercise. Beginning on a unison pitch in all voices (the same octave for males and females), the singers raise the pitch one half step over sixteen slow breath pulses on a neutral syllable. Invariably the singers arrive too early. This exercise shows the amount of room between half steps and causes singers to really listen to the subtle gradations that can be made in altering pitch.

• TUNING INTERVALS. Shaw used another intonation exercise in which a pattern of ascending and descending intervals was sung beginning with minor seconds, major seconds, etc. (see Example 15.1). If students learn to sing only minor and major seconds in tune, they will solve many of the intonational problems that occur in singing.

doo - doo - *etc.*

Example 15.1. Vocalise: Tuning intervals.

• MOVING BY HALF STEPS. Direct all students to sing *loo* beginning on middle C. On repeated cues from the director, sopranos and tenors move up by half steps, while altos and basses down by half steps. Movement continues up or down a major third until the interval of a minor sixth is reached. The interval progression is unison, major second, major third, tritone, and minor sixth. This exercise requires much concentrated effort from the choir members.

• DOMINANT SEVENTH MOVEMENT. This exercise involves dominant seventh resolutions and changing tonality through the circle of fifths (see Example 15.2). Perform it rather slowly in cut time. Accurate whole step and half step movement is critical to accurate intonation. ⋆Intonation exercise⋆

- 3½ steps lower
- 2½ steps higher

Example 15.2. Vocalise: Dominant seventh resolutions.

• TONAL PATTERNS. Sing basic tonal patterns using numbers or solfège sylla-bles and have students echo (underlined numbers indicate the lower octave): 1–3–5–3–1, 1–4–6–4–1, 7–4–5–4–7, 1–3–5–3–1; 1–3–5, 5–8–7, 6–4–2, 3–5–1. After some practice, sing the patterns on *loo* and have the students echo with numbers or solfège syllables.

• FOUR-PART MOVEMENT. This exercise requires the outer parts to hold true to one pitch as the inner parts move against them (see Chapter 14). Move up by half steps.

ENERGIZE THE VOICE

If the body, breath, and ear have been properly energized, the voice will be free to bloom and resonate. The properly produced voice floats on the breath; it is never forced. An energized voice is rich in timbre, projects easily, sings over a wide range, and sounds open and free.

The ideal choir should be a group of soloists whose voices blend because of their richness. Most choirs do not meet this ideal, but choral directors can do much to improve the sounds of their choirs if they are willing to spend the time to cultivate every voice in the ensemble. A little time in each rehearsal given to vocal skills development will produce enormous benefits.

Regarding the sound of high school choirs, Alderson (1979) states,

> High school voices can be rich without strain. With the proper vocal approach high school students are capable of singing without breathiness, nasality, stridency, or other unaccept-able qualities. Of course teenage voices are not as tough as they will be in ten or twenty years, but neither are they as fragile and weak as they were five years before. With today's nutrition and hygiene standards, teenage voices are as healthy as teenage bodies. If high school students can be good athletes, they can be strong singers. (Alderson, 1979, p. 195)

It is true that high school singers often can produce more vocally than might be expected. The choral director should proceed cautiously, however, when energizing the voice. Very loud dynamics are to be avoided, as are vocalises involving extremes of range. Humming and stac-cato vocalises make excellent choices for initial vocalization. These are especially good early in the morning or when students seem to be lacking energy.

Humming

There are three basic physical characteristics of the correctly produced hum: teeth apart and jaw relaxed, lips lightly touching, and tongue forward with tip resting behind the lower front teeth. Humming vocalises are gentle and a good way of massaging the voice. They also per-mit students to listen to their own voices from the inside.

• DOWN FIVE HUM. Perform this simple, descending five-note scale slowly and on one breath (see Example 15.3, line 1). Modulate upward by half steps. Students may use a light abdominal pulsing the first time, checking for connection of the voice to the breath.

• HUMMING MOVEMENT. These simple vocalises add variety to the first vo-calise (see Example 15.3, lines 2 and 3). The last vocalise calls for greater extension of the breath.

Staccato Articulation

The light breath pulse of the staccato vocalise is an excellent means of inducing proper breath support and tonal onset. The support is turned on and off in mini-contractions. The following vocalises aid the development of staccato articulation.

• STACCATO ARPEGGIO. The two vocalises in Example 15.4 are basic to the singer's vocabulary of warm-up techniques. The singer must work to keep the pitches accurate while skipping lightly over the musical triad.

• LIGHTEN UP. Direct students to lighten up when singing from the lower to the upper part of the vocalise in see Example 15.5. Transpose upward a major third by half steps. Listen for accurate tuning of the triad.

• "HO-HO CHORUS." This chorus from *Dido and Aeneas* by Henry Purcell is delightful and fun to use as a warm-up that connects breath to voice (see Example 15.6). It is easy to memorize, very short, and flows one beat to the bar.

Example 15.3. Vocalise: Humming movement.

Example 15.4. Vocalise: Arpeggios.

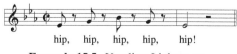

hip, hip, hip, hip, hip!

Example 15.5. Vocalise: Lighten up.

Example 15.6. Vocalise: "Ho-Ho Chorus" from *Dido and Aeneas* (H. Purcell).

Example 15.6. (*continued*)

Legato Articulation

Learning to sing with a sustained line is the basis for fine choral singing. It requires the technique of portamento, in which any given vowel is slurred lightly over two or more pitches. Breath control is especially important when singing long phrases.

• CHANT. The singing of highly sustained Gregorian chant is an excellent way to develop a legato line. The *Alleluia* in Example 15.7 requires three styles of articulation: syllabic (one note per syllable), neumatic (two notes per syllable), and melismatic (three or more notes per syllable).

• LEGATO MOVEMENT. Sing the vocalise in Example 15.8 with either long or short vowels (see Chapter 14). Glide from vowel to vowel with as little "chewing" of the vowels as possible. Sing on one breath, and modulate up by half steps.

• PORTAMENTO. This classic vocalise by Seiber (see Chapter 14) is excellent for teaching portamento. The second note of each two-note grouping should be sung lighter each time.

Example 15.7. Vocalise: Chant "Alleluia."

Example 15.8. Vocalise: Legato movement.

• HYMNS AND CHORALES. The classic hymn and chorale literature is excellent for building strong legato singing. The hymn "When I Survey the Wondrous Cross" by Lowell Mason (see Example 15.9) has four phrases, each sung to one breath. The slow tempo encourages a sustained style.

Marcato Articulation

The correct singing of marcato (accented) articulation requires that each note be pulsed from the abdominal support, and that each accented note be slightly separated from the note that precedes it. This brief space between notes allows for a more accented quality much as might be heard when beating a drum. The strokes from the support mechanism can then be heard in the voice. While not to be overdone, good marcato articulation adds a certain excitement to singing that is dramatic and colorful. The following exercises and vocalises aid in the development of marcato articulation.

• HELP! Direct singers to exclaim the word *Help!* several times, noting the abdominal contraction that occurs each time. (Do not permit student to shout from the throat.) Follow this by speaking the word five times in a row, first in a sustained manner without breath pulses (i.e., *Help—Help—Help—Help—Help*), and second by separating each exclamation with a breath pulse (i.e., *Help / Help / Help / Help / Help*). Note the more accented quality when the words are separated and pulsed. Now sing the five repetitions on one pitch, sustaining the final pitch. Pulse and separate all pitches.

• SFORZANDO (SFZ). The *sforzando* is a forceful accent built on the marcato technique. Unlike marcato articulation, which may occur for a phrase or more, this type of accent most often occurs briefly. It requires a stronger pulse from the support musculature, and the notes must be well separated. To aid students in developing this technique, direct them to count softly *1 an' 2 an' 3 an' 4 an'* for two measures. In the second measure, choose a beat which will have the *sforzando* accent, and have students stand for that count, speaking with "reinforcement." (Do not permit students to shout). Some fun may be had with this exercise by not announcing the accented beat ahead of time. The director gestures "thumbs down" for the softer counting, quickly moving to "thumbs up" for the accent and "thumbs down" for a quick return to softer counting.

When I Survey the Wondrous Cross

Isaac Watts
Lowell Mason

Example 15.9. Vocalise: *When I Survey the Wondrous Cross* (L. Mason).

• MARCATO THRUST. The vocalise in Example 15.10 calls for firm application of the breath upon the vocal onset of beats 1 and 3. This "stroke of the glottis" technique brings the vocal cords together at the onset of pitch; it should not be confused with "shock of the glottis," where the vocal folds close before vocal onset. The use of a light aspirate promotes clean glottal closure. When as the vocalise is secure, repeat without the aspirate.

HA, HA, HA, HA, HA,___ *etc.*
(H)A (H)A (H)A (H)A (H)A

Example 15.10. Vocalise: Marcato thrust.

Glo - - - - - - - - ri-a in ex-cel-sis De - o.

Glo - - - - - - - - ri-a in ex-cel-sis De - o!

Example 15.11. Vocalise: "Gloria" (traditional).

Martellato Articulation

The Italian term *martellato* means "to hammer." It is a technique used in melismatic singing, especially of the Baroque era, to make the fast-running sixteenth-notes passages clean and bright. "Hammering" is perhaps excessive for describing how melismatic passages should be sung. A better term may be "to pulse." The old way of singing runs in Handel's *Messiah*, for example, was to interpolate an *h* for each sixteenth note. This slows the tempo and creates a heavier sound than is now associated with Baroque music. Today, choral directors teach the *martellato* technique, which is characterized by light singing, a mental repetition of the vowel for each note, and individual pulses from the breathing musculature. This is an advanced technique but well worth practicing. The following vocalises help to develop this type of articulation.

- GLORIA. The refrain of the carol "Angels We Have Heard on High" (Example 15.11) is a good way in which to introduce students to melismatic or *martellato* singing. Sing the eighth-note melismas on *doh-doh-doh-doh*. Then remove the *d* consonant, encouraging students to articulate the separate *oh* vowel cleanly from the breath pulse. Slight manual pulsing of the abdominal area can assist the learning process. Direct students to think the *oh* vowel for each eighth note and to keep the singing light.

- PULSING SIXTEENTHS. Direct students in the vocalise in Example 15.12; begin slowly and gradually increase the tempo. Use the syllable *doo* to begin, and as technique improves, remove the *d* consonant. Keep the singing light, rethink the vowel on each note, and lightly pulse each note from the breathing musculature. Manual pulsing of the abdominal area helps to develop the pulsing technique. Be sure that students do not interpolate an *h* for each note; this will only slow the tempo. Transpose upward a minor third by half steps.

- BUMP AND PULSE. The vocalise in Example 15.13 is a more challenging use of martellato technique as the vocal range is expanded. Begin practice by singing on the syllable *doo*. Once the pitches are secure, use only the *ah* vowel, pulsing each note from the abdominal musculature. Remember to keep the singing light.

Example 15.12. Vocalise: Pulsing sixteenths.

Example 15.13. Vocalise: Bump and Pulse.

Vowel Uniformity

Authentic choral literature, that is, music written originally for chorus, uses a type of diction that is modified from that which is used for daily speaking. The purpose of this "singers diction" is to produce greater resonance and beauty of choral tone. One characteristic of this style of production is that vowels are shaped in a uniform fashion so that movement from one vowel to the next is smooth and flowing. Vowels that are "chewed" create an uneven vocal line. Vowels that are uniform result in a uniform vocal quality. Vocal quality is enhanced when vowels assume the same general shape.

Most vocal teachers believe that all vowels, long and short, should be vertically produced. These "tall" vowels all have sufficient height, as if the roof of the mouth were the vaulted ceiling in a cathedral. The lips are never spread as in a smile but are oval shaped and flare slightly forward as for the *oo* vowel. Jaw depth varies a little for each vowel, but the jaw is relaxed for all vowels. To summarize, uniform vowels are vertical ("tall" or "north and south" as opposed to "east and west"), the lips are oval shaped and slightly flared, and the jaw is relaxed.

- OO-OH-AH. This vocalise (see Chapter 14) uses the *oo* vowel as the basis of production for the *oh* and *ah* sounds. The *oo* naturally flares the lips forward, a shape that should be maintained throughout the following vowels. The jaw relaxes for the *oh* vowel, and relaxes even more for the *ah*. Caution: students should not sing *aw* for *ah*. The *aw* sound tends to be too dark and can depress the vowel formants, causing a pitch to sound flat. The *ah* in this vocalise is as that in the word *father*.

- OO-ĒH-EE. This vocalise (see Chapter 14) again uses the *oo* vowel as the basis of production for the *ēh* (*ay* without the diphthong) and *ee* vowels. Developing a vertical *eh* and *ee* position is challenging, as these "east-west" vowels naturally destroy the tall or oval positioning needed for uniform vowels. Singers must not pull the lips back into the smile position but maintain the slight flare of the *oo* as the jaw relaxes.

- UNISON MOVEMENT: LONG VOWELS. Work to maintain a smooth flow from one vowel to the next in this vocalise (see Chapter 14). Maintain the slight flare of the *oo* vowel for all following vowels.

• UNISON MOVEMENT: SHORT VOWELS. Short vowel uniformity is as necessary as that for long vowels. Again, maintain a smooth flow in this vocalise from one vowel to the next (see Chapter 14), and maintain the flare and oval production for all vowels.

• FOUR-PART MOVEMENT. As with the unison-movement vocalises, this vocalise (see Chapter 14) may be sung with long or short vowels. Flowing from vowel to vowel with a uniform vowel shape will enhance the quality of the choral sound.

• SINGING DIPHTHONGS. The correct production of diphthongs involves maintaining vowel uniformity and timing of the primary and vanishing vowel sounds. The phrases in this vocalise (see Chapter 14) are easily memorized and serve as a model for how diphthongs are to be sung.

Vocal Quality

The human voice has the potential to be a beautiful instrument, but poor singing habits can and do rob the voice of its richness. Enhancing the vocal quality of a choir, then, is one of the greatest challenges for the choral director.

Beauty of tone is characterized by uniformity of vowels, rich resonance, and projection. A resonant voice has depth and is able to vary the color from shades of bright to dark. Increasing resonance is dependent upon the "open throat" concept, where the vocal tract is free to resonate like a finely tuned acoustical hall. The pharynx, when open and relaxed, is the primary acoustical chamber that adds depth and richness to vocal tone. Projection or focus involves the process of moving the tone forward from the pharynx through the oral cavity, where it picks up brightness and "spin." A beautiful tone, then, has both depth and brightness and moves forward with energy. The following exercises and vocalises aid in the development of a more resonant and projected vocal quality.

• VOICE IMITATION. Direct students to sing a song phrase as it might have sounded when they were in elementary school. Then sing it as an opera singer might. Discuss how the voice can change its vocal color by changes within the vocal tract. Ventriloquists change their voices doing this same thing—they change the position of the various articulators. Students must understand that the voice need not be monochromatic, with only one sound or color. It is possible to sing with many variations of vocal quality.

• LARYNGEAL MOVEMENT. Lightly touch the larynx with the fingertips. Swallow and note the upward movement of the larynx. Yawn and note the downward movement of the larynx. Speak an *uh* with the elevated larynx and note the overly bright sound. Now speak an *aw* with a depressed larynx noting the dark or hooty quality. Both positions of the larynx are to be avoided when singing. The larynx should remain in an "at rest" position for vocalization. Sing a "down five" vocalise (see Chapter 14) while lightly touching the larynx; work to maintain the "at rest" position.

• PHARYNGEAL OPENERS. Direct students to sigh gently in a descending vocal glissando. Note the relaxation of the larynx and open-throat feeling. Sing the "down five" vocalise (see Chapter 14) through a feeling of vocal sigh. Inhale in such a way as to form a cool spot at the rear of the soft palate, again noting the open-throat feeling. Sing easy vocalises while maintaining this arched-palate openness. Make an inner smile by smiling "inside" the mouth with lips lightly closed and teeth parted (like a sti-fled yawn). Note how the inner smile opens the throat and lifts the soft palate. Sing easy vocalises with this feeling of an inner smile.

• JAW EXERCISES. Drop the jaw and massage the large masseter muscles, which cover the jaw bones. Next, place the tips of the index fingers on either side of the head just in front of the ears at the base of the pinna, the spot where the jaw hinges to the synovial cavity. Place the thumbs under the rear of the jaw and drop the jaw from the hinge; feel the indentations when the jaw opens. Direct students to check their jaw-drop position while vocalizing. Sing the "no-ah no" vocalise (see Chapter 14) to de-velop jaw flexibility. Prop the jaw open while vocalizing with two fingers of each hand pressing the flesh of the cheeks between the teeth. Place the thumbs under the chin to check for undue tension of the mylohyoid and geniohyoid muscles.

• TONGUE FLEXIBILITY. Direct students to sustain an American *r* sound. Note how the tongue stiffens and pulls back. Now move the tongue forward by relaxing it and note the difference in the forward tongue position. Place the tip of the tongue at the base of the lower front teeth and sing the unison movement vocalise (see Chapter 14). The tongue should remain relaxed and forward for all vowels. With the tongue anchored at the based of the lowered front teeth, move the tongue forward and back without moving the jaw. Sing a sustained pitch using this tongue flex exercise. Begin the flex movement slowly and gradually increase in speed. The tongue must be free of rigidity if the tone is to be free and resonant.

• M AND N. The sustained continuants *m* and *n* help to develop a tone that has forward focus balanced with pharyngeal openness. Sing the vocalise in Example 15.14 with a very sustained sounding of the consonants, and carry this quality into the vowels.

• HUNG-A H. The vocalise in Example 15.15 causes the soft palate to lower and touch the tongue while the *ng* sound is held. The action relaxes the swallowing mus-

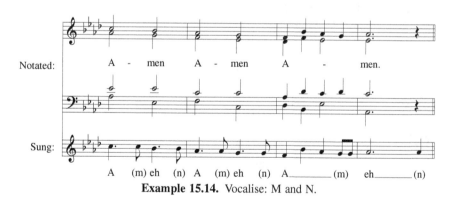

Example 15.14. Vocalise: M and N.

Hung- ah_____

Example 15.15. Vocalise: Hung-ah.

cles. When the *ng* changes to the vowel, the soft palate moves up quickly, helping the student to feel an open throat position.

• DONA NOBIS PACEM. The well-known melody in Example 15.16 makes for an excellent warm-up and voice-building vocalise. Care must be taken that the pure Latin vowels be used; for example, the final syllable in *Dona* is sung *nah*, and not *nuh*. Work to keep all vowels "tall" by relaxing the law sufficiently. A warmer, more resonant sound can be developed by keeping the lips slightly flared. Lips that are too rounded will create a dark, hooty color that is often flat.

Vocal Projection

An energized voice is one that has focus "in the mask." Whether loud or soft, the tone has a center that is alive and exciting. While pharyngeal resonance is desired in a voice, a voice that remains in the throat does not carry or project to the audience. Pop singers need little vocal projection, as they rely on electric amplification to be heard. Choral singers, however, typically sing without the use of microphones. Projection should not be confused with singing too loudly or oversinging, which ruins blend. A voice that projects has an energy in the tone that carries it forward. When all voices are energized, the choral tone has a presence that holds the attention of the listeners.

• OCTAVE LIFT. This vocalise (see Chapter 14, Example 14.4) employs the *n* sound as a means of moving the tone forward into the mask. Direct students to resonate the *n* vigorously each time know is sung, and keep the tone flowing in that forward direction.

• VOWEL FOCUS. Precede this vocalise (see Chapter 14, Example 14.12) by buzzing the lips several times on a sustained *vvvvv* sound. Notice the strong forward placement of the sound. Now sing the vocalise, changing to the vowel sound on the ascending vocal line. Maintain the forward placement of the *vvvv* through the vowel.

• FOCUS IN THE MASK. Direct students to sustain the sound *hmmmmm* down in the throat (teeth parted but lips pressed together). Now repeat the *hmmmmmm* sound

Dona Nobis Pacem (Give Us Peace)

Traditional Round

Example 15.16. Vocalise: *Dona Nobis Pacem* (traditional).

up in the nose (teeth clenched with lips together). Note the poor focus of both these sounds. Now relax the jaw with teeth parted but lips lightly touching, and again sustain the *hmmmmmm* sound. The lips should lightly tingle and the mouth should feel full of sound. Repeat this last position for the *hmmmmmm*, and open the mouth to a selected vowel. The vowel sound should flow naturally forward when the breath support is firm.

• SUBITO FORTE-PIANO. Direct the chorus to sing a tonic chord loudly on *ah*, noting how they automatically firm their breath support when singing *forte*. Now repeat the chord singing softly, but direct students to maintain the same firm breath support. Singers commonly "go off the breath" when singing softly, that is, back off from using the breathing musculature. This causes a devitalized tone that lacks focus. It is more difficult to sing softly than loudly when done correctly. The breath support must remain firm for both dynamic levels. A soft and supported tone is exciting to hear.

Range Extension

The average human voice with some training is capable of singing a two-octave range. With extensive instruction, a range of three octaves is possible. In rare cases, ranges of more than three octaves are known. Singing with an extended range of at least two octaves is necessary for a variety of choral music. Vocalises that stretch the range must be sung lightly and never forced.

• HOW LOW CAN YOU GO? Sing the "down five" vocalise (see Chapter 14, Example 14.2) on the words *low-low-low-low-low*. Transpose downward by half steps, and do not force the voice. At some point, each voice must shift into the pure lower register if the bottom of the voice is to sound. Singers often carry a mixed type of registration below middle C, which results in a weak lower register. Even sopranos should exercise the chest register.

• ARPEGGIO EXTENSION. This vocalise (see Chapter 14, Example 14.3) extends the upper voice. It should be sung lightly and rather quickly. Direct students to drop the jaw a little more on the top notes.

• ROLLING ALONG. The vocalise in Example 15.17 is another exercise for extending the upper voice. Repeat *loo* for each pitch, and "roll along" up and down the scale in a light and floating manner. Men will sing the exercise an octave lower, and must shift to a male alto sound near the top of the range. Altos also should sing this vocalise as a good means of keeping their upper voices active. When sung lightly, altos and basses will hardly know they are singing "high."

Consonant Clarity

Vowels are the basis of beautiful tone, but clear consonants are necessary for intelligible pronunciation of words. Attention to the proper execution of consonants during the choral warm-up can save much time when dealing with the texts of choral music. The general guidelines for most consonants are: (1) sing with exaggeration, (2) sing them quickly, and (3) sing initial consonants slightly ahead of the beat. The following exercises are found in Chapter 14: echo consonant drill, tongue twisters, karate chop, hissing sibilants, and the three *R*s. Students must be reminded periodically that languages are not sung in the manner of daily speech. A "singers diction" must be learned and practiced.

Example 15.17. Vocalise: Rolling Along. (from C. J. Johnson, *The Training of Boys' Voices* [Boston: Ditson, 1906]).

Expression

Elements of expression are typically not thought of as something that choristers can practice. On the contrary, the following elements can be practiced in the warm-up, and are presented in Chapter 14: meaning and mood, facial posture, body posture, spin the phrase, dynamic variation, tempo variation, messa di voce, and portamento. When such elements are stressed in the warm-up, they alert choristers to the application of these techniques to the choral music being sung.

Discussing the meaning and mood of a composition will lend insight into what the choir members are thinking about the music and how they should sing it. Often, singers give little thought to the meaning of a text and go about the process of singing as if on autopilot. This practice is sure to result in a dull and lifeless performance. Time taken to discuss the meaning of a text is well worth the end result.

Music does not happen by itself. It requires the human mind and inspiration to lift the music from the page. Many popular singers who have terrible voices are successful because they know how to make music; that is, they know how to "reach out and touch someone." It is easy for choral singers to hide behind the ensemble; they must be challenged to be expressive. It is not easy, but expression can be taught.

SUMMARY

The development of vocal skills cannot be a haphazard process. The choral director must have a plan of action to use effectively the brief amount of time available for nurturing students' voices. The following outline is suggested for helping to plan a systematic process of vocal skills development. It entails a minimum of six exercises or vocalises and should not take more than five to six minutes. When performance preparations are not immediate, more time can be allowed for initial explanations of the exercises and vocalises. As concerts approach, less time will be given to this phase of the rehearsal. An effective warm-up flows uninterrupted from element to element, without lengthy explanations.

The choral director must take care not to fall into the trap of repeating the same vocalises over and over until a mindless routine avails little in the form of vocal improvement. Some directors are known to use only one exercise repeatedly for every rehearsal; students seldom have a clue as to why they are singing it and often grow to hate it. The warm-up requires some in-depth planning if voices are to reach their potential. A good plan is rather simple: energize the body, energize the breath, energize the ear, then energize the voice.

VOCAL SKILLS DEVELOPMENT OUTLINE: ENERGIZING THE WARM-UP

1. **Energize the body** (1–2 exercises)
   a. Physical conditioning
   b. Posture development
2. **Energize the breath** (1–2 exercises)
   a. Breathing motion
   b. Breath control
   c. Breath support
3. **Energize the ear** (1 exercise)
   a. Inner hearing
   b. Intonation
4. **Energize the voice** (3–4 exercises)
   a. Humming
   b. Staccato articulation

    c. Legato articulation

    d. Marcato articulation

    e. Martellato articulation

    f. Vowel uniformity

    g. Vocal quality

    h. Vocal projection

    i. Range extension

    j. Consonant clarity

    k. Expression

STUDY AND DISCUSSION QUESTIONS

1. What is the difference between a vocal warm-up and a vocal skills development time?
2. Why should a variety of exercises and vocalises be used for vocal skills development?
3. What is involved in energizing the body?
4. What seven postural elements are involved in posture practice?
5. What are the three areas of energizing the breath? Define each.
6. How does the diaphragm act during controlled exhalation for singing?
7. What is the natural link between the breath and the singing voice?
8. What is meant by the term "audiation," and why is this skill important to singing?
9. What techniques can be used to develop inner hearing and audiation?
10. Robert Shaw believed that almost 50 percent of poor intonation is due to what?
11. What should be avoided in vocalises when working with high school singers?
12. What are the basic characteristics of producing the proper humming technique?
13. What is meant by *portamento*, and how is this technique sung?
14. What is *martellato* articulation, and when is it used?
15. What are the characteristics of uniform vowels?
16. What are the characteristics of the resonant voice?
17. What does singing "in the mask" mean?
18. On the average, the well-trained voice has how wide a singing range?
19. Why should the choral director discuss the meaning and mood of a composition with the choir members?
20. What are the four "energized" parts of the vocal skills development outline?

REFERENCES

Alderson, R. (1979). *Complete handbook of voice training*. West Nyack, NY: Parker.

Decker, H. A., and J. Herford (1988). *Choral conducting symposium* (2d ed.). Englewood Cliffs, NJ: Prentice Hall.

Doscher, B. M. (1991). Exploring the whys of intonation problems. *Choral Journal, 32*(4), 25–30.

Ehmann, W., and F. Haasemann (1981). *Voice building for choirs*. Chapel Hill, NC: Hinshaw Music.

Gordon, E. E. (1999). All about audiation and music aptitudes. *Music Educators Journal, 86*(2), 41–44.

Haasemann, F., and J. M. Jordan (1995). *Group vocal technique*. Chapel Hill, NC: Hinshaw Music.

Nesheim, P., and W. Noble (1995). *Building beautiful voices*. Dayton, OH: Roger Dean.

Neuen, D. (1988). The sound of a great chorus. *Music Educators Journal, 75*(4), 43–45.

Phillips, K. H. (1992). *Teaching kids to sing*. New York: Schirmer Books.

Robinson, R., and J. Althouse (1995). *The complete choral warm-up book*. Van Nuys, CA: Alfred.

16 | Teaching Sight-Singing Skills

It is common knowledge among music educators that choral singers generally sight-sing poorly. Unlike their instrumental counterparts, who often learn to read music from the time of their first instrumental lesson, singers continue to sing by rote and seem never to catch up in reading notes. Has it always been this way? Must it be this way?

This chapter presents a historical overview of sight-singing in the schools, suggests an approach and integration of that approach into the choral rehearsal, and concludes with ways of assessing sight-singing skills. The vital importance of music reading for developing choral musicianship is the basic tenet of this chapter.

HISTORICAL OVERVIEW

Developing students who can sight-sing has been a long-established goal of music education in the United States. Lowell Mason included materials for its study in his first manual of instruction (1832), and in the 1960s the MENC committee on general education stated: "The generally educated person is literate. He understands musical symbols. He is able to respond to the musical notation of unison and simple part songs. He can follow the scores of instrumental compositions" (Ernst and Gary, 1965, p. 5). Today, the importance of sight-singing in the curriculum again is affirmed by its inclusion as the fifth of the nine national standards (MENC, 1994). To reach the "proficient" level of this fifth standard for high school chorus, "students demonstrate the ability to read an instrumental or vocal score of up to four staves by describing how the elements of music work" (Swiggum, 1998, p. 43). They also need to "sightread, accurately and expressively, music with a level difficulty of 3, on a scale of 1 to 6" (p. 46). Could most high school students achieve these goals today? Probably not. Why not? Why can't singers sight-sing, when it has been and continues to be such an important goal for music education?

One great difficulty in the teaching of sight-singing is that no one accepted method has been adopted by which to teach music reading. Despite a variety of different systems currently in use, Demorest (1998), in a review of the research regarding sight-singing practice, reports that no modes of instruction or materials were found to predominate.

A second major difficulty in the teaching of sight-singing is that choral directors, as a whole, give little time for it in the rehearsal. Research shows that where it is required as an element of state contests, directors seem to spend more time (Demorest, 2001). The following goal of the Maryland Choral Directors Association defines the importance that this organization gives to sight-singing:

> The MCEA has made sight-reading a fundamental aspect of the choral festival. We strive to make sight-reading both meaningful, as well as highly attainable. We want every choral student in Maryland to feel confident and comfortable sight-reading. (Crarey, 2001, p. 26)

Likewise, in 1992 "choral sight-reading officially became a required part of the Ohio Music Education Association's (OMEA) district and state-level adjudicated events" (Armstrong, 2001, p. 21). Demorest comments:

> Perhaps the requirements for music literacy in the National Standards will encourage more teachers to devote time to music-reading instruction. For now, teachers who want sight-singing taught in their part of the country might push for the inclusion of sight-singing as a required component of district and state choir contests. (2001, p. 27)

Guido d'Arezzo

Sight-singing in the Western world developed when a systematic means of music notation became necessary for unifying the practice of Gregorian chant. Guido d'Arezzo (c. 995–1050), an eleventh-century monk, devised a technique of solmization from the syllables of the successive phrases of the *Hymn to St. John the Baptist*. The syllabes *ut*, *re*, *me*, *fa*, *sol*, and *la* were used with a system of overlapping hexachords. Guido provided the model for the system of Western solmization syllables, which, with slight modification, remain in use today (Phillips, 1984).

In addition to the use of syllables as mnemonic devices (memory aids), Guido linked the use of solmization to the Guidonian hand (see Chapter 1). Each joint and the tip of the left hand represented one of the twenty notes of the system. The pupils thus learned to sing various intervals as the teacher pointed with the index finger of the right hand to the different places on the open left hand. "No late Medieval or Renaissance music textbook was complete without a drawing of this hand" (Grout, 1980, p. 61).

Guido's influence was great, not only for the use of sight-singing syllables, but also for the use of the "hand staff" (see Figure 16.1). Demorest (2001) presents this as a technique that some teachers continue to use for teaching lines and spaces (p. 68).

Movable *Do* and Fixed *Do*

The solmization employed by Guido made use of the movable *do* system. (The tonic or first note of the scale or mode is always *do*.) "Whenever a melody went beyond the range of one hexachord, the singer moved to another by changing syllables on a note common to both, a process known as 'mutation'" (Hoppin, 1978, p. 64). Thus the movable *do* system as used today has a strong precedent in Guido's model.

Little is known about sight-singing in the Medieval or Renaissance periods. The scale was increased to seven notes, *ut* was changed to *do*, and *si* was added for the seventh step.

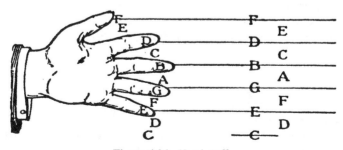

Figure 16.1. Hand staff.

The addition of key signatures firmly established the use of movable *do*, and additional clefs (C, F, G) made music reading easier. Guido's system remained unaltered until the sixteenth century.

The expanding chromaticism and use of transposition in the seventeenth century made Guido's movable *do* more difficult to use. One experiment had compound syllables as a basis for a fixed *do* terminology. Such terms as *D-sol-re* and *C-fa-ut* were used to represent, simultaneously, letter and syllable names. Circa 1600 the Guidonian syllables were adapted by French musicians to a fixed *do* system, which gained acceptance in Italy by the eighteenth century. Fixed *do* to this day has been called the European system.

The fixed *do* technique assigns one of seven syllables to each pitch of the diatonic C major scale. To express sharps or flats, the singer uses the same syllable names but adjusts the pitch. For example, the key of G major is sung from *sol* to *sol*, with the seventh scale degree being sung *fa*, but a half step higher. There is a revised fixed *do* that adds syllables names for sharps and flats. The ascending and descending chromatic scales in fixed *do* are given in Example 16.1. The traditional system of fixed *do* was later adapted to the revised form at the end of the nineteenth century by the famous French educator Émile Jaques-Dalcroze. Both movable *do* and fixed *do* systems continue to be used around the world today, thus contributing to a general lack of uniformity in approaches to sight-singing.

Singing Schools

An adaptation of the movable *do* technique called *tonic solfa* was established in England and brought to the American colonies by the early settlers. Because church singing was poor among the colonists, singing schools were established for the instruction of voice and the reading of music. These schools were popular with the youth as a means of social interaction. The programs were held evenings, usually at the church, where an itinerant singing master would give instruction over a period of four to six weeks.

The Reverend John Tufts, of Newbury, Massachusetts, published a twenty-three-page manual titled *An Introduction to Singing of Psalm-Tunes, in a Plain and Easy Method, with Collection of Tunes in Three Parts* (1721) for use in the singing schools. This method used the *fasola* technique of sight-singing, based on the English tonic solfa system, which made no use of a staff. Both systems used only four syllables, with *mi* as the leading tone (*fa, sol, la, fa, sol, la, mi, fa*). Tufts's system used a staff, but he put the syllables on the staff in place of note heads (see Example 16.2). His book became the first means of organized music education in the United States.

Another popular publication of 1721 was *The Grounds and Rules of Musick Explained* by the Reverend Thomas Walter. Also for singing school use, it was the first music publication in the United States to make use of printed bar lines and the then common diamond-head notes. It used only the four syllables *fa, sol, la,* and *mi,* which were found in all similar American publications for a hundred years (Lowens, 1954, p. 89).

do di re ri mi fa fi sol si la li ti do ti teh lah leh sol seh fa mi meh re rah do

Example 16.1. The chromatic scale in revised fixed *do*.

Example 16.2. "America" (H. Carey) as written in regular and Tuft's syllable notation.

Shape Notes

The singing school movement in the South adopted the use of *shape notes,* in which shapes (oval, rectangle, diamond, triangle) were used instead of regular note heads. This mnemonic device was quite successful, and Andrew Law is given credit for its invention. His publication *The Art of Singing* made no use of a staff; it used only *fasola* and shape notes. Law's partners William Little and William Smith later published *The Easy Instructor, or A New Method of Teaching Sacred Harmony*, which used the *fasola* and shape note system but placed the shape notes on the staff. Shape notes gradually expanded to a seven-syllable form that embraced all seven of the traditional solfège syllables (see Figure 16.2).

Publication of *The Sacred Harp* (1844) by B. F. White and E. J. King brought about tremendous growth in the southern singing school movement. Typical singing schools were held for twenty days at a local church, where a singing teacher would instruct young and old from eight in the morning until four in the afternoon. Pupils were taught major and minor scales, various meters, and use of the shape note system. Large singing conventions were held under tents (these continue today in the South), where the great hymns from *The Sacred Harp* were sung first by syllable and then with words. Four-part harmony was common, and good sight-singing skills were fostered among the people.

Lowens and Britton (1953) state that American music education might be better if shape notes been adopted in the public schools. "No one who has witnessed the astonishing sight-singing virtuosity of the rural South today, trained with what is basically the *Easy Instructor* method, can possibly doubt the effectiveness of the device" (p. 32).

Lowell Mason

The urban attitude in the North became more sophisticated in the early nineteenth century, and people looked to adopt European ways of living. The singing school was gradually discarded for more formal educational settings, and with the founding of the Boston Academy of Music in 1832 by Lowell Mason, the use of the seven-syllable/seven-note movable *do* system became basic in northern music instruction.

Lowell Mason (1792–1872) was a famous instructor in the singing school movement before establishing a private academy. He was known as a fine musician, successful composer,

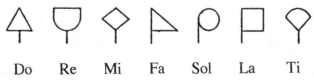

Figure 16.2. Scale of seven syllables and shapes by Jesse B. Aikin as used in the *Christian Minstrel* (Philadelphia, 1846).

conductor, and pedagogue. His belief that all children could learn to sing (with the proper instruction) paved the way for his being named Boston's first public school music teacher (1838). The publication of his *Manual of the Boston Academy of Music, for Instruction in the Elements of Vocal Music, on the System of Pestalozzi* in 1834 set the standard in music pedagogy for a hundred years. Other publications by Mason, such as the *Song Garden* series, became basic texts for public school music programs.

Mason believed in the "rote to note" process; children first sing easy songs by rote before engaging in visual notation. He very much believed in sight-singing; two of three parts of his *Manual* were given to instruction in reading pitch (movable *do*) and rhythm. But he strongly believed that the theory of music should follow a strong aural awareness of sound. Many of the "old" singing school masters were opposed, as their approach had been to teach notes from the beginning. Thus began the famous "rote versus note" controversy, an issue that continues today. It is important to remember for Mason, "rote *to* note" did not mean "rote *or* note." Mason taught "rote *before* note."

Lowell Mason taught countless numbers of children to sing, and he trained numerous teachers of music who went on to establish successful school music programs. Sight-singing and development of the singing voice were the two central objectives of school music instruction. For a hundred years his efforts helped to make sight-singing a valued and central part of American school music education.

The Great Publishing Era

The late nineteenth and early twentieth centuries witnessed a great outpouring of vocal music series. Spurred on by the music publishing industry, the "rote versus note" controversy raged. On the "note" side, Hosea Holt wrote the popular *Normal Music Course* (1883), with structured "scientific" sight-reading exercises. Luther Whiting Mason wrote the *National Music Course* (1870), which favored the rote to note ("song method") approach. The first nationally prominent graded series, it was extremely popular. Thus the debate between advocates of "note" and "rote to note" became fueled by numerous publications on each side of the issue. In conflict, also, were the solmization systems. Some teachers adopted the Curwen (English) tonic solfa system, some favored fixed *do*, but most favored movable *do*. Whatever the approach, music teachers continued to value and teach sight-singing skills.

Changing Philosophies

Two basic educational movements emerged at the beginning of the twentieth century: (1) progressivism, which emphasized the instructional side of teaching, including recitation, and (2) child study pragmatism, which stressed "spirit" rather than method. This latter philosophy was championed by John Dewey, who believed that the arts were essential to the school experience. Dewey did not believe in a music class that emphasized drill and the "mechanics" of music making. He emphasized the "beautiful" or aesthetic nature of music. Children were to learn about music by making music.

Some music series also signaled this change of direction in music instruction. Two in this genre were the *Hollis Dann* music series (1914–17) and the *Universal* music series (Gehrkens, Damrosch, Garllan, 1920–23). Fueled by the child study movement, these music texts placed a new emphasis on the quality of the musical experience. Music reading became secondary to students' sheer musical enjoyment. The time spent on sight-singing skills was questioned. The song approach (rote teaching with little instruction on how to sing or read notes) emerged as the leading philosophy in music teaching.

Karl Gehrkens, in his influential book *Music in the Grade School* (1934), was among the first to advocate moving from formal instruction and vocalises to a new "song approach."

> Believing that vocal training could be fostered through the aesthetic experience, he suggested that the old idea of using exercises for training the voice, which involved a considerable amount of class time, should be replaced by a modern approach designed to teach the child through the singing of beautiful songs. The lack of information on child vocal pedagogy in methods texts from Gehrken's publication to the present demonstrates that this song approach became very popular among public school teachers. (Phillips, 1992, p. 10)

James Mursell and Mabelle Glenn (1938), leading figures of the time, also cautioned against drill in the music classroom. Singing skills were to be taught only by the singing of songs. By 1956, however, Mursell was warning against the omission of vocal skills development in music classes. It was too late—the demise of singing confidence among the general populace had begun.

Singing in the high schools was dramatically affected in America by the a cappella choir movement. Begun at the college level in the 1920s, this type of choral organization quickly found favor in high schools throughout the country, especially the midwest.

> The a cappella choir movement, based on the model of F. Melius Christiansen, was advancing in the nation's high schools at the very time the song approach was becoming common at the elementary level. In numerous high schools, a cappella choir programs began to rival their instrumental counterparts (Kegerreis, 1970).

> The emphasis of the a cappella choir was on performance, and the limited repertoire produced a polished perfection heretofore unknown among high school singers. While choral music was given a new prestige by this movement, it also thrived via the song approach. Little attention was given to music-reading skills, and music was taught largely by rote. (Phillips, 1992, p. 11)

While the a cappella movement had waned by midcentury, there remained strong high school choral programs throughout the country. These choirs sang a variety of choral literature made possible by a proliferation of music publishing. However, the lack of instruction in sight-singing skills generally resulted in a rote approach to choral music teaching. The end product became far more important than the process of learning. Still, there is no doubt that the a cappella choir movement greatly improved the status of choral music in America's schools.

Educational Reform

The year 1957 was momentous for the world, as the former Soviet Union launched into earth's orbit the satellite Sputnik. Scientists and educators in the United States complained of the weak quality of American education. Meetings such as the Woods Hole Conference (1959) and the Yale Seminar (1963) were convened to discuss the restructuring of American education, including the music curriculum. In 1965 the Manhattanville Music Project was launched, which signaled the beginning of concept-based music education.

While much support for a more "academic" approach to music teaching became evident, no unified or basic system of music instruction appeared. Listening activities with analysis of music became prominent in general music classes, while the other skills of the earlier "pentad" (singing, moving, playing, and creating) became less important. Music series again contained sight-singing materials, but authors on the subject did not commit themselves to any specific method of syllables, numbers, letters, and so forth. Choral students, in general, continued to be taught by rote.

Three Europeans emerged and changed the focus of music education during the 1960s: Zoltán Kodály, Carl Orff, and Émile Jaques-Dalcroze. The Kodály method, as developed by Kodály for his native Hungary, emphasized sight-singing with movable *do*, solfège, and hand signs as a mnemonic device prior to reading notation. Carl Orff developed a national music curriculum in Germany that also focused on music reading skills using the pentatonic mode, solfège syllables, movable *do*, and tuned percussion instruments. Jaques-Dalcroze, a Swiss educator, developed a system of movement he called eurhythmics to improve the general musicianship of college music students, especially as it pertained to rhythm. He taught solfège with the fixed *do* system, as he believed it possible to develop a sense of perfect pitch. The Dalcroze approach became a popular means for teaching movement.

All three systems of teaching music literacy were adapted and adopted by American elementary teachers; the use of all three together (in varying degrees) became known as the "eclectic" curriculum. Today, many teachers are certified as Kodály, Orff, or Dalcroze specialists, and sight-singing in these curricula is at the center of music education. Unfortunately, Kodály, Orff, and Dalcroze are typically viewed as elementary music curricula. Secondary teachers seem to disregard them, "but it is important for secondary choral directors to have some familiarity with them so that they know something of the means by which their students have been trained to that point" (Demorest, 2001, p. 52).

Another name stands out among twentieth-century reformers of music teaching—Edwin Gordon. An American music educator and music psychologist, Gordon is widely known for his tests of music aptitude (see Chapter 3) and for his theory of how people learn music. He reaffirms the principle set forth by Lowell Mason more than a century ago—rote experiences with music must precede instruction in notation. Gordon (1993) has coined the term *audiation* for the ability to hear and comprehend music internally. He asserts the major weakness in music-reading instruction to be the teaching of theory before aural understanding (audiation). Gordon believes that using notation too early in the instructional sequence only serves to frustrate the learner. His learning theory is reflected in a music-learning sequence that moves from aural and oral learning, at the discrimination learning level, to theoretical understanding at the inference learning level. His ideas are reflected in a published method for teaching sight-singing (Gordon and Woods, 1986), and while it is not widely used with secondary choral classes, the learning theory is transferable and easily adapted.

Current Practices

Steven Demorest is a leading expert in the field of sight-singing and choral singers. In chapter 2 of his book *Building Choral Excellence: Teaching Sight-Singing in the Choral Rehearsal* (2001), Demorest presents a summary of research about sight-singing practices in America's secondary choirs. The following are the main findings.

- A great many pitch-reading systems are in use. Most common are movable *do*, numbers, fixed *do*, and intervals.

- Many commercial publications are available; no preference stands out. Directors are more apt to use their own exercises and those based on music being rehearsed.

- Results of comparing the effectiveness of different systems of sight-singing reveal little evidence of superiority.

- Little relationship exists between a student's choral participation and his or her sight-singing success.

- Instrumental background, especially piano, is positively related to sight-singing achievement.

- Sight-singing achievement by group does not mean that all individual choir members can sight-sing well.

- Regular individual testing and feedback in connection with group instruction yield significant improvement in sight-singing performance.

- Many choral directors are unwilling to devote much rehearsal time to sight-singing skills because of performance pressures.

- Choral directors devote more rehearsal time to sight-singing skills when the ensemble will be tested on this skill at contest or festival.

While the above results are based on few studies, Demorest does summarize his presentation with three recommendations worth considering: (1) commit rehearsal time to teaching sight-singing, perhaps advocating its use in choral contests; (2) attempt to incorporate the benefits of both keyboard and instrumental training into a more comprehensive curriculum; and (3) make provision for systematic evaluation of students' ability (p. 32). These three guidelines, if followed by choral directors, might help to assure that current practices in sight-singing would improve. Comprehensive musicianship requires it.

HOW TO TEACH SIGHT-SINGING

How should the choral director teach sight-singing? Research suggests that no single best way to teach sight-singing is known. "All sight-singing methods are a means to an end, not an end in themselves" (Demorest, 2001, p. 36). Demorest recommends that teachers "choose an approach with which they are comfortable and employ it on a consistent basis. If this is done, the students will become better readers" (p. 36).

An abundance of commercial sight-singing materials are available from music publishers (see Appendix E). Each provides a ready-made manual of sequential exercises for each choral member, which can be carried in the choral folio. The choral director need not purchase a "known" package. However, teachers can write their own and distribute them to the choir, or exercises can be placed on the chalkboard. Most important to the choice of materials, published or unpublished, is the learning sequence supporting the approach or method used to teach sight-singing.

Building Aural Awareness

Most published sight-singing methods begin with the reading of notation, putting the eye before the ear. These systems do not follow the logical sequence of rote to note. The learning sequence for language is similar to that for music.

> A useful analogy to learning sequence in music is the sequence of events by which we acquire language facility as children. Learning to read and comprehend language has many corollaries to learning to read and comprehend music. It should be noted, however, that research does not support similarities in brain activity in language and music acquisition. Nevertheless, the overt parallels are obvious. Acquiring verbal skills is dependent mainly on the ability to hear and discriminate sounds and then attach meaning to them. Acquiring musical skill and understanding is also dependent mainly on the ability to hear and discriminate sounds and attach meaning to them.

If every paragraph you read first had to be rote-taught to you, you would be a very in-efficient reader. You not only would read a minimum of material, but you would gain lit-tle or no meaning from the symbols. In addition, you would have great difficulty transfer-ring your reading skills to unfamiliar materials. We do not expect children to learn to speak without first hearing speech. In addition, children gain vocabulary and verbal facility over a long time period through speech alone and without a symbol system. (Schleuter, 1997, pp. 34–35)

The Kodály Method (Choksy, 1988), *Jump Right In: The Music Curriculum* (Gordon and Woods, 1986), *Making the Transition from Ear to Voice to Music Reading: Vocal Connec-tions* (Whitlock, 1992), and an instrumental methods book, *A Sound Approach to Teaching Instrumentalists* (Schleuter, 1997), are examples of texts that present aural skills development before the teaching of visual notation.

The choral director need not have a mastery of any sight-singing approach to begin a program of aural skills instruction. Steps in the development of aural acuity or audiation include:

- **Sense of tonality.** Students are able to recognize songs in major, minor, and other mo-dalities by singing tonic and dominant triads, the building blocks of Western music. Listening experiences also facilitate modality recognition.

- **Inner hearing.** Students enhance audiation skills by "singing on the inside" and rec-ognizing "same or different" patterns (see Chapter 14).

- **Aural recognition of tonal patterns.** Students aurally recognize standard tonal pat-terns (two to five tones) by correctly echo-singing them with movable *do* syllables. Patterns sung by the director at first using syllables should eventually be sung using *loo-loo-loo*, with students continuing to echo with syllables.

- **Aural recognition of tonal patterns in songs.** Students recognize tonal patterns in simple songs and sing with appropriate syllables (e.g., "Twinkle, Twinkle, Little Star," *do do sol sol la la sol, fa fa mi mi re re do*).

- **Aural recognition of beat and meter.** Students tap to the steady beat of aural exam-ples, and show recognition of basic meters by conducting patterns of two, three, and four.

- **Aural recognition of rhythm patterns.** Students echo-clap short rhythm patterns, led by the director, and eventually respond using some type of counting or syllable sys-tem (e.g., "1–2–3&–4").

Cooper and Kuersteiner (1965), in the once-popular methods book *Teaching Junior High School Music*, present two chapters on the development of sight-singing and ear-train-ing skills. The chapter devoted to ear training, a rarity among general methods texts, hear-kens back to an era when it was generally believed that all children could learn to sing and read music.

Learning to Read Notation

Once an aural understanding of sound patterns is established—that is, when students can echo-sing patterns with correct syllables—it is time to introduce notation. At first, the ele-ments of rhythm and pitch may be approached separately but concurrently. Once a visual un-derstanding of both is connected to the brain, the two are combined. Steps in the develop-ment of notation reading include the following stages of visual recognition:

- **Staff, clefs, bar line, and meter signature.** Students can identify verbally from visual representation the basic elements underlying the system of music notation and can interpret the meaning of each.

- **Rhythm patterns.** Students verbally sound (with numbers, syllables, neutral syllable, etc.) short notated rhythm patterns. Flash cards are especially helpful at this step. Patterns of visual notation are linked to aural patterns learned earlier and should progress from simple quarter-eighth combinations to more complex rhythms. The concept of meter as it relates to rhythm is sometimes difficult to establish among younger students. A helpful technique for making this connection can be found in the article "Teaching Singers to Sight-Read" (Phillips, 1996).

- **Tonal patterns.** Students sing (solfège, numbers, pitch names, etc.) basic notated tonal patterns. Rhythm should be kept to even quarter notes. The use of flash cards is recommended. The patterns should be those that were sung earlier by rote. The names of lines and spaces also should be introduced, and when changed male voices are in the ensemble, the bass clef should be included.

- **Combined tonal and rhythm patterns.** Students sing (solfège, numbers, pitch names, etc.) notated tonal and rhythm patterns. The use of flash cards is recommended. These patterns should reflect those that students have in their aural vocabulary. When changed male voices are in the ensemble, the bass clef should be included.

- **Notational patterns in music scores.** Students practice sight-singing skills at ever increasing levels of difficulty by locating familiar patterns in their parts and silently audiating them. Simple, homophonic selections work best at the beginning, and tonality and key must be established. After a study time, the chorus sings the new work from sight. Reading skills can then be transferred to performance music as sight-singing technique improves. The director must permit students to read some or all of each composition as it is being learned. One thing is for certain, sight-singing skills will not improve unless students are provided the opportunity to practice reading new material.

A Panoply of Practices

- **Intervals.** Teaching intervals is a common practice. Roe (1983) gives a number of well-known songs categorized by the first melodic interval (e.g., perfect fourth: "Here Comes the Bride"). While students ought to know the basic intervals, sight-singing by interval is a questionable practice (Schleuter, 1997). When students read language, they read by word groupings and not word by word. Similarly, when students read music, their facility is enhanced when reading by patterns rather than note to note. Teach patterns, and then extract the intervals.

- **Music dictation.** Having students take music dictation is an excellent means by which to develop aural skills. Patterns can be dictated for rhythm, pitch, or both. Unfortunately, there is so little time in the choral rehearsal for warm-ups and sight-singing that time for dictation is rarely possible. Nevertheless, block schedules permit more time for activities other than rehearsing; including dictation makes a lot of sense.

- **Speaking words in rhythm.** Bertalot (1993) recommends that students speak the words of their music in rhythm before they add pitch (p. 101). This is a good technique, but care must be taken that students don't drone while counting. Insist on an elevated voice when speaking. This technique also helps to improve articulation.

- **Count singing.** The late Robert Shaw regularly practiced *count singing* in rehearsals. Using the "1-e-and-a, 2-e-and-a, ti-e-and-a, 4-e-and-a" measure-based counting system (Shaw replaced "3" with "ti"), singers employ the count syllables to sing instead of the text. Much of Shaw's reputation for rhythmical clarity and precision is due to this one exercise.

- **Physical movement.** The use of physical movement is an asset for underlying the rhythm of music. Again, Robert Shaw would ask singers to walk in a circle to the pulse of the music, or to subdivide the pulse. Having singers "finger tap" (two fingers of one hand tapping into the palm of the other hand) is another way to use movement to highlight rhythm. Directing students to lean forward into phrases also is helpful. While physical movement in the choral setting is limited, explore what is possible.

- **Rhythm syllables.** Some systems for reading rhythm advocate the use of rhythm syllables as an aid: Kodály (*ta, ti, ri*), Chevé (*ta, te, fa*), and Gordon (*du, de, du, di*). Orff uses words whose syllables correspond to rhythms, e.g., four sixteenth notes could be said "Mississippi" because it has four syllables. The Dalcroze approach, which is rhythm-centered, does not use rhythm syllables.

- **Hand signs.** Hand signs were first developed by the English clergyman John Curwen. Adapted by Zoltán Kodály, these visual signs have become a popular inclusion with solfège instruction. While used predominantly with elementary students, there is no reason not to use them with secondary choristers.

- **Movable *do* and fixed *do*.** Research shows that most teachers use movable *do* for solfège (Demorest, 2001). It has the advantage of being an aural system that adapts readily from key to key; that is, the interval from *do* up to *mi* is always a major third in all major modes. Critics say that movable *do* breaks down when singing music with much chromaticism, e.g., contemporary art music. They also say that fixed *do* is a better visual system in that each syllable corresponds to only one pitch name, such as, *sol* is always G, and *fi* is always F#. The G major scale is sung *sol* to *sol*, with F (fa) altered to F# (fi). Perhaps a combination of movable *do* for aural skills instruction and fixed *do* for visual reading is warranted? There is little research comparing the two systems. Therefore choral directors need to experiment a little to determine what works for them and their students.

- **Letter names, numbers, neutral syllables.** Some teachers (especially instrumental teachers) prefer to use actual letter names when singing notes. This is a type of fixed *do* system and is not conducive to aural skills training. Singing by numbers makes it possible to indicate actual scale degrees. This is a type of movable *do* system as 1 is always the first degree of any scale. Some people prefer to use a neutral syllable, such as, *doo*. This appears to be a type of interval reading; neither aural nor visual prompts seem to be important.

Do Something!

The challenge before the choral director is to do something, and to do it consistently. The choice of an approach or method may depend heavily upon the director's background and what he or she is comfortable teaching. It also will depend upon trying different ways to develop both aural and visual skills. Once some system is chosen, it has to be used regularly in the choral rehearsal. Progress may be slow, but it will be rewarding.

SCHEDULING TIME FOR SIGHT-SINGING

Once the decision is made to integrate sight-singing into the rehearsal, choral directors must decide if they want to adopt the "rote to note" approach or the "note" approach. This chapter has shown the benefits of using a "rote to note" or "aural to visual" system. Train the ear, and then bond the visual representation to the aural image. Next, the director must decide upon materials to use: published sight-singing manuals (see Appendix E), a "named" method (e.g., Kodály), or self-written materials. Whatever is chosen, it must reflect the philosophy decided upon earlier. If aural skills are first to be developed, then visual materials are not needed until later in the program, when flash cards can be used.

An Opening Routine

Research shows that most choral directors teach sight-singing following the vocal warm-up (Demorest, 2001, p. 31) as a direct extension of the warm-up routine. However, aural skills instruction fits nicely into the "energize the ear" segment of the vocal skills development time (see Chapter 15). So, whether it is part of the warm-up routine or immediately follows it, the sight-singing component works well near the beginning of the rehearsal, when students are fresh. The establishment of an opening routine is important for a well-organized rehearsal.

As students learn enough to permit the sight-singing of new choral literature, the director may wish to limit the sight-singing instruction component of the rehearsal. This could take place in an advanced choir where members are reading at a high level. The frequent return to aural and visual exercises keeps skills sharpened, however, especially when sight-singing is adjudicated by group or individually.

The applicability of sight-singing skills to reading choral music is the ultimate goal of music reading instruction. Therefore the director needs to give students the opportunity to sight-read new music early after visual notation has been introduced. This may require the inclusion of some simple repertoire that may not be programmable. Simple, four-part, homophonic pieces (e.g., hymns, folk songs) are good for this purpose. As students become more able to sing by sight, they should be challenged to read at least part of each new selection. Students must be given time to study and hear the piece on the "inside" before asking for a response on the "outside." Using something other than words the first time through facilitates the reading process. Key and tonality are important to establish at the beginning.

How Much Time?

How much time can be given to a sight-singing lesson? Not much, especially the closer to concert time it becomes. Probably no more than 10 percent of the rehearsal should be used, which for a fifty-minute period is only five minutes! If the warm-up takes another 10 percent, only forty minutes remain for rehearsing music. When choirs are younger and there is less pressure to perform, more time can be spent on the fundamentals of voice production and music reading. The middle school years are when these foundational skills should be developed. But when they are not, the senior high school choral director will need to extend the time, at least initially, for sight-singing instruction.

Those schools that have block schedules provide an opportunity for some students to receive more in-depth instruction in sight-reading. Ideally, all students should receive the same amount of time, but that is not always possible. And if the choir is sharing the block with the band, then band students are less likely to need help in learning to read music. The block schedule has some advantages.

ASSESSING SIGHT-SINGING SKILLS

Both group and individual sight-singing skills need to be assessed frequently by the choral director to determine the progress being made by students learning to sight-read. Especially important is the assessment of individual skills, as research has shown that weaker sight-singers can be masked by leaders in the choir who sing out and cover the deficiencies of the weaker readers (Bennett, 1984; Demorest and May, 1995; Henry and Demorest, 1994). Surveys show that prior to the publication of the national standards (MENC, 1994), among choral directors, "as few as 1 in 10 do any kind of regular formal evaluation of their students' sight-singing ability" (Demorest, 2001, p. 106).

Guidelines for Assessment

The following Guidelines for assessment have been adapted from *Performance Standards for Music* (MENC, 1996, pp. 7–9). They present six ways in which music teachers should think about shaping the assessment process.

- *Assessment should be standards-based and should reflect the music skills and knowledge that are most important for students to learn.* Achievement should reflect the accomplishment of specific criteria set forth for each area of the curriculum.
- *Assessment should support, enhance, and reinforce learning.* It should not be seen as an intrusion into the learning environment.
- *Assessment should be reliable.* Measurement tools produce similar or same results when used repeatedly, and from person to person.
- *Assessment should be valid.* Measurement tools assess the knowledge or skills they are supposed to assess.
- *Assessment should be authentic.* Authentic assessment involves a demonstration of the essential nature of the skill or knowledge being assessed.
- *The process of assessment should be open to review by interested parties.* Students, parents, school administrators, and the public should be aware of the assessment process and its content and be given the opportunity to provide feedback.

While assessment of sight-singing skills may be just one more thing a choral director has to do, the benefits will be heard in a choir that no longer has to be spoon-fed every note. Greater security and sophistication will be heard when students can read notes.

> Music exalts the spirit. It enhances the quality of life. It brings joy, satisfaction, and fulfillment to every human being. It is one of the most powerful, compelling, and glorious manifestations of human culture. It is the essence of civilization itself. Music learning would deserve to be included in the curriculum even if it could not be assessed. But music learning based on explicit standards can be assessed. Music should never be neglected in the school merely because its assessment may be difficult, time-consuming, or costly. (MENC, 1996, p. 9)

Assessing the Choir

Group sight-singing assessment should be an ongoing process in the choral rehearsal (Armstrong, 2001). If students are not challenged to sight-read, their skills will not develop. To be done correctly, however, students must be given time to study the new music to identify problem spots. They should be encouraged to audiate before singing, with tonality and key being established first. The use of a syllable, letter, or number system, instead of words, is encouraged on the first read. If students break down, a brief explanation can be given, but students should be encouraged to correct their own errors and try again. If the rhythm is particularly difficult, it can be read separately before the pitch is added. Repeated readings yield multiplied rewards.

Should group choral assessment take place? Yes, because group evaluation is common at festivals and contests. Also, the choral director can provide a form of motivation for singers by assigning a rating (e.g., 1–5) to each ensemble effort. Sight-singing "challenges" among sections of the choir can foster a spirit of friendly competition and at the same time encourage teamwork and effort. Directors must remember to provide adequate time for students to study the music before an attempt at sight-singing is made. Singers also should be given the opportunity of a second reading.

Assessing Individuals

Individual testing of sight-singing skills should be a basic part of any school choral music program, and at least part of a student's grade should reflect sight-reading achievement (see Chapter 5, "Grading for Choirs"). While it is time consuming to do so, students will place greater value on developing sight-singing skills if they know that achievement in this area is important enough to be part of their grade in chorus. Research has shown that students who receive individual assessment improve significantly more than those who receive only group instruction (Demorest, 1998a).

Testing is done in a number of ways. First, students can be asked to sing individually within the choral ensemble, or in quartets. This practice can be intimidating to students who are not used to singing alone in front of others. If the choir cannot be monitored some way by the choral director, however, sight-singing assessment may have to be carried out in groups.

Demorest (2001) recommends "taped assessment" of sight-singing achievement. A tape recorder (or two) is located in a separate room from the choir, and students are on their own to use the equipment and do what they are asked to do. Demorest outlines both evaluative and practice procedures. The *evaluative assessment procedure* involves the following:

- The student enters the room with two tape recorders. Tape 1 contains directions; tape 2 is for recording his or her sight-singing.
- The student presses "Play" on tape recorder 1, the instruction tape.
- The student is asked to open the folder with the test example; the tape then plays the tonic chord and a starting pitch and instructs the student to study the example for thirty seconds.
- The student is then told to press "Record" on tape recorder 2 and say his or her name. The key and starting pitch are given again on tape 1, followed by another thirty seconds of silence for the student to sing the melody.
- The instruction tape then tells the student to turn off recorder 2 and rewind the instruction tape for the next student. (p. 111)

The outline of steps for the *practice assessment procedure* is as follows:

- In the hallway outside the testing room is a music stand with a folder. The student opens the folder and looks at the sight-singing example.
- When the previous student is finished, the student enters the practice room and opens the folder in the practice room that contains the same example.

- The student presses the "Record" button on the tape recorder and gives his or her name.
- The student then sings the tonic triad or some other solfège or number patterns to establish the key; he or she taps two measures in tempo and begins singing the melody.
- When the student is finished, he or she presses the "Stop" button and leaves. (p. 112)

Students can be tested individually by the director, as long as the choir can be monitored or kept singing during the testing period. This is an excellent opportunity for a student director to gain experience. One director is known to test students in the janitor's closet outside the music room. It is quieter than the rooms off the rehearsal area and close enough to the choir room to monitor the rehearsal. Students come and go quickly from a preannounced order, and actual testing time for an entire vocal exam is no more than five minutes. Still, it takes several days to test all students.

Sight-singing need not be tested every grading period. Sometimes students are tested only three times a year (first six weeks, third six weeks, and end of year). Special appointments can be made available whenever a student desires to raise his or her grade through a sight-reading test.

The use of computer technology may be the way to go in the future. Demorest (2001) gives one program that can record a student's sight-singing and score it on percentages of correct rhythm and pitch: Musicware's *Music Lab Melody*, version 3.0d. While current technology is still developing, "the program offers many worthwhile features" (p. 115).

Assessment Tools

Some type of evaluation measure is needed if results of sight-singing are to be computed as part of students' grades. Among the most commonly used is the *rating scale*, an example of which follows:

1. *Deficient:* sight-sings with little or no accuracy.
2. *Below average:* sight-sings with some accuracy.
3. *Average:* sight-sings with fair accuracy but not with consistency.
4. *Good:* sight-sings with few mistakes and consistent accuracy.
5. *Excellent:* sight-sings with advanced and consistent accuracy.

Rather than just a rating of 1–5, the rating scale above also has a "rubric" or explanation of what the rating means. The above scale is "global" in nature; more specific scales might contain separate rubrics for pitch, rhythm, and expression (see Demorest, 2001, p. 118).

The problem with most rating scales is that they tend to be necessarily vague. This may be a plus, however, as directors are able to adjust the scale for use with different grade levels. The scale provides a number (1–5) that can be averaged with the student's final grade. Schleuter (1997) states:

> Objectivity of rating scales may often be improved if they are used with tape-recorded performances rather than during the live performance. This eliminates distracting visual observations during test performances that may influence rater consistency. Students in class lessons and rehearsals may individually leave the room to tape-record a test performance in a separate recording location. The instructor may then listen to the tape at a later time. (p. 187)

Another option for a tool to assess sight-singing is that of *criterion scoring*. A particular criterion is stated, and students pass or fail. Demorest (2001, p. 116) gives the following example:

1. Retained the original key throughout the example.   _____
2. Kept a steady tempo throughout the example.   _____
3. Majority of pitches were accurate and in tune.   _____
4. Majority of rhythms were accurate.   _____
5. Expressive markings were realized in performance.   _____

Total Score: _____

Each criterion represents a broad category of observation. Criteria also may be additive, yielding a total score (each statement being worth 1 point).

A third type of assessment measure is *numerical scoring*. In this case, the director actually counts the number of pitches and rhythms sung correctly. Each note in the given phrase is worth one point (one-half pitch, one-half rhythm) in the total score, which depends upon the number of notes in the phrase. This type of scoring is objective and reliable; it is also more difficult to use. It is hard for the director to catch all the mistakes on one hearing. A simpler version assigns one point per measure, rather than one point per note.

Students deserve to know how well they perform on any test, including sight-singing. Such feedback can take a number of forms: the measurement tool itself (often does not contain much information), written comments (time consuming), checklists (relatively easy to use), computerized responses (immediate feedback from computer program), and taped comments (student turns in cassette tape with his or her singing; teacher evaluates and responds on tape). Whatever mode the choral director chooses, students need to understand their progress in becoming competent sight-readers. Sight-singing also takes on more importance when it is practiced regularly and students know that achievement in this area is part of their regular choral grade. Remember: you can't test something you don't teach. Teach students to sight-read!

STUDY AND DISCUSSION QUESTIONS

1. What have been some of the obstacles to the teaching of sight-singing in the contemporary choral rehearsal?

2. What were the contributions of Guido d'Arezzo to the development of sight-reading?

3. How do movable *do* and fixed *do* differ? Which is more commonly used by music teachers in the United States?

4. When, where, and why were singing schools established? How did the northern version differ from the southern version?

5. Who was Lowell Mason, and what was his position on teaching kids to sight-read?

6. What was the "rote versus note" debate, when did it occur, and who was fueling the debate for more note reading?

7. How did the a cappella choir movement influence the teaching of sight-singing?

8. How do Kodály, Orff, Dalcroze, and Gordon differ in their teaching of sight-reading?

9. Among Demorest's findings regarding sight-singing practice today, what is the relationship between students' choral participation and sight-singing success?

10. Among Demorest's findings regarding sight-singing practices today, what is the relationship among individual testing, feedback, and students' sight-singing performance?

11. What three general guidelines does Demorest give as the result of research on sight-singing?

12. What are the components of developing singers' aural acuity?

13. What are the components of learning to read notation?

14. What is more efficient, sight-reading by intervals or by patterns? Why?

15. When and how long should sight-singing be taught in the choral rehearsal?

16. Should group sight-singing achievement be assessed? What is the danger in group-only assessment?

17. What are different ways in which individual assessment of sight-singing can take place?

18. What steps does the evaluative assessment procedure involve?

19. What steps does the practice assessment procedure involve?

20. What are the various assessment tools that can be used to evaluate sight-singing?

REFERENCES

Armstrong, M. (2001). Adjudicated sight-reading for the choral ensemble: An incentive for musical literacy. *Choral Journal, 41*(10), 21–30.

Bennett, P. (1984). Tricks, masks, and camouflage: Is imitation passing for music reading? *Music Educators Journal, 71*(3), 62–63, 65–69.

Bertalot, J. (1993). *Five wheels to successful sight-singing. A practical approach to teach children (and adults) to read music.* Minneapolis: Augsburg Fortress.

Cooper, I., and K. O. Kuersteiner (1965). *Teaching junior high school music.* Boston: Allyn and Bacon, Inc.

Crarey, N. L. (2001). Our goal. *Maryland Music Educator, 47*(3), 26–27.

Demorest, S. M. (1998a). Improving sight-singing performance in the choral ensemble: The effect of individual testing. *Journal of Research in Music Education, 46*(2), 182–92.

——— (1998b). Sight-singing in the secondary choral ensemble: A review of the research. *Bulletin of the Council for Research in Music Education*, 137, 1–15.

——— (2001). *Building choral excellence: Teaching sight-singing in the choral rehearsal.* New York: Oxford University Press.

Demorest, S. M., and W. V. May (1995). Sight-singing instruction in the choral rehearsal: Factors related to individual performance. *Journal of Research in Music Education, 43*(2), 156–67.

Ernst, K. D., and C. L. Gary (eds.) (1965). *Music in general education.* Washington, DC: Music Educators National Conference.

Gehrkens, K. (1934). *Music in the grade school.* Boston: Birchard.

Gordon, E. E. (1993). *Learning sequences in music.* Chicago: G.I.A.

Gordon, E. E., and D. Woods (1986). *Jump right in: The music curriculum.* Chicago: G.I.A.

Grout, D. J. (1980). A history of Western music (3d ed.). New York: Norton.

Henry, H., and S. M. Demorest (1994). Individual sight-singing achievement in successful school ensembles: A preliminary study. *Update: Applications of Research in Music Education, 13*(1), 4–8.

Hoppin, R. H. (1978). *Medieval music.* New York: Norton.

Kegerreis, R. I. (1970). History of the high school a cappella choir. *Journal of Research in Music Education, 28*(4), 319–29.

Lowens, I. (1954). John Tufts's introduction to the singing of Psalm-tunes (1721–1744): The first American music textbook. *Journal of Research in Music Education, 2*(2), 89.

Lowens, I., and A. P. Britton (1953). The easy instructor (1798–1831): A history and bibliography of the first shape note tune book. *Journal of Research in Music Education, 1*(1), 32.

MENC (1994). *National standards for arts education: What every young American should know and be able to do in the arts.* Reston, VA: MENC/CNAEA.

——— (1996). *Performance Standards for Music.* Reston, VA: MENC.

Musicware (1997). *Music lab melody* (version 3.0d). Computer software. Redmond, WA: Music Lab Systems.

Mursell, J. L. (1956). *Music education: principles and programs.* Morristown, N.J.: Silver Burdett.

Mursell, J. L., and M. Glenn (1938). *The psychology of school music teaching.* New York: Silver Burdett.

Phillips, K. H. (1984). Sight singing: Where have we been? Where are we going? *Choral Journal, 24*(6), 11–17.

——— (1992). *Teaching kids to sing.* New York: Schirmer Books.

——— (1996). Teaching singers to sight-read. *Teaching Music, 3*(6), 32–33.

Roe, P. F. (1983). *Choral music education* (2d ed.). Prospect Heights, IL: Waveland Press.

Schleuter, S. L. (1997). *A sound approach to teaching instrumentalists.* New York: Schirmer Books.

Swiggum, R. (ed.) (1998). *Strategies for teaching high school chorus.* Reston, VA: Music Educators National Conference.

17 | Rehearsing the Choir

Directing a choir rehearsal can be a most exciting and rewarding event. It represents the culmination of years of music preparation and instruction. The rewards will depend greatly upon the amount of planning that has been done and the ability to communicate effectively as a leader. Effective communication is enhanced by an authoritative—not authoritarian—manner; the conductor must look and act the part. No one wants to sing for a person who cannot take charge and get the job done.

The development of an effective speaking voice is part of the conductor's package. Speaking to the choir in an everyday, conversational tone often denotes lack of confidence. The conductor need not shout to be heard, but projection of the speaking voice is paramount to effective communication as a choral director. The support and projection of the speaking voice are the same for singing and speaking. Slightly raising the pitch of the voice helps to preserve the vocal folds and protect them from abuse. Long rehearsals are tiring and wearing on the voice.

The conductor also must look the part of a leader. This means acting the role, even when scared to death. The younger children are, the more they seem to sense when the director is not confident. Discipline problems quickly develop when children suspect that the young conductor is vulnerable. A type of mob psychology can develop as loud and boisterous activity erupts. The old adage "don't smile until Christmas" is applicable when the new choral director begins his or her career. Being businesslike does not require being mean or nasty. It means being in charge. The conductor must have rules, announce them, enforce them, and proceed through the rehearsal in an orderly and objective fashion (see Chapter 8). Experience greatly helps the process, but "plan your work, and work your plan" is always a good guideline.

Chapter 15 presents the outline for the choral warm-up, which begins each rehearsal. The goals are to energize the body, breath, ear, and voice. This is typically followed by sight-reading exercises (Chapter 16). Sight-singing should be fostered throughout the rehearsal, but research shows that most directors who include sight-reading instruction do so near the beginning of the rehearsal (Demorest, 2001). The remainder of the time is for the learning of music. Becoming a good rehearsal director takes much experience, but certain general principles are applicable, the first two of which have been discussed previously: maintaining a businesslike attitude and speaking authoritatively. The sections that follow detail how to introduce new music, the use of a whole-part-whole strategy, directing efficient rehearsals, and correcting common ensemble problems.

INTRODUCING A NEW CHORAL WORK

Each new choral composition should be introduced so as to generate interest in it from the outset. The deadliest way is just to start in with no idea of what the music is about or its background. Also, if the conductor says something like, "This is a great piece of music, I love it, and so will you," the piece may be doomed for failure. Students should be given the chance to form their own opinions about the value of the music and whether they like it or not. This doesn't mean that the music chosen must be up for a popularity vote; remember, the choral director is a music educator. Following is an eight-step process that insures that a choir will learn new music faster and with greater understanding than with more haphazard approaches.

Comprehensive Musicianship

Applying the concept of comprehensive musicianship (Hylton, 1995), the director will, as a first step, introduce each new piece of music with enough background to give the students a broad understanding of the following:

- **Title of the composition.** If the title is in a foreign language, how does it translate? If the chorus is from a larger work, what is the title of that work?

- **Composer/arranger.** Who wrote or arranged the music? What is his/her nationality?

- **Era of composer and style of composition.** When was this music written, and when did the composer live? What are a few characteristics of this time period?

- **Meaning and mood.** Where does the text come from? What is this composition about in general? What is the general feeling to be conveyed?

- **Structure or form.** What is the overall design of the composition (e.g., AB, ABA, rondo, through-composed, strophic)? Are there sections that repeat or contrast?

All of the above information should be presented as briefly as possible. Students will not be taking notes, so long lectures are discouraged. The better technique is to draw the information from the students by the use of questions. Students should be able to look at the music and determine almost everything in the above list except, perhaps, the form. They may not know the era of the composer and composition, but then again, if a comprehensive approach is used repeatedly, their knowledge will be expanding.

Each time a selection of choral music is returned to, the rehearsing of it should begin with a few questions drawn from the input of the previous practice. This is real teaching as, without written notes, students must rely on their memory. In general, the director should refrain from asking the chorus, "Who knows the composer of this composition?" This tends to give students the freedom to speak out at random, and discipline often relaxes when students speak out at will. Instead, the director should ask, "Does anyone know who composed this work?" (signal to put hand up) or "Bill, do you know who the composer is?" Not all points need to be reviewed each time. One way to review without questioning is for the director to say, "Please take out the piece we are working on by Palestrina," or "The next selection is the one from Handel's *Messiah*." This takes some forethought but is well worth the planning effort.

Each subsequent rehearsal also should include at least one new element about the composition. Examples could include key, meter, tonality, interesting words or concepts in the text, points of interest about the composer or style period, meanings of character terms and dynamic indications, and so forth. By the time all choral selections are ready for performance, a rich and varied core of knowledge will have been developed for each piece of music. This information can be provided on a handout and used as the basis for a written test following the concert. Such a test also could include students' observations about how well they performed the music and what they thought of it. This latter content can be evaluated by "seriousness of purpose" rather than a "right or wrong" standard.

The comprehensive musicianship portion of each rehearsal must necessarily be short. Students do not join choir to learn about music history and theory. Nevertheless, when done correctly, students can learn a lot about these topics as part of the regular rehearsal routine. Music has a large and complex body of knowledge. Choral directors should include at least some of this knowledge-based learning in rehearsals.

Overview of the Music

Some type of overview of the entire composition is the second step in introducing a new work. At minimum, the text should be read aloud and discussed. If in a foreign language, a good translation is needed. A phonetic reading of the text is not necessary at this step. Rather, the overview is to give a complete picture of the piece.

Many directors play a recording at this step. If the performance is a good one, this may be the quickest way to introduce the whole piece to the choir. Some directors object to the use of recordings, as they fear a negative result if the choir tries to imitate what they hear. But if the recording is excellent, imitation may not be so bad. Also, one exposure to a recorded performance will have little effect on the eventual outcome of a choir's singing. There is a tremendous library of choral recordings today, and choral directors are encouraged to be informed, if only for their own edification.

If use of a recording is undesirable or unavailable, the composition may be played, at least in part, at the piano. Major themes can be outlined, and the director may wish to sing the important melodies. If the accompanist can play from an open score, the parts themselves should be played rather than any independent accompaniment.

It is important that the overview step not take too long. Students want to sing, and the sooner they sing the better. Nevertheless, at least a cursory overview helps the singer understand where the composition begins and ends, and what happens in between.

Sight-Read All or Part

If the chorus members have good sight-reading skills, have them sing through the entire piece, either using solfège or on a neutral syllable such as *loo* or *doo*. The rehearsal should be under tempo so the most accurate reading can take place. If the selection is long, sight-singing only a section at a time is beneficial. It is not necessary to begin at the beginning of the piece; an easier, more manageable section often is preferable to starting from the beginning. Roe (1983) suggests students hum parts while listening to the piano (p. 256).

A choir that has minimal sight-singing skills will necessarily skip this third step. If students are to learn to sight-sing, however, they must be given the opportunity to apply their developing skills to new music. Using the techniques presented in Chapter 16, choir members will learn to teach themselves rather than having their parts spoon-fed.

If the rhythm is particularly challenging, rehearsing only the rhythm by itself is encouraged. Students can "count-sing" or apply any approach the director wants. Tapping the pulse or beat note also helps to unify the rhythm. Students should not be allowed to tap the pulse with the foot or in ways that are audibly distracting. Tapping two fingers of one hand into the palm of the other is a suitable technique.

Mark the Score

Depending upon the age level of the choir, score markings will be minimal to numerous. At this fourth step, the director should dictate those markings that will be necessary for accurate presentation of the music and text, such as, breath marks, phrasings, and articulations. Highlighting or circle dynamic markings, character terms, and tempos, especially if they are likely to be overlooked by the singers. Not all of the choral selection need be marked at one time, especially if the piece is long. Marking section by section is often preferable.

When the directives are given, the choir director must be sure to announce the page first, then the system, measure number, and beat. Work from the largest parameter to the smallest. All too often a director will say, "Staccato the third beat in measure six, second system, on page two." Since the choir has no idea what page the director is referring to until the end of the directive, the singers become lost from the outset and the whole process falls apart.

If directives are given clearly and orderly, students' pencils should be flying. Sometimes there are students who just can't keep up to the dictation process. If they are permitted to interrupt and ask questions, the process becomes bogged down and ends up taking too much time. The choir should be told that if members miss a directive or get lost, they should ask their section leader following rehearsal. This practice will cause students to become more attentive when markings are given.

Finally, music markings should be done only in pencil. Frequently a director will change his or her mind about a breath mark or dynamic level. When music is marked with ink it becomes difficult to change. A pencil in every choir folder is required.

Model the Text

Directors typically skip this fifth step, but it is an important part of the process. If the style of the music requires rhythmic diction, then vowels must be modified and consonants exaggerated. An excellent chorus will do this automatically, but most singers need constant reminders about good diction.

If the director begins to rehearse a new piece with pitches and words simultaneously, it is almost certain that in all but the best of groups, the diction will suffer. That is why step two requires singing with solfège or a neutral syllable and no words. When the words are pronounced wrong from the beginning, they become difficult to change as the learning process continues.

Once the notes are learned by syllable, the words should then be modeled by the director. Demonstrations of particularly difficult vowels may need numerous repetitions, especially when diphthongs are involved. The consonants, also, must be given attention. Models of final consonant placement, double consonants, initial consonants, tuned consonants, and so forth should be demonstrated by the director and echoed by the choir. This approach greatly helps to beautify the sound and make the text intelligible.

An additional way to teach correct pronunciation of the text, especially when the rhythm is demanding, is to have the choir speak the words in rhythm. The singers should not be permitted to speak in a droning voice. Elevating the speaking pitch of the voice helps to protect the vocal cords. Good choral speaking makes the same demands as singing when it comes to proper breath support, pitch of the voice, and projection.

The director cannot accurately model the text if the text has not been studied in depth before the rehearsal. Modeling diction forces the director to think about the pronunciation of the text as it relates to vowel and consonant production. Again, text modeling is best done by section if there is much text involved. In the Baroque era, where much textual repetition is common, modeling text may involve only one phrase of words.

If the style of the music does not require rhythmic diction, then rehearsing the words without the music is unnecessary. Music of a popular nature typically requires pronunciation that reflects common language usage.

Put Words and Music Together

The director now rehearses words and music together in step six. All parts should be practiced simultaneously, especially if the first section rehearsed is not difficult. Having the accompanist play the parts while the choir mentally sings the section is a helpful aid. Next, the choir should attempt singing the passage; the singing should move ahead, regardless of breakdowns. Students should be challenged to read the music.

If students have practiced the pitches on a syllable or syllables, isolated the rhythm, and rehearsed the words separately, then putting together these three component parts should be easier than if all three were practiced simultaneously from the start. While this process may seem to be time consuming, it actually speeds the pace and produces greater accuracy.

Young or inexperienced groups who lack sight-reading skills may have trouble staying on their parts when the three elements of pitch, rhythm, and words are put together. This is all the more reason to isolate these elements before combining them.

Isolate and Combine Parts

It is best at step seven, especially with young singers, to teach the melody last. Inexperienced singers who have trouble carrying a part often become confused if they first hear the melody line. A general guide for the teaching of parts is as follows:

- Play or sing the bass part (or lowest part).
- Play or sing the tenor part.
- Combine the bass and tenor parts.
- Play or sing the alto part.
- Combine alto part with tenor and bass parts.
- Play or sing the soprano part.
- Combine soprano with other parts and listen for accuracy of all parts together.

Some directors will have all singers sing each of the parts as it is rehearsed. This greatly helps in maintaining student interest and discipline. The technique works especially well with people who read music. Students who have minimal sight-singing achievement, however, easily can be confused by singing parts other than their own. One thing is clear: no section should be rehearsed for too long a duration while other sections just sit and listen. This produces boredom and often results in talking and a breakdown of discipline.

Another strategy for rehearsing parts is to determine if voices have the same part. If this is the case, they can be rehearsed simultaneously, saving much time. Also, the above strategy can be varied by changing the various group combinations in the learning process, e.g., soprano and tenor.

Sally Herman, author of *Building a Pyramid of Musicianship* (1988), relates the practice of using tapes in the choral rehearsal. She advocates the making of rehearsal tapes for each part of a new selection. Students gather by vocal part at the corners of the choir room, listen to the tape, and learn their parts as they sing with it. This, she states, works well if there is a substitute teacher for the day. It would seem that different tapes playing at the same time would be distracting, but Herman relates that students learn to block out the parts other than their own. Herman does not recommend this activity for every piece of music and believes strongly in the development of literacy skills. She gives this piece of advice:

> There is nothing more boring to the student than having to sit while one part at a time is gone over and over. Discipline problems are usually a direct result of boredom. You are setting yourself up for problems when three-fourths of your students have nothing to do. Do you really think they are going to study the music while you work with another section? How do they know what to study when they are not yet that familiar with the music? Give them something definite to study. Tell them to try to find their own part on a light vowel sound as you work with one part. Hand them a sheet with the phonetic pronunciation to the German text of that particular piece to study during the time you work with another section. Give them a study guide to the piece of music so that they can be marking their music with the appropriate articulation. Have them search for diction problems and note them in the music. Find something constructive for them to do. (p. 93)

Herman's advice is on the mark. Students left to their own while others are rehearsing are quick to become bored. They need to have something to do.

Another use of the tape recorder, as given by Herman, is for assessment purposes. On a given day, as many students who have battery-operated tape recorders are to bring them to class. As selections are sung, each student tape records his or her own singing. Tape recorders are passed to others as needed for additional tapings. As the students leave the class they deposit their tapes (with a name label) in a box near the door. Listening to the tapes helps the director determine vocal development, part security, correct placement, changing voices, and so forth. Herman then writes each student a letter with a voice assessment. "I can compliment all that I want to in the letters without the fear of hurting another student's feelings" (1988, p. 94).

Herman makes another important point: "Don't sing along with your students. How can you hear them if you are singing?" (p. 94). Another point is worth considering also: Don't mouth the words when you are conducting. Students become accustomed to watching your mouth more than your conducting gestures. If you stumble on the words, they might stumble as well.

Put It All Together

In step eight, all parts and sections are combined into a complete work. Sometimes it is necessary to work more on the transitions between sections, for here is where the singing often will break down. Once the choir can sing though a composition, they must be challenged to improve some element each time they repeat it. Simply saying "sing it again" does little to aid improvement. Always sing with objectives.

WHOLE-PART-WHOLE STRATEGY

The "whole-part-whole" strategy is another of the most commonly used and most effective means of rehearsing. This strategy involves three steps rather than eight: (1) a preview of the big picture, (2) focusing on parts, and (3) a refinement of the whole.

Initial instruction involves conveying an understanding of the big picture, a sense of the whole. This stage is identical to "comprehensive musicianship," step one of the eight-step procedure discussed above.

The second stage involves what is sometimes called "woodshedding." The various vocal parts are checked for accuracy and corrections made as needed. When pitch or rhythm problems are heard, the error must be isolated in the problematic voice part and corrected. Often the problem stems from the transition into the offending note, and the passage must be rehearsed accordingly. Sometimes the problem may be in relation to other vocal parts; holding the note against the other parts helps to secure its place. When the problem is corrected, the passage should be sung in context with the other parts to determine if it has been secured. Of vital importance is that the passage be sung without accompaniment; if students can hold the part without the piano, they know it.

Learning to rehearse parts takes time and requires the skill of "vocal conducting" or, using the voice to guide the process. The objective is to drill the notes quickly, with a minimum amount of verbal instruction. However, leading students vocally to repeated action requires that commands be given, as "I'll give you 1–2, and you come in on 3," or "I'll count one measure before you enter." Sometimes, merely saying "again" in rhythm will bring about the desired repetition without a wasted break. As students become more comfortable with their parts, less verbal instruction is needed, and the director becomes more of an actual conductor.

Beginning conductors often have difficulty with error detection. They have not developed the ears for hearing parts other than the one they sing. Unfortunately, research in this area (Giersch, 1994) is scant and only seems to verify what is already known. One observation is worth noting, however, directors seem to improve at this task over time. One way to improve this facility is to know all of the parts before rehearsing begins. By learning and singing each part, the conductor is better able to place it into the context of the whole. The only way to improve is through experience.

As each section is learned, it must be connected to the others so that transitions will be smooth. Each time a larger unit of the piece is rehearsed, interpretive elements such as tempo and dynamics should be monitored. Never must a phrase, section, or entire composition be repeated without some directive for improvement. As each composition is refined, it should be coming closer to the ideal that the choral director has in mind.

Finally, the whole arrives; the entire composition is sung from beginning to end. It was previewed, taken apart, and now it is put back together again. Though the final result represents much learning, it must not sound that way. Great choral singing sounds effortless. All the hard work must remain under the surface if the beauty of the music is to emerge. In the end, the aesthetic payoff is worth the hours of rehearsing when the rehearsals have been businesslike and focused.

Pacing the Rehearsal

Learning to pace a rehearsal is of vital importance. If singers become bored because of the slow pace, the rehearsal will drag. Likewise, if the pace is too fast and driven, singers will become bewildered and exhausted. Finding an even, forward-moving pace is something learned from experience. Some general guidelines are as follows:

- Do not teach a new composition all in one rehearsal.
- Generate a time line for the rehearsal and stick with it as much as possible.
- Keep the rehearsal moving. If something is not working, abandon it until another time.
- Begin and end the rehearsal with something the choir knows.
- Rehearse more difficult music nearer the beginning than the end of the period.

- Keep talking to a minimum. Sing.
- Speak clearly and project the voice.
- Have singers alternate sitting and standing.
- Begin and end the rehearsal on time.
- Allow for times of levity but immediately return to serious business.
- Use written transmissions as much as possible for announcements.
- Do not rehearse demanding passages to great length.
- Do not rehearse passages with high tessituras to great length.
- Beware of overrehearsing, which may take the edge off a performance.
- Vary the rehearsal routine. Be creative.
- Insist that singers get their heads out of the music.
- Make the most of eye contact.

Providing Reinforcement

Singers are human beings who need to be "stroked" like everyone else. When they feel good about what they are doing, they will forgive many of the conductor's faults. But when they feel poorly—watch out! It is therefore to the choral director's great advantage to keep the singers happy.

When the singers do a good job, they should be told. That doesn't mean that gushing is necessary; it just means that nicely spaced compliments are in order when they are in order. On the other hand, if everything the choir sings is "good," it will never improve. Phrases like "that's improving," or "I heard a better blend that time," are ways of offering positive reinforcement without saying it was "good." The proper reinforcement during a rehearsal can greatly help move the rehearsal forward.

Likewise, negative comments can be deadly to motivation. The use of sarcasm is never appropriate, and yelling at a choir only serves psychologically to turn the members as a group against the director. A stern look, a warning, even silence are appropriate when needed. There is an old saying that has truth: "It is easier to attract flies with honey than with vinegar." The choral director should remain cool, calm, and positive. Rehearsals can at times be stressful. When this occurs, the best advice is to back off, slow down, inject some levity, and move forward.

Working with the Accompanist

The director should avoid accompanying whenever possible. Being trapped behind the piano blocks the conductor's efficiency of hearing and often results in the conductor's pounding out the parts. The director will listen much better if he or she is away from the piano.

Student accompanists should be used whenever available. "The director has a responsibility to further the pianistic and musical development of the piano students by providing some training in accompaniment" (Roe, 1983, p. 275). More than one accompanist can be used for each choir, giving opportunity for the one not playing to sing. Music should be assigned by difficulty level and corresponding technique.

The director needs to work with the accompanist to provide some basic instruction in rehearsal procedures. These may include: (1) learning to play parts from an open score, (2) giving pitches (from the bottom upward), (3) playing with confidence without banging, (4) warm-up procedures, (5) when to play and when not to play, and (6) how to follow the director's gestures. These elements should not be taken for granted; inexperienced accompanists need guidance. Regarding the use of accompaniment, Pfautsch (1988) states:

> Some choral conductors argue that the piano should never be used in a choral rehearsal. They emphasize the dangers of constant use, of complete dependency on the piano by singers, and of retarded sight reading. They also point to the differences between tempered pitches produced by the piano and the nontempered pitches produced by the voice. Most choral directors recognize these dangers, but they would also add that, when used with discretion, the piano can be of great assistance. Excessive dependence on the piano . . . can be a detriment, yet this does not mean that, just because the piano is used, the singers cannot learn to hear each other and make efforts to produce a homogenous ensemble sound. (p. 86)

Conductors have overcome the temptation of using the piano constantly by occasionally doing without it for an entire rehearsal. This forces singers to become much more reliant on their sight-reading skills, and it inevitably benefits intonation. Also, directing students to sing their parts without accompaniment is a valuable means of determining if they really know the parts or are just relying upon the piano. The conductor who learns to rehearse the choir with minimal piano playing creates a more musically independent ensemble.

The use of commercially available accompaniment tapes is widespread. Conductors of elementary and middle school choirs often turn to this device when a live accompanist is unavailable. Tapes also are chosen because of their enhanced instrumental sound, which is appealing to students. A number of problems can develop when using such tapes, however: (1) balance between singers and tape output is hard to control, (2) the "canned" tape allows for little individual interpretation from the conductor, (3) it sometimes is difficult to coordinate the tape with the live singing, (4) students follow the tape and not their conductor, and (5) if the sound equipment fails, the show is over. Conductors are admonished to study any tape carefully; there are good tapes and poor ones. In any case, the use of accompaniment tapes should not preclude the use of regular instrumentalists, whenever possible.

Assessing the Rehearsal

The best time to evaluate any rehearsal is immediately following it. While this is often difficult with singers lingering to ask questions, make small talk, and so forth, the conductor begins the next rehearsal where the one before ended. An evaluation of each rehearsal as close as possible to its completion greatly aids in guiding the plan for the next.

It is helpful if the director tape-records rehearsals. This practice reveals many elements of the singing and rehearsing that can be missed during the rehearsal itself. Also, it gives the conductor an opportunity to sample the sound and determine what needs to be done to improve it. Even more helpful is to have the choir occasionally listen to a tape of their singing. Each member hears mainly his or her part during practice; how that part fits into the whole ensemble is often not understood. Waiting to listen to the concert tape, while rewarding, is really too late if the choir is to be advanced in their singing throughout the rehearsal period.

All conductors, especially those just beginning, would benefit from seeing themselves on videotape. The camera doesn't lie, and "what you see is what you get." What is heard may not be accurate, however, as video camcorders are not known to have excellent sound reproduction. Nevertheless, when students view their poor posture or lack of facial expression, they can be motivated to do something about it. If the conductor's gestures are unclear or imprecise, the videotape will indicate that improvement is needed.

A great part of the choral director's job is to assess the rehearsal as it is progressing. Listening for balance, blend, errors, consonants, vowels, and so forth is a never-ending process. However, the conductor must bring a good "mental set" to the rehearsal to which comparisons are constantly made. This is where beginning conductors often fail—their preconceptions are weak, and they have no model in mind by which to evaluate the choir's responses. Careful planning, preparation, and experience are the antidotes to making correct judgments in the rehearsal process.

Assessment brings the cycle of "whole-part-whole" full circle—the beginning whole is based on the concluding whole, and the conclusions lead back to the beginning. During the "part" phase, assessment also is vitally important. Learning to assess and provide proper feedback are two of the conductor's principal responsibilities.

DIRECTING AN EFFICIENT REHEARSAL

The universal complaint of choral directors is the lack of rehearsal time. "If we only had time for one more run through" is a common expression. The late Margaret Hillis, director of the Chicago Symphony Chorus, once was asked why the chorus took so long to prepare a concert when the orchestra could do it in a few rehearsals. "Language" was her response. It is true that choirs have to deal with words as an added layer of music making. However, orchestral directors, who often conduct members of a union, know that rehearsal efficiency is the only way to prepare a concert in the limited time available. If the conductor runs over the designated time, the musicians are paid overtime. Since most choristers are not paid, this is not a big problem. Nevertheless, choral conductors should act as if it were, and learn to run a tight ship. Directing efficient rehearsals means using every minute to its intended advantage—the learning of music.

Fifty Ways to Be Efficient

Charles Heffernan, the author of *Choral Music Technique and Artistry* (1982), presents fifty excellent guidelines to assist the choral director in developing efficient rehearsals (pp. 105–8). While many of these techniques have been discussed here and in other chapters, the list is so comprehensive as to warrant a full presentation in an abridged version. Both new and experienced choral directors would do well to ponder the application of these techniques to their choral rehearsal strategies.

1. Before the first rehearsal, you must thoroughly digest the music that is to be presented. Allow a period of time to permit the composition to mature in your thought.

2. Go over the music with the rehearsal pianist before the singers assemble. The rehearsal is not the place to correct the pianist's wrong notes or lack of understanding of the style.

3. Arrive early for each rehearsal and ascertain that all logistics are in order.

4. All singers must be aware that they have a definite contribution to make to the choral body and that their invariable presence is vital to every rehearsal.

5. All singers should have their own music. If several compositions are being rehearsed, they should be in a folder marked with the chorister's name. Each singer needs a pencil with which to notate the conductor's directions.

6. Indicate on a chalk board or bulletin board the compositions that are to be studied at each rehearsal. Choristers should get the compositions in order before the rehearsal begins.

7. Someone besides the conductor should take the attendance, distribute the music, set up chairs, and so on. Assigning these important duties to members of the choir can provide a sense of active participation to those involved.

8. Begin and conclude the rehearsal exactly at the appointed hours. Do not tolerate chronic tardiness or early leaving.

9. Usually, vocalize the choir with various exercises before starting to rehearse the music. However, occasionally use an easy composition in the warm-up.

10. Routines can be deadly. Work for variety in the warm-ups and rehearsal procedures.

11. Try to begin each rehearsal with something that will go well.

12. Practice having the choir respond vigorously and audibly to your preparation beat until everyone understands the necessity for breathing together in the tempo and character of what is to follow.

13. It is vital for every performer and the conductor to be in eye contact during the preparatory beat.

14. Develop in your singers the ability to understand the technical language of music. Teach them music terminology.

15. Guard against overconducting or attempting to inspire your singers to great artistic heights during the initial study of a composition. Learn the notes first.

16. You must have eye-to-eye contact with your singers constantly. Do not bury your head in the score, and do not permit your singers to do so either.

17. Train your choir to locate quickly the spot you wish to rehearse; say, for example, "Page 20, third system, second measure, fourth beat."

18. Initially, insist that the singers learn to observe every mark on the printed page. Many choristers look only at the words. Use pencils freely!

19. When learning parts, especially in music of the Baroque and Renaissance periods where a sectional sound is desirable, separate the four sections of the choir into the four corners of the room. Have each section stand in a circle and sing across to the person opposite.

20. Train the choir to be able to start at any point on the page.

21. After the initial reading of a new work, immediately begin to correct mistakes. Do not allow errors to be rehearsed into the music. Beware singing through, time and time again, the parts that are well learned and secure.

22. Sing for your group. Demonstrate your wishes.

23. As far as possible, scrutinize the four sections of the choir equally. Do not be guilty of ignoring the altos, picking on the tenors, and so on.

24. Urge the choir members to begin to memorize at once.

25. Never become passive; you must constantly take action. Transmit constantly; do not coast.

26. Do not be a bluffer. Admit your mistakes. Too many blunders may be an indication of insufficient preparation.

27. Encourage your singers to free themselves from the printed notes as soon as possible. After learning the notes, sing the music. There is a difference.

28. Frequently have the choir stand up, stretch, and move about. Be alert to physical lethargy in your choir.

29. Ask the choir to sing something from memory at each rehearsal. Try to conduct as long as possible without looking at your score.

30. During every rehearsal you must have eye-to-eye contact with every singer and player.

31. When rehearsing, do not try to hear everything at the same time unless you have an extremely keen ear and extensive conducting experience. It is better to listen for specifics.

32. A short recess in the middle of rehearsal may be beneficial. Guard against losing the momentum, however.

33. For fun and reading experience, occasionally have sections sing other parts.

34. Do not harangue your choir. Give praise when praise is due.

35. Try to have at least one good laugh at each rehearsal.

36. Read new music regularly. Constantly refresh the weary spirit of your singers by bringing them stimulating literature.

37. If you use instrumentalists with your choir, get them up to the level of the singers. Rehearse the players separately if possible.

38. The orchestra players must breathe, in their minds, at the upbeat. The orchestra and the choir will then attack together.

39. The orchestra must respond to the conductor's downbeat; if it does not, the attacks will become later and later.

40. Maintain a good dynamic balance between the players and singers at all times. Mark down the dynamic levels in the brass parts. If the strings are too loud, instruct the players to bow closer to the fingerboard rather than near the bridge.

41. Regularly record your rehearsals. Study the tapes. If possible, videotape your rehearsal. Show the results to your choir.

42. At the core of every great ensemble is the ability to play and sing in a chamber style, with extreme sensitivity to one another. Therefore, regularly break the choir down into small ensembles or quartets. Have these small groups demonstrate for each other.

43. Occasionally, spread the entire choir in a scrambled formation around the perimeter of a large room. Singing in this arrangement builds confidence and sonority.

44. Do not overrehearse. Excessive rehearsal may cause a composition to deteriorate.

45. Do not talk too much.

46. At times, walk around through the various sections of the choir while they are singing. You may be pleasantly surprised or dismayed at what you hear.

47. Occasionally, let someone else conduct. Sit back and listen objectively to your own choir.

48. At dress rehearsal, try to simulate the actual performance conditions. Leave nothing to chance.

49. Record your concerts for future study. Do not play the tapes immediately after the performance, however; it is often a letdown to do so. Do not hold a long, boring postmortem at the rehearsal following a concert. A few words of appreciation to your forces may be in order, but extended analysis of past disasters or triumphs accomplishes little.

50. Either love your choir or leave it.

Singing Is Hard Work

Choir members need to be challenged to work hard at every rehearsal. Something is wrong with singers' attitudes when the conductor is the hardest-working member of the group. The choir should be on task and disciplined, making good use of every efficient moment of rehearsal time. Also, choir members should be expected to study their music between rehearsals. They can review what has been rehearsed and, if able, work ahead on new music. This is especially important when choirs rehearse only once a week.

The late choral conductor Robert Shaw made a practice of sending a letter to his choir members following rehearsals. These "Dear People" letters (Musselman, 1979) have become a model for corresponding with choir members on such matters as phrasing, articulation, dynamics, and so forth. Shaw was a deeply insightful conductor, and his letters were strewn with the philosophical views that guided his inspiring performances. Known for efficient rehearsing, he knew that corresponding outside of rehearsal could save much time in rehearsal. This is a valuable practice and should be considered by all conductors as a means to improving rehearsal efficiency. The use of e-mail makes this type of correspondence much less cumbersome than in the past.

Working with Instruments

Occasionally the choral conductor will have the opportunity to work with instrumentalists for choral accompaniment. While this topic is beyond the scope of the present text, the author recommends to the reader Part 3 (Chapters 13–16), "Conducting Instruments," of *The Complete Conductor* (Demaree & Moses, 1995), and *Face to Face with an Orchestra* (Moses & Demaree, 1987). Elizabeth Green's classic *The Modern Conductor* (1997) is an excellent guide to working with strings.

Working with Soloists

Professional soloists typically are paid for their services. They often appear only before the performance at the dress rehearsal. These people are highly skilled musicians and need to be shown respect by the conductor. Their musical preferences for tempos, dynamics, phrasing, and so forth, should be carefully considered. The conductor has the final responsibility, however, for determining overall musical interpretation.

When a soloist is an amateur or student, the conductor will spend much more time coaching and teaching the solo. The singer will be guided mainly by the direction of the conductor and will rely heavily upon the conductor's directives. When in performance, these soloists may lean heavily upon the conductor for cues and assurances. Eye contact with the conductor is of paramount importance in this setting.

Whether a soloist is amateur or professional, contact before the dress rehearsal is necessary to work out problems in the music. Usually a "piano rehearsal" is scheduled with the soloist, keyboard accompanist, and conductor prior to rehearsing with the choir and orchestra. It is embarrassing and a waste of time if corrections must be made in the dress rehearsal. Professional soloists require little help in the performance from the conductor, but all soloists must be positioned so they can see the conductor for tempos and cues.

Sectional Rehearsals

Some choral directors use sectional rehearsals to save time and maximize part learning. This is a good practice if the other persons conducting the sectionals are well versed in what the conductor wants from the music. If sectionals become merely "note beating," little may be gained if the conductor must correct interpretive elements once the sections are joined. The most common division for sectionals is men and women.

Considerations for including sectionals in the rehearsal strategy include: (1) availability of another rehearsal accompanist, (2) availability of another rehearsal room, (3) sufficient time in the rehearsal schedule, (4) time available for the conductor to communicate clearly to the other sectional leader what is to be covered, and (5) availability of a person with the skills to conduct the sectional. To be done correctly, a sectional rehearsal takes much time to plan, and for this reason, directors often do not use this strategy.

COMMON ENSEMBLE PROBLEMS

Most choral ensembles consist of amateur singers who have had minimal music instruction. Therefore, the choral director must be able to detect and analyze ensemble problems, as well as apply techniques to remedy them. The following is a list of common problems found in choirs, probable causes, and suggested remediations.

Poor Tone Quality

Although choral tone quality is based primarily on vowel production, many other vocal faults may interfere with timbre. The most common faults are described here.

BREATHY TONE.   A breathy tone, caused by too much air slipping between the vocal folds upon phonation, is a common phenomenon among adolescent singers. Students must work on improving their breath control (slow emission of the air column) by maintaining an expansive rib cage while singing. They also should work on firm glottal closure (see exercises in Chapter 15).

HARD OR DRIVEN TONE.   A hard tone is caused by overdriving the voice with too much effort. Without relaxing the support muscles, the singer must use more control by keeping the ribs out. A relaxed jaw helps to relax tone, and staccato vocalises also help to relax muscles.

SHRILL TONE.   An overly bright tone is caused by an elevated larynx and "smiling" position of the lips for vowel production. Singers must maintain an at-rest position of the larynx for all pitches and should gently flare the lips as for the darker vowels (e.g., *oo*).

DARK OR COVERED TONE.   An overly dark tone sounds hooty and often gives a false maturity to young voices. It is caused by a depressed larynx and lack of projection in the vowel. The larynx must be at rest for all pitches and never artificially lowered. This requires a relaxed and forward-positioned tongue. Work with brighter vowel sounds also helps to balance the resonance of overly dark voices.

WOBBLE.   A voice begins to wobble when the breathing musculature loses strength. The tone varies in dynamic level as the breath support column varies in intensity. Singers with this problem must work on restoring muscle tone to their abdominal muscles so support can be firm and consistent.

TREMOLO.   Unlike the wobble, which is a variation of intensity, the tremolo or "bleat" is caused by a high laryngeal position and by muscle constriction in the laryngeal area. Singers must work on maintaining firm breath support while keeping the neck and swallowing muscles relaxed. The "tongue flex" (see chapter 15) helps to alleviate the tremulous voice with excessive vibrato.

NASAL TONE.   The nasal tone is pinched and overly resonates in the nose. The singer needs to maintain the open throat position (use of a "sigh") and a relaxed larynx. Working with darker vowels helps to lower the larynx. A high, forward placement in the mask also helps to focus the tone forward.

STRAIGHT TONE.   Many European choirs today sing with a straight tone, that is, with no vibrato. To sing without vibrato means to sing with some type of external control over the laryngeal mechanism, thus stifling the voice's natural capacity for vibrato. It also may mean that vocal technique is underdeveloped, which results in too little breath support and too much pressing at the laryngeal level. While it may help intonation for the choir to control or lessen the vibrato (especially sopranos), total elimination of the vibrato is not recommended.

Poor Intonation

Choirs that sing out of tune make audiences uncomfortable. Sharping or flatting of pitch originates either psychologically or physically, or it may be due to external factors.

PSYCHOLOGICAL ORIGINS.   If a poor sense of pitch is psychological in nature, the singer is not mentally alert or audiating pitch. Calling attention to "singing on the inside" (Chapter 15) will help when singers are not matching the sung pitches to the model "inside." Regular "inner hearing" exercises aid in developing aural skills (see Chapter 15).

PHYSIOLOGICAL ORIGINS.   If the problem is physical in origin, it can be due to the breathing musculature's being either under- or overdriven, with ensuing throat constriction and rigidity of the swallowing muscles. If a tone is overdriven, it is likely to be sharp; underdriven pitch is often flat. Moreover, different shaping of vowels among singers may cause the resultant vowel formants to beat against one another, thus producing out-of-tune singing. Good intonation results from vowel uniformity. Room temperature and fatigue also may influence the physical alertness of the singer and cause pitch to sag. It is especially important that singers rest and not become overly tired on the day of a concert. They must be physically and mentally alert at concert hour.

KEY OF COMPOSITION.   Occasionally a conductor may find that the key of the choral work does not feel right in the voice. The tessitura may be poor for the group, or the range could be excessive. When this occurs, and it seems more frequent in music of the Renaissance, the conductor is justified in raising or lowering the key a half step or more. Often, when singing goes flat, it is better to raise the key higher rather than lower it to where it seems to be heading. Lowering the key a half step may result in even flatter singing.

SCOOPING AND SLURRING.   Sliding up to pitch can be a mental habit, often caused by laziness, or it can be the adaptation of a pop style of singing to choral music. Remediation involves singing the music being rehearsed all in a staccato fashion, thus eliminating the time for the slur to occur. Working a phrase staccato and then legato teaches the singer to aim for the center of each pitch without the preliminary glide.

Lack of Rhythmic Vitality

Orienting choir members to the basic rhythmic pulse and its relationship to the various rhythm patterns is essential for rhythmic vitality. Art music, unlike popular music, uses an underlying beat that is perceived rather than heard. It is good for singers to physically relate to the beat and its support of the rhythmic texture.

MARKING THE BEAT.   Having choristers quietly clap or tap the beat is a common way to create pulse consciousness. A rolling motion of a hand is another way to create a beat that is moving forward.

MARKING THE OFFBEAT.   Another approach to pulse awareness is to snap fingers on the offbeats. This permits a clean subdivision of the pulse and raises awareness of the inner pulse.

TAPPING THE BEAT, SPEAKING THE RHYTHM.   Tapping the pulse while speaking the rhythm is a way to "layer" rhythm over pulse. Any method of counting can be used.

COUNT-SINGING.   Pitches can be sung using the count-singing procedure (see Chapter 16). This approach, made popular by Robert Shaw, requires a secure understanding of rhythm and its component parts.

Poor Phrasing

The musical phrase is like the ebb and flow of an ocean wave—always coming and going, building and breaking. Singers must be aware of phrase length, composition, peak, and flow. Unless the conductor has analyzed the composition for phrase construction, no clear evidence of phrasing will be heard from the choir.

MUSICAL SENTENCES.   Phrases are identified by placing breath marks in the score. Singers need to place a comma ['] at the end of each phrase as directed by the conductor. In polyphonic music the breaths typically will occur at different places in the music.

MUSICAL FLOW.   Every phrase needs a forward motion, or a sense of flow. Singers can gain an understanding of phrase movement by "painting" phrases in the air with horizontal "paint brush" strokes of one hand. One phrase is a sweeping gesture from left to right, right to left, or both for longer phrases. Music is movement, and this external action needs to be internalized for helping phrases to come alive.

MUSICAL PEAK.   Every phrase has a focus where the music builds to a peak and then subsides. Sometimes this peak may build over several phrases. Awareness of this peak can be felt by students in combination with the musical flow gesture. Sweeping across the horizontal plane (left to right, right to left), incidates the peak by closing the hand in preparation to the peak, and opening it at the moment the peak occurs.

Poor Diction

Choirs are notorious for poor diction. This problem may be due to the acoustics of the hall, but often it is caused by lack of attention from the choral director. Primary to the teaching of diction skills, the choristers must understand what type of diction they should be using.

SUNG-SPEECH DICTION.   Most folk and popular songs, including spirituals, use sung-speech pronunciation, where syllables glide from one to the next. No attempt is made to keep the individual notes or syllables separate. Neither is it proper to place emphasis on final consonants. In fact, to do so sounds strange and unnatural.

RHYTHMIC DICTION.   Art music of a highly rhythmic nature (especially that of the Baroque and Classical eras) requires that the integrity of each note and syllable be maintained. Double consonants are articulated separately, and nonvocal consonants are often vocalized to be heard. The speaking of text in rhythm aids the development of this choral technique.

LATE INITIAL CONSONANTS.   If singers do not execute initial consonants slightly ahead of the beat, the tone will sound late. This is true especially when singing with instrumentalists, who have no consonants to delay the tone. The conductor can overcome this problem by directing singers to initiate pitches with words beginning with consonants and listening for the quick onset of tone. The troublesome continuants *l* and *r* must not scoop up to the pitch.

SLOPPY FINAL CONSONANTS.   Final consonants must sound at a given point in the rhythm of a phrase. A kinesthetic feeling for this point can be developed by having singers make a "karate chop" gesture of one hand against the other at the directed point of final consonant sounding. Once a feel for this action is developed, the choir should respond to the conductor's karate chop gesture. Finally, the conductor can execute this gesture with only one hand lightly chopping in the air at the appropriate final consonant point. This gesture is made directly in front of the conductor using a downward stroke of the hand. The hand is raised upward at the wrist for preparation of the downward chop, which occurs in time with the final consonant.

Boring Interpretation

The author once heard the late Robert Shaw say, "Ladies and gentlemen, inspiration begins with all the right notes—go learn some." How true. The notes have to be secure before musical meaning can emerge. If the performance involves nothing more than a correct rendition of all the right notes, however, the audience will be bored. Music is about the communication of thoughts, ideas, and feelings. The choir must be constantly challenged to lift the notes from the page and to make the music come alive.

MEANING AND MOOD.   Choral directors need to take the time to discuss with their choirs the meaning and mood of each selection being sung in a concert. In addition, the quality of choral tone has to be chosen that is appropriate for each piece. The choir that sings with a glum face, "What a joy to be here, on this wonderful occasion," is doing little to inspire the audience.

ENERGIZE.   A boring choral performance often lacks energy. The choral conductor must work to energize body, breath, ear, and voice (see Chapter 16) if a live performance is to sound alive and exciting. This is the ultimate goal of the choral director—to present a chorus that makes music through an energized and stimulating performance. Such choirs rightfully deserve to hear "Bravo!" Even the occasional standing ovation may be justified.

STUDY AND DISCUSSION QUESTIONS

1. What are the two basic elements of the conductor's package for effective communication?
2. Why should a choral director not introduce a new choral work to a choir by saying, "This is a great work and you're going to love it"?
3. What information pertaining to comprehensive musicianship should be introduced when a new choral work is begun? Why should this section of the rehearsal be short?
4. What are the eight steps given for introducing and rehearsing a new work?
5. What are techniques for giving an overview of a new work?
6. Why is modeling of text by the conductor an important step in rehearsing music?
7. How can audio tapes be used in the choral rehearsal?
8. What is the "whole-part-whole" strategy of rehearsing?
9. How can beginning conductors become better at error detection?
10. Of the numerous guidelines given for pacing a rehearsal, which three do you think are the most important?
11. Why is positive reinforcement needed for the choir?
12. Why is it important to communicate with the accompanist before rehearsing?
13. When should assessment of the rehearsal take place?
14. Of the fifty ways to efficiency in a choral rehearsal, which three do you think are the most important?
15. What should be the distribution of work in a rehearsal?
16. How can a conductor work to correct a breathy choral tone?
17. What is the danger of using a totally straight tone?
18. What are four causes of poor intonation, and how can these be remedied?
19. What are some techniques for overcoming poor musical phrasing?
20. How can a choir keep from giving a boring choral presentation?

REFERENCES

Demaree, R. W., and D. V. Moses (1995). *The complete conductor.* Englewood Cliffs, NJ: Prentice Hall.

Demorest, S. M. (2001). *Building choral excellence: Teaching sight-singing in the choral rehearsal.* New York: Oxford University Press.

Giersch, D. P. (1994). Choral diagnostic model: A self-administered and self-scored instrument for high school choral teachers to evaluate their skills in identifying and solving rehearsal problems (doctoral diss. Temple University). *Dissertation Abstracts International, 54*(7), 2501A.

Green, E. (1997). *The modern conductor* (6th ed.). Upper Saddle River, NJ: Prentice Hall.

Heffernan, C. W. (1982). *Choral music technique and artistry.* Englewood Cliffs, NJ: Prentice Hall.

Herman, S. (1988). *Building a pyramid of musicianship.* San Diego: Neil A. Kjos Music.

Hylton, J. B. (1995). *Comprehensive choral music education.* Upper Saddle River, NJ: Prentice Hall.

Moses, D. V., R. W. Demaree Jr., and A. F. Ohmes (1987). *Face to face with an orchestra.* Princeton, NJ: Prestige.

Musselman, J. A. (1979). *Dear people . . . Robert Shaw.* Bloomington, IN: Indiana University Press.

Pfautsch, L. (1988). The choral conductor and the rehearsal. In H. A. Decker and J. Herford (eds.), *Choral conducting symposium* (2d ed.). Englewood Cliffs, NJ: Prentice Hall.

Roe, P. (1988). *Choral music education* (2d ed.). Prospect Height, IL: Waveland Press.

18 | Understanding Styles and Performance Practices

Musicologists who have studied the choral field have discovered a wealth of knowledge applicable to contemporary choral musicians, especially in the area of styles and performance practices. Therefore, it is the choral director's responsibility to gain an understanding of stylistic practices and to apply this knowledge to choral music making. For example, before it was known that Baroque tempo terms were more descriptive of the character of a composition (e.g., *allegro* translated as "cheerful") rather than the actual speed, presentations of Handel's *Messiah* were typically slow and ponderous. With the knowledge of historical style practice, today's performances of *Messiah* are usually faster and livelier. Knowing about authentic practices of the past guides the choral conductor in giving a more accurate and satisfying performance, especially when programming art music from the major eras of choral composition.

An in-depth knowledge of performance practices is typically a topic undertaken by experienced conductors. Therefore, a thorough presentation of this area is not covered in this book. The beginning conductor should have a basic understanding of each of the major style periods, and that is what is attempted in this chapter. Books such as *The Complete Conductor* (Demaree and Moses, 1995), *The Choral Experience* (Robinson and Winold, 1976) and *Choral Music: History, Style, and Performance Practice* (Garretson, 1993) offer a more in-depth presentation; books and articles devoted to specific performance practice details are listed at the end of this chapter.

MEDIEVAL ERA (c. 500–1450)

Medieval times in Europe also were known as the "Dark Ages." Three classes of people existed: the poor, or serfs; the nobility, who were wealthy landowners, and the clergy. There was no middle class until late in the period, when a middle class of tradesmen, merchants, and traders gradually evolved. The peasants were, as a whole, illiterate; no system of public education was known. Their status was maintained by the powerful religious and political body—the Roman Catholic Church. Unable to read, the peasants were kept "in the dark" about the value of education and how it could better their status in this life. They were led to believe that fulfillment came in life after death. This attitude, maintained for centuries, began to change only during the Renaissance, when enlightened thinking was reborn.

Music in medieval Europe was advanced by the church, where religion was the center of life and culture. Early in the era monophonic chant dominated and was later codified by Pope Gregory as a standard for use by the church throughout Europe (Gregorian chant). Beginning in the year 900, two-voice polyphony was introduced (organum), which later evolved into two significant types of polyphonic composition: the motet and the mass. Motets were written for unaccompanied choir and based on a sacred, nonliturgical Latin text. These short pieces were generally inserted into the regular church mass. The early mass was put together from various single movements by anonymous composers. Beginning in 1360, however, the entire Ordinary of the mass (Kyrie, Gloria, Credo, Sanctus, Benedictus, Agnus Dei) was composed by one person, in this case, Guillaume de Machaut in the *Messe de Notre Dame*. The Cathedral of Notre Dame in Paris emerged during this time as the most important music center in Europe. Choral music was the dominant form of music making; organs, strings, and wind instruments gradually became more acceptable.

Secular vocal musicians emerged in the south of France and were called *troubadours*. These singers and storytellers traveled from town to town entertaining people. In northern France they were known as *trouvères*, and in Germany they were called *minnesingers*. These minstrels sang in the vernacular, and the music was folklike. The linking of poetry, music, and dancing was common, and this type of entertainment flourished in the feudal courts.

Schools of Composition

Three schools of composition were dominant in the Middle Ages, that of Notre Dame, the Ars Nova, and that of Burgundy.

The *School of Notre Dame* in Paris emerged as the musical center of Europe around 1175 and became known as the *Ars Antiqua* ("old art") of the late twelfth and thirteenth centuries. Polyphonic composition developed from two-part to three- and sometimes four-part writing. Six rhythmic modes brought about regular rhythm patterns in a form known as measured organum (usually in triple time in deference to the Trinity). Dissonance and consonance also became more pronounced. The *conductus* was the first compositional form free of Gregorian chant. Composers were Leonin and Perotin.

In the *Ars Nova* ("new art"), centered in fourteenth-century France and Italy, duple rhythm was introduced and became as important as triple had been in the preceding generation; music composition became more florid and complex in general. The motet and mass evolved as the major forms of composition. Composers included Vitry and Machaut.

The composers of the *Burgundian School* (Burgundian courts in first half of fifteenth century; included eastern France, Belgium and the Netherlands) developed precursors to polyphonic music in organum style and also developed secular music including the *rondeau*, *ballade*, and *chanson*. Composition was a reaction to the more formal academic style of the previous century and resulted in sweeter, less austere writing. The instrumental ensemble became important, and dissimilar instruments such as recorders, viols and trombones were combined for the first time. Composers included Binchois and Dufay.

Style Elements

MELODY.   Early melodies were pentatonic in structure; later, eight church modes or scales were employed (e.g., a to a on the white keys of the piano was aeolian). Movement was mostly conjunct, with small skips and limited range.

HARMONY.   There was no harmony in chant; later, organum used parallel fourths, fifths, and octaves. In late polyphonic composition, melodic ornamentation occurred in added parts, but open intervals still dominated.

TONALITY. Music was modal; each mode had certain characteristics of range, style, melodic formula, and tonal center. Ionian (major) and aeolian (natural minor) were part of the modal system.

RHYTHM. The pace was steady, gentle, and unmetered in chant, with the eighth-note the pulse. Early organum was free and melismatic until the Ars Antiqua, when measured organum employed short and accented rhythm patterns. In the Ars Nova, duple rhythm was introduced along with a system of proportional notation.

TEXTURE. Monophonic texture (a single line) existed before 900, and polyphony (two or more melodic lines) was dominant from 900 to 1600.

TIMBRE. The sound of medieval music was rather transparent. Both voices and instruments were folklike, and no "heavy" singing or playing was known.

DYNAMICS. No intensity levels were marked in the music. Given the small ensemble sizes for both singers and instrumentalists, music making was probably rather moderately sounded, with little variation within pieces.

TEMPO. No indications of tempo were marked. Church music was typically slow paced, the *tactus* set by the speed of the human pulse (fifty to sixty beats per minute). Secular dance music moved at a lively pace.

FORM. Early sacred forms consisted of chants, organum, clausulae, and conductus. Later sacred forms included complete settings of the mass and motets. Secular writing included the minstrel song, caccia, ballata, and dance forms.

Sources for Further Study

Those wishing a more in-depth understanding of medieval music may consult the following sources: *Medieval Music* (Hoppin, 1978), *Music in the Middle Ages* (Reese, 1940), *Music in the Medieval World* (Seay, 1965), and *The Interpretation of Early Music* (Donington, 1963).

RENAISSANCE ERA (c. 1450–1600)

The Renaissance ("rebirth") represents a time in western European history when humankind awoke from the darkness of the medieval ages to a period of hope in life on this earth. No longer were people bound to religious beliefs that focused more on life after death than the present life. This enlightenment was fueled by the Protestant Reformation of the sixteenth century. Sacred music, heretofore sung only in Latin, was now sung in the vernacular, and commoners were welcomed to participate in singing. The invention of the printing press by Gutenberg in 1450 and the printing of music made it possible to disseminate music on a greater scale. The Renaissance marked a period of intense musical growth, especially that of choral music. The Golden Era of polyphony reached its peak in the music of the Roman School, headed by Giovanni Pierluigi da Palestrina (c. 1525–94).

Schools of Composition

A number of important schools or centers of composition flourished during the Renaissance.

The *Flemish School*, in the southern part of Belgium known as Flanders, developed a new polyphonic style ("points of imitation") where all voice parts were equal. Composers included Josquin Desprez, Lasso (Lassus), Isaac, Jacobus Clemens (Clemens non Papa), Ockeghem, Obrecht, Willaert, Gombert, and Regnart.

The *Roman School*, centered at the Vatican in Rome, developed polyphonic sacred writing to its greatest heights. Composers included Morales, Palestrina, and Victoria (Vittoria).

The *Venetian School*, centered at the Cathedral of St. Mark's in Venice, developed the polychoral style (multiple choirs, including instrumental choirs), with a blend of homophonic and polyphonic textures. Composers included Croce, Andrea Gabrieli, and Giovanni Gabrieli (uncle and nephew).

The *German School* continued polyphonic writing but also used more homophonic texture as in the chorale. Composers included Hassler, Jacobus Handl (Gallus), Luther, and Praetorius.

The *English School* continued the polyphonic Roman style and developed the anthem form. Composers included Byrd, Dunstable, Gibbons, Tallis, Taverner, and Tye.

The *English Madrigal School* developed a secular musical language of excellent verse, one or two singers on a part, simplicity of texture, "fa-la-la" refrains (ballet), and lively dance rhythms. Composers included Bennett, Byrd, Dowland, Farmer, Gibbons, Morley, Weelkes, Wilbye, and Ravenscroft.

The *Italian Madrigal School* developed an art form based on counterpoint and equal voices; parts were often played on instruments. Composers included Arcadelt, Lasso, Gesualdo, Marenzio, and Monteverdi.

Style Elements

The Renaissance was a period of intense growth in the melodic characteristic of musical composition. The music was primarily linear, each part being equally important. The term *a cappella* is often associated with the Renaissance. Literally interpreted, it means "in the church style," and singing was not necessarily performed without accompaniment (except in the Sistine Chapel, where instruments were banned). The use of instruments or the organ to double voice parts was a familiar practice in the Renaissance. Common stylistic elements included the following:

MELODY.   Melodic style included conjunct, diatonic motion, a smooth contour, narrow range (often high tessitura), motivic repetition (points of imitation), and text painting (melodic figures represent certain declamations of the text, e.g., "sorrow" is painted in a descending melodic figure). Melismatic passages were also common, and instruments often doubled voices.

HARMONY.   Tertian harmony dominated, but the interval of the third often was omitted in final chords. Suspensions (dissonance) were prepared and resolved naturally. The emphasis was on linear or horizontal sonorities. The bass voice was added to the choral ensemble around 1450, resulting in four equal voices.

TONALITY.   The church modes were employed, with major and minor used more at the end of the era. The "Picardy third" was a common device whereby a composition in minor ended on a tonic major chord.

RHYTHM. The rhythm, even and nonmetrical, has been characterized as "freedom from the bar line." The basic pulse was often the half note.

TEXTURE. Polyphonic texture dominated, with occasional passages in homophonic style ("familiar" writing). Polychoral and antiphonal writing were practiced at St. Mark's in Venice.

TIMBRE. Church choirs were typically small and comprised men and boys. The sound was balanced and rather light, with little vibrato. Secular ensembles employed one or two voices on a part.

DYNAMICS. Loud and soft were limited, *mp* to *mf*, and were unmarked before 1597, when Giovanni Gabrieli first used *p* to indicate *solo* and *f* to indicate *tutti*. Subtle contrasts were indicated by the rise and fall of the vocal lines. Agogic accents (longer notes) received the most weight, and tonic accent was important in well-written compositions.

TEMPO. Tempos were generally not marked (metronome markings are editorial). Each tempo was dictated by the text and the time signature (the "proportional" sign), which signified *tempus* (time, each measure divided into two or three beats), and *prolationis* (prolation, the division of the beat into two or three subdivisions). In general, the *tactus* (beat) was the half note and moved between forty-eight and eighty beats per minute, depending upon the clarity of the fastest notes and the use of ornamentation (the more ornamented the slower the tempo). Sacred music of the Renaissance was generally slow. When the basic metric pattern moved from two to three beats per measure, however, the indication was to conduct three notes in the new section in the space of two in the previous section, which caused the music to move faster in the triple section.

TEXT. There was much textual repetition in sacred music. Therefore, the text often was obscured in polyphonic writing. Sacred texts (most from Holy Scripture) were devout, worshipful, and universal. Secular texts were often frivolous and mostly based on love or pastoral themes.

FORM. The common sacred forms were mass, motet, canticle, *piae cantiones* (sacred songs), anthem, and hymn (chorale). Common secular forms were madrigal, chanson, ballata, canzonetta, lied, and freemen's songs.

Sources for Further Study

For those wishing to explore in-depth sources on Renaissance performance practice, the following are cited fully in the reference section at the end of the chapter: Beckmann-Collier, 1988; Brown and Sadie, 1990; Brown and Stein, 1999; Dorian, 1981; Fenlon, 1990; Haberlen, 1972; Kite-Powell, 1989.

BAROQUE ERA (c. 1600–1750)

The term "Baroque" originated from the Portuguese word *barocca*, which indicated an irregularly shaped pearl. It was adopted by later generations as a way of making fun of Baroque art, which came to be considered exaggerated and in poor taste. Characteristics of Baroque music, later ridiculed, included its highly ornamented nature (trills, appoggiaturas, etc.), virtuosity, dramatic nature, and specific musical expressiveness (known as the "doctrine of affections"). The Baroque love of decoration flowed through the period's painting, sculpture, and architecture, as well as its music. The names of Bach and Handel are synonymous with Baroque music.

The music of the Baroque era represented a radical shift from that of the Renaissance. While the music of the earlier period was predominantly vocal and choral, instrumental music now came to rival the voice because of advancements in instrument development, and because the courts of the nobility and royalty demanded secular entertainments. The length of compositions also was extended in the Baroque, and multimovement forms became common. A cappella music quickly faded as instruments were used to accompany and play independently. The era also saw the beginning of a new form—opera.

Schools of Composition

The following schools and composers are representative of Baroque music:

The *German School* developed the *concertato* style, which contrasted voices with instruments. Composers included J. S. Bach, Buxtehude, Hammerschmidt, Handel, Pachelbel, Praetorius, Schütz, and Telemann.

The *Italian School*, centered around the Vatican in Rome, originated the oratorio. Composers included Carissimi, Lotti, Marcello, Monteverdi, Pergolesi, Pitoni, A. Scarlatti, and Vivaldi.

The *English School*, which included the last of the great English composers until the twentieth century, continued to develop church and cathedral music and opera. Composers were Blow, Handel (who became an English citizen), and Purcell.

The *French School*, centered in Paris and Versailles, the palace of Louis XIV, developed opera, in which the chorus played a major role. Composers included Charpentier and Lully.

Style Elements

The common stylistic elements of choral music in the Baroque were as follows:

MELODY.   Melismatic passages became common, as did melodic leaps and chromatic pitches. Melodies were greatly ornamented, and included those both written and improvised by soloists. Ranges were moderately wide and often exceeded the octave.

HARMONY.   Whereas the Renaissance focused on the melody, the Baroque focused on the harmony and its functional nature (tertian, with some seventh chords, augmented sixths, etc.). Modulations were common (circle of fifths), as were sequences.

TONALITY.   The establishment of the major-minor system was confirmed. Standard pitch level was about a half step lower than that of today. For minor tonality, melodic minor was used when the melody was the main consideration, and harmonic minor was employed when vertical harmony was the main consideration.

RHYTHM.   The "tyranny of the bar line" was common as consistent metrical organization dominated. Characteristic was an unflagging rhythm (*fortspinnung*) that moved forward with constancy and even tempo. Dotted rhythms were common but were not played strictly as written. The French style increased the length of the dotted note and shortened the complimentary note. In the Italian style, dotted notes conformed to the basic "swing" of the music; that is, if the underlying feeling was in triplets, dotted notes took on the triplet characteristic of long-short, as in "Jesu Joy of Man's Desiring" by J. S. Bach. For an in-depth but concise discussion of this topic, see *The Choral Experience* (Robinson and Winold, 1992, pp. 381–88).

TEXTURE.   Homophonic texture became extensively used, as well as a more fluid type of polyphonic writing. This newer form of polyphony was highly imitative and fugal in nature. Monody (solo with homophonic accompaniment) also was introduced in the early Baroque period by composers such as Monteverdi.

TIMBRE.   Vocals works were generally accompanied by instruments. Larger works contained *ritornello* sections for instruments alone; the *basso continuo* provided the harmonic support with a chordal keyboard part (usually harpsichord or organ) and lower string instruments doubling the bass line (usually cello). The composer rarely wrote out the continuo parts but employed a shorthand technique known as *figured bass*. Choirs became slightly larger in the Baroque, with sixteen to twenty singers being common, and continued to comprise only men and boys. Instrumental compositions often used contrasting effects between a small group of instruments (*concertino*) and a full group (*ripieno*). This form of writing became known as the *concertato* or concerted (contrasting) style, which became the forerunner of the concerto in the Classical period.

DYNAMICS.   "Terraced" dynamics resulted in blocks of contrasting louds and softs. The use of *crescendo* and *decrescendo* was not common except as *messa di voce* for long notes. Varying stages of loudness over long phrases were indicated by use of dynamic terms in sequence (i.e., *pianissimo, piano, forte, fortissimo*).

TEMPO.   The "doctrine of affections" indicated one mood (tempo) per movement or section. Contrast was achieved between sections or movements and not within. Tempos were deliberate and steady with little variation. They are believed to have been faster than contemporary interpretations of tempo terminology.

TEXT.   *Musica poetica* emphasized expression and emotion, which was accomplished through text (word) painting. Sacred music incorporated religious writing and poetry as well as continued use of scripture.

FORM.   Single-movement forms included the motet, anthem, and chorale. Multimovement sacred forms were the mass, cantata, oratorio, passion, and Magnificat. Secular forms included opera, solo song, and madrigal.

Sources for Further Study

For those wishing to explore in-depth sources on Baroque performance practice, the following are cited fully in the reference section at the end of the chapter: Brown and Sadie, 1989; Dart, 1963; Donington, 1982; Mann, 1992; and Neumann, 1978, 1993).

CLASSICAL ERA (c. 1750–1825)

The Classical era in music was one of grace and elegance. Formality was at its core and was reflected in the mannerisms of royal courts and nobility. The highly decorative Baroque manner was abandoned for a simpler style of musical writing. This style, first known as the *stile galant,* evolved into more intricate forms such as *sonata allegro*, which gave birth to the Classical symphony. Austria and Germany were the centers where instrumental music came to dominate. Composers moved from working under the patronage system (Haydn), to defying the system (Mozart), and finally to breaking loose as independent musicians (Beethoven). Choral music continued its importance in the sacred rites of the church, but instrumental music and opera advanced greatly as concerts for the public were made available. Continued improvements in music printing made the dissemination of composers' works easier, and a wider audience developed for art music. The age of the public concert took root in this era.

One place where the Classical giants' music traveled was to a small group of Moravians, a religious sect who traveled to and settled in the areas of Bethlehem, Pennsylvania, and Winston-Salem, North Carolina. Most American colonists had little schooling, and art music events were rare. The Moravians, however, were a well educated group who brought string and wind instruments with them to the New World. Choral music was central to their form of worship, but they also cultivated the use of strings and winds. Children were expected to learn an instrument and read music. Some of the earliest renditions of Beethoven's symphonies were given by the Moravians in the new colonies.

Schools of Composition

One major school of composition dominated the Classical era—the Viennese. It and other minor schools were as follows:

The *Viennese School* developed the symphony to great heights and also contributed masses, motets, oratorios, and part-songs. Composers included L. van Beethoven, F. J. Haydn, and W. A. Mozart.

The *Italian School*, centered in Rome, continued to write liturgical music for the Roman rite. Composers included Boccherini, Cherubini, Gasparini, and Zingarelli.

The *English School*, centered in London, continued development of the sacred anthem form. Composers included Attwood, Callcott, and Wesley.

The *Early American School*, centered in the New England colonies, developed the "fuguing tune," a simple contrapuntal form for voices. Composers included Billings, Hopkinson, Ingalls, Law, Morgan, and Read.

The *Moravian School*, centered in Pennsylvania and North Carolina, developed no new forms of music but composed anthems and imported European works. Composers included Antes, Geisler, Gregor, and Herbst.

Style Elements

The common stylistic elements of choral music in the Classical era were as follows:

MELODY.   The structure of the melody was often motivic, characterized by short melodic fragments and little embellishment. Melodies were typically scalewise, with occasional chromatic notes, and often melismatic. Lyricism and smooth contours dominated the melodic outline.

HARMONY. A simple, functional harmonic vocabulary was employed, with use of seventh chords and secondary dominants. Organized key relationships were formal and predictable between movements. Continuo writing was abandoned for full part writing except in some sacred choral music.

TONALITY. A strong and conservative tonal system of major and minor was employed. Key changes often were expressed only by accidentals in the parts.

RHYTHM. Music was metrically conceived and moved by the bar rather than by the beat. Simple and constant rhythm patterns were clearly marked with strong cadences and a certain liveliness. Silence (notated rests) became an important part of the rhythmic structure. The standard appoggiatura was performed as a long-short figure.

TEXTURE. Both homophony and polyphony were used individually and in combination. Grand fugues and double fugues were written in polyphonic texture.

TIMBRE. Choral forces became larger and sometimes were very large. A richer orchestral sound developed as instruments improved in quality. An orchestra of eighteen to twenty strings and winds in pairs was common. The following adjectives are generally characteristic of Classical sound: crystalline, bright, polished, clear, easy, crisp, and elegant.

DYNAMICS. Intensity levels were regularly marked with dynamic markings, and *crescendo* and *decrescendo* markings were gradually developed. Dynamic contrasts were employed within movements as well as various dynamic accents.

TEMPO. Classical tempos were generally moderate, and extremes were avoided, although a wide range of tempos was employed, including *tempo rubato* (used with discretion) and occasional changes of tempo within movements. Beethoven was the first composer to use metronome markings (the metronome being invented by Mäzel).

TEXT. Literary sources were used as well as that of the Holy Scriptures. Words showed emotional restraint and were rather objective. Text painting continued to be employed.

FORM. The formal structure of Classical music was in evidence through great symmetry (ABA) and balance between repetition and contrast. Phrase structure was mostly regular and cadences well defined. The opera chorus was more effectively used than in the Baroque as opera became more realistic. Larger choral forms included oratorio, cantata, mass, Te Deum, Magnificat, Stabat Mater, and vespers. Smaller works included offertories, motets, antiphons, and part-songs.

Sources for Further Study

For those wishing to explore in-depth sources on Classical performance practice, the following are cited fully in the reference section at the end of the chapter: Brown and Sadie, 1990; Larsen, 1988; Neumann, 1989; and O'Neal, 1991.

ROMANTIC ERA (c. 1825–1900)

The restraint and objectivity of the Classical era dissolved into overt emotion and great sub-jectivity in the Romantic era. This movement began with the literature of the eighteenth cen-tury, particularly with such writers as Rousseau and Goethe, and climaxed in the works of the late Romantic composers such as Brahms, Wagner, and Strauss. These composers wrote to communicate depth of emotion, and formal design became less important as musical com-position spilled over its boundaries. Choruses grew very large, and orchestras expanded to include families of instruments: strings, woodwinds, brass, and percussion. Orchestral color was enhanced as composers wrote for these families and individual solo instruments. Opera took on enormous proportions, and opera choruses became operatic in nature with full-throated, soloistic singing. Nationalism took on great importance as schools of composition reflected nationalistic flavor.

It was in the nineteenth century that the conductor, as we know the role today, became a standard part of the music ensemble. Public audiences for music concerts were filled with middle-class citizens who came to view the conductor as a celebrity. Artists, in general, now had the option of making a living at their art, and many chose to do so. The Romantic era made the world of music making a public arena; the concert hall took the place of the church for many composers, singers, players, and conductors. Great choral works such as the *Deutsches Requiem* of Brahms were composed not for a religious service but for a concert-going audience. Choral music transcended the chapel, the church, the drawing room, and the palace to assume a new life in the role of the public concert hall.

Schools of Composition

The numerous schools of choral composition active in the nineteenth century included the following:

The *German School*, centered in Bayreuth, Berlin, Dresden, Frankfurt, Hamburg, Leipzig, and Munich, adopted new instruments to the orchestra and colorful orchestrations, organized singing societies, and created music dramas (Wagnerian opera). Important composers included Brahms, Mendelssohn, Schumann, and Wagner.

The *Italian School*, centered in Milan, Rome, and Turin, developed *verismo* (realistic) opera in which realism was emphasized. Large-scale choral works for chorus and orchestra also were important. Prominent composers included Bellini, Donizetti, Puccini, Rossini, and Verdi.

The *Austrian School*, centered in Vienna, placed great emphasis on solo singing (art song) and smaller choral works, while continuing to set larger forms such as the mass. Composers included Bruckner, Schubert, Strauss, and Wolf.

The *French School*, centered in Paris, developed everything from huge spectacles (Berlioz) to smaller church works. Prominent composers included Adam, Berlioz, Dubois, Fauré, Gounod, Offenbach, and Saint-Saëns. The later *Impressionist School* added further to the dissolving of functional harmonic writing; prominent composers included Debussy and Ravel.

The *Russian School*, centered in Moscow and St. Petersburg, concentrated on sacred mu-sic for the liturgy, larger works for chorus and orchestra, and opera. Composers included Bort-niansky, Gretchaninov, Ippolitov-Ivanov, Kopylov, Leontovich, Mussorgsky, Rachmaninoff, Tchaikovsky, and Tschesnokov.

The *English School*, centered in London, Cambridge, and Oxford, concentrated on cathe-dral music, glees, part-songs, and some larger works for chorus and orchestra. Gilbert and

Sullivan operettas were extremely popular. Composers included de Pearsall, Elgar, Gaul, Noble, Stainer, Sullivan, and S. S. Wesley.

The *Czech-Hungarian School*, centered in Prague and Brno, composed large works for chorus and orchestra. Composers included Dvořák and Janáček.

The *American School*, centered in Boston, Philadelphia, and New York, wrote smaller choral works, folk songs, spirituals, and oratorios. Composers included Beach, Burleigh, Buck, De Koven, Foster, MacDowell, Mason, and Parker.

Style Elements

The common stylistic elements of choral music in the Romantic era were as follows:

MELODY.   Melodic variation, from flowing and smooth to fragmented and irregular, was dictated by personal feeling, with dynamic peaks and changes. Melodies tended to grow out of harmonic progressions, becoming less independent than previously.

HARMONY.   Romantic composers made great use of chromaticism, nonharmonic tones, altered chords, and ninth and thirteenth chords to build harmonic tension. Strong, formal cadences were usually avoided in favor of deceptive cadences used to give a sense of tension and movement. Modal harmonies for folk songs, especially those of nationalistic origin, served to open new avenues of harmonic expressivity.

TONALITY.   Major-minor tonality continued, but a weaker sense of key center developed, leading to a gradual disintegration of the major-minor system. Tonality was further weakened by the fusion of major and minor modes, using chords typical of one mode in the other. Key relationships became less formalized, with modulations to distant keys; sudden moving in and out of key for short periods of time added to the weakening of a strong feeling for a particular key.

RHYTHM.   In the early Romantic period, rhythm remained much as it had in the Classical period. By the middle of the nineteenth century, rhythm came to be more irregular and more interesting, with changes in meter, cross-rhythms, and syncopations. Later, rhythm was often complex and rhapsodic, sometimes avoiding strong stresses to increase the sense of tension, especially in slower movements.

TEXTURE.   The texture was largely homophonic, with a mixture of vertical and horizontal elements. Polyphonic texture became more of a device than a style. Thick textures often resulted in divided choral parts.

TIMBRE.   Choruses and orchestras were often large, producing a big sound and much drama. Choral singing was more soloistic, operatic, fuller, and heavy, emphasizing the bass voice. Small choral ensembles also existed, mostly of amateurs, who gathered together in homes to sing part-songs. This singing was lighter and more folklike.

DYNAMICS.   A full range of intensity was explored from *ppp* to *fff*. Wide changes were frequent, with subtle shadings and minute gradations. Many accents added to the dynamic tension.

TEMPO.   Metronome markings were used extensively. Wide variations were employed in tempos, from *largo* to *presto*. There was much use of *tempo rubato*.

TEXT. Composers used outstanding literature and poetry as texts for choral music. These were often highly emotional and sensitive, adding to the musical tension. Folklore also was used as a textual source, especially in opera.

FORM. Formal structure was often unclear. Sections of works would overlap without strong cadences and lacked symmetry. Contrasting theme groups were employed, but sometimes only motives were pitted against each other. Larger choral forms included cantata, oratorio, mass, Te Deum, and choral symphony. Smaller forms were part-song, motet, opera chorus, sacred piece, and anthem.

Sources for Further Study

For those wishing to explore in-depth sources on Romantic performance practice, the following are cited fully in the reference section at the end of the chapter: Delisi, 1991; Moerk, 1974; Sadie, 1986; and Young, 1962.

CONTEMPORARY ERA (c. 1900–PRESENT)

Art music in the twentieth century continued the dissolution of traditional compositional practice begun in the nineteenth century. Serial techniques replaced tonality with atonality. Melody was often fractured into small, disjunct units, and rhythm at times became intense and powerfully dominant. Forms were anything from the miniature to the huge, and techniques such as minimalism used constant and varying repetition as a unifying device. Electronic instruments were explored, and composers used prerecorded tapes in addition to live music making. In short, the contemporary era moved in many directions, throwing off the old and experimenting with the new, with no one style representing a new mainstream. Many composers wrote in a rather eclectic style, sampling various new compositional techniques without totally abandoning the past.

Choral singing advanced somewhat in the twentieth century, although early pointillistic works by Webern are unheard today and compositions like *Friede auf Erden* of Schoenberg are too difficult for most choirs. The choral art remains that of the amateur, and most composers who want their music performed compose in some form of tonal structure that is comfortable for amateur singers. This is not to say that great choral music has not been composed in the contemporary era. Benjamin Britten's *War Requiem* is a notable example. But even Britten's work, while rhythmically challenging, is accessible to most adult choral singers.

The choral world depends greatly upon the past and its rich heritage of choral literature for the bulk of its repertoire. Non-Western music has made inroads, but the canon of great choral singing continues to be from composers of the Renaissance, Baroque, Classical, and Romantic periods. Nevertheless, conductors today need to be responsible for programming contemporary music that stretches their singers and challenges traditional views of the choral art. Who knows when the next Bach or Mozart may appear? A new and great composer will emerge only when his or her music is given the opportunity to be heard. And learning to understand the language of contemporary composers often takes time. The profession must be willing to experiment if it is to move forward in the twenty-first century with vision and hope.

Schools of Composition

A number of schools of composition developed early in the twentieth century and are outlined as follows:

The *Expressionist School*, centered in Germany in the first half of the twentieth century, appeared as a reaction to French Impressionism. Expressionist music was characterized by great intensity, much use of dissonance, angular melodic fragments, varying tempos, and complex rhythms. The expression of the inner self in concrete forms was central. Composers included Berg, Krenek, Schoenberg, and Webern.

The *Neo-Classical School*, which appeared worldwide after World War I, returned to the eighteenth-century ideal of formal balance and craftsmanship rather than emotional expression, which became a secondary factor. Composers included Britten, Fine, Foss, Hindemith, Milhaud, Persichetti, Poulenc, Schuman, and Stravinsky.

The *Neo-Romantic School*, which appeared worldwide after World War II, returned to the nineteenth-century style of rich sonorities, tonality, and subjective writing. Composers included Barber, Bernstein, Creston, Dello Joio, Hanson, Menotti, Orff, Rutter, and Toch.

Various *National Schools*, appeared worldwide and made use of folk music. Composers included Bloch, Chávez, Copland, Holst, Hovhaness, Ives, Kodály, Thompson, Vaughan Williams, and Villa-Lobos.

The *Avant-Garde School* developed nontraditional means of composing such as speaking on pitch (*Sprechstimme*), inclusion of environmental sounds, body sounds (e.g., tongue clicking), nonsynchronized speech sounds, electronic tape, computer-generated sound, improvisation, and so on. Composers included Cage, Felciano, Gaburo, Glass, Hennagin, Jenni, and Stockhausen,

The *Eclectic School* combined techniques from a number of past schools, resulting in no one particular style. Numerous choral composers wrote and continue to write in this manner.

Style Elements

The following elements were generally characteristic of twentieth-century music, although styles varied greatly:

MELODY.   Some composers continued to use traditional melodic structures, but others departed radically, with instrumentally conceived melodies of jagged contour, wide ranges and skips, and irregular phrasing. Contours expressive of the text were used even to the extent of losing specific tonal designation, as in the technique of *Sprechstimme* (speaking on pitch).

HARMONY.   Traditional harmony continued, albeit with freer use of dissonance, but some composers increased dissonance greatly. Nonfunctional chordal progressions were freely used.

TONALITY.   Traditional tonality continued, but polytonality and atonality also evolved. There was renewed interest in modes and an exploration of whole-tone scales and nontraditional scale patterns.

RHYTHM.   In addition to traditional rhythms, mixed meters, asymmetry, polyrhythms, syncopation, and cross-accents were employed. Intense rhythm dominated some compositions.

TEXTURE.   Polyphony returned and was equal to homophony. Twelve-tone and serial composers exploited a thin, almost ephemeral, contrapuntal texture in which notated silence tended to play as important a part as the notated sounds. Neo-Romantic composers used a rather thick and heavy sound—full, rich, and chordal.

DYNAMICS. Extreme contrasts were used with great variety. Indications were very explicit. Much use was made of accents.

TEMPO. Extreme contrasts and freedom were employed with great variety. Nontraditional means of timing by seconds rather than meter were explored. Tempo indications were very explicit.

FORM. The tendency was toward brevity in all elements. Compositions were tightly organized but not often symmetrical. Renewed interest was shown in Classical and Baroque forms such as the mass, cantata, oratorio, and anthem.

Sources for Further Study

The following sources are given for those who wish to explore practices in contemporary music to greater depth: Brown and Sadie, 1989; Clark, 1975; Folstrom, 1974; Hansen, 1967; Moe, 1988; Lang, 1977; Salzman, 1988; Sanders, 1970; and White, 1982.

STUDY AND DISCUSSION QUESTIONS

1. Why is a knowledge of historical performance practices important for the choral conductor today?

2. What are the approximate dates for each of the major eras of choral composition?

3. Where was music making centered in Medieval Europe, and what famous cathedral was most important?

4. How did the Ars Antiqua, Ars Nova, and Bergundian School differ musically?

5. What is the overall performance style of Medieval music, and how appropriate is this style of singing for high school singers? Explain your answer.

6. Why is the year 1450 often designated as the beginning of the Renaissance?

7. What type of musical composition did the Venetian school become famous for in the Renaissance? Where did this take place? Who were the most famous composers of this style of music making, and how were they related?

8. Of all the style elements given for the Renaissance, which one most characterized sacred music of the period?

9. What was the compositional device known as the "Picardy third"?

10. What were the main compositional differences between Baroque and Renaissance music?

11. Which school of composition dominated the Baroque era? Who were the major composers?

12. What do the following expressions mean? *fortspinnung*, terraced dynamics, doctrine of affections, *musica poetica*, *basso continuo*, melismatic, tyranny of the bar line, monody, *concertato* style.

13. What was music like in the American colonies, and how did it differ from that found among the Moravians?

14. Which school of composition dominated the Classical era, and who were its major composers?

15. What was the dominant style characteristic of Classical music, and in what major musical form was this clearly manifested?

16. What were the sizes of the chorus and orchestra in the Classical period?

17. How were harmony and tonality handled by composers of the Romantic era?

18. In what ways has contemporary choral music advanced the choral art?

19. What responsibility does the contemporary choral conductor have to program contemporary music?

20. Why is Stravinsky considered a Neo-Classical composer?

REFERENCES

Beckmann-Collier, A. (1988). Performance practices of sacred polyphony in Rome and Madrid at the time of Tomás Luis de Victoria, *Choral Journal, 28*(7), 13–20.

Brown, H. M., and S. Sadie (eds.) (1989). *Performance practice: Music after 1600.* New York: Norton.

———— (1990). *Performance practice: Music before 1600.* New York: Norton.

Brown, H. M., and L. K. Stein (1999). *Music in the renaissance* (2d ed.). Upper Saddle River, NJ: Prentice Hall.

Clark, W. J. (1975). Problems in contemporary choral music. *Journal of Church Music, 17*(7), 11–14.

Dart, T. (1963). *The interpretation of music.* New York: Harper and Row.

Delisi, D. (1991). Mendelssohn's *Elijah*: Dramatic and musical structure, possible cuts and excerpts. *Choral Journal, 31*(10), 27–32.

Demaree, R. W., and D. V Moses (1995). *The complete conductor.* Upper Saddle River, NJ: Prentice Hall.

Donington, R. (1963). *The interpretation of early music.* London: Faber and Faber.

———— (1982). *Baroque music: Style and performance.* New York: Norton.

Dorian, F. (1981). *The history of music in performance: The art of musical interpretation from the Renaissance to our day.* Westport, CT: Greenwood Press.

Fenlon, I. (1990). *The Renaissance.* Upper Saddle River, NJ: Prentice Hall.

Folstrom, R. (1974). The choral warmup: A look at avante-garde music. *Choral Journal, 14*(8), 22–23.

Garretson, R. L. (1993). *Choral music: History, style, and performance practice.* Upper Saddle River, NJ: Prentice Hall.

Haberlen, J. B. (1972). Microrhythms: The key to vitalizing Renaissance music. *Choral Journal, 8*(3), 11–14.

Hansen, P. (1967). *An introduction to twentieth century music* (2d ed.). Boston: Allyn and Bacon.

Hoppin, R. H. (1978). *Medieval music.* New York: Norton.

Kite-Powell, J. T. (ed.). (1989). *A practical guide to historical performance practice: The Renaissance.* New York: Early Music Press.

Lang, P. H. (1977). Choral music in the twentieth century. *American Choral Review, 19*(2), 7–18.

Larsen, J. P. (1988). *Handel, Haydn, and the Viennese Classical style.* Trans. Ulrich Kramer. Ann Arbor, MI: UMI Research Press.

Mann, A. (1992). *Bach and Handel: Choral performance practice.* Chapel Hill, NC: Hinshaw Music.

Moe, D. (1988). The choral conductor and twentieth-century choral music. In H. A. Decker and J. Herford (eds.), *Choral conducting symposium* (2d ed.). Englewood Cliffs, NJ: Prentice Hall.

Moerk, A. A. (1974). The musicologist looks at style in the interpretation of choral music. *Choral Journal, 25*(1), 5–11.

Neumann, F. (1978). *Ornamentation in Baroque and post-Baroque music with special emphasis on J. S. Bach.* Princeton, N.J.: Princeton University Press.

—— (1989). *New essays on performance practice*. Ann Arbor, MI: UMI Research Press.

—— (1993). *Performance practices of the seventeenth and eighteenth centuries*. New York: Schirmer Books.

O'Neal, M. (1991). An introduction to performance practice considerations for the Mozart Requiem. *Choral Journal, 31*(9), 46–56.

Reese, G. (1940). *Music in the Middle Ages*. New York: Norton.

Robinson, R., and A. Winold (1976). *The choral experience: Literature, materials, and methods*. New York: Harper and Row.

Sadie, S. (1991). *Music guide: An introduction*. Upper Saddle River, NJ: Prentice Hall.

Salzman, E. (1988). *Twentieth century music: An introduction* (3d ed.). Upper Saddle River, NJ: Prentice Hall.

Sanders, H. (1970). Sprechstimme in choral music. *Choral Journal, 11*(2), 7–10.

Seay, A. (1965). *Music in the medieval world*. Upper Saddle River, NJ: Prentice Hall.

White, J. P. (1982). *Twentieth-century choral music: An annotated bibliography on music suitable for use by high school choirs*. Metuchen, NJ: Scarecrow Press.

19 | Presenting the Performance

All of the work involved in rehearsal preparation comes down to this—the concert. There would be few choirs without performances. Imagine a football team and no game. It is the performance that motivates the choir to disciplined action. The payoff from even a mediocre performance can be a heady experience. While much of a director's educational goals are met during the rehearsal phase, the concert works as a final exam, one in which the combined work of everyone in the performance results in the final grade. A choir is a totally cooperative effort—no one sits on the bench.

THE CONCERT PROGRAM

Putting a program together is an art, and it takes time to learn how. A good program should develop much like a drama: the audience's interest is focused with something interesting at the beginning (a processional, antiphonal event, special introduction, upbeat first selection, etc.), and then the music develops and builds to a climactic end. The audience leaves with a good feeling—wanting more, not looking at their watches. Robinson and Winold (1976) state:

> Many conductors build choral programs in a vacuum: they approach this responsibility from the standpoint of the ideal as opposed to the practical point of view. They will program one difficult work after another until they have exhausted the choir vocally. Or they will put together a program that is perfectly fine from a musical standpoint but one that wears out the audience. (p. 172)

Length of Program

How long should the school concert last? An hour and fifteen minutes to an hour and a half is all most school audiences can muster. A concert over an hour and forty-five minutes is often tiring, no matter how good it is. It is far better for a concert to be shorter and sung better than for it to be longer and sung poorly. Less time is better.

Should a concert have an intermission? School audiences often appreciate the break (when sitting for more than twenty minutes at a time in front of the television is taxing). If parents need to leave after their children have sung, an intermission is a good spot for this to happen. If there is more than one choir on the program, a break also provides time for the choirs in the second half to warm up and line up. The intermission should be kept to no more than fifteen minutes, and some type of signal (flashing lights, chime) is needed five minutes before the intermission ends. A program that lasts one hour and forty-five minutes, including a fifteen-minute intermission, should be considered a maximum length. A program of two hours or more is doomed. A program that lasts an hour or less does not require an intermission. On this matter of time, Roe (1983) states:

> There must be a consideration of the audience's endurance and span of attention. Most programs should not exceed one hour and fifteen minutes to one hour and a half. Be sure to include applause and entrances and exits in the program's total length. A program must not last longer than the audience can endure. It is a real compliment to a program when the audience leaves the auditorium audibly wishing the program had lasted longer. It is no compliment when the audience is heard to remark, "That was a fine program, but it was too long." (pp. 315–16)

Programming the Choirs

The concert should begin with something "up," and it should be good. First impressions are lasting impressions, and the audience wants to be glad that it has come. In classroom learning theory, Madeline Hunter calls this the "anticipatory set." It brings the audience to attention and focuses eyes and ears on the program. This may take the form of an energetic, upbeat number, or even an appropriate welcome from the principal. It is probably not the best time to do a slow Renaissance motet, unless the audience is musically sophisticated.

The weakest choir must not begin the program. It should probably come second in order. Opening with the best singers for even a couple of numbers begins the concert on a "high." This will whet the audience's appetite for more of this group later on. When the weakest (often the youngest) choir follows, they will be challenged, having heard good singing before their appearance. This often helps them to focus and try harder. Their portion of the program should be relatively short.

The time for the heaviest music comes at the third spot, or early in the program. This is when the concert choir presents its masterworks section. The audience is still relatively fresh and will tolerate music in foreign languages, especially if translations are provided. This section should last fifteen to twenty minutes. Most parents are in attendance to hear their own children sing, and many leave upon hearing that choir. After these first three groups (forty-five minutes or so), it may be a good time for an intermission.

Following the break is the place for another more general chorus, such as a ninth-grade mixed chorus or nonselect high school chorus. These groups should be good and the music not too demanding. The fifth slot can be filled by a special ensemble, such as a madrigal group, trio, solo, or octet. People like to hear talented students sing solos or perform in small groups, and this brings a certain variety to the program. Perhaps an all-state ensemble can sing a selection from their festival, or the chorus and soloists from a recent Broadway musical production can be featured performing a medley from the show.

The final section of the program should be mostly spirited and uplifting. It may consist of combined choirs, or include instrumentalists as accompanists. Singalongs with audience participation are a good way to end. Patriotic numbers or spirituals are perennial favorites with which to close concerts. Unless the audience really knows music, the final selection of the program will determine whether or not they want to keep coming back. At this point, the conductor becomes part educator and part entertainer. Educating and entertaining the audience go hand in hand.

Being aware of the audience for whom the performance is to be given is extremely important and should help guide the music being programmed (see Chapter 9):

> Knowledge of the audience is perhaps the most important element in program building. Many choral concerts have turned out to be utter fiascoes because the conductor failed

to consider the nature of the audience. The conductor who presents a full program of sixteenth- and seventeenth-century Italian and German music for a concert of teenagers in a Romanian youth hostel is doomed to failure. A collection of American spirituals, nineteenth-century Brahms folksongs, or sixteenth-century English and Italian madrigals would be much more effective if sung with expression and vitality. (Robinson and Winold, 1976, p. 172)

There are many variations to orchestrating the program layout. In general, the program wants to begin strong, then move quickly through the weakest groups, followed by the heaviest music. Subsequent music should be lighter but excellent and move to a peak at the end. The choosing of music for the school term is governed greatly by the need for the final concert program to be well structured.

Music placement within each of the choir sections also needs to be thought through; juxtaposing a silly song next to a serious sacred piece is not a good idea. Each section should have both unity and enough variety to provide contrast. Too much contrast, however, ruins the effect of coherence.

The Printed Program

Most concerts have some form of written program that audience members receive upon entering the concert hall. The program helps the audience follow the order of the performance and can provide additional information, such as dates of forthcoming concerts. The program also serves as a souvenir of the event and marks the time, place, and music presented for historical reference. Many students save their programs in scrapbooks and keep them for a lifetime.

QUALITY AND SIZE OF THE PROGRAM. The quality of the printed program and the number of pages vary widely. Some programs are little more than a single sheet of paper containing just the basics; others are multipage folders with textured paper for the cover. Time, talent, and budget usually decide how simple or elaborate the program will be.

Desktop publishing has made the production of a program rather easy. Different fonts and sizes provide a variety of scripts, and the inclusion of pictures and symbols (e.g., clefs, notes, etc.) is possible through the use of scanners and clip art. Color printing can make for an attractive appearance.

THE COVER. If a cover is used on the program, it should be appealing to the eye. It need not be multicolored, but something other than white is typical. If the concert has a theme, a good place to display it is on the program cover. Some types of commercial covers (e.g., church bulletins) have artwork on the front already. Detailed information regarding the concert need not appear until the beginning of the inside pages. If the cover is the front of one folded sheet of paper, then the concert particulars need to appear on the cover. In either case, the information usually contains the following:

- Name of the organization (school, church, community chorus, etc.)
- Name(s) of the choir(s) performing (if different from name of the organization)
- Theme (if any, e.g., Thirtieth Anniversary Gala Concert)
- Name of conductor (with no titles indicated, such as Ms., Mrs., Mr., Dr.)
- Name of accompanist(s) (optional, can also be placed inside)

- Date and time
- Place (city included when not apparent)

ORDER OF THE PROGRAM.   The program itself begins on a new page, and the word PROGRAM often appears centered at the beginning. The music is listed by groupings or by choirs. Roman numerals often are used to separate these sections of the program, and if there is more than one choir singing, the name of the choir can be placed under the numeral. The music selections are then listed in order on the left margin, and the composers on a right, justified margin. Caution should always be taken to include the correct spellings of titles and composers. Sometimes only the last name of each composer is given, and at other times the full first and last names are given. Also seen are the use of initials, such as "J. S. Bach" and "G. F. Handel." This is at the discretion of the choral director. Dates of birth and death are frequently listed in parentheses below the composers' names. When a selection is an arrangement, the composer is given first, followed by the arranger, with "arr." preceding the latter. The same is true when an editor's name is given ("ed."), although the names of editors are frequently omitted from the program.

Selections sometimes are grouped by theme within sections. For example, all of the sacred pieces might appear together, followed by the secular. In this case, the works with a common quality might be single spaced, indicating a commonality. Choruses in a foreign language often have the translation placed directly under the title and indented. If the translation is a long one, or of multiple movements, the translation can appear later in the program. The names of soloists appear directly under the pieces containing solos. Names of major soloists for an entire work often appear on the front of the program. When a chorus has multiple movements, the names of those parts are listed directly under the main title and indented. This should signal the audience to hold applause until the end of the entire grouping.

EDUCATING THE AUDIENCE.   When a number of short choruses are presented within one section of the concert, the audience can become worn out from so much applauding. Frequently interjected applause also breaks the continuity of the concert. In this case, the following directive can be printed in the program following the last group: *"The audience is requested to refrain from any response until the completion of each section of the program marked by a numeral."* The director also can ask the audience not to applaud until the end of an entire multisection work if they suspect that the audience will respond following each part. A little education of the audience can greatly improve audience deportment.

Additionally, pictures taken with flashes during a concert are annoying and can cause performers to stumble or become distracted. Again, a simple directive in the program will help curb this practice: *"The taking of flash pictures is disturbing to performers and not permitted while the choirs are singing."*

Finally, audience members frequently go and come while choirs are singing. This is rude behavior, and most do not realize how distracting such travel becomes during the program. Parents taking kids to the bathroom need to tell their children to go before the concert begins or to hold it. This next directive has been found helpful in cutting down unnecessary traffic: *"The audience is requested not to enter nor leave the auditorium except between sections of the program when the lights are raised. Thank you."*

It is a shame to have to write such admonishments in concert programs, but school audiences often have poor deportment (e.g., the parents who do not take a crying child out of the performance venue), and the preceding short statements are courteous, to the point, and improve the performance environment significantly.

ACKNOWLEDGMENTS.   When space permits in the program, it is a good idea to acknowledge those people who assisted in bringing the concert to fruition. Such persons include administrators, custodians, ushers, publicity personnel, program arrangers, photographers, ticket handlers, and so forth. It is also proper to thank the news media—TV, radio stations, and newspapers that have provided free announcements. Some directors acknowledge the school's administration separately, and the entire music area staff is listed together. People can never be acknowledged enough for their help and cooperation.

GREETINGS.   Blank pages are a waste in a program. Such space provides the director the opportunity to greet the audience and to reflect upon the goals and objectives of the choral music program. Consider the following:

> *Good evening. We are glad to have you with us tonight. Our concert brings to a close a busy year for the music department. In counting we find that some or all of our students have participated in over thirty parades, concerts, and other musical events this year. That is a lot of music making! And when you count the hours of preparation for each performance, you realize the vast amount of energy consumed in what we hope you find a worthy pursuit. For it is through your continued support that our hard work finds fulfillment. Although it is our main goal as music educators to educate students in terms of a wide variety of music, the performance provides the students with the final test of their classroom experience. It can be compared to the final exam in a regular academic course, except that here all students are working toward a common goal—the best possible concert.*

> *One role of the music educator is to help students learn to make discriminating choices. We are in an age of environmental pollution and sound pollution. Music of all types bombards us continually, whether we desire it or not. And like all things that become commonplace, we begin to lose our ability to discriminate between the poor, the mediocre, the good, and the great. It is along these lines that we hope to educate the student, not so much to tell them what music they should like, but rather to give them guidelines by which to arrive at informed decision making.*

> *We hope you will continue to support music in your school, not as a "frill" but as a vital part of the children's lives. Many will never have another opportunity once they pass through our doors, and they will pass on to their children only what they have learned. What music heritage will we leave to them?*

ANNOUNCEMENTS OF FUTURE EVENTS.   Another section of the program can feature announcements of future school events. This may be for the entire music area, for all of the arts, or for school events in general. Other faculty appreciate having their events publicized in the concert program. It is a good way in which to build bridges among curricular and noncurricular areas.

CHOIR PERSONNEL.   If space permits, the names of students by choir should be listed in the program. It helps if these names are in alphabetical order, or by section. Students' names should be proofread closely. People in general do not like to have their names misspelled. Besides, it's a mark of shoddy preparation when misspellings of any kind appear in the concert program.

PROGRAM NOTES.   A program that is large enough can contain informative notes about the music in the concert. This is not the place for overly detailed information. Instead, the notes should help the listener to grasp the salient points that will help them to appreciate the music more fully.

Dr. Alfred Mann, professor emeritus of the Eastman School of Music, has provided the accompanying program notes for Handel's *Messiah*. He has given permission to any and all choral directors who care to use these notes when performing *Messiah* to do so with the proper credit included; the wording of the credit should read: "From *Directing the Choral Music Program* by Kenneth H. Phillips, and used by permission of Alfred Mann and Oxford University Press, copyright © 2004."

PROGRAM NOTES
Messiah — G. F. Handel

Handel's *Messiah* holds an extraordinary place, both among the composer's works and in the history of Western music. No other work has met with the same wide and enduring response. It also holds an extraordinary place in the history of performance: it is the only work of its time that has seen a continuous sequence of revivals—for almost two decades under the direction of the composer, for two further decades under conductors who had shared Handel's work on the London scene, for the following two centuries through the devotion of generation after generation—and our warm wishes accompany today's performance for which these notes were written.

For a long time, and until quite recently, the work was generally known not as *Messiah* but as *The Messiah*. While this seems indeed to be a small error, it is actually indicative of a greater misunderstanding. The original form of the title was to express that Handel's oratorio deals not with "the," the person, but the idea, the mission of *Messiah*—redemption. Contrary to the opinion that links *Messiah* to such oratorios as *Elijah* or *Saul*, it is not the dramatic presentation of a heroic figure but rather a contemplation. The story moves essentially from one reflective aria to the next, in spite of its lively imagery.

It goes without saying that Handel remains the experienced dramatist, and that key phrases of the Savior's life become vivid in the composer's language—but they are vivid as reflections more so than real scenes. True, the touching story of the Nativity is set apart, even with a little overture of its own—a Pifa, as Handel calls it—a piece evoking the *pifferari* (the Italian word referring to the players of the shepherd's pipes), who intone a pastoral Neapolitan melody. But this overture is only eleven measures long— only the suggestion of a piece. The vision of the Heavenly Host appears and disappears again into heaven, but then the image of the shepherd remains and is profoundly reinterpreted.

The story of the Lord's Passion is similarly introduced—though it begins not with an overture but directly, with the words of the evangelist, sung in the traditional tenor role. But the actual death scene is rendered in a small accompanied recitative, merely five measures long. A reflection of the Ascension follows, and a brief scene in heaven. But the veritably dramatic tone is reserved for the story of the Gospel, that is "gone out into all the lands unto the ends of the world"—"the Lord gave the Word"—"the kings of the earth rise up, and the rulers take counsel together against the Lord and His Anointed."

The Last Part, with its thoughts of eternity—the eternal life of the Redeemer and of mankind redeemed—its allegory of the Last Judgment, and its anthem of thanksgiving, forms an epilogue, just as the prophecy of the beginning formed a prologue.

The compiler of the wordbook, Charles Jennens, a well-to-do squire, had been a friend of Handel's for quite some time. A somewhat self-assured man of letters, he had already acted as Handel's librettist on occasion. Handel appreciated his work, and sessions at Jennens's country estate gave rise to an extended collaboration of considerable influence upon the design of Handel's texts.

The year in which Handel composed *Messiah* was also the year in which he wrote his last opera. A brilliant operatic career, for which Handel had in fact come to England, had lasted exactly thirty years, but in spite of overwhelming successes, opera had remained essentially foreign to the spirit of the British—an "exotic and irrational entertainment," in the famous words of Dr. Samuel Johnson. Handel had given up a gigantic effort, and rumors began to circulate that he intended to leave England and return to Germany.

A letter Jennens wrote at this time, and rediscovered recently, contains the remark:

> Handel says he will do nothing next Winter, but I hope I shall persuade him to set another Scripture collection I had made for him, and perform it for his Benefit in Passion week. I hope he will lay out his whole Genius and Skill upon it, that the Composition may excel all his former Compositions, as the Subject excels every other Subject. The Subject is *Messiah*.

Yet Handel had other plans. He had received the invitation from the Lord Lieutenant of Ireland, the Duke of Devonshire, to spend the next season at Dublin, and he accepted, announcing that he would plan a series of subscription concerts for December and February, aside from other occasional performances; but he saved the performance of the principal work, *Messiah*, for the end of the season and scheduled it for the benefit of three charitable institutions.

Messiah remained to be set aside for the support of charity. Returned the following season, Handel concentrated on performance of oratorio, the form he had developed in his work on the side, and he introduced *Messiah* to the London audience. But much of his work thereafter was devoted to the public benefit.

He became a governor of the "hospital"—shelter, home—for abandoned children and orphans and endowed the completion of its chapel, where in succeeding years he gave annual benefit performances of the work. In his will he made provisions for their perpetuity, and for these performances he had a new score and orchestral as well as vocal parts written out, which still guide today's performers in the way the composer wanted the work presented. He conducted his last *Messiah* performance at Covent Garden on April 6, 1759, with the announcement of a benefit performance to follow on May 3 at the Foundling's Hospital. He died a week later, on April 14.

Thus Handel stayed directly connected with the continued course of the work—an exception in his performing career. As he conducted it year by year, it was never in the same manner, nor did the music remain unaltered, and thus posterity looks in vain for a "definitive version"—we can only try moving closer to Handel's intentions. The composer of Handel's time, in fact, did not think in terms of definitive versions—he might make changes even in the published form, and Handel never had the work printed.

That the music was subjected to changes was above all for a very obvious reason: Handel worked with performers of different quality and ability from season to season, and the choice of soloists and intense individual work with them were matters of his eminent concern. Some of his greatest changes were actually made in preparation of the first performance, at Dublin. As a rule, he engaged more than one artist for each solo role, and he had brought with him from London the principal soprano and alto soloists. Detained by unfavorable weather in Chester, he had asked the local church music director to gather some singers for him, so that he might check for any problems in his performance materials, and he also engaged a secondary soprano soloist and an organist to assist him as choirmaster in preparing the choral forces in Dublin. He knew none of the musicians there, except the concertmaster, and he relied on the professional singers from Dublin's Christ Church and St. Patrick's cathedral to furnish his men soloists. At the Cathedral, the writer Jonathan Swift served as dean and only grudgingly consented to have the choirboys involved in the concert performance.

"I have form'd another Tenor Voice which gives great Satisfaction," wrote Handel to Jennens in high spirits some time after his arrival in Dublin, but the basses proved to be a disappointment. Thus Handel rewrote some of the bass arias; they became tasks— arias or recitatives—for tenor, alto, at times even soprano, and have left conscientious performers with problems even today. In other portions of the work Handel made changes evidently preferred in his writing, though at times he returned to the original version in later years.

The soloist who acquired the most fame was Suzanne Cibber, principal alto. We have touching documentations of her qualities, of which the passage quoted here from a book published at that time serves as an example:

> No person of sensibility, who has had the good fortune to hear Mrs. Cibber sing in the oratorio of the Messiah, will find it very difficult to give credit to accounts of the most wonderful effects produced from so powerful an union. And yet it was not to any extraordinary powers of voice (whereof she has but a very modest share) nor to a greater degree of skill in musick (wherein many of the Italians must be allowed to exceed her) that she owed her excellence, but to expression only; her acknowledged superiority in which could proceed from nothing but skill in her profession.

She was not a trained singer but an actress, a celebrated tragedienne, and it must have been this capacity that prompted Handel for the first performance to take away the final aria from the work even from Signora Christina Avoglio, his distinguished principal soprano soloist, for whom he had written the aria "Rejoice," and assign it to Mrs. Cibber.

Since the budgets and performance parts for the Foundling Hospital performance have been preserved, we are informed of the modest size of Handel's vocal and instrumental forces. The choir numbered less than thirty singers, but the soloists sang with them—at least, all the choral music appears in their parts. The size of the orchestra was what likewise seems to us unusually small. To a modest string group were added oboes, bassoons, trumpets, horns (to double the trumpet parts in some passages), and harpsichord, from which the conductor—the composer—directed the performance.

The changed expense account for the performance on May 3, 1759, less than three weeks after Handel's death, leaves us with a moving impression. The name of Thomas Bramwall, Handel's servant who had guided the blind composer to the harpsichord, was crossed out, and his fee was deducted from the total with the laconic note: "Th^s Mr. Handel's man absent." The place of the assistant conductor at the organ, John Christopher Smith, the son of Handel's life-long friend and amanuensis and Handel's student from earlier years, was taken by Samuel Howard, who had sung in Handel's earliest oratorio performance, and John Christopher Smith took the conductor's chair at the harpsichord. The legacy of Handel had gone to posterity.

Alfred Mann
Professor Emeritus, the Eastman School of Music

TECHNICAL MATTERS

A number of technical provisions must be taken care of by the choral director before the actual concert date. These include the following.

TIMING SHEET.   A list of all the selections in the program and the length of each is needed to determine the total time of the concert. Added to this must be time for choirs to enter and leave the performing area, and time for applause, comments, and so forth.

NEWS RELEASE.   News releases are often handled by someone designated to that job within the school. All of the pertinent information, however, must be supplied by the choral director: school, choirs, conductor, soloists, accompanists, date, place, time, and any admission costs. Include also any type of theme being used and how it will be developed in the program. Newspapers like pictures of soloists or small groups (not entire choirs) and often will supply a photographer if given enough lead time.

REHEARSAL SCHEDULE.   The director needs to lay out the rehearsal schedule for the period leading up to the concert, by months, weeks, and days. The approximate amount of time to rehearse each piece should be indicated. Often, in making this schedule the director will realize that there is too little time and too much music.

USHERS.   People are needed who will serve as ushers for the program, especially when there is reserved seating. A school club may serve this need. Some type of preconcert instructions are needed for these people so they will know how to carry out their responsibilities. This may be in the form of a written memo or a brief meeting between the director and ushers. Besides taking tickets and handing out programs, ushers should know to ask late arrivers to await being seated until a break in the program occurs. Ushers also should know where the restrooms are and where the closest telephone is found. They also should have some type of hard candy (wrapped) to offer to people who are coughing. Ushers can make or break a concert.

TICKETS.   If an admission is being charged, tickets will need to be made. When reserved seating is used, tickets indicate side, row, and seat number. The ushers must know how to interpret these indicators. Tickets can be one of the best sources of advertising for a concert. If students are to help in ticket sales, some process for the orderly distribution of tickets and collection of money must be in place.

PIANO TUNING.   The piano (if used) should be tuned before the dress rehearsal. It must be moved to the concert location at least a day before the tuner visits so the piano will have adjusted to the new environment. Care must be taken that the piano not be moved after it has been tuned. School pianos typically are not the best and go out of tune quickly.

STUDENT DRESS.   Most choirs wear some type of garment that brings a uniform look to the group. Many high schools have gone to having boys wear tuxedos and girls wear dresses that match in style and color. Choir robes remain popular, and younger choirs often wear dark bottoms and white tops, or even dark bottoms and look-alike T-shirts. All of these wardrobe requirements must be carefully planned long before the concert.

SOUND SYSTEM.   The director must determine whether or not to use a sound system. If speaking occurs, a sound system may be warranted. A young soloist's voice may need to be amplified to be heard. If the sound system hisses, cracks, and pops, it is better not to use it. Amplification of choral singing is discouraged.

STAGE CREW.   Concerts often involve special staging needs, and a stage crew helps tremendously in facilitating the movement of curtains, props, lighting, and so forth. Lights should be adjusted before the dress rehearsal and care taken not to blind students with harsh spotlights. If a school club provides these services, it must be contacted in advance. What is not wanted is a group of people fooling around during the program and making noise backstage. The members of the stage crew must be responsible people, and a stage manager (ideally an adult) should be in charge.

EQUIPMENT.   Choral concerts usually involve choral risers, a piano, a conductor's podium and music stand, and perhaps a conductor's box on which to stand. If instrumentalists are involved, there will be seats and music stands needed. Special props and stage decorations also are frequently used. Accounting for and moving all of this equipment takes coordinated effort, but it should not be the final responsibility of the choral director, who will have enough on his or her mind. A stage manager needs to be appointed to check on and insure that everything on the director's list of equipment is in place at the time of the dress rehearsal.

DRESS REHEARSAL

The term *dress rehearsal* is commonly used for the final rehearsal before any performance. Where plays and musicals are concerned, the actors and singers do wear the costumes that will be worn in the production. In choral concerts, the choirs typically do not wear in the dress rehearsal what they will wear in performance. Some inexperienced singers (at any age) may need to be informed of this distinction. The author actually had an adult male come to a dress rehearsal in his tuxedo. He had taken the term *dress rehearsal* literally!

Musical Considerations

The objective of the dress rehearsal is to run the show, to bring together all of the parts that need to coalesce for a public performance. Lloyd Pfautsch (1988) states:

> This final rehearsal is the time when the chorus realizes its capabilities and experiences an added or a heightened sense of involvement. If they are ready for this realization and experience, then they have been well prepared during all other rehearsals. If they are not ready, then it is too late for the conductor to recoup the time that has been lost. (p. 109)

Most experienced choral conductors would agree with Pfautsch's words. It is too late to use the dress rehearsal for the teaching of notes. This should be a time when the choristers are challenged one last time to make music and move beyond the written page.

It is best not to overrehearse music at the dress rehearsal. In fact, some conductors do not run entire selections, especially if the concert is the same day. Overrehearsing often robs singers of spontaneity and enthusiasm; their presentation can become dull and lifeless. Likewise, underrehearsing will result in a concert that sounds insecure. The conductor must develop a good sense of knowing how to pace the dress rehearsal for the maximum benefit of the singers and those technical crew.

The dress rehearsal should proceed without interruption, with brief pauses to correct details occurring only when absolutely necessary. Stopping to converse with the stage crew about lighting, sound, and so forth, is kept to a minimum or the choir will become tired and restless.

If every selection is to be sung through, then it is extremely important that each be sung without interruption. While it is tempting for the conductor to interrupt and make corrections, this should be done either before or after each piece is sung in its entirety. If a piece breaks down, it often will be at a weak transition point. Singing the chorus through in its entirety is the only way to check for such weak spots, if they still exist. Again, the dress rehearsal is not the place when such learning should be taking place.

The accompanist must be able to see the conductor with ease and needs adequate lighting. Also, the choir must be able to hear the accompaniment. If a piano is used and the sound board is facing the audience, the choir may be unable to hear the instrument. In such cases, subtle amplification of the piano may be needed, using "fall back" speakers directed toward the choir. When possible, place the the piano so as to direct its sound toward the choir.

Using instrumentalists besides the accompanist for a concert requires a rehearsal order that does not keep them waiting around while they are not needed. Rehearsing out of order may be necessary to let the instrumentalists go first. Alternatively, the players may be given a time to report that is close to the time they will play.

Nonmusical Matters

Numerous nonmusical matters must be coordinated during the dress rehearsal. In addition to the technical matters already mentioned, the following also need consideration.

DISCIPLINE. Firm discipline is needed during the dress rehearsal. Students are expected to act as they would at the concert. Audience members are often more critical of the way students act while singing than of the singing itself. It is a good idea to have a code of deportment for the dress rehearsal and concert. These rules should be covered before the dress rehearsal, but reminders of specific parts may be needed that day. The following can be adapted as needed.

- Be on time ("call time").
- Know where your choir is to report for warm-up.
- Remember to bring what you will wear on the day of the concert.
- Bring no concert ticket money on the day of the performance. It may get lost.
- Be sure to sign in for attendance purposes.
- Valuables (especially money) should be left at home.
- Refrain from eating a heavy meal before singing, but do eat something.
- Gum chewing is not permitted.
- Talking is not permitted in the concert hall except between sections of the program when lights are up. Do not talk when entering or exiting the performance area.
- Keep your eyes on the conductor at all times. Do not look at the announcer, soloist, accompanist, audience, other singers, and so forth.
- Leave concert music at home. Bringing it to the performance may result in its being lost. If music is used, place it in some type of black folder.
- Do not react to your mistakes or those of others (roll your eyes, look at someone, heave and sigh). The audience rarely knows when mistakes are made unless you tell them.
- When the concert is over, take pride in your work. Do not react negatively when others congratulate you, even if it was not a great performance. Thank your parents, grandparents, siblings, and so forth, for coming.
- The concert represents many weeks of cooperative effort—it is the final exam for the choir. Determine to make your best contribution so everyone can experience the success and rewards of a job well done. Remember: make music.

SEATING.   School concerts are a valuable place for students' education to continue. Being seated in the auditorium where the concert is taking place allows younger choirs to hear the singing of the older groups. Motivating students to improve their singing is easier when they experience hearing other choirs sing. However, students have to be disciplined listeners; they must not be permitted to talk while others are singing. They need to be reminded before the concert to show the other groups the respect with which they wish to be treated. Having students seated during the concert also helps to keep them focused and quiet before it is their turn to sing. With younger students, having adult supervisors seated among the singers lends some visible authority to necessary discipline.

If it is not possible to seat the choirs in the performance hall, then other rooms have to be designated for the purpose. One of the biggest problems with this arrangement is that students, especially younger boys, will horse around and become overheated. Also, students talk, and then talk louder to be heard. This is hard on the voice. Some type of activity needs to be provided for students who must wait until others have sung. The need for adult supervision goes without saying. Students are never to be left on their own without being supervised.

STAGE CREW.   Although a meeting with the stage crew or stage manager should precede the dress rehearsal, it may become necessary while rehearsing to stop and change a light cue or sound level. These stops must be brief and the rehearsal should move forward. Stage equipment such as risers, acoustical shell, music stands, chairs, and decorations need to be in place before the final rehearsal begins. The dress rehearsal must come as close as possible to the actual concert. If the stage crew is responsible for opening the house on the day of the concert, they must know what time it is to happen and how the lights are to be set for people entering the auditorium. Following the concert, it is a nice idea to send a letter of thanks to the crew for their good work.

When the rehearsal or concert is over it is necessary that the building be secured. The director must know who locks the doors. It should not be the director's responsibility, but sometimes in small schools it is. The details of bringing off a successful concert are far greater than just preparing the music.

CONDUCTING THE CONCERT

Every year thousands of choirs present countless numbers of concerts in all types of settings. They bring tremendous satisfaction to themselves and their audiences through disciplined and polished singing. The hours of rehearsals result in positive, life-enhancing experiences. Choral singers do a good thing. It is the choral conductor, however, who ultimately is responsible for it all, as musician, educator, psychologist, technician, business manager, party planner, and more. It all takes much, much planning to arrive successfully at the day of the concert (see Unit 2).

Preconcert Activities for the Choir

The singers must know what the "call" or report time is for the concert, and where they are to meet. Different choirs often report to different rooms, which means that some adult assistance will be needed. If the concert is to begin at 3:00 P.M., a call time of 2:00 P.M. is typical. Attendance must be taken in some form, and students should sit or stand in concert formation. Adrenaline will be flowing and excitement in the air. The conductor must be sure not to stifle this energy while channeling it in the proper direction.

WARM-UP. The warm-up period follows the traditional pattern for this activity: energize the body, breath, ear, and voice. Now is not the time to be learning new vocalises. This warm-up routine should be calm and slow-paced. If it is too energetic, the singers can begin to oversing and tire their voices. The conductor may wish for a student director to handle this warm-up activity.

NOTES. The conductor should make a list of notes or brush-up needs for each piece following the dress rehearsal (title, page, measure, problem). These are the most problematic areas and should be rehearsed in order. Such things might include a bad cutoff, problem pitch, diction problem, and so forth. There is no time for the rehearsing of complete passages.

STARTS. The conductor then begins each piece with the choir singing just a few measures. This activity serves as a reminder of the order of the concert.

CHARGE. The last part of the choir's preconcert activity is to remind students to make music and not advertise their mistakes. If time permits, last-minute pit stops may be made (drink and restroom), and then it is time to line up or sit in the auditorium.

The conductor must be "up" for all of this preconcert activity. Even if the conductor is not feeling well, he or she must fake wellness. Students are sensitive to their director's feelings and typically reflect his or her moods in performance. A conductor who is nervous or hesitant must put on a good act to cover up such feelings. The general must never waiver in front of the troops!

Preconcert Activities for Assistants

While the choirs are warming up, ushers, stage crew, sound technicians, and so forth, should be doing their jobs.

USHERS.   The ushers typically open the house forty-five minutes to an hour before the performance. Someone should be designated for the purpose of placing the box of programs at the rear of the auditorium. The head usher assigns others to the different doors as they arrive. Ushers then greet people, take tickets if appropriate, hand out programs, and if necessary, direct people to their seats. Ushers close the doors when the lights first lower and remain at their posts to keep latecomers from interrupting the program. If lights come on between sections, ushers will not need flashlights to guide latecomers to seating. At the end of the concert, the head usher takes any remaining programs to the choral room.

STAGE CREW.   The members of the stage crew should open the house at the predetermined time. House lights but not stage lights should be on. A check should be made that all equipment is correctly placed and working. If students are sitting as choirs in the auditorium, their seating area needs to be marked off with masking tape; each choir removes the tape as it enters. If a sound system is being used, it also should be tested.

AUDIO TAPING.   Directors often tape their concerts for after-concert study. Some even employ professionals to do the recording. This latter practice saves the choral director from one more job. If it is not possible to obtain professional recording services, the director ought to have someone else responsible (perhaps a colleague) for the setting up of equipment and the recording of the concert.

The Big Event

Two minutes before the concert is to begin, the lights are flashed to warn people to be seated. As the first choir enters the performance area, the lights should be lowered but not extinguished. Sufficient light must be present so that the audience can follow the program.

When the choir is in place, the conductor enters. The pace of walking should be quick but not hurried, and the head should be level. Upon arriving at the podium, the conductor turns to the audience and bows in recognition of the applause. He or she then turns around and places the music on the music stand. (Some directors prefer to have their music on the stand before they enter the auditorium.) If there is a box, the conductor steps up on it, which signals the choiristers to raise their music (a prearranged cue), if they are using music. The conductor scans the group for eye contact, does the same with instrumentalists or the accompanist (if used), and the concert begins.

DEALING WITH EMERGENCIES.   All kinds of things can go wrong during a concert: babies cry at inappropriate times, students faint, someone throws up, the choir forgets the words, lights blow out, sound systems crackle, risers collapse. You name it—it's happened. When discussing the handling of such emergencies, Demaree and Moses (1995) indicate the key to be *concentration*:

The first thing you and your musicians must fight to maintain is a clear focus on the music at hand. **Your worst enemy in a crisis is distraction. When one realizes that one is facing an emergency, one's tendency is to hurry to a solution. Don't let that happen. Take time!** The second priority is flexibility. Almost any emergency (even in performance) can be survived if you keep your composure, take your time, and *think what are your real requirements—the absolute essentials of the music.* Maintain those. (p. 429)

This is good advice. Some problems will solve themselves given enough time. Some will not, however, and you and your students must be prepared to keep your cool.

The author once was giving a performance of a Lenten cantata with a choir, and things were going well. When the baritone soloist intoned, "Come, and see the place where He lay," however, the biggest bass in the back row (Gary) fainted, as if on cue, and pitched forward, taking altos and sopranos on his plunge. He collapsed at the feet of the conductor, and the music momentarily paused. The conductor had been taught somewhere in the gray past (probably in a choral methods class) that the best place for someone who has fainted is on the floor, where the air is coolest. The choir had been told this, and no one moved to help the fallen bass. The conductor's wife, however, had not been given this bit of advice, and she dashed forward to help the passed-out singer, only to realize quickly that one of Gary's legs was bigger than her whole body, and she couldn't begin to move this dead weight. So the concert went on, and eventually Gary came to, got up on his own accord, and sat down in a front pew. The moral of the story: when people faint, unless they are injured, leave them alone. They will come to when they are ready and can help themselves. By the way, the young man in this story turned out to have low blood pressure. To elevate it, his doctor told him to run laps before a performance.

Another true story comes to mind. The seventh-grade choir was lined up to go on for a school assembly when up came running a small girl who had been sick the previous week and did not know where to stand. "Stand on the end of the first row," said the conductor, and into the auditorium they went. The singers were doing well when from the audience came a commotion. Hearing a disturbing sound to the right, the conductor turned his head just in time to capture the small girl, who had been throwing up like a fountain. The smell could have knocked you over. At that point there was nothing more to be done—the show stopped! All of the choir exited stage right while the custodian came out and cleaned up the mess. That event happened many years ago, but it will remain forever etched in the mind of the author.

ACKNOWLEDGING APPLAUSE.   When the audience applauds, it is saying thank you to the performers. It is rude not to acknowledge applause, but some conductors always look ill at ease when doing so. The gracious acknowledgment of applause is a necessity for bringing closure to a presentation.

An audience can tire quickly from applauding after every two-minute selection. Better that they hold their applause to the end of each complete section of the concert. A simple statement in the program requesting that any response be held to the end of each multi-movement piece or section will cut down on wasted time and activity.

When the applause begins, the conductor turns to the audience, smiles, and bows. The conductor should not look at the audience while bowing but rather look down as the head moves forward and downward. The second bow is usually for soloists and accompanist. It is good for these people to be moving forward during the first bow. The third bow is for the chorus. The conductor steps quickly to the side and gestures with one hand toward the choir. If there are instrumentalists, the conductor indicates for them to stand. If the applause is strong the conductor may join with the soloist for a final bow, or the conductor may take a solo bow if there are no soloists. The soloists and conductor exit the stage quickly (or the soloists may return to the choir if singing in it); women exit first, followed by men. If there is sustained applause, the conductor and soloists return for a final bow. Bowing is an important part of the conductor's technique and should be practiced in conducting classes.

Some directors want their choirs to bow. This can be effective if the singers do it right and look good. It is something that has to be rehearsed. One way to do this is for the conductor to face the choir, extend both arms in recognition, turn back to the audience with arms extended, and then drop the arms inward while bowing with the singers. The dropping of the arms is the cue for the choir to bow. Another cue for the choral bow is for the conductor to move to one side, extend one arm toward the choir, and with a flick of the wrist indicate the bowing routine. Students standing behind others cannot move much from the waist and should be taught to execute a slight nod with the head.

NARRATIONS OR COMMENTS.   The use of a narrator is a common practice for choral concerts. Typically the narration weaves a common theme throughout the performance. Narrations should be kept short and not sound like dry history lessons.

Sometimes, comments from the conductor or a choir member may help the audience to understand the piece to be sung, especially if the selection is not easily accessible. These comments should be short and objective and not point out the obvious. Neither does the audience need a history lesson at this time—they can read the program notes. Comments should help guide the listeners to find something in the music to which they can relate. A chorister chosen to give comments should have a strong voice that projects easily.

SHOWING APPRECIATION.   Singers deserve a pat on the back. The conductor needs to tell the choirs at the end of the concert that he or she appreciates their hard work. By standing at the stage exit door when the singers exit, the conductor can smile and thank students in groups as they are leaving. This immediate contact after the concert makes everyone feel good. Also, the conductor should be available backstage for those making the effort to extend congratulations.

Assessing the Concert

Choral directors often have choristers listen to the tape or CD of the concert in a following rehearsal. Students sometimes become bored with this activity. Therefore, it is recommended that some type of formal, written assessment be required of students as they listen to their portion of the concert. Questions might include:

- What was your favorite selection from your portion of the concert? Why?
- What was your least favorite selection and why?
- Make a list of titles and beside each write the general mood (e.g., sad, happy, lively) and the general tempo (e.g., slow, fast, very fast).
- Which piece do you think the choir sang the best?
- Which piece do you think the choir sang the poorest?
- On a scale of 1 (lowest) to 5 (highest), how good was the diction?
- Where do you think that we as a choir need to improve?
- On a scale of 1 (lowest) to 5 (highest), how would you rate our overall performance?

Assessment is central to education. Students need to evaluate themselves, and they need to hear from their conductor how he or she thought they did. Every performance is another step to becoming better, but students will not improve unless they have set for them clear goals and expectations. The written assessment following any concert is a time for growth— it should not be missed.

Millions of people have fond memories of concerts organized and conducted by choral directors. Concerts require much work, and the effort is worth it. Let's sing!

STUDY AND DISCUSSION QUESTIONS

1. How long should the typical school concert last? Why?
2. Why should the order of the concert be developed like a drama?
3. Why is knowledge of the audience important when selecting a program?
4. Why should a concert have a well-written program for the audience?
5. What information should be contained on the cover or first page of the program?
6. How can the audience be educated about proper concert deportment?
7. What types of additional information can be placed in the concert program?
8. What are some guidelines for writing program notes?
9. What types of technical matters does the conductor have to organize for the concert?
10. How does dress rehearsal differ between a stage musical and a choral concert?
11. What are some general guidelines for the dress rehearsal?
12. Why is it important to speak to students about concert deportment before the dress rehearsal and concert?
13. Where is the preferred place for students to wait before they sing? Why?
14. What kinds of things does the stage crew do?
15. What are the preconcert activities for the choir?
16. Why is it important for the choral conductor to be "up" for the concert?
17. What are the responsibilities of the ushers?
18. What is the correct way to bow?
19. What is the best advice for preparing choirs for concert emergencies?
20. Why is postconcert assessment valuable, and how can it be done?

REFERENCES

Demaree, R. W., and D. V. Moses (1995). *The complete conductor*. Englewood Cliffs, NJ: Prentice Hall.

Mann, A. (2001). Program notes: Messiah—G. F. Handel. Unpublished manuscript.

Pfautsch, L. (1988). The choral conductor and the rehearsal. In H. A. Decker and J. Herford, *Choral conducting symposium* (2d ed), 69–111. Englewood Cliffs, NJ: Prentice Hall.

Robinson, R., and A. Winold (1976). *The choral experience*. New York: Harper's College Press.

Roe, P. F. (1983). *Choral music education* (2d ed.). Englewood Cliffs, NJ: Prentice Hall.

20 | Directing Other Choral Organizations

The focus of this book is on directing the high school choral program. There are, however, a number of other venues outside the school setting where choral organizations need expert direction. These groups include community or civic choirs, church choirs, children's choirs, and other nontraditional choirs. Professional choruses are not discussed, as they are few in number and typically directed by nonschool personnel, that is, persons who make a living by directing professional ensembles (e.g., the Dale Warland Singers) or choruses attached to other organizations (e.g., a symphony chorus).

Few choral directors can earn a living outside of a school setting. There are those churches large enough to support a full-time director of music, but most church jobs are part-time. The same can be said for community choral organizations, in which some directors volunteer their time when funds are lacking. For the most part, choral directors earn a living directing school, college, and university choirs and supplement that income with earnings from outside organizations.

Directing choral groups in the community can have very positive rewards. Because the same singers often return year after year, it is possible to build lasting friendships and a solid musical core of singers who sing well. Conducting nonschool groups presents the opportunity of doing a greater variety of repertoire and more mature literature. Choirs for adult singers provide a setting for life-long learning in music, an ever growing trend in music education. It is safe to say that most school choral director will, at some time in their career, also conduct another choir in their community.

THE COMMUNITY OR CIVIC CHORUS

The singing schools of colonial America generated an interest in choral singing that gave birth to both church and community choirs. "The Stoughton (Massachusetts) Musical Society, the oldest enduring community choral organization in the United States, was founded in 1786 because of the influence of the singing school" (Collins, 1999, p. 33). The most famous of the early community choirs was that of the Handel and Haydn Society of Boston, founded in 1815. Lowell Mason served a time as its director.

> Choral societies were important to the development of American choral music because they set very high standards for other musically minded individuals and groups to emulate. Not only did they bring outstanding choral works before the public, but they also provided commercial and professional opportunities for concert singers (and amateurs as well) and conductors. (Collins, 1999, p. 33)

This early community chorus movement began in the East and spread quickly throughout the country. Today, community choirs can be found even in small towns and villages; these civic ensembles are a solid foundation for choral singing in America.

An excellent publication for organizing and operating a professional and volunteer choral ensemble is published by Chorus America: *The Chorus Handbook* (Page, Greenberg, and Leise, eds., 1999). This monograph includes fifteen chapters from different authors, ranging from "The Legal Aspects of Establishing Your Chorus" (Floyd Farmer) and "Volunteer and Professional Singers, Auditions, Performance Schedules" (Paul Hill), to "The Board of Directors" (Constance J. Bernt), "Multiculturalism and Diversity" (Albert J. McNeil), and "Commissioning a Musical Work" (Alice Parker). The handbook may be ordered from Chorus America, 1156 15th Street, N.W., Suite 310, Washington, DC 20005. E-mail: service@chorusamerica.org. Phone: (202) 331–7577.

Board of Directors

A community chorus typically has a board of directors that oversees the policies and governance of the group. Elected by the chorus membership, the members and officers serve for terms specified in the bylaws of the organization. This board is extremely important to the health of the group, as it often bears the greatest amount of work. Its major activities vary but include fund-raising, budgeting, publicity, ticket sales, calendar approval, hiring of paid personnel (director, accompanist, soloists, instrumentalists, etc.), planning for social events and after-concert parties, and so forth.

The conductor's relationship to the group must be one of mutual respect. A clear delineation of expectations from both parties is necessary to keep smooth working order. It is good for the director to have a signed contract that clearly sets forth expectations and duties. The board will expect much input from the director and will value that input if the director does not become dictatorial. In the end, the director is hired (usually) by the board, and the board has the final word in decision making.

Who has the final word on the choice of music for concerts? If the conductor is also the music director, then the director has the last word. If, however, the conductor is not designated as music director, then the board has final approval of music matters. This should be clearly stipulated in the bylaws and in the director's contract.

The organization needs a constitution and bylaws. These are important for the legal status of the group when applying for tax exemption. Both documents should be updated from time to time and kept current. This is the job of the board.

Finances

The financial needs of a community chorus can be substantial. Expenses typically include salary for the conductor, salary for the accompanist, rental of performance venues, program costs, advertising, fees of soloists, instrumental fees, costs of music, and so forth. Income sources can include membership fees, concert income, donations, program advertising, endowment interest, and so forth. A good treasurer is required to maintain accurate financial records. Also, a nonprofit group can be required to file a yearly report with the IRS (based on income).

Members

Membership typically is open to adult singers in the community above a set age. High school students may or may not be permitted to join, depending upon the desire of the group. Membership requirements need to be published as part of the audition announcement. Such requirements often include membership fee, cost of music, regular attendance at rehearsals and concerts, concert attire, and so forth. It should be known from the first rehearsal that a strict attendance policy will be enforced. Section leaders often serve as attendance "watch dogs."

A balanced membership among vocal parts is typically sought. However, finding enough male singers to balance the number of female singers is usually a problem. It is not recommended that women be assigned to the tenor part. A woman singing what is alto 2 has little carrying power, and the voice does not sound like a tenor. The director must remember that balance does not come by having a "square" choir, that is, equal numbers of voices in each part. It takes only a few good tenors to balance a whole choir. Likewise, a few strong basses will possess enough sound to create a firm foundation. Weak voices on any part will add little to the overall balance. The director should consider achieving balance by counting the number of strong voices in each section rather than the total number of singers. The lack of males is then not always such a big problem.

Auditions

Community choirs often require that new people as well as returning members audition each year. The time of the audition is publicly announced for an evening when those who work are available. As people phone, the secretary schedules the audition times. Audition materials may include a song the person knows (for new people) or a sample of the literature sung from the previous season. It also may include some vocalizing, especially for establishing vocal range. If sight-reading ability is to be checked, then some type of sight-singing exercise or music is needed. A sight-singing check for returning members may not be necessary. The director usually serves as the auditioner; others may be included at the discretion of the board.

Returning members can present a problem. Older adults with aging voices sometimes develop vocal problems that cause their voices to stick out in the ensemble. What does the director do with a soprano whose wobble is beyond help, but whose dedication to the choir over the years has been outstanding? The director cannot ignore the problem—it will not go away. Moving the soprano to alto can help, but it also may offend the soprano. Discussing the situation with the board is important. If the bylaws give the board the ultimate authority to decide who stays and who does not stay, then it will be their ultimate decision. If it is with the director that final decisions about choir personnel are made, then a frank discussion with the person about his or her vocal problem is necessary. Moving a soprano to alto or a tenor to bass is a partial solution and may permit the singer to fade out gracefully without being terribly hurt. Choral directors always must be conscious of the human condition and sensitive to the feelings of their singers. Without singers there would be no need for choral directors!

Concert Venues

The community chorus sings in a variety of places: auditoriums of local high schools and colleges, hospitals, museums, banquet rooms of hotels, malls, churches, and so forth. It usually has no performing venue of its own and must seek out other places in the community to sing. While this widens exposure of the group, many halls have poor acoustics for singing. It is best when a group can find one performance venue that will present them in the best acoustic possible.

Some civic organizations are fortunate to be able to sing regularly with an orchestra. Singing with instruments can create balance problems, and these must be anticipated before the dress rehearsal. For example, in the *German Requiem* of Brahms, the women's parts are sometimes low when the woodwind choir is high. There is no way that the women can sing softly and be heard over the bright-sounding instruments. Such balance adjustments require careful consideration. Also, singers must be conscious to sing vowels on the beat, initiating tone at the same time as the instruments. Early consonants are extremely important when singing with an orchestra.

Music Programming

Community choirs often choose a theme around which to build their concerts: "The Glorious Baroque," "A Grand Night for Singing," "A Sampler of Folksongs and Spirituals," "An American Portrait," "Bach Festival 22." A theme is good for publicity purposes and brings a certain amount of cohesion to the program.

Because civic choirs comprise adult voices, it is sometimes harder to do music of the Renaissance with this group. An older adult choir often sounds better when singing full-throated music such as that of the Romantic period. Opera choruses and arias make an excellent source for programming. If a director and choir wants to perform music from earlier periods, it must realize that a concentrated effort will be required to modify the tone color of the ensemble to fit the style of the period and the music.

A number of community choruses present Handel's *Messiah* each holiday season. Some have developed a singalong concert where audience members are invited to bring their copies of the oratorio and sing along. Typically, the entire *Messiah* is not presented, but only Part 1 and portions of Parts 2 and 3. This has proven to be a popular event that builds bridges to the community at large.

Some choirs use special events to fund-raise, such as an invitation-only wine and cheese-tasting party followed by a special program featuring the choir. A dessert theme can be successful, again followed by a private concert. Singing at banquets is another way to advertise and raise funds. Care must be taken, however, that too many special events not be scheduled. When busy people become concerned that the choir is taking too much time, they drop out. The director needs to maintain a good balance between the number of regular concerts and the number of special events the group presents. Too much of a good thing can be harmful.

Intrinsic and Extrinsic Benefits

Most people who choose to participate in a community or civic chorus are seeking an excellent musical experience through great choral literature. The intrinsic value of the music is enough to keep them returning year after year. If the musical payoff begins to decrease, they will lose interest and drop out. Others find the extrinsic social benefits to be as equally rewarding and maintain membership through good times and bad. A choir cannot remain strong, however, when its singing begins to suffer. The size of the audience will decrease, and the choir may have trouble paying its bills. When the choir maintains high musical standards and the members have a great sense of success, then everything else is an added bonus.

One extrinsic benefit of the civic chorus is community identity and recognition. When the civic chorus performs, it brings a feeling of pride to the residents of the area, and when the choir sings outside of its town, it brings recognition for the whole community. A civic chorus is a community of people, a microcosm of the place that people call home. What better way to represent the corporate nature of people working and living together than through a community chorus?

CHURCH CHOIRS

The church throughout history has been the foundation of the choral movement, and choral singing has been the center of the worship service. From simple chants to the complexities of modern choral composition, choral music has had a secure home in the church. Choirs have provided countless people with opportunities to sing and express themselves in a unique way. Likewise, choral directors have honed their art while adding to their sustenance. The choral professional is forever indebted to church leaders through the centuries for allowing choral music to flourish as part of its ministry.

Church Choir Beginnings

Choral singing in colonial America had a slow growth. Singing schools were organized to improve the vocal technique and music reading of the colonists, but the emphasis was on congregational singing. The Moravians imported their love of choirs from Europe, but their fine choral singing was a notable exception. In nineteenth-century America, church choral music began to develop in the Northeast under the leadership of Lowell Mason, who conducted at several churches in Boston. Mason's program became a model for others, and his insistence on good choral literature, good singing technique, and sight-singing skill was emulated. These three standards of traditional church music became characteristic of choral singing in mainline churches and continue today.

The formal choral tradition, begun in Europe and imported to America by Mason and others, is the same on both sides of the ocean—choirs, in the truest sense of the word, sing the finest choral music. The music is void of modernisms and hearkens to a day when popular-style church music was unknown. Whatever period of music is used, it reflects a high level of sanctity and formality. For the professional choral musician, it is the true choral art form. Choral music is choir music, composed for a number of equal voice parts that compliment and support one another. Good choral singing results in a blend of these parts where each vocal line is critical to the balance of the whole. Choral music is not a solo arranged for a choir. Choral music is music written for a choir. For those wanting a a greater understanding of a formal church music program, John Bertalot's *Immediately Practical Tips for Choral Directors* (1994) presents in a narrative form what this traditional approach looks like today.

Contemporary Christian Music

The roots of contemporary Christian music are found in nineteenth-century Methodism and their frontier camp meetings, whose hymns, spirituals, gospel songs, and Sunday school songs represented a more informal, personal, and sentimental approach to texts and singing. Revival songs by Dwight L. Moody and Ira D. Sankey became popular, and in the early twentieth century, the gospel hymns of Billy Sunday and Homer Rodeheaver prepared the way for the crusade hymns of Billy Graham and Cliff Barrows. None of this music, however, would have been confused with pop music. Ralph Carmichael in the 1940s used a variety of techniques associated with Fred Waring's Pennsylvanians, but it had a distinctive quality that identified it as religious music. In the 1960s John Peterson's music was extremely popular; it used a contemporary style and salvation message. There was no doubt, however, that Peterson's music was church music. The world of popular music and church music remained separate.

All of this began to change in the 1960s as pop music began to invade the church. Robert Mitchell (1978) states,

The most noteworthy initial impetus came from Geoffrey Beaumont's *20th Century Folk Mass*, which was released in England late in the 1950's. This quickly crossed the ocean and received attention in the country as the "Jazz Mass" (although the musical idiom used was that of the swing of the late 1930's). Within the next decade there emerged explosively an incredible variety of ventures in the experimental use of various pop idioms for the purpose of worship and evangelism. These ventures included as many kinds of pop sounds as can be identified across the spectrum of varieties of entertainment music. Furthermore, such experiments were carried out by virtually all segments of the church. . . . Catholic and Protestant, American and European, liturgical and free churches, liberal and conservative . . . all of these participated. (p. 131)

The world of popular music invaded church music, while at the same time the church invaded popular music.

Starting with the 1950's, folk musicians such as Bob Dylan began to write and sing songs that, while not overtly religious, were focused on various moral issues—the kind of issues with which the church appropriately should be concerned. Soon songs began to appear that were based on expressions or passages of Scripture—for example, "Turn, Turn, Turn," or Leonard Cohen's "Story of Isaac." This was followed by the rising popularity of specific hymn materials such as the Hawkins Singers' "O Happy Day" or Judy Collins' "Amazing Grace." Finally, such overtly Christian things as *Godspell, Jesus Christ Superstar*, and Leonard Bernstein's *Mass* began to be created for and find acceptance in society completely outside the church. Thus, the categories of sacred and secular, each of which had been so impervious to the other in 1950, had penetrated each other in a substantial way by 1975. (Mitchell, 1978, pp. 132–33)

The world in the church and the church in world—a merging of music styles during the second half of the twentieth century. The results have not always been happy ones.

The Dilemma

Today's choral directors are often faced with a dilemma. Trained in the traditional classic choral style, conductors often find themselves at odds with evangelical Christian worship and its popular music idioms. For example, most contemporary, evangelical church music is about one's own personal testimony and salvation. Unlike the texts of Martin Luther, which stress the plurality of worship (e.g., "Now Thank *We* All Our God," "A Mighty Fortress Is *Our* God"), popular evangelical music stresses the personal pronouns "I" and "me," as in John Newton's *Amazing Grace*:

Amazing grace! how sweet the sound,
That saved a wretch like me!
I once was lost, but now am found,
Was blind, but now I see.

Perhaps the greatest problem that traditional choral musicians have with so much contemporary church music is that the latter is not really choral music. It is typically conceived as a good tune and then arranged for chorus. The song may sound just as good if sung by a soloist with backup accompaniment. It takes little molding, and dynamic nuance is uncommon. The traditional choral sound of blend and resonance does not exist, as voices are valued for their individual quality. In short, it is popular music in a choir robe.

There is no doubt about the impact of popular music on church music ministries. Many mainline churches have gone to Saturday evening "contemporary" worship services. Evangelical churches have all but abandoned traditional music, and even the hymnbooks are gone. In these churches the music is often loud and upbeat, with lots of hand clapping, repetitive, and accompanied by a "worship band." It is the voice of a youth-oriented people who, being raised in a pop culture, identify with this type of music. The music is easy to sing, easy to remember, and simplistic.

An Age of Pluralism

So what is the contemporary church choral director to do? First, the choral musician must recognize that pluralism in church music is a fact. Many churches are finding that to hold on to their people they must speak in the vernacular. Second, trained choral musicians must make a choice: (1) seek employment only in mainline churches that continue to value traditional choral music, (2) adapt to the evangelical popular form of music making and forget tradition, or (3) recognize that pluralism exists and work for a balanced program. The third position is not always possible when the minister of the church wants only a youth-oriented music style. Unfortunately, it is this third position that truly recognizes the plurality of membership in so many churches today.

For those choral directors working in an evangelical church and trying to find some balance in the musical offerings, two books by Donald Hustad (1981; 1993) are recommended. In the foreword to the 1981 edition, "The Pilgrimage of a Schizophrenic Musician," Hustad speaks of the inner conflicts he has known living in the "two very different worlds of art music and traditional evangelical church music" (p. vii). He presents how he has come to blend the broad spectrum of contemporary church music.

Some choral directors cannot abandon their traditional choral art, and they should not. Every church is a culture, and to each its own. Those churches that remain committed to true choral music continue to need choral directors who are highly trained in the traditional sense. For those who choose to work in an evangelical church, a different set of skills is needed, many of which are learned on the job. And for those walking the line, knowledge of and facility with both styles is a big job. The choice is personal and based on one's own education, background, and faith. Each choral director must conduct in a setting in which he or she is comfortable.

Church Music Organization

The music program within any church has certain organizational structures that may vary slightly, but a certain commonality does exists as follows:

CHURCH GOVERNING BODY.   Every church has some type of elected governing body that is ultimately responsible for policy, personnel, and finances. This group sets the music budget and has final authority over hiring and terminating musicians. It is good to know who these people are and to win their commitment to the music program.

MINISTER.   The senior minister is responsible for running the daily activities of the church. Coordination with the minister is essential for planning service music. The minister will have much influence on the philosophy of music and worship. The choral director should discuss with the minister the style of worship music expected before signing a contract.

MUSIC COMMITTEE.   The music committee comprises church members elected or appointed. The chair calls regular meetings to approve requests by the choir director and to oversee special events, such as the purchase of new choir robes. The choir director reports directly to the music committee in the chain of command.

CHOIR DIRECTOR.   In some large churches the choir director is called the director of music. This is often a full-time position and requires overseeing multiple personnel. Most churches have a choir director who is part-time. This person conducts the adult church choir and sometimes other choirs such as youth, children's, bell, and so forth. In some churches the choir director is also the organist.

ORGANIST.   The church organist accompanies all rehearsals and performances by the adult choir and serves as organist for the church services. It is important that the choir director and organist have a good working relationship.

OTHER SERVICE PERSONNEL.   Some churches with large programs employ choir directors for youth, children's, bell choirs, and so forth. Smaller churches typically have these positions filled by volunteers. Additional volunteer help can be used for care of robes, taking attendance, accompanying, and maintaining the choral library.

Graded Choirs

Many churches have what are known as "graded" choir programs, which include a number of choirs for children through adults. Depending upon the number of children in the church, the number of children's choirs will vary. In a smaller church, there may be only one choir for children encompassing grades one through six. Such a choir presents a broad level of abilities, and it is a challenge for any director to find music easy enough for the younger children but not "babyish" for the older. Dividing children into three groups by two grades each or into two groups by three grades each is preferable to all children in one choir. The kindergarten age is very young for children to be in a formal choir, and this activity is not recommended for them.

There are a number of good resources for directing children's choirs. *Children Sing His Praise*, edited by Donald Rotermund (1985), presents a number of excellent articles by specialists over a broad range of topics. *Directing the Children's Choir*, by Shirley McRae (1991), is a comprehensive resource with *Orff-Schulwerk* integrated into the teaching approach. The Choristers Guild (2834 W. Kingsley Rd., Garland, TX 75041) has long been the leading publisher of materials for children's choirs in the mainline church.

Children in the middle school or junior high grades are organized into what have been called youth choirs or junior choirs. Grades encompass five through eight, or just seven through eight and sometimes nine. Keeping students interested in singing through these adolescent years is as demanding for the church musician as it is for the school music teacher. John Yarrington's *Building the Youth Choir* (1990) is recommended reading for anyone working with teenagers in youth choirs. Few churches have separate high school choirs for students in grades nine through twelve. Most often, high school students begin to sing at this time in the adult choir.

The choral program in most churches focuses on the adult choir. Known as the senior choir or chancel choir, its membership comprises volunteers who have a love for singing. Because of its volunteer nature, church choirs vary widely in their singing ability and difficulty of literature they are able to perform. The new director is wise to pick music on the easy side when beginning a new job, especially if the ability level of the choir is unknown. The level of most of the music in the choral library is not always an accurate indicator of the choir's proficiency in singing.

A lack of male participants is a constant complaint about church choirs, and directors must recruit constantly. The size of the church choir in the average church of several hundred members varies between twenty-five and thirty members. The choir typically rehearses one evening a week, sings the special service music on Sunday morning, and leads the congregational singing. Special presentations for the Advent and Lenten seasons are common. Many churches perform an annual service of lessons and carols at Christmastide, which is based on an old English tradition.

Because church choirs are volunteer organizations, the choral director has to be willing to work with all types of voices. Adult church choirs often contain persons with problem voices, and while vocal exercises should be practiced to help all voices improve, the likelihood of making dramatic changes in the sound of older singers is not great. In this case, directors must work with what they have while continuing to encourage good singing technique.

The orientation of the adult choir is not to perform but rather to lead worship. When an anthem is performed, the offering must be judged by the sincerity of its presentation and not by quality standards that are applied to an auditioned group. This is not to say that church choral directors should not aim for high musical presentation. It does say that church choir directors must have realistic expectations, taking into consideration the nature of the choir's membership.

The church choral director has a big job preparing special music for each Sunday. Those who go into church music either part-time or full-time must know the difficulties and challenges that await them in working with amateur singers and not become discouraged. The rewards can be very satisfying in many ways.

CHILDREN'S CHOIRS

The last two decades of the twentieth century experienced a tremendous growth in children's choirs, both in and out of school settings. This movement became the fastest-growing area of choral development in America. Many reasons can be cited for this boom: (1) parents and children became dissatisfied with the singing in school general music, which had become mostly recreational; (2) materials and techniques for instructing children's voices became more readily available; (3) high-quality vocal literature for children was published; (4) the ACDA became a focal point for exciting choral directors about children's choirs; (5) performances by superior children's choirs from America and Europe were heard at the national conferences of MENC and ACDA; (6) recordings by outstanding American and European children's choirs were widely disseminated; and (7) new research in the development of children's singing voices made this a hot area of interest for teachers of vocal music. There came about a new legitimacy to the belief that all children could be taught to sing and that it was not harmful to do so.

Choir Structure

Many children's choirs are, in structure, similar to adult community choirs. The members are auditioned, attend weekly rehearsals, pay a membership fee, present public concerts, and so forth. They are conducted most often by experienced vocal music teachers who also may be choral directors. These choirs wear special performance attire and often travel on choir tours. It is a complex business and requires a board to help govern and finance the group.

Choirs in elementary schools have existed since Lowell Mason's time. The quality of literature varies but typically is not challenging. These types of choirs meet on school time, usually during music class, and classes are combined for a final massed-group rehearsal before a performance. The fact that these choirs involve all students is important.

Numerous elementary school vocal teachers have become interested in doing more advanced work with those students who really want to sing. For them, an honors or out-of-school choir represents an auditioned group where only the best singers are chosen. When large numbers are auditioning, a system of feeder choirs is established to enable more students to participate. In one school district in Iowa, the superintendent of schools believes so strongly in this program that a bus travels from school to school one morning a week, picking up children and delivering them to a central site for honor choir practice. The directing job is handled by two music teachers who accompany for each other. This group makes an annual trip to a university where they perform in a choral clinic. It is exciting to see the enthusiasm elementary students have for singing. Likewise, it is rewarding to see how the parents respond so positively to a nonsports activity. The honors choir is definitely the "in" group at this school district.

Yet children's choirs that involve an audition raise an important concern. Children at an early age should not be discouraged about singing by not passing an audition. Having a choir for all children to sing in is very important at the elementary level. By the intermediate years, however, children tend to know whether or not they want to sing, and an auditioned group can be special for those children who really want to sing. It is possible to have auditioned choirs and still meet the needs of all students for singing through general music and "all-grade" choirs.

Resources for working with children's choirs have become widely available and include the following: *Lifeline for Children's Choir Directors* (Bartle, 1993), *Teaching Kids to Sing* (Phillips, 1992), *Teaching Children through Choral Music Experience* (Rao, 1991), and *Teaching the Elementary School Chorus* (Swears, 1985).

The Curriculum

Directing a children's choir often means working at the grassroots level. Many children who audition may show potential but rarely have good singing technique. Therefore, they need to be taught to sing and read music in the choral rehearsal. This takes time, and the director's challenge is to build voices, develop reading skills, and prepare the music for performance.

The first area of the choir curriculum is the same as that for older students—building confident singing voices. Two of the biggest problems that directors encounter in teaching children proper vocal production are incorrect breathing and singing only in the chest voice. Once children learn to breathe properly and discover the use of the head voice, the technique for singing begins to align and function automatically. Until that time, a conscious effort must be made to have students use the vocal mechanism correctly.

SINGING LESSONS.   Every rehearsal for children should begin with a singing lesson, where clearly stated objectives are accomplished through the practice of vocal exercises and vocalises. The outline for this rehearsal segment is the same as that presented in Chapter 15: energize the body, energize the breath, energize the ear, and energize the voice. The body is the student's instrument—each child must learn to carry it so as to maximize its output. The breath is the foundation or motor of the singing process. Children who breathe incorrectly are more likely to sing inaccurately (Phillips, 1992). Since singing is a psychomotor skill, children must be able to hear, discriminate among, identify, and remember pitches. They also must be able to identify their own voices in relationship to an aural image of sound and the voices around them. Young children often sing inaccurately in a group because they lose their own voice in the crowd about them. Energizing the voice requires application of the breath to phonation, and experiencing the upper voice is the biggest step. Singing like Mickey Mouse is not that difficult, but many children seem to make it through school music without having discovered the upper vocal register, or head voice.

Numerous vocal exercises and vocalises are presented in Chapters 13, 14, and 15 and are as applicable to children, however, as to older students and adults. With young children, however, the director must be careful not to spend so much time on singing lessons as to tire the young voices. Children are unable to endure long periods of vocal instruction without developing vocal fatigue, but some time for vocal instruction is required if students are to find confidence in their singing and maximize their vocal potential.

MUSIC LITERACY.   Children who do not learn to read music grow up to be handicapped singers. It is the shame of the choral profession that so many choirs continue to be taught by rote. The remedy for this problem begins at the elementary level with a consistent program of sight-singing skills instruction.

A rote-to-note approach to sight reading is presented in Chapter 16 of this text. The basic rationale is that children first become comfortable with learning good singing technique, while at the same time develop aural skills, which results in the ability to audiate (Gordon, 1999), or understand what they hear musically. A child who hears and identifies "Twinkle, Twinkle, Little Star," has not reached the audiation stage until he or she can sing: *do-do-sol-sol-la-la-sol, fa-fa-mi-mi-re-re-do.* Once children are able to identify and label the pitches, they are ready to see what the pitches look like when notated. A bond or association is then created by what is heard in the mind with what is seen by the eyes.

Probably the greatest flaw in attempts to teach sight-singing is that the eye relates to nothing preexisting in the child's mind. Children are introduced to all types of theoretical elements—clefs, lines and spaces, key signatures, and so forth—but most of it becomes a meaningless jumble because it relates to little that the child has experienced. When written notes relate to nothing aurally, students do not become facile music readers.

Three major curricular approaches use the rote-to-note process: Gordon, Kodály, and Suzuki. However, the children's choir director need not have an in-depth knowledge of or use any of these excellent methods to successfully teach children to sight-sing. The steps laid out in Chapter 16 are sufficient to develop a sight-singing component of the rehearsal based on the rationale of rote-to-note. It is important to lay the aural foundation early in the child's singing career so that visual recognition will become more and more accurate. Regular, consistent instruction in sight-singing skill forms the second component of the children's choir rehearsal.

HIGH-QUALITY LITERATURE.   Learning to sing well and sight-sing accurately are just building blocks for making music. The actual singing of songs is what the choir is all about, and choosing literature to reinforce and continue to develop good singing technique is a demanding job for the choral director. A lot of junk music is published every year. Some of it is cute, some of it is catchy, and most of it is just of poor quality.

What makes a good children's choir selection? First, the text needs to relate to children, and it should be well written. It does not have to be serious, but it needs to have literary merit. The melody must be original and appealing, and it helps if it sometimes appears in voices other than the top part. Tessitura should be about a fifth in primary grades and an octave in the upper grades. The form should have some element of contrast, and the harmony must enrich the tonal fabric. It there is an accompaniment it should be creative and mildly independent. Most of all it must be musical, that is, beautiful. Leading children to an aesthetic experience through wonderful choral singing can be accomplished only through using high-quality literature. That is not to say that using some music for its purely entertainment value is not justified. But a steady diet of pop schlock will never fulfill the objectives of a true music education curriculum.

Finding superior children's choir literature has become easier as publishing houses have created new series for children's choir music. Learning about these sources takes a while but is worth the effort. Both the Bartle (1993) and Swears (1985) books contain excellent lists of recommended octavos. *We Will Sing!* by Doreen Rao (1993) is a choral curriculum for classroom choirs. There are three performance projects of ever increasing difficulty, which are available in three student booklets. This is first-class literature, and all of it is available on a CD or cassette tape format. Rao also has edited an MENC monograph called *Choral Music for Children: An Annotated List* (1990), which presents an annotated description of many pieces, helpfully graded as beginner, intermediate, or advanced.

The Director

The director of a children's choir must have a thorough knowledge of the child voice—what to expect and how to develop it. Most importantly, the director must have an aural knowledge of correct tone production for children's singing. This aural model will guide everything he or she does in the way of vocal technique development. It is amazing that any person would undertake to direct a children's choir who did not have the sound of correctly produced children's voices in mind. It is different from the sound of pop singers today, which is an unhealthy form of voice production. Those who would undertake to work with children should spend some time reading in-depth books like *Teaching Kids to Sing* (Phillips, 1992) and attend workshops and classes on child vocal production. Most importantly, they should seek to hear excellent models of children's singing. A good resource in this area is the video *Vocal Techniques for the Young Singer* (1997), by Henry Leck.

It goes without saying that the director of a children's choir must be an excellent musician. More than technical proficiency, however, is needed. To inspire children to do their best, the director must have a great love for music and understand how music can improve the quality of life for the children.

Lastly, the director must be a great teacher. Part of this involves knowing how to structure a rehearsal so that it flows and accomplishes the objectives outlined. Part of it involves being an effective communicator, using the voice and eye contact to motivate students and maintain control. And finally, the teacher must be well organized and task oriented. "Flying by the seat of the pants" or "winging it" are expressions not applicable to fine choral musicians. The children's choir, or any choir, will succeed only to the degree that the director plans the work and works the plan. When that happens, a great musical experience is primed and waiting to unfold, no matter what the age of the singers. A quality musical experience can be had just as profoundly with children as with adults. There is much fulfillment to be gained in working with kids.

NONTRADITIONAL CHOIRS

Choral directors can find the opportunity to use their talents in a number of other places. These include working in nontraditional settings such as prisons and senior centers, and working with the disabled. Wherever people congregate, the potential exists for choral singing.

A Prison Choir

One of the benefits in belonging to the ACDA is receiving the monthly publication of the *Choral Journal*, in which a wide range of articles regularly appear. In the August 1997 issue, Ann Waters presents an interview with Elvera Voth, conductor of the East Hill Singers, a male chorus in the Lansing Correctional Facility (minimum security), in Lansing, Kansas. The article presents a challenge to choral directors to consider taking choral music to an ever expanding prison population. Concerning her work with prisoners, Voth states:

> When I began working at Lansing, I quickly realized that prison life produces men who are tense and wary about expressing themselves. I had to work to establish a trusting and relaxed atmosphere so that they would accept criticism for musical errors without feeling threatened. I tried to keep the rehearsals lighthearted and encouraged a give-and-take atmosphere. Laughter and humor assume a sense of trust. It took a long time before these men trusted me enough to risk a laugh when I combined humor with musical discipline. Musical discipline, exacting and consistent, is a concept new to many of the singers, but it instills patterns and habits that can establish a model for other kinds of success. (p. 17)

Ninety-minute rehearsals are held in the prison chapel two nights a week. Voth works with soloists, instrumentalists, and sections prior to the main rehearsals. The chapel has an old, untuned upright piano. Since most of the singers envision themselves as soloists, it takes time to orient to the idea of choral blend. Also, sight-singing instruction is necessary, as most inmates have little sight-reading skills.

Voth combines a group of men from a local church choir with the inmate singers once or twice a month for rehearsals and for concerts:

> Friendship and mutual respect quickly develop when we sing together. With the secure support of the Rainbow men, the inmates are able to grasp the concept of good choral sound and the relationship of exact pitch and rhythm to the musical experience. They could not have the same choral experience without that help. (p. 19)

Regarding the choice of choral repertoire, Voth relates:

> Choosing repertoire for the East Hill Singers is an especially difficult process. Which pieces will work given such a wide variety of musical talent and experience? Will this literature stimulate an often bored, deadened mind? Will it be a window to new ways of thinking about their lives? Will it reach some place deep inside them that has become dormant? Will it help them feel that they are part of humankind and not outcasts looking in? Surely, texts and music written from the heart of human experience can offer these things. (pp. 19–20)

Voth goes on to relate that while most of the inmates sing contemporary Gospel music, "our music is chosen from the standard sacred and secular choral repertoire" (p. 20). Assessing the effects of choral music in the prison, Voth concludes, "I now know that people in prison receive the same social and spiritual benefits from choral singing that have so blessed our own lives. I know without doubt that this work is one of the most humbling, disturbing, and consuming experiences of my career" (p. 21).

What a challenge Elvera Voth presents to the choral profession—to move beyond the familiar and safe to working with a literally captive audience. If choral music has the power to transform lives and enhance the quality of living, where else is it needed more than in prisons?

A Choir for Seniors

Roy Ernst, professor of music education at the Eastman School of Music, is the founding director of a program for senior citizens he calls "Music for Life." It began in 1991 with the New Horizons Band project, a model program for adults aged fifty and above for entry and reentry to instrumental band playing. Fifty such programs now exist in the United States and Canada. The program has expanded to include other kinds of adult music making, including choirs. Concerning choral groups, Ernst (2001) states,

> There are some special challenges for adult choral groups. One choral conductor told me, "I think bands and orchestras for senior adults are great, but senior choruses can never be successful because voices worsen as they age." I don't believe that. I believe voices become *different* with age. We need to define the special strengths of older singers and then create new arrangements, compositions, and methods that take advantage of what they can do. In many cultures, the oldest singers are the most revered because of the wisdom and years of life experience that they bring to making music. A seniors' vocal group in Iowa City alludes to that by calling itself "The Voice of Experience." I love hearing this group sing because they really do offer something special. (p. 50)

The Iowa City choir to which Ernst makes reference is directed by Glenn Jablonski, a retired high school choral director. The choir has been in existence for eighteen years and rehearses twice a week at the senior center. No audition is required for membership, and all seniors are encouraged to participate. No membership fee is required. The typical enrollment is about fifty persons, and the average age is seventy-five. Three past members have sung into their nineties. The music that the group sings is from the standard choral literature, mostly easy to medium pieces. Two concerts are presented each year, along with numerous other social engagements. The choir presents a valuable time for interaction with other seniors and permits the members to give voice to their love for music.

Another of the benefits of senior adult music ensembles is that "people who become involved in adult ensembles support music education in the schools by their example of choosing to be active music makers. They tend to admire and support music teachers. One senior adult musician told me, 'I heard the elementary concert in my district. Wow! Those kids are good, and the teacher is wonderful!' " (Ernst, 2001, p. 50).

Roger Hoel (1998) tells of his desire to keep singing as he grew older resulting in the founding of the Minnetonka Senior Chorale and later the Minnesota Senior Choral Association. As of 1998 there were nine senior choirs in the Twin Cities area. Hoel comments that "the ensemble often meets the special needs of newly widowed seniors, who may not have the social opportunities they once enjoyed" (p. 44). He concludes:

> I believe music so lovingly placed in our hearts early in our lives should be heard, played, and sung all our lives. The wobbles, pitch problems, loud basses, and memory lapses may be daunting, but they're not insurmountable. In fact, those problems are often the greatest sources of fun and laughter. May the joy of singing remain with us all our lives. (p. 45)

The challenge is before the profession to expand the senior choir movement. While it is true that a unified blend is more difficult to achieve among older voices, Ernst's idea of thinking differently about tone quality at this age is a point well taken. Instrumental directors seem to be leading in planning for life-long music making for seniors, but Roy Ernst's conception is to find a place for all seniors to make music, including singers.

A Choir for the Disabled

The Individuals with Disabilities Act of 1990/1997 (formerly Public Law 94-142) directs that all children with disabilities be given equal access to educational programs in the public schools. Vicki Lind, in her article "Adapting Choral Rehearsals for Students with Learning Disabilities" (2001), indicates numerous ways in which choral directors can make their rehearsals more productive for disabled students. She concludes,

> Singers with specific learning disabilities can participate successfully in all aspects of music learning if the information is presented in a variety of ways. Educators have found that using kinesthetic, visual, and aural teaching strategies can help singers with specific learning disabilities participate more fully in the classroom. Rehearsals designed to incorporate a variety of activities can help singers with SpLD stay focused and participate fully. (p. 30)

While the Disabilities Act does direct that all children with disabilities be given equal access to education, it does not mandate that all children be mainstreamed. What it states is that disabled children be placed in the "least restrictive environment." This environment has to be determined for each individual student according to the school's policy. In one case it may be determined that a severely disabled child will do better in a regular chorus, while in another it could be that a moderately disabled person will do better in a chorus for disabled children. It all depends upon the individual and how he or she is functioning mentally and physically.

Patricia Coates, in the article "Enabling the Disabled Choral Singer" (1988), suggests that a choir for disabled students is appropriate when it will better meet the students' needs:

> Some educators question the advisability of grouping handicapped people together, expressing concern that a choir of this type might stigmatize the students. However, more often than not, handicapped students suffer social isolation when they are placed among the general school population. Viewed from a different perspective, the handicapped choir provides a peer group that may be otherwise unavailable. Severely handicapped students are better able to develop their performing abilities in a climate of peer acceptance. (p. 47)

Coates states that performance standards must be set high, and attention paid to improving vocal production. It is not unreasonable, she relates, to expect the students to learn to follow the conductor and interpret the music. "It is the rule rather than the exception that an idea will have to be modified over time until the desired outcome is accomplished" (pp. 47–48). Coates gives a number of suggestions for recruiting, auditioning, rehearsal rules, limitations, and potential. "Gradually the group will evolve into a polished performing organization. The extra effort it takes will provide handicapped students with an opportunity to perform that they might not otherwise have had" (p. 48).

Alumni Choir

An alumni choir at the high school or college level is typically a once-a-year event. It may be as simple as coming together to sing during a homecoming event, or it may involve a European trip. Some colleges have sponsored tours abroad for their alumni, and this can be a special time or it can be stressful if arrangements break down and people grumble. It is one thing to take a group of students on tour who require little more than a cot to sleep, and another to take a group of adults who are used to all of the amenities of life. Nevertheless, directing an alumni choir can be rewarding as old friendships are reestablished and new ones made through music. High school reunions are a perfect time for former choral students to enjoy making music together once again.

Intergenerational Choir

The parent-child gap has troubled psychologists and educators for years. Some attempts have been made to bridge this chasm, and attempts have shown bright prospects for intergenerational programs in music.

Paul Schilf (2001) directed an intergenerational study in which students and parents played together in a Saturday band program. Students attended weekly band rehearsals with those parents brave enough to volunteer for this combined ensemble. Most of the parents had not played since high school and were nervous about sitting next to students who were playing well. Nevertheless, initial nervousness gave way, and students and parents soon began interacting and enjoying one another's company. The study ended with a successful public concert, and positive reactions from students, parents, and other family members were received. Music, once again, was shown to be a catalyst for cooperative learning—this time, between generations.

Intergenerational choirs might have great success, given that many people continue to sing as they grow older. Little research has been done in this area, and only two studies are known. A study by Bowers (1997) investigated the attitudes of senior citizens and university students in a mixed intergenerational chorus. Members of each group were matched as "buddies" for a year-long program, which culminated in a final concert. Results of the study indicated that positive interaction can improve stereotypical attitudes between intergenerational singers.

Similiar results were found in a study by Darrow, Johnson, and Ollenberger (1994) when teenagers and older adults were combined in an intergenerational choir:

> It seems possible that intergenerational programming can serve as a viable means of communication between generations. Because the extended family is less intact today, many young people do not know their grandparents; and because of the mobility of today's society, older persons often become estranged from their children and grandchildren. The surrogate relationships that frequently develop through intergenerational activities can fulfill a need for family contact and dissuade isolation. (p. 132)

Intergenerational choirs provide an opportunity for personal and musical growth. "It seems possible that music, along with the experience of age and the enthusiasm of youth, can help to bridge the generation gap" (p. 133).

STUDY AND DISCUSSION QUESTIONS

1. What are some of the benefits of directing nonschool choral groups?
2. Who publishes an excellent guide for organizing a community chorus? What do you know about this group?
3. What are the responsibilities of a board of directors for a community chorus?
4. What are the responsibilities of the conductor of a community chorus?

5. How are members chosen for most community choirs? What is involved in this process?

6. For what reason do most people choose to sing in a community chorus?

7. What is the dilemma in which church choral directors often find themselves today? In what ways can this dilemma be resolved?

8. Why is it important to know the musical tastes of a minister before taking a job as a church choral director?

9. What does a church's "graded choir" system involve?

10. What problems arise when church choir members are not auditioned?

11. What has contributed to the boom in the children's choir movement?

12. What reasons can be given in favor of select and nonselect children's choirs?

13. What three areas make up the children's choir curriculum?

14. What general principle should govern the teaching of music literacy to children?

15. Why is high-quality choral literature so important for children's choirs?

16. What are the basic qualifications for the children's choir director?

17. What are some difficult challenges to starting a choir for prisoners?

18. What is the main objective of the "Music for Life" program?

19. Where does the Individuals with Disabilities Act say that students with disabilities be placed in the school setting?

20. What are the personal and musical benefits that can happen as the result of an intergenerational choral experience?

REFERENCES

Bartle, J. A. (1993). *Lifeline for children's choir directors* (rev. ed.). Toronto: Gordon V. Thompson Music.

Bertalot, J. (1999). *Immediately practical tips for choral directors*. Minneapolis: Augsburg Fortress.

Coates, P. (1988). Enabling the disabled choral singer. *Music Educators Journal, 73*(5), 46–48.

Bowers, J. (1997). *Public school partnerships in teacher education: The adopt-a-choir program and the senior singers.* Paper presented at the National Symposium for Research in Music Behavior, Minneapolis, May 1997.

Collins, D. L. (1999). *Teaching choral music* (2d ed). Upper Saddle River, NJ: Prentice Hall.

Darrow, A. A., C. M. Johnson, and T. Ollenberger, (1994). The effect of participation in an intergenerational choir on teens' and older persons' cross-age attitudes. *Journal of Music Therapy, 31*(2), 119–133.

Ernst, R. (2001). Music for life. *Music Educators Journal, 88*(1), 47–51.

Gordon, E. E. (1999). All about audiation and music aptitudes. *Music Educators Journal, 86*(2), 41–44.

Hoel, R. S. (1998). Keeping the songs alive: Working with senior singers. *Choral Journal, 38*(7), 43–45.

Hustad, D. P. (1981). *Jubilate! Church music in the evangelical tradition.* Carol Stream, IL: Hope.

Hustad, D. P. (1993). *Jubilate II: Church music in worship and renewal.* Carol Stream, IL: Hope.

Leck, H. (1997). *Vocal techniques for the young singer* (video). Ft. Lauderdale, FL: Plymouth Music (available from Colla Voce, Indianapolis, IN).

Lind, V. R. (2001). Adapting choral rehearsals for students with learning disabilities. *Choral Journal, 41*(7), 27–30.

McRae, S. W. (1991). *Directing the children's choir.* New York: Schirmer Books.

Mitchell, R. H. (1978). *Ministry and music.* Philadelphia: The Westminster Press.

Page, R., L. Greenberg, and F. Leise (eds.) (1999). *The chorus handbook: Chorus 101: The "how-to" book for organizing and operating a professional and volunteer choral ensemble.* Washington, DC: Chorus America.

Phillips, K. H. (1992). *Teaching kids to sing.* New York: Schirmer Books.

Rao, D. (1991). *Teaching children through choral music experience.* New York: Boosey and Hawkes.

——— (1993). *We will sing! Choral music experience for classroom choirs.* New York: Boosey and Hawkes.

——— (ed.) (1990). *Choral music for children: An annotated list.* Reston, VA: Music Educators National Conference.

Rotermund, D. (1985). *Children sing his praise: A handbook for children's choir directors.* St. Louis: Concordia.

Schilf, P. (2001). An analysis of interactions between teenagers and their parents in an intergenerational concert band (doctoral diss., University of Iowa).

Swears, L. (1985). *Teaching the elementary school chorus.* West Nyack, NY: Parker.

Waters, A. W. (1997). Conducting a prison chorus: An interview with Elvera Voth. *Choral Journal,* *38*(1), 17–21.

Yarrington, J. (1990). *Building the youth choir: Training and motivating teenage singers.* Minneapolis: Augsburg Fortress.

Unit 3

OPTIONAL PROJECTS

1. Planning and Leading a Warm-Up Routine

a. Review the elements that are important items for the choral warm-up (body, breath, ear, voice). Plan a five- to six-minute warm-up routine that includes representative exercises and vocalises; share it with the class. Be able to discuss the objective of each item and its importance to vocal development.

b. Lead the class in the warm-up routine developed in the first part of this project. Spend as little time talking as possible. Have your plan memorized so the routine will flow from item to item without hesitation. Repeat this exercise if time permits.

2. Planning and Leading a Sight-Singing Exercise

a. Review the components (aural and visual) for the teaching of sight-singing. Plan a four- to five-minute sight-singing lesson that includes both aural and visual components, and which assumes that students are in the beginning stages of using written notation.

b. Lead the class in the sight-singing exercises. Written copy should be available for each class member, when applicable. Repeat this project if time permits.

3. Rehearsing the Choir (Microteaching)

a. Plan and direct a choral rehearsal segment for five minutes in which you introduce a new piece of music. Structure this segment based on a comprehensive musicianship approach: title, composer, era, meaning and mood, and overall structure. Don't just lecture. Draw answers from students whenever possible.

b. Repeat the microteaching experience by building on the first part of this project. Review and add something new to the historical or theoretical knowledge of the choral piece. Study the techniques for helping students gain a concept of a piece as a whole, and then direct students in doing so.

c. Other microteaching sessions include the teaching of text, rhythm, melody, and parts as a layering process. Microteaching for problems in pitch, rhythm, intonation, blend, diction, and so forth will help you begin hearing problem spots within the whole texture of sound. If time permits, teach for longer segments of time and the polishing of each choral selection.

4. Developing a Concert Program

a. Develop a program for a spring concert at the high school where you are the choral director. The performance should include four choirs: a concert choir (the best students), a general high school chorus, a junior choir of seventh and eighth graders, and a small ensemble of your choosing (madrigal group, show choir, etc.). Choose approximately five selections for each group, and be sure to consider range, tessitura, and level of difficulty when selecting the music. The selections for the concert choir should be of the masterworks style. Be sure that music for the junior choir has a part singable by boys with changing voices. The total length of the concert should be no more than ninety minutes, which includes applause and change of choirs. The intermission, if any, must be included as part of the ninety minutes. Choice of a theme is optional.

b. Prepare written materials as follows.

1. Design a written program for the concert as it will appear when duplicated. The cover needs to include pertinent information such as school, date, time, place, and conductor. Lay out the program (usually two pages on the inside) in a logical order; spelling of choral titles and composers is <u>very</u> important. Include also the names of any soloists and accompanists, and an acknowledgment section for those you wish to thank. Names of students may be included by choir, but this is optional.

2. Write a news release to be sent out for advertising the concert. Highlight something about the program that will arouse the public's interest. Newspapers always like to include the names of soloists.

3. Prepare a weekly rehearsal schedule in preparation for this concert. How long will the total preparation period last? Show when the rehearsal of each piece will begin and for how many weeks it will be rehearsed. Note the time of the dress rehearsal in the schedule.

4. Prepare a timing sheet to show the time (in minutes and seconds) of each selection, the time allowed for applause and changing of choirs, any announcements, and so forth. The total time of the concert is to be no more than ninety minutes.

5. Prepare a technical sheet to address the following: printed program, piano tuning, ushers, stage crew, risers, acoustical shell, sound system, special lighting, decorations, student attire, and tickets. If any of the preceding do not apply, mark as N/A.

c. Package this project in a large envelope and include the music. All music should be returned by the end of the course.

MOVING INTO THE WORKPLACE

21 | Planning for Success

EUGENE F. BECHEN

The final step in preparing to become a choral director involves making the transition from student to educator. As for all phases of this preparation, planning is of critical importance. A great amount of frustration and stress can be avoided if the student takes a proactive approach to planning for success.

CREATING A SUCCESSFUL STUDENT TEACHING EXPERIENCE

The student teaching experience plays a vital role in the development of the music educator. It serves as the bridge between the undergraduate music education program and the real world of public school teaching. Although many view this period as important, many student teaching experiences fail to give beginning teachers the tools they need to develop into successful music educators.

Ideally, the student teaching experience should serve as the culmination of several years of preparation, with well-executed lesson plans, frequent supervision, and high-quality mentoring. Often the opposite is true. Svengails states, "Unfortunately, this critical experience is often a patchwork, at best, with many of the essential components seemingly left to chance" (1992, p. 31). Many student teachers must fend for themselves at the end of their undergraduate programs, not having an understanding of the issues that will affect their student teaching experience and the beginning of their career.

Five basic issues affect the quality of the student teaching experience and, in turn, the classroom performance of the beginning teacher: (1) the student teacher, (2) the school site, (3) the cooperating teacher, (4) interpersonal relationships, and (5) the process of student teaching.

The Student Teacher

Student teachers are often unaware that they cause many of their own problems when student teaching. Many of these problems have to do with personality characteristics, role identity, and personal concerns.

Eugene F. Bechen, Ph.D., is a graduate of The University of Iowa and is currently Assistant Professor of Music at Indiana State University, Terre Haute.

Student teachers often lack an understanding of the personality characteristics needed to be successful in the classroom and fail to work on developing these characteristics prior to student teaching. This lack of understanding results in student teachers who are shy, timid, passive, and permissive in the classroom, resulting in management and discipline problems.

Brand (1983) identifies six attributes found in successful music teachers based on a review of the research literature: (1) enthusiasm; (2) warmth and personal interest; (3) a rehearsal technique combining clarity, brevity, fast pace, and variety; (4) a balance of praise and meaningful criticism; (5) a discipline technique focusing on communication; and (6) the desire to improve and learn. Many student teachers can identify the importance of this list of attributes, but few develop these practices before student teaching. Beginning teachers can improve their chances for success in the classroom by observing and emulating master teachers. Developing these attributes in advance will allow for greater success during student teaching.

Role identity also affects the beginning teacher's performance. Concerns with role identity initially manifest themselves in classroom management techniques. "Future teachers come to the university program and student teaching with many of their classroom management beliefs and styles in place, based in part on their own personalities and past teacher role models" (Snyder, 1998, p. 38). Student teachers have watched teachers teach for years and have had time to decide in their own minds what teaching personality or identity they want to present in their classroom. Snyder states, "Student teachers tend to accept or reject techniques that will or will not work for them, according to their personalities" (1998, p. 38). As a result, many student teachers end up presenting a teaching personality based on a role identity from the past rather than one appropriate for their present teaching environment. Student teachers often grow frustrated when their dated identity does not seem to work with the students in their classroom. Preservice and beginning teachers can help improve their adaptability to different teaching environments by familiarizing themselves with a variety of instructional settings prior to the student teaching experience.

Personal concerns of student teachers (housing, transportation, money, student teaching location, etc.) are most on their minds prior to student teaching. Such problems are often not addressed early enough to keep from becoming hindrances. These factors often limit student teachers geographically, forcing them to teach in an environment that is not conducive to their success. Attempts to save money or lessen commuting time often result in trouble later on, as student teachers realize that their student teaching environment does not fit them as well as they would like it to, nor does it allow them to succeed. While personal concerns are important, the student teacher must remember that a high-quality student teaching experience will be the basis for launching a successful teaching career.

The School Site

The school site is usually chosen for its proximity to the college or university, and because most university teacher preparation programs have regular student teaching seminars in which attendance is required. When a student needs to teach at a site outside of the university's area of supervision, a sponsoring school and supervisor must be found. While this may not be the best practice, it is an acceptable one carried out by many schools. It is important that some type of student teaching seminar be included for students in this situation.

Another reason that choice of school sites may be limited is the student's need to finish coursework, prepare a recital, or participate in an ensemble. These types of activities are not recommended for student teachers, as they invariably interfere with the student teaching process. Students find themselves living two lives at the same time—that of college student and public school teacher. While the site may be convenient, the negative effect on the student's work is almost guaranteed.

The willingness of school administrators and cooperating teachers to host student teachers also affects the availability of choices for student teaching assignments. Compensation for cooperating teachers to host a student teacher is minimal in comparison to the demands of the job, and many overburdened music teachers are not willing to take on the extra responsibility of hosting a student teacher. In addition, the preservice teacher needs to be aware that while some schools may look upon hosting the student teacher as an opportunity, others may view it as a burden.

The most unfortunate problem with the limited availability of school sites is the prevention of student teachers from teaching in environments that are culturally diverse. Students need to teach in as many diverse situations as possible to prepare them adequately for the world of school teaching. Some universities now have midsemester practicum placements in inner-city schools for students who would not normally receive this type of placement.

Other site-based factors that might affect the quality of the student teaching experience could involve scheduling (e.g., block scheduling versus a seven-period day), inadequate or poor facilities, the school's attitude toward its arts programs, and the overall quality of discipline and student management throughout the school. Students should consider all of these factors when requesting a student teaching site.

The Cooperating Teacher

Not all cooperating teachers have the same attitude toward hosting a student teacher. Some view the experience as an opportunity to learn new ideas and are enthusiastic about making a contribution to the field of music education. Others see the experience as another demand on their busy, overbooked schedule. Many student teachers fail to investigate the attitudes of potential hosts and often are stuck with cooperating teachers whose attitudes do not meet their needs.

Another concern regarding cooperating teachers is their experience in dealing with student teachers. The cooperating teacher may be eager to help the student teacher develop his or her teaching skill, but may lack the experience and ability to provide adequate solutions to some of the difficulties of student teaching. Potential student teachers need to research the abilities of a potential cooperating teacher by talking to previous student teachers who have taught at that school. Working with or teaching for a particular teacher prior to placement in a school provides the best opportunity to assess the ability of the cooperating teacher.

Many student teachers do not think about the amount of time the cooperating teacher will have to interact with them. Music teachers are so overextended that they rarely have time to stay on top of all the administrative tasks in running their program, let alone find time each day to work with their student teacher. Students often realize this is the case after it is too late and are often frustrated with the lack of time they are able to spend with their cooperating teacher. It is important for the student teacher to receive feedback and still be empathetic to the demands of the music schedule. Student teachers benefit from scheduling regular daily or weekly times with their cooperating teachers to talk about classroom performance.

Student teachers also need to be concerned about cooperating teachers' attitudes toward providing adequate teaching opportunities. Will the student teacher be allowed to teach in all aspects of the program or just a select few? Is the cooperating teacher willing to allow the student teacher to conduct at public performances? Will the student teacher be allowed to spend as much time with the select ensembles as with the younger, less-visible ensembles? How much time will the student teacher be allowed to work with small groups and ensembles? How much time will the student teacher spend in teaching the show choir, jazz choir, or madrigal singers? These are important questions to answer before the student teaching experience.

When student teachers do not seek this information prior to school placement, they may be disappointed to learn that cooperating teachers will not let them work with their select ensembles. Student teachers often take this lack of student contact personally and let it affect their relationships with the cooperating teachers. Many fail to realize the pressure on cooperating teachers to have their ensembles ready to perform and compete. Once again, talking to former student teachers will provide information to answer these questions.

The student teacher needs to talk to the cooperating teacher before the student teaching process to make a list of anticipated responsibilities and activities. Such an outline will help the student and the cooperating teacher to think about what is appropriate and when it should be implemented.

Problems sometimes arise during student teaching when a difference in philosophies exists between the cooperating and the student teacher. Most often these differences are centered on attitudes toward competition, program management, teaching style, and pedagogical approaches. Beginning teachers can benefit greatly by networking with and getting to know their potential cooperating teachers before being assigned to them. However, when conflicts of attitude arise between the student teacher and cooperating teacher, the student teacher must respect the position of the cooperating teacher, who is in authority.

Interpersonal Relationships

The student teaching experience depends greatly on interpersonal relationships among several key people. Obviously, the relationship with the cooperating teacher is of the utmost importance. Many student teachers underestimate the importance of this relationship. They falter and do not work hard enough to keep the lines of communication open. Student teachers must do everything they can to keep this two-way relationship healthy and positive. They must never underestimate the value of the cooperating teacher and his or her ability to help after student teaching. If the student has worked hard on keeping this relationship healthy, it could last long after the letters of recommendation have been written and a job has been found.

Student teachers also must be concerned about their relationship with the university supervisor, especially in the areas of grading and evaluation. The supervisor is usually in charge of evaluating and assigning grades. Problems arise when the expectations of the university supervisor are not met by the student teacher or the cooperating teacher. Although the student may not work with the supervisor as much as the cooperating teacher, everything must be done to foster a positive relationship with this person. Also, the supervisor can be an excellent resource for help should a problem arise between the student teacher and cooperating teacher.

In addition to fostering the above relationships, the student teacher will want to develop relationships with all of the music department staff. They, too, can be an excellent resource during the student teaching experience. The student should take advantage of their expertise and use their feedback as often as possible. Although these music teachers may not be as "official" as the cooperating teacher, they can benefit the student in many ways. In addition, administrators, secretaries, custodians, and other members of the faculty often provide the student teacher with much support and various perspectives on teaching in the school environment.

The Student Teaching Process

The student teaching process is complex and is affected by a number of factors that are out of the student teacher's control. Svengalis states, "The process of the internship [student teaching] abounds with potential problems" (1992, p. 32).

The length of student teaching will have an important effect on the quality of the experience. Student teachers benefit greatly from longer experiences, as they are able to see the long-term process of teaching—from an organizational and motivational beginning to a polished performance. Longer student teaching experiences also allow student teachers to develop more meaningful relationships with their students and colleagues, making the process more rewarding. A longer experience also provides the student teacher with a more realistic view of what it takes to be a successful music educator. Student teachers with shorter internships often comment on how their experience was lacking.

The timing of the student teaching experience also affects the quality of the internship. Different semesters or quarters bring different challenges and activities for the choral program. The difference between student teaching in the fall during the production of the school musical and student teaching in the spring during show choir season provides two completely different sets of experiences. Shorter internships occurring at the first or second half of the semester also affect what the student teacher sees and does not see in regard to the complete teaching process.

Another concern involves the assessment and evaluation of teaching. Student teachers often do not receive enough feedback from those responsible for the assessment and evaluation of their teaching. Visits from university supervisors may be sparse and sporadic, with the possibility of the supervisor's having little or no musical background. Differences in evaluation and performance expectations between the cooperating teacher and the university supervisor also can be a problem. Evaluation and grading forms are often provided by colleges of education and lack the musical specificity needed for the student teacher to improve his or her teaching. All of this can cause great concern for the student teacher wanting to succeed.

Student teachers can enhance the evaluation process through a variety of analysis and assessment strategies. Daily journal writing allows student teachers to reflect on their teaching for the day and to see patterns in their teaching that are successful or unsuccessful. Video and audio taping of classroom presentations provide an enormous amount of information to help improve speaking, nonverbal communication, classroom management, rehearsal technique, and conducting skills. Having the cooperating teacher (or other music teachers) regularly take notes on presentations provides high-quality feedback that can serve as a catalyst for discussion with the cooperating teacher or university supervisor. Unfortunately, many student teachers do not take the initiative to collect this information and lose out on many valuable learning opportunities.

Increasing awareness of possible problems before student teaching begins will help in being better prepared for the student teaching experience. By taking a proactive approach, the student teacher can deal with many of these problems before entering the classroom. The student needs to take the initiative to work for the best assignment possible. By making a list of strengths and weaknesses in advance and finding the school environment that is most suitable, the student teacher is planning for success.

Kimberly Welch (1993) took control of her student teaching placement and considered five major factors in her search. She looked for:

- An experience in a region different from her childhood and college background in order to broaden her views in and out of the classroom

- A school system that would have a variety of students—culturally, economically, and academically—so she would be better prepared to handle mixed student populations in future job situations

- An experience that would give equal emphasis to the elementary, middle, and high school levels—one that would provide her with the knowledge needed to be capable of any music position, K–12

- The most experienced and most highly motivated cooperating teachers possible—individuals who were currently making great strides in their field

- A school system that would lend itself to good job opportunities upon completion of student teaching and graduation

Welch suggests the following to other students who are entering the student teaching experience:

- Write letters and call college officials, school superintendents, principals, and teachers regarding student teaching possibilities.

- Organize your own schedule to fit in the experiences you want.

- Cultivate professional contacts and draw on them to choose your cooperating teachers.

- Work with your college or university officials for maximum flexibility. (p. 40)

Many student teachers rely too heavily on a university system of placing student teachers that is focused more on convenience than quality. Welch points out that "all you really need as a student is a positive attitude toward your career—an attitude that calls for taking an active part in designing your student teaching experience" (p. 41). By considering the above factors, student teachers can give themselves a successful and meaningful student teaching experience that will influence their teaching for years to come.

THE JOB SEARCH

Another important "to do" for the beginning music educator is the job search. This process takes a great deal of organization, time, preparation, determination, and persistence. For many, this process needs to occur during the student teaching experience, making it doubly tough to keep up with the demands of student teaching and job hunting.

Using the Internet

The job search, however, is now easier than ever. The advent of the personal computer and the Internet allows faster access to job listings, applications, school district information, and even online books that teach how to find and apply for jobs. One of the most valuable resources for the first-year teacher is Barbara Payne's "A Career Guide to Music Education" (1997; located at ⟨http://www.menc.org/industry/job/career.html⟩). This online book is an invaluable resource for music educators about to embark on their first job search. The chapters in the book are as follows:

1. Starting Your Job Search
2. Locating Your Job Search
3. Résumés, Cover Letters, and Application Forms
4. Interviewing

5. Graduate School

6. Appendix: Sample Power Verbs for Résumés

This excellent resource contains examples of many of the necessary documents needed for the job search. It also has an excellent list of sample interview questions and references for additional sources of information.

The computer and Internet have increased the accessibility of information involved in the job search. One result is an increased level of competition for jobs, as more people from a wider geographical base can apply for teaching jobs. People also are getting their information to school administrators more quickly via the Internet. E-mail, attachments, and online student teaching portfolios allow administrators fast access to a potential employee's résumé. The technological influences on the job search are profound and place much higher demands on potential teachers to create electronic versions of their documentation.

Another important use for the Internet is to find job listings. Becoming familiar with websites on the Internet helps to guide a person to job listings, vacancy bulletins, and information about school districts. It is worth the effort to become familiar with how to use various search engines on the Internet to find the information needed. This takes a bit of practice (depending on a person's skill level at the computer), as each search engine works differently. At this point in time some of the more popular Internet search engines are:

- Google ⟨http://www.google.com⟩
- HotBot ⟨http://www.hotbot.com⟩
- Yahoo ⟨http://www.yahoo.com⟩
- Alta Vista ⟨http://altavista.com⟩
- Lycos ⟨http://www.lycos.com⟩

Literally hundreds of websites are devoted to helping educators find jobs on the Internet. Some current websites posting job vacancies for choral music educators are:

- Music Educators National Conference ⟨www.menc/industry/job/joblist.html⟩
- The American Choral Directors Association ⟨www.acdaonline.org/⟩
- ChoralNet Job Board ⟨http://choralnet.org/jobs/⟩

Other current job sites for educators include:

- Academic Employment Network ⟨www.academploy.com⟩
- K12jobs ⟨www.k12jobs.com⟩
- AfterCollege ⟨www.aftercollege.com⟩

Other sources of listings on the Internet include classified sections of newspaper web pages, web pages from music stores, and regional choral and music education association sites.

The Internet also offers a great deal of information on job search strategies, as well as how to build résumés and write cover letters. Student teachers who start building and developing their cover letters, résumés, online portfolios, and so forth, prior to student teaching have a much greater chance of developing high-quality documents that will help them find a job. Students need to analyze their skills, gather the necessary tools, and begin to put the necessary materials together as early as possible. This will put them ahead of the majority of job seekers and lessen the demands on their time during the student teaching experience.

Job Search Tips

Payne's book also provides excellent information to begin creating job search documents and offers important advice for interviewing and executing a successful job search. In addition to Payne's advice, the following list of tips may be helpful when carrying out the first job search.

- Start early. Set goals for yourself in preparing and completing your materials and then carry them out. A good friend once told me, "Procrastination kills."

- Make sure you have the necessary skills to run a computer, word processor, and web browser prior to the job search. You will save a great deal of time and frustration if you are not having to learn software applications along the way.

- Know what kind of job you want. Know what type of an environment you can or cannot live with. What geographical region do you want to live in? What types of communities do you enjoy? Make lists of your preferences and keep this list up to date. These lists will help you clarify what you are looking for during the search.

- Don't limit yourself geographically. Although you may know what you want and where you want to teach, a job may not be available in that particular region or town. Accept the fact that teaching is a nomadic profession and that you may have to compromise your standards a bit to become employed at the beginning of your career.

- Never underestimate the value of networking with fellow music educators. Make as many contacts as you can before, during, and after student teaching. Network with people who know what is going on in the music education community. Officers of district and state music associations and sales representatives from music stores are excellent sources of information. The contacts you have made may help you land that first job.

- Collect résumés and cover letters from other music educators. Find out how other people constructed these documents and what content they decided was important to include.

- Show your paperwork (résumé, cover letter, portfolios) to fellow music educators and have them give you comments and suggestions before you begin to send these materials to employers. After you have collected everyone's opinions, pick those that work best for you.

- Always present yourself as professionally as possible while creating your documents. Many administrators throw résumés and cover letters into the circular file when they see a typographical or grammatical error. Constantly look for errors in your documents.

- Create and organize a system that allows you to keep track of what materials have been sent to each school district. Keep a log of phone calls and names of contacts, when documents were sent, and copies of responses to short-answer questions on job applications. You will find that many school district job applications will ask the same questions. You can save yourself a great deal of work by developing good responses to these questions and keeping them on hand for the next application.

- Collect videotapes of your teaching in the classroom during student teaching. Pick the best presentations, put them on videotape, and take the tape along with you to each job interview. The tape may help convince an administrator to hire you.

- Practice interviewing as much as possible. Go to job fairs and on-campus interviews as much as possible, even if you are not interested in a particular job. Interviewing is a lot like sight-reading or auditioning—the more you do it, the better you will be at it.

- Be prepared for all types of interview situations. Don't be afraid to ask about the format of the interview before you arrive. Will it be a one-on-one situation or will you be interviewed by a panel? Will you be interviewed by parents or students? Will you have to perform in any way (conduct, sing, play the piano)? It is very important to know this information before the interview.

The job search can be educational, rewarding, and stressful. Relationships with the cooperating teacher, university supervisor, and others will prove to be beneficial to the job search. Students should seek out advice from colleagues and ask for their opinions often. These people will help to guide the student through the process, offering valuable advice and perspectives along the way. All of this information should be used to help make the best career decisions possible.

PROFESSIONAL GROWTH AND DEVELOPMENT

One of the great things about a career in music is that learning is never-ending. Even as a teacher in a public or private school, learning occurs on a daily basis. The field of music education constantly changes over time, and it is vital for music teachers to consistently work on growing and developing as a professional educator. Participation in professional development activities helps teachers to be more effective in the classroom and to feel better about what they do and the influence they have on their students. Teachers need to remain in contact with the outside world.

Professional Organizations

Although there are many ways in which to develop and grow professionally, it is vital that music teachers become members of professional organizations and associations in the field of music education and education in general. Memberships in state, regional, and national associations keep members abreast of the most recent developments in their field. Belonging to the American Choral Directors Association, Music Educators National Conference, and the National Education Association provides many professional development opportunities. By getting involved in these organizations at the state and national levels, the music educator will learn a great deal by networking with some of the top educators in the field.

Professional organizations also provide a variety of educational materials and publications to read and study. Associations and organizations present numerous conventions and clinics to attend, allowing members to see new developments in music education firsthand. Attending conferences and clinics also allows teachers to survey and investigate new literature, classroom materials and equipment, curriculum approaches, and dozens of other important topics in the field of music education. Many music educators find conferences and clinics to be a shot in the arm, as they share many of their ideas and concerns with other music teachers.

Mentoring, Performing, Graduate School

Some music education associations provide mentoring services for beginning teachers. Experienced master teachers are assigned to mentor beginning teachers new to the area and then help the new teachers through their first year of teaching. Mentor programs often have the beginning teacher visit and observe the mentor in their classroom environment, allowing the first-year teacher to collect ideas on how to handle certain instructional situations. Other mentors visit the classroom of the beginning teacher, taking a supervisory role to help the teacher improve. Mentoring programs are currently growing and are of great benefit to the beginning music educator.

Maintaining a life as a performer is also an excellent way to grow and develop professionally, as is becoming an adjudicator, guest performer, soloist, or festival conductor. In addition, working on a graduate degree in music can be one of the most intellectually invigorating activities in which one can participate. It is vitally important that teachers continue to grow and develop throughout their careers. Master teachers who have had excellent longevity in the field of music education are often the educators who are deeply committed to their own professional growth and development.

DEALING WITH STRESS AND BURNOUT

Many would agree that being a music educator in the public schools can be stressful. After dealing with all of the problems and concerns described earlier for the student teaching experience, most students agree that student teaching is very stressful.

Reality Shock

Student teachers often find the amount of stress in teaching to be greater than they perceived it would be. For many, this stress is a result of reality shock during their first teaching experience. Veenman (1984) defines "reality shock" as "the collapse of the missionary ideals formed during teacher training by the harsh and rude reality of everyday classroom life" (p. 143). Jelinek (1986) reports that student teachers experience reality shock when they encounter too many changes in their environment in a short time. The reality shock of student teaching makes stress far more negative than positive, as it begins to take its toll on the beginning teacher. Jelinek adds that stress pushes some student teachers beyond their ability to adapt, which causes mental disturbance and disorientation. The student teaching experience is often the first real taste of the stressful demands of teaching for the beginning teacher.

During student teaching it becomes evident that a wide variety of factors can affect the stress and anxiety levels of beginning educators. The research literature has found numerous factors that contribute to preservice educator stress: (1) classroom management, (2) discipline, (3) relationship with cooperating teacher, (4) teaching environment, (5) reality of teaching, (6) instructional behavior, (7) personal characteristics, (8) job search, (9) time management, and (10) level of organization. These factors affect the development of preservice educators and often influence their attitudes toward teaching as they begin their careers. Becoming aware in advance of the stressors of teaching can ease some of the stress experienced while student teaching.

Unrealistic Optimism

Many beginning teachers enter the profession with an unrealistic optimism regarding their ability to teach, rehearse, and manage the classroom. Bechen (2000) found that preservice music educators exhibited higher levels of confidence in their ability to teach than their first-year colleagues. He also found preservice music educators to have higher confidence levels in their teaching than experienced music educators. This surplus of confidence often makes new teachers unprepared for the demands of the first year of teaching. As a result, their perceptions about teaching are shattered and stress levels rise. Many find it difficult to deal with the reality shock of having complete responsibility for the music program when there is no cooperating teacher or university supervisor on whom to lean. Widely recognized stress factors associated with daily teaching responsibilities (classroom management, discipline, time management) often reach such levels that beginning teachers find it difficult to cope. Unfortunately, many promising music educators let the stress overwhelm them and leave the profession after a few years.

Stress is defined as "the physical, mental, or emotional reaction resulting from an individual's response to environmental tensions, conflicts, pressures, and other stimuli" (Greenburg, 1984, p. 2). Different people will react to stress in many different ways. Some will be motivated by stress, while others will react negatively. Beginning educators should analyze how they will deal with the stressful situations that will arise in their classrooms. Greater awareness of the stress involved in teaching can help educators to improve the longevity of their careers.

Burnout

Music educators often hear of colleagues who burn out and leave the profession. After years of hard work these stressed-out individuals decide that they can no longer remain in their current positions. Some leave the profession altogether, while others transfer to less visual, less stressful jobs. Christina Maslach (1996), a leading psychologist in the area of educator burnout, defines it as "a phenomenon related to job stress where individuals spend considerable time in close encounters with others under conditions of chronic tension and stress" (p. 4). Many music educators are profoundly affected by burnout without really knowing what it is or how they might combat it.

Scrivens (1979) describes teacher burnout as "the big click"—the point where one suddenly "turns off" and adopts a more practical, ego-satisfying lifestyle (p. 34). He discusses burnout as an active phenomenon, "because even if teachers are only vaguely aware of a feeling of exhaustion, their psychological defense mechanisms are sending a poignant and urgent message: 'Get out before you've used yourself up'" (p. 34).

Hamann, Daugherty, and Mills (1987) investigated burnout symptoms in public school music educators. Their study contains a thorough review of the literature that focuses on the physical and psychological symptoms of burnout, and specifically on burnout among music educators, listing both major and minor symptoms. Some of the more serious physical symptoms of burnout include: (1) peptic ulcers, (2) high blood pressure, (3) rheumatoid arthritis, (4) thyroid disease, (5) rise in cholesterol level, (6) chronic back pain, and (7) migraine headaches. Less serious physical symptoms are: (1) minor weight loss or gain, (2) inability to get rid of colds, and (3) fatigue. Psychological symptoms include: (1) detachment, (2) boredom, (3) cynicism, (4) a sense of impotence, (5) paranoia, (6) disorientation, (7) psychosomatic complaints, (8) depression, (9) denial of feelings, (10) frustration, (11) irritability, (12) impatience, and (13) worry (p. 129).

Rosenman and Friedman (1983) believe that burnout is more likely associated with individuals who display personality and behavior traits known as Type A behaviors. Type A behavior is characterized by twenty-three traits and includes behaviors such as: (1) aggressiveness, (2) hostility, (3) ambitiousness, (4) competitiveness, (5) tenseness, (6) impatience, (7) inability to relax away from work, (8) suppressed hostility, (9) orientation toward achievement, and (10) denial of failure. This is in contrast to individuals with Type B behavior personalities, in which easygoing personality traits predominate. Type A individuals often feel pressured, are engaged in multiple activities, are overly conscious of time in relation to their output, are influenced by criticisms, and are in need of constant social approval.

In addition to finding that certain personality types are more prone to burnout, numerous studies have established that individuals who are often the most productive, dedicated, and committed to their fields are frequently most affected by burnout. According to Spradley and Veninga, as cited in Hamann, Daugherty, and Mills (1987, p. 129), burnout among individuals in the helping professions follows a five-step pattern:

1. The "Honeymoon" is the beginning stage. High energy levels, enthusiasm, and job satisfaction start to wear off.

2. The "Fuel Shortage" stage includes the early symptoms of inefficiency at work: dissatisfaction with the job, fatigue, sleepless nights, increased smoking or drinking, or other means of escape.

3. The "Chronic Symptoms" stage involves one's awareness of the physical and psychological symptoms of burnout—chronic exhaustion, physical illness, anger, and depression.

4. In the "Crisis" stage the symptoms of burnout have reached an acute phase and cause the individual to obsess with problems.

5. "Hitting the Wall" is the stage of total professional deterioration and dysfunction of physical and psychological health.

Many music educators move from one of the above stages to another and back many times throughout the course of their career. The key is never to reach levels 4 or 5.

In focusing on teacher burnout among musicians, the authors (Hamann, Daugherty, and Mills, 1987) summarize the findings of numerous studies by Hamann (1985, 1986, 1989, 1990) and Hamann and Daugherty (1984), on the effects of burnout among music educators. Hamann's studies have led to the following conclusions concerning burnout among music educators:

- Public school music educators have significantly higher burnout levels than public school general classroom teachers.

- Younger subjects (20–29 years) have significantly higher burnout levels than did older music teachers (50–70 years).

- Music teachers with few years of experience (1–5 years) have significantly higher levels of burnout than teachers with high total years of teaching experience (21–40 years).

- Music teachers who indicate that they work 40–50 hours or more per week in their jobs have significantly higher burnout levels than subjects who indicate they work 39 or less hours per week.

- Single or divorced teachers have significantly higher levels of burnout than married subjects.

- Music teachers who teach only in a middle school, a K–12 situation, a high school, or a 4–12 setting have significantly higher levels of burnout than subjects teaching in 1–8, elementary, junior high, or junior high plus high school settings. (p. 130–31)

Additionally, several factors were found to contribute significantly to music teacher burnout levels:

- Lack of recognition by administration, other teachers, peers, parents, and students

- Unclear goals from general administration, music administration, and fellow music teachers

- Lack of coordination between levels in the curriculum
- Lack of goals in personal planning
- Lack of cooperation among music teachers in the district and building
- Too much work and not enough salary or time to do it, and not enough equipment, room, or budget (p. 131)

Hamann (1987) concludes by stating,

> If, based on the research literature findings, it can be assumed that it is the most dedicated and effective individuals that are most affected by burnout, then the findings in this study should be of great concern to all; for it may be our most dedicated and effective music teachers that are considering leaving the profession. It is therefore recommended that methods of dealing with, coping, preventing, and/or reducing burnout symptoms be discussed within the educational setting. (p. 139)

Knowing that burnout is the result of long-term stress, music educators would be well served by becoming aware of its beginnings and how to cope with it in their careers.

How can a teacher begin to cope with stress and keep it under control during his or her career? In analyzing perceptions and reactions to stressful events, the teacher must try to discriminate between good stress and bad stress. Good stress results in motivating factors that bring about an improvement in behavior. For some, stress serves to improve performance, whereas in others it has the opposite effect—pushing some people beyond their limits, causing negative physical, mental, and emotional reactions. The overall goal should be to reduce stress levels to prevent burnout.

What are some ways to control stress levels and reduce potential burnout? Monitoring and controlling perceptions and attitudes toward stressful events is a good place to start. Stress level is determined by one's beliefs about events and how one reacts to them. Keeping a journal is an excellent way to increase awareness of reactions to stress and how to deal with them from day to day. Resistance to stress is increased by an openness to change, a willingness to make commitments, and an appreciation that a person can control his or her life.

Personal Strategies to Lower Stress

Developing and carrying out stress management strategies also will help you to manage stress more effectively. The following is a list of common strategies involved in controlling stress and some methods of implementing each strategy.

- Avoid or reduce stressors.
  - Leave the environment or area of conflict.
  - Leave the job.
  - Take time away from teaching.
- Modify stress-inducing behaviors.
  - Change Type A behaviors.
  - Eliminate Type A behaviors.
- Develop resources for coping.
  - Physical improvements: Improve your physical health, improve your nutritional habits, exercise regularly, get enough rest.
  - Psychological improvements: Gain a sense of control, believe in yourself, be confident.

- Emotional improvements: Network with other music educators, make new friends, learn techniques for time management and relaxation, improve assertiveness levels.

- Self-monitoring: Keep a daily journal. Look for patterns of reactions. Self-monitoring will probably reveal that you increase your level of stress by (1) telling others stories about your stresses and (2) telling yourself over and over how stressful life is.

- Lower your stress arousal: Participate in activities that will help you relax. Hobbies, activities outside of music education, leisure activities, etc., will help you to unwind.

- Adjust to stress by using cognitive approaches: Try to eliminate negative self-talk and catastrophic thinking. Eliminate negative self-programming by changing the meaning that stressful situations hold for you. Be less self-critical when you do not have perfect performances and by convincing yourself that you are not alone in facing stress.

Job-Related Strategies to Lower Stress

A teacher can do numerous things to lower stress on the job. Music educators should consider the following:

- Make lists of tasks that need to be accomplished (daily, weekly, short-term, long-term, etc.).

- Set goals and develop a plan for reaching that goal. Have goals and plans for your career and your personal life.

- Thin out your schedule. Eliminate activities that are less important to you. Take a sabbatical from certain activities so you can create a schedule that is better suited to you.

- Avoid procrastination. Many people create a great deal of stress for themselves by putting things off.

- Eliminate distracters in your environment that cause stress. Turn off the phone or stereo and close the office door. Help your students to understand that teachers need "study time."

- Learn to delegate. You cannot do it all by yourself. Many beginning teachers take a "If it is to be, it is up to me!" approach to teaching. Many tasks in your program can be delegated to students and parents.

- Give yourself idle time during the teaching day. Do not feel guilty for giving yourself some down time away from the music department.

- Be as efficient as possible. Work out a plan so you only do a task once.

- Learn to say no. Be careful not to take on too many commitments.

- Keep a balance between your career and personal life.

Although a career in music education can be stressful, it also can be a most rewarding professional life. By becoming aware of stressors and stress-managing strategies, the music educator should keep from becoming a negative statistic. Constant self-monitoring and a healthy lifestyle will help the music educator to have a long and successful career.

STUDY AND DISCUSSION QUESTIONS

1. What are the five problem areas involved in the student teaching experience?

2. What are the attributes necessary for the choral music educator to be successful in the classroom? Which of these attributes do you see in yourself? Which attributes do you need to develop and work on?

3. How would you describe an ideal choral music educator? What personality does he or she present in the classroom? What characteristics does he or she exhibit?

4. What are some personal concerns that might affect your student teaching experience?

5. What are some concerns for the student teacher that involve the school site?

6. Why is the cooperating teacher important to a successful student teaching experience?

7. Why is it so important for the student teacher to develop and foster quality relationships during the student teaching experience?

8. What are some of the concerns involved in the process of student teaching? Which problems are you most concerned about?

9. What are some of the benefits of controlling your student teaching placement?

10. How would you evaluate your current technological skills? What skills will you need to improve in order to launch a successful job search? What is your ability in using a word processor, web browser, Internet search engine, and so on?

11. Why is it important to start the job search process early?

12. How would you describe the perfect job for your first year of teaching?

13. Why is networking so important during the job search?

14. What are three ways to develop and grow professionally once you have started your first teaching job? How will these activities help you to grow professionally?

15. What is reality shock? What is meant by "unrealistic optimism"? Why is it important for a beginning teacher to know about these?

16. What are some factors that affect the stress and anxiety levels of beginning teachers?

17. How are *stress* and *burnout* defined?

18. What are three physical and three psychological symptoms of burnout?

19. How would you describe someone who has a Type A personality?

20. What are some stress reduction strategies you plan to put into action? How might they help you in the future?

REFERENCES

Bechen, E. F. (2000). Sources of stress as perceived by preservice and inservice Iowa music educators (doctoral diss., The University of Iowa). *Dissertation Abstracts International, DAI-A 61(11)*, 4318.

Brand, M. (1983). Characteristics of effective music teachers. Unpublished paper. ERIC Document Reproduction Service No. ED 237 400.

Greenburg, S. (1984). *Stress and the teaching profession.* Baltimore: Brooks.

Hamann, D. (1985). Teacher burnout. *Dialogue in Instrumental Music Education, 9*(2), 53–61.

———— (1986). Burnout and the public school orchestra director. *Update: Applications of Research in Music Education, 4*(3), 11–14.

———— (1989). Burnout assessment and comparison among general public school, public school music, and university music instructors. *Dialogue in Instrumental Music Education, 13*(2), 49–64.

———— (1990). Burnout: How to spot it, how to avoid it. *Music Educators Journal, 77*(2), 30–33.

Hamann, D., and E. Daugherty (1984). Teacher burnout: The cost of caring. *Update: Applications of Research in Music Education, 2*(3), 7–10.

Hamann, D., E. Daugherty, and C. Mills (1987). An investigation of burnout assessment and potential job related variables among public school educators. *Psychology of Music, 15*(2), 128–40.

Jelinek, C. A. (1986). Stress and the pre-service teacher. *Teacher Educator, 22*(1), 2–9.

Maslach, C., S. Jackson, and M. Leiter (1996). *Maslach burnout inventory manual* (3d ed.). Palo Alto, CA.: Consulting Psychologists Press.

Payne, B. (1997). *A career guide to music education.* ⟨http://www.menc.org/industry/job/career.html⟩.

Rosenman, R. H., and M. Friedman (1983). Relationship of Type A behavior pattern to coronary heart disease. In H. Seyle (ed.), *Seyle's guide to stress research*, vol. 2. New York: Scientific and Academic Editions.

Scrivens, R. (1979). The big click. *Today's Education, 68*(4), 34–35.

Snyder, D. (1998). Classroom management for student teachers. *Music Educators Journal, 84*(4), 37–40.

Svengalis, J. (1992). Partnership: The key to student teaching. *Music Educators Journal, 79*(2), 31–34.

Veenman, S. (1984). Perceived problems of beginning teachers. *Review of Educational Research, 54*(2), 143–78.

Welch, K. (1993). Taking control of your student teaching. *Teaching Music, 1*(2), 40–41.

Appendix A

Music Publishers and Distributors

Nearly all of the following music publishers and distributors have websites that can be reached through the Internet by originating a search using the name of the dealer. The following sites also are helpful: ⟨http://www.ensemble.org/assoc/acdapa/chorlink.htm⟩ (Choral Sites and Resources), ⟨http://mpa.org/publist.html⟩ (Directory of Music Publishers), and ⟨http://www.choralnet.org/⟩ (ChoralNet).

Aberdeen Music (distributed by Plymouth Music Co.)

Addington Press (distributed by Hinshaw Music, Inc.)

Agape (distributed by Hope Publishing Co.)

Alexandria House, 468 McNally Dr., Nashville, TN 37211

Alfred Publishing Co., PO Box 10003, Van Nuys, CA 91410

Allegro Music Service, 1398 Lamberton Dr., Silver Springs, MD 20902

Alliance Music Publications, PO Box 131977, Houston, TX 77007

Altram Music Corp., 9301 Wilshire Blvd., Beverly Hills, CA 90210

Antara Music Group, PO Box 210, Alexandria, IN 46001

Arista Music Co., 8370 Wilshire Blvd., Beverly Hills, CA 90211

Art Masters Studio (AMSI), 1599 SE 8th St., Minneapolis, MN 55414

Associated Music Publishers, 24 E. 22nd St., New York, NY 10010

Augsburg Fortress Press, 426 5th St., Box 1209, Minneapolis, MN 55440

AVI Music Publishing Group, 10116 Riverside Dr., Suite 200, Toluca Lake, CA 91602

Axelrod Music Inc., 251 Weybosset St., Providence, RI 02903

Bärenreiter Music Publishers (distributed by Foreign Music Distributors)

Beckenhorst Press, PO Box 14273, Columbus, OH 43214

Belmont Music Publishers, PO Box 231, Pacific Palisades, CA 90272

Belwin Music Publishers (distributed by Warner Bros.)

Benson Music Co., 365 Great Circle Road, Nashville, TN 37228

Irving Berlin Music Corp., 29 W. 46th St., New York, NY 10019

Big 3 Music Corp. (distributed by Belwin Music)

Birch Tree Group Ltd., 180 Alexander St., Princeton, NJ 08540

Fred Bock Music Co., PO Box 570567, Tarzana, CA 91357

Boekle-Bomart, Inc. (distributed by Jerona Music Corp.)

Boosey & Hawkes, Inc., 35 E. 21st St., New York, NY 10010

Boston Music Co., 116 Boylston St., Boston, MA 02116

Bote & Bock Musikverlag (distributed by Hal Leonard)

Bourne Co./International Music Co., 5 W. 37th St., 6th Floor, New York, NY 10018

Breitkopf & Härtel (distributed by Hal Leonard)

Brentwood Music Publishing, 1 Maryland Farms, Suite 200, Brentwood, TN 37027

Broadman Press, 127 9th Ave. N., Nashville, TN 37234

Brodt Music Co., PO Box 9345, Charlotte, NC 28299

Alexander Broude, 575 8th Ave., New York, NY 10018

Broude Brothers Ltd., PO Box 547, Williamstown, MA 01267

Cambiata Press, PO Box 1151, Conway, AR 72032

Carlin America, Inc., 126 East 38th St., New York, NY 10016

Carus-Verlag (distributed by Mark Foster Music Co.)

Canyon Press (distributed by E. C. Kerby, Ltd.)

Chantry Music Press, 32–34 N. Center St., Springfield, OH 45501

Chappell & Co. (distributed by Hal Leonard)

Charter Publications (distributed by J. W. Pepper & Son, Inc.)

Cherith Publishing Co., PO Box 72, Placentia, CA 92670

Charter Publications (distributed by J. W. Pepper)

Cherry Lane Music Co., (distributed by Alfred Music)

ChoralWeb Publishing, Inc., PO Box 9164, Moscow, ID 83843

Choral Workbook Series, 449 6th St., Struthers, OH 44471

Choristers Guild, 2834 W. Kingsley Rd., Garland, TX 75041

John Church Music Co. (distributed by Theodore Presser)

Clarus Music Ltd., 340 Bellevue Ave., Yonkers, NY 10703

Columbia Pictures (distributed by CPP/Belwin Music)

Franco Columbo Publishing Co. (distributed by Belwin Music)

Concordia Publishing House, 3558 S. Jefferson Ave., St. Louis, MO 62118

Consolidated Music Publishers (distributed by Music Sales Corp.)

Consort Press, PO Box 50413, Santa Barbara, CA 93150

Coronet Press (distributed by Theodore Presser)

CPP/Belwin (distributed by Warner Bros. Publications, Inc.)

Creative World Music Publications (distributed by Warner Bros.)

Curtis Music Press (distributed by Kjos Music)

Curwen & Sons (distributed by Hal Leonard)

Dartmouth Collegium Musicum (distributed by Shawnee Press)

Roger Dean Publications (distributed by Lorenz)

Dickson-Wheeler, 208 1st St., Scotia, NY 45401

Oliver Ditson (distributed by Theodore Presser)

Doxology Music, PO Box M, Aiken, SC 29802

Eble Music Co., 115 S. Linn St., Iowa City, IA 52240

Eckroth Music Co., 1132 28th Ave. South, Moorhead, MN 56560

earthsongs, 220 N. W. 29th St., Corvallis, OR 97330

Editio Musica (distributed by Boosey & Hawkes)

Edition Musicus, PO Box 1341, Stamford, CT 06904

Editions Salabert (distributed by Hal Leonard)

Edizione Suvini Zerboni, Milan (distributed by Boosey & Hawkes)

Educator's Music Annex, 13618 Detroit Ave., Cleveland, OH 44107

ELCA Publishing House, 426 S. 5th St., Box 1209, Minneapolis, MN 55440

Elkan-Vogel (distributed by Theodore Presser)

European American Music Distributors Corp., Box 850, Valley Forge, PA 19482

Evangel Press (distributed by Art Masters)

Faber Music Co., 50 Cross St., Winchester, MA 01890

Carl Fischer LLC, 65 Bleecker St., New York, NY 10012

J. Fischer & Bros. (distributed by Belwin Mills)

H. T. Fitzsimons Co. (distributed by Antara Music Group)

Harold Flammer (distributed by Shawnee Press)

Foreign Music Distributors, 13 Elkay Dr., Chester, NY 10918

Mark Foster Music Co., PO Box 4012, Champaign, IL 61820

Sam Fox Music Sales Corp. (distributed by Plymouth Music Co.)

Frangipani Press, 1928 Arlington Rd., PO Box 669, Bloomington, IN 47402

Frank Music Corp. (distributed by Hal Leonard)

Friends of Jewish Music, 10 Strauss Lane, Olympia Fields, IL 60461

Galaxy Music Corp. (distributed by E. C. Schirmer)

Galleria Press (distributed by Plymouth Music)

Galleon Music, Inc. (distributed by Altram Music Corp.)

Genesis III Music Corp. (distributed by Plymouth Music)

Genevox Music Group, 127 9th Ave., Nashville, TN 37234

Gentry Publications (distributed by Antara Music Group)

G.I.A. Publications, 7404 S. Mason Ave., Chicago, IL 60638

Glory-Sound Publications (distributed by Shawnee Press)

H. W. Gray Co. (distributed by Belwin Mills)

Greystone Press (distributed by Plymouth Music)

Hal Leonard Corp., 7777 W. Bluemound Rd., Milwaukee, WI 53213

Hamblen Music, PO Box 210, Alexandria, IN 46001

Hansen House, 1820 West Ave., Miami Beach, FL 33139

Hänsler Music/USA, 3773 W. 95th St., Leawood, KS 66206

Harmonia (distributed by Foreign Music Distributors)

T. B. Harms Co. (distributed by Warner Bros.)

Frederick Harris Music Co., Ltd., 340 Nagle Dr., Buffalo, NY 14225

Henle USA, Inc., PO Box 1753, Maryland Heights, MO 63043

Heritage Music Press (distributed by Lorenz)

Heugel et Cie (distributed by Theodore Presser Co.)

Highland Music Co., 1311 N. Highland Ave., Hollywood, CA 90028

Hinrichson Edition (distributed by C. F. Peters Corp.)

Hinshaw Music, PO Box 470, Chapel Hill, NC 27514

Raymond Hoffman Co. (distributed by Intrada Music Group)

Charles Homeyer & Co. (distributed from Carl Fischer)

Hope Publishing Co., 380 S. Main St., Carol Stream, IL 61088

Intrada Music Group, PO Box 1240, Anderson, IN 46012

Ione Press (distributed by E. C. Schirmer)

Intuit Music Group, PO Box 121277, Nashville, TN 37212

Jenson Publications (distributed by Hal Leonard)

Jerona Music Corp., PO Box 5010, Hackensack, NJ 07606

Joclem Music Publishing (distributed by Boosey & Hawkes)

Edwin F. Kalmus & Co., 6403 W. Rogers Circle, Boca Raton, FL 33431

Kenbridge Music (distributed by Jerona Music Corp.)

Kendor Music, PO Box 278, Main and Grove Sts., Delevan, NY 14042

E. C. Kerby, Ltd. (distributed by Hal Leonard)

Neil A. Kjos Music Co., 4380 Jutland Dr., San Diego, CA 92117

Laurel Press (distributed by Lorenz)

Lawson-Gould Music Publishers, 250 W. 57th St., #1005, New York, NY 10107

Lexicon Music, PO Box 2222, Newbury Park, CA 91320

Lillenas Publishing Co., 2923 Troost, Box 527, Kansas City, MO 64141

Lorenz Corp., 501 E. 3d St., Dayton, OH 45401

Ludwig Music Publishing Co., 557 E. 140th St., Cleveland, OH 44110

Magnamusic Distributors, 74 Amenia Union Rd., Sharon, CT 06069

Malecki Music, PO Box 150, Grand Rapids, MI 49501

Manna Music, PO Box 218, Pacific City, OR 97135

Maranatha! Music, PO Box 31050, Laguna Hills, CA 92654

Margun/Gunmar Music, Inc. (distributed by Jerona Music Corp.)

Edward B. Marks Music Corp. (distributed by Hal Leonard)

Masters Music Publications, PO Box 810157, Boca Raton, FL 33481

MCA Music Publishing (distributed by Hal Leonard)

McKinney Music, 127 9th Ave., Nashville, TN 37234

McLaughlin & Reilly (distributed by Warner Bros. Publications)

Mel Bay Publications, PO Box 66, #4 Industrial Ave., Pacific, MO 63069

Mercury Music Corp. (distributed by Theodore Presser)

Merion Music Corp. (distributed by Theodore Presser)

MMB Music, 10370 Page Industrial Blvd., St. Louis, MO 63132

Morningside Publishers, 1727, Larkin Williams Rd., Fenton, MO 63026

Edwin H. Morris & Co. (distributed by Hal Leonard)

Musik Innovations, 9600 Perry Highway, Pittsburgh, PA 15237

Musiclenders.org, 1511 Skyview, Wichita, KS 67212

Music Mart, Inc., PO Box 4280, Albuquerque, NM 87106

Music Press (distributed by Theodore Presser)

Music Sales Corp., 225 Park Ave. South, New York, NY 10003

Music 70 Publishers, 170 N. E. 33rd St., Ft Lauderdale, FL 33334

National Music Publishers, PO Box 868, Tustin, CA 92680

Novello Publications (distributed by Theodore Presser)

Orpheus Music Co. (distributed by Theodore Presser)

Oxford University Press, 198 Madison Ave., New York, NY 10016

Paterson's Publications, Ltd. (distributed by Carl Fischer)

Paragon Press, PO Box 210, Alexandria, IN 4600

Paull Pioneer Publications (distributed by Shawnee Press)

Peer Southern Music (distributed by Theodore Presser)

J. W. Pepper & Sons, PO Box 850, Valley Forge, PA 19482

Performers' Editions (distributed by Broude Bros.)

C. F. Peters Corp., 70–30 80th St., Glendale, NY 11385

Plymouth Music Co., 170 N.E. 33rd St., Ft. Lauderdale, FL 33334

Poppler's Music, Inc., 123 DeMers Ave., Grand Forks, ND 58201

Power and Glory Music Co. (distributed by Malecki Music)

Theodore Presser Co., 1 Presser Place, Bryn Mawr, PA 19010

Pro-Art Publications (distributed by Belwin Music)

Providence Press (distributed by Hope Publishing Co.)

Richmond Music Press, PO Box 465, Richmond, IN 47374

Richmond Organization (TRO), (distributed by Plymouth Music)

G. Ricordi & Co. (distributed by Hal Leonard)

Robbins Music (distributed by CPP/Belwin)

Roberton Publications (distributed by Theodore Presser)

Rongwen Music (distributed by Broude Bros.)

R. D. Row Music Co. (distributed by Carl Fischer)

Sacred Music Press (distributed by Lorenz)

Santa Barbara Music Publishing, 260 Loma Media, Santa Barbara, CA 93103

E. C. Schirmer Music Co., 138 Ipswich St., Boston, MA 02215

G. Schirmer (distributed by Hal Leonard)

Arthur P. Schmidt Co. (distributed by Warner Bros.)

Schmitt, Hall & McCreary (distributed by Belwin Music)

Schott & Co. (distributed by European American Music Distributors)

Shapiro, Bernstein Organization (distributed by Plymouth Music)

Shawnee Press, 49 Waring Dr., Delaware Water Gap, PA 18327

John Sheppard Music Press, PO Box 6784, Denver, CO 80206

Somerset Press (distributed by Hope Publishing Co.)

Southern Music Co., PO Box 329, San Antonio, TX 78292

Southwestern Music Co., 223 S. Custer, Weatherford, OK 73096

Spratt Music Publishers (distributed by Plymouth Music Co.)

Staff Music Publishing (distributed by Plymouth Music Co.)

Stainer & Bell, Ltd. (distributed by E. C. Schirmer)

Stanton's Sheet Music, S. Fourth Street, Columbus, OH 43215

Studio 4 (distributed by Alfred Music)

Studio P/R, Inc. (distributed by Warner Bros.)

Summa Productions (distributed by Arts Masters Studio)

Summy-Birchard Music (distributed by Warner Bros.)

Tabernacle Publishing Co. (distributed by Hope Publishing Co.)

Templeton Publications (distributed by Shawnee Press)

Tempo Music Publications, 3773 W. 95th St., Leawood, KS 66206

Tetra-Continuo Music Group (distributed by Plymouth Music Co.)

Thomas House Publications, PO Box 1423, San Carlos, CA 94070

Gordon V. Thompson Music (distributed by Oxford University Press)

Transcontinental Music Publications/New Jewish Press, UAHC 633, 3rd Ave., 6th Floor, New York, NY 10017

Triune Music (distributed by Lorenz)

TRO (The Richmond Organization), 11 W. 19th St., New York, NY 10011

Tuskegee Music Press (distributed by Kjos Music Co.)

Twin Elm Publishing, 1626 27th Ave. Court, Greeley, CO 80631

Universal Edition (distributed by European American Music Distributors Corp.)

Van Ness Press, 127 9th Ave. N., Nashville, TN 37234

Volkwein Music, 138 Industry Dr., Pittsburgh, PA 15275

Nels Vogel 1132 28th Ave., Moorehead, MN 56560

Walton Music Corp. (distributed by Plymouth Music Co.)

Ward-Brodt Music Co., PO Box 259810, Madison, WI 53701

Warner Bros. Publications, 15800 N. W. 48th Ave., Ft. Lauderdale, FL 33014

Joseph Weinberger, Ltd. (distributed by Boosey & Hawkes)

Wesleyan Music Press, PO Box 1072, Fort George Station, New York, NY 10040

West Music, 1212 5th St., Coralville, IA 52241

Wide World Music, Box B, Delaware Water Gap, PA 18327

Williamson Music, 598 Madison Ave., New York, NY 10019

Willis Music Co., 7380 Industrial Rd., Florence, KY 41042

Wingert-Jones Music, PO Box 419878, Kansas City, MO 64141

Witmark and Sons (distributed by Warner Bros.)

Word Music, 3319 West End, #200, Nashville, TN 37228

Zondervan Corp., 365 Great Circle Rd., Nashville, TN 37228

Appendix B

Manufacturers of Equipment, Supplies, and Attire

Academic Choir Apparel, 6867 Farmdale Ave. N., Hollywood, CA 91605

C. M. Almy & Son, Inc., 37 Purchase St., Rye, NY 10580

The Black Folder, 6900 Marconi St., Huntington Park, CA 90255

Cousin's Uniform & Tux, 18 Denise Place, Stamford, CT 06905

Collegiate Cap and Gown Co., 100 N. Market St., Champaign, IL 61820

DeMoulin/Monticello Gown Co., 1809 W. Bernice Ave., Chicago, IL 60613

Formal Fashions, Inc., 1500 W. Drake, Tempe, AZ 85283

Gamble Music Co., 312 S. Wabash, Chicago, IL 60604

Humes and Berg Manufacturing Co., 4801 Railroad Ave., E. Chicago, IN 46312

Lyric Choir Gown Co., PO Box 16954, Jacksonville, FL 32216

Master Professional Performers, 315 Federal Plaza West, Youngstown, OH 44503

Mollard Conducting Batons, Inc., PO Box 178, Bath, OH 44210

E. R. Moore Co., 1810 W. Grace St., Chicago, IL 60613

Music Manager Software, PO Box 9244, Greensboro, NC 27429

Peery Products Co., Box 22434, Portland, OR 97222

Radio Matic of America, PO Box 250, Maplewood, NJ 07040

Sico, Inc., 7525 Cahill Rd., Minneapolis, MN 55440

Southeastern Apparel, 142 Woodburn Dr., Dothan, AL 36301

Southern Music Co., PO Box 329, San Antonio, TX 78292

Stage Accents, 234 Industrial Parkway, Northvale, NJ 07647

Tuxedo Wholesaler, 15636 N. 78th St., Scottsdale, AZ 85260

C. E. Ward, Inc., New London, OH 44851

Wenger Corporation, 555 Park Dr., Owatonna, MN 55060

Appendix C

Lists of Recommended Choral Repertory

Each list of music has appeared in publication as a recommended source of choral repertory. Each citation is used by permission and given in the corresponding footnote.

Selected Choral Literature for Junior High Choirs

BY SANDRA CHAPMAN[1]

(Those selections marked by an asterisk * have been especially successful.)

SA and Two-Part

*Alleluia, Sing With Joy	Perry	Shawnee	EA-71
All the Pretty Little Horses	arr. Artman	Studio PR	V-7932
Ave Maria	Arcadelt/Eilers	Jenson	402-01162
A-Wassailing	Bennett	Jenson	423-23122
Baloo, Baloo	Arr. Rhein	G. Schirmer	12515
Ca' the Yowes	arr. Goetze	Boosey & Hawkes	PC2B6258
Carol of the Cuckoo	C. Jennings	Choristers Guild	CGA-228
Christmas Dance of the Shepherds	Kodály	European American	UE 10878NJ
The Cuckoo Bird	Berkowitz	G. Schirmer	52206
*Dance of the One-Legged Sailor	Pierce	Plymouth	BP-502
Der Engel	Rubenstein	Choral Art	R182
Dream a Dream	Robertson	Studio PR	SV 7716
Festive Madrigal	Perry	Shawnee	EA-113
From a Railway Carriage	Rinter	MCA	00124012
A Gental Alleluia	Monteverdi	Fischer	12011 & 5743
The Gift of Love	arr. Hopson	Hope	CF 148
Gute Nacht	arr. Kjelson	Belwin	2092
*A Hymn of Praise	Kirk	C. Fischer	CM8151
I Work upon the Railway	Crocker	Jenson	423-09062
Let's Sing about the Promised Land	Lightfoot	Heritage	H5798
*Lilacs	Rachmaninoff	Mark Foster	MF856
The Lord to Me a Shepherd Is	Bach/Wyatt	Pro Art	Pr Ch 3029
Lying in a Manger	Carter	Jenson	405-12014
Mio Bambino	Cotton	Mark Foster	MF 855
No Golden Carriage, No Bright Toy	Martin	Heritage	H 5006
*O Music	Mason/Rao	Boosey & Hawkes	OC3B6352
O Who's That Yonder?	arr. Wilson	Hope	JW 7781
Piercing Eyes	Haydn/Hines	Music 70	M70-482
Sleep, Gently Sleep	Brahms/Harris	Jenson	416-19022

[1]S. Chapman (1991), Selected choral literature for junior high choirs, *Choral Journal, 31*(7), 23–29. (Used with kind permission of the ACDA, Lawton, Okla.).

SA and Two-Part (*continued*)

Signs of the Time	Beebe	Hinshaw	HPC-7026
Some Folks	Foster/Kirk	Pro Art	ProCH 3027
Something to Sing About	Silver	McAfee	DMC 8010
Song of the Stars	Raminsh/Rao	Boosey & Hawkes	6270
Spring Song	Paulus	C. Fischer	CM 8035
Three Winds	Hagemann	Presser	312-41021
The Trout	Schubert	Jenson	416-20032
Velvet Shoes	Thompson	E. C. Schirmer	ECS 114
Welcome Hanukah	Kahn	McAfee	DMC 8193
Winter Song	Paulus	C. Fischer	CM 7970
*With Songs of Rejoicing	J. S. Bach	C. Fischer	CM 8086

SAB and Three-Part

Adoramus Te	Gasparini	Jenson	423-01060
Agnus Dei	Butler	C. Fischer	CM 8191
Agnus Dei	Pergolesi	Mark Foster	MF 220
Alfred Burt Carols	Burt/Ades	Shawnee	C-113
Alleluia	Bach/Emerson	Jenson	403-01010
Alleluia	Boyce/Kirk	Belwin	ProCh 203
Alleluia	Brenchley	Shawnee	D-260
Alleluia	Harris	Hinshaw	HMC 372
Alleluia	Nichol	Jenson	443-01030
Alleluia	McLendon	Kjos	5751
Alleluia	Mozart/Ehret	Cambiata	M979124
Alleluia, Praise!	Cherubini	Hope	MW 1223
*All Praise to God	Vulpius/Ehret	G.I.A.	G-2215
*All Ye Who Music Love	Donato	Bourne	B23680-356
American Folk Collage	arr. Grier	Heritage	HV118
Although You Are So Tiny	arr. Ehret	Lawson-Gould	51232
Angeles del Cielo	arr. Rumery	Thomas House	C28-8503
April Is in My Mistress' Face	Morley	Bourne	B230763-356
As Fair as Morn	Wilbye	Mark Foster	MF 338
Ave Maria	Arcadelt/Eilers	Jenson	402-01020
*Ave Verum	Fauré	Heritage	HV 116
Ave Verum	Mozart/Eilers	Jenson	402-01030
Ave Verum Corpus	Josquin	G. Schirmer	11606
Awake the Trumpet's Lofty Sound	Handel	Hal Leonard	08401436
Barbara Allen	arr. Spevacek	Hal Leonard	0870562
Be Glad, You Righteous	Powell	C. Fischer	CM 8139
Behold How My People Prosper	Peter/Kroeger	C. Fischer	CM 8079
Benedictus	Butler	C. Fischer	CM 8201
Benedictus	di Lasso	Studio PR	SV 8613
Bist du bei mir	J. S. Bach	Jenson	437-02030
Blessing, Glory, and Wisdom	J. S. Bach	Elkan-Vogel	362-03118
Blow Thy Horn, Hunter	Cornyshe	Studio	SV8638
*Boatmen Stomp	arr. Gray	G. Schirmer	12396
Born Today	C. Gray	Heritage	HV 123
Bow Down Thine Ear	Mozart	Plymouth	SC 408
Born This Day	Emerson	Jenson	403-02190
Canon (Fuga à tre)	Praetorius	Studio PR	SV 8568
Canon of Praise	Pachelbel	Somerset	MW 1226
*Cantata Domino	Asola/McCray Music 70	M70-350	

SAB and Three-Part (*continued*)

Cantate Domino	Hassler	Bourne	B236836-356
Cantate Domino	Pitoni	Bourne	ES 5C
Cantate Domino	Sleeth	Hinshaw	HMC 900
Cease Sorrows Now	Weelkes	Thomas House	C28-8510
A Celebration of Bach	arr. Jennings	Heritage	HV 175
*Carols Around	arr. Nygard	Hinshaw	HMC-703
*Christmas Gloria	Lovelace	Hope	CF 159
Charlie Is My Darling	Beethoven	Lawson-Gould	51762
Cherubim Song	Bortniansky	Presser	312-40426
Come Let Us Sing	Bennett	Jenson	423-03070
Come Bless Ye the Lord	Telemann	Shawnee	D-5229
Cover Him, Joseph	Martin	Hinshaw	HMC-884
Come, Labor On	Noble	H. W. Gray	GCMR 3457
Come, Let Us This Day	J. S. Bach	Boosey & Hawkes	5469
Confitemini Domino	Constantini	Pro Art	ProCh 3002
Dies ist der Tag	Telemann	Mark Foster	HV 39.010
*Didn't My Lord Deliver Daniel	Thygerson	Heritage	HV 206
Dona Nobis Pacem	Reese	Kimmel	1178-304
*Dream-Land	Vaughan Williams	Boosey & Hawkes	OC3B6484
Drop Drop Slow Tears	Williams	Staff	968
Dream with Your Eyes Wide Open	McKinney	Heritage	HV 125
*Due Pupille Amabili	Mozart	NMP	CMS-103
Early in the Morning	arr. Carter	Jenson	405-05020
Echo Song (SAB/SAB)	di Lasso	Heritage	HV 209
Every Night When the Sun Goes In	arr. Vance	G. Schirmer	12556
Eight Nights, Eight Lights	Emerson	Jenson	403-05220
*Exultate Justi	Viadana	C. Fischer	CM 8083
Ezekiel Saw the Wheel	arr. Martin	Hinshaw	HMC-473
Fare You Well	arr. Kent	Lawson-Gould	51470
Fear Not, Good Shepherds	Smith	Lawson-Gould	12303
Festival Alleluia	Emerson	Jenson	403-06100
Folk Song Trilogy	arr. Ray	Alfred	7368
*Follow the Drinking Gourd	arr. Hoffman	Somerset	Sp782
Free I Am Once More	Regnart	Studio PR	SV8615
From Scotland with Love	arr. Kirk	Pro Art	ProCh 3003
From Sea to Shining Sea	Althouse	Alfred	7301
Gaelic Rhapsody	arr. Lojeski	Hal Leonard	08403132
*Give Me the Splendid Silent Sun	Butler	Hinshaw	HMC-694
Gloria Alleluia	Crocker	Jenson	423-07033
*Gloria (*Heiligmesse*)	Haydn	Walton	W4004
Gloria Dei Patris	Crocker	Jenson	471-07030
Gloria in Excelsis	Lotti	Presser	392-41401
Gloria Patri	Palestrina	Bourne	ES46B
The Glory of the Lord	Marcello	C. Fischer	CM 7978
God of Mercy	J. S. Bach	Augsburg	11-1698
Go and Tell John	Pfautsch	Hope	CY 3342
*Goin' to Boston	arr. Kirk	Pro Art	ProCh 2896
Go 'way from My Window	Reese	Hal Leonard	08602918
The Good News Is in the Music	Carter	Hal Leonard	08602975
Gypsy Heart	Dvořák	Galleon	GSS 4003
*The Gypsy Rover	arr. Porter	Boosey & Hawkes	OC3B6383
Hallelujah, Amen	Handel	Cambiata	M17312
Halleluia	Granito	Alfred	7036
Hava Nagila	arr. Eilers	Jenson	402-08080

SAB and Three-Part (*continued*)

Hear Thou My Prayer	Arcadelt	Spratt	SCC 573
The Heavens Are Telling	Haydn	Hal Leonard	0858351
The Heavens Are Telling	Haydn	Presser	392-41318
Heaven-Haven	Wagner	Heritage	HV 329
Hey, for the Dancing!	Bárdos	Shawnee	D-248
Holy, Holy, Holy	Haydn/Coggin	Presser	312-40735
The Holly Bears a Berry	Thygerson	Beckenhorst	BP 1144
Homeward Bound	Olson	C. Fischer	CM 8143
Hosanna	Gregor	Presser	312-40928
Hosanna in Excelsis	dI Lasso	Studio PR	SV 8613
*Hosanna to the Son	Harris	Hinshaw	HMC-623
How Excellent Thy Name	Handel	G. Schirmer	11504
How Merrily We Live	Este-Razey	Plymouth	PCS-409
I Am a Traveler	Harris	Hinshaw	HMC-582
I Am So Glad Each Christmas Eve	arr. Wood	Augsburg	11-0919
If Ye Love Me	Tallis/Ehret	Richmond	SAB-2
It Was a Lover and His Lass	Morley	Hal Leonard	08603329
I Will Lift up My Eyes	Carter	Hinshaw	HMC-810
I Will Touch the Sky	Loughton	Hal Leonard	08704053
The Jesus Gift	Martin	Hinshaw	HMC-479
Joshua-Jericho	arr. Blevins	Jenson	456-10010
Keepin' Life Simple	Kunz	Jenson	407-11010
Kyrie	Butler	C. Fischer	CM8177
Kyrie	Klouse	Hal Leonard	08704233
Kyrie	Schubert	Hal Leonard	MC 4520
*Kyrie Eleison	Ashton	Cambiata	C 979125
Lift Up Your Heads, Ye Gates	Hammerschmidt	Presser	312-41211
Like Someone in Love	Van Heusen	Boosey & Hawkes	OC3B6386
*Lisbon	Gray	G. Schirmer	12558
Lobet den Herrn, all Heiden	Telemann	Mark Foster	HE 39.007
Lobet den Herrn	Vierdanck	G. Schirmer	12572
Lo, How a Rose E're Blooming	Carter	Somerset	AD 2017
*Lord Jesus Christ, Be Present Now	Byrd/Hopson	Shawnee	D.5246
Madrigals from the XVIIth Century	arr. McKinney	G. Schirmer	9455 & 9612
Maker of All, Be Thou My Guard	Haydn	Broude	CR2
Mango Walk	Pierce	Plymouth	BP-402
Mary Don't Weep, Don't Mourn	arr. Blevins	Jenson	423-13060
Mary Had a Baby	Emerson	Jenson	403-13040
Mighty Lord, Thy Faithfulness	Lotti	E. C. Schirmer	1716
My Soul Longs for You	Beethoven	Gray	GCMR 3442
Now with One Accord	Constantini	Mark Foster	MF 159
Now Is the Month of Maying	Morley	Mus/Publishers	ES 104
Of All the Birds That I Have Heard	Mundy	Thomas House	C28-8511
Old Joe Clark	arr. Johnson	Jenson	423-15030
Ol' Dan Tucker	arr. Johnson	Jenson	446-15020
One Candle	Reese	Hal Leonard	08704722
O Remember Not	Battishill	E. C. Schirmer	2615
O Shepherds, Come Running	arr. Avalos	Belwin	ProCh 2995
O Praise Ye the Lord	Wood	Shawnee	D-5222
Pat-a-Pan	arr. Willet	Heritage	HV 263
The Peace	Emerson	Jenson	403-16060
*Peter Gray	arr. Parker	Hinshaw	HMC-660
Praise Ye the Lord of Hosts	Saint-Saëns	Jenson	402-16020
Praise the Lord	Carter	Hope	JC 285

SAB and Three-Part (*continued*)

Praise the Lord	Handel	Flammer	D-5225
Plenty Good Room	arr. Horman	Somerset	SP 815
Raise a Ruckus	arr. Wyatt	Pro Art	ProCh 2780
Resurrexit Sicut Dixit	Sweelinck	Unicorn	1.0015.2
Ring the Bell	Kirk	Curtis	7930
The Road Not Taken	Klouse	Hal Leonard	08704934
Rock-a My Soul	arr. Blevins	Jenson	456-18010
Sanctus	Butler	C. Fischer	CM 81856
*Sanctus	Schubert	Somerset	SP767
See on Mary's Arm	Harch	Hinshaw	HMC-739
Shenandoah	arr. Porter	Boosey & Hawkes	OC3B6282
Since Robin Hood	Weelkes	NMP	NMP-100
*Sing and Be Joyful	Wilson	Studio PR	SV 7832
Sing a New Song	M. Haydn	Flammer	D-5306
Sing Forth, Believers	Lotti/Hopson	Jenson	433-19050
Sing Me a Plain Old Simple Song	Kunz	Jenson	407-19020
Sing Me Home	Nygard	Hinshaw	HMC-909
*Sing We All Merrily	Russell	Music 70	M70-270
Skye Boat Song	arr. Rodgers	Shawnee	D-281
Snow	Horman	Shawnee	D-139
So My Sheep May Safely Graze	McKuen	Silver Burdett	7012719
Song of the Open Road	Butler	Hinshaw	HMC-850
Sound the Trumpet	Purcell/Ehret	Elkan Vogel	362-03332
Sound the Trumpet	Schubert	Plymouth	SC-405
Sounds of Christmas	arr. Thygerson	Heritage	HV 134
Strike It Up, Tabor	Weelkes	Studio PR	SV 8639
Sweet Are the Charms	Butler	Richmond	DMC 8173
Sweet Love Doth Now Invite	Dowland	Bourne	B236828-356
Sussex Carol	arr. Young	Bechenhorst	BP1242-2
Tell Us, Shepherd Maids	arr. Caldwell	H. W. Gray	2358
Templa bras es Psalterio	arr. Rumery	Thomas House	C28-8501
*There Is a Lady	Eddleman	C. Fischer	CM7999
This Little Light of Mine	arr. Johnson	Jenson	423-20010
Three Cautionary Tales	Frackenpohl	Marks	15124-9
*Three Folk Songs	Brahms	Marks	MC4096
Three French Carols	arr. Kockanek	Heritage	MV 122
Three German Carols	arr. Kockanek	Heritage	HV 199
Three Noels	Grundman	Boosey & Hawkes	5736
Three Polish Carols	arr. Kochanek	Heritage	HV 148
Three Songs from *A Shropshire Lad*	Rhein	G. Schirmer	12346-8
Three Spirituals	arr. Thygerson	Heritage	H 6509
Time Gone	Emerson	Jenson	403-20140
To Us Is Born	Praetorius	Hope	APM-486
Trav'ler	Wilson	Studio PR	SV 7920
Tree of Peace	Bock	Presser	C-134
Troika	Perry	Shawnee	D-337
The Turtle Dove	arr. Spevacek	Jenson	437-20070
Two Chorales (*Christmas Oratorio*)	Bach/Weck	Somerset	SP774
Veni, Jesu	Cherubini	Somerset	SP764
Veni Sanctus Spiritus	Viadana	Concordia	98-2444
A Virgin Unspotted	Billings	Plymouth	TR-403
Wachset in der Gnade	Telemann	Mark Foster	HV 39.003
*We Be Three Poor Mariners	Ravenscroft	Studio PR	SV 8569
Welcome the Spring	Stensaas	Heritage	HV 282

SAB and Three-Part (*continued*)

Westminster Carol	arr. Nygard	Hinshaw	HMC-860
*When Johnny Comes Marching Home	arr. Grier	Heritage	HV 168
When Sleighbells Ring	Kerchner	Hal Leonard	08603835
Where Is the Star?	McGlohon	GlorySound	D-5290
White	Nelson	Boosey & Hawkes	OC3B6429
Who Has Seen the Wind?	Snyder	Studio PR	SV8728
Winter Carol	Wilson	Jenson	409-23030
*Ye Watchers and Ye Holy Ones	arr. Treharne	Boston Music	BMC09379
You Know It's Christmas	Johns	Gentry	G-493

SATB and Four-Part

The Accommodation Stage Line	Brandon	Thomas House	C11-7809
The Alfred Burt Carols	Burt	Shawnee	A-450
Ain't Got Time to Die	arr. Burger	Studio PR	V-7949
All Ye Who Music Love	Donato	Bourne	B200303-357
An American Trilogy	arr. Newbury	Chappell	0044032-357
At This Holiday Time	Averre	Hinshaw	HMC-747
*Ave Verum Corpus	Byrd	Cambiata	D978121
Beautiful Savior	arr. Fettke	Belwin	AN-240
Blessed Is the Man	Butler	Cambiata	C 97203
Canticle of Christmas	Mahler/Wood	Heritage	H 138
Carol of the Bells	Leontovich	Cambiata	U983176
*The Colorado Trail	arr. Vance	Schimtt	7745
Come All Ye Fair and Tender Ladies	arr. Collins	Cambiata	ARS 980152
Contemporary Carols for Choir I & II	Grier	Heritage	H332
Da Pacem Domine	Franck/Goetze	Boosey & Hawkes	OC2B6187
David's Lamentation	Billings	Silver-Burdett	7612701
*Die Musici	arr. Swift	Hinshaw	HMC-4717
English Street Cry	arr. Kicklighter	Cambiata	U978110
Es Steht Ein Lind	Ahrold	Warner Bros.	W3616CH0017
Fanfare	McKinney	Jenson	455-06014
Fa Una Canzona	Vecchi	Lawson-Gould	556
Football (speech chorus)	Dobbins	Shawnee	A-1623
For the Freedom of Man	North	Cambiata	P978111
Glory to God	Handel	G. Schirmer	52249
Glory to Thee, My God, This Night	Tallis	Oxford	40.922
Hallelujah, Amen	Handel	Plymouth	C.C.7
Hi-Ho the Holly	arr. Calkins	Music 70	M70-347
I Am But a Small Voice	Coates	Shawnee	A-1644
If the World Learned How to Sing	Hughes	Jenson	423-09030
In These Delightful Pleasant Groves	Purcell	Silver-Burdett	7612712
Introit and Kyrie (*Requiem*)	Fauré	Cambiata	M117692
Joy Fills the Morning	Lotti	Cambiata	M983177
Jubilate Deo	Young	Shawnee	A-857
Kyrie Eleison	Lotti	Belwin	2204
Let's Begin Again	Rutter	Hinshaw	HMC-513
A Lincoln Log	Butler	Hal Leonard	08041950
Little David, Play on Your Harp	arr. Hairston	Hal Leonard	08601000
*The Man in the Arena	Porter	Boosey & Hawkes	OC4B6385
Mary, Mary	Avery	Curtis	C7943
A Medley of Four French Carols	arr. Mansfield	Lorenz	B381
My Love Is Like a Red, Red Rose	Cutter	Alfred	7319

SATB and Four-Part (*continued*)

*Neighbor's Chorus	Offenbach	Broude	BB130
*The New Promise of Love	Martin	Hinshaw	HMC-690
Noel! The Savior Is Born	Wetzler	Hope	CF 165
Now Let the Heavens Adore Thee	Bach/Collins	Cambiata	D978122
Now Thank We All Our God	Bach/Haberlen	Kjos	Ed. 5975
O Mary, Where Is Your Baby?	arr. Kalbach	Silver-Burdett	7012721
Panis Angelicus	Casciolini	Belwin	ProCh3005
Peace Life a River	Carter	Jenson	405-16024
Praise Ye the Lord, Ye Children	Tye	Oxford	43.241
The Praties They Grow Small	arr. Oliver	Witmark	W3710
The Savior of the World Is Born	Holst	Concordia	98-2184
Scaramella Va alla Guerra	Josquin	McAfee	DMC 1099
Send Out Thy Light	Farrell	Cambiata	C980 149
*She Is So Dear	Praetorius	Presser	332-14558
Sing to the Lord	Tye	C. Fischer	H056
Sing to the Lord	arr. Parker	Lawson-Gould	51322
Six Folk Songs	Brahms	Marks	12597-9
Sleep Little Dove	Thygerson	Richmond	MI 142
Slumber, O Holy Jesu	Wood	SMP	S-188
A Song to Sing	Kirk	Belwin	ProCh 3007
Song of the Sea	Hannisian	Studio PR	SV 7802
Surely He Hath Borne Our Griefs	Handel	Cambiata	M97201
Tan, Tan, Tan	arr. Nichols	Schmitt	8056
Tenebrae factae sunt	Ingegneri	Cambiata	D988155
*Three Madrigals	Diemer	Boosey & Hawkes	5417
Three Madrigals from Royalty	Butler	Gentry	C-118
*Tournament Galop	Gottschalk	McAfee	M1075
Two Hymns	Mozart	Augsburg	11-2069
Upon Her Grave	Mendelssohn	Lawson-Gould	52368
Venite Exultemus	Crocker	Jenson	471-22014
Wachet auf, ruft uns die Stimme	Bach/Wilson	Somerset	MW1225
Wenn Ich ein Vöglein Wär	Schumann	NMP	WHC-97
When the Saints Go Marching In	arr. Shaw	Hal Leonard	08665921
When I Survey the Wondrous Cross	arr. Martin	Presser	312-40785

SSA

Abbe Stadler	Beethoven	Boosey & Hawkes	OC3B6368
As It Fell Upon a Night	arr. Davis	Galaxy	1.1380
Awake the Trumpet's Lofty Sound	Handel	Marks	MC 4527
A Bird in Spring	Atkinson	Schmitt	354
*Cantata Domino	Hassler	Bourne	B201863-354
Come In	Thompson	E. C. Schirmer	ECS 2539
A Girl's Garden	Thompson	E. C. Schirmer	ECS 2540
*Gloria Alleluia	Crocker	Jenson	423-07033
Hotaru Koi	arr. Ogura	Presser	312-415-20
*Jabberwocky (*A Fit of Carroll*)	Carter	Beckenhorst	BP 104
Lift Thine Eyes	Mendelssohn	Studio PR	V7918
Many Gifts One Spirit	Pote	Presser	392-41466
The May Day Carol	arr. Bertaux	Boosey & Hawkes	OC3B6358
My Heart Is Offered Still to You	di Lasso	Lawson-Gould	51071
A New Year Carol	Britten	Boosey & Hawkes	OCFB5848
*Rain Dance	Nygard	Hinshaw	HMC-620

SSA (*continued*)

The River	Davidson	McAfee	DMC 8185
Scarborough Fair	arr. Goetze	Boosey & Hawkes	OC3B6390
Shady Grove	arr. Bertaux	Boosey & Hawkes	OC3B6239
The Snow	Elgar	National	CMS-128
Three Renaissance Pieces	Morley	Shawnee	B-407
Tomorrow Shall Be My Dancing Day	Rutter	Oxford	44.084
*Two Songs of Longing	Crocker	Jenson	471.20013
*You Stole My Love	MacFarren	Bourne	B239061-353

T(T)BB

Bound for Jubilee	Eilers	Studio PR	V7904
*Carols for Caroling	arr. Crouch	Studio PR	V8120
*Easy Folk Songs for Male Voices	Grotenhuis	Jenson	436-05011
It's the Christmas Time of the Year	Kunz	Jenson	407-09031
*My Love Is Like a Rose	Butler	Heritage	H2879
*Reflections of a Lad at Sea	Besig	Shawnee	E-267
Take Me Out to the Ball Game	Tilzer/Harris	Jenson	416-20051
This Train	Emerson	Jenson	403-20031
*A Whale of a Tail	Hoffman	Hall Leonard	08598348

Repertoire Performed by ACDA Honor/Festival Choirs, 1983–94

COMPILED BY GUY B. WEBB[2]

Children

A Child Said	McCray	National	1-130
A Menagerie of Songs	Jennings	G. Schirmer	12434, 12438
A-Tisket, a-Tasket	Fitzgerald/Feldman	Boosey & Hawkes	6456
A Trumpet Song	Purcell	Oxford	54.309
African Celebration	arr. Hatfield	Boosey & Hawkes	C-1991
Agnus Dei	Raminsh	Plymouth	HL-507
Agnus Dei (*Messe Basse*)	Fauré	Theodore Presser	312-40598
Ah! Si mon moine voulait	arr. Ridout	G. V. Thompson	G-182
Alleluia	Mozart	Broadman	4557-62
And God Shall Wipe Away All Tears	Daley	Hinshaw	HMG 1284
At the River	arr. Copland	Boosey & Hawkes	5511
Aviary, The	Bennett	Universal/Presser	312-40662
Away from the Roll of the Sea	Calvert	G. V. Thompson	VG340
Bashana Haba-a	Hirsh	Posthorn	C1019
Birds, The	Britten	Boosey & Hawkes	OCTB6524
Bist du bei mir	J. S. Bach	G. V. Thompson	VG-183
Bless the Lord, O My Soul	Henderson	Hinshaw	HMS 1171
Boston Trot	Elliott	Boosey & Hawkes	OCTB6588
Carol of the Rose	Thompson	E. C. Schirmer	2800

[2]G. B. Webb (1994), Repertoire performed by ACDA honor/festival choirs, 1983–94, *Choral Journal*, *35*(2), 25–40. Note: college repertoire has been omitted from this listing. (Reprinted by permission of the ACDA.)

Children (*continued*)

Cat and Mouse	Jennings	G. Schirmer	3241
Ching-a-Ring-Chaw	arr. Copland	Boosey & Hawkes	5025
Creation's Praise	Henderson	G. V. Thompson	G-241
Christmas Dance of the Shepherds	Kodály	Universal Ed.	10878 NJ
Dance with Me	arr. Davidson	MCA	00124038
Die Meere	Brahms	National	WHC-57
Dodi li	Chen	Boosey & Hawkes	OCT 6679
Domine Deus	J. S. Bach	Boosey & Hawkes	OC2B6552
Du bist die Ruh	Schubert	G. V. Thompson	G1002
Duet from Cantata no. 15	J. S. Bach	Boosey & Hawkes	OC2B6454
E Oru O (Nigerian chant)	Anonymous	Plymouth	HLTBP
Evening Song	Kodály	Boosey & Hawkes	5771
The Father's Love	Lole	Hinshaw	RSCM-519
Feel Good	Baker/Elliot	Boosey & Hawkes	OCTB6711
Fire	Goetze	Boosey & Hawkes	OC3B6482
The Heavenly Aeroplane	Rutter	Oxford	T114
Herr, du siehst statt guter werke auf	J. S. Bach	Boosey & Hawkes	6362
How Beautiful Are the Feet (*Messiah*)	Handel	Boosey & Hawkes	OCTB6702
Hush My Little White Shell (Navajo)	Mann	Posthorn	C1005
Hymn to Freedom	Peterson	Walton	WW-1135
I Will Lift Up My Eyes to the Hills	Boman	Boosey & Hawkes	OCT6550
Innoria (Huron dance)	Patriquin	earthsongs	EW-7A
In Paradisum	Willcocks	Oxford	E148
In the Mornin'	Ives	Associated	AMP 6736-38
Jabberwocky	Jennings	Boosey & Hawkes	OCT6555
Join the Dance	Jennings	Boosey & Hawkes	OCTB6553-5
Jubilate Deo	Praetorius	Boosey & Hawkes	OCUB6350
Kalanta of the New Year	Dalglish	Plymouth	HL-208
Kikkehihi	Schein	Boosey & Hawkes	6103
Laudate Dominum	Mozart	Boosey & Hawkes	OCTB6537
Laudate pueri	Mendelssohn	E. C. Schirmer	ECS 1839
Let Beauty Awake	Vaughan Williams	Boosey & Hawkes	OCTB6591
Little Horses, The	arr. Copland	Boosey & Hawkes	5508
Long, Long Ago	Floyd	Boosey & Hawkes	5648
The Lord Bless You and Keep You	Rutter	Hinshaw	1169
May the Road Rise to Meet You	Hamilton	Plymouth	HL-207
Mid the Oak Trees	Kodály	Boosey & Hawkes	5870
Nodel Kangboyon	arr. Hornady	earthsongs	W-12
Noël des enfants	Debussy	Durand/Presser	D&F 9418
Non nobis, Domine	Byrd	Hinshaw	HMC 1161
Old Dan Tucket	McRae	Plymouth	HL-205
Oliver Cromwell	Britten	Boosey & Hawkes	OCTB5893
Orkney Lullaby	Schultz	Boosey & Hawkes	6569
Path to the Moon	Thiman	Boosey & Hawkes	6114
Psalm 100	Henderson	G. V. Thompson	HMC 1170
Psalm 150	Britten	Boosey & Hawkes	OC4B5584
Psalm 150	Kodály	Oxford	83.072
Psallite	Praetorius	Bourne	ES 21A
Quando Corpus & Amen (*Stabat Mater*)	Pergolesi	Oxford	46.102
Reel a Bouche	Dalglish	Plymouth	HL-205
The Rides-by-Night	Britten	Oxford	OCS 116

Children (*continued*)

Shade of Night (*Songs of Awakening*)	Runyan	Boosey & Hawkes	OCTB6562
Siyahamba	arr. Rao	Boosey & Hawkes	OCTB6656
Side Show	Ives	Peer/Presser	61109-122
Simple Simon	Freedman	G. V. Thompson	G-330
Singabahambayo (South African)	Anonymous	Walton	HLTBP
Song for the Mira	MacGillivray	G. V. Thompson	G-327
Sound the Trumpet	Purcell	Novello	16001706
This Little Babe (*Ceremony of Carols*)	Britten	Boosey & Hawkes	5138
This Train Is Bound for Glory	arr. Hayes	Hinshaw	HMC 1303
Three Rhymes (sets 1 & 2)	Bouman	earthsongs	W-13, W-23
Three Settings of the Moon	Nelson	Boosey & Hawkes	6100
The Tree Toad & Don't Ever Seize a Weasel (*Musical Animal Tales*)	Henderson	G. V. Thompson	166, 168
Water under Snow Is Weary	Wessman	Walton	WF-701
Wenn des Kreuzes bitter keiten	J. S. Bach	Hinshaw	HMC 1190
Where'er You Walk	Handel	Boosey & Hawkes	6510
Wild Geese	Dalglish	Plymouth	HLTBP
Who Can Sail	Agnestig	Walton	WGK-120
Yonder Come Day (Georgia Sea Islands)	Anonymous	World Music	10

Junior High/Middle School

Abendlied	Mendelssohn	National	NMP 144
Adoramus te	Clement	Mercury	352-00126
Agnus Dei	Butler	C. Fischer	CM8191
All My Trials	arr. Swenson	Galaxy	1.2824.1
Am Bodensee	Schumann	Sam Fox	RC 6
America	arr. Hunter	C. Fischer	CM 7947
An American Hymn	Effinger	G. Schirmer	11522
Band of Angels	arr. Hairston	Bourne	W3671
Old Man Noah	Bartholomew	G. Schirmer	HL 50397330
Calypso Serenade	Oliver	Plymouth	PCS-24
Canon of Praise	Pachelbel	Somerset	MW 1226
Cindia	Pascanu	Santa Barbara	SBMP 44
Comic Duet for Two Cats	Rossini	Plymouth	PCS538
Consecrate the Place and Day	Pfautsch	Lawson-Gould	51420
Corner of the Sky	Schwartz	Belwin	OCT 228
Der Tanz	Schubert	Hinshaw	HMC-247
Dreams	Snyder	CPP/Belwin	SV9125
Fa-la-la Fantasie	Sleeth	C. Fischer	7800
Festival Sanctus	Leavitt	CPP/Belwin	SV8821
Gentle Annie	arr. Parker/Shaw	Lawson-Gould	859
Getting It Together	arr. Red	Trigon	TGO 108
Give Us Men, America	Daniels	Warner Bros.	485-10126
Gloria in excelsis (*Gloria*)	Vivaldi	Walton	W2043
The Glory Train	Spevacek	Hal Leonard	08752552
Go Out with Joy	Beebe	Hinshaw	HMC-117
Hae Tsuki Bushi	arr. Baxter	Santa Barbara	SBMP 59
Here's One	arr. Hayes	Hinshaw	HMC-501
hist wist	Jones	Shawnee	1076

Junior High/Middle School (*continued*)

Homeward Bound	Olson	C. Fischer	CM 8143
I Hear America Singing	Thomas	Heritage	15/1067
I Know Where I'm Goin'	arr. Moore	Beckenhorst	111
I'll Say It Anyway	Certon	Hinshaw	HMC 512
Jamaican Market Place	Farrow	Gentry	JG 2092
Jesu dulcis memoria	Victoria	G. Schirmer	2995
Jubilate Deo	di Lasso	G. Schirmer	11410
Kyrie	Leavitt	CPP/Belwin	SV8904
Kyrie	Lotti	Hal Leonard	08681420
Kyrie (*Mass in G*)	Schubert	Kjos	5989
Kyrie eleison	Mozart	C. Fischer	8149
Let All the Nations Praise the Lord	Leisring	Shawnee	A-94
Liebster Herr Jesu	Buxtehude	Marks	4508
Life Has Loveliness to Sell	Mulholland	Plymouth	JM2000
The Lord Is My Shepherd	Pote	Choristers Guild	CGA-551
Misty Morning	Nygard	Hinshaw	HMC 270
Music We Recall	arr. Tolmage	Staff	989
My Heart Is Offered Still to You	di Lasso	Lawson-Gould	563
My True Love Has My Heart	Butler	Hinshaw	HMC-621
O Music, Thou Most Lovely	Jeep	Hinshaw	934
O Praise the Mighty Lord	Handel	C. Fischer	CM 8384
Pålpåhaugen	arr. Ellingboe	Kjos	8719
Pie Jesu (*Requiem*)	Webber	Hal Leonard	08603519
Psallite	Praetorius	Bourne	ES21
Praise Ye!	Bach/Walker	Hal Leonard	08681655
Praise Ye the Lord	Telemann	CPP/Belwin	SV8926
Psallite	Praetorius	Bourne	106586
Praise We Sing to Thee (TTBB)	Haydn	Kjos	2505
Radiator Lions	Jothen	Kendale	NMA-217
Rainy Day	Hannisian	Studio PR	V7705
Ride the Chariot	arr. Smith	Kjos	1015
Riu, riu, chiu	arr. Greenberg	G. Schirmer	HL 50232820
Rosalee	Perry	Jenson	423-18041
Sanctus (*Mass*)	Bernstein	Boosey & Hawkes	OCTB6353
See the World through Children's Eyes (SSA)	Carter	Hope	SP 788
Shenandoah	arr. Goetze	Boosey & Hawkes	6257
Sicut cervus	Palestrina	Hal Leonard	HL50296560
Sing Praise to God Who Reigns Above	Mudde	Augsburg	11-1214
Sing, Sing Ye Muses	Blow	Dean	HCC 102
Sure on this Shining Night	Barber	G. Schirmer	10864
Swell the Full Chorus (*Solomon*)	Handel	Galaxy	1.2144(417)
Three American Lyrics	Rutter	Hinshaw	HMC-811
Three Madrigals	Diemer	Boosey & Hawkes	5417
Three Palestrina Chorals	arr. Tolmage	Staff Music	726
Thou Visiteth the Earth	Green	Novello	88.0013.08
Turtle Dove, The	arr. Spevacek	Hal Leonard	08752552
Ubi caritas	Leavitt	Studio 24	SV9113
The Water Is Wide	arr. Clausen	Foster	MF 3038
Welcome Sweet Pleasure	Weelkes	CPP/Belwin	OCT02560
What Is a Heart	Duson	Hinshaw	HMC-146
What Kind o' Shoes You Gonna Wear?	arr. Hairston	Bourne	1031
When I Survey the Wondrous Cross	arr. Martin	Presser	312-40785
While by My Sheep	arr. Jungst	Plymouth	XM-114
Younger Generation	Copland	Boosey & Hawkes	1723

Senior High School

A Red, Red Rose	Mulholland	European American	EA 445
African Sanctus	Fanshawe	Hal Leonard	11346005
Ain'a That Good News	Dawson	Tuskegee Music	103
Ave Maria	Biebl	Hinshaw	HMC-1255
All Breathing Life	J. S. Bach	G. Schirmer	7470
Ave Maria	Victoria	Mercury	352-00079
The Banks O'Doon	Mulholland	European American	EA 447
Canite tuba	Palestrina	Broude	ABC 4
Canticle of Praise	Beck	Theodore Presser	312-40588
Come to Me, My Love	Dello Joio	Belwin	MC 4609
Crucifixus	Lotti	G. Schirmer	6396
Der Abend	Brahms	G. Schirmer	10134
Der Gang zum Liebchen	Brahms	E. C. Schirmer	391
Down by the Riverside	arr. Rutter	Oxford	X248
Elijah Rock	arr. Hairston	Bourne	S-1017
Exultate Deo	Scarlatti	Marks	MC 76
Gloria	Rutter	Oxford	3380625
High Flight	Jackson	Alliance	AMP0033
Hospodi Pomilui	Lvov	C. Fischer	CM 6580
Hosanna in excelsis	Pierce	Plymouth	BP-122
Heart, We Will Forget Him	Mulholland	National	WHC 153
I Hear America Singing	Thomas	Heritage	15/1067
I'm Gonna Sing	Hunter	C. Fischer	CM 7971
If Ye Love Me	Tallis	Oxford	42.601
In Virtute tua	Gorczycki	Foster	2008
Jabberwocky	Pottle	Trigon	TGM 103
Jamaican Market Place	Farrow	Gentry	JG2092
The Last Words of David	Thompson	E. C. Schirmer	2294
Long Time Ago	Copland	Boosey & Hawkes	1906
Lonesome Dove	arr. Hall	National	WHC 24
Love Songs	Parker	Hinshaw	HMC 366
Lux aeterna	Fissinger	Walton	WW 1124
Music, Dear Solace	Pilkington	Broude	DEE9
Music Spread Thy Voice Around	Handel	G. Schirmer	12063
My Romance	Rodgers	Shawnee	A-1491
Nächtens	Brahms	G. Schirmer	10133
Non nobis, Domine	Quilter	Boosey & Hawkes	MFS461
Over the Rainbow	arr. Emerson	Jensen	403-15104
Placido e il mar (*Idomeneo*)	Mozart	Lawson-Gould	841
Regina coeli	Rogier	Foster	MF 414
Requiem	Duruflé	Durand/Presser	———
Requiem	Rutter	Hinshaw	HMB 164
San Sereni	arr. Terri	Lawson-Gould	51234
Set Me as a Seal	Clausen	Foster	MF2047A
Set Me as a Seal upon Thine Heart	Walton	Oxford	43.043
Shenandoah	arr. Erb	Lawson-Gould	51846
Sicut cervus	Palestrina	E. C. Schirmer	2988
Sing a Mighty Song	Gawthrop	Alliance	AMP0032
Sing We Merrily	Campbell	Novello	19147
Six Chansons	Hindemith	Schott & Co.	10453-8
Song for the Mira	McGillivray	G. V. Thompson	VEI.1080
Song of Exultation	Beck	G. Schirmer	11487
Songs of the Nativity	Montaine	Gray	GCMR 2374
Space Age Canons	Hagemann	C. Fischer	CM8152

Senior High School (*continued*)

Stabat Mater	Verdi	Peters	4256
Steal Away	arr. Simpson	Bourne	B231324-358
Three Choruses (*Family Reunion*)	Parker	C. Fischer	7991-3
Three Lenten Poems	Pinkham	E. C. Schirmer	2693
Two American Folk Songs	arr. Rutter	Oxford	X247
Ubi caritas	Duruflé	Durand	312-41253
Vesperae solemnes de confessore	Mozart	Breitkopf	1533
Walkin' down That Glory Road	Hayes	Hinshaw	HMC-474
What Is a Heart?	Duson	Hinshaw	HMC-146
Who Is He in Yonder Stall	Young	Plymouth	XM302
Wondrous Love	Christiansen	Augsburg	11-140
Zum Schluss	Brahms	G. Schirmer	10135

Women

A Child Said	McCray	National	1-130
A Jubilant Song	McCray	Santa Barbara	SBMP 31
Abenlied	Mendelssohn	National	NMP-145
Ah, si mon moine voulait danser	arr. Patriquin	earthsongs	W7-C
Artsah Alinu	arr. Schwadron	Plymouth	PCS 229
Ave Maria	Holst	Belwin	GMOD 00312
Bury Me beneath the Willow	Palmer	National	NMP 170
Choral Hymns from the Rig-Veda	Holst	Galaxy	1.5091
Clap Yo' Hands	Gershwin	Warner Bros.	H2205
Come, All Musicians, Come	Hassler	Lawson-Gould	51937
Darr kom die Alabama	Haskell	Shawnee	B-335
Circus Band	Ives/Tagg	International/Presser	093576-101
Dormi, Dormi	Goetze	Boosey & Hawkes	OCUB6128
Eucaristica (Deep in My Heart)	Casals	Tetra-Continuo	155
Four Songs for Women's Choir	Brahms	Peters	6617
Fragments from the Mass	Diemer	Marks/Hal Leonard	0007605/MC96
Gloria sei dir gesungen	J. S. Bach	G. V. Thompson	VG-195
Hashivenu	arr. Rao	Boosey & Hawkes	OC3B6430
Heart We Will Forget Him	Mulholland	National	153
Herbstlied	Mendelssohn	National	NMP-145
Hodie	Leavitt	Hal Leonard	0862125
How Excellent Is Thy Name	Snyder	Columbia	SV8556
In Evangolium	Bingen	Hildegard	no. 4
Johnny Has Gone for a Soldier	arr. Jeffers	earthsongs	EW-2
Kyrie (*Missa Brevis*)	Telfer	Lenel	LSC 105
Laetatus sum	Porpora	Marks	MC 4552
Laudi alle vergine Maria	Verdi	Peters	4256c
Le Sommeil de l'enfant Jesus	arr. Jeffers	earthsongs	C-09
L'entend le moulin	Patriquin	earthsongs	W-10
Little Bird, Little Bird	Kubik	Southern	73-12
Lord, See the Good Works of My Heart	J. S. Bach	Boosey & Hawkes	CO2B6362
Love Songs in the Round	Biggs	Consort	CP21
The Maker of Dreams	Rosaenz	Aberdeen Music	1469
Messa basse pour voix de femmes	Fauré	Broude	CR 37
Missa Brevis	Raminsh	Plymouth	———
Missa Brevis in D	Britten	Boosey & Hawkes	LCB-54
Music Spread Thy Voice Around	Handel	Marks	4476
My Heart's Friend	Raminsh	Boosey & Hawkes	OCTB6576
My True Love Hath My Heart	Land	Plymouth	PCS-252

Women (*continued*)

No, di voi non vo Fidarmi	Handel	Greystone	GRP2000
Noel des enfants qui n'ont plus de maisons	Debussy	Durand	———
Now I Walk in Beauty	Smith	G. Schirmer	12374
Now's the Time to Sing	Kirk	G. Schirmer	12109
O Aula nobilis	Mathias	Oxford	W106
O Sacrum convivium	Victoria	Joseph Boonin	B.157
O Waly, Waly	arr. Phillips	Presser	312-41269
Psalm 100	Carter	Walton	2932
Psalm 100	Clausen	Foster	917
Pueri Hebraeorum	Thompson	E. C. Schirmer	492
Four Sacred Songs for the Night	Bright	Shawnee	B-190
Shells	Nystedt	Associated	A-715
Singet dem Herrn	Praetorius	Columbia	SV 8640
So I Let Him Lead Me Home	Mulholland	National	152
Sometimes	Mancini	Shawnee	B-443
Songs Mein Grossmama Sang	Pfautsch	Lawson-Gould	50120
Stabat Mater	Pergolesi	Kalmus	6375
They Say That Susan Has No Heart for Learning	Harris	Associated	A-231
Three Madrigals	Krenek	Music RM	3507
Three Sixteenth-Century Madrigals	Marenzio	Shawnee	B-457
Torches	Hugh-Jones	Oxford	W-97
Vem kan segla Foruntal vind	Agnestig	Walton	WKG-120
Zion's Walls	Copland	Boosey & Hawkes	OCTB6071

Men

A Dirge for Two Veterans	Holst	G. Schirmer	8323
A-Rovin'	arr. Jeffers	earthsongs	EM-1
Alexander's Ragtime Band	Berlin	Berlin Music	S.P.E.B.S.Q.S.A. 93
An Irish Airman Forsees His Death	Adams	earthsongs	M-11
As Beautiful as She	Butler	Jenson	488-10017
Ballad of Little Musgrave and Lady Barnard	Britten	Boosey & Hawkes	17159
Be Thou My Vision	arr. Hunter	Hinshaw	HMC-375
Blessed Be the Lord	Tallis	Associated	NYP 1730
Brothers, Sing On	Grieg	J. Fischer	6927
Cantique de Jean Racine	Fauré	Hinshaw	HMC-714
Chorus of the Pirates	Sullivan	Boston Music	9426
Colorado Trail	arr. Luboff	Walton	W1005
Come, Peace of God	Butler	Sacred	S-2859
Die Nacht	Schubert	Dean	HRD 178
Down in the Valley	arr. Mead	Galaxy	1.1716
Exultate justi	Viadana	CP/Belwin	FCC 01720
Five Foot Two, Eyes of Blue	Henderson	Feist	S.P.E.B.S.Q.S.A. 129
Gaudeamus	arr. Bartholomew	G. Schirmer	11279
Gloria (*Missa mater patris*)	des Prez	G. Schirmer	11012
The God Who Gave Us Life	Thompson	E. C. Schirmer	2139
Got a Mind to Do Right	Morrow	Lawson-Gould	52502
I Hear America Singing	Thomas	Heritage	15-1067
I Hear a Voice a-Prayin'	Bright	Shawnee	C-155
I Shall Not Be Moved	arr. Parker	Lawson-Gould	51297
I Shall Not Die without a Hope	Thompson	E. C. Schirmer	2139
If I Could Write a Song	Sedaka	Warner Bros.	S.P.E.B.S.Q.S.A. 93

Men (*continued*)

If the Rest of the World Don't Want You	Dreyer-Gerber	Bourne	119
Jonah's Song	Schickele	Elkan-Vogel	362-03303
La Pastorella	Schubert	Lawson-Gould	512
Liebe	Schubert	Foster	MF 1059
Little Innocent Lamb	Bartholomew	G. Schirmer	9907
Loch Lomond	arr. Duson	Kjos	5564
The Lord Is My Strength and Song	Morgan	Kjos	5558
The Minstrel Boy	arr. Jeffers	earthsongs	EM-4
Nachtgesang im Walde	Schubert	Breitkopf	OB4919
Nocturnal Serenade	Schubert	Walton	7500
Non nobis, Domini	Quilter	Boosey & Hawkes	MFS 348
Now Let Every Tongue Adore Thee	J. S. Bach	Boston Music	2816
O Be Joyful	Ramsfield	Flammer	C-5006
O Come Let Us Sing unto the Lord	Diemer	C. Fischer	CM8014
O How Amiable	Vaughan Williams	Oxford	42.056
O Magnum Mysterium	Handl	J. Fischer	FEC 7539
The Old Chisholm Trail	arr. Luboff	Walton	1012
The Pasture (*Frostiana*)	Thompson	E. C. Schirmer	2181
Pilgrims Chorus (*Tannhauser*)	Wagner	G. Schirmer	8017
Promised Land	arr. Richardson	Foster	MF 1005
Rhythm of Life	Coleman	Shawnee	C-255
Rise Up, O Men of God	Jennings	Augsburg	00800645731
She Is My Slender Small Love	Thiman	G. Schirmer	10671
Sigh No More, Ladies	Washburn	Oxford	95.109
Somebody's Calling My Name	arr. Whalum	Lawson-Gould	51932
Sometimes I Feel Like a Motherless Child	arr. Heath	G. Schirmer	10567
Song of Peace	Persichetti	Elkan-Vogel	363-00130
Ständchen	Schubert	Lawson-Gould	521
Star-Spangled Banner, The	arr. Dvořak	Kerby	14366
Stouthearted Men	arr. Scotson	Warner Bros.	C10363
Thanks Be to Thee	Handel	Galaxy	1.2221
They Call the Wind Maria	Lerner/Lowe	Chappell	HL 003469-62
This Old Hammer	arr. Ehret	Shawnee	CO183
Vive l'amour	arr. Shaw/Parker	Lawson-Gould	50126
Waltzing Matilda	Cowan	C. Fischer	CM7091
Yes Sir, That's My Baby	Kahn/Donaldson	Bourne	YMIH2

Selected List of Published Multicultural and Ethnically Inspired Choral Music[3]

COMPILED BY LAWRENCE KAPTEIN[4]

Latin America

A la Nanita Nana (Mexico)	arr. Folstrom	Foster	MF-547
Alma Llanera	Guitenaz/Sauce	earthsongs	S-37
Antigua (Guatemala)	Ortega	Alliance	AMP 0064

---

[3] SATB unless otherwise noted.

[4] L. Kaptein (1995), Selected list of published multi-cultural enthnically inspired choral music, *Melisma*, *13*(2), 14–15. (Updated list reprinted by permission of the author and NCACDA.)

Latin America (*continued*)

Antologia coral (Latin Am. Anthology)	Ricordi	Buenos Aires	———
Canciones de Amor	ed. Hansen	Roger Dean Music	15/1333
Coenantibus autem illis (Mexico)	Lienas	Instituto Nacional de Bellas Artes	———
Como Tu (SSSAAA)	Grau	earthsongs	W-41
Congori Shango	arr. Brenas	Twin Elm Music	Greely, CO
El Jarabe Tapatio	Noble	Alliance	AMP-0024
Erat Jesus ejicien saemonium Diecbat Jesus turbis Judaeorum (Mexico)	arr. Navarro	Mapa Mundi	#57
Four 17th Century Latin American Folk Songs	arr. Wilkins	C. C. Birchard	Boston
Jamaican Market Place	Farrow	Gentry	JG2092
La Sandunga (Mexico)	arr. Reyes	Ricordi	———
Las Americas Unidas	Mechem	G. Schirmer	HL50481182
Mata del Anima Sola	Estevez	earthongs	S-38
Missa Criolla (Hispanic Folk Mass)	Ramirez	G. Schirmer	51362
Missa Quilomos (South Am. Indian)	arr. Lyon	Cultural Bridge Innovations, Boulder	———
Noche de Paz	arr. Carrillo	Santa Barbara Music	SBMP-184
Quisiera (Cuba)	arr. Valera	Ward Music	Vancouver
Requiem (Argentina)	Garia	Hänssler Music	———
Riqui, Riqui, Riqurran (Venezuela)	arr. Smith	G. Schirmer	11299
Romance de Roman Castillo	Noble	Alliance	AMP-0027
Salmo 150	Aguiar	earthongs	S-40
Son de La Loma (Cuba)	arr. Castillo	Alliance	AMP-0150
Shut De Do (Jamaica)	Stonehill/Hayes	Word Music	3010262167
Tangueando	Escalada	Lawson-Gould	52729
Te Quiero	Cangiano	earthsongs	S-49
Three Latin America Folk Songs	arr. Sandi	Peer International	60674-121
Tres Cantos Nativos Dos Indios Krao	arr. Leite	earthsongs	S-68
Tumbando Cana (Cuba)	arr. Roberts	Lawson-Gould	51685

Philippines

Dahil sa lyo	arr. Veneracio	University of the Philippines	———
Iddem dem Mallida	Makil/Gomez	Lawson-Gould	52215

Indonesia

Chan Mali Chan (from Three Maly Folksongs)	arr. Tan	Kjos	8782
Gamelan (4 equal voices)	Schafer	Arcana Editions	Canada
Suliram	De Cormier	Lawson-Gould	51755

Russia/Baltic States

Bceholihow Baehne	Rachmaninoff	Music Rusica	MRSMRA028
Behnkn (Brooms)	Rubtsov	Musica Russica	FS 002
Blazenni jaze izbral	Tchaikovsky	Carus-Verlag	CV 40-177/60
Birch Tree Variations	Porter	Alliance Music	AMP 0013
Bo Poje Oepesohbka Ctoria (In the Field a Birch Tree Is Standing)	arr. Chesnokov	Musica Russica	FS-022

Russia/Baltic States (*continued*)

The Estonia Calender Songs	Tormis	Frazer Music	Helsinki
Kalinka	arr. Pitfield	Oxford	81.112
Latvian Boat Song	arr. Kemp	Waterloo Music	Canada
Neslegtais Gredzens	Karlsons	earthsongs	S-23
Metelitsa (Snow Flurries)	Varlamov	Musica Russica	FS011
Smieklis Man (SSAA)	Latvia	Santa Barbara Music	SBMP 165
Songs of the Ukraine (folk songs; 7SSA & 27 SATB)		Witmark & Sons	
Sulle Mulle (Estonia)	Ritsing	Santa Barbara Music	SBMP 182
Three Latvian Carols (2 sets)	Jansons	earthsongs	C-15, C-22
Treputé Mar Tela	Augustinas	Alliance Music	AMP 0043
Trumpet's Dawn	Sviridov	Russian Society of Choirs	K-9
Two Latvian Carols (SSAA)	Jansons	earthsongs	C-14
Two Latvian Carols (TTBB)	Jansons	earthsongs	M-19
Two Russian Folk Songs	arr. Briggs	Consort Press	CA 91350
Vanka 'n Tanka	arr. Kibalchich	Witmark & Sons	————
Varpas (SSAA) (Lithuania)	Vasiliauskaite	Santa Barbara Music	SBMP142
Zoriu Byut (Reveille)	Sviridov	Musica Russica	CMR004-7

Native Americans

Haliwa-Saponi Canoe Song	arr. Burton	World Music	————
Ho hiyuwaye	Lukasik	University of Colorado	(Boulder)
Native Circles	McCray	Colorado State Univ.	(Ft. Collins)
Skidegate Love Song	arr. Chatman	Gordon V. Thompson	VEI 1082
Three Native American Chants	ed. Reid	Twin Elm Music	98-01
Willows by the Waterside	Kreutz	Shawnee	A-1323

Africa

African Mass	Luboff	Walton	WM-110
Andeleli Obodus	arr. Vujic	Alliance Music	AMP 0059
Bandari (Inside These Walls)	Allaway	Santata Barbara	SBDD 66
Betelehemu	arr. Brooks	Lawson-Gould	52744
Freedom Is Coming	ed. Nyberg	Walton	WB-528
Hombe	arr. Ekwneme	G. Schirmer	51807
Kah Behneh Kah	arr. Nebo	G. Schirmer	51464
Kaung'a Yachee	Mganga	earthsongs	S-67
Missa Afro-Brasileria	Fonseca	G. Schirmer	51948
Ngulu	Mganga	earthsongs	S-66
O, Desayo	arr. Levin/Leck	Plymouth	WWIC-500
South African Suite (treble)	arr. Leck	Plymouth	HL-200
Three South African Folk Songs	arr. Lyon	Alliance Music	AMP-0093
Two South African Ceremonial Songs	arr. Kaptein/Lyon	Alliance Music	AMP-0266
Urukumbuzi	arr. Vujic	Alliance Music	AMP 0058

Slavic Countries

Ave Regina coelorum	Zelenka	Carus-Verlag	CV 40.465-01
Cantec de Pace	Pop	Musica Romanica	WRCR0012B
Cantemus!	Bardos	Editio Musica	Z8539
Chindia	Pascanu	Santata Barbara	SBMP-44

Slavic Countries (*continued*)

Credo quod Redemptor meus vivit	Zelenka	Carus-Verlag	CV 40.462-01
Eli, Eli	Bardos	Shawnee	A-1352
Kas Tie Tadi	arr. Samtez	Alliance Music	AMP-0087
Matraszentimrei Dolok (treble)	Ligeti	Schott & Co.	C45593
Mazu Biju, Neredzeju (SSA)	arr. Melngailis	Santa Barbara	SBMP 170
Miezu Varpa Un Apinitis (SSA)	Kalnins/Wolverton	Santa Barbara	SBMP 164
Suita Scruta (Short Suite)	Pascanu	Musica Romanica	XRCM-0010
Tambur	arr. Bardos	Editio Musica	———
Trepute Martela (Lithuania)	Augustinas	Musica Russica	MRSMRA0043
Ungheresca	arr. Bardos	Editio Musica	———
Vine Hulpe di la Munte (SSA)	Pop	Musica Romanica	XRCM-0013
Yugoslav Folk Songs	Seiber	Boosey & Hawkes	229

Asia

A Set of Chinese Folk Songs	arr. Yi	Presser	312-41732
Arirang (SSAA) (Korea)	arr. Park	Alliance Music	AMP-0092
Chinese Love Lyrics	Baker	G. V. Thompson	EI 1016
Crescent Moon Now Floating	ed. Larson	Lawson-Gould	52357
Dravidian Dithyramb (India)	Paranjoti	earthsongs	S-42
Eight Japanese Haiku	Pierce	Walton	2911
Five Haiku ((SSAA) Japan)	Whittemore	Alliance Music	AMP-0201
Jasmine Flower (China)	arr. Tam	Alliance Music	AMP-0183
Kokiriko Bushi	arr. Stuart	Music 70	M70-670
Pengyou Ting (China)	arr. Jennings	earthsongs	C-25
Rising Sun, The (Japan)	Pooler/Pierce	Somerset Press	CE-4328
Sakura	arr. Luboff	Walton	3041

Israel

Al Shlosha D'Varim (SA)	Naplan	Boosey & Hawkes	OCTB6783
Arise and Be Free: A Chanukah Suite	arr. Barnett	Transcontinental	991292-5
Avinu Malkeynu	Janowski	Transcontinental	G-030
Azi Vezimrat Yah	Allen	Transcontinental	991041
Erev Shel Shoshanim	arr. Klebanow	World Music Press	H-001
Four Palestinian Folk Songs	arr. Binder	Marks	2004
Hal'Iluhu (Psalm 150)	Schiller	Transcontinental	991280
Hanukkah Madrigal	Fromm	Transcontinental	991024
Hashivenu (unison, canon)	arr. Rao	Boosey & Hawkes	OC3B6430
Hatikvah	arr. Goldman	Ludwig Music	OH L1185
Hiney Mah Tov	arr. Levine	Mark Foster	MF 3025
Mi Zeh Y'Maleil	arr. Jacobson	Transcontinental	992016
Mi Yitneni Of	arr. Snyder	Hal Leonard	08742404
Oyf'n Prip'chok	arr. Rubin	G. Schirmer	11355
S'Vion	arr. Shields	earthsongs	W-16
Tehum Bi-Ri Tchum	arr. Goldman	G. Schirmer	51888
Three Sephardic Folksongs (SSA)	arr. Western Wind/Leck	Plymouth	WWIC-200
Three Songs for Israel	arr. Browda	Shawnee	A-956
Two Hymns from the Hebrew	arr. Adler	Hope Music	SA-1401
Ya Ba Bom	arr. Goldman	Lawson-Gould	51814
Y'Susum Midbar	arr. Parker	Transcontinental	991420
Yom Seh Le-Yisrael	arr. Cohen	Boosey & Hawkes	W.155

New Zeland/Australia/Maori

Carol to St. Stephen	Body	SOUNZ (Wellington, NZ)	———
Childhood	McLeod	SOUNZ (FAX 64-7-834-3374)	———
Faleula E!	arr. Marshall	Alliance Music	AMP-0239
Ghosts, Fire, Water	Mews	SOUNZ (see above)	———
Hine e Hine	arr. Cooper	SOUNZ (see above)	———
Kapiti	Patterson	SOUNZ (see above)	———
The Last Ones	Marshall	SOUNZ (see above)	———
La'U Lupe (SSAA)	arr. Marshall	Alliance Music	AMP-0239
Minoi, Minoi	Marshall	Alliance Music	AMP-0100
Moemoe Pepe (SSAA)	arr. Marshall	Alliance Music	AMP-0240
Pusi Nofo (SSAA)	arr. Marshall	Alliance Music	AMP-0241
Three Folksongs from the Strait Islands	arr. York	Kelly Sebastian Music	———
Three Maroi Songs	arr. Mews	SOUNZ (see above)	———
To the Horizon	Marshall	SOUNZ (see above)	———
Visions	Rimmer	SOUNZ (see above)	———

Accessible Choral Works for the Developing High School Choir[5]

BY LARRY TORKELSON[6]

Renaissance

Adoramus te	Palestrina	Hal Leonard	08677710
Adoramus te Christe	di Lasso	C. Fischer	CM8273
Agnus Dei	Hassler	Shawnee	A-1482
All Ye Who Music Love	Donato	Kjos	8745
Cantata Domino	Hassler	Bourne	ES18
El Grillo	des Prez	Oxford	95 P 300
Enatus est Emmanuel	Praetorius	Concordia	98-1868
Exaudi Deus	Croce	C. Fischer	CM8347
Innsbruck, I Now Must Leave Thee	Isaac	Tetra-Broude	AB251-3
Kyrie (SAB)	Hassler	Concordia	98-2443
Lo, How a Rose E'er Blooming	Praetorius	Hinshaw	HMC-638
O Bone Jesu	Palestrina	C. Fischer	CM8299
O Domine Jesu	Palestrina	Shawnee	A-1473
O Vos Omnes	Croce	Shawnee	A-1661
Psallite	Praetorius	Bourne	106586
Two di Lasso Classics	di Lasso	Shawnee	A-1888

Baroque

Alleluia (from Cantata 142)	Kuhnau[7]	Mark Foster	MF544H
Canon of Praise (SAB)	Pachelbel	Somerset	MW1226
Cantate Domino	Pitoni	Bourne	ES 5
Come and Sing Forth Your Joyful Praises (SAB)	Vivaldi	Concordia	98-2858
Cum Sancto Spiritu (SAB)	Lotti	CPP/Belwin	SV9112

---

[5]SATB unless otherwise noted.

[6]L. Torkelson (1994), Accessible choral works for the developing high school choir, *Melisma*, *13*(1), 12–13. (Used by permission of the author and NCACDA.)

[7]Formerly attributed to J. S. Bach.

Baroque (*continued*)

Gloria in Excelsis (*Gloria*)	Vivaldi	Walton	2043
Glory to God, Alleluia (SAB)	J. S. Bach	Flammer	D-5404
Hallelujah, Amen (*Judas Maccabaeus*)	Handel	G. Schirmer	9835
Jesu, Joy of Man's Desiring	J. S. Bach	Mark Foster	MF214
Miserere Mei	Lotti	Boosey & Hawkes	B1938
O All Ye Nations	Schütz	Presser	332-13992
Praise the Lord (*Judas Maccabaeus*)	Handel	Flammer	A-5714
Praise We the Name of God	Kuhnau	Mark Foster	M 544D
Praise! Praise! (*Solomon*) (SAB)	Handel	Alfred	4259
Rejoice in the Lord (SAB)	Steffani	Concordia	98-2217
Sing Out Your Joy to God (*Joshua*)	Handel	Hope	AA-1688
Sing unto the Lord (Cantata 196)	J. S. Bach	Mark Foster	MF242
Surely He Hath Borne Our Griefs	Graun	Hinshaw	HMC-583
Wake, Awake for Night Is Flying	J. S. Bach	Somerset	MW1225
(4th mov. and final chorale)			
With Songs of Rejoicing	J. S. Bach	C. Fischer	CM8086
Zion Hears the Watchmen's Voices	J. S. Bach	Oxford	X212

Classical

Adoramus Te	Gasparini	CPP/Belwin	2148
Adoramus Te (SAB)	Gasparini	Hal Leonard	4301060
Agnus Dei (*Missa Brevis St. Joannis de Deo*)	Haydn	Mark Foster	MF282
Agnus Dei (*Missa Brevis in G*)	Haydn	Alfred	5834
The Heavens are Praising (SAB)	Beethoven	Mark Foster	MF2062
Ave Verum	Mozart	Hinshaw	HMC-190
Gloria in Excelsis (*Harmoniemesse*)	Haydn	Hal Leonard	08679600
Gloria (*Heiligmesse*)	Haydn	Walton	2031
Kyrie (*Missa Brevis St. Joannis de Deo*)	Haydn	G. Schirmer	11442
O Praise the Lord with Heart and Voice	Haydn	Flammer	A-5832
(*The Creation*)			
Sanctus (*Heiligmesse*)	Haydn	Plymouth	PCS-138
Sanctus (*Mariazeilermesse*)	Haydn	Alfred	4790
Sanctus (*Missa Brevis in D*)	Mozart	Marks	4183
The Heavens Are Telling	Haydn	Coronet	CP-318
(*The Creation*) (SAB)			
Three Nocturnes (SAB or SSA)	Mozart	Plymouth	PXW-100
Other Nocturne Editions			
Ecco quel fiero istante, K.436	Mozart	G. Schirmer	11851
Mi lagnero tacendo, K.437	Mozart	G. Schirmer	11850
Due pupille amabili, K.439	Mozart	National	CMS-103
Piu non si trovano, K.549	Mozart	National	CMS-101
Two Motets	M. Haydn	G. Schirmer	11045
Two Mozart Kyries (ed. Liebergen)	Mozart	Alfred	7999
Two Mozart Kyrie Settings (McCray)	Mozart	Shawnee	A-1798

19th Century/Romantic

Alleluia, Praise!	Cherubini	Somerset	MW1223
Ave Verum (3-part mixed)	Fauré	Heritage	SV116
Come, Redeemer, Come to Us	Cherubini	C. Fischer	CM8199
Gloria in Altissimus Deo (SAB)	Saint-Saëns	Shawnee	A-1811
Herbstlied (SA or TB)	Schumann	National	WHC-54

19th Century/Romantic (*continued*)

Herbstlied (SA or TB)	Schumann	National	WHC-54
He, Watching over Israel (*Elijah*) (SAB)	Mendelssohn	Hope	AA1690
How Lovely Are the Messengers (*St. Paul*) (SAB)	Mendelssohn	Hope	AA1691
In Stiller Nacht (SAT)	Brahms	Somerset	SP780
Kyrie (*Mass in G*)	Schubert	Kjos	8729
Lebenslust	Schubert	Hinshaw	HMC-425
Liebesgram (SA or TB)	Schumann	National	WHC-82
Lift Thine Eyes (*Elijah*) (3-part)	Mendelssohn	Cambiata Press	M117322
Praise Ye the Lord of Hosts (*Christmas Oratorio*)	Saint-Saëns	Hal Leonard	08681662
Six Folk Songs (First Series)	Brahms	E. B. Marks	No. 9
The May Night (Die Mainacht)	Brahms	E. B. Marks	MC4241
Wondrous Cool, Thou Woodland Quiet	Brahms	G. Schirmer	9335
Wenn Ich Ein Voglein War	Schumann	National	WHC-97
Zum Sanctus (Holy, Holy, Holy)	Schubert	Lawson-Gould	51850

20th Century/Contemporary

A Boy Was Born	Britten	Oxford	84.092
A Christmas Carol	Ives	Merion/Presser	342-10116
Agnus Dei	Leavitt	CPP/Belwin	SV9007
All Things Bright and Beautiful	Rutter	Hinshaw	HMC-663
A Red, Red, Rose	Mulholland	European American	EA445
A Rose Touched by the Sun's Warm Rays	Berger	Augsburg	953
Beau Soir	Debussy	Aberdeen/Plymouth	1023
Dance of the One-Legged Sailor	Pierce	Plymouth	PB-502
For God So Loved the World (SAB)	Distler	Concordia	98-2239
For the Beauty of the Earth	Rutter	Hinshaw	HMC-169
Kyrie	Leavitt	CPP/Belwin	SV8904
Long Time Ago	Copland/Fine	Boosey & Hawkes	1906
maggie and milly and mollie and may	Persichetti	Elken-Vogel	362-01224
Old Abram Brown	Britten	Boosey & Hawkes	1786
Oliver Cromwell	Britten	Boosey & Hawkes	1786
Praise to the Lord	Distler	J. Fischer/Belwin	FEC9694
Rise Up, My Love, My Fair One	McCray	National	WHC-77
Serenity	Ives	Associated (AMP)	A-377
Six Chansons	Hindemith		
The Doe (La Biche)	Hindemith	Schott/Belwin	A-504
A Swan (Un Cygne)	Hindemith	Schott/Belwin	A-505
Sure on This Shining Night	Barber	G. Schirmer	10864
Sweet Day (No. 1 of Three Elizabethan Part Songs)	Vaughan Williams	Galaxy	1.5011
The Earth Adorned	Ahlen	Walton	WH-126
The Glory of the Father	Hovland	Walton	2973
The Prayer of St. Francis	Clausen	Foster	MF2087
The Shepherd to His Love	Diemer	Marks/Belwin	MC97
Three Choral Pastiches (SAB)	Hellden	Walton	2717
Three Hungarian Folk Songs	Bartok	Boosey & Hawkes	5326
Three Madrigals	Diemer	Boosey & Hawkes	5417
Ubi Caritas	Leavitt	CPP/Belwin	SV9113

Appendix D

Voice Class Resources

Christy, V. A., and J. G. Paton (1997). *Foundations in singing: A basic text in vocal technique and song interpretation* (6th ed.). Madison, WI: Brown and Benchmark.

Goleeke, T. (1984). *Literature for the voice: An index of songs in collections and source books for teachers of singing.* Metuchen, NJ: Scarecrow Press.

Harlow, B. (1985). *You, the singer.* Chapel Hill, NC: Hinshaw.

Harpster, R. W. (1984). *Technique in singing: A program for singers and teachers.* New York: Schirmer Books.

Kenney, J. (1987). *Becoming a singing performer: A text for voice classes.* Dubuque, IA: Wm. C. Brown.

Lightner, H. (1991). *Class voice and the American art song: A source book and anthology.* Metuchen, NJ: Scarecrow Press.

Lindsley, C. E. (1985). *Fundamentals of singing for voice classes.* Belmont, CA: Wadsworth.

Miller, K. E. (1983). *Principles of singing: A textbook for first-year singers.* Upper Saddle River, NJ: Prentice Hall.

Sable, B. K. (1982), *The vocal sound.* Upper Saddle River, NJ: Prentice Hall.

Schmidt, J. (1994). *The basics of singing* (3d ed.). New York: Schirmer Books. Audio cassette accompaniment available.

Stanton, R. (1983). *Steps to singing for voice classes* (3d ed.). Prospect Heights, IL: Waveland Press.

Trusler, I., and W. Ehret (1972). *Functional lessons in singing.* Upper Saddle River, NJ: Prentice Hall.

Ware, C. (1995). *Adventures in singing.* New York: McGraw-Hill.

Appendix E

Sight-Singing Materials

Most of the following sight-singing materials are reviewed in Chapter 8 of Steven Demorest's *Building Choral Excellence: Teaching Sight-Singing in the Choral Rehearsal* (New York: Oxford University Press, 2001). A summary chart on page 160 of Demorest's text is especially helpful.

Anderson, T. (1992). *Sing choral music at sight*. Reston, VA: MENC.

Arkis, S., and H. Shuckman (1968–70). *Introduction to sight-singing and the choral sight singer*. New York: Carl Fischer Music.

Bacak, J. E., and E. Crocker (1988–89). *Patterns of sound*. Milwaukee: Jenson (Hal Leonard).

Baugess, D. (1984/85). *Jenson sight singing course*. Student and teacher editions with instructional cassettes. 2 vols. Milwaukee: Jenson (Hal Leonard).

Bertalot, J. (1993). *Five wheels to successful sight-singing*. Minneapolis: Augsburg Fortress Press.

Boyd, J. (1981). *Choral sight-reading*. Champaign, IL: Mark Foster Music.

Cole, S., and L. Lewis (1909). *Melodia: A comprehensive course in sight-singing*. 4 vols. Bryn Mawr, PA: Oliver Ditson (Theodore Presser).

Cooper, I., and K. Kuersteiner (1965). *Teaching junior high school music*. Boston: Allyn and Bacon.

Crocker, E., and J. Eilers (1990). *Patterns of sound series: The choral approach to sight singing*. Milwaukee: Jenson (Hal Leonard).

———. (1994). *Patterns of sound series: Sight-singing for SSA*. Milwaukee: Jenson (Hal Leonard).

Crocker, E., and, J. Leavitt (1995–98). *Essential musicianship*. 3 vols. Milwaukee: Hal Leonard.

Crowe, E., A. Lawton, and W. Whittaker (eds.) (1933/61). *The folk songs sight singing series*. New York: Oxford University Press.

Edstrom, R. (1978). *The independent singer*. San Diego: Curtis Music (distributed by Kjos).

Gardner, M. (1977). *Choral reader*. Ft. Lauderdale, FL: Staff Music (Plymouth Music).

Gordon, E. E., and D. Woods (1986). *Jump right in: The vocal music program*. Chicago: G.I.A.

Hemmenway, J., M. B. Leach, M. N. Wehrung, and M. Carlisle (1977–91). *The keys to sight reading success*. Houston: AMC (a division of Alliance Music).

Henry, M., and M. Jones (1987, 1995). *Songs for sight singing*. 2 vols. San Antonio: Southern Music.

Herman, S. (1986). *Building a pyramid of musicianship*. San Diego: Curtis Music (distributed by Kjos).

Hindemith, P. (1949). *Elementary training of musicians* (2d ed.). New York: Associated Music.

Kodály, Z. (1952–65). *Kodály choral method*. Numerous booklets. New York: Boosey and Hawkes.

Munn, V. (1997–98). *Music reading unlimited*. San Antonio: Southern Music.

Peters, C. S., and P. Yoder (1963). *Master theory series*. 6 vols. San Diego: Curtis Music (Kjos).

Snyder, A. (1993). *The sight-singer*. 2 vols. Miami: CPP/Belwin (Warner Bros.).

Telfer, N. (1992). *Successful sight-singing*. 2 vols. San Diego: Niel A. Kjos Music.

Tower, M. (ed.) (1997–99). *Choral connections*. Teacher and student eds. Woodlands, CA: Glencoe/McGraw-Hill.

Vandre, C. W. (1948/56). *Choir trainer series*. 3 vols. Miami: Belwin Music (Warner Bros.).

Whitlock, R. (1992). *Vocal connections*. San Antonio: Southern Music.

Index

Ranges
pg. 253